Conformity and Conflict

FIFTEENTH EDITION

Conformity and Conflict

Readings in Cultural Anthropology

DAVID W. McCURDY
Macalester College

DIANNA SHANDY
Macalester College

JAMES SPRADLEY

PEARSON

Boston   Columbus   Indianapolis   New York   San Francisco   Amsterdam
Cape Town   Dubai   London   Madrid   Milan   Munich   Paris   Montréal   Toronto
Delhi   Mexico City   São Paulo   Sydney   Hong Kong   Seoul   Singapore   Taipei   Tokyo

Editorial Director: Dickson Musslewhite

Publisher: Charlyce Jones Owen

Program Manager: Rob DeGeorge

Editorial Assistant: Maureen Diana

Project Manager: Richard DeLorenzo

Operations Supervisor: Mary Fischer

Operations Specialist: Mary Ann Gloriande

Cover Designer: Maria Lange

Cover Images: (top) Dominic Byrne / Alamy;
(bottom) Hosam Salem/ZUMA Press/Newscom

Full-Service Project Management: Anju Joshi/
Lumina Datamatics, Inc.

Printer/Binder: Edwards Brothers Malloy

Cover Printer: Phoenix Color/Hagerstown

Text Font: New Aster 10/12

Credits and acknowledgments borrowed from other sources and reproduced, with permission, in this textbook appear on page 391.

Library of Congress Cataloging-in-Publication Data

Conformity and conflict: readings in cultural anthropology / [edited by] David W. McCurdy, Macalester College, Dianna Shandy, Macalester College, James Spradley.—Fifteenth edition.
    pages cm
Includes index.
ISBN 978-0-205-99079-5—ISBN 0-205-99079-7 1. Ethnology. 2. Anthropology.
I. McCurdy, David W. II. Shandy, Dianna.
GN325.C69 2015
306—dc23

2014027156

10 9 8 7 6 5 4 3 2 1

ISBN 10: 0-205-99079-7
ISBN 13: 978-0-205-99079-5

Contents

THREE

Ecology and Subsistence   61

FOUR

Economic Systems   107

FIVE

Kinship and Family   141

EIGHT

Religion, Magic, and Worldview   253

NINE

Globalization   293

TEN

Using and Doing Anthropology   335

Preface

More than four decades ago, as they prepared the first edition of this book, Jim Spradley and David McCurdy sought to make the communication of cultural anthropology more effective for both students and instructors. They looked for useful, engaging articles written by anthropologists for non-anthropologists. They encouraged anthropologists to send them articles that fit their design for *Conformity and Conflict*. They sought out material that demonstrated the nature of culture and its influence on people's lives. They included more material on Western, especially North American, cultures so students could make their own cultural comparisons and see the relation between anthropology and their own lives. They chose articles that reflected interesting topics and current issues, but they also looked for selections that illustrated important anthropological concepts and theories because they believed that anthropology provides a unique and powerful way to look at human experience and make sense of the world around us. Finally, they organized the book around topics found in many textbooks and courses.

The original features of *Conformity and Conflict* remain part of its design today, but the book's content has also shifted over the years to reflect changing instructional and disciplinary interests and the needs and suggestions provided by students and instructors. With this edition, Dianna Shandy joins the editorial team, having first encountered *Conformity and Conflict* as an undergraduate herself and then teaching this book since 1999 as a faculty member at Macalester College. Part introductions now include discussion of many basic anthropological definitions for use by instructors who do not want to assign a standard text but find it helpful to provide students with a terminological foundation. Article introductions seek to tie selections to anthropological concepts and explanations in a coherent and systematic way. Articles and section parts have grown to include environmental, global, medical, and practical anthropological subfields as well as traditional interests such as language, gender, kinship, economics, politics, law, and religion.

Several student aids are retained in the fifteenth edition. Lists of key terms accompany each part introduction. Each article is followed by several review questions. Maps locating societies discussed in articles accompany each selection. There is also a glossary and subject index at the end of the book.

What's New to This Edition

The revision of the fifteenth edition includes a number of changes and updates:

- There are **seven new articles,** and five selections have been brought back from previous editions.
- **Eight articles** found in the fifteenth edition have also been revised and updated.
- **Four** of the seven new articles have been written especially for the fifteenth edition making **fifteen** original articles altogether.

- **Part 1, Culture and Ethnography,** has been revised to update definitions and examples. It also includes a revised article by George Gmelch that incorporates an update based on his consultation with the former student described in the article.
- **Part 2, Language and Communication,** has been revised to update definitions and examples.
- **Part 3, Ecology and Subsistence,** contains a new article by Susan Crate on climate change in Siberia. Richard Reed's article on Forest Development is updated. Nathan Williamson's article on illegal logging has been brought back from a previous edition. It has been revised to update definitions and examples. It introduces climate change as a new definition.
- **Part 4, Economic Systems,** contains a new article on technology and gender division of labor in U.S. coal mines. The introduction has been revised to update examples and definitions. The concept of *neo-liberalism* has been introduced, and a link is drawn between this concept and what Sonia Patten describes is happening in Malawi in relation to World Bank interventions.
- **Part 5, Kinship and Family,** contains a new article on how males and females attain social adulthood in Guinea, West Africa. David McCurdy's article on family and kinship in India has been updated. Updates have also been made to definitions and examples.
- **Part 6, Identity, Roles, and Groups,** contains two new articles. The first, an original selection by Mikaela Rogozen-Soltar, looks at how a Catholic, Spanish woman becomes Muslim, through marriage, in Europe. The second by David McCurdy describes the role of groups in American society—both how they function to meet their member's social needs and how the group is maintained—in his article about a motorcycle association. Dianna Shandy and Karine Moe's article is updated to reflect recent trends and the latest economic data in women's decisions about work and family.
- **Part 7, Law and Politics,** contains three new articles. It now includes a selection by Carolyn Nordstorm about illegality and the informal economy. She links the local with larger econo-political processes. Elizabeth Eames's article on navigating Nigerian bureaucracy has been brought back from a previous edition. This article introduces the idea of navigating bureaucracy being about who you know, not what you know. It also introduces Weber's concept of patrimonial authority as it pertains to the form of government organized as a more or less direct extension of the noble household, where official originate as house servants and remain personal dependents of the ruler. Law and Order by Spradley and McCurdy has also been brought back from a previous edition. Zapotec law meets the basic requirement of every legal system but, unlike its American counterpart, seeks compromise between disputants.
- **Part 8, Religion, Magic, and Worldview,** now includes an original selection by Rachel Mueller on lover spirits in Senegal. This article describes the relationship between this belief system and Islam and argues that the belief in rab spirits will endure well into the future. George Gmelch updated his article, Baseball Magic, to reflect new developments in the field. The introduction to this section has been revised to update definitions and examples.
- **Part 9, Globalization,** has been updated to provide new examples. It also introduces and defines the concepts of *social* and *financial remittances* and *diasporas*. Dianna Shandy's article on refugees has also been updated to reflect the recent turn toward violence in newly independent South Sudan.

- **Part 10, Using and Doing Anthropology,** has been re-titled to reflect the new shaping of the content of this section. The introduction has been revised accordingly. In particular, it introduces and defines the field of *business anthropology* and highlights the 2007 *United Nations Declaration on the Rights of Indigenous Peoples,* as it pertains to the work of some anthropologists. Sonia Patten's work on nutrition and applied medical anthropology has been brought back from an earlier edition. Rachael Stryker's chapter on public interest anthropology at work in a study of the health services afforded women inmates in two California prisons has been revised and updated to reflect new developments. David McCurdy's article on Using Anthropology has also been updated to reflect new developments in ways anthropology is being used in business settings.

Support for Instructors and Students

- **Instructor's Manual with Tests**: For each chapter in the text, this valuable resource provides a detailed outline, discussion questions, and suggested readings. In addition, test questions in multiple-choice, and short answer formats are available for each chapter; the answers are page-referenced to the text. For easy access, this manual is available for download at www.pearsonhighered.com/irc.
- **MyTest** (020506454X): This computerized software allows instructors to create their own personalized exams, edit any or all of the existing test questions, and add new questions. Other special features of the program include random generation of test questions, creation of alternate versions of the same test, scrambling question sequence, and test preview before printing. For easy access, this software is available at www.pearsonhighered.com/irc.
- **PowerPoint Presentation Slides for *Conformity and Conflict***: These PowerPoint slides help instructors convey anthropology principles in a clear and engaging way. For easy access, they are available for download at www.pearsonhighered .com/irc.

Meeting the needs of students and instructors has been a goal of *Conformity and Conflict* since its inception. To help with this goal, we encourage you to send your comments and ideas for improving *Conformity and Conflict* to us at dcmccurdy@comcast .net and shandy@macalester.edu. Ideas for future original selections are also welcome.

Many people have made suggestions that guided this revision of *Conformity and Conflict*. We are especially grateful to graduating Macalester College senior Cady Patton for her keen editorial eye, dedication, and invaluable overall support in bringing this edition to fruition. Similarly, we are grateful to the generations of Macalester College students who provide feedback on this book each time we use it to teach our course, Cultural Anthropology. We are indebted to Macalester College for continued support over many, many years. We appreciate the skills, commitment, and expertise of the authors included in this volume. Their willingness and ability to speak not just to other anthropologists, but to the wider world is commendable. We are also grateful to colleagues Arjun Guneratne and Sonia Patten for their advice and help. Thanks also to reviewers of this edition: Julian Brash, Montclair State University; Risa Ellovich, North Carolina State University; Rachel Giraudo, California State University, Northridge; Anna Konstantatos, Adelphi University; Vincent Melomo, Peace College;

Julian M. Murchison, Millsaps College; Rocky Sexton, Ball State University; Bhavani Sitaraman, University of Alabama, Huntsville; Hal Starratt, Western Nevada College; Charles Townsend, CUNY, LaGuardia. We would also like to thank our former editor Jeff Lasser and current editor Charlyce Jones-Owen, Project Managers Richard DeLorenzo, and Brooks Hill-Whilton, and senior assistant at Pearson Maureen Diana and Anju Joshi, Project Manager at Lumina Datamatics for their guidance and work on this volume.

DWM and DS

PART ONE

CULTURE
AND ETHNOGRAPHY

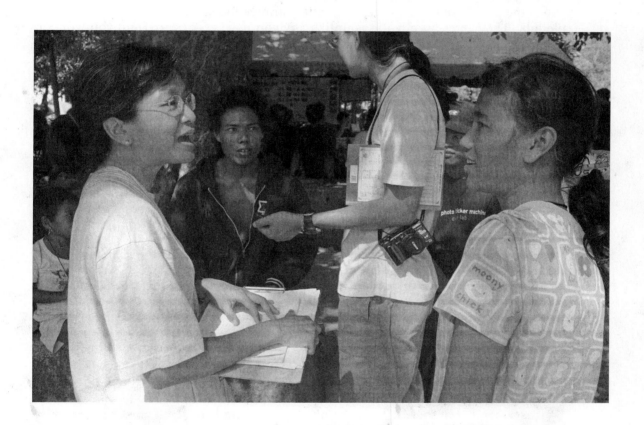

READINGS IN THIS SECTION

Culture, as its name suggests, lies at the heart of cultural anthropology. And the concept of **culture**, along with ethnography, sets anthropology apart from other social and behavioral sciences. Let us look more closely at these concepts.

To understand what anthropologists mean by *culture,* imagine yourself in a foreign setting, such as a market town in India, forgetting what you might already know about that country. You step off a bus onto a dusty street where you are immediately confronted by strange sights, sounds, and smells. Men dress in Western clothes, but of a different style. Some women drape themselves in long shawls that entirely cover their bodies. They peer at you through a small gap in this garment as they walk by. Buildings are one- or two-story affairs, open at the front so you can see inside. Near you some people sit on wicker chairs eating strange foods. Most unusual is how people talk. They utter vocalizations unlike any you have ever heard, and you wonder how they can possibly understand each other. But obviously they do, since their behavior seems organized and purposeful.

Scenes such as this confronted early explorers, missionaries, and anthropologists, and from their observations an obvious point emerged. People living in various parts of the world looked and behaved in dramatically different ways. And these differences correlated with groups. The people of India had customs different from those of the Papuans; the British did not act and dress like the Iroquois.

Two possible explanations for group differences came to mind. Some argued that group behavior was inherited. Dahomeans of the African Gold Coast, for example, were characterized as particularly "clever and adaptive" by one British colonial official, while, according to the same authority, another African group was "happy-go-lucky and improvident." Usually implied in such statements was the idea that group members were born that way. Such thinking persists to the present and in its most malignant extreme takes the form of racism.

But a second explanation also emerged. Perhaps, rather than a product of inheritance, the behavior characteristic of a group was learned. The way people dressed, what they ate, how they talked—all these could more easily be explained as acquisitions. Thus a baby born on the African Gold Coast would, if immediately transported to China and raised like other children there, grow up to dress, eat, and talk like a Chinese. Cultural anthropologists focus on the explanation of learned behavior.

The idea of learning, and a need to label the lifestyles associated with particular groups, led to the definition of culture. In 1871, British anthropologist **Sir Edward Burnett Tylor** argued that "Culture . . . is that complex whole which includes knowledge, belief, art, law, morals, custom, and any other capabilities and habits acquired by man as a member of society."[1] The definition we present here places more emphasis on the importance of knowledge than does Tylor's. We will say that *culture is the learned and shared knowledge that people use to generate behavior and interpret experience.*

Important to this definition is the idea that culture is a kind of knowledge, not behavior. It is in people's heads. It reflects the mental categories they learn from others as they grow up. It helps them *generate* behavior and *interpret* what they experience. At the moment of birth, we lack a culture. We don't yet have a system of beliefs, knowledge, and patterns of customary behavior. But from that moment until we die, each of us participates in a kind of universal schooling that teaches us our native culture. Laughing and smiling are genetic responses, but as infants we soon learn

[1]Edward Burnett Tylor, *Primitive Culture* (New York: Harper Torchbooks, Harper & Row, 1958; originally published by John Murray, London, 1871), p. 1.

when to smile, when to laugh, and even how to laugh. We also inherit the potential to cry, but we must learn our cultural rules for when crying is appropriate and how those rules may differ based on one's role in society.

As we learn our culture, we acquire a way to interpret experience. For example, Americans learn that dogs are like little people in furry suits. Dogs live in our houses, eat our food, share our beds. They hold a place in our hearts; their loss causes us to grieve. Villagers in India, on the other hand, often view dogs as pests that are useful only for hunting (in those few parts of the country where one still can hunt) and as watchdogs. Quiet days in Indian villages are often punctuated by the yelp of a dog that has been threatened or hurt by its master or a bystander.

Clearly, it is not the dogs that are different in these two societies. Rather, it is the meaning that dogs have for people that varies. And such meaning is cultural; it is learned as part of growing up in each group.

There are two basic kinds of culture, explicit and tacit. **Explicit culture** is cultural knowledge that people can talk about. As you grow up, for example, you learn that there are words for things you encounter. There are items such as *clothes*, actions such as *playing*, emotional states such as *sadness*, ways to talk such as *yelling*, and people such as *mother*. Recognizing that culture may be explicit is important to the ethnographic process discussed below. If people have words for cultural categories, anthropologists can use interviews or observations of people talking to uncover them. Because so much culture is explicit, words—both spoken and written—become essential to the discovery and understanding of a culture.

Tacit culture is cultural knowledge that people lack words for. For example, as we grow up we learn to recognize and use a limited number of sound categories such as /d/, /e/, and /f/. Although anthropological linguists have given sound categories a name *(phonemes)*, nonlinguists lack such a term. Instead, we learn our sound categories by hearing and replicating them and we use them unconsciously. No parent said, "Now let's work on our phonemes tonight, dear," to us when we were little.

Anthropologist Edward Hall pioneered the study of tacit culture. He noted, for example, that middle-class North Americans observe four speaking distances—intimate, personal, social, and public—without naming them. (Hall, not his informants, invented these terms.) Hall also noticed that people from other societies observed different tacit speaking distances, so that a Latin American's closer (than North American) personal speaking distance made North Americans uncomfortable because it seemed intimate. Because it is unspoken, tacit culture can be discovered only through behavioral observation.

Ethnography is the process of discovering and describing a particular culture. It involves anthropologists in an intimate and personal activity as they attempt to learn how the members of a particular group see their worlds.

But which groups qualify as culture-bearing units? How does the anthropologist identify the existence of a culture to study? This was not a difficult question when anthropology was a new science. As Tylor's definition notes, culture was the whole way of life of a people. To find it, one sought out distinctive ethnic units, such as Bhil tribals in India or Apaches in the American Southwest. Anything one learned from such people would be part of their culture.

But discrete cultures of this sort are becoming more difficult to find. The world is increasingly divided into large national societies, each subdivided into myriad subgroups. Anthropologists are finding it increasingly attractive to study such subgroups, because they form the arena for most of life in complex society. And this is where the concept of the microculture enters the scene.

Microcultures are systems of cultural knowledge characteristic of subgroups within larger societies. Members of a microculture will usually share much of what they know with everyone in the greater society but will possess a special cultural knowledge that is unique to the subgroup. For example, a college fraternity has a microculture within the context of a university and a nation. Its members have special daily routines, jokes, and meanings for events. It is this shared knowledge that makes up their microculture and that can serve as the basis for ethnographic study. More and more, anthropologists are turning to the study of microcultures, using the same ethnographic techniques they employ when they investigate the broader culture of an ethnic or national group.

More than anything else, it is ethnography that is anthropology's unique contribution to social science. Most scientists, including many who view people in social context, approach their research as **detached observers**. As social scientists, they observe the human subjects of their study, categorize what they see, and generate theory to account for their findings. They work from the outside, creating a system of knowledge to account for other people's behavior. Although this is a legitimate and often useful way to conduct research, it is not the main task of ethnography.

Ethnographers seek out the insider's viewpoint. Because culture is the knowledge people use to generate behavior and interpret experience, the ethnographer seeks to understand group members' behavior from the inside, or cultural, perspective. Instead of looking for a **subject** to observe, ethnographers look for an **informant** to teach them the culture. Just as children learn their native culture from parents and other people in their social environment, ethnographers learn another culture by inferring folk categories from the observation of behavior and by asking informants what things mean.

Anthropologists employ many strategies during field research to understand another culture better. But all strategies and all research ultimately rest on the cooperation of informants. An informant is neither a subject in a scientific experiment nor a **respondent** who answers the investigator's questions. An informant is a teacher who has a special kind of pupil: a professional anthropologist. In this unique relationship a transformation occurs in the anthropologist's understanding of an alien culture. The informant transforms the anthropologist from a tourist into an ethnographer. The informant may be a child who explains how to play hopscotch, a cocktail waitress who shows how to serve drinks and to encourage customers to leave tips, an elderly man who teaches how to build an igloo, or a grandmother who explains the intricacies of Zapotec kinship. Almost any individual who has acquired a repertoire of cultural behavior can become an informant.

Ethnography is not as easy to do as we might think. For one thing, North Americans are not taught to be good listeners. We prefer to observe and draw our own conclusions. We like a sense of control in social contexts; passive listening is a sign of weakness in our culture. But listening and learning from others is at the heart of ethnography, and we must embrace the student role.

It is also not easy for informants to teach us about their cultures. Even explicit culture often lies below a conscious level. A major ethnographic task is to help informants remember their culture.

Naive realism may also impede ethnography. **Naive realism** is the belief that people everywhere see the world in the same way. It may, for example, lead the unwary ethnographer to assume that beauty is the same for all people everywhere or, to use our previous example, that dogs should mean the same thing in India as they do in the United States. If an ethnographer fails to control his or her own naive realism, inside cultural meanings will surely be overlooked.

Culture shock and ethnocentrism may also be stumbling blocks for ethnographers. **Culture shock** is a state of anxiety that results from cross-cultural misunderstanding. Immersed in another society, the ethnographer understands few of the culturally defined rules for behavior and interpretation used by his or her hosts. The result is anxiety about proper action and an inability to interact appropriately in the new context.

Ethnocentrism can be just as much of a liability. **Ethnocentrism** is the belief and feeling that one's own culture is best. It reflects our tendency to judge other people's beliefs and behavior using values of our own native culture. Thus if we come from a society that abhors painful treatment of animals, we are likely to react with anger when an Indian villager hits a dog with a rock. Our feeling is ethnocentric.

It is impossible to rid ourselves entirely of the cultural values that make us ethnocentric when we do ethnography. But it is important to acknowledge and manage our ethnocentric feelings in the field if we are to learn from informants. Informants resent negative judgment.

Finally, the role assigned to ethnographers by informants affects the quality of what can be learned. Ethnography is a personal enterprise, as all the articles in this section illustrate. Unlike survey research using questionnaires or short interviews, ethnography requires prolonged social contact. Informants will assign the ethnographer some kind of role and what that turns out to be will affect research.

The selections in Part One illustrate several points about culture and ethnography. The first piece, by the late James Spradley, takes a close look at the concept of culture and its role in ethnographic research. The second, by Richard Lee, illustrates how a simple act of giving can have a dramatically different cultural meaning in two societies, leading to cross-cultural misunderstanding. In the third selection, Claire Sterk describes how she conducted ethnographic field research under difficult circumstances. She sought to learn the culture of prostitutes working in New York City and Atlanta as part of a broader research interest in the spread and control of AIDS. The fourth article, by George Gmelch, explores how naive realism nearly ended a student's field research in Barbados.

Key Terms

culture p. 2	informant p. 4
culture shock p. 5	microcultures p. 4
detached observers p. 4	naive realism p. 4
ethnocentrism p. 5	respondent p. 4
ethnography p. 3	subject p. 4
explicit culture p. 3	tacit culture p. 3

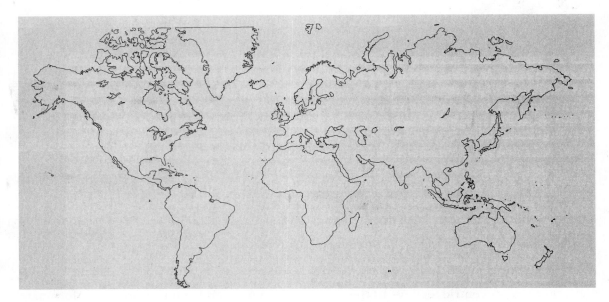

1

Ethnography and Culture

James P. Spradley

Most Americans associate science with detached observation; we learn to observe whatever we wish to understand, introduce our own classification of what is going on, and explain what we see in our own terms. In this selection, James Spradley argues that cultural anthropologists work differently. Ethnography is the work of discovering and describing a particular culture; culture is the learned, shared knowledge that people use to generate behavior and interpret experience. To get at culture, ethnographers must learn the meanings of action and experience from the insider's or informant's point of view. Many of the examples used by Spradley also show the relevance of anthropology to the study of culture in the United States. *

((•─Listen to the **Chapter Audio** on **myanthrolab.com**

Ethnographic fieldwork is the hallmark of cultural anthropology. Whether in a jungle village in Peru or on the streets of New York, the anthropologist goes to where people live and "does fieldwork." This means participating in activities, asking questions, eating strange foods, learning a new language, watching ceremonies, taking field notes, washing clothes, writing letters home, tracing out genealogies, observing play, interviewing informants, and hundreds of other things. This vast range of activities often obscures the nature of the most fundamental task of all fieldwork: doing ethnography.

*"Ethnography and Culture" from *Participant Observation* by James P. Spradley. Copyright © 1980 by Holt, Rinehart, and Winston, Inc. Reprinted by permission of Barbara Spradley.

Ethnography is the work of describing a culture. The central aim of ethnography is to understand another way of life from the native point of view. The goal of ethnography, as Malinowski put it, is "to grasp the native's point of view, his relation to life, to realize *his* vision of *his* world."[1] Fieldwork, then, involves the disciplined study of what the world is like to people who have learned to see, hear, speak, think, and act in ways that are different. Rather than *studying people*, ethnography means *learning from people*. Consider the following illustration.

George Hicks set out, in 1965, to learn about another way of life, that of the mountain people in an Appalachian valley.[2] His goal was to discover their culture, to learn to see the world from their perspective. With his family he moved into Little Laurel Valley, his daughter attended the local school, and his wife became one of the local Girl Scout leaders. Hicks soon discovered that stores and storekeepers were at the center of the valley's communication system, providing the most important social arena for the entire valley. He learned this by watching what other people did, by following their example, and slowly becoming part of the groups that congregated daily in the stores. He writes:

> At least once each day I would visit several stores in the valley, and sit in on the groups of gossiping men or, if the storekeeper happened to be alone, perhaps attempt to clear up puzzling points about kinship obligations. I found these hours, particularly those spent in the presence of the two or three excellent storytellers in the Little Laurel, thoroughly enjoyable. . . . At other times, I helped a number of local men gather corn or hay, build sheds, cut trees, pull and pack galax, and search for rich stands of huckleberries. When I needed aid in, for example, repairing frozen water pipes, it was readily and cheerfully provided.[3]

In order to discover the hidden principles of another way of life, the researcher must become a *student*. Storekeepers and storytellers and local farmers become *teachers*. Instead of studying the "climate," the "flora," and the "fauna" that made up the environment of this Appalachian valley, Hicks tried to discover how these mountain people defined and evaluated trees and galax and huckleberries. He did not attempt to describe social life in terms of what most Americans know about "marriage," "family," and "friendship"; instead he sought to discover how these mountain people identified relatives and friends. He tried to learn the obligations they felt toward kinsmen and discover how they felt about friends. Discovering the *insider's view* is a different species of knowledge from one that rests mainly on the outsider's view, even when the outsider is a trained social scientist.

Consider another example, this time from the perspective of a non-Western ethnographer. Imagine an Inuit woman setting out to learn the culture of Macalester College. What would she, so well schooled in the rich heritage of Inuit culture, have to do in order to understand the culture of Macalester College students, faculty, and staff? How would she discover the patterns that made up their lives? How would she avoid imposing Inuit ideas, categories, and values on everything she saw?

First, and perhaps most difficult, she would have to set aside her belief in *naive realism*, the almost universal belief that all people define the *real* world of objects, events, and living creatures in pretty much the same way. Human languages may differ

---

[1]Bronislaw Malinowski, *Argonauts of the Western Pacific* (London: Routledge, 1922), p. 22.

[2]George Hicks, *Appalachian Valley* (New York: Holt, Rinehart, and Winston, 1976).

[3]Hicks, p. 3.

from one society to the next, but behind the strange words and sentences, all people are talking about the same things. The naive realist assumes that love, snow, marriage, worship, animals, death, food, and hundreds of other things have essentially the same meaning to all human beings. Although few of us would admit to such ethnocentrism, the assumption may unconsciously influence our research. Ethnography starts with a conscious attitude of almost complete ignorance: "I don't know how the people at Macalester College understand their world. That remains to be discovered."

This Inuit woman would have to begin by learning the language spoken by students, faculty, and staff. She could stroll the campus paths, sit in classes, and attend special events, but only if she consciously tried to see things from the native point of view would she grasp their perspective. She would need to observe and listen to first-year students during their week-long orientation program. She would have to stand in line during registration, listen to students discuss the classes they hoped to get, and visit departments to watch faculty advising students on course selection. She would want to observe secretaries typing, janitors sweeping, and maintenance personnel plowing snow from walks. She would watch the more than 1,600 students crowd into the post office area to open their tiny mailboxes, and she would listen to their comments about junk mail and letters from home or no mail at all. She would attend faculty meetings to watch what went on, recording what professors and administrators said and how they behaved. She would sample various courses, attend "keggers" on weekends, read the *Mac Weekly,* and listen by the hour to students discussing things like their "relationships," the "football team," and "work study." She would want to learn the *meanings* of all these things. She would have to listen to the members of this college community, watch what they did, and participate in their activities to learn such meanings.

The essential core of ethnography is this concern with the meaning of actions and events to the people we seek to understand. Some of these meanings are directly expressed in language; many are taken for granted and communicated only indirectly through word and action. But in every society people make constant use of these complex meaning systems to organize their behavior, to understand themselves and others, and to make sense out of the world in which they live. These systems of meaning constitute their culture; ethnography always implies a theory of culture.

Culture

When ethnographers study other cultures, they must deal with three fundamental aspects of human experience: what people do, what people know, and the things people make and use. When each of these is learned and shared by members of some group, we speak of them as *cultural behavior, cultural knowledge,* and *cultural artifacts.* Whenever you do ethnographic fieldwork, you will want to distinguish among these three, although in most situations they are usually mixed together. Let's try to unravel them.

Recently I took a commuter train from a western suburb to downtown Chicago. It was late in the day, and when I boarded the train, only a handful of people were scattered about the car. Each was engaged in a common form of *cultural behavior: reading.* Across the aisle a man held the *Chicago Tribune* out in front of him, looking intently at the small print and every now and then turning the pages noisily. In front of him a young woman held a paperback book about twelve inches from her face. I could see her head shift slightly as her eyes moved from the bottom of one page to the top of the next. Near the front of the car a student was reading a large textbook and using a pen to underline words and sentences. Directly in front of me I noticed a man looking at the ticket he had purchased and reading it. It took me an instant to survey this scene, and then I settled back, looked out the window, and read a billboard advertisement for a plumbing service proclaiming it would open any plugged drains. All of us were engaged in the same kind of cultural behavior: reading.

This common activity depended on a great many *cultural artifacts,* the things people shape or make from natural resources. I could see artifacts like books and tickets and newspapers and billboards, all of which contained tiny black marks arranged into intricate patterns called "letters." And these tiny artifacts were arranged into larger patterns of words, sentences, and paragraphs. Those of us on that commuter train could read, in part, because of still other artifacts: the bark of trees made into paper; steel made into printing presses; dyes of various colors made into ink; glue used to hold book pages together; large wooden frames to hold billboards. If an ethnographer wanted to understand the full cultural meaning in our society, it would involve a careful study of these and many other cultural artifacts.

Although we can easily see behavior and artifacts, they represent only the thin surface of a deep lake. Beneath the surface, hidden from view, lies a vast reservoir of *cultural knowledge.* Think for a moment what the people on that train needed to know in order to read. First, they had to know the grammatical rules for at least one language. Then they had to learn what the little marks on paper represented. They also had to know the meaning of space and lines and pages. They had learned cultural rules like "move your eyes from left to right, from the top of the page to the bottom." They had to know that a sentence at the bottom of a page continues on the top of the next page. The man reading a newspaper had to know a great deal about columns and the spaces between columns and what headlines mean. All of us needed to know what kinds of messages were intended by whoever wrote what we read. If a person cannot distinguish the importance of a message on a billboard from one that comes in a letter from a spouse or child, problems would develop. I knew how to recognize when other people were reading. We all knew it was impolite to read aloud on a train. We all knew how to feel when reading things like jokes or calamitous news in the paper. Our culture has a large body of shared knowledge that people learn and use to engage in this behavior called *reading* and make proper use of the artifacts connected with it.

Although cultural knowledge is hidden from view, it is of fundamental importance because we all use it constantly to generate behavior and interpret our experience. Cultural knowledge is so important that I will frequently use the broader term *culture* when speaking about it. Indeed, I will define culture as *the acquired knowledge people use to interpret experience and generate behavior.* Let's consider another example to see how people use their culture to interpret experience and do things.

One afternoon in 1973 I came across the following news item in the *Minneapolis Tribune:*

Crowd Mistakes Rescue Attempt, Attacks Police

Nov. 23, 1973. Hartford, Connecticut. Three policemen giving a heart massage and oxygen to a heart attack victim Friday were attacked by a crowd of 75 to 100 persons who apparently did not realize what the policemen were doing.

Other policemen fended off the crowd of mostly Spanish-speaking residents until an ambulance arrived. Police said they tried to explain to the crowd what they were doing, but the crowd apparently thought they were beating the woman.

Despite the policemen's efforts the victim, Evangelica Echevacria, 59, died.

Here we see people using their culture. Members of two different groups observed the same event, but their *interpretations* were drastically different. The crowd used their cultural knowledge (a) to interpret the behavior of the policemen as cruel and (b) to act on the woman's behalf to put a stop to what they perceived as brutality. They had acquired the cultural principles for acting and interpreting things in this way through a particular shared experience.

The policemen, on the other hand, used their cultural knowledge (a) to interpret the woman's condition as heart failure and their own behavior as a life-saving effort and (b) to give her cardiac massage and oxygen. They used artifacts like an oxygen mask and an ambulance. Furthermore, they interpreted the actions of the crowd in an entirely different manner from how the crowd saw their own behavior. The two groups of people each had elaborate cultural rules for interpreting their experience and for acting in emergency situations, and the conflict arose, at least in part, because these cultural rules were so different.

We can now diagram this definition of culture and see more clearly the relationships among knowledge, behavior, and artifacts (Figure 1). By identifying cultural knowledge as fundamental, we have merely shifted the emphasis from behavior and artifacts to their *meaning*. The ethnographer observes behavior but goes beyond it to inquire about the meaning of that behavior. The ethnographer sees artifacts and natural objects but goes beyond them to discover what meanings people assign to these objects. The ethnographer observes and records emotional states but goes beyond them to discover the meaning of fear, anxiety, anger, and other feelings.

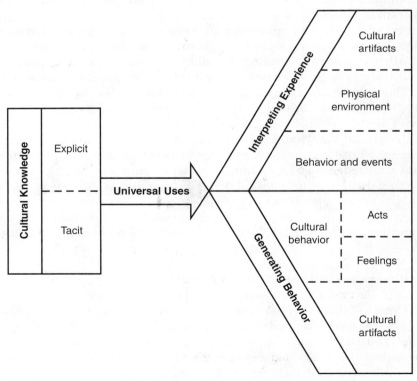

FIGURE 1

As represented in Figure 1, cultural knowledge exists at two levels of consciousness. *Explicit culture* makes up part of what we know, a level of knowledge people can communicate about with relative ease. When George Hicks asked storekeepers and others in Little Laurel Valley about their relatives, he discovered that any adult over fifty could tell him the genealogical connections among large numbers of people. They knew how to trace kin relationships and the cultural rules for appropriate behavior among kins. All of us have acquired large areas of cultural knowledge such as this, which we can talk about and make explicit.

At the same time, a large portion of our cultural knowledge remains *tacit*, outside our awareness. Edward Hall has done much to elucidate the nature of tacit cultural knowledge in his books *The Silent Language* and *The Hidden Dimension*.[4] The way each culture defines space often occurs at the level of tacit knowledge. Hall points out that all of us have acquired thousands of spatial cues about how close to stand to others, how to arrange furniture, when to touch others, and when to feel cramped inside a room. Without realizing that our tacit culture is operating, we begin to feel uneasy when someone from another culture stands too close, breathes on us when talking, touches us, or when we find furniture arranged in the center of the room rather than around the edges. Ethnography is the study of both explicit and tacit cultural knowledge. . . .

The concept of culture as acquired knowledge has much in common with symbolic interactionism, a theory that seeks to explain human behavior in terms of meanings. Symbolic interactionism has its roots in the work of sociologists like Cooley, Mead, and Thomas. Blumer has identified three premises on which this theory rests.

The first premise is that "human beings act toward things on the basis of the meanings that the things have for them."[5] The policemen and the crowd in our earlier example interacted on the basis of the meanings things had for them. The geographic location, the types of people, the police car, the policemen's movements, the sick woman's behavior, and the activities of the onlookers—all were *symbols* with special meanings. People did not act toward the things themselves, but to their meanings.

The second premise underlying symbolic interactionism is that the "meaning of such things is derived from, or arises out of, the social interaction that one has with one's fellows."[6] Culture, as a shared system of meanings, is learned, revised, maintained, and defined in the context of people interacting. The crowd came to share their definitions of police behavior through interacting with one another and through past associations with the police. The police officers acquired the cultural meanings they used through interacting with other officers and members of the community. The culture of each group was inextricably bound up with the social life of their particular communities.

The third premise of symbolic interactionism is that "meanings are handled in, and modified through, an interpretive process used by the person dealing with the things he encounters."[7] Neither the crowd nor the policemen were automatons, driven by their culture to act in the way they did. Rather, they used their cultural knowledge to interpret and evaluate the situation. At any moment, a member of the crowd might

[4]Edward T. Hall, *The Silent Language* (Garden City, NY: Doubleday, 1959); *The Hidden Dimension* (Garden City, NY: Doubleday, 1966).

[5]Herbert Blumer, *Symbolic Interactionism* (Englewood Cliffs, NJ: Prentice-Hall, 1969), p. 2.

[6]Blumer, p. 2.

[7]Blumer, p. 2.

have interpreted the behavior of the policemen in a slightly different way, leading to a different reaction.

We may see this interpretive aspect more clearly if we think of culture as a cognitive map. In the recurrent activities that make up everyday life, we refer to this map. It serves as a guide for acting and for interpreting our experience; it does not compel us to follow a particular course. Like this brief drama between the policemen, a dying woman, and the crowd, much of life is a series of unanticipated social occasions. Although our culture may not include a detailed map for such occasions, it does provide principles for interpreting and responding to them. Rather than a rigid map that people must follow, culture is best thought of as

> a set of principles for creating dramas, for writing script, and of course, for recruiting players and audiences. . . . Culture is not simply a cognitive map that people acquire, in whole or in part, more or less accurately, and then learn to read. People are not just map-readers; they are map-makers. People are cast out into imperfectly charted, continually revised sketch maps. Culture does not provide a cognitive map, but rather a set of principles for map making and navigation. Different cultures are like different schools of navigation to cope with different terrains and seas.[8]

If we take *meaning* seriously, as symbolic interactionists argue we must, it becomes necessary to study meaning carefully. We need a theory of meaning and a specific methodology designed for the investigation of it.

✓●─ **Study** and **Review** on **myanthrolab.com**

Review Questions

1. What is the definition of *culture?* How is this definition related to the way anthropologists do ethnographic fieldwork?

2. What is the relationship among cultural behavior, cultural artifacts, and cultural knowledge?

3. What is the difference between tacit and explicit culture? How can anthropologists discover these two kinds of culture?

4. What are some examples of naive realism in the way Americans think about people in other societies?

---

[8]Charles O. Frake, "Plying Frames Can Be Dangerous: Some Reflections on Methodology in Cognitive Anthropology," *Quarterly Newsletter of the Institute for Comparative Human Development* 3 (1977): 6–7.

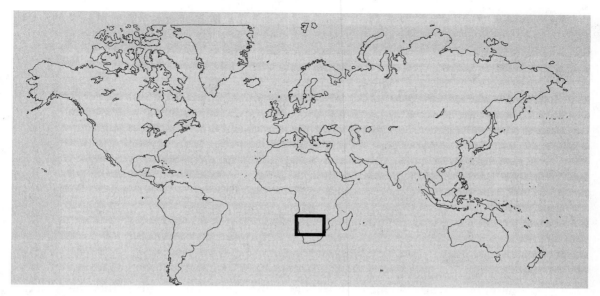

2

Eating Christmas in the Kalahari

Richard Borshay Lee

What happens when an anthropologist living among the !Kung of Southern Africa decides to be generous and to share a large animal with everyone at Christmastime? This compelling account of the misunderstanding and confusion that resulted takes the reader deeper into the nature of culture. Richard Lee carefully traces how the !Kung perceived his generosity and taught the anthropologist something about his own culture. *

((•—[**Listen** to the **Chapter Audio** on **myanthrolab.com**

The !Kung Bushmen's knowledge of Christmas is thirdhand. The London Missionary Society brought the holiday to the southern Tswana tribes in the early nineteenth century. Later, native catechists spread the idea far and wide among the Bantu-speaking pastoralists, even in the remotest corners of the Kalahari Desert. The Bushmen's idea of the Christmas story, stripped to its essentials, is "praise the birth of white man's god-chief"; what keeps their interest in the holiday high is the Tswana-Herero custom of slaughtering an ox for his Bushmen neighbors as an annual goodwill gesture. Since the 1930s, part of the Bushmen's annual round of activities

*From Richard Borshay Lee, "Eating Christmas in the Kalahari," *Natural History*, December 1969, pp. 14–22, 60–64. Reprinted from *Natural History* December 1969; copyright © Natural History Magazine, Inc., 1969.

has included a December congregation at the cattle posts for trading, marriage brokering, and several days of trance dance feasting at which the local Tswana headman is host.

As a social anthropologist working with !Kung Bushmen, I found that the Christmas ox custom suited my purposes. I had come to the Kalahari to study the hunting and gathering subsistence economy of the !Kung, and to accomplish this it was essential not to provide them with food, share my own food, or interfere in any way with their food-gathering activities. While liberal handouts of tobacco and medical supplies were appreciated, they were scarcely adequate to erase the glaring disparity in wealth between the anthropologist, who maintained a two-month inventory of canned goods, and the Bushmen, who rarely had a day's supply of food on hand. My approach, while paying off in terms of data, left me open to frequent accusations of stinginess and hardheartedness. By their lights, I was a miser.

The Christmas ox was to be my way of saying thank you for the cooperation of the past year; and since it was to be our last Christmas in the field, I was determined to slaughter the largest, meatiest ox that money could buy, insuring that the feast and trance dance would be a success.

Through December I kept my eyes open at the wells as the cattle were brought down for watering. Several animals were offered, but none had quite the grossness that I had in mind. Then, ten days before the holiday, a Herero friend led an ox of astonishing size and mass up to our camp. It was solid black, stood five feet high at the shoulder, had a five-foot span of horns, and must have weighed 1,200 pounds on the hoof. Food consumption calculations are my specialty, and I quickly figured that bones and viscera aside, there was enough meat—at least four pounds—for every man, woman, and child of the 150 Bushmen in the vicinity of /ai/ai who were expected at the feast.

Having found the right animal at last, I paid the Herero £20 ($56) and asked him to keep the beast with his herd until Christmas day. The next morning word spread among the people that the big solid black one was the ox chosen by /ontah (my Bushman name; it means, roughly, "whitey") for the Christmas feast. That afternoon I received the first delegation. Ben!a, an outspoken sixty-year-old mother of five, came to the point slowly.

"Where were you planning to eat Christmas?"

"Right here at /ai/ai," I replied.

"Alone or with others?"

"I expect to invite all the people to eat Christmas with me."

"Eat what?"

"I have purchased Yehave's black ox, and I am going to slaughter and cook it."

"That's what we were told at the well but refused to believe it until we heard it from yourself."

"Well, it's the black one," I replied expansively, although wondering what she was driving at.

"Oh, no!" Ben!a groaned, turning to her group. "They were right." Turning back to me she asked, "Do you expect us to eat that bag of bones?"

"Bag of bones! It's the biggest ox at /ai/ai."

"Big, yes, but old. And thin. Everybody knows there's no meat on that old ox. What did you expect us to eat off it, the horns?"

Everybody chuckled at Ben!a's one-liner as they walked away, but all I could manage was a weak grin.

That evening it was the turn of the young men. They came to sit at our evening fire. /gaugo, about my age, spoke to me man-to-man.

"/ontah, you have always been square with us," he lied. "What has happened to change your heart? That sack of guts and bones of Yehave's will hardly feed one camp, let alone all the Bushmen around /ai/ai." And he proceeded to enumerate the seven camps in the /ai/ai vicinity, family by family. "Perhaps you have forgotten that we are not few, but many. Or are you too blind to tell the difference between a proper cow and an old wreck? That ox is thin to the point of death."

"Look, you guys," I retorted, "that is a beautiful animal, and I'm sure you will eat it with pleasure at Christmas."

"Of course we will eat it; it's food. But it won't fill us up to the point where we will have enough strength to dance. We will eat and go home to bed with stomachs rumbling."

That night as we turned in, I asked my wife, Nancy, "What did you think of the black ox?"

"It looked enormous to me. Why?"

"Well, about eight different people have told me I got gypped; that the ox is nothing but bones."

"What's the angle?" Nancy asked. "Did they have a better one to sell?"

"No, they just said that it was going to be a grim Christmas because there won't be enough meat to go around. Maybe I'll get an independent judge to look at the beast in the morning."

Bright and early, Halingisi, a Tswana cattle owner, appeared at our camp. But before I could ask him to give me his opinion on Yehave's black ox, he gave me the eye signal that indicated a confidential chat. We left the camp and sat down.

"/ontah, I'm surprised at you; you've lived here for three years and still haven't learned anything about cattle."

"But what else can a person do but choose the biggest, strongest animal one can find?" I retorted.

"Look, just because an animal is big doesn't mean that it has plenty of meat on it. The black one was a beauty when it was younger, but now it is thin to the point of death."

"Well, I've already bought it. What can I do at this stage?"

"Bought it already? I thought you were just considering it. Well, you'll have to kill it and serve it, I suppose. But don't expect much of a dance to follow."

My spirits dropped rapidly. I could believe that Ben!a and /gaugo just might be putting me on about the black ox, but Halingisi seemed to be an impartial critic. I went around that day feeling as though I had bought a lemon of a used car.

In the afternoon it was Tomazo's turn. Tomazo is a fine hunter, a top trance performer . . . and one of my most reliable informants. He approached the subject of the Christmas cow as part of my continuing Bushman education.

"My friend, the way it is with us Bushmen," he began, "is that we love meat. And even more than that, we love fat. When we hunt we always search for the fat ones, the ones dripping with layers of white fat: fat that turns into a clear, thick oil in the cooking pot, fat that slides down your gullet, fills your stomach and gives you a roaring diarrhea," he rhapsodized.

"So, feeling as we do," he continued, "it gives us pain to be served such a scrawny thing as Yehave's black ox. It is big, yes, and no doubt its giant bones are good for soup, but fat is what we really crave, and so we will eat Christmas this year with a heavy heart."

The prospect of a gloomy Christmas now had me worried, so I asked Tomazo what I could do about it.

"Look for a fat one, a young one . . . smaller, but fat. Fat enough to make us //gom (evacuate the bowels), then we will be happy."

My suspicions were aroused when Tomazo said that he happened to know a young, fat, barren cow that the owner was willing to part with. Was Tomazo working on commission, I wondered? But I dispelled this unworthy thought when we approached the Herero owner of the cow in question and found that he had decided not to sell.

The scrawny wreck of a Christmas ox now became the talk of the /ai/ai water hole and was the first news told to the outlying groups as they began to come in from the bush for the feast. What finally convinced me that real trouble might be brewing was the visit from u!au, an old conservative with a reputation for fierceness. His nickname meant spear and referred to an incident thirty years ago in which he had speared a man to death. He had an intense manner; fixing me with his eyes, he said in clipped tones:

"I have only just heard about the black ox today, or else I would have come here earlier. /ontah, do you honestly think you can serve meat like that to people and avoid a fight?" He paused, letting the implications sink in. "I don't mean fight you, /ontah; you are a white man. I mean a fight between Bushmen. There are many fierce ones here, and with such a small quantity of meat to distribute, how can you give everybody a fair share? Someone is sure to accuse another of taking too much or hogging all the choice pieces. Then you will see what happens when some go hungry while others eat."

The possibility of at least a serious argument struck me as all too real. I had witnessed the tension that surrounds the distribution of meat from a kudu or gemsbok kill, and had documented many arguments that sprang up from a real or imagined slight in meat distribution. The owners of a kill may spend up to two hours arranging and rearranging the piles of meat under the gaze of a circle of recipients before handing them out. And I knew that the Christmas feast at /ai/ai would be bringing together groups that had feuded in the past.

Convinced now of the gravity of the situation, I went in earnest to search for a second cow; but all my inquiries failed to turn one up.

The Christmas feast was evidently going to be a disaster, and the incessant complaints about the meagerness of the ox had already taken the fun out of it for me. Moreover, I was getting bored with the wisecracks, and after losing my temper a few times, I resolved to serve the beast anyway. If the meat fell short, the hell with it. In the Bushmen idiom, I announced to all who would listen:

"I am a poor man and blind. If I have chosen one that is too old and too thin, we will eat it anyway and see if there is enough meat there to quiet the rumbling of our stomachs."

On hearing this speech, Ben!a offered me a rare word of comfort. "It's thin," she said philosophically, "but the bones will make a good soup."

At dawn Christmas morning, instinct told me to turn over the butchering and cooking to a friend and take off with Nancy to spend Christmas alone in the bush. But curiosity kept me from retreating. I wanted to see what such a scrawny ox looked like on butchering, and if there *was* going to be a fight, I wanted to catch every word of it. Anthropologists are incurable that way.

The great beast was driven up to our dancing ground, and a shot in the forehead dropped it in its tracks. Then, freshly cut branches were heaped around the fallen carcass to receive the meat. Ten men volunteered to help with the cutting. I asked /gaugo to make the breast bone cut. This cut, which begins the butchering process for most large game, offers easy access for removal of the viscera. But it also allows the hunter to spot-check the amount of fat on an animal. A fat game animal carries a white layer up to an inch thick on the chest, while in a thin one, the knife will quickly cut to bone. All eyes fixed on his hand as /gaugo, dwarfed by the great carcass, knelt to the breast. The first cut opened a pool of solid white in the black skin. The second and third cut widened and deepened the creamy white. Still no bone. It was pure fat; it must have been two inches thick.

"Hey /gau," I burst out, "that ox is loaded with fat. What's this about the ox being too thin to bother eating? Are you out of your mind?"

"Fat?" /gau shot back. "You call that fat? This wreck is thin, sick, dead!" And he broke out laughing. So did everyone else. They rolled on the ground, paralyzed with laughter. Everybody laughed except me; I was thinking.

I ran back to the tent and burst in just as Nancy was getting up. "Hey, the black ox. It's fat as hell! They were kidding about it being too thin to eat. It was a joke or something. A put-on. Everyone is really delighted with it."

"Some joke," my wife replied. "It was so funny that you were ready to pack up and leave /ai/ai."

If it had indeed been a joke, it had been an extraordinarily convincing one, and tinged, I thought, with more than a touch of malice, as many jokes are. Nevertheless, that it was a joke lifted my spirits considerably, and I returned to the butchering site where the shape of the ox was rapidly disappearing under the axes and knives of the butchers. The atmosphere had become festive. Grinning broadly, their arms covered with blood well past the elbow, men packed chunks of meat into the big cast-iron cooking pots, fifty pounds to the load, and muttered and chuckled all the while about the thinness and worthlessness of the animal and /ontah's poor judgment.

We danced and ate that ox two days and two nights; we cooked and distributed fourteen potfuls of meat and no one went home hungry and no fights broke out.

But the "joke" stayed in my mind. I had a growing feeling that something important had happened in my relationship with the Bushmen and that the clue lay in the meaning of the joke. Several days later, when most of the people had dispersed back to the bush camps, I raised the question with Hakekgose, a Tswana man who had grown up among the !Kung, married a !Kung girl, and who probably knew their culture better than any other non-Bushman.

"With us whites," I began, "Christmas is supposed to be the day of friendship and brotherly love. What I can't figure out is why the Bushmen went to such lengths to criticize and belittle the ox I had bought for the feast. The animal was perfectly good and their jokes and wisecracks practically ruined the holiday for me."

"So it really did bother you," said Hakekgose. "Well, that's the way they always talk. When I take my rifle and go hunting with them, if I miss, they laugh at me for the rest of the day. But even if I hit and bring one down, it's no better. To them, the kill is always too small or too old or too thin; and as we sit down on the kill site to cook and eat the liver, they keep grumbling, even with their mouths full of meat. They say things like, 'Oh, this is awful! What a worthless animal! Whatever made me think that this Tswana rascal could hunt!'"

"Is this the way outsiders are treated?" I asked.

"No, it is their custom; they talk that way to each other, too. Go and ask them."

/gaugo had been one of the most enthusiastic in making me feel bad about the merit of the Christmas ox. I sought him out first.

"Why did you tell me the black ox was worthless, when you could see that it was loaded with fat and meat?"

"It is our way," he said, smiling. "We always like to fool people about that. Say there is a Bushman who has been hunting. He must not come home and announce like a braggart, 'I have killed a big one in the bush!' He must first sit down in silence until I or someone else comes up to his fire and asks, 'What did you see today?' He replies quietly, 'Ah, I'm no good for hunting. I saw nothing at all [pause] just a little tiny one.' Then I smile to myself," /gaugo continued, "because I know he has killed something big."

In the morning we make up a party of four or five people to cut up and carry the meat back to the camp. When we arrive at the kill we examine it and cry out, 'You mean to say you have dragged us all the way out here in order to make us cart home your pile of bones? Oh, if I had known it was this thin I wouldn't have come.' Another one pipes up, 'People, to think I gave up a nice day in the shade for this. At home we may be hungry, but at least we have nice cool water to drink.' If the horns are big, someone says, 'Did you think that somehow you were going to boil down the horns for soup?'

"To all this you must respond in kind. 'I agree,' you say, 'this one is not worth the effort; let's just cook the liver for strength and leave the rest for the hyenas. It is not too late to hunt today and even a duiker or a steenbok would be better than this mess.'"

"Then you set to work nevertheless; butcher the animal, carry the meat back to the camp and everyone eats," /gaugo concluded.

Things were beginning to make sense. Next, I went to Tomazo. He corroborated /gaugo's story of the obligatory insults over a kill and added a few details of his own.

"But," I asked, "why insult a man after he has gone to all that trouble to track and kill an animal and when he is going to share the meat with you so that your children will have something to eat?"

"Arrogance," was his cryptic answer.

"Arrogance?"

"Yes, when a young man kills much meat he comes to think of himself as a chief or a big man, and he thinks of the rest of us as his servants or inferiors. We can't accept this. We refuse one who boasts, for someday his pride will make him kill somebody. So we always speak of his meat as worthless. This way we cool his heart and make him gentle."

"But why didn't you tell me this before?" I asked Tomazo with some heat.

"Because you never asked me," said Tomazo, echoing the refrain that has come to haunt every field ethnographer.

The pieces now fell into place. I had known for a long time that in situations of social conflict with Bushmen I held all the cards. I was the only source of tobacco in a thousand square miles, and I was not incapable of cutting an individual off for noncooperation. Though my boycott never lasted longer than a few days, it was an indication of my strength. People resented my presence at the water hole, yet simultaneously dreaded my leaving. In short I was a perfect target for the charge of arrogance and for the Bushman tactic of enforcing humility.

I had been taught an object lesson by the Bushmen; it had come from an unexpected corner and had hurt me in a vulnerable area. For the big black ox was to be the one totally generous, unstinting act of my year at /ai/ai and I was quite unprepared for the reaction I received.

As I read it, their message was this: There are no totally generous acts. All "acts" have an element of calculation. One black ox slaughtered at Christmas does not wipe out a year of careful manipulation of gifts given to serve your own ends. After all, to kill an animal and share the meat with people is really no more than the Bushmen do for each other every day and with far less fanfare.

In the end, I had to admire how the Bushmen had played out the farce—collectively straight-faced to the end. Curiously, the episode reminded me of the *Good Soldier Schweik* and his marvelous encounters with authority. Like Schweik, the Bushmen had retained a thoroughgoing skepticism of good intentions. Was it this independence of spirit, I wondered, that had kept them culturally viable in the face of generations of contact with more powerful societies, both black and white? The thought that the Bushmen were alive and well in the Kalahari was strangely comforting. Perhaps, armed with that independence and with their superb knowledge of their environment, they might yet survive the future.

✓●─ **Study** and **Review** on **myanthrolab.com**

Review Questions

1. What was the basis of the misunderstanding experienced by Lee when he gave an ox for the Christmas feast held by the !Kung?

2. Construct a model of cross-cultural misunderstanding, using the information presented by Lee in this article.

3. Why do you think the !Kung ridicule and denigrate people who have been successful hunters or who have provided them with a Christmas ox? Why do Americans expect people to be grateful to receive gifts?

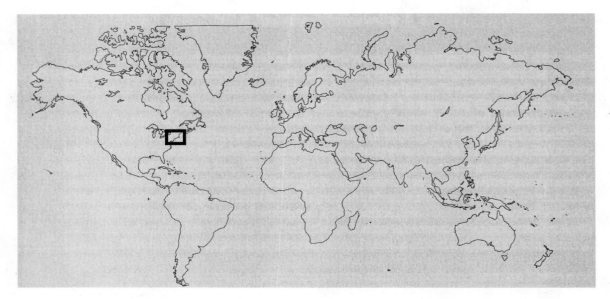

3

Fieldwork on Prostitution in the Era of AIDS

Claire E. Sterk

Many Americans associate social research with questionnaires, structured interviews, word association tests, and psychological experiments. They expect investigators to control the research setting and ask for specific information, such as age, income, place of residence, and opinions about work or national events. But ethnographic fieldwork is different. Cultural anthropologists may administer formal research instruments such as questionnaires, but largely their goal is to discover culture, to view the actions and knowledge of a group through the eyes of its members. In this sense, ethnographers are more like students; cultural informants are more like teachers. To implement ethnographic research, anthropologists must often become part of the worlds they seek to understand. They arrive as strangers, seek entrance into a group, meet and develop relationships of trust with informants, and wrestle with the ethical dilemmas that naturally occur when someone wants to delve into the lives of others.

These are the challenges Claire Sterk discusses in this selection. Working inside the United States, as many anthropologists do these days, she engaged in a long-term study of prostitutes in New York City and Atlanta. Her research required her to discover the places where her informants worked and hung out, introduce herself, develop rapport, and conduct open-ended interviews that permitted informants to teach her about their lives. During this process, she learned not to depend too much on contacts (gatekeepers) she met initially, that it was helpful to know something about respondents but to avoid an "expert" role, to refrain from expressing her own opinions about the culture and lives of her subjects, and

20

*to negotiate a variety of ethical questions. She ends by listing six themes that emerged from her ethnographic study.** *

―――――――――――――――――――――

Prostitution is a way of life. IT IS THE LIFE.

We make money for pimps who promise us love
*   and more,*

but if we don't produce, they shove us out the door.

We turn tricks who have sex-for-pay.

They don't care how many times we serve
*   every day.*

The Life is rough. The Life is tough.

We are put down, beaten up, and left for dead.

It hurts body and soul and messes with
*   a person's head.*

Many of us get high. Don't you understand it is
*   a way of getting by?*

The Life is rough. The Life is tough.

We are easy to blame because we are lame.

*   —Piper, 1987*[1]

((•— **Listen** to the **Chapter Audio** on **myanthrolab.com**

One night in March of 1987 business was slow. I was hanging out on a stroll with a group of street prostitutes. After a few hours in a nearby diner/coffee shop, we were kicked out. The waitress felt bad, but she needed our table for some new customers. Four of us decided to sit in my car until the rain stopped. While three of us chatted about life, Piper wrote this poem. As soon as she read it to us, the conversation shifted to more serious topics—pimps, customers, cops, the many hassles of being a prostitute, to name a few. We decided that if I ever finished a book about prostitution, the book would start with her poem.

This book is about the women who work in the lower echelons of the prostitution world. They worked in the streets and other public settings as well as crack houses. Some of these women viewed themselves primarily as prostitutes, and a number of them used drugs to cope with the pressures of the life. Others identified themselves more as drug users, and their main reason for having sex for money or other goods was to support their own drug use and often the habit of their male partner. A small group of women interviewed for this book had left prostitution, and most of them were still struggling to integrate their past experiences as prostitutes in their current lives.

The stories told by the women who participated in this project revealed how pimps, customers, and others such as police officers and social and health service

*From *Tricking and Tripping* by Claire E. Sterk (Putnam Valley, NY: Social Change Press, 2000), pp. 14–20. Reprinted by permission.

[1]The names of the women who were interviewed for this study, as well as those of their pimps and customers, have been replaced by pseudonyms to protect their privacy.

providers treated them as "fallen" women. However, their accounts also showed their strengths and the many strategies they developed to challenge these others. Circumstances, including their drug use, often forced them to sell sex, but they all resisted the notion that they might be selling themselves. Because they engaged in an illegal profession, these women had little status: their working conditions were poor, and their work was physically and mentally exhausting. Nevertheless, many women described the ways in which they gained a sense of control over their lives. For instance, they learned how to manipulate pimps, how to control the types of services and length of time bought by their customers, and how to select customers. While none of these schemes explicitly enhanced their working conditions, they did make the women feel stronger and better about themselves.

In this [article], I present prostitution from the point of view of the women themselves. To understand their current lives, it was necessary to learn how they got started in the life, the various processes involved in their continued prostitution careers, the link between prostitution and drug use, the women's interactions with their pimps and customers, and the impact of the AIDS epidemic and increasing violence on their experiences. I also examined the implications for women. Although my goal was to present the women's thoughts, feelings, and actions in their own words, the final text is a sociological monograph compiled by me as the researcher. . . .

The Sample

. . . The research was conducted during the last ten years in the New York City and Atlanta metropolitan areas. One main data source was participant observation on streets, in hotels and other settings known for prostitution activity, and in drug-use settings, especially those that allowed sex-for-drug exchanges. Another data source was in-depth, life-history interviews with 180 women ranging in age from 18 to 59 years, with an average age of 34. One in two women was African-American and one in three white; the remaining women were Latina. Three in four had completed high school, and among them almost two-thirds had one or more years of additional educational training. Thirty women had graduated from college.

Forty women worked as street prostitutes and did not use drugs. On average, they had been prostitutes for 11 years. Forty women began using drugs an average of three years after they began working as prostitutes, and the average time they had worked as prostitutes was nine years. Forty women used drugs an average of five years before they became prostitutes, and on the average they had worked as prostitutes for eight years. Another forty women began smoking crack and exchanging sex for crack almost simultaneously, with an average of four years in the life. Twenty women who were interviewed were ex-prostitutes.

Comments on Methodology

When I tell people about my research, the most frequent question I am asked is how I gained access to the women rather than what I learned from the research. For many, prostitution is an unusual topic of conversation, and many people have expressed surprise that I, as a woman, conducted the research. During my research some customers indeed thought I was a working woman, a fact that almost always amuses those who hear about my work. However, few people want to hear stories about the women's struggles and sadness. Sometimes they ask questions about the reasons why women become prostitutes. Most of the time, they are surprised when I tell them that the prostitutes as well as their customers represent all layers of society. Before presenting the findings, it seems important to discuss the research process, including gaining access to the women, developing relationships, interviewing, and then leaving the field.

Locating Prostitutes and Gaining Entree

One of the first challenges I faced was to identify locations where street prostitution took place. Many of these women worked on strolls, streets where prostitution activity is concentrated, or in hotels known for prostitution activity. Others, such as the crack prostitutes, worked in less public settings such as a crack house that might be someone's apartment.

I often learned of well-known public places from professional experts, such as law enforcement officials and health care providers at emergency rooms and sexually transmitted disease clinics. I gained other insights from lay experts, including taxi drivers, bartenders, and community representatives such as members of neighborhood associations. The contacts universally mentioned some strolls as the places where many women worked, where the local police focused attention, or where residents had organized protests against prostitution in their neighborhoods.

As I began visiting various locales, I continued to learn about new settings. In one sense, I was developing ethnographic maps of street prostitution. After several visits to a specific area, I also was able to expand these maps by adding information about the general atmosphere on the stroll, general characteristics of the various people present, the ways in which the women and customers connected, and the overall flow of action. In addition, my visits allowed the regular actors to notice me.

I soon learned that being an unknown woman in an area known for prostitution may cause many people to notice you, even stare at you, but it fails to yield many verbal interactions. Most of the time when I tried to make eye contact with one of the women, she quickly averted her eyes. Pimps, on the other hand, would stare at me straight on and I ended up being the one to look away. Customers would stop, blow their horn, or wave me over, frequently yelling obscenities when I ignored them. I realized that gaining entree into the prostitution world was not going to be as easy as I imagined it. Although I lacked such training in any of my qualitative methods classes, I decided to move slowly and not force any interaction. The most I said during the initial weeks in a new area was limited to "How are you" or "Hi." This strategy paid off during my first visits to one of the strolls in Brooklyn, New York. After several appearances, one of the women walked up to me and sarcastically asked if I was looking for something. She caught me off guard, and all the answers I had practiced did not seem to make sense. I mumbled something about just wanting to walk around. She did not like my answer, but she did like my accent. We ended up talking about the latter and she was especially excited when I told her I came from Amsterdam. One of her friends had gone to Europe with her boyfriend, who was in the military. She understood from her that prostitution and drugs were legal in the Netherlands. While explaining to her that some of her friend's impressions were incorrect, I was able to show off some of my knowledge about prostitution. I mentioned that I was interested in prostitution and wanted to write a book about it.

Despite the fascination with my background and intentions, the prostitute immediately put me through a Streetwalker 101 test, and apparently I passed. She told me to make sure to come back. By the time I left, I not only had my first conversation but also my first connection to the scene. Variations of this entry process occurred on the other strolls. The main lesson I learned in these early efforts was the importance of having some knowledge of the lives of the people I wanted to study, while at the same time refraining from presenting myself as an expert.

Qualitative researchers often refer to their initial connections as gatekeepers and key respondents. Throughout my fieldwork I learned that some key respondents are important in providing initial access, but they become less central as the research evolves. For example, one of the women who introduced me to her lover, who was also her pimp, was arrested and disappeared for months. Another entered drug treatment soon after she facilitated my access. Other key respondents provided access to only a segment of the players on a scene. For example, if a woman worked for a pimp, [she] was unlikely . . . to introduce me to women working for another pimp. On one stroll my initial contact was with a pimp whom nobody liked. By associating with him, I almost lost the opportunity to meet other pimps. Some key respondents were less connected than promised—for example, some of the women who worked the street to support their drug habit. Often their connections were more frequently with drug users and less so with prostitutes.

Key respondents tend to be individuals central to the local scene, such as, in this case, pimps and the more senior prostitutes. Their function as gatekeepers often is to protect the scene and to screen outsiders. Many times I had to prove that I was not an undercover police officer or a woman with ambitions to become a streetwalker. While I thought I had gained entree, I quickly learned that many insiders subsequently wondered about my motives and approached me with suspicion and distrust.

Another lesson involved the need to proceed cautiously with self-nominated key respondents. For example, one of the women presented herself as knowing everyone on the stroll. While she did know everyone, she was not a central figure. On the contrary, the other prostitutes viewed her as a failed streetwalker whose drug use caused her to act unprofessionally. By associating with me, she hoped to regain some of her status. For me, however, it meant limited access to the other women because I affiliated myself with a woman who was marginal to the scene. On another occasion, my main key respondent was a man who claimed to own three crack houses in the neighborhood. However, he had a negative reputation, and people accused him of cheating on others. My initial alliance with him delayed, and almost blocked, my access to others in the neighborhood. He intentionally tried to keep me from others on the scene, not because he would gain something from that transaction but because it made him feel powerful. When I told him I was going to hang out with some of the other people, he threatened me until one of the other dealers stepped in and told him to stay away. The two of them argued back and forth, and finally I was free to go. Fortunately, the dealer who had spoken up for me was much more central and positively associated with the local scene. Finally, I am unsure if I would have had success in gaining entrance to the scene had I not been a woman.

Developing Relationships and Trust

The processes involved in developing relationships in research situations amplify those involved in developing relationships in general. Both parties need to get to know each other, become aware and accepting of each other's roles, and engage in a reciprocal relationship. Being supportive and providing practical assistance were the most visible and direct ways for me as the researcher to develop a relationship. Throughout the years, I have given countless rides, provided child care on numerous occasions, bought groceries, and listened for hours to stories that were unrelated to my initial research questions. Gradually, my role allowed me to become part of these women's lives and to build rapport with many of them.

Over time, many women also realized that I was uninterested in being a prostitute and that I genuinely was interested in learning as much as possible about their lives. Many felt flattered that someone wanted to learn from them and that they had knowledge to offer. Allowing women to tell their stories and engaging in a dialogue with them probably were the single most important techniques that allowed me to develop relationships with them. Had I only wanted to focus on the questions I had in mind, developing such relationships might have been more difficult.

At times, I was able to get to know a woman only after her pimp endorsed our contact. One of my scariest experiences occurred before I knew to work through the pimps, and one such man had some of his friends follow me on my way home one night. I will never know what plans they had in mind for me because I fortunately was able to escape with only a few bruises. Over a year later, the woman acknowledged that her pimp had gotten upset and told her he was going to teach me a lesson.

On other occasions, I first needed to be screened by owners and managers of crack houses before the research could continue. Interestingly, screenings always were done by a man even if the person who vouched for me was a man himself. While the women also were cautious, the ways in which they checked me out tended to be much more subtle. For example, one of them would tell me a story, indicating that it was a secret about another person on the stroll. Although I failed to realize this at the time, my field notes revealed that frequently after such a conversation, others would ask me questions about related topics. One woman later acknowledged that putting out such stories was a test to see if I would keep information confidential.

Learning more about the women and gaining a better understanding of their lives also raised many ethical questions. No textbook told me how to handle situations in which a pimp abused a woman, a customer forced a woman to engage in unwanted sex acts, a customer requested unprotected sex from a woman who knew she was HIV infected, or a boyfriend had unrealistic expectations regarding a woman's earnings to support his drug habit. I failed to know the proper response when asked to engage in illegal activities such as holding drugs or money a woman had stolen from a customer. In general, my response was to explain that I was there as a researcher. During those occasions when pressures became too severe, I decided to leave a scene. For example, I never returned to certain crack houses because pimps there continued to ask me to consider working for them.

Over time, I was fortunate to develop relationships with people who "watched my back." One pimp in particular intervened if he perceived other pimps, customers, or passersby harassing me. He also was the one who gave me my street name: Whitie (indicating my racial background) or Ms. Whitie for those who disrespected me. While this was my first street name, I subsequently had others. Being given a street name was a symbolic gesture of acceptance. Gradually, I developed an identity that allowed me to be both an insider and an outsider. While hanging out on the strolls and other gathering places, including crack houses, I had to deal with some of the same uncomfortable conditions as the prostitutes, such as cold or warm weather, lack of access to a rest room, refusals from owners for me to patronize a restaurant, and of course, harassment by customers and the police.

I participated in many informal conversations. Unless pushed to do so, I seldom divulged my opinions. I was more open with my feelings about situations and showed empathy. I learned quickly that providing an opinion can backfire. I agreed that one of the women was struggling a lot and stated that I felt sorry for her. While I meant to indicate my genuine concern for her, she heard that I felt sorry for her because she was a failure. When she finally, after several weeks, talked with me again, I was able to explain to her that I was not judging her, but rather felt concerned for her. She remained cynical and many times asked me for favors to make up for my mistake. It took me months before I felt comfortable telling her that I felt I had done enough and that it was time to let go. However, if she was not ready, she needed to know that I would no longer go along. This was one of many occasions when I learned that although I wanted to facilitate my work as a researcher, that I wanted people to like and trust me, I also needed to set boundaries.

Rainy and slow nights often provided good opportunities for me to participate in conversations with groups of women. Popular topics included how to work safely, what to do about condom use, how to make more money. I often served as a health educator and a supplier of condoms, gels, vaginal douches, and other feminine products. Many women were very worried about the AIDS epidemic. However, they also were worried about how to use a condom when a customer refused to do so. They worried particularly about condom use when they needed money badly and, consequently, did not want to propose that the customer use one for fear of rejection. While some women became experts at "making" their customers use a condom—for example, by hiding it in their mouth prior to beginning oral sex—others would carry condoms to please me but never pull one out. If a woman was HIV positive and I knew she failed to use a condom, I faced the ethical dilemma of challenging her or staying out of it.

Developing trusting relationships with crack prostitutes was more difficult. Crack houses were not the right environment for informal conversations. Typically, the atmosphere was tense and everyone was suspicious of each other. The best times to talk with these women were when we bought groceries together, when I helped them clean their homes, or when we shared a meal. Often the women were very different when they were not high than they were when they were high or craving crack. In my conversations with them, I learned that while I might have observed their actions the night before, they themselves might not remember them. Once I realized this, I would be very careful to omit any detail unless I knew that the woman herself did remember the event.

In-Depth Interviews

All interviews were conducted in a private setting, including women's residences, my car or my office, a restaurant of the women's choice, or any other setting the women selected. I did not begin conducting official interviews until I developed relationships with the women. Acquiring written informed consent prior to the interview was problematic. It made me feel awkward. Here I was asking the women to sign a form after they had begun to trust me. However, often I felt more upset about this technicality than the women themselves. As soon as they realized that the form was something the university required, they seemed to understand. Often they laughed about the official statements, and some asked if I was sure the form was to protect them and not the school. None of the women refused to sign the consent form, although some refused to sign it right away and asked to be interviewed later.

In some instances the consent procedures caused the women to expect a formal interview. Some of them were disappointed when they saw I only had a few structured questions about demographic characteristics, followed by a long list of open-ended questions. When this disappointment occurred, I reminded the women that I wanted to learn from them and that the best way to do so was by engaging in a dialogue rather than interrogating them. Only by letting the women identify their salient issues and the topics they wanted to address was I able to gain an insider's perspective. By being a careful listener and probing for additional information and explanation, I as the interviewer, together with the women, was able to uncover the complexities of their lives. In addition, the nature of the interview allowed me to ask questions about contradictions in a woman's story. For example, sometimes a woman would say that she always used a condom. However, later on in the conversation she would indicate that if she needed drugs she would never use one. By asking her to elaborate on this, I was able to begin developing insights into condom use by type of partner, type of sex acts, and social context.

The interviewer becomes much more a part of the interview when the conversations are in-depth than when a structured questionnaire is used. Because I was so integral to the process, the way the women viewed me may have biased their answers. On the one hand, this bias might be reduced because of the extent to which both parties already knew each other; on the other, a woman might fail to give her true opinion and reveal her actions if she knew that these went against the interviewer's opinion. I suspected that some women played down the ways in which their pimps manipulated them once they knew that I was not too fond of these men. However, some might have taken more time to explain the relationship with their pimp in order to "correct" my image.

My background, so different from that of these women, most likely affected the nature of the interviews. I occupied a higher socioeconomic status. I had a place to live and a job. In contrast to the nonwhite women, I came from a different racial background. While I don't know to what extent these differences played a role, I acknowledge that they must have had some effect on this research.

Leaving the Field

Leaving the field was not something that occurred after completion of the fieldwork, but an event that took place daily. Although I sometimes stayed on the strolls all night or hung out for several days, I always had a home to return to. I had a house with electricity, a warm shower, a comfortable bed, and a kitchen. My house sat on a street where I had no fear of being shot on my way there and where I did not find condoms or syringes on my doorstep.

During several stages of the study, I had access to a car, which I used to give the women rides or to run errands together. However, I will never forget the cold night when everyone on the street was freezing, and I left to go home. I turned up the heat in my car, and tears streamed down my cheeks. I appreciated the heat, but I felt more guilty about that luxury than ever before. I truly felt like an outsider, or maybe even more appropriate, a betrayer.

Throughout the years of fieldwork, there were a number of times when I left the scene temporarily. For example, when so many people were dying from AIDS, I was unable to ignore the devastating impact of this disease. I needed an emotional break.

Physically removing myself from the scene was common when I experienced difficulty remaining objective. Once I became too involved in a woman's life and almost adopted her and her family. Another time I felt a true hatred for a crack house owner and was unable to adhere to the rules of courteous interactions. Still another time, I got angry with a woman whose steady partner was HIV positive when she failed to ask him to use a condom when they had sex.

I also took temporary breaks from a particular scene by shifting settings and neighborhoods. For example, I would invest most of my time in women from a particular crack house for several weeks. Then I would shift to spending more time on one of the strolls, while making shorter and less frequent visits to the crack house. By shifting scenes, I was able to tell people why I was leaving and to remind all of us of my researcher role.

While I focused on leaving the field, I became interested in women who had left the life. It seemed important to have an understanding of their past and current circumstances. I knew some of them from the days when they were working, but identifying others was a challenge. There was no gathering place for ex-prostitutes. Informal networking, advertisements in local newspapers, and local clinics and community settings allowed me to reach twenty of these women. Conducting interviews with them later in the data collection process prepared me to ask specific questions. I realized that I had learned enough about the life to know what to ask. Interviewing ex-prostitutes also prepared me for moving from the fieldwork to writing.

It is hard to determine exactly when I left the field. It seems like a process that never ends. Although I was more physically removed from the scene, I continued to be involved while analyzing the data and writing this book. I also created opportunities to go back, for example, by asking women to give me feedback on parts of the manuscript or at times when I experienced writer's block and my car seemed to automatically steer itself to one of the strolls. I also have developed other research projects in some of the same communities. For example, both a project on intergenerational drug use and a gender-specific intervention project to help women remain HIV negative have brought me back to the same population. Some of the women have become key respondents in these new projects, while others now are members of a research team. For example, Beth, one of the women who has left prostitution, works as an outreach worker on another project.

Six Themes in the Ethnography of Prostitution

The main intention of my work is to provide the reader with a perspective on street prostitution from the point of view of the women themselves. There are six fundamental aspects of the women's lives as prostitutes that must be considered. The first concerns the women's own explanations for their involvement in prostitution and their descriptions of the various circumstances that led them to become prostitutes. Their stories include justifications such as traumatic past experiences, especially sexual abuse, the lack of love they experienced as children, pressures by friends and pimps, the need for drugs, and most prominently, the economic forces that pushed them into the life. A number of women describe these justifications as excuses, as reflective explanations they have developed after becoming a prostitute.

The women describe the nature of their initial experiences, which often involved alienation from those outside the life. They also show the differences in the processes between women who work as prostitutes and use drugs and women who do not use drugs.

Although all these women work either on the street or in drug-use settings, their lives do differ. My second theme is a typology that captures these differences, looking at the women's prostitution versus drug-use identities. The typology distinguishes among (a) streetwalkers, women who work strolls and who do not use drugs; (b) hooked prostitutes, women who identify themselves mainly as prostitutes but who upon their entrance into the life also began using drugs; (c) prostituting addicts, women who view themselves mainly as drug users and who became prostitutes to support their drug habit; and (d) crack prostitutes, women who trade sex for crack.

This typology explains the differences in the women's strategies for soliciting customers, their screening of customers, pricing of sex acts, and bargaining for services. For example, the streetwalkers have the most bargaining power, while such power appears to be lacking among the crack prostitutes.

Few prostitutes work in a vacuum. The third theme is the role of pimps, a label that most women dislike and for which they prefer to substitute "old man" or "boyfriend." Among the pimps, one finds entrepreneur lovers, men who mainly employ streetwalkers and hooked prostitutes and sometimes prostituting addicts. Entrepreneur lovers engage in the life for business reasons. They treat the women as their employees or their property and view them primarily as an economic commodity. The more successful a woman is in earning them money, the more difficult it is for that woman to leave her entrepreneur pimp.

Most prostituting addicts and some hooked prostitutes work for a lover pimp, a man who is their steady partner but who also lives off their earnings. Typically, such pimps employ only one woman. The dynamics in the relationship between a prostitute and her lover pimp become more complex when both partners use drugs. Drugs often become the glue of the relationship.

For many crack prostitutes, their crack addiction serves as a pimp. Few plan to exchange sex for crack when they first begin using; often several weeks or months pass before a woman who barters sex for crack realizes that she is a prostitute.

Historically, society has blamed prostitutes for introducing sexually transmitted diseases into the general population. Similarly, it makes them scapegoats for the spread of HIV/AIDS. Yet their pimps and customers are not held accountable. The fourth theme in the anthropological study of prostitution is the impact of the AIDS epidemic on the women's lives. Although most are knowledgeable about HIV risk behaviors and the ways to reduce their risk, many misconceptions exist. The women describe the complexities of condom use, especially with steady partners but also with paying customers. Many women have mixed feelings about HIV testing, wondering how to cope with a positive test result while no cure is available. A few of the women already knew their HIV-infected status, and the discussion touches on their dilemmas as well.

The fifth theme is the violence and abuse that make common appearances in the women's lives. An ethnography of prostitution must allow the women to describe violence in their neighborhoods as well as violence in prostitution and drug-use settings. The most common violence they encounter is from customers. These men often assume that because they pay for sex they buy a woman. Apparently, casual customers pose more of a danger than those who are regulars. The types of abuse the women encounter are emotional, physical, and sexual. In addition to customers, pimps and boyfriends abuse the women. Finally, the women discuss harassment by law enforcement officers.

When I talked with the women, it often seemed that there were no opportunities to escape from the life. Yet the sixth and final theme must be the escape from prostitution. Women who have left prostitution can describe the process of their exit from prostitution. As ex-prostitutes they struggle with the stigma of their past, the challenges of developing a new identity, and the impact of their past on current intimate relationships. Those who were also drug users often view themselves as ex-prostitutes and recovering addicts, a perspective that seems to create a role conflict. Overall, most ex-prostitutes find that their past follows them like a bad hangover.

✓●┤**Study** and **Review** on **myanthrolab.com**

Review Questions

1. Based on reading this selection, how is ethnographic research different from other social science approaches to research?

2. What can ethnographic research reveal that other forms of research cannot? What can the use of questionnaires and observational experiments reveal about people that ethnographic research might miss?

3. What were some of the techniques Sterk used to enter the field, conduct her research, and leave the field? What problems did she face?

4. What advice does Sterk have for aspiring ethnographers?

5. What are some of the ethical issues faced by anthropologists when they conduct ethnographic research?

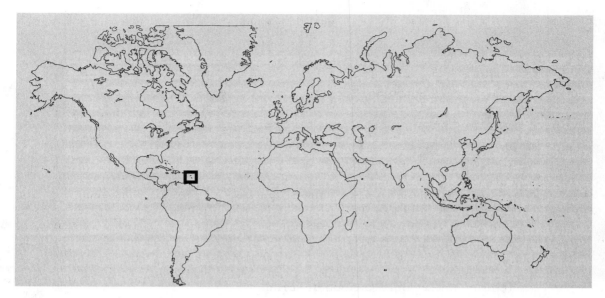

4

Nice Girls Don't Talk to Rastas

George Gmelch

We all are subject to naive realism. It's only natural that the cultural knowledge we learn as we grow up and live in our society shapes the way we see the world and behave in it. It is normal for us to accept our cultural perspective as an accurate portrayal of the way the world really is. Although our naive realism usually goes unnoticed as we function inside our own society, it becomes more obvious when we attempt to communicate with outsiders who possess a different cultural view of reality. Anthropologists attempt to consciously control their own naive realism, but even they sometimes must learn about their own naiveté by making mistakes when they do fieldwork in foreign settings.

This article by George Gmelch, updated for the fifteenth edition of Conformity and Conflict, describes a case of cross-cultural misunderstanding involving an American student living in a Barbadian village as part of a study abroad program. She unwittingly assumes that villagers are a homogeneous group of which Rastafarians (a religious sect) are members. By interacting with them, she finds herself shunned by everyone. Her American vision of equality causes her to assume that villagers accepted everyone as equal. She overlooks the existence of class distinctions in this small community characterized by face-to-face relationships. The article includes a post-script where the student describes the impact of this experience on her life over time.*

---

*From George Gmelch, "Nice Girls Don't Talk to Rastas." Used by permission of George Gmelch.

For the past thirty years I have been taking American undergraduates to the field on anthropology training programs in Ireland, Tasmania, and Barbados. It's been no surprise that when my students—young and inexperienced—venture into cultures different from their own they sometimes violate local norms. Professional anthropologists are not immune from making such mistakes; in fact there is a small but lively literature about fieldwork in which anthropologists recount their cultural blunders and the revealing consequences that followed.[1]

In this essay I describe the predicament of a female American student, Hanna, living in a rural village on the Caribbean island of Barbados. The trouble, which stems from her associating with people—Rastafarians—her community regards as undesirables, speaks to common shortcomings of American students living abroad for the first time. Namely, their failure to understand social class and their assumption that others see the world the same way they do—what anthropologists call *naïve realism*. I will return to these points later, but first Hanna's story.

* *

"George, telephoooone," called out my Barbadian neighbor from the house next door early one morning. "It's Hanna, your student, she say it important." Hanna's voice was full of emotion. "I'm in trouble and I really need to talk to you." I told her to start walking toward Josey Hill and that I would set out toward her village, and that we would meet at the pasture where many families grazed cattle and sheep and boys played cricket and soccer.

When I arrived Hanna—tall, green eyed, and pretty—was already there. "They've turned against me. When I walk by, they turn their heads the other way. Someone in the rum shop called me the 'devil's child.'"

Hanna, from a college town in upstate New York where her father taught theater and her mother taught English, had made many friends in her village. In fact, she was enjoying her time in Freeman Hill so much that she fantasized about settling there and teaching school at St. Margaret's, the small elementary school where she had been doing research.[2]

Slowly, the story emerged. Hanna revealed that she had been seeing a Rastafarian named Joseph, and that some villagers had seen her walking with him into the hills beyond the village. In a rugged area an hour's walk down the coast from Freeman Hill a small group of Rastas—orthodox Rastas who wore no clothes and subsisted off the land—lived in caves. That morning Hanna's homestay mother, Thelma, had entered the bedroom, shut the door tightly, and breathing hard told Hanna that people in the village were saying that she was smoking marijuana and bathing naked with the Rastas. Some thought she must be a drug addict.

Rastafari is a movement and way of life more than an organized religion. It was inspired by the teachings of Marcus Garvey, the Jamaican-born founder of the Universal Negro Improvement Association, in the 1920s and 1930s. Garvey denounced the colonial mentality that had taught blacks to be contemptuous of their African heritage; he advocated self-reliance for blacks and a "back to Africa" consciousness. From Jamaica, the Rastafari movement spread throughout the Caribbean, into parts

---

[1]See, for example, Barbara Anderson, *First Fieldwork: The Misadventures of an Anthropologist*, and Philip DeVita, *The Naked Anthropologist: Tales from Around the World*.

[2]The name of the student, Hanna, and the Rasta, Joseph, are real; the names of all other persons and places are pseudonyms.

of Africa, the US, England and beyond. Rastafari arrived in Barbados in the 1970s and in urban areas gained many followers among local black youths, who saw it as an extension of their adolescent rebellion from school and parental authority, as well as among some mainstream artists, academics, musicians, and even sports figures.

The Rastas' long dreadlocks, green, gold, and red colors, distinctive caps, and reggae music became common on the streets of Barbados's capital city of Bridgetown. By the 1990s, a colony of thirty orthodox Rastas who rejected all the trappings of Western society (which they call "Babylon"), even clothes, had begun living in caves just down the coast from Hanna's village. Although the subject of considerable local comment, most of the nearby villagers knew very little about them or their beliefs.

"I had no idea people would react this way," said Hanna defensively, wiping tears from her cheeks. "Joseph said he was a 'bush doctor.' I mean what is the harm? He's a nice guy, he wouldn't harm anyone. Aren't anthropologists supposed to be interested in everyone? Anthropologists don't ignore people just because some people don't like them. Right?"

Hanna assured me that she hadn't gone naked with the Rastas or become sexually involved. At first, I thought this an unnecessary declaration, but then I recalled the talk my anthropologist wife, Sharon, had with the female students about problems created by romantic involvements with local men. In the past, such liaisons had upset the students' homestay families and damaged the students' reputations and rapport, as often the men involved had been considered disreputable characters—beach bums—who were beneath the social status of the host families.

With much anguish, Hanna recounted that Thelma wanted her to move out, to leave the village. Hanna had only three weeks left in Barbados. There wasn't time for her to start over somewhere else, nor did I know of another family who had space to take her in. I told her to go back to the village and that I would call on her that evening. When I got home I looked through my copy of Hanna's field notes (the students turned in a copy of their notes every week). A reference to Rastas took on new meaning:

> [February 21] I went to Janice's primary school today and on the way out I started talking to a Rastaish looking dude with a leather Crocodile Dundee hat on just standing on the roadside. I was aware that I could be seen by the children on the playground. When Janice got home, she reprimanded me for talking to him. Janice: "We don't live the way Rastas do. It's not right just to go and talk to anyone you feel like. That man is a killer. Once you left all the children said, 'Look, he is going to carry her away into the hills and kill her.' I am serious. Even teacher told me to tell you not to talk to him. And teachers know about these things."

Later, Hanna described her encounters with the Rastas in more detail. After walking home from the school yard with Joseph, she had agreed to meet him the following week at the small village shop. It wasn't a good choice, as the shop is located where the village's three roads meet, and its veranda is a social gathering place. There wasn't a more conspicuous place in all of Freeman Hill. A little discretion might have prevented her liaisons with Joseph from ever being known. Hanna described what happened in her journal:

> When I saw Joseph coming down the road, I hopped off the porch to go meet him, and every person within the viewing distance did a double take. On the days that I've spent with Joseph, we meet at ten, arrive at his place in the later morning, and usually begin cooking right away. His single meal a day usually takes three hours to prepare, so he likes to get it started as soon as possible so he can relax once it gets dark. His place is so simple

and relaxing. It's set up on a ridge, and well hidden. You ascend a steep rock incline and step onto a ledge with a panoramic view of the Atlantic. On one side is a looming two story rock with an opening in the center; this is Joseph's bedroom. You step down in a dark, cool, homey cave, about 10 by 20 feet with smooth rocks on the floor, a slender little bed on one side, and a natural stone bench coming out of the wall. Joseph's "dresser" is a jutting piece of rock where he rests his Bible, a broken fragment of a mirror, and his shell necklace. He said it took three months process of burning and chipping away at the floor and walls of his cave to make the place livable. "Yeah, it was rough," he said, "but I want my place to be just right when I have a wife come live with me. Because no woman is going to want to come live in a cave she can't stand up in, right?" He grinned.

My usual response to the occasional problems that students unwittingly create is to visit the parties involved—first, to better understand the issue and then try to resolve the misunderstanding by explaining each side's custom to the other. I hoped Hanna's situation would be no different, although it involved a large number of people and I didn't know much about the villagers' relationship with the local Rastas. I was friendly with two respected elders in Freeman Hill, so I decided to go to them for advice. I went first to Ezra Cumberbatch a Pentecostal preacher whose daughters had befriended Hanna; and then to Randall Trotman, a return migrant who had recently resettled in Barbados after a dozen years in England—he had the perspective that comes with having lived in another society.

Reverend Cumberbatch told me that the Rastas Hanna had been visiting were well known to the village, and that most people, especially the old ones, viewed them as lazy layabouts, who smoked marijuana and stole fruit and vegetables from their gardens. I remembered that one of my neighbors in Josey Hill had cut down his banana tree after Rastas had repeatedly taken the fruit, or so he claimed. He said he'd rather not have the tree than have Rastas around his house.

Randall Trotman had a more balanced view. "Some are good and some are bad. Some of them steal your coconuts and aloe, but others are school teachers and craftsman and good citizens." He explained how some Barbadians, especially in town, respected them for their knowledge of plants and herbs, for their vegetarianism and healthy lifestyle, and their rejection of materialism and the false values of "Babylon" (the outside world). But he also noted that in rural places like Freeman Hill all Rastas were tarred with the same brush—not unlike the attitudes toward Muslims among some Americans after 9/11. Before I left the Trotman home, I asked about a rumored crime I had heard earlier, but had found villagers unwilling to say much about it. Apparently a villager, furious about the theft of his crops (which could have been taken by monkeys as easily as Rastas), had put poison in some cucumbers. Randall said two Rastas had died and that the police investigation was inconclusive. In the end, both preacher and returnee were sympathetic to Hanna's plight, but neither had any practical advice on what she could do to repair her reputation and save her field work.

Thinking I should meet the Rastas themselves, I set out to visit them. With the vaguest of directions, I hiked down the steep and rugged coastline looking for the area the Rastas called "Creation." I lost the trail and worked my way through the dense brush on a steep hillside that rose directly from the sea. Remembering Hanna's account, I climbed up several steep inclines to the openings in the rock wall looking for the Rastas' caves. The erosion caused by water trickling down through the coral capstone which overlays nearly all of Barbados had created dozens of large caves. The view was magnificent, down the green cliffs and out across the blue Atlantic.

I called out several times but nothing came back. The place was eerily quiet, and I began to question what I was doing there. What was I going to say if I did find them?

That I was there to check them out for the safety of my student? That they shouldn't let my student go naked or smoke marijuana with them? Feeling that I was intruding in their living space, I turned and trekked for home, and then to Hanna's homestay.

Thelma, Hanna's homestay mother, listened patiently to my explanations of what anthropologists do and of Hanna's naiveté. I told Thelma that students sometimes innocently violate local norms, but that these misunderstandings were usually easily cleared up and that in the end no one was the worse for it. She responded that my students would all be returning to the United States, leaving behind whatever ill will they created, and that she was the one that would be living in Freeman Hill for the rest of her life. "I don't want my children exposed to these Rastas," she said, adding that she would be implicated in the minds of many villagers if Hanna's "friends" brought harm to anyone.

After sincere assurances from Hanna that she would stay away from the Rastas, Thelma agreed to let her stay. Although Hanna remained, the villagers had little to do with her during her last weeks there. "It's like I have something contagious and they don't want to get too close to me," she wrote. "The road workers who verbally harassed me at the beginning of my stay but finally stopped after I made friends in the village, have now begun to treat me, once again, as a sexual object." To do successful field research anthropologists must have good rapport with local people; if that is damaged data collection can be impossible. In an assessment of her field experience, Hanna concluded, "I learned the power of a societal norm. Nice girls don't talk to Rastas. Exceptions: none." As I began to reflect on Hanna's experience, it became clear that she had not fully appreciated social class distinctions (and the prejudices that go with them) in Barbadian society or the communal nature of village life. Compared to their English counterparts, American students generally have little understanding of social class (they perceive the great majority of their fellow Americans as all belonging to the middle-class). Similarly, even after weeks in the field, my students typically view the inhabitants of their villages as being fairly homogeneous–all of the same social class. They are not. The students only gradually become aware of class differences from comments by their homestay families about other villagers. It takes time for students to understand the workings of life in a small-scale, face-to-face society where people pay close attention to the actions of neighbors, where gossip is recreation, and where, with the slightest provocation, rumor can affect a family's reputation. And like Hanna, sometimes they also learn about class and status by making mistakes— by violating norms concerning relationships between different categories of people. I doubted that the English university students I once taught, steeped in the meaning of class, would have made the same mistake as Hanna.

But it was not just a lack of awareness; rather, American students often operate on an assumption of personal autonomy. That is, if they can see "the truth" in a situation or view their actions as harmless, then they feel entitled to act without regard for what others might think. Such an attitude sometimes stems more from what anthropologists call *naïve realism*, the mistaken view that deep down everyone perceives the world in basically the same way. And why shouldn't they think this way. Most were raised in fairly homogeneous suburbs and on college campuses where they typically have little contact with the international students, or even minorities, who might challenge their assumptions. For students like Hanna, Barbados is the first time they have ever lived in another culture, and they arrive with their naïve realism fairly intact. The words Hanna used in defense of her actions were revealing, "Joseph wouldn't harm anyone. Rastas are just spiritual people, they don't want anything to do with modern society, they just want to be left alone to do their own thing. Why can't they [the villagers] see that?" Typically it takes my students some weeks before they begin to appreciate that they, like the Rastas, simply cannot always "do their own thing," at least not without repercussions.

I now use Hanna's story as a lesson for other field school students: communities are never as homogeneous as they seem; be sensitive to class differences and local prejudices; think about how your actions and relationships could be viewed by others because not everybody sees the world the way you do.[3]

Postscript

In 2013 I contacted Hanna to say hello but equally curious what, years later, she remembered of her experience in Barbados. "At the time the blow-up happened," she said in our phone conversation and a later e-mail, "The only thing I cared about was what the villagers thought, how my homestay mother felt, and how it might affect you [the field program], but now that time has gone by and I've learned that no long term damage was done, I realize that meeting and getting to know Joseph was the most important thing that happened to me. I don't regret it. You see, having been invited into Joseph's world was mind blowing. His simple life—waking up every day to the sunrise, bathing in a beautiful waterfall, gathering fresh vegetables and herbs that he grew in his hillside garden, cooking on an outdoor fire, walking on the seashore, praying, reading his Bible, and meditating—for me was to encounter the polar opposite of what I knew at the time. In the crazy, hectic world we live in, where we no longer seem to have time for anything, Joseph had time for everything: time for conversation, time for singing, time for deep thought, time for appreciating nature and time for praising his God.

In the beginning, I only meant to interview Joseph, but then when I discovered how fascinating it all was, he became the focus of my research. In my studying his way of life, we formed a close bond of friendship. But it wasn't like what people imagined; whenever in his company, I was either tape recording or taking notes, and although I was, admittedly, naive, I tried never to conduct myself in a way that was incongruent with my goals as a student anthropologist. For the record, I can assure you that nothing inappropriate ever happened between us. I still find it sad that because Joseph's lifestyle was unorthodox, because he was "different," he was deemed threatening to people in my village . . . I learned so much about Bajan culture that I could never have learned in any other way. I saw firsthand the prejudice and discrimination that the Rastas dealt with all the time. And I think it is that experience that has made me very open-minded toward people of different cultures and different religions today."

✓● ⎯[**Study** and **Review** on **myanthrolab.com**

Review Questions

1. What does the term *naive realism* mean? Give some examples from your own experience.

2. What behavior by an American study abroad student offended the Barbadian villagers she lived with? Why was she surprised by their reaction?

3. What did George Gmelch do to mediate the cross-cultural misunderstanding? How successful was it?

4. What part does social class play in this event?

5. Why is this story a good example of naïve realism?

[3]Thelma, Hanna's homestay mother, has since housed several other students.

PART TWO

LANGUAGE
AND COMMUNICATION

READINGS IN THIS SECTION

Culture is a system of symbols that allows us to represent and communicate our experience. We are surrounded by symbols: the American flag, a new automobile, a diamond ring, billboard pictures, and, of course, spoken words.

A **symbol** is anything that we can perceive with our senses that stands for something else. Almost anything we experience can come to have symbolic meaning. Every symbol has a referent that it calls to our attention. The term *lawn,* for example, refers to a field of grass plants. When we communicate with symbols, we call attention not only to the referent but also to numerous connotations of the symbol. In U.S. culture we associate lawns with places such as homes and golf courses; actions such as mowing, fertilizing, and raking; and activities such as backyard games and barbeques. Human beings have the capacity to assign meaning to anything they experience in an arbitrary fashion, which allows limitless possibilities for communication.

Symbols greatly simplify the task of communication. Once we learn that a word such as *barn,* for example, stands for a certain type of building, we can communicate about a whole range of specific buildings that fit into the category. And we can communicate about barns in their absence; we can even invent flying barns and dream about barns. Symbols make it possible to communicate the immense variety of human experience, whether past or present, tangible or intangible, good or bad.

Many channels are available to human beings for symbolic communication: sound, sight, touch, and smell. Language, our most highly developed communication system, uses the channel of sound (or, for some deaf people, sight). **Language** is a system of cultural knowledge used to generate and interpret speech. It is a feature of every culture and a distinctive characteristic of the human animal. **Speech** refers to the behavior that produces vocal sounds. Our distinction between language and speech is like the one made between culture and behavior. Language is part of culture, the system of knowledge that generates behavior. Speech is the behavior generated and interpreted by language.

Every language is composed of three subsystems for dealing with vocal symbols: phonology, grammar, and semantics. Let's look briefly at each of these.

Phonology consists of the categories and rules for forming vocal symbols. It is concerned not directly with meaning but with the formation and recognition of the vocal sounds to which we assign meaning. For example, if you utter the word *bat,* you have followed a special set of rules for producing and ordering sound categories characteristic of the English language.

A basic element defined by phonological rules for every language is the phoneme. **Phonemes** are the minimal categories of speech sounds that serve to keep utterances apart. For example, speakers of English know that the words *bat, cat, mat, hat, rat,* and *fat* are different utterances because they hear the sounds /b/, /c/ (represented as /k/ by linguists), /m/, /h/, /r/, and /f/ as different categories of sounds. In English, each of these is a phoneme. Our language contains a limited number of phonemes from which we construct all our vocal symbols.

Phonemes are arbitrarily constructed, however. Each phoneme actually classifies slightly different sounds as though they were the same. Different languages may divide up the same range of speech sounds into different sound categories. For example, speakers of English treat the sound /t/ as a single phoneme. Hindi speakers take the same general range and divide it into four phonemes: /t/, /tʰ/, /T/, and /Tʰ/. (The lowercase *t*s are made with the tongue against the front teeth, while the uppercase *T*s are made by touching the tongue to the roof of the mouth further back than would be normal for an English speaker. The *h* indicates a puff of air, called *aspiration,* associated with the *t* sound.) Americans are likely to miss important distinctions among Hindi words because they hear these four different phonemes as a single one. Hindi speakers, on the other hand, tend to hear more than one sound category as they listen to English speakers pronounce *t*s. The situation is reversed for /w/ and /v/. We treat these as two phonemes, whereas Hindi speakers hear them as one. For them, the English words *wine* and *vine* sound the same.

Phonology also includes rules for ordering different sounds. Even when we try to talk nonsense, we usually create words that follow English phonological rules. It would be unlikely, for example, for us ever to begin a word with the phoneme /ng/—usually written in English as "ing." It must come at the end or in the middle of words.

Grammar is the second subsystem of language. **Grammar** refers to the categories and rules for combining vocal symbols. No grammar contains rules for combining every word or element of meaning in the language. If this were the case, grammar would be so unwieldy that no one could learn all the rules in a lifetime. Every grammar deals with *categories* of symbols, such as the ones we call *nouns* and *verbs*. Once you know the rules covering a particular category, you can use it in appropriate combinations.

Morphemes are the categories in any language that carry meaning. They are minimal units of meaning that cannot be subdivided. Morphemes occur in more complex patterns than you may think. The term *bats,* for example, is actually two morphemes, /bat/ meaning a flying mammal and /s/ meaning plural. Even more confusing, two different morphemes may have the same sound shape. /Bat/ can refer to a wooden club used in baseball as well as a flying mammal.

The third subsystem of every language is semantics. **Semantics** refers to the categories and rules for relating vocal symbols to their referents. Like the rules of grammar, semantic rules are simple instructions for combining things; they instruct us to combine words with what they refer to. A symbol can be said to *refer* because it focuses our attention and makes us take account of something. For example, /bat/ refers to a family of flying mammals, as we have already noted.

Language regularly occurs in a social context, and to understand its use fully it is important to recognize its relation to sociolinguistic rules. **Sociolinguistic rules** combine meaningful utterances with social situations into appropriate messages.

Although language is the most important human vehicle for communication, almost anything we can sense may represent a **nonlinguistic symbol** that conveys meaning. The way we sit, how we use our eyes, how we dress, the car we own, the number of bathrooms in our house—all these things carry symbolic meaning. We learn what they mean as we acquire culture. Indeed, a major reason we feel so uncomfortable when we enter a group from a strange culture is our inability to decode our host's symbolic world.

Anthropological linguists also focus on the ways people use metaphors and frame discourses when they speak. **Metaphors** represent a comparison, usually linguistic, that suggests how two things that are not alike in most ways are similar in another. For example, we often link passion (affection and hatred) with temperature, as in affection is warm and hatred is cold. **Frames** are social constructions of social phenomena. Social frames are often created by media sources, political movements, or other social groups to present a particular point of view about something. People can construct frames to advance a particular message they want listeners to hear. Advertisers are expert at creating frames consisting of metaphors that project a message they hope will sell products. For example, a TV ad for a sleep aid is set with a dark background (night), with a luminescent green Luna moth gently flitting through it, and a quiet soothing voiceover. They create a sleep frame by linking darkness, a delicate and soft animal, and quietness, all suggesting restfulness, with the drug they are trying to sell. In short, they put the sleep aid in the frame we normally associate with sleep.

The articles in Part Two illustrate several important aspects of language and communication. The first article, by Laura Bohannan, illustrates a case of cross-cultural miscommunication. When she tells the story of Hamlet to African Tiv elders, the story takes on an entirely different meaning as the Tiv use their own cultural knowledge in its interpretation. The second article, by Sarah Boxer, describes how the U.S. military tries to frame military operations by naming them with positive metaphors. However, she notes how difficult the task is as metaphors can have both positive and negative images. In the final article, Deborah Tannen, illustrates another aspect of language—conversation styles. Focusing on the different speaking styles of men and women in the workplace, she describes and analyzes how conversational styles themselves carry meaning and unwittingly lead to misunderstanding.

Key Terms

frames p. 39
grammar p. 39
language p. 38
metaphors p. 39
morphemes p. 39
nonlinguistic symbol p. 39

phonemes p. 38
phonology p. 38
semantics p. 39
sociolinguistic rules p. 39
speech p. 38
symbol p. 38

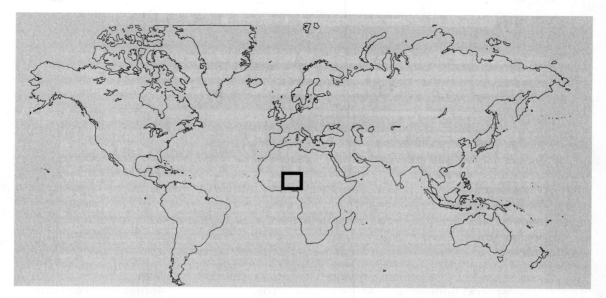

5

Shakespeare in the Bush

Laura Bohannan

All of us use the cultural knowledge we acquire as members of our own society to organize our perception and behavior. Most of us are also naive realists: we tend to believe our culture mirrors a reality shared by everyone. But cultures are different, and other people rarely behave or interpret experience according to our cultural plan. In this article, Laura Bohannan describes her attempt to tell the story of Hamlet to Tiv elders in West Africa. At each turn in the story, the Tiv interpret the events and motives in Hamlet using their own cultural knowledge. The result is a very different version of the classic play and an excellent example of cross-cultural miscommunication.*

((•⌐**Listen** to the **Chapter Audio** on **myanthrolab.com**

Just before I left Oxford for the Tiv in West Africa, conversation turned to the season at Stratford. "You Americans," said a friend, "often have difficulty with Shakespeare. He was, after all, a very English poet, and one can easily misinterpret the universal by misunderstanding the particular."

I protested that human nature is pretty much the same the whole world over; at least the general plot and motivation of the greater tragedies would always be clear—everywhere—although some details of custom might have to be explained and difficulties of translation

---

*From Laura Bohannan, "Shakespeare in the Bush." Used by permission.

might produce other slight changes. To end an argument we could not conclude, my friend gave me a copy of *Hamlet* to study in the African bush: it would, he hoped, lift my mind above its primitive surroundings, and possibly I might, by prolonged meditation, achieve the grace of correct interpretation.

It was my second field trip to that African tribe, and I thought myself ready to live in one of its remote sections—an area difficult to cross even on foot. I eventually settled on the hillock of a very knowledgeable old man, the head of a homestead of some hundred and forty people, all of whom were either his close relatives or their wives and children. Like the other elders of the vicinity, the old man spent most of his time performing ceremonies seldom seen these days in the more accessible parts of the tribe. I was delighted. Soon there would be three months of enforced isolation and leisure, between the harvest that takes place just before the rising of the swamps and the clearing of new farms when the water goes down. Then, I thought, they would have even more time to perform ceremonies and explain them to me.

I was quite mistaken. Most of the ceremonies demanded the presence of elders from several homesteads. As the swamps rose, the old men found it too difficult to walk from one homestead to the next, and the ceremonies gradually ceased. As the swamps rose even higher, all activities but one came to an end. The women brewed beer from maize and millet. Men, women, and children sat on their hillocks and drank it.

People began to drink at dawn. By midmorning the whole homestead was singing, dancing, and drumming. When it rained, people had to sit inside their huts: there they drank and sang or they drank and told stories. In any case, by noon or before, I either had to join the party or retire to my own hut and my books. "One does not discuss serious matters when there is beer. Come, drink with us." Since I lacked their capacity for the thick native beer, I spent more and more time with *Hamlet*. Before the end of the second month, grace descended on me. I was quite sure that *Hamlet* had only one possible interpretation, and that one universally obvious.

Early every morning, in the hope of having some serious talk before the beer party, I used to call on the old man at his reception hut—a circle of posts supporting a thatched roof above a low mud wall to keep out wind and rain. One day I crawled through the low doorway and found most of the men of the homestead sitting huddled in their ragged cloths on stools, low plank beds, and reclining chairs, warming themselves against the chill of the rain around a smoky fire. In the center were three pots of beer. The party had started.

The old man greeted me cordially. "Sit down and drink." I accepted a large calabash full of beer, poured some into a small drinking gourd, and tossed it down. Then I poured some more into the same gourd for the man second in seniority to my host before I handed my calabash over to a young man for further distribution. Important people shouldn't ladle beer themselves.

"It is better like this," the old man said, looking at me approvingly and plucking at the thatch that had caught in my hair. "You should sit and drink with us more often. Your servants tell me that when you are not with us, you sit inside your hut looking at a paper."

The old man was acquainted with four kinds of "papers": tax receipts, bride price receipts, court fee receipts, and letters. The messenger who brought him letters from the chief used them mainly as a badge of office, for he always knew what was in them and told the old man. Personal letters for the few who had relatives in the government or mission stations were kept until someone went to a large market where there was a letter writer and reader. Since my arrival, letters were brought to me to be read.

A few men also brought me bride price receipts, privately, with requests to change the figures to a higher sum. I found moral arguments were of no avail, since in-laws are fair game, and the technical hazards of forgery difficult to explain to an illiterate people. I did not wish them to think me silly enough to look at any such papers for days on end, and I hastily explained that my "paper" was one of the "things of long ago" of my country.

"Ah," said the old men. "Tell us."

I protested that I was not a storyteller. Storytelling is a skilled art among them; their standards are high, and the audiences critical—and vocal in their criticism. I protested in vain. This morning they wanted to hear a story while they drank. They threatened to tell me no more stories until I told them one of mine. Finally, the old man promised that no one would criticize my style "for we know you are struggling with our language." "But," put in one of the elders, "you must explain what we do not understand, as we do when we tell you our stories." Realizing that here was my chance to prove *Hamlet* universally intelligible, I agreed.

The old man handed me some more beer to help me on with my storytelling. Men filled their long wooden pipes and knocked coals from the fire to place in the pipe bowls; then, puffing contentedly, they sat back to listen. I began in the proper style, "Not yesterday, not yesterday, but long ago, a thing occurred. One night three men were keeping watch outside the homestead of the great chief, when suddenly they saw the former chief approach them."

"Why was he no longer their chief?"

"He was dead," I explained. "That is why they were troubled and afraid when they saw him."

"Impossible," began one of the elders, handing his pipe on to his neighbor, who interrupted, "Of course it wasn't the dead chief. It was an omen sent by a witch. Go on."

Slightly shaken, I continued. "One of these three was a man who knew things"—the closest translation for scholar, but unfortunately it also meant witch. The second elder looked triumphantly at the first. "So he spoke to the dead chief, saying, 'Tell us what we must do so you may rest in your grave,' but the dead chief did not answer. He vanished, and they could see him no more. Then the man who knew things—his name was Horatio—said this event was the affair of the dead chief's son, Hamlet."

There was a general shaking of heads around the circle. "Had the dead chief no living brothers? Or was this son the chief?" "No," I replied. "That is, he had one living brother who became the chief when the elder brother died."

The old men muttered: such omens were matters for chiefs and elders, not for youngsters; no good could come of being behind a chief's back; clearly Horatio was not a man who knew things.

"Yes, he was," I insisted, shooing a chicken away from my beer. "In our country the son is next to the father. The dead chief's younger brother had become the great chief. He had also married his elder brother's widow only about a month after the funeral."

"He did well," the old man beamed and announced to the others, "I told you that if we knew more about Europeans, we would find they really were very like us. In our country also," he added to me, "the younger brother marries the elder brother's widow and becomes the father of his children. Now, if your uncle, who married your widowed mother, is your father's full brother, then he will be a real father to you. Did Hamlet's father and uncle have one mother?"

His question barely penetrated my mind; I was too upset and thrown too far off balance by having one of the most important elements of *Hamlet* knocked straight out of the picture. Rather uncertainly I said that I thought they had the same mother, but I wasn't sure—the story didn't say. The old man told me severely that these genealogical details made all the difference and that when I got home I must ask the elders about it. He shouted out the door to one of his younger wives to bring his goatskin bag.

Determined to save what I could of the mother motif, I took a deep breath and began again. "The son Hamlet was very sad because his mother had married again so quickly. There was no need for her to do so, and it is our custom for a widow not to go to her next husband until she has mourned for two years."

"Two years is too long," objected the wife, who had appeared with the old man's battered goatskin bag. "Who will hoe your farms for you while you have no husband?"

"Hamlet," I retorted without thinking, "was old enough to hoe his mother's farms himself. There was no need for her to remarry." No one looked convinced. I gave up. "His mother and the great chief told Hamlet not to be sad, for the great chief himself would be a father to Hamlet. Furthermore, Hamlet would be the next chief: therefore he must stay to learn the things of a chief. Hamlet agreed to remain, and all the rest went off to drink beer."

While I paused, perplexed at how to render Hamlet's disgusted soliloquy to an audience convinced that Claudius and Gertrude had behaved in the best possible manner, one of the younger men asked me who had married the other wives of the dead chief.

"He had no other wives," I told him.

"But a chief must have many wives! How else can he brew beer and prepare food for all his guests?"

I said firmly that in our country even chiefs had only one wife, that they had servants to do their work, and that they paid them from tax money.

It was better, they returned, for a chief to have many wives and sons who would help him hoe his farms and feed his people; then everyone loved the chief who gave much and took nothing—taxes were a bad thing.

I agreed with the last comment, but for the rest fell back on their favorite way of fobbing off my questions: "That is the way it is done, so that is how we do it."

I decided to skip the soliloquy. Even if Claudius was here thought quite right to marry his brother's widow, there remained the poison motif, and I knew they would disapprove of fratricide. More hopefully I resumed, "That night Hamlet kept watch with the three who had seen his dead father. The dead chief again appeared, and although the others were afraid, Hamlet followed his dead father off to one side. When they were alone, Hamlet's dead father spoke."

"Omens can't talk!" The old man was emphatic.

"Hamlet's dead father wasn't an omen. Seeing him might have been an omen, but he was not." My audience looked as confused as I sounded. "It *was* Hamlet's dead father. It was a thing we call a 'ghost.'" I had to use the English word, for unlike many of the neighboring tribes, these people didn't believe in the survival after death of any individuating part of the personality.

"What is a 'ghost'? An omen?"

"No, a 'ghost' is someone who is dead but who walks around and can talk, and people can hear him and see him but not touch him."

They objected. "One can touch zombis."

"No, no! It was not a dead body the witches had animated to sacrifice and eat. No one else made Hamlet's dead father walk. He did it himself."

"Dead men can't walk," protested my audience as one man.

I was quite willing to compromise. "A 'ghost' is a dead man's shadow."

But again they objected. "Dead men cast no shadows."

"They do in my country," I snapped.

The old man quelled the babble of disbelief that rose immediately and told me with that insincere, but courteous, agreement one extends to the fancies of the young, ignorant, and superstitious, "No doubt in your country the dead can also walk without being zombis." From the depths of his bag he produced a withered fragment of kola nut, bit off one end to show it wasn't poisoned, and handed me the rest as a peace offering.

"Anyhow," I resumed, "Hamlet's dead father said that his own brother, the one who became chief, had poisoned him. He wanted Hamlet to avenge him. Hamlet believed this in his heart, for he did not like his father's brother." I took another swallow of beer. "In the country of the great chief, living in the same homestead, for it was a very large one, was an important elder who was often with the chief to advise and help him. His name was Polonius. Hamlet was courting his daughter, but her father and her brother . . . [I cast hastily about for some tribal analogy] warned her not to let Hamlet visit her when she was alone on her farm, for he would be a great chief and so could not marry her."

"Why not?" asked the wife, who had settled down on the edge of the old man's chair. He frowned at her for asking stupid questions and growled, "They lived in the same homestead."

"That was not the reason," I informed them. "Polonius was a stranger who lived in the homestead because he helped the chief, not because he was a relative."

"Then why couldn't Hamlet marry her?"

"He could have," I explained, "but Polonius didn't think he would. After all, Hamlet was a man of great importance who ought to marry a chief's daughter, for in his country a man could have only one wife. Polonius was afraid that if Hamlet made love to his daughter, then no one else would give a high price for her."

"That might be true," remarked one of the shrewder elders, "but a chief's son would give his mistress's father enough presents and patronage to more than make up the difference. Polonius sounds like a fool to me."

"Many people think he was," I agreed. "Meanwhile Polonius sent his son Laertes off to Paris to learn the things of that country, for it was the homestead of a very great chief indeed. Because he was afraid that Laertes might waste a lot of money on beer and women and gambling, or get into trouble by fighting, he sent one of his servants to Paris secretly, to spy out what Laertes was doing. One day Hamlet came upon Polonius's daughter Ophelia. He behaved so oddly he frightened her. Indeed"—I was fumbling for words to express the dubious quality of Hamlet's madness—"the chief and many others had also noticed that when Hamlet talked one could understand the words but not what they meant. Many people thought that he had become mad." My audience suddenly became much more attentive. "The great chief wanted to know what was wrong with Hamlet, so he sent for two of Hamlet's age mates [school friends would have taken long explanation] to talk to Hamlet and find out what troubled his heart. Hamlet, seeing that they had been bribed by the chief to betray him, told them nothing. Polonius, however, insisted that Hamlet was mad because he had been forbidden to see Ophelia, whom he loved."

"Why," inquired a bewildered voice, "should anyone bewitch Hamlet on that account?"

"Bewitch him?"

"Yes, only witchcraft can make anyone mad, unless, of course, one sees the beings that lurk in the forest."

I stopped being a storyteller, took out my notebook and demanded to be told more about these two causes of madness. Even while they spoke and I jotted notes, I tried to calculate the effect of this new factor on the plot. Hamlet had not been exposed to the beings that lurk in the forest. Only his relatives in the male line could bewitch him. Barring relatives not mentioned by Shakespeare, it had to be Claudius who was attempting to harm him. And, of course, it was.

For the moment I staved off questions by saying that the great chief also refused to believe that Hamlet was mad for the love of Ophelia and nothing else. "He was sure that something much more important was troubling Hamlet's heart."

"Now Hamlet's age mates," I continued, "had brought with them a famous storyteller. Hamlet decided to have this man tell the chief and all his homestead a story about the man who had poisoned his brother because he desired his brother's wife and wished to be chief himself. Hamlet was sure the great chief could not hear the story without making a sign if he was indeed guilty, and then he would discover whether his dead father had told him the truth."

The old man interrupted, with deep cunning. "Why should a father lie to his son?" he asked.

I hedged: "Hamlet wasn't sure that it really was his dead father." It was impossible to say anything, in that language, about devil-inspired visions.

"You mean," he said, "it actually was an omen, and he knew witches sometimes send false ones. Hamlet was a fool not to go to one skilled in reading omens and divining the truth in the first place. A man-who-sees-the-truth could have told him how his father died, if he really had been poisoned, and if there was witchcraft in it; then Hamlet could have called the elders to settle the matter."

The shrewd elder ventured to disagree. "Because his father's brother was a great chief, one-who-sees-the-truth might therefore have been afraid to tell it. I think it was for that reason that a friend of Hamlet's father—a witch and an elder—sent an omen so his friend's son would know. Was the omen true?"

"Yes," I said, abandoning ghosts and the devil; a witch-sent omen it would have to be. "It was true, for when the storyteller was telling his tale before all the homestead, the great chief rose in fear. Afraid that Hamlet knew his secret, he planned to have him killed."

The stage set of the next bit presented some difficulties of translation. I began cautiously. "The great chief told Hamlet's mother to find out from her son what he knew. But because a woman's children are always first in her heart, he had the important elder Polonius hide behind a cloth that hung against the wall of Hamlet's mother's sleeping hut. Hamlet started to scold his mother for what she had done."

There was a shocked murmur from everyone. A man should never scold his mother.

"She called out in fear, and Polonius moved behind the cloth. Shouting 'A rat!' Hamlet took his machete and slashed through the cloth." I paused for a dramatic effect. "He had killed Polonius!"

The old men looked at each other in supreme disgust. "That Polonius truly was a fool and a man who knew nothing! What child would not know enough to shout, 'It's me!'" With a pang, I remembered that these people are ardent hunters, always armed with bow, arrow, and machete; at the first rustle in the grass an arrow is aimed and ready, and the hunter shouts "Game!" If no human voice answers immediately, the arrow speeds on its way. Like a good hunter Hamlet had shouted, "A rat!"

I rushed in to save Polonius's reputation. "Polonius did speak. Hamlet heard him. But he thought it was the chief and wished to kill him to avenge his father. He had meant to kill him earlier that evening. . . ." I broke down, unable to describe to these pagans, who had no belief in individual afterlife, the difference between dying at one's prayers and dying "unhousell'd, disappointed, unaneled."

This time I had shocked my audience seriously. "For a man to raise his hands against his father's brother and the one who has become his father—that is a terrible thing. The elders ought to let such a man be bewitched."

I nibbled at my kola nut in some perplexity, then pointed out that after all the man had killed Hamlet's father.

"No," pronounced the old man, speaking less to me than to the young men sitting behind the elders. "If your father's brother has killed your father, you must appeal to your father's age mates; *they* may avenge him. No man may use violence against his senior relatives." Another thought struck him. "But if his father's brother had indeed been wicked enough to bewitch Hamlet and make him mad, that would be a good story indeed, for it would be his fault that Hamlet, being mad, no longer had any sense and thus was ready to kill his father's brother."

There was a murmur of applause. *Hamlet* was again a good story to them, but it no longer seemed quite the same story to me. As I thought over the coming complications of plot and motive, I lost courage and decided to skim over dangerous ground quickly.

"The great chief," I went on, "was not sorry that Hamlet had killed Polonius. It gave him a reason to send Hamlet away, with his two treacherous age mates, with letters to a chief of a far country, saying that Hamlet should be killed. But Hamlet changed the writing on their papers, so that the chief killed his age mates instead." I encountered a reproachful glare from one of the men whom I had told undetectable forgery was not merely immoral but beyond human skill. I looked the other way.

"Before Hamlet could return, Laertes came back for his father's funeral. The great chief told him Hamlet had killed Polonius. Laertes swore to kill Hamlet because of this; and because his sister Ophelia, hearing her father had been killed by the man she loved, went mad and drowned in the river."

"Have you already forgotten what we told you?" The old man was reproachful. "One cannot take vengeance on a madman; Hamlet killed Polonius in his madness. As for the girl, she not only went mad, she was drowned. Only witches can make people drown. Water itself can't hurt anything. It is merely something one drinks and bathes in."

I began to get cross. "If you don't like the story, I'll stop."

The old man made soothing noises and himself poured me some more beer. "You tell the story well, and we are listening. But it is clear that the elders of your country have never told you what the story really means. No, don't interrupt! We believe you when you say your marriage customs are different, or your clothes and weapons. But people are the same everywhere; therefore, there are always witches and it is we, the elders, who know how witches work. We told you it was the great chief who wished to kill Hamlet, and now your own words have proved us right. Who were Ophelia's male relatives?"

"There were only her father and her brother." Hamlet was clearly out of my hands.

"There must have been many more; this also you must ask of your elders when you get back to your country. From what you tell us, since Polonius was dead, it must have been Laertes who killed Ophelia, although I do not see the reason for it."

We had emptied one pot of beer, and the old men argued the point with slightly tipsy interest. Finally one of them demanded of me, "What did the servant of Polonius say on his return?"

With difficulty I recollected Reynaldo and his mission. "I don't think he did return before Polonius was killed."

"Listen," said the elder, "and I will tell you how it was and how your story will go, then you may tell me if I am right. Polonius knew his son would get into trouble, and so he did. He had many fines to pay for fighting, and debts from gambling. But he had only two ways of getting money quickly. One was to marry off his sister at once, but it is difficult to find a man who will marry a woman desired by the son of a chief. For if the chief's heir commits adultery with your wife, what can you do? Only a fool calls a case against a man who will someday be his judge. Therefore Laertes had to take the second way: he killed his sister by witchcraft, drowning her so he could secretly sell her body to the witches."

I raised an objection. "They found her body and buried it. Indeed Laertes jumped into the grave to see his sister once more—so, you see, the body was truly there. Hamlet, who had just come back, jumped in after him."

"What did I tell you?" The elder appealed to the others. "Laertes was up to no good with his sister's body. Hamlet prevented him, because the chief's heir, like a chief, does not wish any other man to grow rich and powerful. Laertes would be angry, because he would have killed his sister without benefit to himself. In our country he would try to kill Hamlet for that reason. Is this not what happened?"

"More or less," I admitted. "When the great chief found Hamlet was still alive, he encouraged Laertes to try to kill Hamlet and arranged a fight with machetes between them. In the fight both the young men were wounded to death. Hamlet's mother drank the poisoned beer that the chief meant for Hamlet in case he won the fight. When he saw his mother die of poison, Hamlet, dying, managed to kill his father's brother with his machete."

"You see, I was right!" exclaimed the elder.

"That was a very good story," added the old man, "and you told it with very few mistakes. There was just one more error, at the very end. The poison Hamlet's mother drank was obviously meant for the survivor of the fight, whichever it was. If Laertes had won, the great chief would have poisoned him, for no one would know that he arranged Hamlet's death. Then, too, he need not fear Laertes's witchcraft; it takes a strong heart to kill one's only sister by witchcraft.

"Sometime," concluded the old man, gathering his ragged toga about him, "you must tell us some more stories of your country. We, who are elders, will instruct you in their true meaning, so that when you return to your own land your elders will see that you have not been sitting in the bush, but among those who know things and who have taught you wisdom."

✓●─[**Study** and **Review** on **myanthrolab.com**

Review Questions

1. In what ways does Bohannan's attempt to tell the story of Hamlet to the Tiv illustrate the concept of naive realism?

2. Using Bohannan's experience of telling the story of *Hamlet* to the Tiv and the response of the Tiv elders to her words, illustrate cross-cultural misunderstanding.

3. What are the most important parts of *Hamlet* that the Tiv found it necessary to reinterpret?

4. Building off of Bohannan's experience, can you think of ways in which cross-cultural misunderstandings shape interactions in other settings?

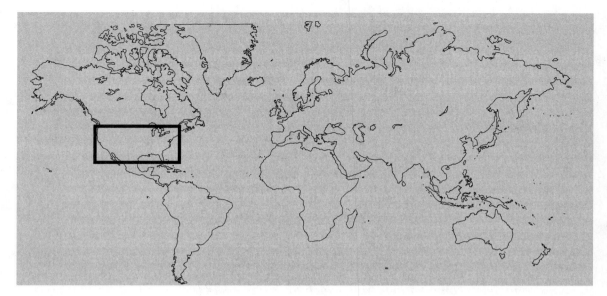

6

Manipulating Meaning: The Military Name Game

Sarah Boxer

It's easy to take the act of conversation for granted. After all, one simply says what one means. But talk is much more complicated than that. For one thing, what you say depends on your social identity and that of the people you are addressing. For example, you normally would not greet the president of your college or university by saying, "How's your ass, Bob?" Social situations also might require particular forms of speech. U.S. Senators do not refer to each other by name when they are on the Senate floor. Instead they will address each other as "the junior Senator from Minnesota," depending on seniority and state.

Talking is made even more complex by the use of metaphors, the linking of one thing with another. Synonyms carry slightly different meanings, and we often choose one over another to frame a discourse about something in a particular way. Framing might stem from a variety of motivations related to the impression we wish to give listeners. For example, because the word cripple seems harsh—one associated with deformity, lameness, and absence of ability—we regularly substitute the milder word disabled in its place.

Framing is a regular feature of advertising and is also especially prevalent in politics. For example, in an effort to repeal a tax on the assets of deceased Americans, Republicans substituted the term death tax for the original estate tax. To tax inanimate estates is one thing but to tax death seems especially cruel. Or take the word war. Democratic president Lyndon Johnson used the term to emphasize the importance of winning the fight (notice the associated metaphors) against poverty. The resultant "war on poverty" phrase became a model for naming other important policy initiatives. We engaged (and still fight) the "war on drugs," "the war on cancer," and recently, "the war on terrorism." In the last case, the term war has been taken more literally to mean actual war (conflict between states) in regard to Iraq.

Especially articulate individuals can create word images on their feet, but corporations and government agencies often institutionalize the process of framing. This selection, by Sarah Boxer, traces the history of one such bureaucratic process—the naming of military operations by members of the U.S. armed forces. Challenged by the need to generate public support for military actions, the naming process has taken on grand proportions. First used by the Germans in World War II, operations naming changed from a secret code to a positive statement designed to generate public support by 2001. At first, commanders chose the military operations' names. When these names were later revealed to the public, naming came to be seen as a form of public relations. By the Vietnam War, the U.S. military had created a computer program called "Code Word, Nickname, and Exercise Term System" or "NICKA" for short. Today each major military command has rights to certain letter combinations from which to create names for operations, but higher authorities may discard these names. Boxer concludes by noting that an unanticipated pitfall of the process is the potential for almost any word to offend some members of the national audience. For that reason, some of the best names may be those that have no meaning at all.*

((•— **Listen** to the **Chapter Audio** on **myanthrolab.com**

For a few days in September [2001] it looked as if the United States would be fighting a war named Infinite Justice. By late September the name was gone. The Council on American-Islamic Relations had found the name offensive because it sounded too much like Eternal Retribution. In other words the United States seemed to be assuming God's role. On Sept. 25 Defense Secretary Donald H. Rumsfeld announced that the military operation would be called Enduring Freedom.

Never mind that Enduring Freedom presented its own troubling ambiguities: Is "enduring" supposed to be taken as an adjective, like long-lasting? Or as a present participle, as in "How long are we going to be enduring this freedom?"

This is not the first time that the name of a military operation has been floated then grounded. The history of naming such operations shows how an art that was once covert has slowly become bureaucratic propaganda.

As Lt. Col. Gregory C. Sieminski points out in his classic short history, "The Art of Naming Operations," published in 1995 in *Parameters*, the quarterly of the United States Army War College, the name of the 1989 United States invasion of Panama, Just Cause, was originally Blue Spoon, until the commander of the Special Operations Command, Gen. James Lindsay, asked an operations officer on the Joint Staff, Lt. Gen. Thomas Kelly, "Do you want your grandchildren to say you were in Blue Spoon?"

So who does create nicknames for military operations these days? There are 24 Defense Department entities, each of which is assigned "a series of two-letter alphabetic sequences," Colonel Sieminski explains. For example, AG-AL, ES-EZ, JG-JL,

QA-QF, SM-SR, and UM-UR belong to the Atlantic Command. In order to name the invasion of Granada in 1983, the Atlantic Command started with the letters UR and came up with Urgent Fury. Once the name was generated, it was sent to the Joint Chiefs of Staff, who sent it to the Defense Secretary for the ultimate decision.

But all this can be overridden if the naming seems important enough. And that seems to be happening more and more. "Since 1989 U.S. military operations have been nicknamed with an eye toward shaping domestic and international perceptions," Colonel Sieminski notes.

A huge effort, for example, went into choosing the right name for the operation to defend Kuwait from Iraq. Gen. H. Norman Schwarzkopf wanted the name Peninsula Shield, even though the letters PE were not assigned to his command. Then Crescent Shield was proposed, with an eye to local sentiment. Finally it became Desert Shield. And then the word "desert" bloomed and multiplied: Desert Storm, Desert Saber, Desert Farewell, Desert Share.

The naming game began with the Germans. In World War II they seem to have been the first to give military operations code names, Colonel Sieminski writes. They ransacked mythology and religion for ideas: Archangel, St. Michael, St. George, Roland, Mars, Achilles, Castor, Pollux, and Valkyrie. Hitler himself named the invasion of the Soviet Union Barbarossa for the "12th-century Holy Roman Emperor Frederick I, who had extended German authority over the Slavs in the east," Colonel Sieminski writes.

Churchill, like Hitler, was partial to names that came from "heroes of antiquity, figures from Greek and Roman mythology, the constellations and stars, famous race-horses, names of British and American war heroes," Colonel Sieminski writes. And he set naming etiquette. Names should not "imply a boastful or overconfident sentiment," Churchill said; they should not have "an air of despondency"; they should not be frivolous or ordinary; and they should not be a target for fun. No widow or mother, Churchill said, should have "to say that her son was killed in an operation called 'Bunnyhug' or 'Ballyhoo.'"

For all of Churchill's pains with nomenclature, the names of British and American operations were originally designed to be secret, not meant for public ears until the war or operation was finished.

The United States named its first operations after colors. When the colors began to run out, the War Department drew up a list of "10,000 common nouns and adjectives," avoiding "proper nouns, geographical terms, and names of ships" that might give military clues away to the enemy, Colonel Sieminski writes. And each theater had its own blocks of code words; "the European Theater got such names as Market and Garden, while the Pacific Theater got names like Olympic and Flintlock."

Soon after World War II ended, the Pentagon began creating operation names that were especially designed for public ears. The first nickname was Operation Crossroads, for the 1946 atomic bomb tests conducted on Bikini Atoll. And then things opened up more. During the Korean War Gen. Douglas MacArthur "permitted code names to be declassified and disseminated to the press once operations had begun, rather than waiting until the end of the war," Colonel Sieminski writes.

What followed were some very "aggressive nicknames" for counteroffensives in China: Thunderbolt, Roundup, Killer, Ripper, Courageous, Audacious, and Dauntless.

The bloody names kept flowing in Vietnam, but public relations concerns soon stemmed the tide. The most controversial name, Colonel Sieminski notes, was Masher, the nickname for a "sweep operation through the Bong Son Plain." President Lyndon B. Johnson "angrily protested that it did not reflect 'pacification emphasis.'"

In other words Masher somehow did not say "peace" to the world, Colonel Sieminski writes. Masher was reborn as White Wing. After 1966, operations tended to be named for towns and figures: Junction City, Bastogne, Nathan Hale. To rouse the troops at the Khe Sanh garrison, a "round-the-clock bombing attack" was called Operation Niagara, "to invoke an image of cascading shells and bombs," Colonel Sieminski notes.

By the end of the Vietnam War the process of naming had grown baroque. So in 1975 the Joint Chiefs of Staff created a computer system, the Code Word, Nickname, and Exercise Term System. "The NICKA system is not, as some assume, a random word generator for nicknames," Colonel Sieminski writes; "it is in fact merely an automated means for submitting, validating and storing them."

There is plenty of room for drama. But the fashion now, he writes, is "to make the names sound like mission statements by using a verb-noun sequence: Promote Liberty, Restore Hope, Uphold Democracy, Provide Promise." They are boring, unmemorable names.

Despite the monotonous trend, names are more important than they have ever been. With "the shrinking scale of military action," Colonel Sieminski writes, the nickname of an operation now may well become the name for the whole war and its rationale. Maybe that is the problem.

Robin Tolmach Lakoff, a professor of linguistics at the University of California, Berkeley, and the author of *The Language War*, a book about the unintentional overtones of language, said, "Whoever gives the name has control over it." Naming an operation is like naming a baby, she added. "Your creation is opaque, but the name suggests what you hope it will be." What then was the hope with Infinite Justice and then with Enduring Freedom?

The nouns in the name of the operation, she said, were no problem: freedom and justice. It was the adjectives that presented problems. The name had to please so many different kinds of people that every adjective seemed fraught with offensive overtones. "It is a virtue in times of peril," Ms. Lakoff said, "to find words without meaning."

✓● Study and Review on myanthrolab.com

Review Questions

1. Why do military commanders and public officials take the naming of military actions so seriously?

2. How has the procedure for naming military actions changed since campaigns were first given names in World War II?

3. What pitfalls are there in choosing names for military actions in the United States today? Are there solutions to such problems?

4. What evidence supports or challenges the belief held by many in authority that the way something is portrayed in words does actually affect how people will understand it?

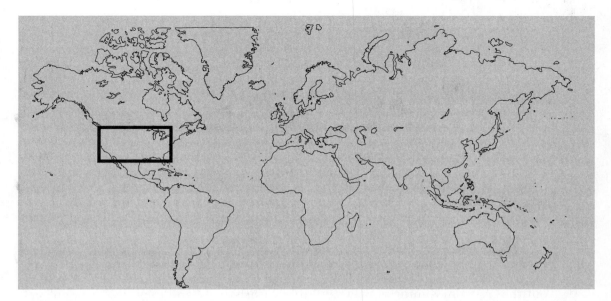

7

Conversation Style: Talking on the Job

Deborah Tannen

In this piece excerpted from her book about conversation in the workplace, Deborah Tannen discusses a tacit dimension of communication, conversation style. Looking at the different ways men and women approach or avoid asking for help on the job, she argues that gender differences in conversation style are responsible not only for miscommunication but also for misguided evaluations and moral judgments about the performance and character of coworkers.*

((•—⌐**Listen** to the **Chapter Audio** on **myanthrolab.com**

People have different conversational styles, influenced by the part of the country they grew up in, their ethnic backgrounds and those of their parents, their age, class, and gender. But conversational style is invisible. Unaware that these and other aspects of our backgrounds influence our ways of talking, we think we are simply saying what we mean. Because we don't realize that others' styles are different, we are often frustrated in conversations. Rather than seeing the culprit as differing styles, we attribute troubles to others' intentions (she doesn't like me), abilities (he's stupid), or character (she's rude, he's inconsiderate), our own failure (what's wrong with me?), or the failure of a relationship (we just can't communicate). . . .

*Reuse of text from Introduction and first chapter from "Women and Men Talking on the Job" (pp. 21–42), from *Talking from 9 to 5* by Deborah Tannen. Copyright © 1994 by Deborah Tannen. Reprinted by permission of HarperCollins Publishers.

Although I am aware of the many influences on conversational style and have spent most of my career studying and writing about them . . . style differences influenced by gender receive particular attention [here]. This is not only because these are the differences people most want to hear about (although this is so and is a factor), but also because there is something fundamental about our categorization by gender. When you spot a person walking down the street toward you, you immediately and automatically identify that person as male or female. You will not necessarily try to determine which state they are from, what their class background is, or what country their grandparents came from. A secondary identification, in some places and times, may be about race. But, while we may envision a day when a director will be able to cast actors for a play without reference to race, can we imagine a time when actors can be cast without reference to their sex?

Few elements of our identities come as close to our sense of who we are as gender. If you mistake people's cultural background—you thought they were Greek, but they turn out to be Italian; you assumed they'd grown up in Texas, but it turns out they're from Kentucky; you say "Merry Christmas" and they say, "we don't celebrate Christmas; we're Muslim"—it catches you off guard and you rearrange the mental frame through which you view them. But if someone you thought was male turns out to be female—like the jazz musician Billy Tipton, whose own adopted sons never suspected that their father was a woman until the coroner broke the news to them after his (her) death—the required adjustment is staggering. Even infants discriminate between males and females and react differently depending on which they confront.

Perhaps it is because our sense of gender is so deeply rooted that people are inclined to hear descriptions of gender patterns as statements about gender *identity*—in other words, as absolute differences rather than a matter of degree and percentages, and as universal rather than culturally mediated. The patterns I describe are based on observations of particular speakers in a particular place and time: mostly (but not exclusively) middle-class Americans of European background working in offices at the present time. Other cultures evince very different patterns of talk associated with gender—and correspondingly different assumptions about the "natures" of women and men. I don't put a lot of store in talk about "natures" or what is "natural." People in every culture will tell you that the behaviors common in their own culture are "natural." I also don't put a lot of store in people's explanations that their way of talking is a natural response to their environment, as there is always an equally natural and opposite way of responding to the same environment. We all tend to regard the way things are as the way things have to be—as only natural.

The reason ways of talking, like other ways of conducting our daily lives, come to seem natural is that the behaviors that make up our lives are ritualized. Indeed, the "ritual" character of interaction is at the heart of this book. Having grown up in a particular culture, we learn to do things as the people we encounter do them, so the vast majority of our decisions about how to speak become automatic. You see someone you know, you ask "How are you?," chat, then take your leave, never pausing to ponder the many ways you could handle this interaction differently—and would, if you lived in a different culture. Just as an American automatically extends a hand for a handshake while a Japanese automatically bows, what the American and Japanese find it natural to say is a matter of convention learned over a lifetime.

No one understood the ritual nature of everyday life better than sociologist Erving Goffman, who also understood the fundamental role played by gender in organizing our daily rituals. In his article "The Arrangement Between the Sexes,"

Goffman pointed out that we tend to say "sex-linked" when what we mean is "sex-class-linked." When hearing that a behavior is "sex-linked," people often conclude that the behavior is to be found in every individual of that group, and that it is somehow inherent in their sex, as if it came hooked to a chromosome. Goffman suggests the term "genderism" (on the model, I assume, of "mannerism," not of "sexism") for "a sex-class linked individual behavioral practice." This is the spirit in which I intend references to gendered patterns of behavior: not to imply that there is anything inherently male or female about particular ways of talking, nor to claim that every individual man or woman adheres to the pattern, but rather to observe that a larger percentage of women or men *as a group* talk in a particular way, or individual women and men *are more likely* to talk one way or the other.

That individuals do not always fit the pattern associated with their gender does not mean that the pattern is not typical. Because more women or men speak in a particular way, that way of speaking becomes associated with women or men—or, rather, it is the other way around: More women or men learn to speak particular ways *because* those ways are associated with their own gender. And individual men or women who speak in ways associated with the other gender will pay a price for departing from cultural expectations.

If my concept of how gender displays itself in everyday life has been influenced by Goffman, the focus of my research—talk—and my method for studying it grow directly out of my own discipline, linguistics. My understanding of what goes on when people talk to each other is based on observing and listening as well as tape-recording, transcribing, and analyzing conversation. In response to my book *You Just Don't Understand*, I was contacted by people at many companies who asked whether I could help them apply the insights in that book to the problem of "the glass ceiling": Why weren't women advancing as quickly as the men who were hired at the same time? And more generally, they wanted to understand how to integrate women as well as others who were historically not "typical" employees into the increasingly diverse workforce. I realized that in order to offer insight, I needed to observe what was really going on in the workplace. . . .

Women and Men Talking on the Job

Amy was a manager with a problem: She had just read a final report written by Donald, and she felt it was woefully inadequate. She faced the unsavory task of telling him to do it over. When she met with Donald, she made sure to soften the blow by beginning with praise, telling him everything about his report that was good. Then she went on to explain what was lacking and what needed to be done to make it acceptable. She was pleased with the diplomatic way she had managed to deliver the bad news. Thanks to her thoughtfulness in starting with praise, Donald was able to listen to the criticism and seemed to understand what was needed. But when the revised report appeared on her desk, Amy was shocked. Donald had made only minor, superficial changes, and none of the necessary ones. The next meeting with him did not go well. He was incensed that she was now telling him his report was not acceptable and accused her of having misled him. "You told me before it was fine," he protested.

Amy thought she had been diplomatic; Donald thought she had been dishonest. The praise she intended to soften the message "This is unacceptable" sounded to him like the message itself: "This is fine." So what she regarded as the main point—the needed changes—came across to him as optional suggestions, because he had already registered her praise as the main point. She felt he hadn't listened to her. He thought she had changed her mind and was making him pay the price.

Work days are filled with conversations about getting the job done. Most of these conversations succeed, but too many end in impasses like this. It could be that Amy is a capricious boss whose wishes are whims, and it could be that Donald is a temperamental employee who can't hear criticism no matter how it is phrased. But I don't think either was the case in this instance. I believe this was one of innumerable misunderstandings caused by differences in conversational style. Amy delivered the criticism in a way that seemed to her self-evidently considerate, a way she would have preferred to receive criticism herself: taking into account the other person's feelings, making sure he knew that her ultimate negative assessment of his report didn't mean she had no appreciation of his abilities. She offered the praise as a sweetener to help the nasty-tasting news go down. But Donald didn't expect criticism to be delivered in that way, so he mistook the praise as her overall assessment rather than a preamble to it.

This conversation could have taken place between two women or two men. But I do not think it is a coincidence that it occurred between a man and a woman. . . . Conversational rituals common among men often involve using opposition such as banter, joking, teasing, and playful put-downs, and expending effort to avoid the one-down position in the interaction. Conversational rituals common among women are often ways of maintaining an appearance of equality, taking into account the effect of the exchange on the other person, and expending effort to downplay the speakers' authority so they can get the job done without flexing their muscles in an obvious way.

When everyone present is familiar with these conventions, they work well. But when ways of speaking are not recognized as conventions, they are taken literally, with negative results on both sides. Men whose oppositional strategies are interpreted literally may be seen as hostile when they are not, and their efforts to ensure that they avoid appearing one-down may be taken as arrogance. When women use conversational strategies designed to avoid appearing boastful and to take the other person's feelings into account, they may be seen as less confident and competent than they really are. As a result, both women and men often feel they are not getting sufficient credit for what they have done, are not being listened to, are not getting ahead as fast as they should.

When I talk about women's and men's characteristic ways of speaking, I always emphasize that both styles make sense and are equally valid in themselves, though the difference in styles may cause trouble in interaction. In a sense, when two people form a private relationship of love or friendship, the bubble of their interaction is a world unto itself, even though they both come with the prior experience of their families, their community, and a lifetime of conversations. But someone who takes a job is entering a world that is already functioning, with its own characteristic style already in place. Although there are many influences such as regional background, the type of industry involved, whether it is a family business or a large corporation, in general, workplaces that have previously had men in positions of power have already established male-style interaction as the norm. In that sense, women, and others whose styles are different, are not starting out equal, but are at a disadvantage. Though talking at work is quite similar to talking in private, it is a very different enterprise in many ways.

When Not Asking Directions Is Dangerous to Your Health

If conversational-style differences lead to troublesome outcomes in work as well as private settings, there are some work settings where the outcomes of style are a matter of life and death. Healthcare professionals are often in such situations. So are airline pilots.

Of all the examples of women's and men's characteristic styles that I discussed in *You Just Don't Understand,* the one that (to my surprise) attracted the most attention was the question "Why don't men like to stop and ask for directions?" Again and again, in the responses of audiences, talk-show hosts, letter writers, journalists, and conversationalists, this question seemed to crystallize the frustration many people had experienced in their own lives. And my explanation seems to have rung true: that men are more likely to be aware that asking for directions, or for any kind of help, puts them in a one-down position.

With regard to asking directions, women and men are keenly aware of the advantages of their own style. Women frequently observe how much time they would save if their husbands simply stopped and asked someone instead of driving around trying in vain to find a destination themselves. But I have also been told by men that it makes sense not to ask directions because you learn a lot about a neighborhood, as well as about navigation, by driving around and finding your own way.

But some situations are more risky than others. A Hollywood talk-show producer told me that she had been flying with her father in his private airplane when he was running out of gas and uncertain about the precise location of the local landing strip he was heading for. Beginning to panic, the woman said, "Daddy! Why don't you radio the control tower and ask them where to land?" He answered, "I don't want them to think I'm lost." This story had a happy ending, else the woman would not have been alive to tell it to me.

Some time later, I repeated this anecdote to a man at a cocktail party—a man who had just told me that the bit about directions was his favorite part of my book, and who, it turned out, was also an amateur pilot. He then went on to tell me that he had had a similar experience. When learning to fly, he got lost on his first solo flight. He did not want to humiliate himself by tuning his radio to the FAA emergency frequency and asking for help, so he flew around looking for a place to land. He spotted an open area that looked like a landing field, headed for it—and found himself deplaning in what seemed like a deliberately hidden landing strip that was mercifully deserted at the time. Fearing he had stumbled upon an enterprise he was not supposed to be aware of, let alone poking around in, he climbed back into the plane, relieved that he had not gotten into trouble. He managed to find his way back to his home airport as well, before he ran out of gas. He maintained, however, that he was certain that more than a few small-plane crashes have occurred because other amateur pilots who did not want to admit they were lost were less lucky. In light of this, the amusing question of why men prefer not to stop and ask for directions stops being funny.

The moral of the story is not that men should immediately change and train themselves to ask directions when they're in doubt, any more than women should immediately stop asking directions and start honing their navigational skills by finding their way on their own. The moral is flexibility: Sticking to habit in the face of all challenges is not so smart if it ends up getting you killed. If we all understood our own styles and knew their limits and their alternatives, we'd be better off—especially at work, where the results of what we do have repercussions for co-workers and the company, as well as for our own futures.

To Ask or Not to Ask

An intern on duty at a hospital had a decision to make. A patient had been admitted with a condition he recognized, and he recalled the appropriate medication. But that medication was recommended for a number of conditions, in different dosages. He wasn't quite sure what dose was right for this condition. He had to make a quick decision: Would he interrupt the supervising resident during a meeting to check the dose, or would he make his best guess and go for it?

What was at stake? First and foremost, the welfare, and maybe even the life, of the patient. But something else was at stake too—the reputation, and eventually the career, of the intern. If he interrupted the resident to ask about the dosage, he was making a public statement about what he didn't know, as well as making himself something of a nuisance. In this case, he went with his guess, and there were no negative effects. But, as with small-plane crashes, one wonders how many medical errors have resulted from decisions to guess rather than ask.

It is clear that not asking questions can have disastrous consequences in medical settings, but asking questions can also have negative consequences. A physician wrote to me about a related experience that occurred during her medical training. She received a low grade from her supervising physician. It took her by surprise because she knew that she was one of the best interns in her group. She asked her supervisor for an explanation, and he replied that she didn't know as much as the others. She knew from her day-to-day dealings with her peers that she was one of the most knowledgeable, not the least. So she asked what evidence had led him to his conclusion. And he told her, "You ask more questions."

There is evidence that men are less likely to ask questions in a public situation, where asking will reveal their lack of knowledge. One such piece of evidence is a study done in a university classroom, where sociolinguist Kate Remlinger noticed that women students asked the professor more questions than men students did. As part of her study, Remlinger interviewed six students at length, three men and three women. All three men told her that they would not ask questions in class if there was something they did not understand. Instead, they said they would try to find the answer later by reading the textbook, asking a friend, or, as a last resort, asking the professor in private during office hours. As one young man put it, "If it's vague to me, I usually don't ask. I'd rather go home and look it up."

Of course, this does not mean that no men will ask questions when they are in doubt, nor that all women will; the differences, as always, are a matter of likelihood and degree. As always, cultural differences play a role too. It is not unusual for American professors to admit their own ignorance when they do not know the answer to a student's question, but there are many cultures in which professors would not, and students from those cultures may judge American professors by those standards. A student from the Middle East told a professor at a California university that she had just lost all respect for one of his colleagues. The reason: She had asked a question in class, and the offending professor had replied, "I don't know offhand, but I'll find out for you."

The physician who asked her supervisor why he gave her a negative evaluation may be unusual in having been told directly what behavior led to the misjudgment of her skill. But in talking to doctors and doctors-in-training around the country, I have learned that there is nothing exceptional about her experience, that it is common for interns and residents to conceal their ignorance by not asking questions, since those who do ask are judged less capable. Yet it seems that many women who are more likely than men to ask questions (just as women are more likely to stop and ask for directions when they're lost) are unaware that they may make a negative impression at the same time that they get information. Their antennae have not been attuned to making sure they don't appear one-down.

This pattern runs counter to two stereotypes about male and female styles: that men are more focused on information and that women are more sensitive. In regard to classroom behavior, it seems that the women who ask questions are more focused on information, whereas the men who refrain from doing so are more focused on interaction—the impression their asking will make on others. In this situation, it is the men who are more sensitive to the impression made on others by their behavior, although their concern is, ultimately, the effect on themselves rather than on others. And this sensitivity is likely to make them look better in the world of work. Realizing this puts the intern's decision in a troubling perspective. He had to choose between putting his career at risk and putting the patient's health at risk.

It is easy to see benefits of both styles: Someone willing to ask questions has ready access to a great deal of information—all that is known by the people she can ask. But just as men have told me that asking directions is useless since the person you ask may not know and may give you the wrong answer, some people feel they are more certain to get the right information if they read it in a book, and they are learning more by finding it themselves. On the other hand, energy may be wasted looking up information someone else has at hand, and I have heard complaints from people who feel they were sent on wild-goose chases by colleagues who didn't want to admit they really were not sure of what they pretended to know.

The reluctance to say "I don't know" can have serious consequences for an entire company—and did: On Friday, June 17, 1994, a computer problem prevented Fidelity Investments from calculating the value of 166 mutual funds. Rather than report that the values for these funds were not available, a manager decided to report to the National Association of Securities Dealers that the values of these funds had not changed from the day before. Unfortunately, June 17 turned out to be a bad day in the financial markets, so the values of Fidelity's funds that were published in newspapers around the country stood out as noticeably higher than those of other funds. Besides the cost and inconvenience to brokerage firms who had to re-compute their customers' accounts, and the injustice to investors who made decisions to buy or sell based on inaccurate information, the company was mightily embarrassed and forced to apologize publicly. Clearly this was an instance in which it would have been preferable to say, "We don't know."

Flexibility, again, is key. There are many situations in which it serves one well to be self-reliant and discreet about revealing doubt or ignorance, and others in which it is wise to admit what you don't know.

✓●—Study and Review on myanthrolab.com

Review Questions

1. What does Tannen mean by *conversational style?*

2. What is the important style difference in the way men and women ask for directions or help, according to Tannen?

3. What is Tannen's hypothesis about why males avoid asking other people for directions?

4. In Tannen's perspective, what conclusions do men and women draw about each other when they display typically different approaches to asking directions?

PART THREE

ECOLOGY
AND SUBSISTENCE

READINGS IN THIS SECTION

Ecology is the relationship of an organism to other elements within its environmental sphere. Every species, no matter how simple or complex, fits into a larger, intricate ecological system; each adapts to its ecological niche unless rapid environmental alterations outstrip the organism's ability and potential to adapt successfully. An important aim of ecological studies is to show how organisms fit within particular environments. Such studies also look at the effect environments have on the shape and behavior of life forms.

Every species has adapted biologically through genetically produced variation and natural selection. For example, the bipedal (two-footed) locomotion characteristic of humans is one possible adaptation to walking on the ground. It also permitted our ancestors to carry food, tools, weapons, and almost anything else they desired, enabling them to range out from a home base and bring things back for others to share.

Biological processes have led to another important human characteristic, the development of a large and complex brain. The human brain is capable of holding an enormous inventory of information. With it, we can classify the parts of our environment and retain instructions for complex ways to deal with the things in our world. Because we can communicate our knowledge symbolically through language, we are able to teach one another. Instead of a genetic code that directs behavior automatically, we operate with a learned cultural code. Culture gives us the ability to behave in a much wider variety of ways and to change rapidly in new situations. With culture, people have been able to live successfully in almost every part of the world.

Cultural ecology is the way people use their culture to adapt to particular environments. All people live in a **physical environment**, the world they can experience through their senses, but they will conceive of it in terms that seem most important to their adaptive needs and cultural perspective. We call this perspective the **cultural environment**.

All human societies must provide for the material needs of their members. People everywhere have to eat, clothe themselves, provide shelter against the elements, and take care of social requirements such as hospitality, gift giving, and proper dress.

Societies employ several different strategies to meet their material needs, strategies that affect their complexity and internal organization as well as relationships to the natural environment and to other human groups. Anthropologists often use these **subsistence strategies** to classify different groups into five types: hunter-gatherers, horticulturalists, pastoralists, agriculturalists, and industrialists. Let us look briefly at each of these.

People who rely on **hunting and gathering** depend on wild plants and animals for subsistence. Hunter-gatherers forage for food, moving to different parts of their territories as supplies of plants, animals, and water grow scarce. They live in small bands of 10 to 50 people and are typically egalitarian, leading a life marked by sharing and cooperation. Because hunter-gatherer bands are so small, they tend to lack formal political, legal, and religious structure, although members have regular ways to make group decisions, settle disputes, and deal ritually with the questions of death, adversity, social value, and world identification.

Hunter-gatherers tend to see themselves as part of the environment, not masters of it. This view shapes a religious ritual aimed at the maintenance and restoration of environmental harmony. All people lived as hunter-gatherers until about 10,000 years ago, when the first human groups began to farm and dwell in more permanent settlements. Today few hunter-gatherers survive. Most have lost their habitats to more powerful groups bent on economic and political exploitation.

Horticulture represents the earliest farming strategy, one that continues on a diminishing basis among many groups today. Horticulturalists garden. They often use a technique called **slash-and-burn agriculture**, which requires them to clear and burn over wild land and, with the aid of a digging stick, sow seeds in the ashes. When fields lose their fertility after a few years, they are abandoned and new land is cleared. Although horticulturalists farm, they often continue to forage for wild foods and still feel closely related to the natural environment.

Horticulture requires a substantial amount of undeveloped land, so overall population densities must remain fairly low. But the strategy permits higher population densities than hunting and gathering, so horticulturalists tend to live in larger permanent settlements numbering from 50 to 250 individuals. (Some horticultural societies have produced chiefdomships with much larger administrative and religious town centers.) Although they are still small by our standards, horticultural communities are large enough to require more complex organizational strategies. They often display more elaborate kinship systems based on descent, political structures that include headmen or chiefs, political alliances, religions characterized by belief in a variety of supernatural beings, and the beginnings of social inequality. Many of today's so-called tribal peoples are horticulturalists.

Pastoralism is a subsistence strategy based on the herding of domesticated animals such as cattle, goats, sheep, and camels. Although herding strategies vary from one environment to another, pastoralists share some general attributes. They move on a regular basis during the year to take advantage of fresh sources of water and fodder for their animals. They usually congregate in large encampments for part of the year when food and water are plentiful, then divide into smaller groups when these resources become scarce. Pastoralists often display a strong sense of group identity and pride, a fierce independence, and skill at war and raiding. Despite attempts by modern governments to place them in permanent settlements, many pastoral groups in Africa and Asia continue their nomadic lifestyle.

Agriculture is still a common subsistence strategy in many parts of the world. Agriculture refers to a kind of farming based on the intensive cultivation of permanent land holdings. Agriculturalists usually use plows and organic fertilizers and may irrigate their fields in dry conditions.

Agrarian societies are marked by a high degree of social complexity. They are often organized as nation-states with armies and bureaucracies, social stratification, markets, extended families and kin groups, and some occupational specialization. Religion takes on a formal structure and is organized as a separate institution.

The term **industrialism** labels the final kind of subsistence strategy. Ours is an industrial society, as is much of the Western, and more recently, the Asian world. Industrial nations are highly complex; they display an extensive variety of subgroups and social statuses. Industrial societies tend to be dominated by market economies in which goods and services are exchanged on the basis of price, supply, and demand. There is a high degree of economic specialization, and mass marketing may lead to a depersonalization of human relations. Religious, legal, political, and economic systems find expression as separate institutions in a way that might look disjointed to hunter-gatherers or others from smaller, more integrated societies.

The study of cultural ecology involves more than an understanding of people's basic subsistence strategies. Each society exists in a distinctive environment. Although a group may share many subsistence methods with other societies, there are always special environmental needs that shape productive techniques. Andean farmers, for example, have developed approximately 3,000 varieties of potatoes to meet the demands of growing conditions at different elevations in their mountain habitat. Bhil farmers in India have learned to create fields by damming up small streams in their rugged Aravalli hill villages. Otherwise, they would find it difficult to cultivate there at all. American farmers learned to "contour-plow" parallel to slopes in response to water erosion and now increasingly use plowless (no-till) farming to prevent the wind from carrying away precious topsoil.

No matter how successful their microenvironmental adjustments are, most groups in the world now face more serious adaptive challenges. One difficulty is the exploitation of their lands by outsiders, who are often unconstrained by adaptive necessity. A second is the need to overexploit the environment to meet market demand. (See Part Four for articles on market pressures.) A third is **climate change**, a long-term change in the Earth's climate, which includes a long-term increase in the atmospheric temperature as well as rising sea levels. Climate change ushers in a range of new challenges for people around the globe. These impacts are most detectable among people in climate-sensitive regions.

In all of these cases, many local peoples find that their traditional subsistence techniques no longer work. They have lost control of their own environmental adjustment and must struggle to adapt to the influences of outsiders, what is left of their habitat, and, the ground shifting under their feet.

Finally, just as humans adapt culturally to their environments, altering them in the process, environments may biologically adapt to humans. For example, intensive agriculture in the United States provides greater food sources for deer. In response, the number of deer has risen by as much as 400 percent. Animals domesticated by humans, such as cows, pigs, chickens, sheep, goats, dogs, and cats, have also experienced both genetic modification and increased numbers from their association with people.

The !Kung San, described by Richard Lee in the first selection, provide an excellent example of a traditional foraging lifestyle. The updates to this article by Richard Lee and Megan Biesele show that the same band of people who once lived on wild foods in the Kalahari now find themselves confined to small government-mandated settlements. Cattle herders tend their animals on the desert lands once occupied by the !Kung.

The second article, by Nathan Williamson, which is brought back from a previous edition, focuses on illegal logging in Bolivian forests. He notes that conservation efforts designed to prevent the logging have been ineffective. He locates the source of the problem in the international demand for the wood from these forests.

In the third article, which is new to this edition, Susan Crate tackles the complicated phenomenon of climate change, which has the most detectable impacts on people in climate sensitive regions like Siberia.

The final selection, by Richard Reed, which is updated for this volume of Conformity and Conflict, is a sobering reminder of what can happen to a horticultural people who once subsisted in harmony with their tropical forest habitat, but who now find themselves being displaced by colonists who have stripped the forest bare. Reed adds that there are now attempts to save the remaining forest and its native inhabitants by utilizing grassroots strategies to maintain the health of the natural environment while stimulating the collection of forest products.

Key Terms

agriculture p. 63
climate change p. 64
cultural ecology p. 62
cultural environment p. 62
ecology p. 62
horticulture p. 62

hunting and gathering p. 62
industrialism p. 63
pastoralism p. 63
physical environment p. 62
slash-and-burn agriculture p. 63
subsistence strategies p. 62

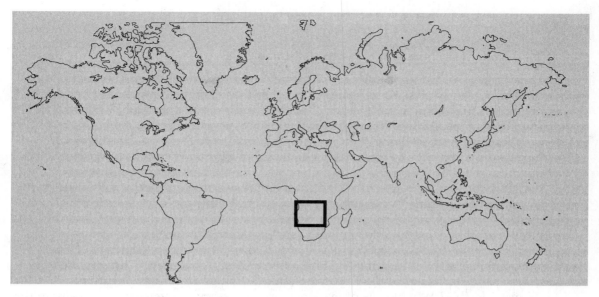

8

The Hunters: Scarce Resources in the Kalahari

Richard Borshay Lee

Until about 10,000 years ago, everyone in the world survived by hunting and gathering wild foods. They lived in intimate association with their natural environments and employed a complex variety of strategies to forage for food and other necessities of life. Agriculture displaced foraging as the main subsistence technique over the next few thousand years, but some hunter-gatherers lived on in the more remote parts of the world. This study by Richard Lee was done in the early 1960s and describes the important features of one of the last foraging groups, the Ju/'hoansi-!Kung living in the Kalahari Desert. It argues against the idea, held by many anthropologists at that time, that hunter-gatherers live a precarious, hand-to-mouth existence. Instead, Lee found that the !Kung, depending more on vegetable foods than meat, actually spent little time collecting food and managed to live long and fruitful lives in their difficult desert home. The update by Lee and Megan Biesele that appears at the end of the article details the events that have led the !Kung to settle down permanently to life as small-scale farmers and cattle raisers.*

*Reproduced by permission of the American Anthropological Association from the General Anthropology Bulletin of the General Anthropology Division, Volume 1, Issue 1, pp. 1, 3–5, 1994. Not for sale or further reproduction.

((••┤**Listen** to the **Chapter Audio** on **myanthrolab.com**

The current anthropological view of hunter-gatherer subsistence rests on two questionable assumptions. First is the notion that these people are primarily dependent on the hunting of game animals, and second is the assumption that their way of life is generally a precarious and arduous struggle for existence.

Recent data on living hunter-gatherers show a radically different picture. We have learned that in many societies, plant and marine resources are far more important than are game animals in the diet. More important, it is becoming clear that, with few conspicuous exceptions, the hunter-gatherer subsistence base is at least routine and reliable and at best surprisingly abundant. Anthropologists have consistently tended to underestimate the viability of even those "marginal isolates" of hunting peoples that have been available to ethnographers.

The purpose of this paper is to analyze the food-getting activities of one such "marginal" people, the !Kung Bushmen of the Kalahari Desert. Three related questions are posed: How do the Bushmen make a living? How easy or difficult is it for them to do this? What kinds of evidence are necessary to measure and evaluate the precariousness or security of a way of life? And after the relevant data are presented, two further questions are asked: What makes this security of life possible? To what extent are the Bushmen typical of hunter-gatherers in general?

Bushman Subsistence

The !Kung Bushmen of Botswana are an apt case for analysis. They inhabit the semi-arid northwest region of the Kalahari Desert. With only six to nine inches of rainfall per year, this is, by any account, a marginal environment for human habitation. In fact, it is precisely the unattractiveness of their homeland that has kept the !Kung isolated from extensive contact with their agricultural and pastoral neighbors.

Fieldwork was carried out in the Dobe area, a line of eight permanent waterholes near the South-West Africa border and 125 miles south of the Okavango River. The population of the Dobe area consists of 466 Bushmen, including 379 permanent residents living in independent camps or associated with Bantu cattle posts, as well as 87 seasonal visitors. The Bushmen share the area with some 340 Bantu pastoralists largely of the Herero and Tswana tribes. The ethnographic present refers to the period of fieldwork: October 1963 to January 1965.

The Bushmen living in independent camps lack firearms, livestock, and agriculture. Apart from occasional visits to the Herero for milk, these !Kung are entirely dependent upon hunting and gathering for their subsistence. Politically they are under the nominal authority of the Tswana headman, although they pay no taxes and receive very few government services. European presence amounts to one overnight government patrol every six to eight weeks. Although Dobe-area !Kung have had some contact with outsiders since the 1880s, the majority of them continue to hunt and gather because there is no viable alternative locally available to them.

Each of the fourteen independent camps is associated with one of the permanent waterholes. During the dry season (May–October) the entire population is clustered around these wells. Table 1 shows the numbers at each well at the end of the 1964 dry season. Two wells had no camp residents and one large well supported five camps. The number of camps at each well and the size of each camp changed frequently during the course of the year. The "camp" is an open aggregate of cooperating persons

TABLE 1 Numbers and Distribution of Resident Bushmen and Bantu by Waterhole*

Name of Waterhole	No. of Camps	Population of Camps	Other Bushmen	Total Bushmen	Bantu
Dobe	2	37	—	37	—
Langwa	1	16	23	39	84
Bate	2	30	12	42	21
!ubi	1	19	—	19	65
!gose	3	52	9	61	18
/ai/ai	5	94	13	107	67
!xabe	—	—	8	8	12
Mahopa	—	—	23	23	73
Total	14	248	88	336	340

*Figures do not include 130 Bushmen outside area on the date of census.

which changes in size and composition from day to day. Therefore, I have avoided the term "band" in describing the !Kung Bushman living groups.

Each waterhole has a hinterland lying within a six-mile radius that is regularly exploited for vegetable and animal foods. These areas are not territories in the zoological sense, since they are not defended against outsiders. Rather, they constitute the resources that lie within a convenient walking distance of a waterhole. The camp is a self-sufficient subsistence unit. The members move out each day to hunt and gather, and return in the evening to pool the collected foods in such a way that every person present receives an equitable share. Trade in foodstuffs between camps is minimal; personnel do move freely from camp to camp, however. The net effect is of a population constantly in motion. On the average, an individual spends a third of his time living only with close relatives, a third visiting other camps, and a third entertaining visitors from other camps.

Because of the strong emphasis on sharing, and the frequency of movement, surplus accumulation of storable plant foods and dried meat is kept to a minimum. There is rarely more than two or three days' supply of food on hand in a camp at any time. The result of this lack of surplus is that a constant subsistence effort must be maintained throughout the year. Unlike agriculturalists, who work hard during the planting and harvesting seasons and undergo "seasonal unemployment" for several months, the Bushmen hunter-gatherers collect food every third or fourth day throughout the year.

Vegetable foods comprise from 60 to 80 percent of the total diet by weight, and collecting involves two or three days of work per woman per week. The men also collect plants and small animals, but their major contribution to the diet is the hunting of medium and large game. The men are conscientious but not particularly successful hunters; although men's and women's work input is roughly equivalent in terms of man-day of effort, the women provide two to three times as much food by weight as the men.

Table 2 summarizes the seasonal activity cycle observed among the Dobe-area !Kung in 1964. For the greater part of the year, food is locally abundant and easily collected. It is only during the end of the dry season in September and October, when

TABLE 2 The Bushman Annual Round

	Jan.	Feb.	Mar.	April	May	June	July	Aug.	Sept.	Oct.	Nov.	Dec.
Season	*Summer Rains*			*Autumn Dry*			*Winter Dry*			*Spring Dry*		*First Rains*
Availability of water	Temporary summer pools everywhere			Large summer pools			Permanent waterholes only					Summer pools developing
Group moves	Widely dispersed at summer pools			At large summer pools			All population restricted to permanent waterholes					Moving out to summer pools
Men's subsistence activities	1. Hunting with bow, arrows, and dogs (year-round) 2. Running down immatures (year-round) 3. Some gathering (year-round)					Trapping small game in snares				Running down newborn animals		
Women's subsistence activities	1. Gathering of mongongo nuts (year-round) 2. Fruits, berries, melons					Roots, bi resins, albs				Roots, leafy greens		
Ritual activities	Dancing, trance performances, and ritual curing (year-round)				Boys' initiation*							
Relative subsistence hardship			Water-food distance minimal			Increasing distance from water to food				Water-food distance minimal		

*Held once every five years; none in 1963–64.
†New Year's: Bushmen join the celebrations of their missionized Bantu neighbors.

desirable foods have been eaten out in the immediate vicinity of the waterholes, that the people have to plan longer hikes of 10 to 15 miles and carry their own water to those areas where the mongongo nut is still available. The important point is that food is a constant, but distance required to reach food is a variable; it is short in the summer, fall, and early winter, and reaches its maximum in the spring.

This analysis attempts to provide quantitative measures of subsistence status, including data on the following topics: abundance and variety of resources, diet selectivity, range size and population density, the composition of the work force, the ratio of work to leisure time, and the caloric and protein levels in the diet. The value of quantitative data is that they can be used comparatively and also may be useful in archeological reconstruction. In addition, one can avoid the pitfalls of subjective and qualitative impressions; for example, statements about food "anxiety" have proven to be difficult to generalize across cultures.

Abundance and Variety of Resources

It is impossible to define "abundance" of resources absolutely. However, one index of relative abundance is whether or not a population exhausts all the food available from a given area. By this criterion, the habitat of the Dobe-area Bushmen is abundant in naturally occurring foods. By far the most important food is the mongongo (mangetti) nut (Ricinodendron rautanenii Schinz). Although tens of thousands of pounds of these nuts are harvested and eaten each year, thousands more rot on the ground each year for want of picking.

The mongongo nut, because of its abundance and reliability, alone accounts for 50 percent of the vegetable diet by weight. In this respect it resembles a cultivated staple crop such as maize or rice. Nutritionally it is even more remarkable, for it contains five times the calories and ten times the protein per cooked unit of the cereal crops. The average daily per capita consumption of 300 nuts yields about 1,260 calories and 56 grams of protein. This modest portion, weighing only about 7.5 ounces, contains the caloric equivalent of 2.5 pounds of cooked rice and the protein equivalent of 14 ounces of lean beef.

Furthermore, the mongongo nut is drought resistant, and it will still be abundant in the dry years when cultivated crops may fail. The extremely hard outer shell protects the inner kernel from rot and allows the nuts to be harvested for up to twelve months after they have fallen to the ground. A diet based on mongongo nuts is in fact more reliable than one based on cultivated foods, and it is not surprising, therefore, that when a Bushman was asked why he hadn't taken to agriculture, he replied: "Why should we plant, when there are so many mongongo nuts in the world?"

Apart from the mongongo, the Bushmen have available eighty-four other species of edible food plants, including twenty-nine species of fruits, berries, and melons and thirty species of roots and bulbs. The existence of this variety allows for a wide range of alternatives in subsistence strategy. During the summer months the Bushmen have no problem other than to choose among the tastiest and most easily collected foods. Many species, which are quite edible but less attractive, are bypassed, so that gathering never exhausts all the available plant foods of an area. During the dry season the diet becomes much more eclectic and the many species of roots, bulbs, and edible resins make an important contribution. It is this broad base that provides an essential margin of safety during the end of the dry season, when the mongongo nut forests are difficult to reach. In addition, it is likely that these rarely utilized species provide important nutritional and mineral trace elements that may be lacking in the more popular foods.

Diet Selectivity

If the Bushmen were living close to the "starvation" level, then one would expect them to exploit every available source of nutrition. That their life is well above this level is indicated by the data in Table 3. Here all the edible plant species are arranged in classes according to the frequency with which they were observed to be eaten. It should be noted that although there are some eighty-five species available, about 90 percent of the vegetable diet by weight is drawn from only twenty-three species. In other words, 75 percent of the listed species provide only 10 percent of the food value.

In their meat-eating habits, the Bushmen show a similar selectivity. Of the 223 local species of animals known and named by the Bushmen, 54 species are classified as edible, and of these only 17 species were hunted on a regular basis. Only a handful of the dozens of edible species of small mammals, birds, reptiles, and insects that occur locally are regarded as food. Such animals as rodents, snakes, lizards, termites, and grasshoppers, which in the literature are included in the Bushman diet, are despised by the Bushmen of the Dobe area.

Range Size and Population Density

The necessity to travel long distances, the high frequency of moves, and the maintenance of populations at low densities are also features commonly associated with the hunting and gathering way of life. Density estimates for hunters in western North America and Australia have ranged from 3 persons/square mile to as low as 1 person/100 square miles. In 1963–65, the resident and visiting Bushmen were observed to utilize an area of about 1,000 square miles during the course of the annual round for an effective population density of 41 persons/100 square miles. Within this area, however, the amount of ground covered by members of an individual camp was surprisingly small. A day's round-trip of twelve miles serves to define a "core" area six miles in radius surrounding each water point. By fanning out in all directions from their well, the members of a camp can gain access to the food resources of well over 100 square miles of territory within a two-hour hike. Except for a few weeks each year, areas lying beyond this six-mile radius are rarely utilized, even though they are no less rich in plants and game than are the core areas.

Although the Bushmen move their camps frequently (five or six times a year), they do not move them very far. A rainy season camp in the nut forests is rarely more than ten or twelve miles from the home waterhole, and often new campsites are occupied only a few hundred yards away from the previous one. By these criteria, the Bushmen do not lead a free-ranging nomadic way of life. For example, they do not undertake long marches of 30 to 100 miles to get food, since this task can be readily fulfilled within a day's walk of home base. When such long marches do occur they are invariably for visiting, trading, and marriage arrangements, and should not be confused with the normal routine of subsistence.

TABLE 3 !Kung Bushman Plant Foods

Food Class	Part Eaten								Total Number of Species in Class	Totals (percentages)	
	Fruit and Nut	Bean and Root	Fruit and Stalk	Root, Bulb	Fruit, Berry, Melon	Resin	Leaves	Seed, Bean		Estimated Contribution by Weight to Vegetable Diet	Estimated Contribution of Each Species
I. Primary Eaten daily throughout year (mongongo nut)	1	—	—	—	—	—	—	—	1	c.50	c.50*
II. Major Eaten daily in season	1	1	1	1	4	—	—	—	8	c.25	c.3†
III. Minor Eaten several times per week in season	—	—	—	7	3	2	2	—	14	c.15	c.1
IV. Supplementary Eaten when classes I—III locally unavailable	—	—	—	9	12	10	1	—	32	c.7	c.0.2
V. Rare Eaten several times per year	—	—	—	9	4	—	—	—	13	c.3	c.0.1‡
VI. Problematic Edible but not observed to be eaten	—	—	—	4	6	4	1	2	17	nil	nil
Total Species	2	1	1	30	29	16	4	2	85	100	—

*1 species constitutes 50 percent of the vegetable diet by weight.
† 23 species constitute 90 percent of the vegetable diet by weight.
‡ 62 species constitute the remaining 10 percent of the diet.

Demographic Factors

Another indicator of the harshness of a way of life is the age at which people die. Ever since Hobbes characterized life in the state of nature as "nasty, brutish and short," the assumption has been that hunting and gathering is so rigorous that members of such societies are rapidly worn out and meet an early death. Silberbauer, for example, says of the Gwi Bushmen of the central Kalahari that "life expectancy … is difficult to calculate, but I do not believe that many live beyond 45." And Coon has said of hunters in general:

> The practice of abandoning the hopelessly ill and aged has been observed in many parts of the world. It is always done by people living in poor environments where it is necessary to move about frequently to obtain food, where food is scarce, and transportation difficult … Among peoples who are forced to live in this way the oldest generation, the generation of individuals who have passed their physical peak, is reduced in numbers and influence. There is no body of elders to hand on tradition and control the affairs of younger men and women, and no formal system of age grading.

The !Kung Bushmen of the Dobe area flatly contradict this view. In a total population of 466, no fewer than 46 individuals (17 men and 29 women) were determined to be over sixty years of age, a proportion that compares favorably to the percentage of elderly in industrialized populations.

The aged hold a respected position in Bushmen society and are the effective leaders of the camps. Senilicide is extremely rare. Long after their productive years have passed, the old people are fed and cared for by their children and grandchildren. The blind, the senile, and the crippled are respected for the special ritual and technical skills they possess. For instance, the four elders at !gose waterhole were totally or partially blind, but this handicap did not prevent their active participation in decision making and ritual curing.

Another significant feature of the composition of the work force is the late assumption of adult responsibility by the adolescents. Young people are not expected to provide food regularly until they are married. Girls typically marry between the ages of fifteen and twenty, and boys about five years later, so that it is not unusual to find healthy, active teenagers visiting from camp to camp while their older relatives provide food for them.

As a result, the people in the twenty to sixty age group support a surprisingly large percentage of nonproductive young and old people. About 40 percent of the population in camps contributes little to the food supplies. This allocation of work to young and middle-aged adults allows for a relatively carefree childhood and adolescence and a relatively unstrenuous old age.

Leisure and Work

Another important index of ease or difficulty of subsistence is the amount of time devoted to the food quest. Hunting has usually been regarded by social scientists as a way of life in which merely keeping alive is so formidable a task that members of such societies lack the leisure time necessary to "build culture." The !Kung Bushmen would appear to conform to the rule, for as Lorna Marshall says:

It is vividly apparent that among the !Kung Bushmen, ethos, or "the spirit which actuates manners and customs," is survival. Their time and energies are almost wholly given to this task, for life in their environment requires that they spend their days mainly in procuring food.

It is certainly true that getting food is the most important single activity in Bushman life. However, this statement would apply equally well to small-scale agricultural and pastoral societies too. How much time is actually devoted to the food quest is fortunately an empirical question. And an analysis of the work effort of the Dobe Bushmen shows some unexpected results. From July 6 to August 2, 1964, I recorded all the daily activities of the Bushmen living at the Dobe waterhole. Because of the coming and going of visitors, the camp population fluctuated in size day by day, from a low of 23 to a high of 40, with a mean of 31.8 persons. Each day some of the adult members of the camp went out to hunt and/or gather while others stayed home or went visiting. The daily recording of all personnel on hand made it possible to calculate the number of man-days of work as a percentage of total number of man-days of consumption.

Although the Bushmen do not organize their activities on the basis of a seven-day week, I have divided the data this way to make them more intelligible. The workweek was calculated to show how many days out of seven each adult spent in subsistence activities (Table 4, Column 7). Week II has been eliminated from the totals since the investigator contributed food. In week I, the people spent an average of 2.3 days in subsistence activities, in week II, 1.9 days, and in week IV, 3.2 days. In all, the adults of the Dobe camp worked about two and a half days a week. Since the average working day was about six hours long, the fact emerges that !Kung Bushmen of Dobe,

TABLE 4   Summary of Dobe Work Diary

Week	(1) Mean Group Size	(2) Adult-Days	(3) Child-Days	(4) Total Man-Days of Consumption	(5) Man-Days of Work	(6) Meat (lbs.)	(7) Average Workweek/ Adult	(8) Index of Subsistence Effort
I (July 6–12)	25.6 (23–29)	114	65	179	37	104	2.3	.21
II (July 13–19)	28.3 (23–27)	125	73	198	22	80	1.2	.11
III (July 20–26)	34.3 (29–40)	156	84	240	42	177	1.9	.18
IV (July 27–Aug. 2)	35.6 (32–40)	167	82	249	77	129	3.2	.31
4-wk. total	30.9	562	304	866	178	490	2.2	.21
Adjusted total*	31.8	437	231	668	156	410	2.5	.23

*See text

Key: Column 1: Mean group size = $\dfrac{\text{total man-days of consumption}}{7}$.

Column 7: Workweek = the number of workdays per adult per week.

Column 8: Index of subsistence effort = $\dfrac{\text{man-days of work}}{\text{man-days of consumption}}$ (e.g., in Week I, the value of "S" = 21,

i.e., 21 days of work/100 days of consumption or 1 workday produces food for 5 consumption days).

despite their harsh environment, devote from twelve to nineteen hours a week to getting food. Even the hardest-working individual in the camp, a man named ≠ oma who went out hunting on sixteen of the twenty-eight days, spent a maximum of thirty-two hours a week in the food quest.

Because the Bushmen do not amass a surplus of foods, there are no seasons of exceptionally intensive activities such as planting and harvesting, and no seasons of unemployment. The level of work observed is an accurate reflection of the effort required to meet the immediate caloric needs of the group. This work diary covers the midwinter dry season, a period when food is neither at its most plentiful nor at its scarcest levels, and the diary documents the transition from better to worse conditions (see Table 4). During the fourth week the gatherers were making overnight trips to camps in the mongongo nut forests seven to ten miles distant from the waterhole. These longer trips account for the rise in the level of work, from twelve or thirteen to nineteen hours per week.

If food getting occupies such a small proportion of a Bushman's waking hours, then how do people allocate their time? A woman gathers on one day enough food to feed her family for three days, and spends the rest of her time resting in camp, doing embroidery, visiting other camps, or entertaining visitors from other camps. For each day at home, kitchen routines, such as cooking, nut cracking, collecting firewood, and fetching water, occupy one to three hours of her time. This rhythm of steady work and steady leisure is maintained throughout the year.

The hunters tend to work more frequently than the women, but their schedule is uneven. It is not unusual for a man to hunt avidly for a week and then do nothing at all for two or three weeks. Since hunting is an unpredictable business and subject to magical control, hunters sometimes experience a run of bad luck and stop hunting for a month or longer. During these periods, visiting, entertaining, and especially dancing are the primary activities of men. (Unlike the Hadza, gambling is only a minor leisure activity.)

The trance dance is the focus of Bushman ritual life; over 50 percent of the men have trained as trance-performers and regularly enter trance during the course of the all-night dances. At some camps, trance dances occur as frequently as two or three times a week, and those who have entered trances the night before rarely go out hunting the following day . . . In a camp with five or more hunters, there are usually two or three who are actively hunting and several others who are inactive. The net effect is to phase the hunting and non-hunting so that a fairly steady supply of meat is brought into camp.

TABLE 5   Caloric and Protein Levels in the !Kung Bushman Diet, July–August, 1964

	Per-Capita Consumption				
Class of Food	Percentage Contribution to Diet by Weight	Weight in Grams	Protein in Grams	Calories per Person per Day	Percentage Caloric Contribution of Meat and Vegetables
Meat	37	230	34.5	690	33
Mongongo nuts	33	210	56.7	1,260	67
Other vegetable foods	30	190	1.9	190	
Total all sources	100	630	93.1	2,140	100

Caloric Returns

Is the modest work effort of the Bushmen sufficient to provide the calories necessary to maintain the health of the population? Or have the !Kung, in common with some agricultural peoples, adjusted to a permanently substandard nutritional level?

During my fieldwork I did not encounter any cases of kwashiorkor, the most common nutritional disease in the children of African agricultural societies. However, without medical examinations, it is impossible to exclude the possibility that subclinical signs of malnutrition existed.

Another measure of nutritional adequacy is the average consumption of calories and proteins per person per day. The estimate for the Bushmen is based on observations of the weights of foods of known composition that were brought into Dobe camp on each day of the study period. The per-capita figure is obtained by dividing the total weight of foodstuffs by the total number of persons in the camp. These results are set out in detail elsewhere and can only be summarized here. During the study period 410 pounds of meat were brought in by the hunters of the Dobe camp, for a daily share of nine ounces of meat per person. About 700 pounds of vegetables were gathered and consumed during the same period. Table 5 sets out the calories and proteins available per capita in the !Kung Bushman diet from meat, mongongo nuts, and other vegetable sources.

This output of 2,140 calories and 93.1 grams of protein per person per day may be compared with the Recommended Daily Allowances (RDA) for persons of the small size and stature but vigorous activity regime of the !Kung Bushmen. The RDA for Bushmen can be estimated at 1,975 calories and 60 grams of protein per person per day. Thus it is apparent that food output exceeds energy requirements by 165 calories and 33 grams of protein. One can tentatively conclude that even a modest subsistence effort of two or three days' work per week is enough to provide an adequate diet for the !Kung Bushmen.

The Security of Bushman Life

I have attempted to evaluate the subsistence base of one contemporary hunter-gatherer society living in a marginal environment. The !Kung Bushmen have available to them some relatively abundant high-quality foods, and they do not have to walk very far or work very hard to get them. Furthermore, this modest work effort provides sufficient calories to support not only active adults, but also a large number of middle-aged and elderly people. The Bushmen do not have to press their youngsters into the service of the food quest, nor do they have to dispose of the oldsters after they have ceased to be productive.

The evidence presented assumes an added significance because this security of life was observed during the third year of one of the most severe droughts in South Africa's history. Most of the 576,000 people of Botswana are pastoralists and agriculturalists. After the crops had failed three years in succession and over 100,000 head of cattle had died on the range for lack of water, the World Food Program of the United Nations instituted a famine relief program which has grown to include 180,000 people, over 30 percent of the population. This program did not touch the Dobe area in the isolated northwest corner of the country, and the Herero and Tswana women there were able to feed their families only by joining the Bushman women to forage for wild foods. Thus the natural plant resources of the Dobe area were carrying a higher proportion of population than would be the case in years when the Bantu harvested crops. Yet this added pressure on the land did not seem to adversely affect the Bushmen.

In one sense it was unfortunate that the period of my fieldwork happened to coincide with the drought, since I was unable to witness a "typical" annual subsistence cycle. However, in another sense, the coincidence was a lucky one, for the drought put the Bushmen and their subsistence system to the acid test and, in terms of adaptation to scarce resources, they passed with flying colors. One can postulate that their subsistence base would be even more substantial during years of higher rainfall.

What are the crucial factors that make this way of life possible? I suggest that the primary factor is the Bushmen's strong emphasis on vegetable food sources. Although hunting involves a great deal of effort and prestige, plant foods provide from 60 to 80 percent of the annual diet by weight. Meat has come to be regarded as a special treat; when available, it is welcomed as a break from the routine of vegetable foods, but it is never depended upon as a staple. No one ever goes hungry when hunting fails.

The reason for this emphasis is not hard to find. Vegetable foods are abundant, sedentary, and predictable. They grow in the same place year after year, and the gatherer is guaranteed a day's return of food for a day's expenditure of energy. Game animals, by contrast, are scarce, mobile, unpredictable, and difficult to catch. A hunter has no guarantee of success and may in fact go for days or weeks without killing a large mammal. During the study period, there were eleven men in the Dobe camp, of whom four did no hunting at all. The seven active men spent a total of 78 man-days hunting, and this work input yielded eighteen animals killed, or one kill for every four man-days of hunting. The probability of any one hunter making a kill on a given day was 0.23. By contrast, the probability of a woman finding plant food on a given day was 1.00. In other words, hunting and gathering are not equally felicitous subsistence alternatives.

Consider the productivity per man-hour of the two kinds of subsistence activities. One man-hour of hunting produces about 100 edible calories, and of gathering, 240 calories. Gathering is thus seen to be 2.4 times more productive than hunting. In short, hunting is a high-risk, low-return subsistence activity, while gathering is a low-risk, high-return subsistence activity.

It is not at all contradictory that the hunting complex holds a central place in the Bushmen ethos and that meat is valued more highly than vegetable foods. Analogously, steak is valued more highly than potatoes in the food preferences of our own society. In both situations the meat is more "costly" than the vegetable food. In the Bushman case, the cost of food can be measured in terms of time and energy expended. By this standard, 1,000 calories of meat "costs" ten man-hours, while the "cost" of 1,000 calories of vegetable foods is only four man-hours. Further, it is to be expected that the less predictable, more expensive food source would have a greater accretion of myth and ritual built up around it than would the routine staples of life, which rarely if ever fail.

Conclusions

Three points ought to be stressed. First, life in the state of nature is not necessarily nasty, brutish, and short. The Dobe-area Bushmen live well today on wild plants and meat, in spite of the fact that they are confined to the least productive portion of the range in which Bushman peoples were formerly found. It is likely that an even more substantial subsistence would have been characteristic of these hunters and gatherers in the past, when they had the pick of African habitats to choose from.

Second, the basis of Bushman diet is derived from sources other than meat. This emphasis makes good ecological sense to the !Kung Bushmen and appears to be a common feature among hunters and gatherers in general. Since a 30 to 40 percent input of meat is such a consistent target for modern hunters in a variety of habitats, is it not reasonable to postulate a similar percentage for prehistoric hunters? Certainly the absence of plant remains on archeological sites is by itself not sufficient evidence for the absence of gathering. Recently abandoned Bushman campsites show a similar absence of vegetable remains, although this paper has clearly shown that plant foods comprise over 60 percent of the actual diet.

Finally, one gets the impression that hunting societies have been chosen by ethnologists to illustrate a dominant theme, such as the extreme importance of environment in the molding of certain cultures. Such a theme can best be exemplified by cases in which the technology is simple and/or the environment is harsh. This emphasis on the dramatic may have been pedagogically useful, but unfortunately it has led to the assumption that a precarious hunting subsistence base was characteristic of all cultures in the Pleistocene. This view of both modern and ancient hunters ought to be reconsidered. Specifically I am suggesting a shift in focus away from the dramatic and unusual cases, and toward a consideration of hunting and gathering as a persistent and well-adapted way of life.

Epilogue: The Ju/'hoansi in 1994[1]

In 1963 perhaps three-quarters of the Dobe Ju/'hoansi were living in camps based primarily on hunting and gathering while the rest were attached to Black cattle posts. Back then there had been no trading stores, schools, or clinics, no government feeding programs, boreholes, or airstrips, and no resident civil servants (apart from the tribally-appointed headman, his clerk, and constable). By 1994 all these institutions and facilities were in place and the Dobe people were well into their third decade of rapid social change; they had been transformed in a generation from a society of foragers, some of whom herded and worked for others, to a society of small-holders who eked out a living by herding, farming, and craft production, along with some hunting and gathering.

Ju villages today look like others in Botswana. The beehive-shaped grass huts are gone, replaced by semi-permanent mud-walled houses behind makeshift stockades to keep out cattle. Villages ceased to be circular and tight-knit. Twenty-five people who lived in a space twenty by twenty meters now spread themselves out in a line village several hundred meters long. Instead of looking across the central open space at each other, the houses face the kraal where cattle and goats are kept, inscribing spatially a symbolic shift from reliance on each other to reliance on property in the form of herds.

Hunting and gathering, which provided Dobe Ju with over 85 percent of their subsistence as recently as 1964, now supplies perhaps 30 percent of their food. The rest is made up of milk and meat from domestic stock, store-bought mealie (corn)

[1]Excerpted from Richard B. Lee and Megan Biesele, General Anthropology, Vol. 1, No. 1, Fall 1994, pp. 1, 3–5.

meal, and vast quantities of heavily-sugared tea whitened with powdered milk. Game meat and foraged foods and occasional produce from gardens make up the rest of the diet. However, for most of the 1980s government and foreign drought relief provided the bulk of the diet . . .

In the long run, Dobe-area Ju/'hoansi face serious difficulties. Since 1975, wealthy Tswana have formed borehole syndicates to stake out ranches in remote areas. With 99-year leases, which can be bought and sold, ownership is tantamount to private tenure. By the late 1980s borehole drilling was approaching the Dobe area. If the Dobe Ju do not form borehole syndicates soon, with overseas help, their traditional foraging areas may be permanently cut off from them by commercial ranching.

✓●─ Study and Review on myanthrolab.com

Review Questions

1. How does Lee assess the day-to-day quality of !Kung life when they lived as foragers? How does this view compare with that held by many anthropologists in the early 1960s?

2. What evidence does Lee give to support his view about the !Kung?

3. According to Lee, !Kung children are not expected to work until after they are married; old people are supported and respected. How does this arrangement differ from behavior in our own society, and what might explain the difference?

4. What was a key to successful subsistence for the !Kung and other hunter-gatherers, according to Lee?

5. In what ways has life changed for the !Kung since 1964? What has caused these changes?

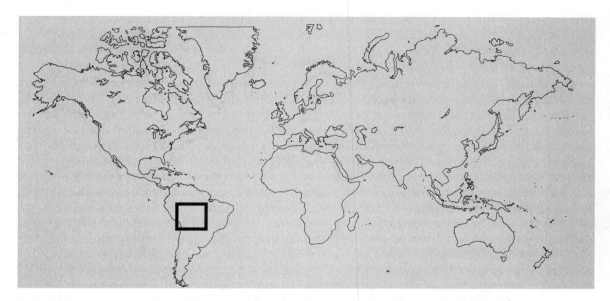

9

Illegal Logging and Frontier Conservation

Nathan Williamson

Conservation policy often seems to be based on a protective ideology and a faith in economic motivational theory. Too often, such policy ignores local reality, such as when the Indian government divided Aravalli Hill forests on the basis of a U.S. model. They designated ranges, lots, and sublots, hired forest guards, and began what was supposed to be a forty-two-year cutting cycle. The policy failed to conserve the forest because it ignored the fact that people lived in and used the forest every day. What is needed is a better understanding of what is actually going on, which, as this article by Nathan Williamson illustrates, is a possible role for anthropologists. Based on two years of field-work in and near the Chimanes forest in the eastern Bolivian lowlands, Williamson argues that forest conservation efforts by the Bolivian government and international organizations such as the International Tropical Timber Organization have largely failed to prevent illegal logging by commercial companies, chain saw gangs, and Chimanes Indians. Major reasons for this are the world demand for quality tropical hardwoods, the poverty of people living on the Bolivian frontier, and the inability of a poor government to control illegal activities in such a remote area. The only solution, he concludes, is for an international agreement to control demand for tropical hardwoods or at least a plan that directs small-scale logging in a sustainable way.

*"Illegal Logging and Frontier Conservation" by Nathan Williamson. Reprinted by permission of the author.

((∙●⌐**Listen** to the **Chapter Audio** on **myanthrolab.com**

I hold up the microphone I am using during an impromptu interview and ask Alfonso Campero if he is worried about hitting the tree that has emerged from the darkness in front of us.[1] He and I are crouched in the bow of a balsa-wood raft that carries his family, piles of green plantains, and bags of unshelled rice down the Maniqui River. The Maniqui is an Amazonian tributary that cuts through Bolivia's tropical lowlands. The river flows through parts of Beni Department (a department is roughly equivalent to a U.S. state), an area about the size of Minnesota. Except for where lush hardwood forests butt up against the Andes Mountains to the west, Beni is flat. This explains why the Maniqui meanders through endless curves and loops and why traveling on it by raft can be painfully slow. Even so, the current is persistent and Alfonso doesn't have time to answer me. The cumbersome raft hits the log and Alfonso and his father, Jorge, swear and grunt as they push us away from the partly submerged hazard.

Navigation on the river is complicated by the fact that the Camperos are also guiding a raft of timber, which they have cut illegally near their homestead in the Chimanes Indian Reserve, down river to San Borja. San Borja is a frontier town defined by unpaved streets, shacks, bars, prostitutes, and lumber mills. It is also headquarters to several lumber companies, and it is to a small-scale lumber buyer that the Camperos will sell their timber. He, in turn, will mill the wood in one of several small lumber mills found in San Borja and probably sell it to a local lumber company. The company will ship it by truck up the perilous, single-track dirt road to the Bolivian highlands, where it will likely be used to make furniture, flooring, or windows. Some of these products end up on the world market.

The Camperos are only a small part of the region's logging industry. Largest are the several logging companies that, with government approval, are supposed to conduct their logging at sustainable levels in forests set aside for managed logging. The timber they cut there is considered to be legally harvested by the Bolivian government. But most of the logging companies are closely tied to small illegal logging operations such as the Camperos' because the companies can increase their profits by buying the valuable illegal timber and claiming that it has come from their own forest ranges. They also buy timber from another small-scale source, the *cuartoneros* (chainsaw gang members), who scout for mahogany (and other hardwoods) found in the Chimanes Reserve, cut it down, chainsaw it into timbers *(cuartones)*, carry it piece by piece to nearby streams, and float it down to San Borja. Working together and motivated by the global demand for fine hardwoods, the logging company owners and workers, sawmill operators, truckers, Chimanes Indians, and *cuartoneros* form a single economic system.

But this system also works within another context, the international movement to conserve natural resources. The Bolivian government and world conservation groups, alarmed by the wholesale destruction of the world's prime forests and also motivated by the specter of lost revenue that accompanies it, have implemented plans designed to achieve sustainable logging in and around the Chimanes forest. On the face of it, their conservation policies appear sensible and workable. But in fact they are not. To be sure, the logging systems found in San Borja are not as destructive as the clear-cutting that goes on in many parts of the world, but they are slowly depleting the forest and will probably eventually lead to its destruction. Why have the carefully

[1]All names have been changed.

planned conservation efforts failed in this case? The answer lies in the geographic, economic, and political realities of frontier life in this part of Bolivia, and the actions of commercial timber companies driven by the high world demand for quality tropical hardwoods.

Conservation Policy

The Bolivian government and several NGOs (nongovernmental organizations) have introduced plans to regulate logging in the Bolivian lowlands at a time when the forests still exist. The Chimanes forest has not yet suffered the effects of clear-cutting and the invasion of farmers and ranchers seen in other parts of the Amazon basin. Loggers are the major threat. With this in mind, Conservation International, a conservation organization based in Washington, D.C., arranged a debt-for-nature swap in the region in 1987. The organization bought (paid off) part of Bolivia's external national debt in exchange for the formation of a trust fund to pay for conservation projects in the region and permanent legal status for a biosphere reserve. Following the 1987 debt-for-nature swap, the International Tropical Timber Organization, an industry association, began funding its own sustainable forestry program inside the conservation and timber production areas. At the time, Conservation International, the International Tropical Timber Organization, and the Bolivian government hoped to demonstrate that economic development could be harmonious with forest conservation. The International Tropical Timber Organization's Chimanes program asked seven timber companies in the conservation area to change their harvesting practices in return for rights to cut in certain designated parts of the forest. They now would cut a variety of commercial species on a rotating schedule that would permit forest regeneration. The Chimanes program hoped to show that the forest could provide timber for the long term and that the forest's enhanced economic value in that role would discourage its destruction for use as pasture, colonization, and farming.

When I arrived in the Chimanes area for the first time in 1999, I quickly realized that what looked promising on paper was difficult to achieve on the ground. Despite an initial investment by the International Tropical Timber Organization of $1,200,000 and subsequent foreign assistance totaling $300,000 to $400,000 a year, the seven timber concessions in the conservation area did little to change their extraction techniques. It was more profitable for them to continue to cut only the most valuable species, primarily mahogany, than to search the forest for the less-valuable species that the sustainable forestry program required them to cut. It also did not work because the seven companies could buy timber from individuals—Chimanes Indians like the Camperos, and *cuartoneros*—who were willing and able to illegally harvest the most valuable trees in forests that were off limits to the big companies and logging altogether. In this way, some companies that were part of the legal economy "laundered" prime wood cut by people who were part of the "shadow," or illegal, economy. It is easy to understand why companies are motivated to do this. Timber extraction costs are high in this part of the world because it is so expensive to ship in equipment and send out the wood. Harvesting just the most valuable hardwoods is more economical; cutting cheaper wood is not. But what motivates the Chimanes Indians and *cuartoneros* to break the law, especially considering how much work it is for them to harvest timber by hand?

Chimanes Economics

Economic necessity is the most obvious answer. About 8,000 Chimanes live in the Chimanes Reserve, which is about the size of Rhode Island. Only one or two logging roads carve up their vast tract of tropical forest and most of the people use the Maniqui River as their highway. The Chimanes seem to relish isolation, and remain hesitant to make strong connections with the rest of Bolivia. Few of them speak Spanish. Although some of them have married colonists, their contacts with outsiders are largely limited to trading, piloting rafts, and searching for the valuable trees that they or *cuartoneros* will cut. The Chimanes have often been mislabeled "nomads" because they move about the forest to hunt and fish. Nevertheless, virtually every Chimanes family has a small agricultural field and a more or less permanently located reed hut. Chimanes are expert fishermen, and, for this reason, most of their villages hug the banks of the Maniqui River.

Besides farming and hunting, many Chimanes produce some goods for sale. They grow and sell rice to river traders and weave two-foot-long shingles out of *jatata*, a small palm (*Genoma deversa*), which are used to roof houses in San Borja and other parts of the frontier.

The Chimanes are self-sufficient in many ways, but they still need to make money. They often buy (or trade for) tools, food, clothing, school supplies (for the children who go to school), and other goods they cannot produce themselves. Although the work is hard and the proceeds are meager, illegal logging is the easiest way to increase income.

The villagers living in Nápoles, a Chimanes settlement of about nineteen huts located up river from San Borja, harvest timber themselves or in partnership with timber buyers from San Borja. Jorge Campero, who, with his family, lives in Nápoles, figures that 50 percent of the villagers are employed in the illegal logging trade "right down to the schoolteacher," his son emphasized. Because the villagers don't have enough money to pay for a tractor to haul trees out of the woods, they use homemade oxcarts to bring the wood to the river.

This is how the Camperos harvested the timber we were rafting down the Maniqui. The Camperos cut four old-growth trees behind their house in late April of 2001 and used their cart to bring the wood to the river. Alfonso figured that he could sell the load for about $400 when they reached San Borja and clear about $220 after expenses. He would split the money with his father. This amount may appear small to many North Americans, especially if they knew how many dollars the wood would bring in the United States, but in Bolivia, where the average daily wage is about $2, the sum is significant. To the Camperos, who depend on illegal logging to earn a living, forest conservation means little.

Cuartoneros

Cuartoneros log illegally for the same reasons that Chimanes do, but they work differently from the Indians. The Nápoles Chimanes community is unique in that many of its villagers are self-employed loggers, meaning they transport the wood themselves and sell it to small lumber mills or timber buyers in San Borja. Most of the other Chimanes villages sell their timber to traders who come up river to get it. In either case, most of their logging is done near the river. But in the more remote areas of the Chimanes Territory, it is the *cuartoneros*, or chainsaw crews, who mine the forest for its most valuable trees. And they do so without the help of mechanized equipment except for chainsaws and outboard motors. Mostly poor men from San Borja, they scout, often with the help of Chimanes Indians, for mahogany trees in the Chimanes Reserve, cut the trees down, saw them up with chainsaws, and carry the timbers to nearby streams. I joined a group of *cuartoneros* on a timber-cutting excursion in April 1999. Before we departed, team members loaded the outboard motor-powered dugout canoe with needed equipment, including a replacement chainsaw bar, a drum of gasoline, and food. The boat was a supply shuttle; its purpose was to drop me and the equipment off near a logging camp and return to town.

The Chimanes forest is well watered. It receives ninety-one inches of rain on average each year, which runs off to form small streams that flow into creeks and wide rivers. Once we were under way, it immediately became clear how important rivers and streams are to the *cuartoneros'* method of timber extraction. When the rivers run high, the timber can be floated to San Borja. When the rivers are low, crews must wait for rain to transport the wood.

Typically, the *cuartoneros* set up camp by a stream in an area where they believe uncut mahogany trees are located. They string up plastic tarpaulins to protect them and their equipment from the rain. They make a fire to cook the food they have brought with them or hunted in the forest. Next they contact local Chimanes Indians and ask them to scout the forest for suitable mahogany and other valuable hardwood trees. The search is more difficult than it might seem because broad-leafed mahogany trees grow at very low densities in Bolivia. Indeed, the loggers may only find one or two large-sized trees every twenty-five acres. If team members have already cut the trees closest to their camp, they may have to walk for several miles to reach the next tree they can fell.

Before they can cut the trees, however, the loggers must clear a trail from them to the nearest large stream or river. To do this, the men use machetes, cutting steps into inclines and chopping the brush back to form paths. Because of the large amount of labor involved in carrying the wood, trails must be as direct and level as possible. Bridges made from wood slabs are also placed over the brooks and streams that often block the way. Finally, the trail is carefully scouted for roots and other objects that might trip the loggers as they carry their heavy loads of wood to the river.

A chainsaw operator, who must work for hours each day with his heavy implement, does the actual cutting and processing of the trees. Mahogany grows up to six and one-half feet in diameter. To fell such a large tree, the chainsaw operator makes several cuts at its base. When the tree drops, the chainsawer's assistant, using wooden wedges and levers cut from smaller trees in the forest, must level it. Then the assistant measures the widths of the *cuartones* to be cut by marking the ends of the tree trunk. Finally, he uses an oil-soaked line to snap sawing guides along the length of the log.

The chainsaw operator, cutting along the snapped lines freehand, divides the tree into *planchones* (slabs) that are typically six and one-half inches thick and as wide as the log. The assistant flips the slabs over and snaps guidelines six or seven inches apart along their lengths. The chainsawer cuts along these lines to produce *cuartones*. Other loggers will carry these timbers, which weigh anywhere from 80 to 200 pounds, to the stream or river. While the carriers transport the wood, the chainsawer continues to saw *cuartones*.

To carry the *cuartones* to the river or stream, the men form a relay, with each worker responsible for his own section of the trail (*tramo*) that, depending on the difficulty of the terrain, is between 20 and 200 feet long. The first *lomero* (timber carrier) sets the pace. He upends a *cuarton*, balancing it horizontally on a shoulder pad. Trotting at a half jog, he plants the *cuarton* point down on the ground at the end of his *tramo*, and the next *lomero* picks it up on his shoulder and trots off toward the end of his section. The process is repeated over and over again until all the *cuartones* reach their final destination.

The work is exhausting. The loggers often have to carry the heavy timbers up steep hills, across narrow makeshift bridges, and down slippery descents. Even on the flat sections, the pace is hard because the *lomeros* run faster there. Despite the hard work, carrying is a slow way to move timber. It may take an entire day to move thirty timbers half a mile. As one logger recalled,

> Shit, my first day I almost fainted. Because they were heavy, those *cuartones*. I was saying it wasn't the kind of work for me because it seemed like they were going to kill me. "You will learn," they said. But all night my arms and legs were so sore. *They* [the other men] were relaxed! The other guys were playing. I said, shit, I am sick.

The work goes on for days until sufficient *cuartones* are cut and moved. Then the men drag the *cuartones* into the stream and wade, float, or push them to the nearest river. There, they lash them together to form rafts (*cayapos*), and float them to San Borja.

Why would anyone do this arduous and illegal work? The answer seems to be that there are few better alternatives for employment on the frontier. Jobs are hard to find in Bolivia, and the San Borja region is no exception. And by local standards (manual laborers, such as brush clearers and cowboys, receive about $33 to $35 a month), *cuartoneros* are paid well. In 1999, the foreman on a *cuartonero* crew made $5.26 a day. The chainsawer received four or five cents for each board foot he milled (I estimated that the crew produced about 2,200 board feet that month), while the timber carriers earned $5.30 a day. The chainsawer's assistant earned $4.38 and the camp cook, $3.50.

It is the lure of higher pay, combined with the fact that most men who work on chainsaw gangs are in debt to their *patrons*, the men who underwrite and organize the operation, which sends them back into the forest time and again. In this debt/peonage system, men are rarely able to earn enough to fully pay off what they owe. As a result, although the Chimanes forest is out of bounds to loggers, the attraction of higher pay and the need to pay off debts draws the men back into the illegal work time and again.

Forest Conservation

Is it possible for industrial logging to be sustainable, to log in a way that permits forests to recover and produce timber for hundreds of years? Sustainable extraction for forests may actually work in some areas of North America. Unfortunately, the story in the tropics is more complex. Here large tracts of virgin rain forest remain, but logging them in a way that would let them recover is very expensive. For example, Bowles et al.[2] estimate that systems of logging that preserve tropical

---

[2]I. A. Bowles et al., "Policy, Logging and Tropical Forest Conservation," *Science* 280 (1998): 1900.

forests' biodiversity cost from 20 to 450 percent more than simply hacking the most valuable trees out of the forest and moving on to other untouched stands of trees.

But is illegal logging in the Chimanes forest and approved logging in other forests near San Borja that destructive? The answer is both yes and no. In the long run, the forest will be denuded of its most valuable trees. In the short run, illegal logging is less destructive than approved commercial logging. However, as markets for more tree species continue to open up for Bolivian logging companies, even approved companies will be tempted to log in more damaging ways.

Similar to slash-and-burn agriculture, which was once viewed as devastating to forests and wasteful but is now felt to permit forest sustainability if done in moderation, *cuartonero* and Chimanes logging have less impact on the forest than one might think. Unlike mechanized logging operations, these small-scale lumbermen do not clear wide skid roads that account for much of the ecological damage caused by logging in Bolivia. The forest quickly overgrows the five-foot-wide trails the *cuartoneros* clear to get timber out of the forest. Chimanes logging is slightly more destructive because the Indians clear oxcart trails, which are much wider than footpaths, to transport the timber they cut and because they cut more trees in the forest near their houses.

Cuartoneros also spare almost all the less valuable rain forest tree species because it is only worth their time and hard labor to cut and carry the most valuable trees. (Wood processed from a single large mahogany tree can bring $1,000 in San Borja and much more in the United States and Europe.) In addition, *cuartonero* timber harvests are limited to an area a few miles wide along large streams, because it does not make financial sense to carry the wood any farther.

Mechanized logging is more destructive. Industrial logging companies may have to cut and market less valuable rain forest species to justify the high cost of installing logging roads. And the roads, cut by bulldozers, are destructive to the forest. Although commercial operations can theoretically rotate their cutting areas to allow for regrowth, these sustainable forest practices still require extensive road networks to reach far into the forest.

But even the least destructive logging practices change the forest. Young mahogany trees do not usually produce seeds. It is the larger trees that regenerate the species and these are the ones that loggers cut down. In the end, the selective practice of cutting the most valuable trees will eliminate these species from the forest. The creation of logging roads, the migration of people into the frontier who are looking for work, and the likely improvement of the road up the mountains linking the region to La Paz in the highlands will all threaten the forest.

Forest Management on the Frontier

In an attempt to stop the prolific illegal logging along the Maniqui River, both by large lumber companies and by the Chimanes and *cuartoneros*, the Bolivian Forestry Service recently approved two timber management plans for the Chimanes Reserve. Both call for local people, the Chimanes and *cuartoneros*, to put down their chainsaws and cooperate with a group of timber companies that have been given exclusive rights to log in the management areas. Unfortunately, these plans provide good examples of what can go wrong with forestry projects in indigenous territories.

First, the Chimanes Indians possess no organized tribal government or agency that can deal effectively with the government or with logging companies. Mindful of this, forestry projects in other areas of Bolivia (one is run by a Bolivian NGO working with the Nature Conservancy) try to establish a Western-style governing body among native groups. This was not necessary for the Chimanes because the New Tribes evangelical missionaries had created something called the Chimanes Council, which is currently negotiating timber deals with outsiders on behalf of the tribe. Unfortunately, most Chimanes are unhappy with the results, and few believe the Council can fairly represent them.

A second problem is the Forest Service's choice of logging companies that have rights to do the work. One timber company that just received legal rights to log in the territory has long been involved in the illegal timber trade. Another is alleged to be a front for a U.S. timber company that is known for breaking Bolivian forestry laws.

A third problem concerns employment. At best, timber companies with new rights to log the Chimanes Territory will employ one or two men from each Chimanes village. The remaining men, who used to log illegally, are supposed to find other ways to earn a living. And although some *cuartoneros* may be hired by logging companies, their wages may be lower. If illegal logging ceases, many will lose their livelihoods.

In sum, it appears that the Bolivian Forest Department's new plan will not prevent current logging practices. Instead, the agreement will give local companies access to the Chimanes forest, which used to be out of bounds for cutting, and it probably won't stop small-scale cutting and smuggling.

Conclusion

The Chimanes forest and other forests near San Borja are attractive natural resources ripe for exploitation by entrepreneurs. International environmental groups have sought ways to preserve the region's old-growth forests by suggesting various plans to promote sustainable logging. The Bolivian government has endorsed these plans or developed its own conservation programs, motivated partly by debt-for-nature agreements and partly by the economic argument that it is better to establish a longer-producing industry. But these programs have not worked well because poor Indians and colonists, driven by the need for work and money, ignore the agreements and because commercial logging companies in search of profits do as well.

On top of it all is the simple fact that logging law and policy cannot be enforced. San Borja and the Chimanes forest area are part of the Bolivian frontier. Just as frontier life in the United States bred lawlessness and opportunism, so does the Bolivian frontier. Located far from centers of government in La Paz in the highlands, the lowlands are barely connected to the rest of the country. The Bolivian nation is perpetually in debt. It does not have the resources, and perhaps, at times, the will, to control illegal frontier activity.

What possible solution is there to this difficult problem? The answer may ultimately lie with the world community. Just as demand drives the illegal international drug trade, the world market for quality old-growth forest hardwoods stimulates illegal logging. Controlling logging will require moderating demand by limiting imports of mahogany. One minor example of this approach is India's long-standing limit on the amount of pith it can produce for conversion into pith helmets. More dramatic are international agreements that limit whale hunting and define seasons on some varieties of fish.

Another approach might be to appeal to people's consciences. Wood produced in a sustainable manner can be labeled as environmentally friendly and priced higher to cover the costs of sustainable management. Conservation groups could run ad campaigns that are similar to those aimed at the fur coat industry. Building a home with unsustainably harvested mahogany paneling could be equated with the death of a priceless tropical forest ecosystem. Or perhaps it is possible to institute a program that permits Chimanes Indians and *cuartoneros* to log but also to replant the species they take. No matter what the approach, the dream of one day having sustainable logging in Bolivia and other parts of the world with tropical forests can only be realized if there is a worldwide determination to support it by using legal agreements, market mechanisms, and good forestry management.

In the meantime, the Camperos lose little sleep about whether their logging is sustainable. Their mission is simple: sell the wood to a small sawmill whose owner will sell the boards to someone with connections to get the shipments to a city where it can be re-sold and exported. Alfonso has his own and his family's life to worry about. Because it rained for several days, it has taken him over a month to harvest wood that will bring him $120. On that kind of money he has to feed, clothe, and school his eight children.

By nightfall the kids have fallen asleep in a big pile in the middle of the raft. They lie all tangled together under a sheet their father has hung over them to keep off the rain. As we near San Borja, he and Jorge become quiet. They are nervous about losing their wood because there have been rumors that local Forest Service agents are confiscating undocumented lumber. It has taken them 32 days to get their wood this far. They don't want to lose it now.

✓●─ **Study** and **Review** on **myanthrolab.com**

Review Questions

1. According to Williamson, what plans and programs have been tried to promote sustainable logging in the Bolivian lowlands? How have they worked?

2. What are the three main types of logging employed by people in the Chimanes and nearby forests? How destructive to the forest is each?

3. What motivates the Chimanes Indians and *cuartoneros* to illegally cut timber in the Chimanes Forest Reserve? What role does the frontier nature of the area play in their ability to get away with these activities?

4. According to Williamson, why have the programs put forward by the Bolivian government and NGOs failed to work in the forests that surround San Borja? What does he suggest might be the way to promote sustainable logging there?

5. How are logging activities in the Bolivian lowlands connected to the world economy?

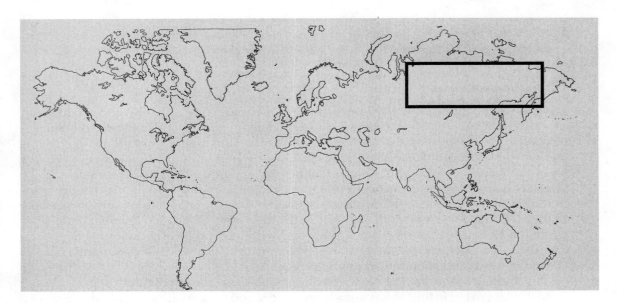

10

We are Going Underwater

Susan A. Crate

Humans are a part of a global ecosystem. A good deal of anthropological literature has focused on the ways in which the most vulnerable, natural-resource dependent groups in the world will disproportionately experience the most harmful effects of climate change. While we know that humans are amazingly adaptive creatures, climate change ushers in a range of new, and as yet, still-untested challenges for people around the globe. While we typically think of climate change specialists as biologists and chemists who study ice cores, tree rings, rocks, and the like, this article, new to this edition of Conformity and Conflict, *by Susan Crate shows the crucial dimension of human-environment interaction and the very real impacts actions by people half a world away can have on indigenous peoples.**

((•⎯Listen to the **Chapter Audio** on **myanthrolab.com**

There are no longer any skylarks. They are gone, and we don't hear them. And now we also don't hear the shaman's drum. Before we had shamans, and the woods rang. . . . Humans are not meant to dig down in the earth, but they started to do mining here in the Soviet time, and now with all the water they want to dig down again, this time to make canals. There is too much water. For example, at Chegde there used to be many families working and haying and keeping animals, and now only one family can get enough hay there, because the rest is flooded.

*From Susan A. Crate, "We are going underwater: Siberian villagers show the world what global climate change means." *Natural History* May 2011: 20+.

But I think all the canals and all the digging will make matters worse. They dug a canal at Tuolbe—a six-meter-deep canal. That is bad; we are not to dig like that. This is a sacred land, and we are not to bother the land so much.

—Bahylai (Vasilii) Nikolaev, Khoro, Suntar District, Republic of Sakha
(Yakutia), Russian Federation, July 10, 2010.

For me, testimony like this from Viliui Sakha, a horse- and cattle-breeding people of northeastern Siberia, is food for thought. I have lived, worked, and conducted ethnographic research in their communities since 1991 and have witnessed many transformations over the years. But Nikolaev, born in 1926, can look back over a long lifetime of drastic changes. Even though the 1917 October Revolution had already occurred, Nikolaev was born early enough to learn and live his people's pre-Soviet adaptations—both physical and spiritual—to the extreme Siberian climate. He also witnessed the Soviet transformation of his people's lifeways and culture through the gradual collectivization and further rapid consolidation of Sakha subsistence practices into sovkhozi (agro-industrial state farm operations). Nikolaev was one of several native Sakha hired as local guides for Soviet geological teams exploring the diamond-rich region during the push for industrialization in the late 1950s. His diverse life experience is richly summarized in his view that Sakha laws of nature have been repeatedly and increasingly broken—to the point where the fundamental sounds, the song of the skylark and the echo of the shaman's drum, are now absent from his homeland.

Nikolaev's homeland is the Republic of Sakha (Yakutia), which takes up one-fifth of the Russian Federation's territory. Ethnically, about 45 percent of the republic's 1 million inhabitants are Sakha, formerly called Yakuts, their Russian designation. Most still speak their native Sakha, a Turkic language (readers accustomed to the transliteration of Russian names and words will notice some nonstandard adaptations). Nikolaev is Viliui Sakha, because he lives in one of the districts that lies in the watershed of the Viliui River, a western tributary of the great Lena River, which flows northward through the center of the republic. Viliui Sakha are distinctive from Sakha inhabiting the republic's central regions, mostly on account of their acclaimed music and dance traditions, personified by the late improvisatory singer Sergei Afanas'evich Zverov.

For more than half a millennium Sakha have raised their cattle and horses in an extreme continental climate. Like all place-based peoples (a term used in anthropology circles to refer to groups who depend directly upon their immediate environment for both their physical and spiritual sustenance), their pioneering ancestors developed adaptations to live and flourish within a specific ecosystem. In their case, they faced a subarctic environment with continuous permafrost and annual temperature swings of 180 Fahrenheit degrees, from -75 in the winter to 105 in summer. Also like most place-based peoples, Sakha refined an ancestral belief system that mediates their interactions with their environment. Theirs is an animistic world view, one that recognizes the sentient quality of all of creation and that requires people to perform specific acts and rituals in order to thrive. Shamans, individuals either born or apprenticed into their calling, are the intermediaries for humans with the spirit worlds. "Black" shamans travel from the middle world, the world of human habitation, to the lower world to fight and negotiate with abaahi (evil spirits) in times of crisis. In contrast, "white" shamans interact with sky spirits, most importantly during the Sakha summer festival, to ensure a plentiful harvest.

Not only have Sakha adapted to an extreme climate and subarctic ecosystem, they have also accommodated outside social pressures. In the mid-1600s, during

Russian imperial expansion eastward, colonizers forced them to pay iasak (fur tribute) and annexed some of their lands. Their holdings were further taken during the Soviet collectivization process; their environment was despoiled by Soviet-era industrialization—in their case, diamond mining—and since the early 1990s they continue to deal with changes following the fall of the Soviet Union. For most Viliui Sakha, daily life continues to be a full-time job of addressing the immediate needs of family, household, income, and food production.

With the turn of the twenty-first century, however, Sakha face a new challenge, one much less announced or recognized: a subtle and gradually increasing change in cycles and patterns of weather and climate.

I began hearing testimonies about this new change in the summer of 2005, the last field research season of a project focused on local definitions of future sustainability. While analyzing surveys, the project research team, made up of my village research assistants and me, found that in answers to the final, open-ended question, 90 percent of the eighty-five participants had expressed concern about changes in weather patterns, temperature, landscape, and the like. In response, we decided to spend part of the final weeks interviewing elders, since they had the longest continuous period of observation of local weather and climate.

Among the thirty-three elders interviewed, ten mentioned that one of the differences between now and before was that now the Bull of Winter was no longer arriving. I knew they were referring to the mythological beast who, according to the Sakha story, comes bringing with him the cold three-month period when it is too dry to snow and all is held in a frozen silence. Such testimony clarified for me how global climate change was affecting not only the villagers' physical environment, but also their mythological or cosmological adaptation to that environment—a ripe subject for further investigation. Before leaving the field that summer, I asked if the communities wanted to participate in a three-year project focused on understanding these changes of concern. With their approval (and a bit of proposal writing), I returned in 2008 to begin documenting their local experiences and adaptive responses.

During our first summer of research, we focused on gathering local people's observations and perceptions of change, their explanations of the causes of those changes, and their opinions about how the near future would unfold if those changes were to continue. We met with Sakha in the four villages where I had been concentrating my field research since 1991, all located in the Suntar district. In each village, we conducted two six-person focus groups and interviewed fifteen people. Our results showed overall consensus on the following nine changes.

Winters are warm. Most agreed that warmer winters are welcome, since people need less wood to heat their homes, and cows can be outside more and can walk to the water hole instead of people having to haul water to the barns for them. "It is good not to be cold," one young man remarked, "and we youth already expect the winter to be warm!" But with further probing, many also commented that warmer winters mean more sickness, especially for elders and children. The same probing also revealed many favorable views of a cold winter. One elder remarked: "In winter the cold makes your body feel lighter, and you work and move better and go about with enthusiasm. In the warmth, it is like your bones have melted, and you can't work and move well." This acceptance of cold is even expressed in time-tested proverbs still in use today. For example:

"Cold is the companion of the young."

"Cold in the cold time, hot in the hot time."

"We are Sakha—so we need cold!"

There is increasing water on the land. Standing water and flooding interfere with the villagers' main rural resource: graze for horses and hay as fodder for cows. "I don't recall anything like the water we have had in the past ten years," said one villager. "Before, we hayed all the fields—now we have to go here and there to hay, because all our haylands are underwater." The increased water also ruins roads needed to access resources, and has even begun inundating foundations of low-lying houses. House-holders have also been accustomed to creating a buluus, or underground freezer, by digging a hole down to the permafrost. In it they store meat, milk products, and even ice for summer drinking water. That natural convenience is increasingly flooded, and more and more households have to do without a buluus or use an electric freezer.

There is too much rain, and it falls at the wrong times. Precipitation patterns have changed so that it not only rains more, but rainfall tends to come not in spring but instead during July and August, interfering with the villagers' haying activities. "When it rains, it rains for very long times and at the wrong times of year," said one villager. "When I was ten and went haying, we would wait for rain—it never rained. Back then it only rained for two or three days during the entire haying season—and when it did rain, we would go berrying. But in the last ten years we have not been able to finish the hay work because of rain."

Summers are cold. Cold summers prevent the full maturing of many staple gar-den and forage plants, not to mention hay. Cold summer weather also makes it less inviting to get all the work done to prepare for the long winter. Sakha have a saying: "One day of summer is worth a week of winter." They also feel robbed of a much-de-served recharge of warmth from the hot, dry summers formerly characteristic of their area. "If it is warm," said one elder, "we feel good and wear light clothes and can work hard—and soak up all the Sun's warm rays." Notably, Sakha say both kinds of unsea-sonable weather—mildness in the cold time and wet chill in the hot time—sap their energy for work.

Seasons come late. The most problematic lagging season is an extended fall, which is interfering with the regular timing of events. For example, the extended periods of freeze and thaw affect the annual cycle of slaughter. Typically, Sakha wait until tem-peratures are below freezing twenty-four hours a day so that they can store the meat in unheated sheds, utilizing the environment as a natural freezer. That would normally be in the middle of November. With the extended fall, however, they are now having to wait an extra two to four weeks—which means feeding the animals intended for slaugh-ter another two to four weeks' worth of hay, and putting off replenishing household meat stores.

The extended fall also interferes with the gathering of oton (cowberry or lin-gonberry), the last berry of the season and the one most highly prized by households for its vitamins. Typically those berries are harvested in large quantities, which are poured into cardboard boxes and stored in unheated sheds to gradually freeze for flesh eating during the winter. With the repeated freezing and thawing that now oc-curs, the skin of the berries is broken, and entire boxes of them turn into unusable mush.

In addition, many natural signs that tell Sakha spring is on its way increasingly appear during the extended fall period. One is n'urguhunnar, or snowdrops, the first spring flower that pushes up through the snow, much as crocuses do in temperate zones of the United States. The formation of icicles and of new needles on larch trees are other "heralds of spring" that, jarringly, are seen in the newly extended fall.

Even as winter finally settles in, problems arise. The extended fall, characterized by cycles of freezing and thawing, often causes formation of a layer of ice beneath the snow that makes it impossible for horses, which forage outside year-round, to continue feeding. Between that and the increase in snowfall, many horse breeders now complain that their herds are suffering. "Horses can't reach their food, so they starve, and many die—and many of the babies inside them die," one villager reported. "Also, this winter some fell through the thin ice."

There is too much snow. Villagers also report that instead of the usual three-month break in snowfall when the Bull of Winter arrived, it now snows all winter, owing to warming. Because of this, they constantly have to clear snow, especially to move it away from their homes before the spring thaw to avoid inundation. As one put it, "With so much snow, falling all winter long, and the winds—we now have to shovel all winter, and sometimes a few times a day."

There are more floods. Inhabitants also talked about how the annual spring flood cycle, characteristic of their ecosystem and resulting from the spring thaw of ice and snow, has increased in volume and duration. This results in broken transportation infrastructure (roads and bridges), sudden inundation of homes and public buildings, and the intensification of the existing problem of increasing water on the land.

Temperatures change suddenly. Many people mentioned this new phenomenon. One elder remarked, "In June it is hot, then very cold and windy. In the fall season it will suddenly snow and then there will be very warm days. In winter it was minus 40 [Celsius], and the next day, very suddenly, it was 3 or 4 degrees [above zero]."

There are fewer birds and animals. The decline was widely noted. "I hunt, and I can tell you that the wild animals are very few—you can count them on your fingers," said one villager. An elder lamented:

> It used to be that you got up in the morning, and your
> ears were filled with the sounds of birds and animals. In
> the summer we waited to hear the skylark's song in the
> hay fields, and in the spring we waited for the cuckoo's
> talking. We lived on the edge of Kuukei lake, and the
> ducks and geese also made a lot of sounds. Now it is totally
> quiet. I miss the birds' singing—they have been my
> friends ever since I was a child, we grew up together.

Hares, an important game species for Sakha, will not nest in wet land, and so, to the extent that water is increasing across the land, they have more than likely changed their range. But a decline in the population of hares, or of other wild animals, should not be attributed solely to global climate change. For example, over the last decade more people have had the time and resources to hunt than in the Soviet period. Not only that, most contemporary youth no longer observe Sakha hunting ethics (as one elder put it, "Young people nowadays kill everything they see"). Such factors play a role in consort with climate-change effects. This dynamic of "multiple stressors" plays a similar role in the other eight changes inhabitants observe.

In discussions of their various observations in the focus groups and in interviews, the increasing water on the land emerged as the inhabitants' greatest concern. But beyond the practical concerns of not enough hay, hampered transportation, and household inundation, Sakha also find the increasing water psychologically unsettling. "I am very scared that we are going underwater," said one villager. "Looking down from a plane you can see that the land has patches of water across it—water is coming up from below. It looks like the land is sinking down." I was reminded how the phrase uuga barabyt ("We are going underwater") had already come up in focus-group and interview discussions. Even I had noticed the increasing water on the land after an absence of three years, and had documented it by taking some snapshots during our 2008 airplane ride to the villages.

As mentioned above, climate change is not the only contributing factor to contemporary local change, and also it is not the first issue Sakha have coped or are coping with. They could be thought of as experts in adapting—to an extreme subarctic climate, to Russian colonization, to sovietization, to post-Soviet times. But how they will adapt to the new changes—particularly the flooding of land and the difficulty of laying up sufficient hay for their herds—remains to be seen. Our 2009 survey revealed that the vast majority do not want to move away, even if it means not keeping cows. Like most place-based peoples, they are tied to their ancestral homelands.

We also know from our investigation that most Sakha do not make the connection between the changes they are seeing locally and global climate change. Their explanations were based on the evidence available to them, which points to contributing factors in the changes they observe, but does not tell the full story. When asked what was the cause, most blamed the Viliui hydroelectric reservoir. Others identified the source as the natural wet and dry cycles of their ecosystem. The third most popular explanation was the recent overabundance of technology and mechanization. The few who mentioned global climate change were either teachers, university students home from the city for the summer, or elders who read every newspaper they could subscribe to.

The unprecedented effects of global climate change—at work to a greater or lesser extent in each of the nine changes—make adaptation a novel challenge for Viliui Sakha, and for all the world's inhabitants. Therefore, finding ways to bring an understanding of that phenomenon into local awareness makes sense as a way to encourage new adaptive strategies, bolster survival, and allay some of the psychological distress. Conversely, the detailed and highly specific observations of place-based peoples such as the Viliui Sakha contribute important information, clarifying the diverse physical and cultural ways that this global phenomenon is having its effect. This kind of local knowledge needs to be brought to the attention of the global community and into the formulation of policy initiatives.

This revelation prompted our team to explore the ways we could both increase local awareness of the role played by climate change and also bring local observations and understanding to the regional science community. Our culminating event for the three-year project was what we called "knowledge exchanges."

One of our regional scientific consultants since the project's outset, Alexander Fedorov, a specialist from the Melnikov Permafrost Institute, quickly agreed to participate in the knowledge exchanges. He himself is Viliui Sakha, from the Nyurba district, which neighbors the Suntar district where our research is based. He told us he was keenly aware of the need to bring scientific information to the affected communities. It was poignant to me that halfway through the knowledge exchange trip, Fedorov shared with me how satisfying the experience was for him—adding that not only was it the first time he had presented his research to a public audience, but also the first time he had done so in his native Sakha language.

In the summer of 2010 we traveled by van from the capital city, Yakutsk, to our four research villages, stopping to hold knowledge exchanges in the four district centers along the way. We began the exchanges by inviting audience participants to talk about changes they had been observing. Here is just one example, from a man who traveled six miles on horseback to attend our event:

> I am a cowboy and hunter—and I see that the land has
> changed. Where there was never a ravine there now is
> a ravine, all has caved in. Around the streams, where
> the flat haylands are located, the same thing is happening—ravines
> have now formed and all the water goes
> away very quickly down those ravines, and the lands
> that never were dry before are now dry. The ducks
> come very late. Mostly I am speaking about changes in
> the land's surface: where there never was a hill, there
> now is a hill; where there never was a hole, there now
> is. The wet lands are now dry, and there are more and
> more ravines. Land that never had water now does, and
> the erosion of our lands is happening very quickly—in
> just the last few years. And horses have a very hard time
> in the warm winter. We thought that warm would be
> good for the horses, but now we understand it is bad for
> them. Overall, we have come to a time when we cannot
> predict the weather. Before, things came in the right
> times, and now they do not.

Alexander Fedorov's sharing of his research was similarly far-reaching. After providing a concise overview of global climate change and its amplified effect in the polar regions, including the Republic of Sakha (Yakutia), he brought his presentation home by focusing on permafrost. He explained that across the world, global climate change is affecting ecosystems in specific ways, and in the Sakha ecosystem the main indicator of it is the degradation of permafrost. He went on to explain that among the many kinds of permafrost, that which made up most of the Viliui regions was the kind with large ice wedges and, consequently, the most susceptible to temperature change and degradation. His comments were illustrated with photographs of familiar village scenes combined with graphed data.

Fedorov also shared newly developed technologies to help preserve permafrost—methods of building new houses and of retrofitting old ones. For new construction, large pipes are laid under the site where the house will be built and are covered with several feet of soil; then the house is built on top. The pipe ends are left open in winter to allow freezing air to maintain the permafrost, and are closed in summer to prevent warm air from thawing it. For an existing home, an auger is used to dig a hole several yards deep alongside the foundation, down to the permafrost. A pipe is then inserted and filled with diesel fuel or kerosene, which keep the soil cold because of their low freezing points.

Overall, the knowledge exchanges were a success: residents participated actively, adding their local knowledge to the scientific understanding of how the global phenomenon is affecting their locales; reciprocally, specific scientific knowledge helped to fill out local perceptions of contemporary change. Our task now is to integrate local and regional knowledge and to share it more broadly among the region's inhabitants and beyond. Our primary goals in this integration are both to bolster Sakha understandings and adaptations and to inform the science and policy communities about how climate change is affecting local environments and cultures.

Some scientists are developing ways to "scale down" global climate models to make them relevant to local communities. In my work on global climate change and place-based peoples, I am repeatedly asked if we plan to "scale up" our findings to have global significance. Although I do believe the knowledge we have gained can have a wider application, it will not be by scaling it up, but rather by giving the world community a local window into the diverse ways global climate change is unsettling and challenging such time-refined adaptations as those of the Viliui Sakha. Those of us who live within consumer societies may believe that the centralized energy, food, and water systems on which we so depend are on much safer ground than Sakha hay-fields, but if our location and technology can delay the full impact of change, they can also make us less adaptable when the floodwaters (figurative or literal) finally reach us. We must recognize our infrastructures'—and our own—ultimate vulnerability to climate impacts, and act in time.

Place-based peoples in climate-sensitive regions, such as the far north, are now feeling the first and most detectable effects of global climate change. We must ask ourselves how we will fare as climate change proceeds to affect the world's temperate zones. We should realize that we are all losing our places. If we can learn to identify, admire, and share the unique adaptive capacities of one another's cultures, we will all have a better chance to weather the storm.

✓•─ **Study** and **Review** on **myanthrolab.com**

Review Questions

1. According to Crate, what are the nine changes induced by climate change in this setting?

2. How does Crate define "place-based peoples"?

3. What are the attributes of a climate-sensitive region?

4. What does a focused study of the Viliui Sakha contribute to our understanding of climate change more broadly?

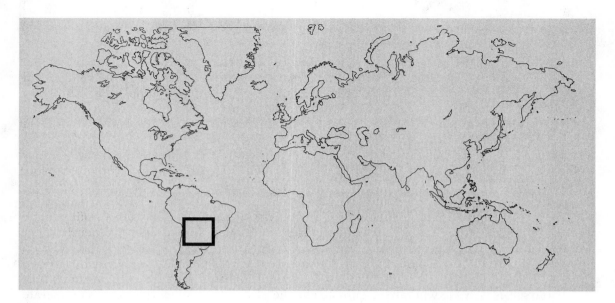

11

Forest Development the Indian Way

Richard K. Reed

To most industrialized peoples, the practice of slash-and-burn agriculture seems wasteful. Horticulturalists use axes and machetes to fell forests, burn the debris, and then plant in the ashes. Within a few short years, the fields are abandoned and the farmer moves on. For people used to thinking of agriculture as intensively planted permanent fields, slash-and-burn agriculture seems destructive. Richard Reed, in this article updated for the fifteenth edition of Conformity and Conflict, *challenges this simplistic notion. Describing the production practices of the Guaraní Indians living in the tropical forests of Paraguay, and detailing the destruction of their original way of life by the infiltration of* colonos *(non-Indian colonists), he shows that Indian slash-and-burn agriculture combined with commercial harvesting of natural products offers a more sustainable and economically sound means for all people to prosper in these fragile forests.* *

((•⎯Listen to the **Chapter Audio** on **myanthrolab.com**

When I arrived in Itanaramí that very first time, it felt like I had left the modern world behind. This small Guaraní Indian village was hidden deep in the Paraguayan forests, surrounded by hundreds of miles of wilderness. I took a jeep to the end of a rutted dirt road and followed

*From Richard K. Reed, "Forest Development the Indian Way." Used by permission of the author.

96

winding footpaths for two days into the heart of one of South America's great natural areas. Trees shaded the trail I took over the low hills, and clear streams offered cool refreshment in the valleys. Entering the community, the path opened into a small clearing and Veraju's small thatch roof jutted up through the tangle of the family's overgrown garden. His family was busy in the house yard, preparing manioc from the garden and game from the hunt. The rest of the settlement was similarly embedded in the forest, each home set in a small clearing along the narrow footpath. Houses seemed isolated from the world, protected from modernity by the high trees and verdant foliage of this vast forest.

I soon discovered that the isolation was illusory. Their house lots were strewn with machetes from Costa Rica and clothes were sewn from Brazilian polyester cloth. Even the most isolated households bought salt and soap and fish hooks from traders.

Guaraní made their living by gardening and hunting, but they also obtained cash by gathering and selling goods from the forest, especially the leaves of the wild yerba-mate plant *(Ilex Paraguaiensis)*, which is brewed in a caffeinated infusion throughout southern South America. And the commercial work was not new. A little research showed that the Guaraní had sold the leaf to Brazilian, Argentine, and Bolivian merchants since at least 1590. They had developed a way to mine the forest for its wealth without destroying the resources on which they depend.

The Threatened Forests

But the Guaraní's environment was threatened even then. The world's great tropical regions had become prime targets for a new kind of economic development. Ranchers and farmers, from Brazil to Indonesia, flocked to the jungle frontiers armed with chainsaws and bulldozers. They built roads, clear-cut timber, and denuded the land of foliage, often burning the trees and brush as they went.

The scope of this human invasion staggers the mind. Intensive development destroys hundreds of square miles of virgin tropical forest each day. In the Amazon alone, an area the size of New Jersey is cleared every year. We are discovering that not only are the forests finite, but they are rapidly disappearing. Almost 80% of Paraguay's deep forests have been cleared or seriously eroded.

The future of this development is as finite as the resources it depends on. The march of progress, which seems so powerful and necessary, will soon destroy the very resources it requires. We can either choose to abandon our current development strategies or we will be forced to change.

As a result, the modern world is searching for models of development that promote growth within the world's finite resources. This *sustainable development* differs from conventional strategies in several important respects. First, it recognizes that resources are finite and protects those resources even as we benefit from them. Second, sustainable development emphasizes the relationship between economic, ecological, and social systems, striving to protect the integrity of all three. Third, sustainable development promotes social stability by distributing the benefits and raising the standard of living of all people.

As the modern world searches for technological solutions to its increasingly obvious problems, I discovered that the Guaraní offered a proven model for sustainable tropical forest development. More than simply providing their subsistence, they had developed a *commercial* system that gave them access to the world marketplace without destroying the forests they depended on.

We may ask what accounts for this successful adaptation. What subsistence strategies permit them to live within the ecological limits of the forest? Can such people provide a model for successful tropical forest management? If so, perhaps indigenous peoples will be as important to our future as the oxygen-giving forests they live in. Let's look at the factors that allowed the Guaraní of eastern Paraguay to prosper in the forest and the lessons we may learn from them.

The Guaraní

Before the encroachment of outsiders, the Guaraní Indians were well adapted to their forest environment. Like most horticulturalists, they lived in small, widely scattered communities. Because their population densities were low, and because they practiced a mixture of slash-and-burn agriculture and foraging, they placed a light demand on forest resources. Small size also meant a more personal social organization and an emphasis on cooperation and sharing. Although of greater size and complexity than hunter-gatherer bands, Guaraní villages contained many of the cultural values found in these nomadic societies.

Since that first visit thirty years ago, I have continued to conduct ethnographic fieldwork in the small group of Guaraní villages that include Itanaramí. The residents of these communities are among the last of the Guaraní Indians still living in the forests of southern South America. They are the remnants of an ethnic group that 400 years ago dominated southern Brazil and Paraguay from the Atlantic Ocean to the Andes. The Guaraní have suffered as disease, slavers, and colonists have invaded their forests. Today, only 30,500 Guaraní remain in isolated settlements where the tropical forest survives-and even these are threatened.

The forests of Itanaramí have high canopies that shelter both animal and human populations. When I first arrived in the region, the expanse of trees was broken only by streams and rivers that drain westward to the broad, marshy valley of the Parana River. Viewed from the ground, the density of the forest growth was matched only by the diversity of plant species.

Itanaramí itself is built along a small stream that gives the settlement its name. To my uninformed eye, it was difficult to recognize the existence of a village at all when I first arrived there. Homesteads-which consisted of a clearing, a thatched hut, and a field-were scattered in the forest, often out of sight of one another. A closer look revealed that pathways through the forest connected houses to each other and to a slightly larger homestead, that of the *tamoi* (literally grandfather), the group's religious leader. As in many small societies, households were tied together by kinship, which wove a tapestry of relations that organized social affairs and linked Itanaramí to other Guaraní communities.

I discovered that Guaraní culture emphasized sharing and cooperation. Sisters often shared work and childcare. Brothers usually hunted together. Food was distributed among members of the extended family, including cousins, aunts, and uncles. Families shared abundance with compatriots who had less and expected the same treatment in return. People emphasized the general welfare, not individual wealth.

The *tamoi*, although in no sense a leader with formal authority, commanded considerable respect in the community. He settled disputes, chastised errant juniors, and led the entire community in evening religious ceremonies where all drank *kanguijy* (fermented corn), danced, and chanted to the gods.

The people of Itanaramí not only lived in the forest, they saw themselves as of it. The forest was basic to indigenous cosmology. The people referred to themselves as *ka'aguygua*, or "people of the forest." Villagers often named their children after the numerous forest songbirds, symbolizing their close personal ties to the environment.

Sustainable Production

Guaraní had lived in their present locale for centuries and had dwelled throughout the tropical forests of lowland South America for thousands of years. During all this time, they exploited flora, fauna, and soils of the forests without undermining the integrity of the forest ecosystem. In fact, Guaraní production seems to promote biodiversity. The secret of their success was their production strategy. The Indians mixed agriculture with gathering, hunting, and fishing in a way that permitted the environment to recover. They even collected forest products for sale to outsiders, again without causing environmental damage. Guaraní farming was well suited to forest maintenance. Using a form of shifting agriculture called slash-and-burn farming, the Indians permitted the forest to recover from the damage of field clearing. The way Veraju, the tamoi of Itanaramí, and his wife, Kitu, farmed provides a typical example. When the family needed to prepare a new field, it was Veraju who did the heavy work. He cut the trees and undergrowth to make a half-acre clearing near his house. Then he, Kitu, and some of their five children burned the fallen trees and brush, creating an ash that provided a powerful fertilizer for the thin forest soils. When the field was prepared, Kitu used a digging stick fashioned from a sapling to poke small holes in the ground, and planted the staple Guaraní crops, beans and manioc root (from which tapioca is made). Interspersed with the basic staples, they added the slower-growing banana, sugar cane, and orange trees to round out their diet. When the crops matured, it was Kitu and her daughters who harvested them.

The secret to successful slash-and-burn agriculture is field "shifting" or rotation. Crops flourish the first year and are plentiful the next, but the sun and rain soon take their toll on the exposed soil. The thin loam layer, so typical of tropical forests, degenerates rapidly to sand and clay. Grasses, weeds, and insect pests, rare in the deep forest, eventually discover the vulnerable crops. By the third year, the poor soils are thick with weeds and grow only a sparse corn crop and few small manioc roots. Rather than replant a fourth time, Veraju and Kitu would clear a new field nearby where soils are naturally more fertile and the forest can be burned for additional ash fertilizer.

Although fallow, their old field was not abandoned. They returned periodically to dig some of the remaining manioc and, while there, tend a small area of banana trees or clear the weeds from around a young orange tree. If Veraju discovered a yerba plant taking root in the tangle of undergrowth he would cut back the surrounding brush and give it room to grow.

The surrounding forest quickly reclaims the old field; roots penetrate the opening from the forest edge and animals wander through it dropping seeds in their path. As the forest returns, the decaying matter once again strengthens the depleted soil. After several years the plot will be distinguished only as one of the citrus groves that are scattered throughout the unbroken forest. In this way, the forest produces a sustained yield without degrading the natural ecosystem.

More than protect the forest, Guaraní production increases the biodiversity of the system. As gardens revert to fallows, and regrowth turns into forest, some of the species planted and tended by the Guaraní survive. The forest that regrows has plants that would have failed but for the attention of Kitu or Veraju.

The forest recovers sufficiently fast for the same plot to be cleared and replanted within ten or fifteen years. This "swidden" system results in the cyclic use of a large area of forest, with a part under cultivation and a much larger portion lying fallow in various stages of decomposition.

If farming formed the only subsistence base, the Guaraní would have had to clear much larger gardens. But they also turned to other forest resources game, fish, and forest products-to meet their needs. Guaraní men often formed small groups to hunt large animals such as deer, tapir, and peccary with guns purchased from outsiders or with the more traditional bows and arrows they make themselves. A successful hunt provides enough meat to share liberally with friends. Men also trapped smaller mammals, such as armadillo and paca (a large rodent). They fashioned snares and deadfall traps from saplings, tree trunks, and cactus fiber twine. These were set near homesteads, along streams, and at the edges of gardens. Traps not only provided meat, but also killed animals that would otherwise eat the crops.

Fish also supplied protein for the Guaraní diet and reduced dependence on agricultural produce. Many rivers and streams flow near Itanaramí on flat bottomland. These watercourses meander in broad loops that may be cut off as the river or stream changes course during a flood. Meanders, called oxbows, make ideal fishing spots. In addition to hook and line, men captured the fish by using a poison extracted from the bark of the *timbo* vine. Floated over the surface of the water, the sap suffocates the fish and allows them to be caught by hand.

The forest also supplied a variety of useful products for the Guaraní. They made houses from tree trunks and bamboo stalks; rhododendron vines secured thatched roofs. Villagers collected wild honey and fruit to add sweetness to their diets. If the manioc in the fields were insufficient, wild tubers provided a basic staple. Even several species of insect larva and ants were collected as tasty and nutritious supplements to the daily meal. Finally, the Indians knew about a wide variety of medicinal plants. They processed roots, leaves, flowers, and seeds to release powerful alkaloids, making teas and poultices for the sick and injured.

But the Guaraní were not isolated from commercial goods. Almost five hundred years ago, White traders entered the forests of the Guaraní and gave Indians access to world markets. The Guaraní continued to produce for most of their needs, but items such as machetes, hooks, soap, and salt were more easily bought than manufactured or collected. As they did with farming and hunting, Guaraní turned to the forest to meet such economic needs. They regularly collected two forest products, yerba-mate and leaves from wild orange trees, which have an oil used in flavorings and perfumes, to raise the necessary funds.

It is important to note the special Guaraní knowledge and values associated with subsistence activities. Because they lived in the forest for such a long time, and because they would have nowhere to turn if their own resources disappeared, they relied on a special and complex knowledge of how the forest works and how it can be used.

For example, Guaraní, such as Veraju, distinguished among a variety of "ecological zones," each with a unique combination of soil, flora, and fauna. They recognized obvious differences between the high forests on the hills, the deep swamps of river basins, and the grassy savannahs of the high plains. But they made more subtle distinctions within these larger regions. For example, they called the low scrub along rivers *ca'ati*. Flooded each year during the rainy season, this region supported bamboo groves that harbored small animals for trapping and provided material for house construction. The forests immediately above the flood plain look like an extension of the ca'ati, but to the Guaraní they differed in important ways. This ecological zone supported varieties of bamboo that were useless in house construction but that attracted larger animals, such as peccary, which they hunted. In all, the Guaraní distinguished among nine resource zones, each with distinctive soils, flora, fauna, and uses. These subtle distinctions among ecological zones enabled the Guaraní to use the forest to its best benefit. By shifting their subsistence efforts from one zone to another, just as they shifted their fields from one spot to the next, the Guaraní assured that the forest environment, with its rich variety of life, would always be able to renew itself.

Rather than undermine the stability of the forest, Guaraní production has increased biodiversity by fostering the growth of useful plants. The evidence is subtle but ubiquitous. The species of bamboo for arrows and palms valued for bows staves are more common in forests near Guaraní communities and, even in the most distance areas, citrus groves and yerba trees signal the existence of long-forgotten gardens. Research shows that this form of subtle agroforestry has increased the biodiversity of forests throughout lowland Latin America.

Anthropologists have come to understand that all of these primordial forests have experienced the gentle hand of human intervention, enough to challenge our belief that any ecosystem is truly "natural."

The Impact of Unsustainable Development

In the last few years, intensive commercial development has come to the region in which Itanaramí lies. Paraguay's deforestation rates are among the highest in the world, raising the specter of complete ecological destruction. White *colonos* (settlers), armed with chain saws and earthmovers, attack the trees. They vandalize the land without awareness of the carefully integrated ecological zones.

As the trees fall, the forest products, such as yerba mate, are destroyed. So are the mammals and fish, the bamboo and the rhododendron vines, the honey and the fruits, and the fallow fields. As these resources disappear, so does the economy of the once self-sufficient Guaraní. Without their traditional mode of subsistence, it has become impossible to maintain their kin-organized society, the influence of the tamoi, and the willingness to share. Indian communities are destroyed by poverty and disease, and the members who remain join the legions of poor laborers who form the lowest class of the national society. In short, the Guaraní lose their ability to survive as an independent ethnic group.

Recent intensive development began near Itanaramí with a road that colonists cut through the jungle to the village. Through this gash in the forest moved logging trucks, bulldozers, farm equipment, and buses. Accompanying the machinery of development were farmers, ranchers, and speculators, hoping to make a quick profit from the verdant land. They descended from their vehicles onto the muddy streets of a newly built frontier town. They cleared land for general stores and bars, which were soon filled with merchandise and warm beer. By day, the air in the town was fouled by truck noise and exhaust fumes; by night it was infused with the glare of electric lights and the noise of blaring loud speakers.

Soon the settlers began to fell the forest for fields for cotton, soybeans, and pasture. Survey teams cleared boundaries and drew maps. Lumber gangs camped in the forests, clear-cutting vast tracts of trees. Valuable timber was hauled off to new lumber mills; everything else was piled and burned. Massive bulldozers created expanses of sunlight in the previously unbroken forest. Within months, pasture, cotton, and soybeans sprouted in the exposed soils. Where once the land had been home for game, it now provided for cattle. Herds often clogged the roads, competing with trucks hauling cotton to market and busses loaded with new colonists. Settlers fenced in the fields and cut lanes through the remaining forest to mark off portions that would be private property (off-limits to Indians).

The road and fields reached Itanaramí in 1994. A cement bridge was built over the stream and chainsaws, logging trucks, and bulldozers assaulted the forests the Guaraní once used for gardens, farming, and hunting. The footpath that once carried Guaraní to the tamoi's house now carries their timber to market in Brazil. The families are left with barren house lots.

Moreover, by destroying the forest resources surrounding the Guaraní villages of the region, colonos set in motion a process that destroyed the native culture and society. Guaraní communities became islands surrounded by a sea of pastures and farm fields. Although the Indians held onto their gardens, they lost the forest resources needed to sustain their original mode of subsistence, which depended on hunting, fishing, and commercial gathering in the forest as well as farming. These economic changes forced alterations in the Indian community.

First, without the forest to provide game, fish, and other products, the Guaraní became dependent on farming alone for their survival. Without wild foods, they had to plant more corn and beans. Without the forest production of yerba mate leaves to collect for sale, they were also forced to plant cash crops such as cotton and tobacco. These changes forced them to clear gardens that were over twice the size of their previous plots.

While the loss of the forest for hunting and gathering increased their dependence on agriculture, the fences and land titles of the new settlers reduced the land available to the Indians for cultivation. Families soon cleared the last of the remaining high forests that they controlled. Even the once forested stream banks were denuded.

After they had cleared their communities' high forest, Indian farmers were forced to replant fields without allowing sufficient fallow time for soils to rejuvenate. Crops suffered from lack of nutrients and yields declined despite additional effort devoted to clearing and weeding. Commercial crops, poorly suited to the forest soils, did even worse. As production suffered, the Indians cleared and farmed even larger areas. The resulting spiral of poor harvests and enlarged farms outstripped the soil's capacity to produce and the Guaraní's ability to care for the crops. Food in the Indian communities grew scarce. The diet was increasingly restricted to non-nutritious manioc as a dietary staple because it was the only plant that could survive in the exhausted soils.

The Guaraní felt the ecological decline in other ways. The loss of game and poor crop yields exacerbated health problems. Settlers brought new diseases such as dengue fever and malaria into the forest. The Guaraní have little inherited resistance to these illnesses and poor nutrition reduced their defenses even further. Disease not only sapped the adults' energy for farming and childcare, it increased death rates at all ages. Tuberculosis, which well-fed Guaraní had rarely contracted, became the major killer in the community.

The environmental destruction took a psychological toll as well. Guaraní began to fall into depression, get drunk on cheap cane liquor, and, all too often, commit suicide. A number of suicides were noted among the Guaraní in Brazil in the 1990s and subsequent research in Paraguay showed that indigenous peoples were killing themselves at almost fifty times the national average. The epidemic hit 15- to 24-year-olds the hardest. These young people saw little future for themselves, their families, and their people.

Deforestation also disrupted social institutions. Without their subsistence base, many Guaraní needed additional cash to buy food and goods. Indian men were forced to seek work as farmhands, planting pastures and picking cotton on land where they once hunted. Women stayed at home to tend children and till the deteriorating soils of the family farms.

The search for wage labor eventually forced whole Guaraní families to move. Work was available on the new farms that had replaced the forest and entire families left home for hovels they constructed on the land of their *patrones*. They were prohibited from planting gardens of their own, so the displaced Indians were forced to buy their provisions, usually from the same patrones at inflated prices. Worse still, as mechanized agriculture replaced farm labor, many Guaraní found themselves dislocated again. Without recourse, they now take refuge in the capital of Asunción, begging on street corners and foraging through garbage for their food. A lonely struggle in urban squalor replaces the mutual interdependence of traditional Guaraní social organization.

As many individuals and families left the Guaraní villages, tamoi leaders lost influence. It became impossible to gather disparate relatives and friends for religious ritual. The distances were too great for the elders' nieces and nephews to seek out counsel and medicines. Moreover, the diseases and problems suffered by the Guaraní were increasingly caused by people and powers outside the forest. The tamoi could neither control nor explain the changing world.

Finally, as the forest disappeared, so did its power to symbolize Guaraní identity. No longer did young Indians see themselves as "people of the forest." Increasingly, they called themselves *indios*, the pejorative slur used by their non-Indian neighbors. Despite suffering dramatic change by powerful forces, Guaraní are proving their resilience. Many of the Guaraní of eastern Paraguay remain in small but impoverished communities in the midst of a frontier society based on soybean farming and cattle ranching. The households that previously were isolated individual plots are now concentrated in one small area without forest for farming or privacy. The traditional tamoi continue to be the center of the social and religious life of the community, but no longer exert influence over village decisions, which are increasingly dominated by affairs external to the local community.

Development and Ecology

Some people might argue that the Guaraní need to learn from their new neighbors, that they need to change their traditional ways and adopt the economy and culture of the more modern, prosperous society. The problems the Guaraní suffer, they claim, are a result of their traditional economy and culture. Change might be painful for today's Indians, but will provide unequaled opportunity for their descendents.

Unfortunately, this argument ignores the fact that recent development is destroying the resources on which the new farming and ranching depend. The long-run ramifications of forest clearing are disastrous, not simply for the Guaraní and other Indians, but for settlers and developers as well. The tropical forest ecosystem is extremely fragile. When the vegetable cover is destroyed, the soil quickly disappears. Erosion clogs rivers with silt and the soils left behind are baked to a hardpan on which few plants can survive. Rainwater previously captured by foliage and soil is quickly lost to runoff, drying the winds that feed the regional rain systems. Although first harvests in frontier areas seem bountiful, long-term farming and ranching are unprofitable as the soils, deprived of moisture and the rejuvenating forces of the original forest, are reduced to a "red desert."

Returning to Itanaramí today, one notices that many of the fields first cleared by ranchers in 1996 have already been abandoned. And even worse, leaving the cleared land fallow does not restore it. Once destroyed, the forest plants cannot reclaim the huge expanses of degraded soils left by unsustainable development.

Nor have developers been interested in husbanding the land. The colonos who clear the forests are concerned with short-term profit. Entrepreneurs and peasant farmers maximize immediate returns on their labor and investment, unaware of the environmental costs that subsidize their earnings. When the trees and soils of one area are exhausted, the farmers, ranchers, and loggers move farther into the virgin forest in search of new resources. The process creates a wave of development that leaves destruction in its wake. Unlike the Guaraní who have developed sustainable systems, developers do not stay and contend with the environmental destruction caused by their activities.

Indigenous Models for Sustainable Development

Rather than forcing the Guaraní to adapt to our models of development, perhaps we need to take a lesson from indigenous peoples. If we hope to survive in the rain forest, we must learn from the people who have not only survived, but prospered commercially in this fragile environment. International agencies and national governments have begun to recognize that our development strategies are doomed to failure. The changes are evident in the remaining forests of the Guaraní.

Although deforestation continues unchecked in many regions of the Amazon Basin, the government of Paraguay recently passed powerful legislation to protect the undamaged forests in the eastern regions. In addition, private enterprises and forest conservation programs are using the experience of indigenous people to promote sustainable development of these forest resources.

Groups like the Guaraní of Itanaramí, so recently threatened by encroaching development, are providing a model for newcomers to earn a profit from the natural resources, while protecting the existing environment. The natural forests of some of the Guaraní are the last remaining undisturbed subtropical forest in eastern Paraguay. With the help of Nature Conservancy, an area of 280 square miles has been set aside as the Mbaracayú Nature Reserve. In addition, the program is attempting to protect a much larger buffer zone around the reserve by promoting rational land use by colonists and native peoples alike.

Aided by anthropologists who have made detailed studies of indigenous commercial harvesting, private entrepreneurs are now integrating the Guaraní models of agro-forestry into new production strategies in this buffer zone. Guayaki Sustainable Rainforest Products, Inc., a business based in California, is working with local Indians to market yerba mate from the forests surrounding the Mbaracayú Reserve. The leaf is sold in the United States in bulk to be used in mate gourds, and in a wide variety of the company's energy drinks and beverages. Not only does this provide a fair wage for the collectors (and a profit for the company), but it increases the value of standing forest, providing an incentive to reforest some of Paraguay's cleared land.

Far from being backward and inefficient, the mixed horticultural subsistence strategies of indigenous forest groups is turning out to be the most practical way to manage the fragile tropical forest environment.

✓●—Study and Review on myanthrolab.com

Review Questions

1. Anthropologists claim that subsistence strategies affect a society's social organization and ideology. Evaluate this assertion in light of reading about the way the Guaraní live in their rain forest environment.

2. Why is horticulture more environmentally sensible than intensive agricultural and pastoral exploitation of the Amazonian rain forest?

3. How does Guaraní intervention increase the biodiversity of the forest ecosystem? Does this change our understanding of "nature" and the "natural world"?

4. Guaraní Indians are largely subsistence farmers and foragers. How do they use their forest environment without destroying it?

5. How have *colonos* disrupted the lives of Guaraní villagers? What does this tell us about the relationship between subsistence and social structure?

6. How can the Guaraní use their rain forest habitat to make money, and what does their experience suggest as a way to integrate forest exploitation into a market economy without environmental destruction?

PART FOUR

ECONOMIC SYSTEMS

READINGS IN THIS SECTION

People everywhere experience wants that can be satisfied only by the acquisition and use of material goods and the services of others. To meet such wants, humans rely on an aspect of their cultural inventory, the **economic system**, which we will define as the provision of goods and services to meet biological and social wants.

The meaning of the term *want* can be confusing. It can refer to what humans *need* for their survival. We must eat, drink, maintain a constant body temperature, defend ourselves, and deal with injury and illness. The economic system meets these needs by providing food, water, clothing, shelter, weapons, medicines, and the cooperative services of others.

But material goods serve more than just our survival needs: they meet our culturally defined *wants* as well. We need clothes to stay warm, but we want garments of a particular style, cut, and fabric to signal our status, rank, or anything else we wish to communicate socially. We need food to sustain life, but we want particular foods prepared in special ways to fill our aesthetic and social desires. Services and goods may also be exchanged to strengthen ties between people or groups. Birthday presents may not always meet physical needs, but they clearly function to strengthen the ties between the parties to the exchange.

Part of the economic system is concerned with **production**, which means rendering material items useful and available for human consumption. Production systems must designate ways to allocate resources. The **allocation of resources** refers to the cultural rules people use to assign rights to the ownership and use of resources. Production systems must also include technologies. Americans usually associate technology with the tools and machines used for manufacturing, rather than with the knowledge for doing it. But many anthropologists link the concept directly to culture. Here we will define **technology** as the cultural knowledge for making and using tools and extracting and refining raw materials.

Production systems also include a **division of labor**, which refers to the rules that govern the assignment of jobs to people. In hunting and gathering societies, labor is most often divided along the lines of gender, and sometimes age. In these societies, almost everyone knows how to produce, use, and collect the necessary material goods. In industrial society, however, jobs are highly specialized, and labor is divided, at least ideally, on the basis of skill and experience. Rarely do we know how to do someone else's job in our complex society.

The **unit of production**, meaning the persons or groups responsible for producing goods, follows a pattern similar to the way labor is divided in various societies. Among hunter-gatherers, there is little specialization; individuals, families, groups of friends, or sometimes bands form the units of production. But in our own complex society, we are surrounded by groups specially organized to manufacture, transport, and sell goods.

Another part of the economic system is **distribution**. There are three basic modes of distribution: market exchange, reciprocal exchange, and redistribution.

We are most conscious of market exchange because it lies at the heart of our capitalist system. **Market exchange** is the transfer of goods and services based on price, supply, and demand. Every time we enter a store and pay for something, we engage in market exchange. The price of an item may change with the supply. For example, a discount store may lower the price of a microwave oven because it has too many of the appliances on hand. Prices may go up, however, if everyone wants the microwaves when there are few available to sell. Money is often used in market systems; it enables people to exchange a large variety of items easily. Barter involves the trading

goods, not money, but it, too, is a form of market exchange because the number of
ms exchanged may also vary with supply and demand. Market exchange appears
human history when societies become larger and more complex. It is well suited
r exchange between the strangers who make up these larger groups. Although we
e not so aware of it, we also engage in reciprocal exchange. **Reciprocal exchange**
volves the transfer of goods and services between two people or groups based on
le obligations. Birthday and holiday gift giving is a fine example of reciprocity. On
these occasions we exchange goods not because we necessarily need or want them,
but because we are expected to do so as part of our status and role. Parents should
give gifts to their children, for example; children should reciprocate. If we fail in our
reciprocal obligations, we signal an unwillingness to continue the relationship. Small,
simply organized societies, such as the !Kung described earlier, base their exchange
systems on reciprocity. Complex ones like ours, although largely organized around
the market or redistribution, still manifest reciprocity between kin and close friends.

Finally, there is **redistribution**, the transfer of goods and services between a central collecting source and a group of individuals. Like reciprocity, redistribution is
based on role obligation. Taxes typify this sort of exchange in the United States. We
must pay our taxes because we are citizens, not because we are buying something.
We receive goods and services back—education, transportation, roads, defense—but
not necessarily in proportion to the amount we contribute. Redistribution may be the
predominant mode of exchange in socialist societies.

Anthropologists also frequently talk about two kinds of economies. In the past,
many of the world's societies had **subsistence economies** organized around the
need to meet material necessities and social obligations. Subsistence economies are
typically associated with smaller groups. They occur at a local level. Such economies
depend most on the non-market-exchange mechanisms: reciprocity and redistribution. Their members are occupational generalists. Most people can do most jobs,
although, as previously mentioned, there may be distinctions on the basis of gender
and age. The !Kung described by Richard Lee in Parts One and Three of this book had
subsistence economies as do most horticulturalists.

Market economies differ from subsistence economies in their size and motive
for production. Although reciprocity and redistribution exist in market economies,
market exchange drives production and consumption. Market economies are larger
(indeed, there is a growing world market economy that includes almost everyone)
and are characterized by high economic specialization, as well as impersonality. The
American economy is market driven, as are most national systems. If they have not
been already, most subsistence economies will, in the near future, be absorbed into
national market systems. Another shift we have seen over the past quarter century or
so is the shift in economic policies in capitalist countries that have moved toward a
philosophy that emphasizes the free movement of goods, capital, and services, with
cuts to public expenditure for social services. This is referred to as **neo-liberalism**.

The selections in Part Four illustrate several of the concepts discussed above.
In the first article, Lee Cronk looks at gift giving, a classic example of reciprocity. He
finds that gifts can cement relationships, confer prestige, and obligate subordinates as
well as be used to attack enemies.

The second article, by Philippe Bourgois, deals with the plight of poorly educated
Puerto Rican men living in New York City. Once able to work at steady, adequately
paid, manufacturing jobs they now can find only minimum wage work in New York's
service economy because manufacturers have left the city. The lack of income and respect they find there makes selling crack cocaine more appealing.

In the next article, new to *Conformity and Conflict,* Jessica Smith Rolston, deals with the increasing number of U.S. women coal miners who work alongside men at similar jobs. She shows how women find ways to strategically shift their identities to adapt to what still remains as a masculine workplace.

The final selection by Sonia Patten details the effect of free-market World Bank and International Monetary Fund policies on the agricultural subsistence economy of Malawi.

Key Terms

allocation of resources p. 108
distribution p. 108
division of labor p. 108
economic system p. 108
market economies p. 109
market exchange p. 108
neo-liberalism p. 109

production p. 108
reciprocal exchange p. 109
redistribution p. 109
subsistence economies p. 109
technology p. 108
unit of production p. 108

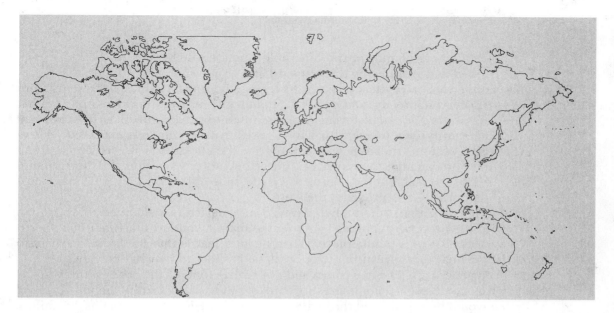

12

Reciprocity and the Power of Giving

Lee Cronk

As we saw in the introduction to Part Four, reciprocity constitutes an important exchange system in every society. At the heart of reciprocal exchange is the idea of giving. In this article, Lee Cronk explores the functions of giving using a variety of examples from societies around the world. Giving may be benevolent. It may be used to strengthen existing relationships or to form new ones. Gifts may also be used aggressively to "fight" people, to "flatten" them with generosity. Givers often gain position and prestige in this way. Gifts may also be used to place others in debt so that one can control them and require their loyalty. Cronk shows that, in every society, from !Kung hxaro exchange to American foreign aid, there are "strings attached" to giving that affect how people and groups relate to each other.*

((•—[**Listen** to the **Chapter Audio** on **myanthrolab.com**

During a trek through the Rockies in the 1830s, Captain Benjamin Louis E. de Bonneville received a gift of a fine young horse from a Nez Percé chief. According to Washington Irving's account of the incident, the American explorer was aware that "a parting pledge was necessary on his own part, to prove that this friendship was reciprocated." Accordingly, he "placed a

*Reprinted with the permission of the New York Academy of Sciences, 7 World Trade Center, 250 Greenwich St., 40th Floor, New York, NY 10007. www.nyas.org

handsome rifle in the hands of the venerable chief; whose benevolent heart was evidently touched and gratified by this outward and visible sign of amity."

Even the earliest white settlers in New England understood that presents from natives required reciprocity, and by 1764, "Indian gift" was so common a phrase that the Massachusetts colonial historian Thomas Hutchinson identified it as "a proverbial expression, signifying a present for which an equivalent return is expected." Then, over time, the custom's meaning was lost. Indeed, the phrase now is used derisively, to refer to one who demands the return of a gift. How this cross-cultural misunderstanding occurred is unclear, but the poet Lewis Hyde, in his book *The Gift*, has imagined a scenario that probably approaches the truth.

Say that an Englishman newly arrived in America is welcomed to an Indian lodge with the present of a pipe. Thinking the pipe a wonderful artifact, he takes it home and sets it on his mantelpiece. When he later learns that the Indians expect to have the pipe back, as a gesture of goodwill, he is shocked by what he views as their short-lived generosity. The newcomer did not realize that, to the natives, the point of the gift was not to provide an interesting trinket but to inaugurate a friendly relationship that would be maintained through a series of mutual exchanges. Thus, his failure to reciprocate appeared not only rude and thoughtless but downright hostile. "White man keeping" was as offensive to native Americans as "Indian giving" was to settlers.

In fact, the Indians' tradition of gift giving is much more common than our own. Like our European ancestors, we think that presents ought to be offered freely, without strings attached. But through most of the world, the strings themselves are the main consideration. In some societies, gift giving is a tie between friends, a way of maintaining good relationships, whereas in others it has developed into an elaborate, expensive, and antagonistic ritual designed to humiliate rivals by showering them with wealth and obligating them to give more in return.

In truth, the dichotomy between the two traditions of gift giving is less behavioral than rhetorical: our generosity is not as unconditional as we would like to believe. Like European colonists, most modern Westerners are blind to the purpose of reciprocal gift giving, not only in non-Western societies but also, to some extent, in our own. Public declarations to the contrary, we, too, use gifts to nurture long-term relationships of mutual obligation, as well as to embarrass our rivals and to foster feelings of indebtedness. And this ethic touches all aspects of contemporary life, from the behavior of scientists in research networks to superpower diplomacy. Failing to acknowledge this fact, especially as we give money, machines, and technical advice to peoples around the world, we run the risk of being misinterpreted and, worse, of causing harm.

Much of what we know about the ethics of gift giving comes from the attempts of anthropologists to give things to the people they are studying. Richard Lee, of the University of Toronto, learned a difficult lesson from the !Kung hunter-gatherers, of the Kalahari Desert, when, as a token of goodwill, he gave them an ox to slaughter at Christmas. Expecting gratitude, he was shocked when the !Kung complained about having to make do with such a scrawny "bag of bones." Only later did Lee learn, with relief, that the !Kung belittle all gifts. In their eyes, no act is completely generous, or free of calculation; ridiculing gifts is their way of diminishing the expected return and of enforcing humility on those who would use gifts to raise their own status within the group.

Rada Dyson-Hudson, of Cornell University, had a similar experience among the Turkana, a pastoral people of northwestern Kenya. To compensate her informants for their help, Dyson-Hudson gave away pots, maize meal, tobacco, and other items. The

Turkana reaction was less than heartwarming. A typical response to a gift of a pot, for example, might be, "Where is the maize meal to go in this pot?" or, "Don't you have a bigger one to give me?" To the Turkana, these are legitimate and expected questions.

The Mukogodo, another group of Kenyans, responded in a similar way to gifts Beth Leech and I presented to them during our fieldwork in 1986. Clothing was never nice enough, containers never big enough, tobacco and candies never plentiful enough. Every gift horse was examined carefully, in the mouth and elsewhere. Like the !Kung, the Mukogodo believe that all gifts have an element of calculation, and they were right to think that ours were no exception. We needed their help, and their efforts to diminish our expectations and lessen their obligations to repay were as fair as our attempts to get on their good side.

The idea that gifts carry obligations is instilled early in life. When we gave Mukogodo children candies after visiting their villages, their mothers reminded them of the tie: "Remember these white people? They are the ones who gave you candy." They also reinforced the notion that gifts are meant to circulate, by asking their children to part with their precious candies, already in their mouths. Most of the youngsters reluctantly surrendered their sweets, only to have them immediately returned. A mother might take, at most, a symbolic nibble from her child's candy, just to drive home the lesson.

The way food, utensils, and other goods are received in many societies is only the first stage of the behavior surrounding gift giving. Although repayment is expected, it is crucial that it be deferred. To reciprocate at once indicates a desire to end the relationship, to cut the strings; delayed repayment makes the strings longer and stronger. This is especially clear on the Truk Islands, of Micronesia, where a special word—*niffag*—is used to designate objects moving through the island's exchange network. From the Trukese viewpoint, to return niffag on the same day it is received alters its nature from that of a gift to that of a sale, in which all that matters is material gain.

After deciding the proper time for response, a recipient must consider how to make repayment, and that is dictated largely by the motive behind the gift. Some exchange customs are designed solely to preserve a relationship. The !Kung have a system, called *hxaro*, in which little attention is paid to whether the items exchanged are equivalent. Richard Lee's informant !Xoma explained to him that "Hxaro is when I take a thing of value and give it to you. Later, much later, when you find some good thing, you give it back to me. When I find something good I will give it to you, and so we will pass the years together." When Lee tried to determine the exact exchange values of various items (Is a spear worth three strings of beads, two strings, or one?), !Xoma explained that any return would be all right: "You see, we don't trade with things, we trade with people!"

One of the most elaborate systems of reciprocal gift giving, known as *kula*, exists in a ring of islands off New Guinea. Kula gifts are limited largely to shell necklaces, called *soulava*, and armbands, called *mwali*. A necklace given at one time is answered months or years later with an armband, the necklaces usually circulating clockwise, and the armbands counterclockwise, through the archipelago. Kula shells vary in quality and value, and men gain fame and prestige by having their names associated with noteworthy necklaces or armbands. The shells also gain value from their association with famous and successful kula partners.

Although the act of giving gifts seems intrinsically benevolent, a gift's power to embarrass the recipient and to force repayment has, in some societies, made it attractive as a weapon. Such antagonistic generosity reached its most elaborate expression, during the late nineteenth century, among the Kwakiutl, of British Columbia.

The Kwakiutl were acutely conscious of status, and every tribal division, clan, and individual had a specific rank. Disputes about status were resolved by means of enormous ceremonies (which outsiders usually refer to by the Chinook Indian term *potlatch*), at which rivals competed for the honor and prestige of giving away the greatest amount of property. Although nearly everything of value was fair game—blankets, canoes, food, pots, and, until the mid-nineteenth century, even slaves—the most highly prized items were decorated sheets of beaten copper, shaped like shields and etched with designs in the distinctive style of the Northwest Coast Indians.

As with the kula necklaces and armbands, the value of a copper sheet was determined by its history—by where it had been and who had owned it—and a single sheet could be worth thousands of blankets, a fact often reflected in its name. One was called "Drawing All Property from the House," and another, "About Whose Possession All Are Quarreling." After the Kwakiutl began to acquire trade goods from the Hudson's Bay Company's Fort Rupert post, in 1849, the potlatches underwent a period of extreme inflation, and by the 1920s, when items of exchange included sewing machines and pool tables, tens of thousands of Hudson's Bay blankets might be given away during a single ceremony.

In the 1880s, after the Canadian government began to suppress warfare between tribes, potlatching also became a substitute for battle. As a Kwakiutl man once said to the anthropologist Franz Boas, "The time of fighting is past. . . . We do not fight now with weapons: we fight with property." The usual Kwakiutl word for potlatch was *p!Esa*, meaning to flatten (as when one flattens a rival under a pile of blankets), and the prospect of being given a large gift engendered real fear. Still, the Kwakiutl seemed to prefer the new "war of wealth" to the old "war of blood."

Gift giving has served as a substitute for war in other societies, as well. Among the Siuai, of the Solomon Islands, guests at feasts are referred to as attackers, while hosts are defenders, and invitations to feasts are given on short notice in the manner of "surprise attacks." And like the Kwakiutl of British Columbia, the Mount Hagen tribes of New Guinea use a system of gift giving called *moka* as a way of gaining prestige and shaming rivals. The goal is to become a tribal leader, a "big-man." One moka gift in the 1970s consisted of several hundred pigs, thousands of dollars in cash, some cows and wild birds, a truck, and a motorbike. The donor, quite pleased with himself, said to the recipient, "I have won. I have knocked you down by giving so much."

Although we tend not to recognize it as such, the ethic of reciprocal gift giving manifests itself throughout our own society, as well. We, too, often expect something, even if only gratitude and a sense of indebtedness, in exchange for gifts, and we use gifts to establish friendships and to manipulate our positions in society. As in non-Western societies, gift giving in America sometimes takes a benevolent and helpful form; at other times, the power of gifts to create obligations is used in a hostile way.

The Duke University anthropologist Carol Stack found a robust tradition of benevolent exchange in an Illinois ghetto known as the Flats, where poor blacks engage in a practice called swapping. Among residents of the Flats, wealth comes in spurts; hard times are frequent and unpredictable. Swapping, of clothes, food, furniture, and the like, is a way of guaranteeing security, of making sure that someone will be there to help out when one is in need and that one will get a share of any windfalls that come along.

Such networks of exchange are not limited to the poor, nor do they always involve objects. Just as the exchange of clothes creates a gift community in the Flats, so the swapping of knowledge may create one among scientists. Warren Hagstrom, a sociologist at the University of Wisconsin, in Madison, has pointed out that papers submitted to scientific journals often are called contributions, and, because no payment is received for them, they truly are gifts. In contrast, articles written for profit—such as this one—often are held in low esteem: scientific status can be achieved only through *giving* gifts of knowledge.

Recognition also can be traded upon, with scientists building up their gift-giving networks by paying careful attention to citations and acknowledgments. Like participants in kula exchange, they try to associate themselves with renowned and prestigious articles, books, and institutions. A desire for recognition, however, cannot be openly acknowledged as a motivation for research, and it is a rare scientist who is able to discuss such desires candidly. Hagstrom was able to find just one mathematician (whom he described as "something of a social isolate") to confirm that "junior mathematicians want recognition from big shots and, consequently, work in areas prized by them."

Hagstrom also points out that the inability of scientists to acknowledge a desire for recognition does not mean that such recognition is not expected by those who offer gifts of knowledge, any more than a kula trader believes it is all right if his trading partner does not answer his gift of a necklace with an armband. While failure to reciprocate in New Guinean society might once have meant warfare, among scientists it may cause factionalism and the creation of rivalries.

Whether in the Flats of Illinois or in the halls of academia, swapping is, for the most part, benign. But manipulative gift giving exists in modern societies, too—particularly in paternalistic government practices. The technique is to offer a present that cannot be repaid, coupled with a claim of beneficence and omniscience. The Johns Hopkins University anthropologist Grace Goodell documented one example in Iran's Khu-zesta-n Province, which, because it contains most of the country's oil fields and is next door to Iraq, is a strategically sensitive area. Goodell focused on the World Bank–funded Dez irrigation project, a showpiece of the shah's ambitious "white revolution" development plan. The scheme involved the irrigation of tens of thousands of acres and the forced relocation of people from their villages to new, model towns. According to Goodell, the purpose behind dismantling local institutions was to enhance central government control of the region. Before development, each Khu-zesta-ni village had been a miniature city-state, managing its own internal affairs and determining its own relations with outsiders. In the new settlements, decisions were made by government bureaucrats, not townsmen, whose autonomy was crushed under the weight of a large and strategically placed gift.

On a global scale, both the benevolent and aggressive dimensions of gift giving are at work in superpower diplomacy. Just as the Kwakiutl were left only with blankets with which to fight after warfare was banned, the United States and the Soviet Union now find, with war out of the question, that they are left only with gifts—called concessions—with which to do battle. Offers of military cutbacks are easy ways to score points in the public arena of international opinion and to shame rivals, and failure either to accept such offers or to respond with even more extreme proposals may be seen as cowardice or as bellicosity. Mikhail Gorbachev is a virtuoso, a master potlatcher, in this new kind of competition, and, predictably, Americans often see his offers of disarmament and openness as gifts with long strings attached. One reason U.S. officials were buoyed last December [1988], when, for the first time since the Second World War, the Soviet Union accepted American assistance, in the aftermath of the Armenian earthquake, is that it seemed to signal a wish for reciprocity rather than dominance—an unspoken understanding of the power of gifts to bind people together.

Japan, faced with a similar desire to expand its influence, also has begun to exploit gift giving in its international relations. In 1989, it will spend more than ten billion dollars on foreign aid, putting it ahead of the United States for the second consecutive year as the world's greatest donor nation. Although this move was publicly welcomed in the United States as the sharing of a burden, fears, too, were expressed that the resultant blow to American prestige might cause a further slip in our international status. Third World leaders also have complained that too much Japanese aid is targeted at countries in which Japan has an economic stake and that too much is restricted to the purchase of Japanese goods—that Japan's generosity has less to do with addressing the problems of underdeveloped countries than with exploiting those problems to its own advantage.

The danger in all of this is that wealthy nations may be competing for the prestige that comes from giving gifts at the expense of Third World nations. With assistance sometimes being given with more regard to the donors' status than to the recipients' welfare, it is no surprise that, in recent years, development aid often has been more effective in creating relationships of dependency, as in the case of Iran's Khūzestān irrigation scheme, than in producing real development. Nor that, given the fine line between donation and domination, offers of help are sometimes met with resistance, apprehension and, in extreme cases, such as the Iranian revolution, even violence.

The Indians understood a gift's ambivalent power to unify, antagonize, or subjugate. We, too, would do well to remember that a present can be a surprisingly potent thing, as dangerous in the hands of the ignorant as it is useful in the hands of the wise.

✓●—**Study** and **Review** on **myanthrolab.com**

Review Questions

1. What does Cronk mean by *reciprocity*? What is the social outcome of reciprocal gift giving?

2. According to Cronk, what are some examples of benevolent gift giving?

3. How can giving be used to intimidate other people or groups? Give some examples cited by Cronk and think of some from your own experience.

4. How does Cronk classify gift-giving strategies such as government foreign aid? Can you think of other examples of the use of exchange as a political device?

5. Consider gift-giving practices in your own life. In what ways do these practices reveal role and status? In what ways is reciprocity present?

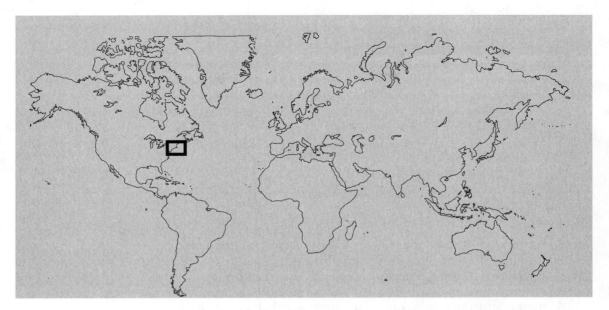

13

Poverty at Work: Office Employment and the Crack Alternative

Philippe Bourgois

There was a time in the United States when people with little education and money could find work in manufacturing plants or other settings requiring manual labor. Many of the skills they needed could be learned on the job and they could make a modest but decent living and support a family. And despite their working-class identity, their jobs gave them dignity and a place in society. But in today's America, manufacturing jobs have often disappeared, leaving thousands of poorly educated people without equivalent work.

In this article, Philippe Bourgois illustrates how this problem has affected unskilled and largely uneducated Puerto Rican men and women in New York City's Spanish Harlem. Manufacturing jobs once provided dignified and stable employment for Puerto Rican men and women. As factories closed beginning in the 1960s, the unemployed could find work only in service industries such as security corporations, law firms, and insurance companies. Because they were uneducated and culturally different, they could hold only minimum-wage jobs in such worlds, as they are usually controlled by educated, largely Anglo people who openly look down on them. In the end, they could achieve higher status and often higher income in their own ethnic community by dealing drugs. The result has been a destructive spiral into addiction, murder, and prison. Bourgois concludes the article with an addendum *noting that high employment in the late 1990s provided more work opportunities for Puerto Ricans in the formal economy and that crack dealing has largely given way to the less visible sale of marijuana and heroin.**

((•─ **Listen** to the **Chapter Audio** on **myanthrolab.com**

For a total of approximately three and a half years during the late 1980s and early 1990s, I lived with my wife and young son in an irregularly heated, rat-filled tenement in East Harlem, New York. This two-hundred-square-block neighborhood—better known locally as *El Barrio* or Spanish Harlem—is visibly impoverished yet it is located in the heart of New York, the richest city in the Western Hemisphere. It is literally a stone's throw from multimillion-dollar condominiums. Although one in three families survived on some form of public assistance in 1990, the majority of El Barrio's 110,600 Puerto Rican and African-American residents fall into the ranks of the working poor.[1] They eke out an uneasy subsistence in entry-level service and manufacturing jobs in one of the most expensive cities in the world.

The public sector (e.g., the police, social welfare agencies, the Sanitation Department) has broken down in El Barrio and does not function effectively. This has caused the legally employed residents of the neighborhood to lose control of their streets and public spaces to the drug economy. My tenement's block was not atypical and within a few hundred yards' radius I could obtain heroin, crack, powder cocaine, hypodermic needles, methadone, Valium, angel dust, marijuana, mescaline, bootleg alcohol, and tobacco. Within two hundred feet of my stoop there were three competing crack houses selling vials at two, three, and five dollars. Several doctors operated "pill mills" on the blocks around me, writing prescriptions for opiates and barbiturates upon demand. In the projects within view of my living-room window, the Housing Authority police arrested a fifty-five-year-old mother and her twenty-two-year-old daughter while they were "bagging" twenty-two pounds of cocaine into ten-dollar quarter-gram "Jumbo" vials of adulterated product worth over a million dollars on the streets. The police found twenty-five thousand dollars in cash in small-denomination bills in this same apartment.[2] In other words, there are millions of dollars' worth of business going on directly in front of the youths growing up in East Harlem tenements and housing projects. Why should these young men and women take the subway downtown to work minimum-wage jobs—or even double minimum-wage jobs—in downtown offices when they can usually earn more, at least in the short run, by selling drugs on the street corner in front of their apartment or schoolyard?

---

*Reprinted by permission of Waveland Press, Inc. from Philippe Bourgois, "Office Work and the Crack Alternative among Puerto Rican Drug Dealers in East Harlem," from *Urban Life: Readings in the Anthropology of the City,* 4th edition, George Gmelch and Walter P. Zenner, eds. (Long Grove, IL: Waveland Press, Inc., 2002). All rights reserved.

[1]According to the 1990 Census, in East Harlem 48.3 percent of males and 35.2 percent of females over sixteen were officially reported as employed—compared to a citywide average of 64.3 percent for men and 49 percent for women. Another 10.4 percent of the men and 5.7 percent of the women in East Harlem were actively looking for legal work. . . . In El Barrio as a whole, 60 percent of all households reported legally earned incomes. Twenty-six percent received Public Assistance, 6.3 percent received Supplemental Security Income, and 5 percent received Medicaid benefits.

[2]Both of these police actions were reported in the local print and television media, but I am withholding the cities to protect the anonymity of my street address.

This dynamic underground economy is predicated on violence and substance abuse. It has spawned what I call a "street culture" of resistance and self-destruction. The central concern of my study is the relationship of street culture to the worlds of work accessible to street dealers—that is, the legal and illegal labor markets that employ them and give meaning to their lives. I hope to show the local-level implications of the global-level restructuring of the U.S. economy away from factory production and toward services. In the process, I have recorded the words and experiences of some unrepentant victims who are part of a network of some twenty-five street-level crack dealers operating on and around my block. To summarize, I am arguing that the transformation from manufacturing to service employment—especially in the professional office work setting—is much more culturally disruptive than the already revealing statistics on reductions in income, employment, unionization, and worker's benefits would indicate. Low-level service sector employment engenders a humiliating ideological—or cultural—confrontation between a powerful corps of white office executives and their assistants versus a younger generation of poorly educated, alienated, "colored" workers. It also often takes the form of a sharply polarized confrontation over gender roles.

Shattered Working-Class Dreams

All the crack dealers and addicts whom I have interviewed had worked at one or more legal jobs in their early youth. In fact, most entered the labor market at a younger age than the typical American. Before they were twelve years old they were bagging groceries at the supermarket for tips, stocking beers off-the-books in local *bodegas*, or shining shoes. For example, Primo, the night manager at a video game arcade that sells five-dollar vials of crack on the block where I lived, pursued a traditional working-class dream in his early adolescence. With the support of his extended kin who were all immersed in a working-class "common sense," he dropped out of junior high school to work in a local garment factory:

> I was like fourteen or fifteen playing hooky and pressing dresses and whatever they were making on the steamer. They was cheap, cheap clothes.
>
> My mother's sister was working there first and then her son, my cousin Willie—the one who's in jail now—was the one they hired first, because his mother agreed: "If you don't want to go to school, you gotta work."
>
> So I started hanging out with him. I wasn't planning on working in the factory. I was supposed to be in school; but it just sort of happened.

Ironically, young Primo actually became the agent who physically moved the factory out of the inner city. In the process, he became merely one more of the 445,900 manufacturing workers in New York City who lost their jobs as factory employment dropped 50 percent from 1963 to 1983. . . .

Almost all the crack dealers had similar tales of former factory jobs. For poor adolescents, the decision to drop out of school and become a marginal factory worker is attractive. It provides the employed youth with access to the childhood "necessities"—sneakers, basketballs, store-bought snacks—that sixteen-year-olds who stay in school cannot afford. In the descriptions of their first forays into legal factory-based employment, one hears clearly the extent to which they, and their families, subscribed to mainstream working-class ideologies about the dignity of engaging in "hard work" rather than education.

Had these enterprising, early-adolescent workers from El Barrio not been confined to the weakest sector of manufacturing in a period of rapid job loss, their teenage working-class dreams might have stabilized. Instead, upon reaching their mid-twenties, they discovered themselves to be unemployable high school dropouts. This painful realization of social marginalization expresses itself across a generational divide. The parents and grandparents of the dealers continue to maintain working-class values of honesty and hard work which conflict violently with the reality of their children's immersion in street culture. They are constantly accused of slothfulness by their mothers and even by friends who have managed to maintain legal jobs. They do not have a regional perspective on the dearth of adequate entry-level jobs available to "functional illiterates" in New York, and they begin to suspect that they might indeed be *"vago bons"* [lazy bums] who do not *want* to work hard and cannot help themselves. Confused, they take refuge in an alternative search for career, meaning, and ecstasy in substance abuse.

Formerly, when most entry-level jobs were found in factories, the contradiction between an oppositional street culture and traditional working-class, masculine, shop-floor culture was less pronounced—especially when the work site was protected by a union. Factories are inevitably rife with confrontational hierarchies. Nevertheless, on the shop-floor, surrounded by older union workers, high school dropouts who are well versed in the latest and toughest street culture styles function effectively. In the factory, being tough and violently macho has high cultural value; a certain degree of opposition to the foreman and the "bossman" is expected and is considered appropriate.

In contrast, this same oppositional street-identity is nonfunctional in the professional office worker service sector that has burgeoned in New York's high-finance-driven economy. It does not allow for the humble, obedient, social interaction—often across gender lines—that professional office workers routinely impose on their subordinates. A qualitative change has occurred, therefore, in the tenor of social interaction in office-based employment. Workers in a mail room or behind a photocopy machine cannot publicly maintain their cultural autonomy. Most concretely, they have no union; more subtly, there are few fellow workers surrounding them to insulate them and to provide them with a culturally based sense of class solidarity.[3] Instead they are besieged by supervisors and bosses from an alien, hostile, and obviously dominant culture who ridicule street culture. Workers like Primo appear inarticulate to their professional supervisors when they try to imitate the language of power in the workplace and instead stumble pathetically over the enunciation of unfamiliar words. They cannot decipher the hastily scribbled instructions—rife with mysterious abbreviations—that are left for them by harried office managers. The "common sense" of white-collar work is foreign to them; they do not, for example, understand the logic for filing triplicate copies of memos or for post-dating invoices. When they attempt to improvise or show initiative they fail miserably and instead appear inefficient, or even hostile, for failing to follow "clearly specified" instructions.

Their "social skills" are even more inadequate than their limited professional capacities. They do not know how to look at their fellow co-service workers, let alone their supervisors, without intimidating them. They cannot walk down the hallway to the water fountain without unconsciously swaying their shoulders aggressively as

---

[3]Significantly, there are subsectors of the service industry that are relatively unionized—such as hospital and custodial work—where there is a limited autonomous space for street culture and working-class resistance.

if patrolling their home turf. Gender barriers are an even more culturally charged realm. They are repeatedly reprimanded for harassing female co-workers.

The cultural clash between white "yuppie" power and inner-city "scrambling jive" in the service sector is much more than a superficial question of style. It is about access to power. Service workers who are incapable of obeying the rules of inter-personal interaction dictated by professional office culture will never be upwardly mobile. Their supervisors will think they are dumb or have a "bad attitude." Once again, a gender dynamic exacerbates the confusion and sense of insult experienced by young, male inner-city employees because most supervisors in the lowest reaches of the service sector are women. Street culture does not allow males to be subordinate across gender lines.

"Gettin' Dissed"

On the street, the trauma of experiencing a threat to one's personal dignity has been frozen linguistically in the commonly used phrase "to diss," which is short for "to disrespect." Significantly, one generation ago ethnographers working in rural Puerto Rico specifically noted the importance of the traditional Puerto Rican concept of *respeto* in mediating labor relations:

> The good owner "respects" (*respeta*) the laborer. . . . It is probably to the interest of the landowner to make concessions to his best workers, to deal with them on a respect basis, and to enmesh them in a network of mutual obligations.[4]

Puerto Rican street-dealers do not find respect in the entry-level service sector jobs that have increased two-fold in New York's economy since the 1950s. On the contrary, they "get dissed" in the new jobs that are available to them. Primo, for example, remembers the humiliation of his former work experiences as an "office boy," and he speaks of them in a race- and gender-charged idiom:

> I had a prejudiced boss. She was a fucking "ho'," Gloria. She was white. Her name was Christian. No, not Christian, Kirschman. I don't know if she was Jewish or not. When she was talking to people she would say, "He's illiterate."
>
> So what I did one day was, I just looked up the word, "illiterate," in the dictionary and I saw that she's saying to her associates that I'm stupid or something!
>
> Well, I am illiterate anyway.

The most profound dimension of Primo's humiliation was being obliged to look up in the dictionary the word used to insult him. In contrast, in the underground economy, he is sheltered from this kind of threat:

> Rocky [the crack house franchise owner] he would never disrespect me that way. He wouldn't tell me that because he's illiterate too. Plus I've got more education than him. I got a GED. . . .

---

[4]Eric Wolf, "San Jose: Subcultures of a 'Traditional' Coffee Municipality," in Julian Stewart (ed.), *The People of Puerto Rico* (Chicago: University of Chicago Press, 1956), p. 235.

Primo excels in the street's underground economy. His very persona inspires fear and respect. In contrast, in order to succeed in his former office job, Primo would have had to self-consciously alter his street identity and mimic the professional cultural style that office managers require of their subordinates and colleagues. Primo refused to accept his boss's insults and he was unable to imitate her interactional styles. He was doomed, consequently, to a marginal position behind a photocopy machine or at the mail meter. Behavior considered appropriate in street culture is considered dysfunctional in office settings. In other words, job requirements in the service sector are largely cultural style and this conjugates powerfully with racism.

> I wouldn't have mind that she said I was illiterate. What bothered me was that when she called on the telephone, she wouldn't want me to answer even if my supervisor who was the receptionist was not there. [Note how Primo is so low in the office hierarchy that his immediate supervisor is a receptionist.]
>
> When she hears my voice it sounds like she's going to get a heart attack. She'd go, "Why are you answering the phones?"
>
> That bitch just didn't like my Puerto Rican accent.

Primo's manner of resisting this insult to his cultural dignity exacerbated his marginal position in the labor hierarchy:

> And then, when I did pick up the phone, I used to just sound *Porta'rrrican* on purpose.

In contrast to the old factory sweatshop positions, these just-above-minimum-wage office jobs require intense interpersonal contact with the middle and upper-middle classes. Close contact across class lines and the absence of a working-class autonomous space for eight hours a day in the office can be a claustrophobic experience for an otherwise ambitious, energetic, young, inner-city worker.

Caesar, who worked for Primo as lookout and bodyguard at the crack house, interpreted this requirement to obey white, middle-class norms as an affront to his dignity that specifically challenged his definition of masculinity:

> I had a few jobs like that [referring to Primo's "telephone diss"] where you gotta take a lot of shit from bitches and be a wimp.
>
> I didn't like it but I kept on working, because "Fuck it!" you don't want to fuck up the relationship. So you just be a punk [shrugging his shoulders dejectedly].

One alternative for surviving at a workplace that does not tolerate a street-based cultural identity is to become bicultural: to play politely by "the white woman's" rules downtown only to come home and revert to street culture within the safety of one's tenement or housing project at night. Tens of thousands of East Harlem residents manage this tightrope, but it often engenders accusations of betrayal and internalized racism on the part of neighbors and childhood friends who do not have—or do not want—bicultural skills.

This is the case, for example, of Ray, a rival crack dealer whose tough street demeanor conflates with his black skin to "disqualify" him from legal office work. He quit a "nickel-and-dime messenger job downtown" in order to sell crack full time in his project stairway shortly after a white woman fled from him shrieking down the hallway of a high-rise office building. Ray and the terrified woman had ridden the elevator together, and, coincidentally, Ray had stepped off on the same floor as her to make a delivery. Worse yet, Ray had been trying to act like a "debonair male" and suspected the contradiction between his inadequate appearance and his chivalric intentions was responsible for the woman's terror:

> You know how you let a woman go off the elevator first? Well that's what I did to her but I may have looked a little shabby on the ends. Sometime my hair not combed. You know. So I could look a little sloppy to her maybe when I let her off first.

What Ray did not quite admit until I probed further is that he too had been intimidated by the lone white woman. He had been so disoriented by her taboo, unsupervised proximity that he had forgotten to press the elevator button when he originally stepped on after her:

> She went in the elevator first but then she just waits there to see what floor I press. She's playing like she don't know what floor she wants to go to because she wants to wait for me to press my floor. And I'm standing there and I forgot to press the button. I'm thinking about something else—I don't know what was the matter with me. And she's thinking like, "He's not pressing the button; I guess he's following me!"

As a crack dealer, Ray no longer has to confront this kind of confusing humiliation. Instead, he can righteously condemn his "successful" neighbors who work downtown for being ashamed of who they were born to be:

> When you see someone go downtown and get a good job, if they be Puerto Rican, you see them fix up their hair and put some contact lens in their eyes. Then they fit in. And they do it! I seen it.
> They turn-overs. They people who want to be white. Man, if you call them in Spanish, it wind up a problem.
> When they get nice jobs like that, all of a sudden, you know, they start talking proper.

Self-Destructive Resistance

During the 1980s, the real value of the minimum wage for legally employed workers declined by one-third. At the same time, social services were cut. The federal government, for example, decreased the proportion of its contribution to New York City's budget by over 50 percent. . . . The breakdown of the inner city's public sector is no longer an economic threat to the expansion of New York's economy because the native-born labor force it shelters is increasingly irrelevant.

New immigrants arrive every day, and they are fully prepared to work hard for low wages under unsavory conditions. Like the parents and grandparents of Primo and Caesar, many of New York's newest immigrants are from isolated rural communities or squalid shanty towns where meat is eaten only once a week and there is no running water or electricity. Half a century ago Primo's mother fled precisely the same living conditions these new immigrants are only just struggling to escape. Her reminiscences about childhood in her natal village reveal the time warp of improved material conditions, cultural dislocation, and crushed working-class dreams that is propelling her second-generation son into a destructive street culture:

> I loved that life in Puerto Rico, because it was a healthy, healthy, healthy life.
>
> We always ate because my father always had work, and in those days the custom was to have a garden in your patio to grow food and everything that you ate.
>
> We only ate meat on Sundays because everything was cultivated on the same little parcel of land. We didn't have a refrigerator, so we ate *bacalao* [salted codfish], which can stay outside and a meat that they call *carne de vieja* [shredded beef], and sardines from a can. But thanks to God, we never felt hunger. My mother made a lot of cornflour.
>
> Some people have done better by coming here, but many people haven't. Even people from my barrio, who came trying to find a better life [*buen ambiente*] just found disaster. Married couples right from my neighborhood came only to have the husband run off with another woman.
>
> In those days in Puerto Rico, when we were in poverty, life was better. Everyone will tell you life was healthier and you could trust people. Now you can't trust anybody.
>
> What I like best was that we kept all our traditions . . . our feasts. In my village, everyone was either an Uncle or an Aunt. And when you walked by someone older, you had to ask for their blessing. It was respect. There was a lot of respect in those days [original quote in Spanish].

The Jewish and Italian-American white workers that Primo's mother replaced a generation ago when she came to New York City in hope of building a better future for her children were largely absorbed into an expanding economy that allowed them to be upwardly mobile. New York's economy always suffered periodic fluctuations, such as during the Great Depression, but those difficult periods were always temporary. The overall trend was one of economic growth. Primo's generation has not been so lucky. The contemporary economy does not particularly need them, and ethnic discrimination and cultural barriers overwhelm them whenever they attempt to work legally and seek service-sector jobs. Worse yet, an extraordinarily dynamic underground drug economy beckons them.

Rather than bemoaning the structural adjustment which is destroying their capacity to survive on legal wages, streetbound Puerto Rican youths celebrate their "decision" to bank on the underground economy and to cultivate their street identities. Caesar and Primo repeatedly assert their pride in their street careers. For example, one Saturday night after they finished their midnight shift at the crack house, I accompanied them on their way to purchase *"El Sapo Verde"* [The Green Toad], a twenty-dollar bag of powder cocaine sold by a new company three blocks away. While waiting for Primo and Caesar to be "served" by the coke seller a few yards away, I engaged three undocumented Mexican men drinking beer on a neighboring stoop in a conversation about finding work in New York. One of the new immigrants was already earning five hundred dollars a week fixing deep-fat-fry machines. He had a straightforward racist explanation for why Caesar—who was standing next to me—was "unemployed":

> OK, OK, I'll explain it to you in one word: Because the Puerto Ricans are brutes! [Pointing at Caesar] Brutes! Do you understand?
>
> Puerto Ricans like to make easy money. They like to leech off of other people. But not us Mexicans! No way! We like to work for our money. We don't steal. We came here to work and that's all [original quote in Spanish].

Instead of physically assaulting the employed immigrant for insulting him, Caesar embraced the racist tirade, ironically turning it into the basis for a new, generational-based, "American-born," urban cultural pride. In fact, in his response, he ridicules what he interprets to be the hillbilly naiveté of the Mexicans who still believe in the "American Dream." He spoke slowly in street-English as if to mark sarcastically the contrast between his "savvy" Nuyorican (New York-born Puerto Rican) identity versus the limited English proficiency of his detractor:

> That's right, m'a man! We is real vermin lunatics that sell drugs. We don't want no part of society. "Fight the Power!"[5]
>
> What do we wanna be working for? We rather live off the system. Gain weight, lay women.
>
> When we was younger, we used to break our asses too [gesturing towards the Mexican men who were straining to understand his English]. I had all kinds of stupid jobs too . . . advertising agencies . . . computers.
>
> But not no more! Now we're in a rebellious stage. We rather evade taxes, make quick money, and just survive. But we're not satisfied with that either. Ha!

Conclusion: Ethnography and Oppression

The underground economy and the social relations thriving off of it are best understood as modes of resistance to subordination in the service sector of the new U.S. economy. This resistance, however, results in individual self destruction and wider community devastation through substance abuse and violence. This complex and contradictory dynamic whereby resistance leads to self-destruction in the inner city is difficult to convey to readers in a clear and responsible manner. Mainstream society's "common sense" understanding of social stratification around ethnicity and class assumes the existence of racial hierarchies and blames individual victims for their failures. This makes it difficult to present ethnographic data from inner-city streets without falling prey to a "pornography of violence" or a racist voyeurism.

The public is not persuaded by a structural economic understanding of Caesar and Primo's "self-destruction." Even the victims themselves psychologize their unsatisfactory lives. Similarly, politicians and, more broadly, public policy ignore the fundamental structural economic facts of marginalization in America. Instead the first priority of federal and local social "welfare" agencies is to change the psychological—or at best the "cultural"—orientations of misguided individuals . . . U.S. politicians furiously debate family values while multinational corporations establish global free-trade zones and unionized factory employment in the U.S. continues to disappear as overseas sweatshops multiply. Social science researchers, meanwhile, have remained silent for the most part. They politely ignore the urgent social problems engulfing the urban United States. The few marginal academic publications that do address issues of poverty and racism are easily ignored by the media and mainstream society. . . .

[5]"Fight the Power" is a rap song composed in 1990 by the African-American group, Public Enemy.

Epilogue

In the six years since this article was first published, four major dynamics have altered the tenor of daily life on the streets of East Harlem and have deeply affected the lives of the crack dealers and their families depicted in these pages: (1) the U.S. economy entered the most prolonged period of sustained growth in its recorded history, (2) the size of the Mexican immigrant population in New York City and especially in East Harlem increased dramatically, (3) the War on Drugs escalated into a quasi-official public policy of criminalizing and incarcerating the poor and the socially marginal, and (4) drug fashion trends among inner-city youth rendered marijuana even more popular and crack and heroin even less popular among Latinos and African Americans.

Crack, cocaine, and heroin are still all sold on the block where I lived, but they are sold less visibly by a smaller number of people. It is still easy to purchase narcotics throughout East Harlem, but much of the drug dealing has moved indoors, out of sight, dealers no longer shouting out the brand names of their drugs. Most importantly, heroin and crack continue to be spurned by Latino and African-American youth who have seen the ravages those drugs committed on the older generations in their community. Nevertheless, in the U.S. inner city there remains an aging hardcore cohort of addicts. In most large cities crack is most visibly ensconced in predominantly African-American neighborhoods on the poorest blocks, often surrounding large public housing projects. In New York City, Puerto Rican households also continue to be at the epicenter of this ongoing, but now more self-contained, stationary cyclone of crack consumption.

In contrast to crack, heroin consumption has increased. Throughout most of the United States, heroin is cheaper and purer than in the early 1990s, belying any claims that the War on Drugs is winnable. Heroin's new appeal, however, is primarily among younger whites outside the ghetto for whom crack was never a drug of choice. It is not a drug of choice among Latino and African-American youth.

To summarize, both heroin and crack continue to be part of a multi-billion-dollar business that ravages inner-city families with special virulence. The younger generations of East Harlem residents, however, are more involved as sellers rather than consumers. Those Latino and African-American youth who do use crack or heroin generally try to hide the fact from their friends.

More important than changing drug-consumption fashions or the posturing of politicians over drug war campaigns has been the dramatic long-term improvement in the U.S. economy resulting in record low rates of unemployment. Somewhat to my surprise, some of the crack dealers and their families have benefited from this sustained economic growth. Slightly less than half have been allowed to enter the lower echelons of the legal labor market. For example, during the summer of 2000: one dealer was a unionized doorman, another was a home health care attendant, another was a plumber's assistant, three others were construction workers for small-time unlicensed contractors, and one was a cashier in a discount tourist souvenir store. Three or four of the dealers were still selling drugs, but most of them tended to be selling marijuana instead of crack or heroin. Three other dealers were in prison with long-term sentences and ironically were probably employed at well below minimum wage in the United States' burgeoning prison-based manufacturing sector. In short, the dramatic improvement in the U.S. economy has forced employers and unions to integrate more formally marginalized Puerto Ricans and African Americans into the labor market than was the case in the late 1980s and early 1990s when the research for this [article] was conducted. Nevertheless, even at the height of the growth in the U.S. economy in the year 2000, a large sector of street youth found themselves excluded. These marginals have become almost completely superfluous to the legal economy; they remain enmeshed in a still-lucrative drug economy, a burgeoning prison system, and a quagmire of chronic substance abuse. From a long-term political and economic perspective, the future does not bode well for inner-city poor of New York. In the year 2000, the United States had the largest disparity between rich and poor of any industrialized nation in the world—and this gap was not decreasing.

✓●─[**Study** and **Review** on **myanthrolab.com**

Review Questions

1. What kinds of jobs in the formal economy could Puerto Ricans living in East Harlem hold forty years ago? How did these jobs enable them to preserve respect as it was defined in their culture?

2. What kinds of jobs are currently available to Puerto Rican men in New York's service economy? How do these jobs challenge the men's self-respect?

3. What structural changes in New York's formal economy have taken place over the past forty years? How have these changes affected the lives of young men living in Spanish Harlem?

4. Why do Puerto Rican men take pride in their street identities?

5. Why does Bourgois claim that the Puerto Rican men's resistance to work in the legal economy leads to "self-destruction" and "wider community devastation"?

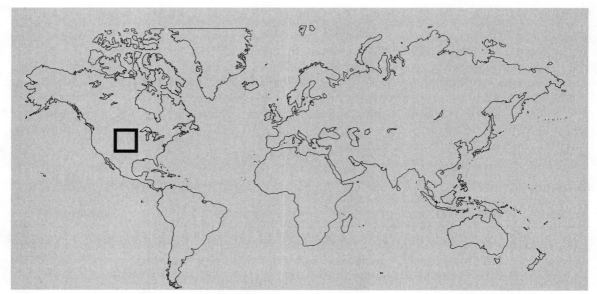

14

Women in the Mine

Jessica Smith Rolston

While mining has always been thought of as a masculine industry, women now make up 20 percent of all production crews in Wyoming's Powder River Basin—the largest coal-producing region in the United States. One of the appeals of this kind of work, particularly for those without college degrees, is the solid pay. Yet the question remains: How do these women fit into a working culture supposedly hostile to females? Anthropologist Jessica Smith Rolston, herself a onetime mine worker and the daughter of a miner, set out to learn more about women working in mines. She draws on years of participant-observation in four mines and extensive interviews with miners, managers, engineers, and the families of mine employees, to provide a nuanced view of gender on the job in coal mines. She suggests that women miners strategically shift between identities to adapt themselves to the workplace.*

((•—[**Listen** to the **Chapter Audio** on **myanthrolab.com**

Melissa faced a dilemma after graduating from college with a teaching degree: teaching jobs would not pay enough to cover her student loans and the cost of raising the child she had recently conceived with a boyfriend she did not wish to marry. "I made one mistake," she recalled. "I didn't need to make another." While she was in college, she had spent the

*This article, "Coal Miners and Changing Division of Labor," was written especially for *Conformity and Conflict*, Copyright © 2014 by Jessica Smith Rolston. Reprinted by permission.

summers back home in Gillette, Wyoming, working for the same coal mine that employed her father. She loved driving the giant mine equipment, such as haul trucks that tower over 20 feet tall, dwarfing even the tallest men. She decided to return to the mines, where I met her while conducting fieldwork research in 2007. The time I spent with her was part of the 22 months I spent conducting participant observation at surface mines and interviewing miners and their families at home. As Melissa drove me around the pit in her favorite haul truck, joking with her coworkers as she showed me the details of her job as an equipment operator, she explained that she loved her coworkers like a family and would probably become a "lifer" and stay at the mines until she made it to retirement. In addition to enjoying the work, she appreciated the money she made as a single mother. Miners like Melissa make between $65,000 and $100,000 annually, depending on experience and overtime work.

Melissa's career may seem surprising for people who see coal mining as a physically strenuous and dirty job performed almost exclusively by men. But she is far from alone. In Wyoming's Powder River Basin, which has been the country's largest producer of coal since the mid-1980s, women represent between 20 and 25 percent of the production crews, with even higher numbers in the engineering and administrative offices. These numbers stand out when compared with the mining industry as a whole, in which women represent between six and eight percent of workers. Women play a larger role in the Wyoming industry for a variety of reasons explored in greater detail below, but key among these are the unique gender relations in the mines. The Wyoming mines present a case in which gendered divisions of labor have become less rigid—almost to the point of disappearing—as men and women craft gender identities that allow them to work productively with one another.

Learning to labor

The majority of the dozen mines currently in operation in the Powder River Basin opened during the mid-1970s and early 1980s, as the United States scrambled to find cheap sources of domestic energy in the midst of the energy crisis. Companies hired large numbers of women to work in all areas of the mines, since they faced a local labor shortage, and many women applied for the high paying mine jobs that offered health care and retirement benefits better than those in unionized mines in other parts of the country. Most of the women who took the jobs had grown up on family farms and ranches in the state or surrounding area, and they recalled that mining "felt natural" to them since they were accustomed to doing physically demanding labor outside with their fathers, uncles, brothers and cousins.

The first challenge for all new miners, including women, is learning how to do their jobs. Surface mines are divided into four main work areas: the pit, where the coal is extracted; the plant, where the coal is processed and loaded onto trains for transportation to power plants; the shop, where equipment is repaired; and the offices, where engineers and administrators do their work. The pits can extend up to 200 feet deep without miners feeling as if they were underground, since they work under the open sky. Equipment operators like Melissa operate a variety of machines to expose and extract the coal and then reclaim the land.

The first step is for scraper operators to remove and specially store the delicate topsoil. After the overburden, the dirt and rock layer covering the coal seam has been drilled and blasted, miners operating draglines, shovels, and haul trucks move it to a pit that has just been emptied of coal and is ready to be reclaimed. A dragline is the size of a comfortable American suburban home but only requires a maintenance technician and an operator to operate. The operator uses a set of controls to maneuver a large bucket to pick up, move, and then drop overburden from the pit that is being excavated into one that has already been mined. This comprises the first phase of reclamation, the final step in the mining process in which the land is restored to similar contours and its previous use. Shovels are also used to remove overburden, but they rely on haul trucks to move the material they dig. In this type of operation, the shovel operator digs the overburden and empties it into the bed of a large haul truck, which can often hold up to three hundred tons of material. The truck driver then hauls it to a dump, where the overburden is placed directly into old pits or stored until needed for reclamation. Once the coal in a large horizontal seam is exposed and blasted, shovel or loader operators extract it in a process similar to removing overburden. The main difference is that the truck driver hauls his or her load of coal to the plant, tipping the truck bed to allow the coal to fall into a series of machines that break it down into manageable chunks for later burning by power plants.

Women participate in all stages of the mining process and operate all of the equipment described above, as well as support machines like large dozers, road graders, and backhoes.

Rank in the pit correlates with the hierarchy of machines used to expose and extract the coal, and women operate the most prestigious loading machines—the draglines, loaders and shovels—alongside men. They also direct entire crews as frontline supervisors. Comparatively fewer women work in the shop as mechanics, perhaps because those jobs are viewed as more physically demanding than operating equipment. The women who do work as mechanics argue that even men use technology and assistance from others rather than pure muscle to do their jobs. Moreover, women mechanics like Barb believe they in some ways have an advantage. She wishes that tools were made lighter for women like her to handle, but she argues that she can get into tight spots such as the area around the belt on a haul truck. "It only takes me twenty minutes because there's so much room in there it's like a football field," she reported, "but it takes guys who can't reach it a lot longer." She can also fit between the tire rim and frame of a rubber tire dozer, whereas many men cannot, and her comparatively thinner and longer fingers can get into places that theirs cannot reach.

Learning to work together

The second challenge, which many miners say is more difficult, is to learn how to relate to other workers. Each crew of workers has unique personality dynamics and sets of expectations for how people manage their work and interact with one another. A common concern for the core group of longtime employees on all of the crews I met was ensuring that everyone pulled their own weight, so that others did not have to do extra work to compensate for someone who was incompetent or lazy. At the same time no one worked so hard that they looked better than the rest and put pressure on others to work beyond their limits. Balancing these expectations takes finesse and has direct implications for the ways in which women both consciously and subconsciously craft their gender identities.

Tomboys

Melissa was like the majority of women miners in identifying as a tomboy. The term almost always refers to women whose attitudes and practices depart from conventional notions of femininity. An equipment operator named Carrie, for example, took pride in describing both herself and her daughter Mandy as tomboys who were "like one of the guys." On her days off she enjoys going hunting, horseback riding, and camping with her kids, just as she did as a child growing up in a farming community in north-central Wyoming. Reflecting on her own childhood, she said, "I was always a tomboy too. I loved doing things with my brothers." Another equipment operator named Wanda clearly linked her childhood experiences and her current life: "I was raised tomboyish with boys. We were always hunting, camping, fishing, whatever." Her coworker Trish agreed, saying, "Tomboys like myself are like one of the guys. They don't mind getting dirty. That means they're mellow and don't get worked up about stupid shit. They don't mind joking around." Melissa was so committed to being one of the guys that she bragged about riding horses eight months into her pregnancy, whereas "sissy pregnant ladies" go on light duty at only three or four months.

The qualities described by the miners—acting like one of the guys, enjoying outdoor physical labor, and not minding dirty workplaces or dirty jokes—are viewed by most men and women miners as making them well-suited for mine labor. Melissa made that point clear during a conversation she had over lunch with her crew. They were discussing the interview process for new hires, and she brought up the story of one woman who seemed like a bad match for the work. "She said that she didn't want to sit on the chair we brought for her because it was dirty," Melissa said incredulously. "I asked her, 'Do you know where you're applying, lady?!' She did not get hired." For Melissa and her coworkers, the woman's discomfort with dirt meant that she would never make it in the mines, not only because dust infiltrated offices as well as equipment cabs, but because she would be too uptight.

Ladies

When describing the social universe of the mines, people always contrasted tomboys with "ladies" or "girly girls." Nicole, a self-identified tomboy, was clear in distinguishing the two when she told me, "I don't want to be a lady out there. I want to be one of the guys." She was like other miners in considering women to be ladies when they attempted to avoid hard work or purposefully emphasized their femininity at the expense of forming friendships with the guys. "They're prissy," complained Trish. "They have nice nails, they wear makeup all the time, and they can't take a joke."

It is telling that long nails and makeup stand out as markers of inappropriate femininity, as they also hinder people from doing the job that is expected of them. After all, women who wish to preserve their makeup or painted nails must avoid the tasks associated with being a "good hand," such as using your own tools and climbing around the equipment to diagnose a potential problem with it. An equipment operator named Greg frequently complained that one of the women on his crew never pulled her own weight. As evidence, he described her long red fingernails and said that he looked at her hands during their meetings, but the polish was never chipped: "Now you tell me, if you're out there doing your job like you are supposed to be doing, do you think your nails are gonna stay pretty like that? I don't think so. So that must mean that she's sitting in her truck all day and can't be bothered to check her own stuff." When he made the observation, we were standing around with Laura waiting for the blast to clear the coal pit, and she nodded and recalled that she stopped wearing her nails long after she broke two of them during her first week at the mine. As a relatively new temporary worker, Laura was anxious to be hired full-time. Making the statement was likely a strategy to "prove herself" to Greg and the rest of the crew that she was a dedicated coworker. Critiques of women's long nails in the basin are not simply about appearance; they are a way to critique women perceived to be overly feminine and thus unable to do a demanding job.

Women who self-identify as ladies often do so to craft more professional identities. Sue, for example, took pride in being a lady at the mine. She was famous on her crew for listening to only Christian radio and refusing to engage in most, if not all, of their joking activities. She thought that practical jokes were unprofessional, so her coworkers stopped playing them on her. On the one hand, she risked alienating herself from her crew since jokes are a key method for crafting close workplace relationships. But on the other hand, the serious demeanor she adopted at work also endeared her to management.

Bitches

Bitch encompasses a wide array of insults at the mine, the majority of which are directed at women. Whereas ladies or girly girls were criticized for being too feminine, the uniting thread of the bitch insult is an accusation that women have pushed the boundary too far in departing from conventional notions of femininity. This may seem surprising given the praise bestowed upon women who "act like the one the guys" by pulling their own weight and not getting offended by swearing or jokes. Delving into the specifics of the insult reveals that accusing a woman of being a bitch is not simply a critique of her departure from conventional expectations of femininity, but of her acting in too masculine a manner as well.

One cardinal sin is swearing too often or in an excessively vulgar manner. Although Nicole wanted to be accepted as one of the guys rather than be viewed as a lady, she said, "At the same time, I do make a very strong point to be careful." She elaborated that being careful meant not crossing the line of acting and speaking too much "like a man" while still being accepted as a friend with whom the guys felt comfortable making jokes. Finding the right balance can be difficult. Laura said she started off at the mines "throwing swear words around" in an attempt to be accepted by the guys, but found that she could not keep up with the one-upmanship and had backed herself into a corner. "If I kept it up, they would have thought I was too crude," she said, and that would mean that they would lose respect for her. A longtime miner named Mary remembered a woman who was upset with a guy on their crew who "had a potty mouth worse than a sailor, even worse than a miner." After work one night they were washing their hands around the large communal sink in the women's locker room, and the other woman "had a hissy fit" complaining about how another coworker was always saying f-ing this and f-ing that. She announced, "I'm not gonna tolerate it, I'm gonna complain," and tried recruiting others to go along with her. Mary and most of the other women refused, partly because they felt that the woman doing the complaining also used language inappropriately. "She says shit all the time and tells off-color jokes without anyone getting upset," Mary said, insinuating that the woman gave up her right to be upset about off-color language when she used it herself.

Mary then shifted our conversation to talk about a rumor that two people from another crew were caught having sex at the fuel station. The guy got fired, she said, because the woman claimed that he was raping her. He said it was consensual, but the mine took her side because they wanted to avoid a potential lawsuit. Although Mary said that no one but the two of them would ever know what really happened, she also leaned toward his side because the woman was "loose and had a reputation." Mary shook her head, knowing that it sounded awful to call out a woman for having a sexual history; logically she knew that even if the woman had a sexual history with that guy or others, it did not give the man in question a free pass to have sex with her then. But she maintained that women had a responsibility to manage their own reputation. "It's bad if you have no credibility," she explained. "It's a catch-22, how to champion women if they don't care enough to take care of themselves."

Mary's segue between swearing and sexuality is telling because women who swear aggressively are also often accused of using their sexuality aggressively. Candace, for instance, told me that she hated the dispatcher on their crew because "she wears tight jeans and low-cut shirts. She has bitch written all over her." Women and men miners recognize the double standard that disadvantages women. "At another mine where I worked there were women screwing guys on the job, too," Wanda explained. "But guys do it, too! They'll point to women doing [sexual] acts, but it takes two. But the guys are studly and the females are sluts. I feel like if they are two consenting adults, they know what they are doing." Wanda, her coworkers, and other crews were equally offended by one of the guys on the crew who bragged about his sexual conquests. But, in general, women still bear the heavier burden for discouraging sexual activity on the crew.

Shifting identities

Though it was frequent for miners to identify themselves and their coworkers *as* tomboys, ladies, or bitches, they also recognized that those identities could change over the course of a conversation, a shift, or a lifetime. Trish, for instance, loved swearing and hanging out with the guys but said, "You still have to watch yourself, like not swear too much. And you can't get away with some of the jokes that they can. You aren't a guy: you're *like* one of the guys." She clarified the difference by saying, "On my days off I like to go out and get dressed up and look nice so that you'd never know I was a coal miner, but when I'm out here it's just jeans and dirt." Molly, who also self-identified as a tomboy, highlighted the strategic importance of being accepted as one of the guys. "Out here you have to act like a guy to make it," she said. "If you're girly you won't make it because no one will respect you." She likes acting tough at work and at the small ranch where she lives with her husband and young son, but brings out her girly side when she deems it appropriate. "I'm still a girly girl, I dress up and put on makeup," she explained, "but you have to adjust to it while you're out here. We can cuss out people like the guys but still act like ladies." She took particular pride in acting so girly on her days off along with other women on her crew that people could not guess their occupation: "You'd never know we're coal miners!"

Women miners can strategically shift between identities to adapt to the workplace. One day when I was riding around with Laura in her haul truck, we started talking about how she and her boyfriend ended up in Gillette. "I'm not a girly girl," she said, "but I never imagined I'd be doing this for money." After we did the safety inspection and climbed up the haul truck, Laura attempted to retract the ladder but found that it was not functioning correctly. When she was finally able to insert herself into the busy radio communication and report the problem, she took care to use the correct procedure and specific terminology that the miners associate with expertise. When the mechanics arrived to investigate the problem, she braved the cold and windy winter morning to join them in their inspection. She told me that doing so was key in order to avoid being labeled a lady. Unable to find a quick fix, the mechanics muscled the ladder back into position so we could drive off and told her to use the completely vertical embedded ladder instead. In her opinion, that was not a real solution because the slipperiness of the embedded ladder made it dangerous. Instead of cursing and becoming aggressive as I had seen some of her coworkers do in similar situations, she tried a different tactic. She began joking with the mechanic she knew the best, making allusions to her own "wussiness" and begging him to fix the ladder as a personal favor to her because she was too afraid of climbing down off of the steeper ladder. He did, and when we returned triumphantly to the cab, she explained the importance of what she called "girl power": "Sometimes it's easier to get stuff done. But you have to be careful, because sometimes it can hurt more than it can help."

Over the course of a few minutes, Laura modified her usual approach to interacting with her coworkers and the machinery in order to strategically invoke a more markedly feminine persona. Strategies and experiences such as these are far more typical than any static categorization of women would suggest. Unpacking what it means when people call themselves or someone else a tomboy or lady reveals strategic shifts in gender performance. The cultural category of tomboy refers less to a specific group of women or a stable identity than a tactic for managing the extent to which gender differences become salient in specific social and technological engagements. When women act like tomboys, they consciously downplay gender difference—but without erasing it completely—in order to craft camaraderie with their coworkers. Conversely, women draw out stereotypically feminine characteristics when they feel that they are at risk of becoming too much like one of the guys or when they seek help by appealing to coworkers who are motivated by dominant notions of femininity.

Conclusion

There is no single type of woman miner in the Powder River Basin, though there are many common themes in the stories that led them to seek work in an industry historically dominated by men. Most women were like Melissa in needing a job that would pay them well. Mining jobs were especially attractive to women without college degrees, since they could earn enough to live solid middle-class lifestyles: own their own houses, go on vacation, drive nice cars and trucks, and send their own children to college. As employment for blue-collar workers becomes increasingly precarious in the United States, the miners may represent the last of what some scholars call the blue-collar middle class.

The majority of women miners were also like Melissa in identifying as tomboys, though there were notable exceptions at every worksite. The prevalence of women who identify as tomboys is partially related to the regional context, since almost all of the women miners grew up in the rural American West or Midwest, where they enjoyed hunting, fishing, and camping alongside their male family members even if they did not live on ranches or farms themselves. Through these activities, they cultivated love for the outdoors, experience with physical labor, and appreciation for bawdy humor—all characteristics that were valued in the mines.

The ways in which women act and position themselves as particular kinds of gendered people do have concrete implications for their job security. Tomboys align themselves horizontally with their crews by participating in activities that craft intense camaraderie and support from their coworkers, but could potentially lead to retribution from management. Ladies align themselves vertically with management by following the rules, but risk losing support from their fellow coworkers. Bitches frequently devalue the importance of alliances, believing that everyone should watch out for themselves above all, though they sometimes form alliances with the ultra macho men onsite. Though these men's aggressive masculinity forms the core of stereotypical images of the industry, they actually comprise a minority of the workforce, which is otherwise dominated by "family men" who place the safety and security of their crew and families at home as their first priority. What is clear is that all of these gendered positions pose particular risks, uncertainties, and rewards, which helps to explain why most women are like Laura in strategically shifting between them. Gender therefore is best understood less as a stable identity and more as a shifting performance.

✓●─[**Study** and **Review** on **myanthrolab.com**

Review Questions

1. What draws women to work in a coal mine?

2. What are some specific ways technological changes have shaped the gender division of labor over time in the coal mine?

3. Which identity works best for women coal miners as they relate to men? Why?

4. What impact, if any, did women miners' family background play in their decision to work in a coal mine?

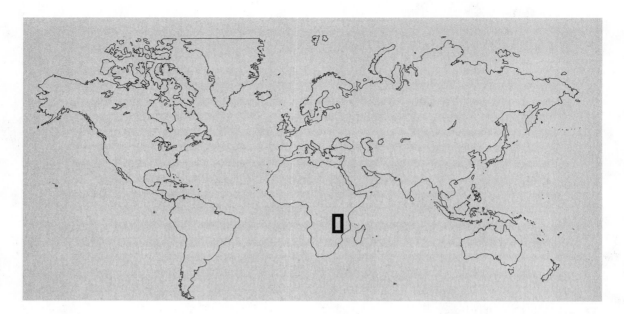

15

Malawi versus the World Bank

Sonia Patten

Market economics rules in most industrialized countries, especially since the decline of communism. In market systems, goods are produced for sale, prices affect demand and vice-versa, and demand drives production. Underlying the system is the profit motive to get the greatest gain for the least cost. The market not only applies to manufacturing and providing services in industrialized societies but also governs agriculture although most governments interfere with it to some extent in that economic sphere. It is no wonder that most economists from industrialized nations believe that the free market system is the key to development in nonindustrialized societies, and this has led institutions such as the World Bank and the International Monetary Fund (IMF) to impose a neo-liberal agenda by dropping social and agricultural support programs in favor of market-based development as a requirement of receiving loans.

There is a problem, however, at least initially, with the market-based approach to development especially as it applies to agriculture. In many nonindustrialized societies, a majority of the people farm small plots of land in order to feed their families and meet social obligations to kin and neighbors. When floods, drought, exhausted soils, and other factors reduce yields and people face starvation, only government aid, not market-based programs, can help them. That is the point Sonia Patten makes in this article as she discusses conditions in the small southeastern African country of Malawi. She notes that international lending agencies required the Malawian government to cease underwriting the cost of fertilizer in favor of a market-based system. As a result, the exhausted land produced less maize and people began to starve. Eventually, the government of Malawi overruled their

136

international lenders and reinstituted a program to provide fertilizer to farm families. The result was a grain surplus, the end of famine, and improved health for the nation's citizens.*

((•─[Listen to the **Chapter Audio** on **myanthrolab.com**

This article is about the impact a group of economic organizations called the "Washington Consensus" has on rural families living in the small southern African nation of Malawi. The "Washington Consensus," which is located in Washington, D.C., as the name implies, and its associated economists and policymakers created a situation in Malawi that forced rural farmers there to trade a day's labor for a day's food, dismantle their homes to sell timbers and roofing for cash so they could purchase food, beg for food, or go hungry. One can challenge statements about the causal relationships between macro-level and micro-level socioeconomic decisions and events, but in this instance the connections seem clear. A review of "Washington Consensus" policy and the information provided by women in ten rural Malawi households over a period of eighteen months helps us understand just how individuals and families struggle to survive when macro-level economic policies have an adverse impact on them.

The "Washington Consensus" refers to a set of economic prescriptions derived from policies of the International Monetary Fund (IMF) and the World Bank (both headquartered in Washington, D.C.) and endorsed by the U.S. Treasury Department. The goal for these policies and prescriptions is to bring about basic economic reform in poor nations, rapidly moving their economies in the direction of capitalism and incorporation into the global marketplace. When a government applies for a loan from these international lending agencies, it must agree to abide by a structural adjustment program (SAP) based on these economic policies and prescriptions. Thus, the conditions for securing a loan include the following: (1) cuts in spending for health, education, and all forms of social welfare; (2) privatization of all state-owned enterprises; (3) opening the economy to foreign competition and direct foreign investment; (4) allowing the market to determine interest rates; (5) managing currency exchange rates to keep them stable. Additionally, governments are to broaden the tax base in order to collect more revenue, deregulate labor markets, and stop using public monies to subsidize commodities, thus increasing the cost to consumers. It is this last point, the withdrawal of subsidies, that I will focus on. The commodity in question is commercial fertilizer, an absolutely essential agricultural input for even the smallest subsistence farmer.

Malawi is one of the poorest nations in the world. It has a population of about thirteen million people, 95 percent engaged in rain-fed agriculture, mostly on smallholdings of about one to four acres. It takes about two-thirds of an acre per person to have a reasonable chance of producing sufficient food to meet subsistence needs for a family. The nation has more or less reached the limit of its possible area of cultivation, and is suffering from the problems that accompany deforestation as people have cut trees to clear land for firewood for cooking and brick-making. There is no longer a fallow period for cropland—farmers plant all of their land every year.

The staple crop is white maize (corn); it is consumed at every meal. Over 90 percent of cultivable land in Malawi is planted to maize. It is hard on the soil, rapidly leaching it of nutrients, especially nitrogen. Presently, if commercial fertilizer high in nitrogen is not applied during the growing season, the amount of maize harvested is greatly diminished. Households are unable to meet their subsistence needs and have no surplus to put on the market. The "season of hunger," that period of time between family consumption of the last store of maize from the previous harvest (any time between early September and late December) and the beginning of the next harvest (in late March or April) grows longer, and families have to find a way to cope.

Fertilizer subsidies have a long history in Malawi. They began in 1952 while the country was still a British colony. The objectives of the subsidy were to ensure distribution of a vital agricultural input at a low cost to even the most geographically remote smallholder farmer, thus increasing output of maize, the priority crop, and to maintain soil fertility. The subsidies continued after independence and into the 1970s. In 1981 the country experienced a balance of payments problem and turned to the World Bank and IMF for assistance in the form of loans. Thus, Malawi has been indebted to and under the influence of these international lending agencies longer than any other African nation, and the involvement continues up to the present. As early as 1984, the World Bank and IMF began attributing problems in the economy to government subsidy policies, particularly with regard to commercial fertilizer. By 1985 the government began progressive reduction of the fertilizer subsidy. By the 1990s, there was complete deregulation and liberalization of the fertilizer and seed markets in Malawi, under the tutelage of the international lending institutions. The process was finalized in 1994/95 with complete removal of all types of subsidies and price controls on all agricultural inputs and products. At the same time there was 40 percent depreciation in the value of the currency and inflation soared from 20 percent to 53 percent.

This was an absolute crisis for small farmers. Harvests fell and malnutrition rose. By the month of June, most rural families were reduced to eating two meals a day. Over a third of rural families were running out of stored maize by September and 80 percent by December. More than 25 percent of under-five children were underweight and more than half were stunted by long-term malnutrition. The country was struggling with the heavy burden of HIV/AIDS, and life expectancy had fallen to 37 years. World Bank economists had begun to get a sense that all was not well, all was not going according to plan, and perhaps a social safety net was needed to "catch" those who were most vulnerable. A number of fertilizer programs were begun to try and meet the needs of smallholders and allow them to have a greater likelihood of producing sufficient food to feed their families.

Government programs like the Starter Pak Initiative and Targeted Input Programme were created to distribute free or subsidized fertilizer. The results were mixed at best.

Big farmers were not eligible for these programs, which relied on the distribution of vouchers to smallholders through village headmen. A voucher could then be exchanged for a 50 kg bag of fertilizer free or at a subsidized price, depending on the program. But headmen sometimes sold the vouchers rather than distribute them. And big farmers would have vendors with coupons buy bags of fertilizer at the subsidized price, then pay the vendors a fee for this service, and re-sell the bags for a handsome profit. The supply of subsidized fertilizer was quickly depleted, long before most small farmers had secured any. Another social safety net program put rural men and women to work building roads, and at the end of several days of work, they were paid with a 50 kg bag of fertilizer. It took so much work to earn a bag that many people refused to participate, saying it seemed like a kind of slavery.

How did individual households cope with these dire circumstances? This is what I learned from ten women in one village where few families could afford a sufficient amount of fertilizer. Some of the families were able to secure one bag, allowing them one application on their maize crop; it takes three applications during a growing season for optimal results. Most of the families used no fertilizer at all. In 2005, all but one family consumed all of their stored food by September, and some as early as August. Normally August is the time of year when weddings take place, when ancestors are honored. These events require contributions of food from each household, but in 2005 the village headman decreed that no household should make these contributions because everyone was suffering from insufficient food.

The first strategy that families turned to in the hunger crisis was to skip meals. When there is sufficient food, people eat *nsima* (maize porridge) three times a day—breakfast, lunch and supper. When there is a food shortage, breakfast is no longer prepared. As the situation continued to deteriorate, women began to mix maize flour, the regular ingredient for *nsima*, with maize bran, which is usually used for animal feed. The next step was to use cassava rather than maize for the noon meal. Cassava is nutrient poor, and most people in the Central Region don't like it. By this time men and women were actively seeking work that they could exchange for food—a day's work in a rich farmer's fields in exchange for enough maize flour to prepare a meal. If such work could not be found, people began to sell off their assets in order to buy maize, which was in short supply and thus very expensive. They sold animals, bricks, sheets of corrugated metal roofing, timbers that had supported their houses—whatever they had that could be sold for money or exchanged for maize. The absolute last resort was to sell land or exchange land for maize. And I was told that some older women who had no family in the vicinity were so desperately hungry that they went door to door begging for something to eat.

It is during this season of hunger that the land must be prepared and the next crop planted and cultivated. When hunger is great, maize will be harvested and cooked while it is still green and other foodstuffs like pumpkins will be cooked when they are small. People can't wait for them to mature—they might starve in the interim.

So how it is that World Bank and IMF economists would mandate a policy that causes so much human suffering? The then president of Malawi, Bingu wa Mutharika, must have asked the same question. He is an economist trained at a prominent U.S. university, and is well aware that Western nations heavily subsidize their farmers. After the disastrous 2005 harvest that required emergency food aid for five million Malawians, he reinstated and deepened fertilizer subsidies over the protests of the U.S. The result? The 2007 maize harvest was so big that Malawi is exporting hundreds of thousands of tons to neighboring countries. The national granaries are full. Acute hunger in children has fallen so sharply that the UN-donated powdered milk stockpiled for treating hungry children has been sent on to other African nations still in need. In sum, it appears that the policies generated by the Washington Consensus may need to be reconfigured when it comes to public investment in African agriculture, especially agriculture practiced by subsistence farmers who are unable to produce enough grain for sale to pay for the fertilizer that will ensure a surplus.

✓●─[**Study** and **Review** on **myanthrolab.com**

Review Questions

1. What is the "Washington Consensus"?

2. What are the five points of the Washington Consensus's structural adjustment program (SAP)? What is the economic theory behind them?

3. What is the history of farm support in Malawi and how did taking loans from the World Bank and IMF change that history?

4. Why is chemical fertilizer so important to farming in Malawi?

5. When it followed SAP guidelines, the government of Malawi ceased to provide fertilizer for its farmers. How did that impact the country's people and agricultural output?

6. What happened when the government of Malawi recently again began to provide fertilizer for its farmers? What does that say about World Bank and IMF policy?

PART FIVE

KINSHIP
AND FAMILY

READINGS IN THIS SECTION

Social life is essential to human existence. We remain in the company of other people from the moment we are born to the time of our death. People teach us to speak. They show us how to relate to our surroundings. They give us the help and the support we need to achieve personal security and mental well-being. Alone, we are relatively frail, defenseless primates; in groups we are astonishingly adaptive and powerful. Yet despite these advantages, well-organized human societies are difficult to achieve. Some species manage to produce social organization genetically. But people are not like bees or ants. We lack the genetically coded directions for behavior that make these insects successful social animals. Although we seem to inherit a general need for social approval, we also harbor individual interests and ambitions that can block or destroy close social ties. To overcome these divisive tendencies, human groups organize around several principles designed to foster cooperation and group loyalty. Kinship is among the strongest of these.

We may define **kinship** as the complex system of culturally defined social relationships based on marriage (the principle of **affinity**) and birth (the principle of **consanguinity**). The study of kinship involves consideration of such principles as descent, kinship status and roles, family and other kinship groups, marriage, and residence. In fact, kinship has been such an important organizing factor in many of the societies studied by anthropologists that it is one of the most elaborate areas of the discipline. What are some of the important concepts?

First is descent. **Descent** is based on the notion of a common heritage. It is a cultural rule tying together people on the basis of reputed common ancestry. Descent functions to guide inheritance, group loyalty, and, above all, the formation of families and extended kinship groups.

There are three main rules of descent. One is **patrilineal descent**, which links relatives through males only. In patrilineal systems, females are part of their father's line, but their children descend from the husband's. **Matrilineal descent** links relatives through females only. Males belong to their mother's line; the children of males descend from the wife's. Bilateral descent links a person to kin through both males and females simultaneously. Americans are said to have **bilateral descent**, whereas most of the people in India, Japan, China and much of Africa are patrilineal. Such groups as the Apache, Asante, and Trobriand Islanders are matrilineal.

Descent often defines groups called, not surprisingly, **descent groups**. One of these is the **lineage**, a localized group that is based on unilineal (patrilineal or matrilineal) descent and that usually has some corporate powers. In the Marshall Islands, for example, the matriline holds rights to land, which, in turn, it allots to its members. Lineages in India sometimes hold rights to land but are a more important arena for other kinds of decisions such as marriage. Lineage mates must be consulted about the advisability, timing, and arrangements for weddings.

Clans are composed of lineages. Clan members believe they are all descended from a common ancestor, but because clans are larger, members cannot trace their genealogical relationships to everyone in the group. In some societies, clans may be linked together in even larger groups called **phratries**. Because phratries are usually large, the feeling of common descent they offer is weaker.

Ramages, or cognatic kin groups, are based on bilateral descent. They often resemble lineages in size and function but provide more recruiting flexibility. An individual can choose membership from among several ramages where he or she has relatives.

Another important kinship group is the family. This unit is more difficult to define than we may think, because people have found so many different ways to organize "familylike" groups. Here we will follow anthropologist George P. Murdock's approach and define the **family** as a kin group consisting of at least one married couple sharing the same residence with their children and performing sexual, reproductive, economic, and educational functions. A **nuclear family** consists of a single married couple and their children. An **extended family** consists of two or more married couples and their children. Extended families have a quality all their own and are often found in societies where family performance and honor are paramount to the reputation of individual family members. Extended families are most commonly based on patrilineal descent. Women marry into such families and must establish themselves among the line members and other women who live there.

Marriage, the socially approved union of two people, is a second major principle of kinship. The regulation of marriage takes elaborate forms from one society to the next. Marriage may be **exogamous**, meaning marriage outside any particular named group, or **endogamous**, indicating the opposite. Bhil tribals of India, for example, are clan and village exogamous (they should marry outside these groups), but tribal endogamous (they should marry other Bhils).

Marriage may also be **monogamous**, where it is preferred that only one individual should be married to one partner at a time, or **polygamous**, meaning that one person may be married to more than one person simultaneously. There are two kinds of polygamy, **polygyny**, the marriage of one man with more than one woman simultaneously, and **polyandry**, the marriage of one woman with more than one man.

Many anthropologists view marriage as a system of alliances between families and descent lines. Viewed in these terms, rules such as endogamy and exogamy can be explained as devices to link or internally strengthen various kinship groups. The **incest taboo**, a legal rule that prohibits sexual intercourse or marriage between particular classes of kin, is often explained as a way to extend alliances between kin groups.

Finally, the regulation of marriage falls to the parents and close relatives of eligible young people in many societies. These elders concern themselves with more than wedding preparations; they must also see to it that young people marry appropriately, which means that they consider the reputation of prospective spouses and their families' economic strength and social rank. Delaying or failing to marry can render an individual suspect in terms of achieving full social adulthood.

The selections in Part Five in this text illustrate several aspects of kinship systems. In the first article, Nancy Scheper-Hughes looks at the relationship that poor Brazilian mothers have with their infants. Because babies die so often, mothers must delay forming attachments to them until their children show that they can survive. The second article, updated for the fifteenth edition, by David McCurdy, looks at the way kinship organizes life for the inhabitants of a Rajasthani Gameti Bhil village. Arranging a marriage requires use and consideration of clans, lineages, families, and weddings. Despite its origin in peasant society, the Indian kinship system is proving useful as people try to cope with a modernizing world. The third article, by Melvyn Goldstein, describes a rare form of marriage—polyandry—and shows why, despite other choices, Tibetan brothers often choose to share a single wife among them. Finally, Susanna Fioratta, in this new article written for *Conformity and Conflict*, looks at the role of marriage in conferring adulthood for both men and women in West Africa.

Key Terms

affinity p. 142

bilateral descent p. 142

clan p. 142

consanguinity p. 142

descent p. 142

descent groups p. 142

endogamy p. 143

exogamy p. 143

extended family p. 143

family p. 143

incest taboo p. 143

kinship p. 142

lineage p. 142

marriage p. 143

matrilineal descent p. 142

monogamy p. 143

nuclear family p. 143

patrilineal descent p. 142

phratry p. 142

polyandry p. 143

polygamy p. 143

polygyny p. 143

ramage p. 142

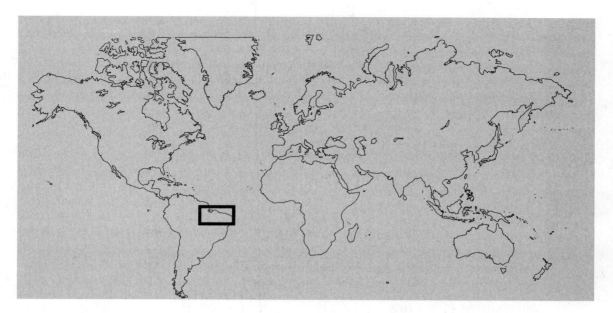

16

Mother's Love: Death without Weeping

Nancy Scheper-Hughes

Kinship systems are based on marriage and birth. Both, anthropologists assume, create ties that can link kin into close, cooperative, enduring structures. What happens to such ties, however, in the face of severe hardship imposed by grinding poverty and urban migration? Can we continue to assume, for example, that there will be a close bond between mother and child? This is the question pursued by Nancy Scheper-Hughes in the following article about the mother–infant relationship among poor women in a Brazilian shantytown. The author became interested in the question following a "baby die-off" in the town of Bom Jesus in 1965. She noticed that mothers seemed to take these events casually. After twenty-five years of research in the Alto do Cruzeiro shantytown there, she has come to see such indifference as a cultural response to high rates of infant death due to poverty and malnutrition. Mothers, and surrounding social institutions such as the Catholic Church, expect babies to die easily. Mothers concentrate their support on babies who are "fighters" and let themselves grow attached to their children only when they are reasonably sure that the offspring will survive. The article also provides an excellent illustration of what happens to kinship systems in the face of poverty and social dislocation. Such conditions may easily result in the formation of woman-headed families and in a lack of the extended kinship networks so often found in more stable, rural societies.

In a current epilogue to this article, Scheper-Hughes notes that political changes in Brazil since the 1980s have led to improved health for mothers and babies. Mothers have *fewer babies and no longer give up on offspring who in the past would have seemed destined to die. Unfortunately, the rise of drugs and gangs along with vigilante death squads have become a major threat to survival and social life in Bom Jesus.**

I have seen death without weeping
The destiny of the Northeast is death
Cattle they kill
To the people they do something worse
                    —Anonymous Brazilian singer (1965)

((•─Listen to the **Chapter Audio** on **myanthrolab.com**

"Why do the church bells ring so often?" I asked Nailza de Arruda soon after I moved into a corner of her tiny mud-walled hut near the top of the shantytown called the Alto do Cruzeiro (Crucifix Hill). I was then a Peace Corps volunteer and a community development/health worker. It was the dry and blazing hot summer of 1965, the months following the military coup in Brazil, and save for the rusty, clanging bells of N.S. das Dores Church, an eerie quiet had settled over the market town that I call Bom Jesus da Mata. Beneath the quiet, however, there was chaos and panic. "It's nothing," replied Nailza, "just another little angel gone to heaven."

Nailza had sent more than her share of little angels to heaven, and sometimes at night I could hear her engaged in a muffled but passionate discourse with one of them, two-year-old Joana. Joana's photograph, taken as she lay propped up in her tiny cardboard coffin, her eyes open, hung on a wall next to one of Nailza and Ze Antonio taken on the day they eloped.

Nailza could barely remember the other infants and babies who came and went in close succession. Most had died unnamed and were hastily baptized in their coffins. Few lived more than a month or two. Only Joana, properly baptized in church at the close of her first year and placed under the protection of a powerful saint, Joan of Arc, had been expected to live. And Nailza had dangerously allowed herself to love the little girl.

In addressing the dead child, Nailza's voice would range from tearful imploring to angry recrimination: "Why did you leave me? Was your patron saint so greedy that she could not allow me one child on this earth?" Ze Antonio advised me to ignore Nailza's odd behavior, which he understood as a kind of madness that, like the birth and death of children, came and went. Indeed, the premature birth of a stillborn son some months later "cured" Nailza of her "inappropriate" grief, and the day came when she removed Joana's photo and carefully packed it away.

More than fifteen years elapsed before I returned to the Alto do Cruzeiro, and it was anthropology that provided the vehicle of my return. Since 1982 I have returned several times in order to pursue a problem that first attracted my attention in the 1960s. My involvement with the people of the Alto do Cruzeiro now spans a quarter of a century and three generations of parenting in a community where mothers and daughters are often simultaneously pregnant.

*From "Death without Weeping," *Natural History,* October 1989. Copyright © 1989 by Nancy Scheper-Hughes, with an update in 2009. Reprinted by permission of the publisher.

The Alto do Cruzeiro is one of three shantytowns surrounding the large market town of Bom Jesus in the sugar plantation zone of Pernambuco in Northeast Brazil, one of the many zones of neglect that have emerged in the shadow of the now tarnished economic miracle of Brazil. For the women and children of the Alto do Cruzeiro the only miracle is that some of them have managed to stay alive at all.

The Northeast is a region of vast proportions (approximately twice the size of Texas) and of equally vast social and developmental problems. The nine states that make up the region are the poorest in the country and are representative of the Third World within a dynamic and rapidly industrializing nation. Despite waves of migrations from the interior to the teeming shantytowns of coastal cities, the majority still live in rural areas on farms and ranches, sugar plantations and mills.

Life expectancy in the Northeast is only forty years, largely because of the appallingly high rate of infant and child mortality. Approximately one million children in Brazil under the age of five die each year. The children of the Northeast, especially those born in shantytowns on the periphery of urban life, are at a very high risk of death. In these areas, children are born without the traditional protection of breast-feeding, subsistence gardens, stable marriages, and multiple adult caretakers that exists in the interior. In the hillside shantytowns that spring up around cities or, in this case, interior market towns, marriages are brittle, single parenting is the norm, and women are frequently forced into the shadow economy of domestic work in the homes of the rich or into unprotected and oftentimes "scab" wage labor on the surrounding sugar plantations, where they clear land for planting and weed for a pittance, sometimes less than a dollar a day. The women of the Alto may not bring their babies with them into the homes of the wealthy, where the often-sick infants are considered sources of contamination, and they cannot carry the little ones to the riverbanks where they wash clothes because the river is heavily infested with schistosomes and other deadly parasites. Nor can they carry their young children to the plantations, which are often several miles away. At wages of a dollar a day, the women of the Alto cannot hire baby sitters. Older children who are not in school will sometimes serve as somewhat indifferent caretakers. But any child not in school is also expected to find wage work. In most cases, babies are simply left at home alone, the door securely fastened. And so many also die alone and unattended.

Bom Jesus da Mata, centrally located in the plantation zone of Pernambuco, is within commuting distance of several sugar plantations and mills. Consequently, Bom Jesus has been a magnet for rural workers forced off their small subsistence plots by large landowners wanting to use every available piece of land for sugar cultivation. Initially, the rural migrants to Bom Jesus were squatters who were given tacit approval by the mayor to put up temporary straw huts on each of the three hills overlooking the town. The Alto do Cruzeiro is the oldest, the largest, and the poorest of the shantytowns. Over the past three decades many of the original migrants have become permanent residents, and the primitive and temporary straw huts have been replaced by small homes (usually of two rooms) made of wattle and daub, sometimes covered with plaster. The more affluent residents use bricks and tiles. In most Alto homes, dangerous kerosene lamps have been replaced by light bulbs. The once tattered rural garb, often fashioned from used sugar sacking, has likewise been replaced by store-bought clothes, often castoffs from a wealthy *patrão* (boss). The trappings are modern, but the hunger, sickness, and death that they conceal are traditional, deeply rooted in a history of feudalism, exploitation, and institutionalized dependency.

My research agenda never wavered. The questions I addressed first crystallized during a veritable "die-off" of Alto babies during a severe drought in 1965. The food and water shortages and the political and economic chaos occasioned by the military coup were reflected in the handwritten entries of births and deaths in the dusty, yellowed pages of the ledger books kept at the public registry office in Bom Jesus. More than 350 babies died in the Alto during 1965 alone—this from a shantytown population of little more than 5,000. But that wasn't what surprised me. There were reasons enough for the deaths in the miserable conditions of shantytown life. What puzzled me was the seeming indifference of Alto women to the death of their infants, and their willingness to attribute to their own tiny offspring an aversion to life that made their death seem wholly natural, indeed all but anticipated.

Although I found that it was possible, and hardly difficult, to rescue infants and toddlers from death by diarrhea and dehydration with a simple sugar, salt, and water solution (even bottled Coca-Cola worked fine), it was more difficult to enlist a mother herself in the rescue of a child she perceived as ill-fated for life or better off dead, or to convince her to take back into her threatened and besieged home a baby she had already come to think of as an angel rather than as a son or daughter.

I learned that the high expectancy of death, and the ability to face child death with stoicism and equanimity, produced patterns of nurturing that differentiated between those infants thought of as thrivers and survivors and those thought of as born already "wanting to die." The survivors were nurtured, while stigmatized, doomed infants were left to die, as mothers say, *a mingua*, "of neglect." Mothers stepped back and allowed nature to take its course. This pattern, which I call mortal selective neglect, is called passive infanticide by anthropologist Marvin Harris. The Alto situation, although culturally specific in the form that it takes, is not unique to Third World shantytown communities and may have its correlates in our own impoverished urban communities in some cases of "failure to thrive" infants.

I use as an example the story of Zezinho, the thirteen-month-old toddler of one of my neighbors, Lourdes. I became involved with Zezinho when I was called in to help Lourdes in the delivery of another child, this one a fair and robust little tyke with a lusty cry. I noted that while Lourdes showed great interest in the newborn, she totally ignored Zezinho who, wasted and severely malnourished, was curled up in a fetal position on a piece of urine- and feces-soaked cardboard placed under his mother's hammock. Eyes open and vacant, mouth slack, the little boy seemed doomed.

When I carried Zezinho up to the community day-care center at the top of the hill, the Alto women who took turns caring for one another's children (in order to free themselves for part-time work in the cane fields or washing clothes) laughed at my efforts to save Ze, agreeing with Lourdes that here was a baby without a ghost of a chance. Leave him alone, they cautioned. It makes no sense to fight with death. But I did do battle with Ze, and after several weeks of force-feeding (malnourished babies lose their interest in food), Ze began to succumb to my ministrations. He acquired some flesh across his taut chest bones, learned to sit up, and even tried to smile. When he seemed well enough, I returned him to Lourdes in her miserable scrap-material lean-to, but not without guilt about what I had done. I wondered whether returning Ze was at all fair to Lourdes and to his little brother. But I was busy and washed my hands of the matter. And Lourdes did seem more interested in Ze now that he was looking more human.

When I returned in 1982, there was Lourdes among the women who formed my sample of Alto mothers—still struggling to put together some semblance of life for a now grown Ze and her five other surviving children. Much was made of my reunion with Ze in 1982, and everyone enjoyed retelling the story of Ze's rescue and of how his mother had given him up for dead. Ze would laugh the loudest when told how

I had had to force-feed him like a fiesta turkey. There was no hint of guilt on the part of Lourdes and no resentment on the part of Ze. In fact, when questioned in private as to who was the best friend he ever had in life, Ze took a long drag on his cigarette and answered without a trace of irony, "Why my mother, of course!" "But of course," I replied.

Part of learning how to mother in the Alto do Cruzeiro is learning when to let go of a child who shows that it "wants" to die or that it has no "knack" or no "taste" for life. Another part is learning when it is safe to let oneself love a child. Frequent child death remains a powerful shaper of maternal thinking and practice. In the absence of firm expectation that a child will survive, mother love as we conceptualize it (whether in popular terms or in the psychobiological notion of maternal bonding) is attenuated and delayed with consequences for infant survival. In an environment already precarious to young life, the emotional detachment of mothers toward some of their babies contributes even further to the spiral of high mortality–high fertility in a kind of macabre lock-step dance of death.

The average woman of the Alto experiences 9.5 pregnancies, 3.5 child deaths, and 1.5 stillbirths. Seventy percent of all child deaths in the Alto occur in the first six months of life, and 82 percent by the end of the first year. Of all deaths in the community each year, about 45 percent are of children under the age of five.

Women of the Alto distinguish between child deaths understood as natural (caused by diarrhea and communicable diseases) and those resulting from sorcery, the evil eye, or other magical or supernatural afflictions. They also recognize a large category of infant deaths seen as fated and inevitable. These hopeless cases are classified by mothers under the folk terminology "child sickness" or "child attack." Women say that there are at least fourteen different types of hopeless child sickness, but most can be subsumed under two categories—chronic and acute. The chronic cases refer to infants who are born small and wasted. They are deathly pale, mothers say, as well as weak and passive. They demonstrate no vital force, no liveliness. They do not suck vigorously; they hardly cry. Such babies can be this way at birth or they can be born sound but soon show no resistance, no "fight" against the common crises of infancy: diarrhea, respiratory infections, tropical fevers.

The acute cases are those doomed infants who die suddenly and violently. They are taken by stealth overnight, often following convulsions that bring on head banging, shaking, grimacing, and shrieking. Women say it is horrible to look at such a baby. If the infant begins to foam at the mouth or gnash its teeth or go rigid with its eyes turned back inside its head, there is absolutely no hope. The infant is "put aside"—left alone—often on the floor in a back room, and allowed to die. These symptoms (which accompany high fevers, dehydration, third-stage malnutrition, and encephalitis) are equated by Alto women with madness, epilepsy, and worst of all, rabies, which is greatly feared and highly stigmatized.

Most of the infants presented to me as suffering from chronic child sickness were tiny, wasted famine victims, while those labeled as victims of acute child attack seemed to be infants suffering from the deliriums of high fever or the convulsions that can accompany electrolyte imbalance in dehydrated babies.

Local midwives and traditional healers, praying women, as they are called, advise Alto women on when to allow a baby to die. One midwife explained: "If I can see that a baby was born unfortuitously, I tell the mother that she need not wash the infant or give it a cleansing tea. I tell her just to dust the infant with baby powder and wait for it to die." Allowing nature to take its course is not seen as sinful by these often very devout Catholic women. Rather, it is understood as cooperating with God's plan.

Often I have been asked how consciously women of the Alto behave in this regard. I would have to say that consciousness is always shifting between allowed and disallowed levels of awareness. For example, I was awakened early one morning in 1987 by two neighborhood children who had been sent to fetch me to a hastily organized wake for a two-month-old infant whose mother I had unsuccessfully urged to breast-feed. The infant was being sustained on sugar water, which the mother referred to as *soro* (serum), using a medical term for the infant's starvation regime in light of his chronic diarrhea. I had cautioned the mother that an infant could not live on *soro* forever.

The two girls urged me to console the young mother by telling her that it was "too bad" that her infant was so weak that Jesus had to take him. They were coaching me in proper Alto etiquette. I agreed, of course, but asked, "And what do *you* think?" Xoxa, the eleven-year-old, looked down at her dusty flip-flops and blurted out, "Oh, Dona Nanci, that baby never got enough to eat, but you must never say that!" And so the death of hungry babies remains one of the best kept secrets of life in Bom Jesus da Mata.

Most victims are waked quickly and with a minimum of ceremony. No tears are shed, and the neighborhood children form a tiny procession, carrying the baby to the town graveyard where it will join a multitude of others. Although a few fresh flowers may be scattered over the tiny grave, no stone or wooden cross will mark the place, and the same spot will be reused within a few months' time. The mother will never visit the grave, which soon becomes an anonymous one.

What, then, can be said of these women? What emotions, what sentiments motivate them? How are they able to do what, in fact, must be done? What does mother love mean in this inhospitable context? Are grief, mourning, and melancholia present, although deeply repressed? If so, where shall we look for them? And if not, how are we to understand the moral visions and moral sensibilities that guide their actions?

I have been criticized more than once for presenting an unflattering portrait of poor Brazilian women, women who are, after all, themselves the victims of severe social and institutional neglect. I have described these women as allowing some of their children to die, as if this were an unnatural and inhuman act rather than, as I would assert, the way any one of us might act, reasonably and rationally, under similarly desperate conditions. Perhaps I have not emphasized enough the real pathogens in this environment of high risk: poverty, deprivation, sexism, chronic hunger, and economic exploitation. If mother love is, as many psychologists and some feminists believe, a seemingly natural and universal maternal script, what does it mean to women for whom scarcity, loss, sickness, and deprivation have made that love frantic and robbed them of their grief, seeming to turn their hearts to stone?

Throughout much of human history—as in a great deal of the impoverished Third World today—women have had to give birth and to nurture children under ecological conditions and social arrangements hostile to child survival, as well as to their own well-being. Under circumstances of high childhood mortality, patterns of selective neglect and passive infanticide may be seen as active survival strategies.

They also seem to be fairly common practices historically and across cultures. In societies characterized by high childhood mortality and by a correspondingly high (replacement) fertility, cultural practices of infant and child care tend to be organized primarily around survival goals. But what this means is a pragmatic recognition that not all of one's children can be expected to live. The nervousness about child survival in areas of northeast Brazil, northern India, or Bangladesh, where a 30 percent or 40 percent mortality rate in the first years of life is common, can lead to forms of delayed attachment and a casual or benign neglect that serves to weed out the worst bets so as to enhance the life chances of healthier siblings, including those yet to be born. Practices similar to those that I am describing have been recorded for parts of Africa, India, and Central America.

Life in the Alto do Cruzeiro resembles nothing so much as a battlefield or an emergency room in an overcrowded inner-city public hospital. Consequently, morality is guided by a kind of "lifeboat ethics," the morality of triage. The seemingly studied indifference toward the suffering of some of their infants, conveyed in such sayings as "little critters have no feelings," is understandable in light of these women's obligation to carry on with their reproductive and nurturing lives.

In their slowness to anthropomorphize and personalize their infants, everything is mobilized so as to prevent maternal overattachment and, therefore, grief at death. The bereaved mother is told not to cry, that her tears will dampen the wings of her little angel so that she cannot fly up to her heavenly home. Grief at the death of an angel is not only inappropriate, it is a symptom of madness and of a profound lack of faith.

Infant death becomes routine in an environment in which death is anticipated and bets are hedged. While the routinization of death in the context of shantytown life is not hard to understand, and quite possible to empathize with, its routinization in the formal institutions of public life in Bom Jesus is not as easy to accept uncritically. Here the social production of indifference takes on a different, even a malevolent, cast.

In a society where triplicates of every form are required for the most banal events (registering a car, for example), the registration of infant and child death is informal, incomplete, and rapid. It requires no documentation, takes less than five minutes, and demands no witnesses other than office clerks. No questions are asked concerning the circumstances of the death, and the cause of death is left blank, unquestioned and unexamined. A neighbor, grandmother, older sibling, or common-law husband may register the death. Since most infants die at home, there is no question of a medical record.

From the registry office, the parent proceeds to the town hall, where the mayor will give him or her a voucher for a free baby coffin. The full-time municipal coffin-maker cannot tell you exactly how many baby coffins are dispatched each week. It varies, he says, with the seasons. There are more needed during the drought months and during the big festivals of Carnaval and Christmas and São Joao's Day because people are too busy, he supposes, to take their babies to the clinic. Record keeping is sloppy.

Similarly, there is a failure on the part of city-employed doctors working at two free clinics to recognize the malnutrition of babies who are weighed, measured, and immunized without comment and as if they were not, in fact, anemic, stunted, fussy, and irritated starvation babies. At best the mothers are told to pick up free vitamins or a health "tonic" at the municipal chambers. At worst, clinic personnel will give tranquilizers and sleeping pills to quiet the hungry cries of "sick-to-death" Alto babies.

The church, too, contributes to the routinization of, and indifference toward, child death. Traditionally, the local Catholic church taught patience and resignation to domestic tragedies that were said to reveal the imponderable workings of God's will. If an infant died suddenly, it was because a particular saint had claimed the child. The infant would be an angel in the service of his or her heavenly patron. It would be wrong, a sign of a lack of faith, to weep for a child with such good fortune. The infant funeral was, in the past, an event celebrated with joy. Today, however, under the new regime of "liberation theology," the bells of N.S. das Dores parish church no longer peal for the death of Alto babies, and no priest accompanies the procession of angels to the cemetery where their bodies are disposed of casually and without ceremony. Children bury children in Bom Jesus da Mata. In this most Catholic of communities, the coffin is handed to the disabled and irritable municipal gravedigger, who often chides the children for one reason or another. It may be that the coffin is larger than expected and the gravedigger can find no appropriate space. The children do not wait for the gravedigger to complete his task. No prayers are recited and no sign of the cross made as the tiny coffin goes into its shallow grave.

When I asked the local priest, Padre Marcos, about the lack of church ceremony surrounding infant and childhood death today in Bom Jesus, he replied: "In the old days, child death was richly celebrated. But those were the baroque customs of a conservative church that wallowed in death and misery. The new church is a church of hope and joy. We no longer celebrate the death of child angels. We try to tell mothers that Jesus doesn't want all the dead babies they send him." Similarly, the new church has changed its baptismal customs, now often refusing to baptize dying babies brought to the back door of a church or rectory. The mothers are scolded by the church attendants and told to go home and take care of their sick babies. Baptism, they are told, is for the living; it is not to be confused with the sacrament of extreme unction, which is the anointing of the dying. And so it appears to the women of the Alto that even the church has turned away from them, denying the traditional comfort of folk Catholicism.

The contemporary Catholic church is caught in the clutches of a double bind. The new theology of liberation imagines a kingdom of God on earth based on justice and equality, a world without hunger, sickness, or childhood mortality. At the same time, the church has not changed its official position on sexuality and reproduction, including its sanctions against birth control, abortion, and sterilization. The padre of Bom Jesus da Mata recognizes this contradiction intuitively, although he shies away from discussions on the topic, saying that he prefers to leave questions of family planning to the discretion and the "good consciences" of his impoverished parishioners. But this, of course, sidesteps the extent to which those good consciences have been shaped by traditional church teachings in Bom Jesus, especially by his recent predecessors. Hence, we can begin to see that the seeming indifference of Alto mothers toward the death of some of their infants is but a pale reflection of the official indifference of church and state to the plight of poor women and children.

Nonetheless, the women of Bom Jesus are survivors. One woman, Biu, told me her life history, returning again and again to the themes of child death, her first husband's suicide, abandonment by her father and later by her second husband, and all the other losses and disappointments she had suffered in her long forty-five years. She concluded with great force, reflecting on the days of Carnaval '88 that were fast approaching:

> No, Dona Nanci, I won't cry, and I won't waste my life thinking about it from morning to night. . . . Can I argue with God for the state that I'm in? No! And so I'll dance and I'll jump and I'll play Carnaval! And yes, I'll laugh and people will wonder at a *pobre* like me who can have such a good time.

And no one did blame Biu for dancing in the streets during the four days of Carnaval—not even on Ash Wednesday, the day following Carnaval '88 when we all assembled hurriedly to assist in the burial of Mercea, Biu's beloved *casula,* her last-born daughter who had died at home of pneumonia during the festivities. The rest of the family barely had time to change out of their costumes. Severino, the child's uncle and godfather, sprinkled holy water over the little angel while he prayed: "Mercea, I don't know whether you were called, taken, or thrown out of this world. But look down at us from your heavenly home with tenderness, with pity, and with mercy." So be it.

Brief Epilogue

Many students write after reading this article asking me whether the situation has changed in the Alto do Cruzeiro. Is life better or worse for mothers and newborn babies? One of the advantages of long-term ethnographic research is seeing history in the making. I began my engagements with the people of the Alto in 1964 at the start of twenty years of military rule, a ruthless regime that produced deep impoverishment among those living in urban *favelas* and in rural areas. The scarcities and insecurities of that era contributed to the death of infants and small babies. By the time I completed my study of mother love and child death in the early 1990s Brazil was well on its way to democratization which ushered in many important changes, most notably a free, public, national health care system (SUS) which guaranteed poor women adequate pre- and post-natal care.

The decade of the 1990s witnessed what population experts call the demographic or epidemiologic transition. As both births and infant deaths declined, mothers began to treat their infants as potentially capable of survival and the old stance of maternal "watchful waiting" accompanied by "letting go" of infants thought of as having no "taste" or "talent" for life, was replaced by a maternal ethos of "holding on" and "holding dear" each infant. Today, young women of the Alto can expect to give birth to three or fewer babies and to see all of them live to adolescence. Many factors produced this reproductive transition: the "modernization" of Catholic beliefs about infant death; the under-the-counter availability of Cytotec, a risky "morning after" pill; the implementation under the national health care system (Serviço Único de Saúde) of local "health agents" who went door to door in poor communities, identifying and rescuing vulnerable infants, toddlers, and old people. The primary cause of the decline in infant mortality on the Alto do Cruzeiro, however, was the "simple" installation of water pipes reaching virtually all the homes in the shantytown with sufficient, clean water. Water = life! It is painful to consider how "culture," "belief," and even "maternal sentiments" follow basic changes in the material conditions—and therefore the possibilities— of everyday life.

Motherhood is not only a social and a cultural construction, but a constellation of embodied practices responding to the requirements and limitations of the political and economic conditions that determine the resilience or vulnerability of infants and their mothers. Today, new problems have beset the people of the Alto do Cruzeiro. Since the publication of "Death without Weeping" drugs and gangs have made their ugly mark on the community and death squads have sprung up to impose a kind of vigilante justice. These anti-social features of life in "Bom Jesus" take some of the pleasure away, as one sees the young men of the Alto who survived that dangerous first year of life, felled by bullets and knife wounds at the hands of gang leaders, *bandidos,* and local police in almost equal measure.

✓●─[**Study** and **Review** on **myanthrolab.com**

Review Questions

1. What did Scheper-Hughes notice about mothers' reactions during the baby die-off of 1965 in Bom Jesus, Brazil?

2. How do poor Brazilian mothers react to their infants' illnesses and death? How do other institutions, such as the church, clinic, and civil authorities respond? Give examples.

3. How does Scheper-Hughes explain the apparent indifference of mothers to the death of their infants?

4. What does the indifference of mothers to the deaths of their children say about basic human nature, especially the mother–child bond?

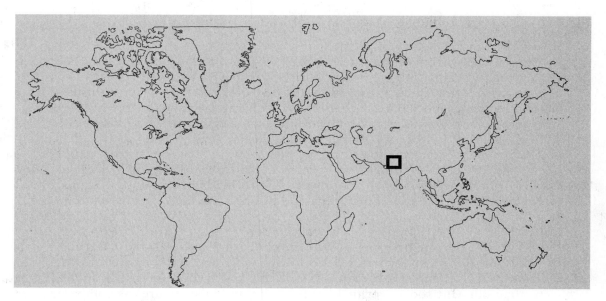

17

Family and Kinship in Village India

David W. McCurdy

Anyone who reads older ethnographic accounts of different cultures will inevitably run across terms such as clan, lineage, avunculocal, levirate, extended family, polyandry, cross-cousin, *and* Crow *terminology. All these terms and many more were created by anthropologists to describe categories, groups, social arrangements, and roles associated with the complex kinship systems that characterized so many of the groups they studied. The importance of kinship for one of these societies, found in an Indian village, is the topic of this article by David McCurdy. He argues that kinship forms the core social groups and associations in rural India in a system well adapted to family-centered landholding and small-scale farming. He concludes by pointing out that Indians have used their close family ties to adapt to life in the emerging cash-labor-oriented modernizing world.* *

((•─┤ **Listen** to the **Chapter Audio** on **myanthrolab.com**

On a hot afternoon in May, 1962, I sat talking with three Gameti (classified as Bhil by the Indian national government) men in the village of Ratakote, located in southern Rajasthan, India.[1]

[1]Ratakote is a Bhil tribal village located 21 miles southwest of Udaipur, Rajasthan, in the Aravalli hills. I did ethnographic research in the village from 1961 to 1963, and again in 1985, 1991, and 1994 for shorter periods of time.

We spoke about the results of recent national elections, their worry over a cattle disease that was afflicting the village herds, and predictions about when the monsoon rains would start. But our longest discussion concerned kin—the terms used to refer to them, the responsibilities they had toward one another, and the importance of marrying them off properly. It was toward the end of this conversation that one of the men, Kanji, said, "Now sāb (Bhili for sāhīb), you are finally asking about a good thing. This is what we want you to tell people about us when you go back to America."

As I thought about it later, I was struck by how different this social outlook was from mine. I doubt that I or any of my friends in the United States would say something like this. Americans do have kin. We have parents, although our parents may not always live together, and we often know other relatives, some of whom are likely to play important parts in our lives. We grow up in families and we often create new ones if we have children. But we also live in a social network of other people whom we meet at work or encounter in various "outside" social settings, and these people can be of equal or even greater importance to us than kin. Our social worlds include such non-kin structures as companies and other work organizations, schools, neighborhoods, churches and other religious groups, and voluntary associations, including recreational groups and social clubs. We are not likely to worry much about our obligations to relatives with the notable exceptions of our children and grandchildren (middle-class American parents are notoriously child-centered), and more grudgingly, our aging parents. We are not supposed to "live off" relatives or lean too heavily on them although we sometimes do.

Not so in Ratakote. Ratakote's society, like many agrarian villages around the world, is kinship-centered. Villagers anchor themselves in their families. They spend great energy on creating and maintaining their kinship system. This actually is not so surprising. Elaborate kinship systems work well in agrarian societies where families tend to be corporate units and where people's social horizons are often limited to the distance they can walk in a day. For the same reasons, families in the United States were also stronger in the past when more of them owned farms and neighborhood businesses.

What may come as a surprise, however, is how resilient and strong Indian kinship systems such as Ratakote's have been in the face of recent economic changes, especially the growth of wage labor. Let us look more closely at the Bhil kinship system, especially at arranged marriage, to illustrate these ideas.

Arranging a Marriage

If there is anything that my American students have trouble understanding about India, it is arranged marriage. They cannot imagine sitting passively by while their parents advertise their charms and evaluate emerging nuptial candidates. The thought of agreeing to make a legal commitment to marry and live with someone they have never met seems out of the question. In our country, personal independence takes precedence over loyalty to family.

Not so in India. There, arranged marriage is still the norm, and most young people, as well as their elders, accept and support the custom. (They often find it sexually exciting, too.) There are many reasons why this is so, but one stands out for discussion here. Marriage constructs alliances between families, lineages, and clans. The resulting kinship network is a pivotal structure in Indian society. It confers social strength and security. People's personal reputations depend on the quality and number of their allied kin. There is little question in their minds about who should arrange marriages. The decision is too important to leave up to inexperienced and impressionable young people.

As an aside I should note that young Indians play a greater part in the process than they used to. Middle-class boys often visit the families of prospective brides, where they manage to briefly "interview" them. They also tap into their kinship network to find out personal information about prospects. Young women also seek out information about prospective grooms. Gameti are no exception. They often conspire to meet those to whom they have been betrothed, usually at a fair or other public event where their contact is likely to go unnoticed. If they don't like each other, they will begin to pressure their parents to back out of the arrangement.

The importance of arranging a marriage was brought home to me several times during fieldwork in Ratakote, but one instance stands out most clearly. When I arrived in the village for a short stay in 1985, Kanji had just concluded marriage arrangements for his daughter, Rupani.[2] What he told me about the process underscored the important role kinship plays in the life of the village.

Kanji started by saying that he and his wife first discussed Rupani's marriage the previous year when the girl first menstruated. She seemed too young for such a union then so they had waited nine months before committing to the marriage process. Even then, Rupani was still only 15 years old. Kanji explained that everyone preferred early marriage for their children because young people were likely to become sexually active as they grew older and might fall in love and elope, pre-empting the arrangement process altogether. Now they figured that the time had come, and they began a series of steps to find a suitable spouse that would eventually involve most of their kin.

The first step was to consult the members of Kanji's *lineage*. Lineage is an anthropological term, not one used by Gameti. But Gameti share membership in local groups of relatives that meet the anthropological definition. Lineages (in this case patrilineages) include closely related men who are all descended from a known ancestor. Kanji's lineage consists of his two married brothers, three married sons of his deceased father's brother (his father is also dead), and his own married son when the latter is home. All are the descendants of his grandfather who had migrated to Ratakote many years earlier. He had talked with all of them informally about the possibility of his daughter's marriage before this. Now he called them together for formal approval.

The approval of lineage mates is necessary because they are essential to the marriage process. Each one of them will help spread the word to other villages that Rupani is available for marriage. They will loan money to Kanji for wedding expenses, and when it comes time for the wedding ceremony, they will provide much of the labor needed to prepare food and arrange required activities. Each family belonging to the lineage will host a special meal for the bride (the groom is similarly entertained in his village) during the wedding period, and one or two will help her make offerings to their lineal ancestors. The groom will also experience this ritual.

The lineage also has functions not directly related to marriage. It has the right to redistribute the land of deceased, childless male members, and it provides its members with political support. It sees to memorial feasts for deceased members. Its

[2]Kanji and Rupani are not real people. Their experiences are a composite of several life histories.

members may cooperatively plow and sow fields together and combine their animals for herding.

With lineage approval in hand, Kanji announced Rupani's eligibility in other villages. (Bhils are village exogamous, meaning they prefer to marry spouses from other communities.) Kanji and his lineage mates went about this by paying visits to feminal relatives in other villages. These are kin of the women, now living in Ratakote, who have married into his family. They also include the daughters of his family line who have married and gone to live in other villages, along with their husbands and husbands' kin.

Once the word has been spread, news of prospective candidates begins to filter in. It may arrive with feminal kin from other villages when they visit Ratakote. Or it may come from neighbors who are acting as go-betweens in Ratakote for kin who live in other villages and who seek partners for their children. Either way, a process of evaluation starts. Does the family of the suggested boy or girl have a good reputation? Are they hospitable to their in-laws? Do they meet their obligations to others? What is the reputation of the boy or girl they are offering in marriage? Is he or she tall or short, light or dark, robust or frail, cheerful or complaining, hardworking or lazy? What about their level of education? Does the family have sufficient land and animals? Have they treated other sons- and daughters-in-law well?

The most fundamental question to ask, however, is whether the prospective spouse is from the right clan. In anthropology, the term *clan* refers to an aggregate of people who all believe they are descended from a common ancestor. In Ratakote this group is called an *arak*. Araks are named and the names are used as surnames when Gameti identify themselves. Kanji comes from the pargi arak and is thus known as Kanji Pargi. There is Lalu Bodar, Naraji Katara, Dita Hiravat, Nathu Airi—all men named for one of the 36 araks found in Ratakote. Women also belong to their father's clan, but unlike many American women who adopt their husband's surname at marriage, they keep their arak name all their lives.

Araks are based on a rule of patrilineal descent. This means that their members trace ancestry through males only. (Matrilineal descent traces the line through females only, and bilateral descent, which is found in U.S. society, includes both sexes.) Patrilineal descent not only defines arak membership, it governs inheritance. (Sons inherit equally from their fathers in Ratakote; daughters do not inherit despite a national law giving them that right.) It says that the children of divorced parents stay with the father's family. It bolsters the authority of men over their wives and children. It supports the rule of patrilocality. It even defines the village view of conception. Men plant the "seeds" that grow into children; women provide the fields in which the seeds germinate and grow.

The arak symbolizes patrilineal descent. It is not an organized group, although the members of an arak worship the same mother goddess no matter where they live. Instead it is an identity, an indicator that tells people who their lineal blood relatives are. There are pargis in hundreds of other Gameti villages. Most are strangers to Kanji but if he meets pargis elsewhere, he knows they share a common blood heritage with him.

It is this sense of common heritage that affects marriage. Gameti, like most Indians, believe that clan (arak) mates are close relatives even though they may be strangers. Marriage with them is forbidden. To make sure incest is impossible, it is also forbidden to marry anyone from your mother's arak or your father's mother's arak, to say nothing of anyone else you know you are related to.

This point was driven home to me during field work in 1962 when a neighbor of Kanji's, Kamalaji Kharadi, who was sitting smoking with several other men, asked me which arak I belonged to. Instead of letting it go at "McCurdy," I said that I didn't have an arak. I explained that Americans didn't have a kinship group similar to this, and that was why I had to ask questions about kinship.

My listeners didn't believe me. After all, I must have a father and you get your arak automatically from him. It is a matter of birth and all people are born. They looked at each other as if to say, "We wonder why he won't tell us what his arak is?" then tried again to get me to answer. My second denial led them to ask, "OK, then what is your wife's arak?" (If you can't get at it one way, then try another.) I answered that she didn't have an arak either. This caused a mild sensation. "Then how do you know if you have not married your own relative?" they asked, secretly, I think, delighted by the scandalous prospect.

The third step that occurred during the arrangement of Rupani's marriage came after the family had settled on a prospective groom. This step is the betrothal, and it took place when the groom's father and some of his lineage mates and neighbors paid a formal visit to Kanji's house. When they arrive, Kanji must offer his guests a formal meal, usually slaughtering a goat and distilling some liquor for the occasion. The bride, her face covered by her sari, will be brought out for a brief viewing, as well. But most of the time will be spent making arrangements—when will the actual wedding take place? Who will check the couple's horoscopes for fit? How much will the bride price (also called bride wealth by many anthropologists) be?

Bride price (*dapa*) deserves special comment. It is usually a standard sum of money (about 700 rupees in 1985), although it may also include silver ornaments or other valuables. The dapa is given by the groom's father and his line to the parents of the bride. Gameti view this exchange as compensation for the loss of the bride's services to her family. It also pays for a shift in her loyalty.

The exchange points at an important strain on families in patrilineal societies, the transfer of a woman from her natal family and line to those of her husband. This transfer includes not only her person, but her loyalty, labor, and children. Although she always will belong to her father's arak, she is now part of her husband's family, not his.

This problem is especially troublesome in India because of the close ties often formed there by a girl and her parents. Parents know their daughter will leave when she marries, and they know that in her husband's house and village, she will be at a disadvantage. She will be alone, and out of respect for his parents her husband may not favor her wishes, at least in public. Because of this, they tend to give her extra freedom and support. In addition, they recognize the strain she will be under when she first goes to live with her new husband and his family. To ease her transition, they permit her to visit her parents frequently for a year or two. They also may try to marry her into a village where other women from Ratakote have married, so that she has some kin or at least supporters.

After her marriage, a woman's parents and especially her brothers find it hard not to care about her welfare. Their potential interest presents a built-in structural conflict that could strain relations between the two families if nothing were done about it.

A solution to this problem is to make the marriage into an exchange, and bride price is one result. Bride price also helps to dramatize the change in loyalty and obligation accompanying the bride's entrance into her new family.

Gameti have also devised a number of wedding rituals to dramatize the bride's shift in family membership. The bride must cry to symbolize that she is leaving her home. The groom ritually storms the bride's house at the beginning of the final ceremony. He does so like a conquering hero, drawing a sword to strike a ceremonial arch placed over the entrance while simultaneously stepping on a small fire (he wears a slipper to protect his foot), ritually violating the household's sacred hearth. At the end of the wedding, the groom, with some friends, engages in a mock battle with the bride's brothers and other young men, and symbolically abducts her. The meaning of this ritual is a dramatic equivalent of a father "giving away the bride" at American weddings.

One additional way of managing possible tension between in-laws is the application of respect behavior. The parents of the bride must always treat those of the groom and their relatives with respect. They must not joke in their presence, and they must use respectful language and defer to the groom's parents in normal conversation. In keeping with the strong patrilineal system, a groom may not accept important gifts from his wife's family except on ritual occasions, such as weddings, when exchange is expected. A groom may help support his own father, but he should not do so with his in-laws. That is up to their sons.

Bride price exchange also sets in motion a life-long process of mutual hospitality between the two families. Once the marriage has taken place, the families will become part of each other's feminal kin. They will exchange gifts on some ritual occasions, open their houses to each other, and, of course, help one another make future marriages.

The Future of Indian Kinship

On a trip to India in 1994, I learned that Rupani had delivered three children since her wedding. Kanji, now over 60 years old, had visited them a few months before I arrived, and said that Rupani was happy and that he had wonderful grandchildren. But he also mentioned that her husband now spent most of his time in the nearby city of Udaipur working in construction there. He sent money home, but his absence left Rupani to run the house and raise the children by herself, although she did so with the assistance of his parents and lineage mates.

Rupani's husband's case was not unusual. Every morning 70 or 80 village men boarded one of the 20 or so buses that travel the road, now paved, that runs through Ratakote to the city. There they waited to be recruited by contractors for day labor at a low wage. Some even had gained special skills that enabled them to acquire more permanent, better-paying jobs and live for weeks at a time in the city.

The reason they have to take this kind of work is simple. Ratakote has more than tripled in population since 1962. (The village had a population of 1,184 in 1963. By 2012 the number was well above 3,000.) There is not enough land for everyone to farm nor can the land produce enough to feed the growing population, even in abundant years. And greater access to the city has also increased villagers' desire for market-based goods. Work in the city is the answer, especially for householders whose land is not irrigated like Kanji's.

But there is a social cost to this growing source of income. Cash labor has a potential to break down the kinship system that Gameti value so highly. It frees men and women from economic dependence on the family, since they make their own money working for someone else. It takes up time, too, making it difficult for them to attend the leisurely eleven-day weddings commonly found in 1962 (now reduced to two days in 2010), and to meet other obligations to kin that require their presence. With cash labor, one's reputation is likely to hinge less on family than on work. For some, work means moving the family altogether. Kamila Katara, one of Kanji's neighbors, has a son who has moved with his wife and children to the central Indian city of Indore. He has a good factory job there, and the move has kept them together. By doing so, however, he and they are largely removed from the kinship loop.

My last trip to India and Ratakote in 2012 revealed an intensification of these changes. A steady stream of buses ply the narrow road that runs through Ratakote to Udaipur. Many if not most of Ratakote's young men (and increasingly some young women) work in the city for cash. Indeed, acquiring money is necessary for family subsistence. Most families need cash to buy grain, oil, and several other food commodities at subsidized government prices in local village shops. Electrification and two cell towers have come to the village. Villagers have bought cell phones and, in a few cases, TVs supported by satellite dishes. These and the acquisition by several people of small motorcycles also require a cash inflow.

Yet despite these economic changes, kinship in Ratakote and for India as a whole remains surprisingly strong. Even though some may live farther away, Gameti sons and daughters still try to visit their families regularly. They send money home, and continue to attend weddings. They talk about their kin, too, and surprisingly, they also continue the long process of arranging marriage for their children.

Perhaps one reason for kinship's vitality is the use to which kinship is put by many Indians. The people of Ratakote and other Indians have never given up teaching their children to respect their elders and subordinate their interests to those of the family. Family loyalty is still a paramount value. They use this loyalty to help each other economically. Family members hire each other in business. They take one another in during hard times. They offer hospitality to each other. Unlike Americans who feel guilty about accepting one-sided help from relatives, Indians look to the future. Giving aid now may pay off with a job or a favor later. Even if it doesn't, it is the proper thing to do.

Instead of breaking up the kinship network, work that takes men and families away from the village has simply stretched it out. An Indian student I know has found relatives in nearly every American city he has visited. He knows of kin in Europe and Southeast Asia too. Anywhere he goes he is likely to have relatives to stay with and to help him. When he settles down he will be expected to return the favor. Another Indian friend also illustrates this point. After attending graduate school and working for a time in the United States, he returned to India where he became CEO of a large international company. He regularly contributes to his father's financial wellbeing and hopes to arrange marriages for his daughters.

When I visited Ratakote again in 2012, I discover that Kanji, along with many villagers I had known well, had died. But the last time I talked with him in 1994, he was not disturbed by the economic changes that were overtaking the quiet agricultural pace of Ratakote. I left him standing in front of his house with a grandson in his arms. His son, who had left the village in 1982 to be a "wiper" on a truck, had returned to run the farm. He was still able to meet his family's obligation to lineage and feminal kin. For Kanji, traditional rules of inheritance had pulled a son and, for the moment at least, a grandson, back into the bosom of the family where they belonged.

✓●—⌐**Study** and **Review** on **myanthrolab.com**

Review Questions

1. What are the main ways that kinship organizes Gameti society in Ratakote, according to McCurdy?

2. What is meant by the terms *clan, lineage, family, patrilineal descent, patrilocal residence, alliance,* and *feminal kin group?* Give examples of each.

3. Why do Gameti parents feel that marriage is too important a matter to be left up to their children?

4. What structural tensions does marriage create in Gameti society? What customs exist to reduce this tension?

5. What attributes do Gameti parents look for in a prospective bride or groom? How do young people try to influence the marriage partner their parents choose for them?

6. Although the U.S. kinship system seems limited by comparison to India's, many argue that it is more important than most of us think. Can you think of ways this might be true?

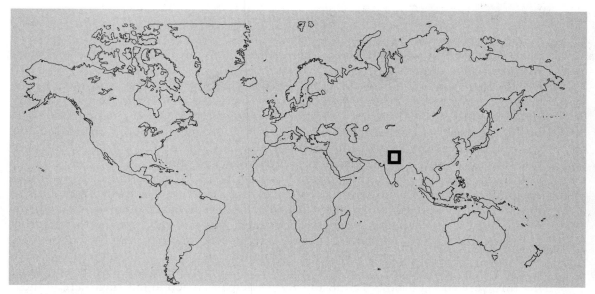

18

Polyandry: When Brothers Take a Wife

Melvyn C. Goldstein

Many of the world's societies permit polygamy, the marriage of an individual to more than one spouse. The most common form of polygamy is polygyny, an arrangement in which a man marries more than one wife. Polygyny may exist for many reasons, not the least of which is its relationship to the substantial economic contributions of women. But there is a second kind of polygamy called polyandry, organized around the marriage of a woman to more than one husband, and its causes may seem less clear. In this article, Melvyn Goldstein describes the fraternal polyandry practiced by Tibetans living in Northern Nepal and seeks to explain why, despite having a choice of marriage forms including monogamy and polygyny, men and women often choose this rare form of marriage. He argues that, by marrying a single wife, a group of brothers can more easily preserve their family resources, whereas monogamous or polygynous marriage usually costs a man his inheritance and requires him to make a fresh start.*

((•—Listen to the Chapter Audio on myanthrolab.com

Eager to reach home, Dorje drives his yaks hard over the seventeen-thousand-foot mountain pass, stopping only once to rest. He and his two older brothers, Pema and Sonam, are jointly marrying a woman from the next village in a few weeks, and he has to help with the preparations.

Dorje, Pema, and Sonam are Tibetans living in Limi, a two-hundred-square-mile area in the northwest corner of Nepal, across the border from Tibet. The form of marriage they are about to enter—fraternal polyandry in anthropological parlance—is one of the world's rarest forms of marriage but is not uncommon in Tibetan society, where it has been practiced from time immemorial. For many Tibetan social strata, it traditionally represented the ideal form of marriage and family.

The mechanics of fraternal polyandry are simple. Two, three, four, or more brothers jointly take a wife, who leaves her home to come and live with them. Traditionally, marriage was arranged by parents, with children, particularly females, having little or no say. This is changing somewhat nowadays, but it is still unusual for children to marry without their parents' consent. Marriage ceremonies vary by income and region and range from all the brothers sitting together as grooms to only the eldest one formally doing so. The age of the brothers plays an important role in determining this: very young brothers almost never participate in actual marriage ceremonies, although they typically join the marriage when they reach their mid-teens.

The eldest brother is normally dominant in terms of authority, that is, in managing the household, but all the brothers share the work and participate as sexual partners. Tibetan males and females do not find the sexual aspect of sharing a spouse the least bit unusual, repulsive, or scandalous, and the norm is for the wife to treat all the brothers the same.

Offspring are treated similarly. There is no attempt to link children biologically to particular brothers, and a brother shows no favoritism toward his child even if he knows he is the real father because, for example, his other brothers were away at the time the wife became pregnant. The children, in turn, consider all of the brothers as their fathers and treat them equally, even if they also know who their real father is. In some regions children use the term "father" for the eldest brother and "father's brother" for the others, while in other areas they call all the brothers by one term, modifying this by the use of "elder" and "younger."

Unlike our own society, where monogamy is the only form of marriage permitted, Tibetan society allows a variety of marriage types, including monogamy, fraternal polyandry, and polygyny. Fraternal polyandry and monogamy are the most common forms of marriage, while polygyny typically occurs in cases where the first wife is barren. The widespread practice of fraternal polyandry, therefore, is not the outcome of a law requiring brothers to marry jointly. There is choice, and in fact, divorce traditionally was relatively simple in Tibetan society. If a brother in a polyandrous marriage became dissatisfied and wanted to separate, he simply left the main house and set up his own household. In such cases, all the children stayed in the main household with the remaining brother(s), even if the departing brother was known to be the real father of one or more of the children.

The Tibetans' own explanation for choosing fraternal polyandry is materialistic. For example, when I asked Dorje why he decided to marry with his two brothers rather than take his own wife, he thought for a moment, then said it prevented the division of his family's farm (and animals) and thus facilitated all of them achieving a higher standard of living. And when I later asked Dorje's bride whether it wasn't difficult for her to cope with three brothers as husbands, she laughed and echoed the rationale of avoiding fragmentation of the family and land, adding that she expected to be better off economically, since she would have three husbands working for her and her children.

Exotic as it may seem to Westerners, Tibetan fraternal polyandry is thus in many ways analogous to the way primogeniture functioned in nineteenth-century England. Primogeniture dictated that the eldest son inherited the family estate, while younger sons had to leave home and seek their own employment—for example, in the military or the clergy. Primogeniture maintained family estates intact over generations by permitting only one heir per generation. Fraternal polyandry also accomplishes this but does so by keeping all the brothers together with just one wife so that there is only one *set* of heirs per generation.

While Tibetans believe that in this way fraternal polyandry reduces the risk of family fission, monogamous marriages among brothers need not necessarily precipitate the division of the family estate: brothers could continue to live together, and the family land could continue to be worked jointly. When I asked Tibetans about this, however, they invariably responded that such joint families are unstable because each wife is primarily oriented to her own children and interested in their success and well-being over that of the children of the other wives. For example, if the youngest brother's wife had three sons while the eldest brother's wife had only one daughter, the wife of the youngest brother might begin to demand more resources for her children since, as males, they represent the future of the family. Thus the children from different wives in the same generation are competing sets of heirs, and this makes such families inherently unstable. Tibetans perceive that conflict will spread from the wives to their husbands and consider this likely to cause family fission. Consequently, it is almost never done.

Although Tibetans see an economic advantage to fraternal polyandry, they do not value the sharing of a wife as an end in itself. On the contrary, they articulate a number of problems inherent in the practice. For example, because authority is customarily exercised by the eldest brother, his younger male siblings have to subordinate themselves with little hope of changing their status within the family. When these younger brothers are aggressive and individualistic, tensions and difficulties often occur despite there being only one set of heirs.

In addition, tension and conflict may arise in polyandrous families because of sexual favoritism. The bride normally sleeps with the eldest brother, and the two have the responsibility to see to it that the other males have opportunities for sexual access. Since the Tibetan subsistence economy requires males to travel a lot, the temporary absence of one or more brothers facilitates this, but there are also other rotation practices. The cultural ideal unambiguously calls for the wife to show equal affection and sexuality to each of the brothers (and vice versa), but deviations from this ideal occur, especially when there is a sizable difference in age between the partners in the marriage.

Dorje's family represents just such a potential situation. He is fifteen years old and his two older brothers are twenty-five and twenty-two years old. The new bride is twenty-three years old, eight years Dorje's senior. Sometimes such a bride finds the youngest husband immature and adolescent and does not treat him with equal affection; alternatively, she may find his youth attractive and lavish special attention on him. Apart from that consideration, when a younger male like Dorje grows up, he may consider his wife "ancient" and prefer the company of a woman his own age or younger. Consequently, although men and women do not find the idea of sharing a bride or a bridegroom repulsive, individual likes and dislikes can cause familial discord.

Two reasons have commonly been offered for the perpetuation of fraternal polyandry in Tibet: that Tibetans practice female infanticide and therefore have to marry polyandrously, owing to a shortage of females; and that Tibet, lying at extremely high altitudes, is so barren and bleak that Tibetans would starve without resort to this mechanism. A Jesuit who lived in Tibet during the eighteenth century articulated this second view: "One reason for this most odious custom is the sterility of the soil, and the small amount of land that can be cultivated owing to the lack of water. The crops may suffice if the brothers all live together, but if they form separate families they would be reduced to beggary."

Both explanations are wrong, however. Not only has there never been institutionalized female infanticide in Tibet, but Tibetan society gives females considerable rights, including inheriting the family estate in the absence of brothers. In such cases, the woman takes a bridegroom who comes to live in her family and adopts her family's name and identity. Moreover, there is no demographic evidence of a shortage of females. In Limi, for example, there were (in 1974) sixty females and fifty-three males in the fifteen- to thirty-five-year age category, and many adult females were unmarried.

The second reason is incorrect because the climate in Tibet is extremely harsh, and ecological factors do play a major role in perpetuating polyandry, but polyandry is not a means of preventing starvation. It is characteristic, not of the poorest segments of the society, but rather of the peasant landowning families.

In the old society, the landless poor could not realistically aspire to prosperity, but they did not fear starvation. There was a persistent labor shortage throughout Tibet, and very poor families with little or no land and few animals could subsist through agricultural labor, tenant farming, craft occupations such as carpentry, or by working as servants. Although the per-person family income could increase somewhat if brothers married polyandrously and pooled their wages, in the absence of inheritable land, the advantage of fraternal polyandry was not generally sufficient to prevent them from setting up their own households. A more skilled or energetic younger brother could do as well or better alone, since he would completely control his income and would not have to share it with his siblings. Consequently, while there was and is some polyandry among the poor, it is much less frequent and more prone to result in divorce and family fission.

An alternative reason for the persistence of fraternal polyandry is that it reduces population growth (and thereby reduces the pressure on resources) by relegating some females to lifetime spinsterhood (see Figure 1). Fraternal polyandrous marriages in Limi (in 1974) averaged 2.35 men per woman, and not surprisingly, 31 percent of the females of child-bearing age (twenty to forty-nine) were unmarried. These spinsters either continued to live at home, set up their own households, or worked as servants for other families. They could also become Buddhist nuns. Being unmarried is not synonymous with exclusion from the reproductive pool. Discreet extramarital relationships are tolerated, and actually half of the adult unmarried women in Limi had one or more children. They raised these children as single mothers, working for wages or weaving cloth and blankets for sale. As a group, however, the unmarried women had far fewer offspring than the married women, averaging only 0.7 children per woman, compared with 3.3 for married women, whether polyandrous, monogamous, or polygynous. When polyandry helps regulate population, this function of polyandry is not consciously perceived by Tibetans and is not the reason they consistently choose it.

If neither a shortage of females nor the fear of starvation perpetuates fraternal polyandry, what motivates brothers, particularly younger brothers, to opt for this system of marriage? From the perspective of the younger brother in a landholding family,

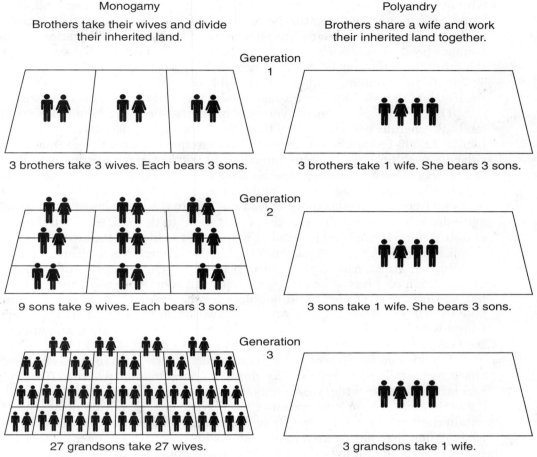

FIGURE 1 Family Planning in Tibet

An economic rationale for fraternal polyandry is outlined in the diagram above, which emphasizes only the male offspring in each generation. If every wife is assumed to bear three sons, a family splitting up into monogamous households would rapidly multiply and fragment the family land. In this case, a rule of inheritance, such as primogeniture, could retain the family land intact, but only at the cost of creating many landless male offspring. In contrast, the family practicing fraternal polyandry maintains a steady ratio of persons to land.

the main incentive is the attainment or maintenance of the good life. With polyandry, he can expect a more secure and higher standard of living, with access not only to his family's land and animals but also to its inherited collection of clothes, jewelry, rugs, saddles, and horses. In addition, he will experience less work pressure and much greater security because all responsibility does not fall on one "father." For Tibetan brothers, the question is whether to trade off the greater personal freedom inherent in monogamy for the real or potential economic security, affluence, and social prestige associated with life in a larger, labor-rich polyandrous family.

A brother thinking of separating from his polyandrous marriage and taking his own wife would face various disadvantages. Although in the majority of Tibetan regions all brothers theoretically have rights to their family's estate, in reality Tibetans are reluctant to divide their land into small fragments. Generally, a younger brother who insists on leaving the family will receive only a small plot of land, if that. Because of its power and wealth, the rest of the family usually can block any attempt of the younger brother to increase his share of land through litigation. Moreover, a younger brother may not even get a house and cannot expect to receive much above the minimum in terms of movable possessions, such as furniture, pots, and pans. Thus a brother contemplating going out on his own must plan on achieving economic security and the good life not through inheritance but through his own work.

The obvious solution for younger brothers—creating new fields from virgin land—is generally not a feasible option. Most Tibetan populations live at high altitudes (above 12,000 feet), where arable land is extremely scarce. For example, in Dorje's village, agriculture ranges only from about 12,900 feet, the lowest point in the area, to 13,300 feet. Above that altitude, early frost and snow destroy the staple barley crop. Furthermore, because of the low rainfall caused by the Himalayan rain shadow, many areas in Tibet and northern Nepal that are within the appropriate altitude range for agriculture have no reliable sources of irrigation. In the end, although there is plenty of unused land in such areas, most of it is either too high or too arid.

Even where unused land capable of being farmed exists, clearing the land and building the substantial terraces necessary for irrigation constitute a great undertaking. Each plot has to be completely dug out to a depth of two to two and a half feet so that the large rocks and boulders can be removed. At best, a man might be able to bring a few new fields under cultivation in the first years after separating from his brothers, but he could not expect to acquire substantial amounts of arable land this way.

In addition, because of the limited farmland, the Tibetan subsistence economy characteristically includes a strong emphasis on animal husbandry. Tibetan farmers regularly maintain cattle, yaks, goats, and sheep, grazing them in the areas too high for agriculture. These herds produce wool, milk, cheese, butter, meat, and skins. To obtain these resources, however, shepherds must accompany the animals on a daily basis. When first setting up a monogamous household, a younger brother like Dorje would find it difficult to both farm and manage animals.

In traditional Tibetan society, there was an even more critical factor that operated to perpetuate fraternal polyandry—a form of hereditary servitude somewhat analogous to serfdom in Europe. Peasants were tied to large estates held by aristocrats, monasteries, and the Lhasa government. They were allowed the use of some farmland to produce their own subsistence but were required to provide taxes in kind and corvée (free labor) to their lords. The corvée was a substantial hardship, since a peasant household was in many cases required to furnish the lord with one laborer daily for most of the year and more on specific occasions such as the harvest. This enforced labor, along with the lack of new land and the ecological pressure to pursue both agriculture and animal husbandry, made polyandrous families particularly beneficial. The polyandrous family allowed an internal division of adult labor, maximizing economic advantage. For example, while the wife worked the family fields, one brother could perform the lord's corvée, another could look after the animals, and a third could engage in trade.

Although social scientists often discount other people's explanations of why they do things, in the case of Tibetan fraternal polyandry, such explanations are very close to the truth. The custom, however, is very sensitive to changes in its political and economic milieu and, not surprisingly, is in decline in most Tibetan areas. Made less important by the elimination of the traditional serf-based economy, it is disparaged by the dominant non-Tibetan leaders of India, China, and Nepal. New opportunities for economic and social mobility in these countries, such as the tourist trade and government employment, are also eroding the rationale for polyandry, and so it may vanish within the next generation.

✓●─Study and **Review** on **myanthrolab.com**

Review Questions

1. What is fraternal polyandry, and how does this form of marriage manage potential conflict over sex, children, and inheritance?

2. Why do many Tibetans choose polyandry over monogamous or polygynous marriage?

3. According to Tibetans, what are some of the disadvantages of polyandry?

4. What is wrong with the theory that Tibetan polyandry is caused either by a shortage of women due to infanticide or is a way to prevent famine by limiting population and land pressure?

5. Why might Tibetan polyandry disappear under modern conditions?

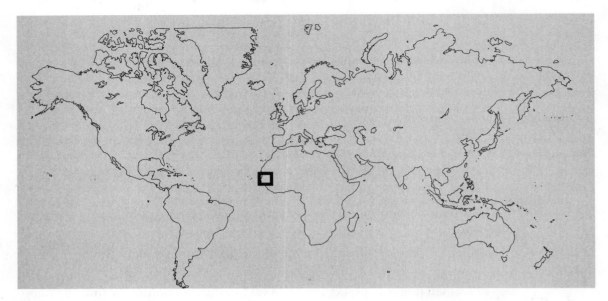

19

Marriage and Adulthood in West Africa

Susanna Fioratta

Americans mostly think of marriage as a more permanent and legal relationship between two people who wish to live together and perhaps raise children. Marriage should confer in us a sense of obligation to one's spouse and offspring and may have some effect on our relations with others. But for us it is not a necessary social condition of adulthood. Such is not the case in some other societies including that of Guinea, which is the topic of this article by Susanna Fioratta. There, only marriage can fully confer adult status on both men and women and give them a normal relationship with others in this West African society. But as Fioratta also shows, becoming and staying married can be difficult there.*

((•─Ⅰ**Listen** to the **Chapter Audio** on **myanthrolab.com**

One day in 2010, I sat in a village café and watched a young man modify a presidential campaign poster with a big, black marker. On one side of the political candidate's smiling face, the young man wrote, "No wife." On the other side, he wrote, "No children." Across the bottom, he wrote, "Alpha Condé rented his wife for 12,000,000 FG [Guinea francs; about $1,800]."

The other lookers-on in the café were highly amused, and called out remarks like, "That's right! He has no wife, no kids! He has no house! How can someone like that govern a country?"

Alpha Condé's marital status had been the subject of much discussion in my fieldwork site in Guinea's Fouta Djallon's highlands. Everyone was taking an active interest in the national presidential campaign, and Condé was among the frontrunners. He was unpopular in the Fouta Djallon for a number of reasons, mostly because another leading candidate hailed from that region. But in everyday conversation, the strongest objection to Alpha Condé's candidacy was that he had no wife—and, by extension, no children and no house.

When I first heard the "no wife" critique of 72-year-old Condé, I assumed that tacit allegations of homosexuality lay behind it. But when I asked questions, a different picture began to emerge. Alpha Condé would make a terrible president, people said, because a man of his age—again, with no wife, children, or house— has not shown himself to be a responsible adult. One informant explained that if such a man lived in the village, he would hardly be treated as a member of society: "People wouldn't visit him, wouldn't invite him to ceremonies, and wouldn't want his advice about problems, because he can't demonstrate that he has done anything. He has nothing to lose." Others claimed that a man with no wife or children of his own should not govern because he would be incapable of sympathy or pity for his subjects: "Given a choice between a child and a rock, he will choose the rock."

At first glance, these critiques may not seem especially remarkable. After all, an unmarried president is also a rarity in United States history (only six, in fact, if you count the widowers), and the wives and families of U.S. politicians often attract public attention. But why should a person's marital status, in the U.S. or in Guinea, matter so much in society?

In the U.S., marriage is a common social and legal relationship, but we rarely think of marriage as something that affects our status as adults. Americans tend to believe that we can achieve economic success and social standing independently of whether or not we are married. And yet, recent debates over the legality of same-sex marriage demonstrate the ongoing significance of marriage as a desirable institution in the U.S., and a spate of news articles in 2013 declared marriage a "luxury good" increasingly inaccessible to people with lower education and income levels.[1] Thus, even in the U.S., marital status holds important social and economic meaning, though we might not always recognize it. But in other countries, including Guinea, marriage is a more explicit mark of social adulthood. It is virtually impossible for an unmarried man or woman to be considered an adult in Guinea.

Examined more closely, the conversations I overheard about Alpha Condé reveal much about the social obligations and responsibilities that many Guineans assumed to be true for any adult. Importantly, these obligations apply to both men and women. I was already used to hearing Fouta Djallon residents talk about marriage as good and necessary for girls and women, but these critiques made it clear that marriage was central to male social adulthood as well.

To understand why marriage is so important, one needs to dig deeper into Guinean society. Marriages usher forth children to raise as the future providers for

---

[1]The *New York Times*, CNBC, the *Atlantic, New York Magazine, Slate*, and others reported similar stories on this issue, citing a sociological study "Intimate Inequalities: Love and Work in a Post-Industrial Landscape," by Sarah Corse and Jennifer Silva.

the family, not just their parents but also their grandparents. Marriage also brings the responsibility to build a house, a place for family members to live and the site of one's future retirement. People could, therefore, visit a married man who had children and a house; they could invite him to weddings, baby naming ceremonies, and other events; and they could ask his advice when they had problems. Marriage was a critical part of responsible adulthood, and responsible adulthood was a status that both men and women needed to achieve (though in different ways, as I explain below) to become respectable members of society. And, as Alpha Condé's situation shows, without marriage, a person cannot be seen as a proper, social adult person.

And yet, despite the importance of marriage in Fouta Djallon society, achieving this ideal can be surprisingly difficult. Married status can be difficult to attain, must be actively maintained, and can be lost through death or divorce. And, furthermore, men and women experience these challenges differently.

Marriage and Other Rites of Passage in the Fouta Djallon

In the Fouta Djallon, children go through several rites of passage on the way to becoming adults. Babies are given naming ceremonies one week after birth. Typically, a family will announce the new baby's name, sacrifice a goat or sheep, and invite friends and neighbors to partake in the feast and pray for the child's health and happiness. An imam or elder man who has studied the Koran may give a special benediction for the baby. At some point during childhood, boys and girls are taken away from home, usually in groups, to remote locations, where the boys are circumcised and the girls are excised (in excision, a girl's clitoris and labia are cut off). These procedures are extremely painful, and, in the case of excision, can result in long-term health complications; nevertheless, most people consider them necessary steps toward adulthood. A girl must be excised in order to become eligible for marriage.

As elsewhere in the world, marriage in the Fouta Djallon is an alliance between families, not merely the individuals involved. The parents of the bride will usually arrange the match either with the parents of the groom or with the groom himself—*if* he is already well established in life, with a wife or wives, children, and a house of his own. Often, the families are already related, because people in the Fouta Djallon practice both cross cousin and parallel cousin marriage. The wedding celebrations may take place over the course of two or three days. The women on both sides of the family will cook great quantities of rice for the occasion, and family members and friends contribute gifts of money or cloth. The groom pays a sum of bride wealth money to the bride's parents, and also presents the bride with one or more suitcases full of cloth. Ostensibly, this cloth is for her to have made into clothes, but in reality she will give much of it away at other ceremonial occasions during the first years of her marriage. After the wedding, the bride goes to live either with her husband or, if he does not yet have his own house, with his parents. Ideally, the newlyweds soon have children, and the husband establishes himself as the head of his own household. Having shown themselves responsible in marriage, both husband and wife may take on further responsibilities in their families and beyond, being sought after for advice, playing roles in ceremonies or community development efforts, or entrusted with sums of money.

However, marriages do not always develop according to this idealized picture, as the following sections demonstrate.

Men and Marriage in the Fouta Djallon

Young men in the Fouta Djallon are at a disadvantage. In a country with limited educational opportunities and few job prospects,[2] they are expected to make enough money to marry, support their parents, future children, and other relatives, and build a house. To fulfill these obligations, many young men must leave their Fouta Djallon villages and seek their fortunes either in Guinea's capital, Conakry, or abroad to Europe, North America, or elsewhere in Africa. Most men I met in the Fouta Djallon had either worked abroad in the past or intended to go abroad in the future. The particular destination was of secondary importance to the primary goal of leaving. Migration is supposed to offer young men opportunities to earn money that they could never get at home, and thus provide them with what many Guineans call in French a *"départ,"* or a start in life: enough money to come home, marry, start a business, build a house, and support a family. But in reality, many men's aspirations go unfulfilled. Tightening visa restrictions have made Europe and North America off-limits to most sub-Saharan African migrants, and even Central African countries like Angola and Congo have deported West African migrants in recent years. Consequently, many Fouta Djallon men seek their fortunes in the nearby West African countries of Senegal, Guinea-Bissau, Sierra Leone, Mali, and Côte d'Ivoire, where they may have only a marginally better chance of earning money than they had at home. For Fouta Djallon migrants everywhere, everyday survival can be difficult. Many men are obliged to stay away longer than they had intended, and some make barely enough money to feed themselves, let alone save for the future. Some men do save up enough money to send their parents, asking them to arrange a marriage on their behalf. The parents will find their absent son a bride and arrange the marriage, whether he is able to return for it or not. But if the groom's income proves unreliable, or if he stays away from his bride too long, the bride's family may well decide to take her back and marry her to a more eligible suitor. Thus, though many young men were among the most vociferous critics of Alpha Condé in the Fouta Djallon, their objections to his lack of wife and house reflected the challenges they themselves faced in both getting married and staying married.

The challenge of saving money for marriage is made even more difficult by the fact that young men must compete for wives with elder men who are members of their fathers' and even their grandfathers' generations. These elder men have had more time to establish themselves, financially and socially, and they are better able to afford marriage. As Muslims, they are also permitted to marry up to four wives, as long as they can support them. As a result, younger men may have difficulty finding available brides. With the relative scarcity of young women and the difficulty of earning money, few men are able to marry their first wife before they reach their thirties. Their brides, however, are much younger.

Women and Marriage in the Fouta Djallon

In her ethnography of female ex-combatants in post-civil war Sierra Leone, Chris Coulter writes of often hearing her informants repeat the adage, "There is no such thing as an unmarried woman."[3] A female person may be either a girl, unmarried

---

[2]Despite abundant natural and mineral resources, Guinea is one of the poorest countries in the world. In 2012, Guinea ranked 178 out of 187 countries on the United Nations Development Programme's Human Development Index, which measures income, education, and health.

[3]Chris Coulter, *Bush Wives and Girl Soldiers,* Cornell University Press 2009.

and ideally a virgin, or she may be a woman, married and ideally a mother. Many of Coulter's informants whose lives had been disrupted by war seemed to fall into an in-between category, neither girls nor women, and this uncertain status made them, their families, and their communities anxious.

Not far from Sierra Leone, in the Fouta Djallon, one may be either *jiwo*, which means girl or virgin in the local Pular language, or *debbo*, woman. People often address a girl as *jiwo*, whether or not they know her name. Calling someone *jiwo* implies little respect; a woman may send a *jiwo* on an errand, and a man may flirt with her. During my time in Guinea, people I met usually asked about my marital status right away, and when they found I was unmarried they often called me *jiwo*. When I first went to Guinea as a twenty-two-year-old Peace Corps volunteer, living with a host family and trying my best to integrate into local life, this did not seem so inappropriate. But years later, as an anthropologist, I began to find the title annoying, especially when used by men around my own age. One day I challenged a group of young men who addressed me as *jiwo*, asking, "Is an unmarried woman *jiwo* even if she's thirty?" "Oh yes, if she's thirty and not yet married, she's called *jiwo*," the men agreed unanimously. "What if she's forty, and still isn't married, then what is she?" I asked desperately. There was a pause, and the men looked at each other. Then one of them said, "In that case, she's smart!" They all burst out laughing.

The idea of an unmarried woman was so anomalous to these men that it probably seemed funny in and of itself. Both men and women in the Fouta Djallon spoke of marriage as an ideal state for women, one that would allow a woman to gain many blessings and lead a virtuous life. But the man's joke that a forty-year-old woman who managed to remain unmarried was "smart" reveals his awareness of the difficulties women faced in marriage. Indeed, perhaps drawing on what they had seen their mothers and sisters experience, these men went on to agree that marriage involved much suffering for women. The very word for "marry" in Pular reflects the inequality of women's experience. For men, the verb is *jombugol*, "to marry," literally "to cover [with a veil]," denoting an action taken. For women, the verb takes a passive construction, *jombegol*, "to be married" or "to be covered." Women had to submit to their husbands in all matters. They must work constantly at whatever their husbands and in-laws wished them to do, often cooking and cleaning for a household of a dozen or more people. They must bear a number of children in an area where medical facilities are few and inadequate. They must take care of their own children as well as any others living in the family compound. They were responsible for maintaining a garden of maize, peanuts, squash, taro, and other vegetables. Their husbands rarely provided enough money to meet household expenses, so most women also tried to earn supplemental income by selling snacks, cloth, or other items at the weekly village market. In a context where hierarchies of gender and generation were both important, women ranked low even years after they were married, obliged to obey both their husbands and their elders. A married woman who succeeded in managing her family's household, despite her relatively low place in the social hierarchy and usually with an insufficient income, demonstrated her own adult capabilities. Her life was difficult, but her friends and relatives recognized her as someone who fulfilled her social responsibilities.

Perhaps an unmarried forty-year-old woman would be "smart" to avoid a life of suffering, but she would have trouble demonstrating her capacity to act as a responsible adult member of society. Furthermore, though an unmarried woman might be "smart" in theory, she was virtually nonexistent in reality. Fouta Djallon girls are considered eligible for marriage as soon as they reach puberty, though in practice marriage may be delayed a few years after that, especially if the girl is in school. Many are married by their late teens, and almost all by their early twenties. Though the unmarried girls I knew had seen the difficulties faced by their mothers and other married female relatives, they nevertheless tended to look forward to their future marriages, especially in the abstract, while the prospective groom was still imaginary. None of them wanted to stay unmarried for long. Several girls informed me that if an unmarried girl or woman died, her body would not be washed and she would not be given a proper burial. Instead, she would be buried in the bush "like a dog." Furthermore, girls believed they would receive blessings in heaven for obeying their parents' wishes, especially in the matter of marriage. A few young married women I knew admitted to me that, as girls, they had fallen in love with local young men who had wanted to marry them. But their parents had not approved these matches, preferring to marry the girls to older men of greater income and social standing. The girls obeyed their parents' wishes, earning blessings and social approval for doing so.

These marriages did not always work out as planned. A twenty-year-old woman I knew had obeyed her parents' wishes in marrying a fifty-year-old man who already had three wives, though she found the idea distasteful. But she had been so unhappy in her husband's house that she had eventually left him, even though she was obliged to leave behind her three-year-old daughter as well. Seeing her unhappiness, her parents did not object to her divorce, but she was not allowed to remain single for long—nor did she want to. Her parents soon arranged another marriage for her, which she accepted. Even women who might appear at first glance to be single were actually married. In particular, widows were often inherited as wives by their deceased husbands' brothers—a practice anthropologists call the levirate. When the women in question were beyond their childbearing years, they often did not live with their new husbands, but they were married nevertheless. Despite the difficulties of marriage, girls and women still desired it, and the social standing that went along with it.

Instability of Marriage

Marriage, as should be clear by now, is a highly coveted state for both men and women in the Fouta Djallon. Though young men face great difficulty in earning money to find a bride and maintain a household, and women are acknowledged to experience suffering within marriage, marriage is still considered ideal, proper, and desirable. Indeed, it is perhaps the challenges associated with marriage that allow individuals to demonstrate responsibility and trustworthiness, effectively achieving adult personhood.

Married status is highly significant in the Fouta Djallon, despite—or perhaps because—achieving it is neither easy nor automatic. Divorce is relatively common in the Fouta Djallon, initiated by both men and women. Premature death is also a grim but real possibility in a country with chronic malnutrition, ubiquitous malaria every rainy season, inadequate sanitation infrastructure, few medical facilities, and notoriously unsafe roads. When a marriage ends, those involved must actively seek to enter or arrange a new one. This is especially true for women, who have only one husband at a time. While the institution of marriage is stable, there is a surprising degree of fluidity, as one's marriage may shift multiple times over the course of a lifetime. Both women and men, as well as their extended families, must rearrange their lives to accommodate to these changes.

These challenges and ideals of married adult personhood underlay the oft-repeated critiques of presidential candidate Alpha Condé in 2010 for having "no wife, no children, and no house." And, in point of fact, the 72-year-old Condé *did* have a young wife, but he had married her shortly before his campaign began, and popular opinion in the Fouta Djallon held that he would divorce her as soon as his campaign ended in defeat. However, contrary to all expectations in the Fouta Djallon, Condé eventually won the election, remains married to his wife, and is the father of an adult son from a former marriage. But though the "no wife, no children" critique of Alpha Condé may have been factually baseless, it continued to circulate. One of my informants, a forty-three-year-old village tailor whose single brief marriage had ended in divorce, expressed his frustration with those who made this critique. "They are not looking at [Condé's] politics, they are attacking him because of his personal life, which has nothing to do with his ability to govern," said the tailor. Having built up a reasonably successful tailoring business despite his lack of wife or children, this man had a different perspective from that of most Fouta Djallon residents. However, his neighbors and family members disagreed. Despite his moneymaking tailoring business, this man was unlikely ever to become a respected elder in the community if he did not soon use that money to remarry, have children, begin building a house, and thereby become generally acknowledged as a responsible adult.

✓●─ **Study** and **Review** on **myanthrolab.com**

Review Questions

1. According to Fioratta, what is the relationship between marriage and recognition as a respected adult in Guinea?

2. In what ways is marriage as a marker of social adulthood in Guinea different for men and women? How is it the same?

3. In what ways is the understanding of marriage in Guinea similar to the understanding of marriage in U.S. society? In what ways is it different?

4. How have the global economy and changes in immigration law in places like Europe and the United States shaped marriage in Guinea?

5. How does Fioratta explain the seeming contradiction of marriage being intensely valued and coveted, at the same time as it places immense demands and difficulties upon those who take part in it?

6. What difficulties do Fouta Djallon men and women face when they seek to marry?

7. What factors lead to divorce among the residents of the Fouta Djallon highlands in Guinea?

PART SIX

IDENTITY, ROLES, AND GROUPS

READINGS IN THIS SECTION

For most of us, social interaction is unconscious and automatic. We associate with other people from the time we are born. Of course we experience moments when we feel socially awkward and out of place, but generally we learn to act toward others with confidence. Yet our unconscious ease masks an enormously complex process. When we enter a social situation, how do we know what to do? What should we say? How are we supposed to act? Are we dressed appropriately? Are we talking to the right person? Without knowing it, we have learned a complex set of cultural categories for social interaction that enables us to estimate the social situation, identify the people in it, act appropriately, and recognize larger groups of people.

Status and roles are basic to social intercourse. **Status** refers to the categories of different kinds of people who interact. The old saying, "You can't tell the players without a program," goes for our daily associations as well. Instead of a program, however, we identify the actors by a range of signs, from the way they dress to the claims they make about themselves. Most statuses are named, so we may be heard to say things like, "That's President Gavin," or "She's a lawyer," when we explain social situations to others. This identification of actors is a prerequisite for appropriate social interaction.

Roles are the rules for action associated with particular statuses. We use them to interpret and generate social behavior. For example, a professor plays a role in large classrooms. Although often not conscious of this role, the professor will stand, use the whiteboard, look at notes, and speak with a slightly more formal air than usual. The professor does not usually wear shorts and a T-shirt, chew gum, sit cross-legged on the podium, or sing. These actions might be appropriate for this person when assuming the identity of "friend" at a party, but they are out of place in front of large audiences.

People also always relate to each other in **social situations**, the settings in which social interaction takes place. Social situations consist of a combination of times, places, objects, and events. For example, if we see a stranger carrying a television set across campus at four o'clock in the afternoon, we will probably ignore the activity. Most likely someone is simply moving. But if we see the same person carrying the set at four in the morning, we may suspect a theft. Only the time has changed, but it is a significant marker of the social situation. Similarly, we expect classrooms to be associated with lectures, and stethoscopes to be part of medical exams. Such places and objects mark the social situations of which they are part.

People also belong to groups. **Social groups** are organized collections of individuals. They are often named—the Republican Party, American Motorcyclist Association, General Motors—although some, such as friends who meet for drinks after work on Fridays, may be anonymous and less formal. Social groups have several attributes. The people who belong to them normally recognize their common membership and share the goals of the group. The group should share an "inside" culture and its members should interact with each other. Groups are also organized internally in some way. Tasks are often divided among members. Finally, groups usually link to one another. For example, when a couple marries, their union connects the families of the bride and groom. There are some collections of people that we might think of as groups that do not fit this definition. "Middle-class" people, for example, are an aggregate, not a social group, because they are not an interacting organized collective. No one says, "I am meeting tonight with my middle-class men's association."

As societies around the world grow larger, it becomes more difficult to identify groups. People may do most of their socializing in **social networks**, the individuals with whom they regularly interact. Networks are not groups; they are defined only in relation to a particular individual. Nonetheless they are important because they may involve a substantial part of an individual's social interaction. A "social messiness" also afflicts interaction worldwide. People freely travel and enter new social situations where culture is not fully shared. Individuals can interact in dozens of different social situations each day.

Groups form around several principles. Every society has kinship groups, the topic of the previous section of this book. Ethnic groups organize around a shared cultural background. Some groups, such as the American Association of Retired Persons, are based on age. Others, such as the National Organization for Women, are based on gender. The Macalester-Groveland Community Council is a territorial group. Many groups, such as the Gold Wing Road Riders Association (a national motorcycle group), Ford Motor Company (an economic group), and Mothers Against Drunk Driving (an interest group) organize around common goals and interests. Many groups are built around several of these design principles at once.

Finally groups can also be organized around social hierarchy. Some degree of **inequality** is part of most human interaction. One spouse may dominate another; a child may receive more attention than his or her siblings; the boss's friends may be promoted faster than other employees. But inequality becomes most noticeable when it systematically affects whole classes of people. In its most obvious form, inequality emerges as **social stratification**, which is characterized by regularly experienced unequal access to valued economic resources and prestige.

Anthropologists recognize at least two kinds of social stratification: class and caste. **Class** stratification restricts individuals' access to valued resources and prestige within a partially flexible system. Although it is often a difficult process, individuals may change rank in a class system if they manage to acquire the prerequisites.

Many sociologists and anthropologists believe that there is an American class system and use terms such as *lower class, working class, middle class,* and *upper class* to designate the unequal positions within it. Americans born into poverty lack access to goods and prestige in this system but can change class standing if they acquire wealth and symbols of higher standing on a continuing basis. Upward mobility is difficult to achieve, however, and few people at the bottom of the system manage to change rank significantly. Indeed, many social scientists feel there is now a permanent underclass in the United States.

Caste defines a second kind of social stratification, one based on permanent membership. People are born into castes and cannot change membership, no matter what they do. In India, for example, caste is a pervasive feature of social organization. South Asians are born into castes and remain members for life; intercaste marriage is forbidden. In the past, castes formed the building blocks of rural Indian society. They were governed by strict rules of deference and served to allocate access to jobs, land, wealth, and power. Cash labor and new industrial jobs have eroded the economic aspect of the system today, but caste persists as a form of rank throughout most of the Indian subcontinent.

Several anthropologists and sociologists have argued that American racial groups are the equivalent of Indian castes. Black and white Americans keep their racial identity for life; nothing can change one's race. Racial identity clearly affects chances for the acquisition of prestige and economic success.

Caste identity, whether Indian or American, tends to preserve and create cultural difference. There is noticeable cultural variation among members of castes in most Indian villages, just as cultural variation occurs among black and white people in the United States.

Using the idea of social stratification, anthropologists have constructed a rough classification of societies into three types: egalitarian, rank, and stratified.

Egalitarian societies lack formal social stratification. They may display inequality in personal relations based on age, gender, or personal ability, but no category of persons within the same sex or age group has special privilege. Hunter-gatherer societies are most likely to be egalitarian.

Rank societies contain unequal access to prestige, but not to valued economic resources. In such societies there may be chiefs or other persons with authority and prestige, and they may gain access to rank by birth, but their positions give them no substantial economic advantage. Horticultural societies, including some chiefdom-ships, fit this category.

Stratified societies organize around formal modes of social stratification, as their name suggests. Members of stratified societies are likely to form classes or castes, and inequality affects access to both prestige and economic resources. Most complex societies, including agrarian and industrialized states, fit into this type.

Inequality may also be based on other human attributes, such as age and gender. In many societies, including our own, age and gender affect access to prestige, power, and resources. It is common for men to publicly outrank women along these dimensions, particularly in societies threatened by war or other adversity.

The articles in this part explore the nature of status, role, and inequality. The first, by anthropologist Dianna Shandy and economist Karine Moe and revised for this edition of *Conformity and Conflict*, looks at a recent trend: the tendency for young, professionally trained women to leave high-paying jobs, once only open to men, to be at home with their children. Stressed by the need to compete full-time at work and faced with significant structural barriers (e.g., child care) yet drawn by the needs and pleasure of being with their children, the move seems a sensible solution if a husband's salary is sufficient or other money is available. Returning to work later when the children are grown is an option but may require a change of career. The second article, by Mikaela Rogozen-Soltar, looks at what happens when people's fundamental identities come into contact by describing the conversion of a Catholic Spanish woman to Islam through her marriage to a Jordanian Muslim immigrant to Spain. The third article, by Jefferson Fish, looks at the way Americans define race. Seen by most Americans as a biologically determined subspecies of human beings, but actually a culturally defined taxonomy based on the classification of one's parents, race in the United States is entirely different from racial categories in Brazil. The final selection is by David McCurdy. He writes about a national motorcycle association, the Gold Wing Road Riders Association, as a micro-culture, identifying the values that bind its members together and the ways they maintain the group over time.

Key Terms

caste p. 179	social groups p. 178
class p. 179	social networks p. 178
egalitarian societies p. 180	social situation p. 178
inequality p. 179	social stratification p. 179
rank societies p. 180	status p. 178
role p. 178	stratified societies p. 180

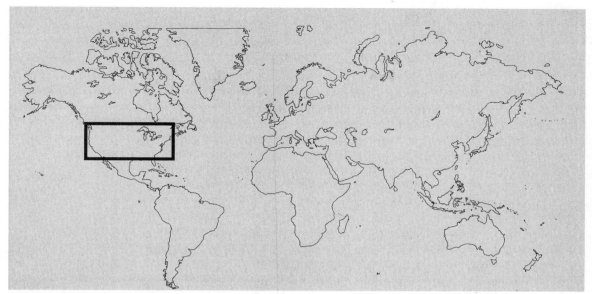

20

Negotiating Work and Family in America

Dianna Shandy and Karine Moe

Successfully employed, college-educated women face a dilemma when they decide to have children. Can they continue to work full-time with the same intensity that has brought them occupational success, or will they have to cut back? What will adjustments required by motherhood and family do to their occupational identity and ability to compete on an equal basis with men? In this article updated for the fifteenth edition of Conformity and Conflict, *anthropologist Dianna Shandy and economist Karine Moe discuss these and other questions concerning how women navigate work and home once they have children. Basing their analysis on extensive interviews with more than 100 women, focus group, and surveys of nearly 1000 college graduates, as well as labor statistics, they argue that younger professional women face significant structural barriers in an attempt to negotiate work and family. Some women choose home over work once they have a family. They devise strategies to maintain their past occupational identity despite their changed circumstances.**

---

*Original article from Dianna J. Shandy and Karine S. Moe, "The Opt-Out Phenomenon: Women, Work, and Identity in America." Used by permission of the authors.

(((●─|**Listen** to the **Chapter Audio** on **myanthrolab.com**

Jennifer, a tall, well-dressed woman in her mid-thirties, fingers the stem of her wine glass and braces herself for the question she will get a dozen times that night at a cocktail party her husband is holding for his clients: *"And what do you do?"*

This question, which most of us might write off as "small talk," is anything but trivial. It reflects the importance we attribute to one's occupation as the primary source of our public social identity. So normally when we answer the what-do-you-do question, we identify ourselves by our occupation. We might say things such as, "I am a college professor at Metro State," or "I'm a wealth management consultant over at Grant and Smith Securities."

Although most North Americans don't like to admit there is a class system (we prefer to believe we accept people for "who they are"), we actually, and often without thinking, rank each other on the basis of our occupational identity. For example, Jennifer's husband is president of an advertising company with both local and regional accounts. The clients at his cocktail party tend to be presidents, vice presidents, or division managers who work for the companies his firm promotes. They represent a more affluent class of people than, say, firefighters, fast food restaurant managers, or administrative assistants although some of these jobs, such as firefighting, confer prestige.

Occupational identity conveys more than just one's class, however. It implies relative status between individuals. When men and women work at the same jobs, their work signifies that they are approximately equal. This assertion gains credence not only from observations of contemporary U.S. society, but also from anthropological fieldwork and cross-cultural comparison. Take a well-known study by Ernestine Friedl, for example.[1] She points out that decades of ethnographic research in a variety of the world's societies have led many anthropologists to conclude that males inherit a predisposition to dominate females everywhere. Friedl argues against this position by citing evidence about gender relations in four contrasting hunting and gathering societies. She asserts that control of publicly (beyond the family) shared resources, especially animal protein, determines the degree to which females are equal to males. First, she notes that among the Washo Indians (a foraging group that lived in the Sierra Nevada Mountains of southern California) both men and women foraged for edible plants and both caught small animals as a source of protein. The result was relative gender equality. Men and women were not segregated in daily activities. Both sexes could take lovers, dissolve marriages, and make decisions for the group. The Hadza of Tanzania, she points out, also display relative gender equality largely because men and women forage separately and work to meet their own individual needs for food.

On the other hand, the Tiwi living on islands off the North Coast of Australia show a more typical hunter-gatherer pattern. The men hunt and the women gather, and the male control of meat (protein), which is shared publicly by the whole group, results in domination over women. Men hunt and control the public distribution of meat; women gather only for family needs.

Finally, in the fourth case represented by the Inuit of the Arctic, males provide virtually all the food by hunting seals, walruses, whales, and fish. As a result, Inuit women are "used, abused, and traded," as Friedl puts it. Friedl also notes that gender inequality continues in many agriculturally based societies where men control

[1]Ernestine Friedl, "Society and Sex Roles," *Human Nature*, April 1978.

most of the food that is publicly exchanged. Anthropologists Jane Collier and Michelle Rosaldo have also argued that although women's roles as gatherers contributed significantly to the food supply, these contributions were symbolically less important than men's hunting activities.[2] Friedl's argument appears to inform what is happening to U.S. women. Women have increasingly gained power and equality as they hold jobs once reserved for men. This has long been a goal for women in our society, and women in America now wield governmental and corporate power at levels never before seen in the history of this country. Women now have unprecedented access to education, jobs, and income.

And that's not all. A large part of the growth in the post–World War II U.S. economy can be attributed to the dramatic increase in the labor force participation by women, especially those who are married. For the first time in U.S. history, women have transitioned to making up half of all workers on U.S. payrolls. Women now serve as the primary breadwinner in roughly forty percent of all families, although only about a quarter of married women earn more than their husbands. And this participation extends to management and leadership positions and the ownership of one-third of all U.S. businesses that employ a quarter of the workforce.

Going hand in hand with this surge in women's contributions to economic productivity, women are at least as well educated as men. Women make up a full 58 percent of the nation's college students and are, overall, the majority in graduate schools and professional schools. They are hired in equal numbers by the country's most prestigious law firms. The majority of veterinarians and accountants are women. Women physicians will soon dominate certain subspecialties within medicine.

In addition, although the number of women in the labor force has increased over the last few decades, fewer males have sought work. Labor economists note that if current trends continue, by 2020 only 70 percent of men will participate in the U.S. labor force, and by 2050, their participation will decline to 66 percent.

To be sure, a wage gap persists between males and females. However, when you look at specific niches within the population, a different picture emerges. Without children, men and women pursue their careers neck and neck in terms of pay when they work similar jobs for similar hours. In fact, once you control for education, occupation, and other demographic characteristics, the gender wage gap for childless people between the ages of 27 and 33 is practically zero. Does this all mean that gender bias is absent in the world of work in America today? No. Although gender discrimination at work continues, women have seen substantial gains in job equality over the past few decades.

Returning Home

And this brings us back to Jennifer's unease about the what-do-you-do question. Like a sizable number of young, married women with children, she decided to give up her career for life as an at-home mother. She did so despite the fact that her personal history fit the trend toward job equality and the growing public influence of women. She graduated from a prestigious eastern college with honors and gained her degree as an attorney at a "top 10" law school. She obtained a high-paying job in a firm specializing

[2]Jane F. Collier and Michelle Z. Rosaldo, "Politics and Gender in Simple Societies," in Sherry B. Ortner and Harriet S. Whitehead (eds.), *On Sexual Meanings: The Cultural Construction of Gender and Sexuality* (Cambridge: Cambridge University Press, 1981).

in mergers and acquisitions where she was in line to become a partner. Then something happened that affected her promising career: she had one, then two children. Now, as an at-home mom, she grapples with the issue of identity in settings such as business cocktail parties where occupational achievement outranks motherhood.

Jennifer is not alone in her decision to leave her career. In our study of college-educated women, we found that a surprising number of young, professional women are leaving work to become "at-home moms." This attorney turned at-home mother is emblematic of a growing number of American women today. In fact, the labor force participation of college educated, married women with children under 18 peaked at 76 percent in 1997, fell steadily and dropped for the first time below 70 percent in 2011. From a labor market perspective, this is a significant and remarkable shift, with dramatic ramifications for economic growth. Having gained a foothold in formerly male-dominated positions, it becomes paradoxical that many highly educated, accomplished women are leaving their careers, often as a consequence of becoming mothers. This article is about why we think this is happening and at least partly, how women are managing to do this without losing status.

Who Drops Out

To better understand this conundrum, an anthropologist joined forces with a labor economist to look at national trends and learn more through interviews, surveys, and focus groups about who is leaving work and for what reasons. We discovered from national labor force participation data that a surprising number of college-educated, especially professional, women were opting out of the labor force. From here we designed interviews and focus groups with women who were making or had made the decision to leave their jobs in order to stay home with their children, as well as those who were continuing to juggle home and office. We also designed an on-line survey that we administered to nearly 1,000 college alumni, who had graduated between 1970 and 2006.

The first thing we discovered was that age counts. We learned that women in their twenties and thirties seemed to approach child birth, child rearing, and employment differently than their mother's and grandmother's generations. This older generation, the so-called Baby Boomers (women in their late forties to mid sixties) were the first large wave of women to compete for prominent positions in the labor force. They entered work with high expectations and demonstrated ability, and like today's younger women, soon found that work conflicted with marriage and the need to raise children. Overall their response has been to attempt to manage both work and family by trying to adjust to both, although with varying degrees of success. Nonetheless, these women were pioneering in their ability to anticipate and overcome obstacles and thereby created inroads for their daughters.

The second thing we discovered was that women in their early thirties to mid forties, usually labeled Gen Xers, benefited from the pioneering work of the earlier generation; however, they were the most likely to report having been "blindsided" by the realities of juggling career and children. Angie, a mother of two children in her mid thirties with an MBA typifies this group. When she considered her own expectations for combining work with motherhood said: "I thought women could do it all but just that my [own] mother did not do it well."

The third thing we discovered was that the youngest group of married and well-educated women with young children, women in their twenties and early thirties often called Millennials, seemed to be far more pragmatic than older women about the conflict between work and family. Accordingly, they were also the most creative in the strategies they had devised to manage this conflict. They were still gunning for top spots educationally, but they reported being more mindful about how they would negotiate career and family. We found that women in their twenties and early thirties were more likely than older women to have reduced their responsibilities at work for family reasons. For some this meant selecting a career that will be more flexible and amenable to the demands of child rearing. Others were planning to have careers and children sequentially. Still others planned to have children first and move into a career at some undefined future point when their children are older. But as we have noted above, many, faced with the need and desire to raise children, have left work behind, at least for the time being.

Finally, men rarely drop out of work to become at-home dads. Among married couples, when one parent leaves the labor force, 97 times out of 100 it is the woman who does so. The phenomenon of at-home dads is a growing trend, but when you look at the bigger picture of labor force participation, the number of men who do this is quite small. In this case couples bend to traditional gender roles—mom quits her job and dad presses even harder in his.

Before we go any further, we should note that by virtue of our focus on college-educated women for both our surveys and our interviews, we are *de facto* conducting a study of elite women. We realize that the notion of having a so-called choice not to work is available to only a narrow slice of American women, whereas most need two incomes to keep their household afloat. Recent turmoil in the economy has brought this issue into even sharper focus. In this respect our study does not tell the story of all women.

However, we argue that it is important to focus on college-educated and therefore relatively elite women because their experiences have the potential to shape the lives of all American women. These women represent the potential leaders, the voices for change. If we don't have a critical mass of women executives, how can we expect the culture of companies to change? How can we expect laws to keep pace with women's lives if they aren't represented in Washington? Therefore, while at first glance middle- and upper-middle-class mothers are targeted most directly by our analysis, we believe the implications of our argument affect all women in America.

Why Do Women "Opt Out"?

So why do women "opt out" now when they have unprecedented access to education, jobs, and income, and potentially suffer the loss of their occupational identity? One suggested answer focuses solely on generation. It says that members of the younger generation, both men and women, are more likely to exit the workforce. Although we don't deny the importance of generation, we feel gender has to be part of the explanation too. In our research, we have grappled with the intersection of gender and generation to understand the outflow of professional women from the labor force. And we agree that younger women approach issues of work and family differently than older women. However, it is important to acknowledge that although gender and generation vie with one another for explanatory power, gender is crucial to what is happening here. Indeed, we believe that gender is more important than generation as a way to understand current intersections of gender, work, and identity in America today.

So if it is not just a generational difference, what are the gender-related factors that bear on women's decision to return home?

What "Pushes" Women to Go Home?

There are several things that "push" women to leave the workforce. Let's look at a few of them.

The 100-Hour Couple

One of the most intriguing explanations for why women leave the workforce is the phenomenon of the 100-hour couple. Let's consider Valerie's situation. Valerie was an English and political science double major in college. A child of a single mother who single-handedly supported and raised five children, Valerie attended a state university and worked her way through school. She went on to attend law school and to work as a real estate attorney. She married her husband, also an attorney, who worked in banking. By the time they had their second child, their careers were at a zenith, with Valerie and her husband each working an average of 75 hours a week. To meet their work obligations, they had a full-time and a part-time nanny. When they discovered they needed yet a third nanny to help out because of work obligations that increasingly spilled over into evenings and weekends, they decided to re-evaluate their situation. They concluded that one of them had to reduce hours at work or quit his or her job altogether. They recognized that they could live on either Valerie's or her husband's salary alone, although her husband's income was significantly larger than hers. Therefore, for financial as well as for other less tangible reasons that could not be tallied on a spreadsheet, Valerie decided to leave her job and to stay home with their children. Valerie described her decision in the following way:

> If we were financially able, one of us needed to quit our jobs. What was the point of having kids if we weren't spending time with them? My children were being raised by strangers—65 hours per week of child care. Deciding to quit my job and stay home with my children was the right thing to do.

Valerie's case illustrates some key points. As women's educational qualifications rise, so too have their occupational aspirations. It's not surprising that well-educated women gravitate toward high-powered, high-paying jobs and marry men who have done the same. Whereas previous generations saw a surplus of professional men relative to women, the educational gap has closed. Instead of the CEO marrying his secretary or the doctor marrying his nurse, the CEO is marrying the CFO and the doctor is marrying the doctor. With this larger pool of well-educated, well-employed women, we have transitioned to high-powered couples resulting in a rapid and significant increase in the percentage of high-earning couples that together work over 100 hours per week.

In Valerie's case, she and her husband surpassed 150-hour workweeks, but when we look across a larger sample of families, 100 hours is a threshold for couples who make a decision for one of them—and as pointed out, it is usually the woman—to alter their work situation.

Child Care

A key structural problem that mothers across socioeconomic groups face is child care. High-quality and affordable child care is hard to find, and even when found, it often has rigid drop off and pick up hours. Many child-care centers charge late parents by the minute and will call child protective services if parents do not arrive within an hour of closing time. Of course, these rules are structured so that the child-care workers can return home to care for their own children. Nevertheless, these constraints don't necessarily mesh with workplace demands for working late or getting a last-minute travel assignment. This dilemma is encapsulated in a shootout at an army base in Texas. Police Sergeant Kimberly Munley managed to shoot the gunman, but was herself shot in the process. When asked what her first thought was following the shooting, she replied that she wanted to grab her cell phone so she could call someone to pick up her kids from child care. Who cares for the children while the parents are at work is an enduring structural dilemma working parents face.

The Second Shift

Another factor pushing women out of the workforce is what sociologist Arlie Hochschild calls the second shift. Here she gives life to the old adage, "A man may work from sun to sun, but a woman's work is never done." The second shift refers to the work women do to maintain and sustain the household in addition to their paid employment. The second shift is commonly seen as a significant stressor for women across socioeconomic groups. It is well-documented that women shoulder a disproportionate percentage of housework. For example, one study reports that women do an average of 27 hours of housework a week, compared with 16 hours a week for men. Important here is that while women have made significant gains in the workplace itself, the gender division of labor at home endures. A recent trend to hire household help is opening possibilities to redefine this aspect of women's lives, but even when families hire people to watch their children or clean their homes, women tend to take on the burden of managing the work that is done in the home and caring for the children.

Although it might strike many as a significant luxury to be able to afford to pay someone to clean their home and watch their children, in our interviews we found that hiring and supervising staff to care for the home and the children placed additional stress on women and was cited by them as part of the decision to quit their jobs. Women also mentioned moral and ethical concerns. Is it "right and fair" to hire women who often have to leave their own children behind to work these jobs? How does one manage the inevitabilities of sick children and/or sick child-care providers?

The women we interviewed did not just describe trying to balance the needs of their children and their jobs, but also their responsibility to manage their homes. For many the solution was to stay home full time.

The Glass Ceiling

Women mentioned a third factor that caused them to consider resigning their jobs. They talked about encountering a "glass ceiling" at work, meaning a form of discrimination that limits a woman's advancement. They felt they were being blocked from moving upward in the institution because of some tacit or unwritten set of norms about women, especially married women with children. The women we interviewed were frustrated by seeing their counterparts without children (or with a spouse at home caring for their children and managing the household) advance more swiftly in their careers than they did. It seemed unfair because these coworkers did not have to take parental leave to care for children and were more available to work longer hours. One woman lamented that her peers who had not taken time off for children were now vice presidents sitting in corner offices. A lack of flexible work options forced many to choose resigning their jobs altogether or embarking on a "mommy track," which does not allow them to devote time to family for a period of their lives and then resume upward mobility in their careers on a par with their male colleagues who are parents.

One way to look at this is that women quit their jobs not because of their families but because the pressures and inflexibility of their work situations actually leave them no way to maintain both. This is why many women we spoke with take issue with the term *opting out*. Work conditions permitting, some of the women we interviewed would have preferred to *opt in*, albeit on terms that better allowed them to both keep their jobs and raise their children.

When we raised the possibility during a focus group of reducing their hours at the job while still remaining employed, one advertising executive summarized the opinion of many of her counterparts when she said, "Part-time is just a joke." Another woman with an MBA said, "My boss was reluctant to let me go part time at all. When I cut my hours, my boss said he'd pay me less per hour."

We should point out that when viewed cross-culturally, different countries manage the intersection of parenting and labor force participation in other ways. When compared with other industrialized countries, the United States rarely accommodates the need for parents to have and care for children. One woman we interviewed who ironically worked for a children's museum took twelve weeks of unpaid leave when her first child was born. The only thing the museum guaranteed was that she would get her job back when she returned from leave. The United States is the only industrialized country that fails to provide paid leave for new mothers, although there are exceptions in some U.S. states. The U.S. Family and Medical Leave Act provides for twelve weeks of job-protected leave, but it only covers those who work for larger companies. The United States ranks with Lesotho, Swaziland, and Papua New Guinea as other countries that do not offer paid leave for mothers of newborns. Sweden is one of the most progressive countries when it comes to parental leave: working parents are entitled to sixteen months paid leave per child. The cost is shared between the state and the employer. What makes Sweden's policy so notable, however, is that it stipulates that at least two months must be used by the "minority" parent, which usually means the dad.

Factors That "Pull" Women Home

Beyond understanding some of the reasons women are "pushed" out of the workforce, it is also important to understand what "pulls" them there.

Being with Their Children

One of the reasons women gave us for why they liked being "at home" revolved around being with their children. Take, for example, the case of Carol. Carol loves being home with her three kids—all in school now—and is thankful that she is able to do this. She loves spending time with the kids, talking with them, being the one they turn to with their questions. And she likes the freedom and flexibility. Last summer she drove across the country with her children to visit her mom for a month. Having the latitude to make this trip was especially meaningful to her when her mother died the following winter after a long battle with cancer.

Sara, a former dancer, introduces a long list of activities her children participate in by saying that Ryan and Aidan "get a lot of mommy time." She notes that she is able to do this because she has "a flexible enough schedule. I can just cart them wherever they need to go." She goes on to describe visits to grandparents in New Mexico and Florida. "When we go, we stay for a week. So, before I quit working at General Mills I would max out my vacation." Having control over their time tended to be a central concern for many of these women.

Lower Stress

Many women seek to pursue a less hectic life. One woman's husband credits her with running "a great back office" such that the family spends their weekends together playing and not running errands. Most were tired of the "juggle and struggle" they encountered when they were still working. They had had to negotiate with their spouse over when, where, who, and how to cover child care. Another woman pointed out that staying at home "made my husband's life easier" and that "he enjoys his children more because he is not worrying about the day-to-day." And women freely point out that this arrangement also allows them to get their needs met by allowing them "time for themselves."

Sense of Responsibility

Women also discussed the moral importance and timing of their decision to head home. One attorney noted, "Conventional wisdom says we need to be there because we have infants. In hindsight, it's absolutely flipped. Now that the kids are getting older, it's more important for me to be there." A bond trader noted that it was easier to hire someone to care for her children when they were "cute naughty" as toddlers, but now that they were not so cute as misbehaving adolescents she felt the need to be more in charge of her kids' care.

Nostalgia

We also found that a longing to reproduce what for them was a pleasant upbringing may pull many women home. Some had at-home mothers who were there for their kids with milk and cookies after school. On the other hand, others may feel the need to redress the rejection they felt as latchkey kids when mothers were not there for them.

Group Support

It seems to be increasingly easier for young women to leave work as other like-minded women make the same choice. In one veterinarian turned at-home mom's words, "I run with a pack of smart women." The result is the formation of social networks of women with their children providing a sense of support, occasions for conversation about domestic matters, and opportunities for their children to play together. Although it's not fun to be an ex-veterinarian who stays home by herself with her kids, it is easier to do so when all your friends are doing it too.

Living within Our Means

Finally, the financial threshold for deciding that one parent will stay home with the kids is a lot lower than one might think. Some of the women we interviewed indicated that their family was making a deliberate choice to live within their means, as determined by one income. Although a somewhat counterintuitive point, having one parent "in reserve" who could join the labor force if the family hit tough financial times instead of taking out a mortgage that relied on both incomes can be a reason women may decide to opt out of the labor force.

Financial Costs

What happens when women give up their paychecks? As one woman aptly noted, "The paycheck gives you a tangible sense of value." Other women we interviewed described how their husband's work time, as the sole income earner, expands as his home effort decreases dramatically. Still other women lament the loss of what they called the "fuck you money," or the financial independence their own earnings afforded them and that potentially allowed them to leave their marriage if they ever felt they needed to. Still others argue that their power did not change because of their husband's appreciation of their efforts at home. The threat that they might return to work and thus destroy the comfortable support system they provide moderates the increased power that husbands might otherwise enjoy. When women leave their jobs for a period of time, they pay a significant financial penalty. Studies show that for every seven years a woman is out of the labor force, she suffers a ten-year penalty in terms of wages and advancement. Women also take significant financial risks when they become financially dependent on their husbands. It is clear that by leaving work and a paycheck, divorce or the death of a husband will likely have a greater impact on their lives.

Returning to Work

A lot has been written about the difficulty of reentering the workforce after significant absences. This is particularly true in a tight economic market. One problem is the limited shelf life of a professional degree. For example, a physician who does not practice for ten years would have to overcome significant hurdles to get back into clinical work. On the other hand, opportunities to work in the medical sector of the economy may still be available.

However, the chance for them to return to their original occupations did not seem to matter to some of our respondents. Many of the women we interviewed said they would prefer to change professions if they returned to work in the future. Some thought of starting their own businesses. Others described transitioning to a caregiving profession. Many of the bond traders, financial managers, and attorneys we interviewed indicated that when, and if, they returned to work they had their eyes on jobs such as elementary school teacher, social worker for the elderly, or advocate for patients in hospitals.

Maintaining Status

So how can Jennifer and many other young at-home mothers manage to maintain the prestige and power that accompanied the upscale jobs they once trained for and held? A traditional way more common in the past was to associate themselves with their husband's status. If she did so, Jennifer might have answered the what-do-you-do question by simply saying, "Oh, I am Paul's wife." But this kind of answer diminishes her past academic and occupational achievements. So she is more likely to mention what she used to do by saying "I am an attorney" or "I was an attorney with Brand and Cockrin, but I am home with the kids for a while."

If they remain outside the workplace for long, women may choose to maintain a sense of occupational worth by serving in "quasi-professional" settings such as membership on the boards of civic associations, positions with nonprofit organizations, and aides at their children's schools.

Finally, it is difficult at this point for us to predict what these young professionals, now turned full-time mothers, will do in the future as their children grow up and they are once again free to work. The move home may only be one phase in a life of shifting pressures, opportunities, and associated identities.

✔●━**Study** and **Review** on **myanthrolab.com**

Review Questions

1. What is the relationship between occupation, class, and social identity in the United States?

2. Shandy and Moe described Ernestine Friedl's work on the degree to which males dominate females. What is Friedl's main argument and what evidence does she use to support it?

3. How does the United States compare with other countries when it comes to supporting motherhood?

4. What factors push women to "head home" instead of continuing to work?

5. What factors pull women to do so?

6. How do women who have left work to raise their children at home deal with the apparent loss of gender equality that comes with their domestic identity over their occupational one?

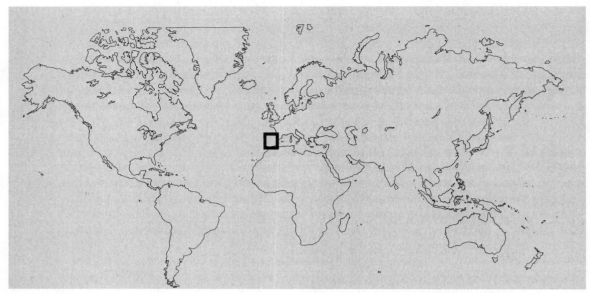

21

Becoming Muslim in Europe

Mikaela Rogozen-Soltar

In this article, written for Conformity and Conflict, *Mikaela Rogozen-Soltar delves into changing Spanish society by examining how a Catholic, Spanish woman decided to convert to Islam. Considering the incompatibility of Islam with Spanish national identity over many centuries, the decision to convert is a loaded one. Her article discusses what happens when people's identities come into contact through globalizing processes like immigration. Through her marriage to a Jordanian Muslim immigrant man, Maria was faced with an unexpected occasion to change her religion. Using Maria as a case study, Rogozen-Soltar explores how Maria is able to inhabit both a Muslim religious identity and a Spanish national identity at the same time, and how she advocates for the ability of others to do so as well.**

((•⌐ **Listen** to the **Chapter Audio** on **myanthrolab.com**

Increasingly, as people from different backgrounds come into contact due to globalization, their basic identities can come into contact as well. This can lead to conflict or to mutual influence, as people create new identities that draw on diverse backgrounds. One place where this is most obvious is in the case of inter-cultural or inter-religious marriage, when people fall in love with someone from a different background and are immediately confronted with a basic difference. For example, in the United States, a frequent confrontation is between Jewish and non-Jewish people who wish to marry or between Catholics and Protestants. But, perhaps, in today's world, the biggest contrast of all is between Muslim and non-Muslim marriage partners. The Mediterranean country of Spain, a majority-Catholic country with a growing Muslim minority, provides us with a key example of this phenomenon.

María Martínez

When I first met María Martínez in 2006, she was a Catholic who could not imagine becoming Muslim. I was a researcher studying Islam in Spain, and by chance we met outside a mosque in Granada, a southern Spanish city famous for its many architectural remnants of Spain's medieval Muslim period (711 to 1492). María told me that her husband was inside the mosque praying. He was Jordanian and Muslim, but she was Catholic, "like all Spaniards," she informed me. A chatty and vivacious woman dressed in a trendy pink and purple pantsuit with perfectly arranged hair, María enthusiastically insisted we walk downtown together. The path through the narrow, winding streets of the Arab-built medieval quarter was long and best traversed with company.

As María and I left, we ran into one of the leaders of the mosque and his wife, both Spanish converts to Islam. The mosque leader wore a long tunic over western-style pants, and his wife wore a headscarf covering her hair. They asked if María was thinking of converting to Islam as well. "No!" María replied emphatically. She was "just too typically Spanish" to consider becoming Muslim. She couldn't possibly give up the Spanish traditions of consuming pork, wine, and beer, all beloved in Granada but prohibited in Islam. "Impossible. I can't even think about it," she concluded. And with that, we headed off toward downtown.

Fast-forward two years. In 2008, I returned to Granada to conduct more field research on Spain's growing Muslim community, including participant observation at NGOs working to promote tolerance of religious, racial, and cultural diversity. To my astonishment, when I knocked on the door of one such organization, María opened it. We had not kept in touch, but I recognized her immediately, and we became fast friends as I worked with her at the NGO where she served as a volunteer lawyer, helping with cases involving Muslims who had experienced religious discrimination. My first day there, María confided that despite her earlier certainty that conversion was not for her, she had in fact become Muslim about one year after our first meeting. She now attended a mosque on a semi-weekly basis, she was studying Arabic in order to read the Koran, Islam's holy book, in its original language, and she was an avid advocate for Islam in Granada, taking every opportunity to explain and defend Islam to her fellow Spaniards. She was quickly becoming an active member of Granada's local Muslim community, made up of European converts to Islam and Muslim migrants from outside of Europe.

María's story raises a number of questions, including: Why did becoming Muslim seem so impossible to her at first? How did she change her mind? In a predominantly Catholic country like Spain, what does it mean to adopt a minority religion like Islam, which is often viewed as inimical, or in opposition to, Western European religious and social values? For María, ultimately it was her marriage to a Muslim man that prompted her to confront these basic questions of personal, religious, and national identity head-on.

Anthropologists are interested in how people in different cultures view their religious identities in relation to other aspects of identity, like their nationality, city, socioeconomic strata, or even group of friends. Sometimes cultural beliefs about the links between religious identities and other kinds of identity become especially clear when people convert to other religions. This is because changes in religion often entail changes in how people identify themselves or how other people view them in ways that go far beyond spiritual beliefs or practices. In Spain, where the vast majority of people have been Catholic for the past several centuries, Catholic identity has been closely tied to how people understand their national identity as Spaniards. For many Spaniards, their culturally specific worldview makes it hard for them to even imagine that Spaniards could be Muslim. As a result, converts to Islam face misunderstandings and judgments from other members of society who see Islam and Spanish identity as mutually exclusive. While many converts to Islam adopt the religion on their own, some convert after falling in love with and marrying Muslims, either fellow Europeans who have already converted, or as in the case of Maria, Muslim migrants from the Middle East or North Africa.

Conversion to Islam in Spain

Conversion to Islam is notable in a number of ways. Globally, conversions to Islam are on the rise. Islam is the world's fastest growing religion, due in part to births in Muslim societies, but also to new Muslims who have adopted the faith. In contrast to some religions, such as Judaism, in which would-be converts must enroll in classes, or receive official acceptance from religious authorities, Islam requires only the recitation of the *Shahada*, a formal declaration of the Islamic faith. This recitation is often done in the presence of Muslim witnesses. María Martínez pronounced the *Shahada* in a mosque in Granada, and now she regularly supports and welcomes others who come to her mosque to recite the *Shahada* and join the Muslim community.

Many people are adopting Islam in places where it is a minority religion, such as in Western Europe and the United States. In these contexts, Islam is sometimes a stigmatized or marginalized religion that many people associate with erroneous stereotypes about fundamentalist terrorism or the oppression of women. Converting from a mainstream religion to a minority religion that is poorly understood and often maligned means that converts to Islam in Europe sometimes face particularly strong political and social challenges. Given such challenges, it is especially important for anthropologists to consider why and how Westerners like Maria are choosing to become Muslim.

In Spain, the compatibility of Islam with Spanish national identity is a long-standing question that has preoccupied religious and political leaders, as well as ordinary people, for centuries. In the middle ages, Spain formed part of a vast Muslim empire that included what today we call North Africa (Morocco, Algeria, Libya, Tunisia, Egypt, and Mauritania). For roughly eight centuries, Spain was predominantly Muslim, with Jewish and Christian minorities. At the turn of the 15th century, Catholic leaders concluded what had been a centuries-long battle to claim southern Spain from Muslim and Arab rule. They then initiated the Spanish Inquisition: a project of ethnic and religious cleansing meant to ensure a uniformly Catholic population for Spain. Over the course of several hundred years, Spain's Jews and Muslims were forced to convert, or be killed or exiled. Since then, Spaniards have struggled to figure out how Muslim Spain should be remembered, and how Muslims might fit into modern Spanish society.

In more recent history, Spain experienced the dictatorship of Francisco Franco from 1939 until 1975. Franco enforced Catholicism as the national religion during his reign. After Franco died in 1975, Spain became a democratic nation in which people are allowed to choose their own religious practices. Some people have chosen to convert to Islam and have formed Muslim communities, especially in southern Spain, the part of the country most associated with the Muslims of Spain's history. Converts report many reasons for adopting Islam, ranging from personal dissatisfaction with Catholicism, to feeling spiritually moved by the beauty and history of Spain's Muslim legacy, to wanting to share a religious identity with their spouses after marriage to Muslims. This last reason largely explains María's conversion, which she felt would align her identity with that of her husband.

Converts to Islam in Granada must face reactions from family, friends, and fellow Spaniards that are shaped by the historical debates in Spain about the relationship between Islam and Spanish national identity. Some people in Granada, including most converts, see Islam as foundational to Spain. They point to buildings like the Alhambra, a prominent castle and fortress built by medieval Muslims that still towers over the city of Granada, as well as the influence of Arabic on the Spanish language, and the fact that Spanish cuisine, music and dance traditions all draw on Arab roots or have parallels in Islamic traditions. Others see Islam as a constant, foreign threat to a Spanish identity they see as fundamentally Catholic, and are fearful of Islam returning to Spain.

Bridging Religious and National Identities

Convert Muslims in Granada often embody this tension themselves. Many converts started out viewing Islam as fundamentally opposed to Spanish identity, and only later came to see the two as compatible. María, who grew up in a rather homogeneous Catholic town several hours' drive from the city of Granada, first encountered Islam in Spain when she met the Jordanian immigrant who later became her husband. She recalled to me humorously how she had believed stereotypes about Islam, assuming all Muslim men were "*machista*" or sexist, and equating Muslims with Arabs, not realizing that many Muslims around the world are not ethnically Arab and that many Arabs are Jewish or Christian. Laughing, she said, "The first thing I said to my husband when we met was, 'So you're Arab? Well they say you Arabs are terrible, you know!' And he said, 'Oh, really?' And I said, 'Yes, they say you treat your women very badly.'" But her now-husband insisted this was not the case. The two began to date, and eventually decided to get married, but because María's family did not approve of her dating a Muslim, Arab man, they were married in secret. Even though María had learned that Muslim men are not necessarily any more "*machista*" than Spanish men, it never crossed her mind to become a Muslim woman.

María's eventual decision to convert to Islam came from both her desire to share a religion with her husband, and her slow realization that it was possible to be both Spanish and Muslim. She only became aware of the possibility of becoming Muslim when she discovered the existence of Spanish converts to Islam in Granada. Prior to this, she saw being Muslim and Spanish as incompatible. But one day she accompanied her husband to the mosque and saw several Spanish women praying there. She later recounted to me:

> I asked the women if I could look around, and I asked one fair-skinned woman where she was from. She said, "I'm Irish." And I said, "And you're *Muslim*?!?" And she goes, "Yeah, yeah, and this woman over here is Spanish, and this one too." And I was shocked, obviously, I was like, "There are Muslims that aren't Arab?" It was the first time I realized that.

With this realization that Spanish women could be Muslim, María felt more free to ponder her own religious future, a topic that had begun to worry her since marrying a man of a different religion than her own. She had begun to wonder what it would be like if she and her husband were to have children. Would it be complicated to have parents of different faiths? The fact that she and her husband came from different religious traditions began to trouble her more and more. At the same time, she was very curious about Islam. Growing up, she was not exposed to information about Islam beyond stereotypes, and as she gained familiarity with the religion through observing her husband's religious practices, she became fascinated. Since her belief that Muslim men all mistreated women had proven false, what else might surprise her about Islam? She began asking her husband to explain Islamic teachings, and to show her how to practice the five pillars of the Islamic faith: the recitation of the *Shahada*, daily prayers, fasting during the month of Ramadan, annual charitable giving, and pilgrimage to Mecca once during the lifetime of those who are able. She was not a very observant Catholic, and she felt saddened by her Catholic family's closed-mindedness about her mixed marriage. Eventually, after periodically attending events at the mosque, reading the Koran, and as she put it, "pestering" her husband with infinite questions about Islam, María decided that she found Islam's central messages of peace and submission to God very beautiful, and not entirely foreign to the values of her Catholic upbringing. So, she decided to convert.

As she learned more about her new religion, María's belief in the links between Muslim religious identity and Spanish national history and identity grew stronger. As someone who had always been part of the mainstream religion of her society, and now found herself in the minority, it was also important to María to promote acceptance of Islam in Spain by educating Spaniards about Islam's compatibility with Spanishness. Over the two years that I worked with her, during interviews, social hours, and downtime at the NGO, she often talked to me about this passion.

María had a three-pronged approach to insisting on the harmony between Islam and Spanish national identity. The first was a new take on Spanish history. While Islam is often seen as coming from outside of Western Europe, María (along with many fellow converts) had come to believe that because of Spain's long Muslim history, Islam is in fact not foreign to Spain, but indigenous to the country, especially to cities like Granada that were originally built by Muslims. Over tea in her apartment one evening, María told me about her participation in local festivals celebrating Spain's Muslim history, saying:

> You know what, Mikaela? It's very strange because, you realize, they were here for 800 years. *800 YEARS, living here, Muslims!* We're not talking about 80 years or five years. No. 800. It's incredible how a country can turn around and renounce its past, its origins. When the Catholic Kings finally captured Granada, they started this promotional campaign to replace Islam with Christianity. So that people would forget Islam. And now it's stuck there in peoples' heads. So now we have a huge job.

María felt that this "huge job" of reminding Catholic and secular Spaniards about their country's Muslim heritage was a crucial remedy to popular assumptions that Islam and Spanishness were diametrically opposed. She believed that if people knew more about the historical role of Islam in Spain, they would come to see Islam as part of, rather than a threat to, Spanish national identity.

In addition to rooting Islam in Spanish history, the second element of María's message was a discourse of Islam's "everydayness." When talking about Islamic practices, she almost always described them using carefully chosen phrases that normalized Islam as part of everyday life. She described how Islamic prayer fit into *la vida quotidiana*, (everyday life), and how Muslim Spanish girls were *"chicas muy normal y corrientes"* (very normal and common girls) who went to Spanish schools, spoke Spanish, and had non-Muslim Spanish friends, a far cry from the image of Muslim women and girls closed off from society, secluded at home. When asked by co-workers about the Muslim headscarf (which she does not wear except when praying at a mosque), she compared the headscarf, known as *hijab*, to scarves worn by pious Catholic women in Spain, who—like some Muslim women—covered their heads out of modesty. When Muslims used the Arabic phrase *Insh'allah* (God willing) in reference to something they hoped for, María would point out that this is just like Spanish-speaking Catholics' penchant for adding *"si Dios lo quiere"* (God willing) to the end of hypothetical statements, such as, "My favorite soccer team will win tonight, God willing!" In this way, María tried to demystify Islam and defuse fears of its foreignness by pointing out that Catholic and Muslim Spaniards actually engage in many similar practices on a daily basis, ranging from the way they talk, to covering for modesty.

Finally, María worked to spread this message of Islam's Spanishness as widely as possible, though she did not try to convert others to Islam. She brought the topic up frequently with her co-workers, happily fielding questions about headscarves, prayers, and the Koran from skeptical or curious colleagues. She also invited the media to events held at the NGO where she worked so that the press would cover stories about Islam in Spain. She even posted YouTube videos of herself wearing a headscarf and talking about how easy and "normal" it is to be a Muslim in Spain, taking on common concerns about Islam, such as the fear that Islam is by nature oppressive to women, and explaining why such stereotypes were not true, one by one.

Despite converts' own firm belief that Islam forms part of Spain's national identity, and that it is thus perfectly possible for Spaniards to embrace Islam, the reactions of other members of society (both non-Muslim Spaniards and non-Spanish Muslim immigrants) illustrate the difficulty of María's task. Because of widespread ideas that pit Europe (understood as Christian or secular) against an imagined Muslim world, the idea of Spanish Muslims is shocking to some people in Granada. Converts face many questions about whether their new religious identity might jeopardize their national identity as Spaniards. Conversion of course does nothing to legally change their identities or membership in the nation-state, but it does raise questions regarding their full social membership as recognized and respected members of Spanish society. At the same time, because they are Spanish, converts sometimes face skepticism from Muslims in Spain who are migrants from Muslim-majority countries, who also are not used to the idea that a person could be both Muslim and of Spanish origin. María and many of her fellow converts told countless stories of social encounters in which someone who knew them to be Spanish refused to believe they were Muslim, or in which someone who met them as a Muslim (for instance, at a mosque) was later shocked to find that they were Spanish.

María's friend and fellow convert Jasmina acutely felt this failure of recognition—that is, people's inability to understand and accept her new identity as both Spanish and Muslim. During an interview over tea, she described an argument she had recently had with a Moroccan woman at a bus stop. Jasmina was waiting for the bus when the Moroccan woman arrived at the bus stop. Seeing Jasmina's headscarf, the woman must have assumed that Jasmina was a fellow Moroccan or an immigrant from another Arabic-speaking Muslim country, and began to speak to Jasmina in Arabic. Jasmina politely explained in Spanish that she was not an Arabic speaker and did not understand the woman. At this, Jasmina recalled, the woman became angry. She continued to speak to Jasmina in Arabic, and shook her head in disbelief when Jasmina insisted that she was from Spain and did not speak Arabic. Finally, exasperated, Jasmina pulled out her Spanish ID card and showed it to the woman, who finally agreed that Jasmina must really be Spanish, and expressed shock. Jasmina was disappointed by this encounter, both because of the unpleasantness of the exchange—the woman had been offended that Jasmina refused to engage her in Arabic—and because she took it as a sign that her deeply felt religious beliefs were not taken seriously by Muslims born into the religion. She said, "The thing is, the Moroccans know that Islam is just a religion, but they still sometimes don't realize that Spaniards can be Muslim."

María Martínez has had a slightly different experience. Because she was married to a lifelong Muslim from an Arab country, she had more contacts with Muslim immigrants, who knew her well and welcomed her as a new Muslim. In contrast to Jasmina, María felt the misrecognition of non-Muslim Spaniards more keenly. Her former co-workers had refused to believe she had become Muslim for weeks after her conversion, until she finally showed them a headscarf she wears to pray at the mosque. Her family proved a further challenge. Given all of her activism on behalf of the Muslim community in Granada, I was surprised to find out about a year into my fieldwork stay that María still had not broken the news of her conversion to her family, who lived far outside the city and therefore were not privy to her role in the conversion movement there. María had already told me about her family's strongly negative reaction to her relationship with a Muslim immigrant. Her mother had half-jokingly threatened to "have a heart attack," and her brother-in-law had banned her from his house, and had even started a brawl with her husband during a family visit. Because of this, María was sure her family was not ready to find out that she herself had become Muslim. She sensed that the idea that she and her future children might not share a religious identity with the rest of the family was beyond the scope of her family's worldview. And so, she took care to hide her new religion when she visited them. She attended Catholic mass, crossed herself, and pretended to eat pork and drink wine, two staples of her family's (and of many Spanish families') meals. In order to fulfill her commitment to her religion without alarming her family, María took fake sips of wine from a wine glass, and cut up pieces of pork on her plate and moved them around so that her food looked partially eaten. She would describe this to me with a heavy sigh, and express hope that in the future, she might be able to tell her family that she was Muslim, that she found spiritual fulfillment in her new religion, and that she was just as Spanish as before.

Conclusion

Like members of all societies, María's family members operated according to social norms and cultural assumptions that are so ingrained that they are often unconscious. According to their cultural logic, if a person is Spanish, then that person is not Muslim, and vice versa. Since María continued to engage in practices seen as "typically Spanish," it did not occur to them that she might have converted to Islam. Her friend Jasmina faced a different situation, but with a similar underlying issue. The Moroccan woman who initially doubted that Jasmina, a Muslim woman in a headscarf, could be Spanish, operated under the same assumption: that people are *either* Muslim *or* Spanish, but not both.

Yet people like María are working hard to show others that they are perfectly able to inhabit Muslim religious identity and Spanish national identity at the same time. For María, these questions of identity were raised by her marriage to a Muslim migrant, which prompted her to reconsider her religious identity. She wanted to share a religious tradition with her husband, but feared becoming Muslim would threaten her national identity. Maria eventually changed her own beliefs about the possibility of incorporating Muslim religious beliefs into her Spanish identity and today she works to convince her fellow Spaniards to accept Islam as a valued part of Spanish history and to incorporate Muslims into Spanish society. Maria and her fellow converts' experiences highlight the complexities of cultural identities and membership in social groups. People are at once constrained by strongly held cultural assumptions about identity, even as they are also sometimes able to modify their own understandings of their identities and the ways they live them.

✓●─[**Study** and **Review** on **myanthrolab.com**

Review Questions

1. What is meant by religious conversion?

2. What historical factors shape the relationship between Islam and a Spanish national identity?

3. What was Maria's family's perception of Islam and how does that differ from the way Maria perceived its meaning?

4. How did Muslims react to Maria's status as a Muslim?

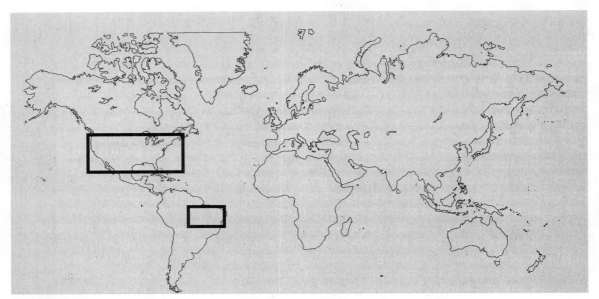

22

Mixed Blood

Jefferson M. Fish

Many Americans believe that people can be divided into races. For them, races are biologically defined groups. Anthropologists, on the other hand, have long argued that U.S. racial groups are American cultural constructions; they represent the way Americans classify people rather than a genetically determined reality. In this article, Jefferson Fish demonstrates the cultural basis of race by comparing how races are defined in the United States and Brazil. In America, a person's race is determined not by how he or she looks, but by his or her heritage. A person will be classified as black, for example, if one of his or her parents is classified that way no matter what the person looks like. In Brazil, on the other hand, people are classified into a series of tipos *on the basis of how they look. The same couple may have children classified into three or four different* tipos *based on a number of physical markers such as skin color and nose shape. As a result, Fish's daughter, who has brown skin and whose mother is black, can change her race from black in the United States to* moreno *(brunette), a category just behind* branca *(blond) in Brazil, by simply taking a plane there.**

((•⊸[Listen to the **Chapter Audio** on **myanthrolab.com**

Last year my daughter, who had been living in Rio de Janeiro, and her Brazilian boyfriend paid a visit to my cross-cultural psychology class. They had agreed to be interviewed about

*"Mixed Blood" by Jefferson M. Fish. Reproduced with permission from *Psychology Today*, copyright © 2008. www.psychologytoday.com

Brazilian culture. At one point in the interview I asked her, "Are you black?" She said, "Yes." I then asked him the question, and he said "No."

"How can that be?" I asked. "He's darker than she is."

Psychologists have begun talking about race again. They think that it may be useful in explaining the biological bases of behavior. For example, following publication of *The Bell Curve*, there has been renewed debate about whether black–white group differences in scores on IQ tests reflect racial differences in intelligence. (Because this article is about race, it will mainly use racial terms, like black and white, rather than cultural terms, like African-American and European-American.)

The problem with debates like the one over race and IQ is that psychologists on both sides of the controversy make a totally unwarranted assumption: that there is a biological entity called "race." If there were such an entity, then it would at least be possible that differences in behavior between "races" might be biologically based.

Before considering the controversy, however, it is reasonable to step back and ask ourselves "What is race?" If, as happens to be the case, race is not a biologically meaningful concept, then looking for biologically based racial differences in behavior is simply a waste of time.

The question "What is race?" can be divided into two more limited ones. The answers to both questions have long been known by anthropologists, but seem not to have reached other social or behavioral scientists, let alone the public at large. And both answers differ strikingly from what we Americans think of as race.

The first question is "How can we understand the variation in physical appearance among human beings?" It is interesting to discover that Americans (including researchers, who should know better) view only a part of the variation as "racial," while other equally evident variability is not so viewed.

The second question is "How can we understand the kinds of racial classifications applied to differences in physical appearance among human beings?" Surprisingly, different cultures label these physical differences in different ways. Far from describing biological entities, American racial categories are merely one of numerous, very culture-specific schemes for reducing uncertainty about how people should respond to other people. The fact that Americans believe that Asians, blacks, Hispanics, and whites constitute biological entities called races is a matter of cultural interest rather than scientific substance. It tells us something about American culture—but nothing at all about the human species.

The short answer to the question "What is race?" is: There is no such thing. Race is a myth. And our racial classification scheme is loaded with pure fantasy.

Let's start with human physical variation. Human beings are a species, which means that people from anywhere on the planet can mate with others from anywhere else and produce fertile offspring. (Horses and donkeys are two different species because, even though they can mate with each other, their offspring—mules—are sterile.)

Our species evolved in Africa from earlier forms and eventually spread out around the planet. Over time, human populations that were geographically separated from one another came to differ in physical appearance. They came by these differences through three major pathways: mutation, natural selection, and genetic drift. Since genetic mutations occur randomly, different mutations occur and accumulate over time in geographically separated populations. Also, as we have known since Darwin, different geographical environments select for different physical traits that confer a survival advantage. But the largest proportion of variability among populations may well result from purely random factors; this random change in the frequencies of already existing genes is known as genetic drift.

If an earthquake or disease kills off a large segment of a population, those who survive to reproduce are likely to differ from the original population in many ways. Similarly, if a group divides and a subgroup moves away, the two groups will, by chance, differ in the frequency of various genes. Even the mere fact of physical separation will, over time, lead two equivalent populations to differ in the frequency of genes. These randomly acquired population differences will accumulate over successive generations along with any others due to mutation or natural selection.

A number of differences in physical appearance among populations around the globe appear to have adaptive value. For example, people in the tropics of Africa and South America came to have dark skins, presumably, through natural selection, as protection against the sun. In cold areas, like northern Europe or northern North America, which are dark for long periods of time, and where people covered their bodies for warmth, people came to have light skins—light skins make maximum use of sunlight to produce vitamin D.

The indigenous peoples of the New World arrived about 15,000 years ago, during the last ice age, following game across the Bering Strait. (The sea level was low enough to create a land bridge because so much water was in the form of ice.) Thus, the dark-skinned Indians of the South American tropics are descended from light-skinned ancestors, similar in appearance to the Eskimo. In other words, even though skin color is the most salient feature thought by Americans to be an indicator of race—and race is assumed to have great time depth—it is subject to relatively rapid evolutionary change.

Meanwhile, the extra ("epicanthic") fold of eyelid skin, which Americans also view as racial, and which evolved in Asian populations to protect the eye against the cold, continues to exist among South American native peoples because its presence (unlike a light skin) offers no reproductive disadvantage. Hence, skin color and eyelid form, which Americans think of as traits of different races, occur together or separately in different populations.

Like skin color, there are other physical differences that also appear to have evolved through natural selection—but which Americans do not think of as racial. Take, for example, body shape. Some populations in very cold climates, like the Eskimo, developed rounded bodies. This is because the more spherical an object is, the less surface area it has to radiate heat. In contrast, some populations in very hot climates, like the Masai, developed lanky bodies. Like the tubular pipes of an old-fashioned radiator, the high ratio of surface area to volume allows people to radiate a lot of heat.

In terms of American's way of thinking about race, lanky people and rounded people are simply two kinds of whites or blacks. But it is equally reasonable to view light-skinned people and dark-skinned people as two kinds of "lankys" or "roundeds." In other words, our categories for racial classification of people arbitrarily include certain dimensions (light versus dark skin) and exclude others (rounded versus elongated bodies).

There is no biological basis for classifying race according to skin color instead of body form—or according to any other variable, for that matter. All that exists is variability in what people look like—and the arbitrary and culturally specific ways different societies classify that variability. There is nothing left over that can be called race. This is why race is a myth.

Skin color and body form do not vary together: Not all dark-skinned people are lanky; similarly, light-skinned people may be lanky or rounded. The same can be said of the facial features Americans think of as racial—eye color, nose width (actually, the ratio of width to length), lip thickness ("evertedness"), hair form, and hair color. They do not vary together either. If they did, then a "totally white" person would have very light skin color, straight blond hair, blue eyes, a narrow nose, and thin lips; a "totally black" person would have very dark skin color, black tight curly hair, dark brown eyes, a broad nose, and thick lips; those in between would have—to a correlated degree— wavy light brown hair, light brown eyes, and intermediate nose and lip forms.

While people of mixed European and African ancestry who look like this do exist, they are the exception rather than the rule. Anyone who wants to can make up a chart of facial features (choose a location with a diverse population, say, the New York City subway) and verify that there are people with all possible admixtures of facial features. One might see someone with tight curly blond hair, light skin, blue eyes, broad nose, and thick lips—whose features are half "black" and half "white." That is, each of the person's facial features occupies one end or the other of a supposedly racial continuum, with no intermediary forms (like wavy light brown hair). Such people are living proof that supposedly racial features do not vary together.

Since the human species has spent most of its existence in Africa, different populations in Africa have been separated from each other longer than East Asians or Northern Europeans have been separated from each other or from Africans. As a result, there is remarkable physical variation among the peoples of Africa, which goes unrecognized by Americans who view them all as belonging to the same race.

In contrast to the very tall Masai, the diminutive stature of the very short Pygmies may have evolved as an advantage in moving rapidly through tangled forest vegetation. The Bushmen of the Kalahari desert have very large ("steatopygous") buttocks, presumably to store body fat in one place for times of food scarcity, while leaving the rest of the body uninsulated to radiate heat. They also have "peppercorn" hair. Hair in separated tufts, like tight curly hair, leaves space to radiate the heat that rises through the body to the scalp; straight hair lies flat and holds in body heat, like a cap. By viewing Africans as constituting a single race, Americans ignore their greater physical variability, while assigning racial significance to lesser differences between them.

Although it is true that most inhabitants of northern Europe, east Asia, and central Africa look like Americans' conceptions of one or another of the three purported races, most inhabitants of south Asia, southwest Asia, north Africa, and the Pacific islands do not. Thus, the 19th century view of the human species as comprised of Caucasoid, Mongoloid, and Negroid races, still held by many Americans, is based on a partial and unrepresentative view of human variability. In other words, what is now known about human physical variation does not correspond to what Americans think of as race.

In contrast to the question of the actual physical variation among human beings, there is the question of how people classify that variation. Scientists classify things in scientific taxonomies—chemists' periodic table of the elements, biologists' classification of life forms into kingdoms, phyla, and so forth.

In every culture, people also classify things along culture-specific dimensions of meaning. For example, paper clips and staples are understood by Americans as paper fasteners, and nails are not, even though, in terms of their physical properties, all three consist of differently shaped pieces of metal wire. The physical variation in pieces of metal wire can be seen as analogous to human physical variation; and the categories of cultural meaning, like paper fasteners versus wood fasteners, can be seen as analogous to races. Anthropologists refer to these kinds of classifications as folk taxonomies.

Consider the avocado—is it a fruit or a vegetable? Americans insist it is a vegetable. We eat it in salads with oil and vinegar. Brazilians, on the other hand, would say it is a fruit. They eat it for dessert with lemon juice and sugar.

How can we explain this difference in classification?

The avocado is an edible plant, and the American and Brazilian folk taxonomies, while containing cognate terms, classify some edible plants differently. The avocado does not change. It is the same biological entity, but its folk classification changes, depending on who's doing the classifying.

Human beings are also biological entities. Just as we can ask if an avocado is a fruit or a vegetable, we can ask if a person is white or black. And when we ask race questions, the answers we get come from folk taxonomies, not scientific ones. Terms like "white" or "black" applied to people—or "vegetable" or "fruit" applied to avocados—do not give us biological information about people or avocados. Rather, they exemplify how cultural groups (Brazilians or Americans) classify people and avocados.

Americans believe in "blood," a folk term for the quality presumed to be carried by members of so-called races. And the way offspring—regardless of their physical appearance—always inherit the less prestigious racial category of mixed parentage is called "hypo-descent" by anthropologists. A sentence thoroughly intelligible to most Americans might be, "Since Mary's father is white and her mother is black, Mary is black because she has black 'blood.'" American researchers who think they are studying racial differences in behavior would, like other Americans, classify Mary as black—although she has just as much white "blood."

According to hypo-descent, the various purported racial categories are arranged in a hierarchy along a single dimension, from the most prestigious ("white"), through intermediary forms ("Asian"), to the least prestigious ("black"). And when a couple come from two different categories, all their children (the "descent" in "hypo-descent") are classified as belonging to the less prestigious category (thus, the "hypo"). Hence, all the offspring of one "white" parent and one "black" parent—regardless of the children's physical appearance—are called "black" in the United States.

The American folk concept of "blood" does not behave like genes. Genes are units which cannot be subdivided. When several genes jointly determine a trait, chance decides which ones come from each parent. For example, if eight genes determine a trait, a child gets four from each parent. If a mother and a father each have the hypothetical genes BBBBWWWW, then a child could be born with any combination of B and W genes, from BBBBBBBB to WWWWWWWW. In contrast, the folk concept "blood" behaves like a uniform and continuous entity. It can be divided in two indefinitely—for example, quadroons and octoroons are said to be people who have one-quarter and one-eighth black "blood," respectively. Oddly, because of hypo-descent, Americans consider people with one-eighth black "blood" to be black rather than white, despite their having seven-eighths white "blood."

Hypo-descent, or "blood," is not informative about the physical appearance of people. For example, when two parents called black in the United States have a number of children, the children are likely to vary in physical appearance. In the case of skin color, they might vary from lighter than the lighter parent to darker than the darker parent. However, they would all receive the same racial classification—black—regardless of their skin color.

All that hypo-descent tells you is that, when someone is classified as something other than white (e.g., Asian), at least one of his or her parents is classified in the same way, and that neither parent has a less prestigious classification (e.g., black).

That is, hypo-descent is informative about ancestry—specifically, parental classifica-tion—rather than physical appearance.

There are many strange consequences of our folk taxonomy. For example, someone who inherited no genes that produce "African"-appearing physical features would still be considered black if he or she has a parent classified as black. The cat-egory "passing for white" includes many such people. Americans have the curious belief that people who look white but have a parent classified as black are "really" black in some biological sense, and are being deceptive if they present themselves as white. Such examples make it clear that race is a social rather than a physical classification.

From infancy, human beings learn to recognize very subtle differences in the faces of those around them. Black babies see a wider variety of black faces than white faces, and white babies see a wider variety of white faces than black faces. Because they are exposed only to a limited range of human variation, adult members of each "race" come to see their own group as containing much wider variation than others. Thus, because of this perceptual learning, blacks see greater physical variation among themselves than among whites, while whites see the opposite. In this case, however, there is a clear answer to the question of which group contains greater physical vari-ability. Blacks are correct.

Why is this the case?

Take a moment. Think of yourself as an amateur anthropologist and try to step out of American culture, however briefly.

It is often difficult to get white people to accept what at first appears to contra-dict the evidence they can see clearly with their own eyes—but which is really the result of a history of perceptual learning. However, the reason that blacks view them-selves as more varied is not that their vision is more accurate. Rather, it is that blacks too have a long—but different—history of perceptual learning from that of whites (and also that they have been observers of a larger range of human variation).

The fact of greater physical variation among blacks than whites in America goes back to the principle of hypo-descent, which classifies all people with one black par-ent and one white parent as black. If they were all considered white, then there would be more physical variation among whites. Someone with one-eighth white "blood" and seven-eighths black "blood" would be considered white; anyone with any white ancestry would be considered white. In other words, what appears to be a difference in biological variability is really a difference in cultural classification.

Perhaps the clearest way to understand that the American folk taxonomy of race is merely one of many—arbitrary and unscientific like all the others—is to contrast it with a very different one, that of Brazil. The Portuguese word that in the Brazilian folk taxonomy corresponds to the American "race" is "*tipo.*" *Tipo*, a cognate of the English word "type," is a descriptive term that serves as a kind of shorthand for a se-ries of physical features. Because people's physical features vary separately from one another, there are an awful lot of tipos in Brazil.

Since tipos are descriptive terms, they vary regionally in Brazil—in part reflect-ing regional differences in the development of colloquial Portuguese, but in part because the physical variation they describe is different in different regions. The Bra-zilian situation is so complex I will limit my delineation of tipos to some of the main ones used in the city of Salvador, Bahia, to describe people whose physical appear-ance is understood to be made up of African and European features. (I will use the female terms throughout; in nearly all cases the male term simply changes the last letter from *a* to *o*.)

Proceeding along a dimension from the "whitest" to the "blackest" tipos, a *loura* is whiter-than-white, with straight blond hair, blue or green eyes, light skin color, narrow nose, and thin lips. Brazilians who come to the United States think that a *loura* means a "blond" and are surprised to find that the American term refers to hair color only. A *branca* has light skin color, eyes of any color, hair of any color or form except tight curly, a nose that is not broad, and lips that are not thick. *Branca* translates as "white," though Brazilians of this tipo who come to the United States—especially those from elite families—are often dismayed to find that they are not considered white here, and, even worse, are viewed as Hispanic despite the fact that they speak Portuguese.

A *morena* has brown or black hair that is wavy or curly but not tight curly, tan skin, a nose that is not narrow, and lips that are not thin. Brazilians who come to the United States think that a *morena* is a "brunette," and are surprised to find that brunettes are considered white but *morenas* are not. Americans have difficulty classifying *morenas*, many of whom are of Latin American origin: Are they black or Hispanic? (One might also observe that *morenas* have trouble with Americans, for not just accepting their appearance as a given, but asking instead "Where do you come from?" "What language did you speak at home?" "What was your maiden name?" or even, more crudely, "What *are* you?")

A *mulata* looks like a *morena,* except with tight curly hair and a slightly darker range of hair colors and skin colors. A *preta* looks like a *mulata,* except with dark brown skin, broad nose, and thick lips. To Americans, *mulatas* and *pretas* are both black, and if forced to distinguish between them would refer to them as light-skinned blacks and dark-skinned blacks, respectively.

If Brazilians were forced to divide the range of tipos, from *loura* to *preta,* into "kinds of whites" and "kinds of blacks" (a distinction they do not ordinarily make), they would draw the line between *morenas* and *mulatas;* whereas Americans, if offered only visual information, would draw the line between *brancas* and *morenas.*

The proliferation of tipos, and the difference in the white–black dividing line, do not, however, exhaust the differences between Brazilian and American folk taxonomies. There are tipos in the Afro-European domain that are considered to be neither black nor white—an idea that is difficult for Americans visiting Brazil to comprehend. A person with tight curly blond (or red) hair, light skin, blue (or green) eyes, broad nose, and thick lips, is a *sarará.* The opposite features—straight black hair, dark skin, brown eyes, narrow nose, and thin lips—are those of a *cabo verde. Sarará* and *cabo verde* are both tipos that are considered by Brazilians in Salvador, Bahia, to be neither black nor white.

When I interviewed my American daughter and her Brazilian boyfriend, she said she was black because her mother is black (even though I am white). That is, from her American perspective, she has "black blood"—though she is a *morena* in Brazil. Her boyfriend said that he was not black because, viewing himself in terms of Brazilian tipos, he is a *mulato* (not a *preto*).

There are many differences between the Brazilian and American folk taxonomies of race. The American system tells you about how people's parents are classified but not what they look like. The Brazilian system tells you what they look like but not about their parents. When two parents of intermediate appearance have many children in the United States, the children are all of one race; in Brazil they are of many tipos.

Americans believe that race is an immutable biological given, but people (like my daughter and her boyfriend) can change their race by getting on a plane and going from the United States to Brazil—just as, if they take an avocado with them, it changes from a vegetable into a fruit. In both cases, what changes is not the physical appearance of the person or avocado, but the way they are classified.

I have focused on the Brazilian system to make clear how profoundly folk taxonomies of race vary from one place to another. But the Brazilian system is just one of many. Haiti's folk taxonomy, for example, includes elements of both ancestry and physical appearance, and even includes the amazing term (for foreigners of African appearance) *un blanc noir*—literally, "a black white." In the classic study *Patterns of Race in the Americas,* anthropologist Marvin Harris gives a good introduction to the ways in which the conquests by differing European powers of differing New World peoples and ecologies combined with differing patterns of slavery to produce a variety of folk taxonomies. Folk taxonomies of race can be found in many—though by no means all—cultures in other parts of the world as well.

The American concept of race does not correspond to the ways in which human physical appearance varies. Further, the American view of race ("hypo-descent") is just one among many folk taxonomies, [none] of which correspond to the facts of human physical variation. This is why race is a myth and why races as conceived by Americans (and others) do not exist. It is also why differences in behavior between "races" cannot be explained by biological differences between them.

When examining the origins of IQ scores (or other behavior), psychologists sometimes use the term "heritability"—a statistical concept that is not based on observations of genes or chromosomes. It is important to understand that questions about heritability of IQ have nothing to do with racial differences in IQ. "Heritability" refers only to the relative ranking of individuals *within* a population, under given environmental conditions, and not to differences *between* populations. Thus, among the population of American whites, it may be that those with high IQs tend to have higher-IQ children than do those with low IQs. Similarly, among American blacks, it may be that those with high IQs also tend to have higher-IQ children.

In both cases, it is possible that the link between the IQs of parents and children may exist for reasons that are not entirely environmental. This heritability of IQ *within* the two populations, even if it exists, would in no way contradict the average social advantages of American whites as a group compared to the average social disadvantages of American blacks as a group. Such differences in social environments can easily account for any differences in the average test scores *between* the two groups. Thus, the heritability of IQ *within* each group is irrelevant to understanding differences *between* the groups.

Beyond this, though, studies of differences in behavior between "populations" of whites and blacks, which seek to find biological causes rather than only social ones, make a serious logical error. They assume that blacks and whites are populations in some biological sense, as sub-units of the human species. (Most likely, the researchers make this assumption because they are American and approach race in terms of the American folk taxonomy.)

In fact, though, the groups are sorted by a purely social rule for statistical purposes. This can easily be demonstrated by asking researchers how they know that the white subjects are really white and the black subjects are really black. There is no biological answer to this question, because race as a biological category does not exist. All that researchers can say is, "The tester classified them based on their physical appearance," or "Their school records listed their race," or otherwise give a social rather than biological answer.

So when American researchers study racial differences in behavior, in search of biological rather than social causes for differences between socially defined groups, they are wasting their time. Computers are wonderful machines, but we have learned about "garbage in/garbage out." Applying complex computations to bad data yields worthless results. In the same way, the most elegant experimental designs and statistical analyses, applied flawlessly to biologically meaningless racial categories, can only produce a very expensive waste of time.

As immigrants of varied physical appearance come to the United States from countries with racial folk taxonomies different from our own, they are often perplexed and dismayed to find that the ways they classify themselves and others are irrelevant to the American reality. Brazilians, Haitians, and others may find themselves labeled by strange, apparently inappropriate, even pejorative terms, and grouped together with people who are different from and unreceptive to them. This can cause psychological complications (a Brazilian immigrant—who views himself as white—being treated by an American therapist who assumes that he is not).

Immigration has increased, especially from geographical regions whose people do not resemble American images of blacks, whites, or Asians. Intermarriage is also increasing, as the stigma associated with it diminishes. These two trends are augmenting the physical diversity among those who marry each other—and, as a result, among their children. The American folk taxonomy of race (purportedly comprised of stable biological entities) is beginning to change to accommodate this new reality. After all, what race is someone whose four grandparents are black, white, Asian, and Hispanic?

Currently, the most rapidly growing census category is "Other," as increasing numbers of people fail to fit available options. Changes in the census categories every 10 years reflect the government's attempts to grapple with the changing self-identifications of Americans—even as statisticians try to maintain the same categories over time in order to make demographic comparisons. Perhaps they will invent one or more "multiracial" categories, to accommodate the wide range of people whose existence defies current classification. Perhaps they will drop the term "race" altogether. Already some institutions are including an option to "check as many as apply," when asking individuals to classify themselves on a list of racial and ethnic terms.

Thinking in terms of physical appearance and folk taxonomies helps to clarify the emotionally charged but confused topics of race. Understanding that different cultures have different folk taxonomies suggests that we respond to the question "What race is that person?" not by "Black" or "White," but by "Where?" and "When?"

✓●─[**Study** and **Review** on **myanthrolab.com**

Review Questions

1. What is Jefferson Fish's main point about the way Americans define race?

2. What is the difference between the way race is defined in the United States and in Brazil? List the Brazilian folk taxonomy of *tipos* and how to translate *tipos* into U.S. racial categories.

3. What evidence challenges the view that races are biologically defined types? What evidence would have to exist to prove that the human species is genetically divided into races?

4. Why does Fish feel it is important to understand that race as Americans define it does not represent a biological reality?

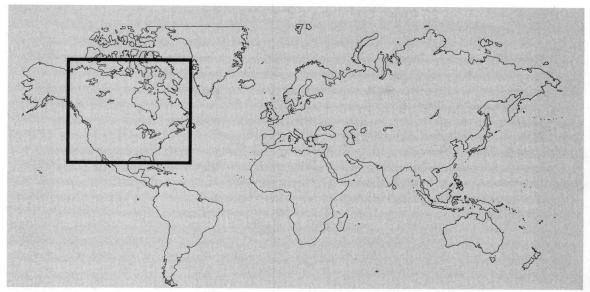

23

Motorcycles, Membership, and Belonging

David W. McCurdy

Many things serve as a basis for human group formation. Kinship is one, as we have seen in the last section. So is territory, as in the case of countries, towns, and neighborhoods. Manufacturing leads to companies, religion to congregations, war experience to veterans' groups, and status to country clubs and fraternal organizations. In this article, David McCurdy looks at a source of social aggregation based on shared interest. Using the example of a large group called the Gold Wing Road Riders Association(GWRRA), he argues that like thousands of other American interest groups, the GWRRA gives its members a comfortable and secure place in which to express their social needs. *

((•─Listen to the **Chapter Audio** on **myanthrolab.com**

If a couple from rural India were to visit the United States for the first time, they might be surprised by American social relations, or more accurately, by an apparent lack of them. Missing are the extended families, caste brotherhoods, close-knit communities, and kin-based inter-village networks that still organize life in many parts of India. Absent, also, is the commanding value, learned from childhood in South Asia, on the importance of social intercourse with and loyalty to kin.

---

*Original article from David W. McCurdy, "Motorcycles, Membership, and Belonging." Used by permission of the author.

Instead, they are likely to find a world predicated on individualism. Most Americans, they discover, grow up in small, nuclear families where both parents, married or divorced, are likely to work away from home. Children seem "cheeky" and often rude as they attempt to assert independence. Neighborhoods lack social cohesion; families guard their privacy and next door neighbors may be strangers. Competition, not cooperation, seems to rule many aspects of social life. People often appear lonely and preoccupied.

Some Americans might agree with this assessment of their social lives. But others might point out that this picture is incomplete, that it obscures a broad range of satisfying social connections that we Americans regularly pursue. For example, although we might work for large corporations, we often form networks of friends and allies within these larger organizations. We also discover friends in other settings, such as neighborhoods, local taverns, ours or spouses' work organizations, and civic groups. Such links draw Americans into wide-ranging personal networks and increasingly, cell phones and computers help keep them there.

Although personal networks are not formally organized groups, they may be all that many of us require to meet our social needs. But organized groups that satisfy personal social needs do exist. Some are voluntary associations organized around such factors as business, social status, and civic endeavors. Others, however, form around people's special interests, such as music, collecting, and sports.

For years I have believed that interest groups such as these are a significant feature of American society. They give their members a comfortable feeling of shared interest. Participation in them provides a sense of achievement and self-worth not available to them in other aspects of their lives. Such groups also represent a flexible arena that allows members to vary their participation as circumstances permit. To illustrate these points, let's take one example, the Gold Wing Road Riders Association (GWRRA or GW for short), which formed around the ownership of a Japanese touring motorcycle, the Honda Gold Wing.

The Honda Gold Wing

Motorcycles first appeared in the United States shortly before the turn of the last century. Used mainly for transportation, they were an alternative to more expensive automobiles. By the early 1920s, however, their popularity declined as cars became cheaper, more comfortable, and more reliable. By 1953 only one US Company, Harley Davidson, made motorcycles and then only for a small number of American consumers. (A few European brands also found their way to market at that time, however.) The motorcycle scene changed dramatically in the late 50s when the Honda Motorcycle Company increased motorcycle popularity by launching a public relations drive to counter what they perceived as motorcycling's outlaw image. Tens of thousands of average Americans responded to the "You Meet the Nicest People on a Honda" ad campaign by buying the company's small, reliable, and inexpensive machines. Once the fun of riding caught on, the demand for larger, faster machines grew, and subsequently, millions of Japanese (and later European and American) motorcycles found their way into American homes and millions of Americans discovered that they enjoyed riding them.

In 1975 Honda introduced a relatively powerful motorcycle called the Gold Wing, which was designed for speed to appeal to sports-minded riders. To make it stand out against competitors, engineers decided on a flat four (cylinder) 1000cc ("boxer") engine design. (Subaru and all the air-cooled VW engines use or used this configuration.) In the opposed four arrangement, cylinders lie on their sides, two on one side and two on the other with the crank shaft in the center. The machine, exhibiting shaft drive, was also easy to maintain. The result was a powerful low-center-of-gravity engine that cancels out engine vibration.

The GWRRA

Although designed for sport riding, the Gold Wing soon came to the attention of riders interested in motorcycle touring. Gold Wings, they discovered, were more comfortable for long distance riding because of their adequate power and lack of vibration. The Gold Wing Road Riders Association was born in 1976 when seven couples living in Phoenix, Arizona, organized a riding club around their newly purchased Gold Wings. The group quickly attracted the attention of other Arizona Gold Wing owners as well as those living in neighboring states. Soon, the GWRRA printed its first edition of a magazine, *Wing World*, containing information about Gold Wing maintenance, accessories, touring, equipment, events, and a variety of other topics of interest to the membership. As the organization gained members throughout the country, it created local riding chapters. Soon, the association divided the United States and Canada into regional and state organizations.

Today, the GWRRA has grown into a large institution almost entirely run by an army of volunteers. Geographically it is divided into 9 US and 3 Canadian *regions*. Regions together contain 49 *districts* (states). Canada has 11. There are now 586 local *chapters* for the US, 36 for Canada, and 10 found in 10 other countries. The organization is led by a director, 10 deputy directors, 9 US and 3 Canadian regional directors, 49 district directors, and 586 chapter directors. Supporting staff includes assistant directors, editors, treasurers, safety educators, leadership trainers, and webmasters. Altogether the Association has well over 70 thousand members. *Wing World*, now a slick, 90-page magazine, is produced by a paid staff. The association organizes an annual national rally called the "Wing Ding," held in a different part of the United States, each year. The event usually draws over 10,000 participants and features a large trade show. Each region also holds an annual rally as does almost every district. Many GWRRA members who have the time go on the "rally circuit," tour the country from one of these events to the next throughout the summer. Local chapters also organize events, including monthly meetings, weekly rides, and yearly fund raisers.

Cultural Themes

To get a clearer idea of what the GWRRA is like, it is useful to look at some of the themes (core values) that are expressed in the way the association is organized and the nature of its activities and symbolism.

GW Members Should Tour

Many Americans like to tour, and for anyone touring can be demanding. But touring on a motorcycle presents extra challenges. Riders must brave rainstorms (and occasionally snow), high winds, and road hazards that four-wheeled vehicles can easily traverse. And riding a motorcycle is more dangerous than driving a car so constant vigilance is required. But for GW members this is part of the excitement of riding. Like physically demanding rites of passage anywhere, the experience creates social solidarity and a warm sense of belonging. It is no wonder that a value on touring is expressed so often in the world of GW riders.

As noted earlier, the Honda Gold Wing seemed made for touring. But since 1975, GW members have played an important role in the machine's evolution. Like native informants, they have addressed what it is like to ride long distances and what motorcycle features would be helpful to meet touring challenges. Like ethnographers, Honda company employees ride with "Wingers" as participant observers. As a result, the machine has been redesigned over the years to meet riders' touring needs. From its original bare form it has transformed into today's 1800cc six-cylinder-engined machine with large built-in cargo space, a front fairing and windshield for wind protection, and wide comfortable seating. Everything is geared to make touring in the open as comfortable, reliable, and safe as possible.

GW members also symbolically emphasize the importance of touring. Map patches of the US and Canada and of one's home state adorn most members' vests. Once visited, states and counties are colored in indicating the extent of a wearer's touring achievements. The more states colored in, the greater the prestige. Vests also display pins indicating safe miles ridden and patches from important places visited. And touring stories abound when *Wingers* get together making for interesting and warm conservation.

Couples Are Valued Members

The GWRRA is largely built around couples. As already noted, the organization was founded by couples and they tended to attract more members like them. And the Gold Wing, which comes with an intercom system installed and its long comfortable seat, is built for two-up riding. Dress also symbolizes the presence of couples. Couples often dress alike, with color matched helmets, jackets, pants, and boots. Quite often a couple's names are lettered on the motorcycle's trunk. The organization has a couples-designed structure. Many chapters, most districts, regions, and the "national" all pick *couples of the year*. Couples may jointly hold single association offices.

Unintentionally, the emphasis on couples has led to an important place for women in the association by encouraging women to become members. Women regularly hold directorships, especially of chapters, and make up a majority of volunteers at rallies and fund raisers. As an aside, although women commonly ride behind their husbands or male partners, more and more of them ride alongside them on their own motorcycles.

Safety Is Essential

Safety is paramount. Almost all members wear helmets all the time. Most wear protective clothing including armored jackets and riding boots that come above the ankles. You won't be likely to see them riding in shorts and tennis shoes. GW members are encouraged to take advanced riding courses and first-aid classes. Many carry first-aid kits and fire extinguishers on their bikes. Every chapter has as an *educator* whose job it is to arrange for safety seminars and emergency first aid classes. Group rides are led by a *ride captain* up front and a *tail gunner* or *tail* bringing up the rear. Bikes ride in a staggered formation rather than side by side. CB radios found on most Gold Wings keep everyone informed about road hazards, cars moving into the formation, and upcoming turns. Riding after drinking alcohol is discouraged. So is aggressive, "show off" riding. Safety is part of the association's motto.

Participation Is Important

The association encourages participation. The members' vests symbolize participation in many ways. Most *Wingers* wear the national association's membership pin, with a ladder of *hangers* dangling below for each year of affiliation. Many also wear the *district* rally pin with a second ladder of hangers for each rally attended. There are special pins for officer positions and for special rides and events held elsewhere in the United States and Canada. There is a national GWRRA patch worn on the back of the vest. Above it is a chapter identification *rocker* and other rockers indicating the wearer's current office and those held in the past if they exist. The front of the vest sports a chapter patch. Many riders wear pins and patches that indicate they have participated in rallies and other events. Wingers joke that it is impossible for GW riders to pass a Dairy Queen without stopping so many wear a Dairy Queen patch. Eating together is a hallmark of the group.

Pride in the Machine

GW members are proud of their motorcycles and are expected to show them off. Some have airbrushed or hand painted scenes adorning their machines. (Bike artists are present at most rallies.) Many buy chrome plated accessories, "accents," and LED lighting strips sold by a number of companies. A regular feature at rallies is the *bike show* where Gold Wings are judged in classes based on model years and kinds of additions. A regular sight at rallies is couples busily washing (host motels are asked to provide outdoor hoses) and polishing their machines. Bikes festooned with extra lighting ride in every rally's specular *light show*. Every district and national rally features a *grand parade*. After coordinating with local community officials, members line up on their Wings to "group ride" over a prearranged route through the community where the rally is held, honking their horns, flashing their emergency lights, and waving to bystanders.

Members Should Have Fun

When GW members get together, they joke and talk about their rides and many know each other well enough to know about home lives, work, and other personal topics. All rallies have organized games, including those *on bike* and *off bike*. Favorites include the slow race where riders attempt to ride a short distance keeping within lines set 16 inches apart. At times, rallies will hold competitive talent shows with humorous skits and musical presentations put on by chapters. Since motorcycling is fun for them, almost every activity meets this requirement. And, of course, complaining should be kept to a minimum and political opinions hidden.

Maintaining the Association

Like many recreational groups, the GWRRA has experienced a relatively high membership turnover. Death, old age, and infirmity have accounted for membership loss. So has declining commitment. There tends to be an inner circle of members who remain active, taking positions of leadership and participating in most events. But recruiting leaders is sometimes difficult because of substantial time requirements. Some chapters have disbanded because no one would or could come forward to head them. Members also move, live too far away from chapter locations, feel left out because they are single, become embroiled in conflicts with other members, find themselves too short of money to buy or maintain a Gold Wing (new Gold Wings now cost around 23,000 dollars), or simply become bored with the same old round of rallies and other events. Despite these problems, the association recruits aggressively and *triking* one's Gold Wing (adding two wheels to the machine's rear end) enables older and "less firm" riders to continue as members. Total membership numbers are steady as a result.

Conclusion

As I look at this US recreational group one thing stands out. The GWRRA is a place where people can find a comfortable home, one in which they can be appreciated and assume respected roles. Despite the fact that they have found enough money to buy an expensive Gold Wing and to tour and participate in association activities, most GW members work at average-paying jobs. They are truck drivers, mail carriers, prison guards, construction foremen, family farmers, apartment managers, church secretaries, production line workers, engineers, and a host of similar jobs that provide them with a living but often little respect or room to express themselves. The GWRRA offers them the support and personal recognition that their occupations lack. The opportunity to hold respected positions, the excitement of riding, ownership of a publically attractive machine, the sense of self-worth that comes from a mild Outward-Bound-like experience and the public and slightly risqué notoriety that stems from riding a motorcycle all meet their personal social needs. For many Wingers, the association is their non-family home.

In 2012 I visited India again. Riding in a friend's car from Gurgaon to downtown Delhi, I spotted a group of about 60 young men standing by an assortment of motorcycles. "They meet here every Sunday to go riding," my host said and I thought "Look-out, in no time the GWRRA's International Director (yes there is one) will be working on you to form a chapter. American society is at your doorstep."

✓●—Study and Review on **myanthrolab.com**

Review Questions

1. What is David McCurdy's main point about what groups like the Gold Wing Road Riders "do" for Americans who participate in them?

2. How are groups in the United States different from _____ ...dy describes in rural India?

3. What other kinds of groups can you think of that knit tog... dents on a college campus or members of a community? H... of maintaining the Gold Wing Road Riders Association m... what happens in these other groups?

4. What applications does an in-depth analysis of a consume... those who make and sell motorcycles?

PART SEVEN

LAW AND POLITICS

READINGS IN THIS SECTION

Ideally, culture provides the blueprint for a smoothly oiled social machine whose parts work together under all circumstances. But human society is not like a rigidly constructed machine. It is made of individuals who have their own special needs and desires. Personal interest, competition for scarce resources, and simple accident can cause nonconformity and disputes, resulting in serious disorganization.

One way we manage social disruption is through the socialization of children. As we acquire our culture, we learn the appropriate ways to look at experience, to define our existence, and to feel about life. Each system of cultural knowledge contains implicit values of what is desirable, and we come to share these values with other people. Slowly, with the acquisition of culture, most people find they *want* to do what they *must* do; the requirements of an orderly social life become personal goals.

Enculturation, however, is rarely enough. Disputes among individuals regularly occur in all societies, and how such disagreements are handled defines what anthropologists mean by the legal system. Some disputes are **infralegal**; they never reach a point where they are settled by individuals with special authority. Neighbors, for example, would engage in an infralegal dispute if they argued over who should pay for the damage caused by water that runs off one's land into the other's basement. So long as they don't take the matter to court or resort to violence, the dispute will remain infralegal. This dispute may become **extralegal**, however, if it occurs outside the law and escalates into violence. Had the neighbors come to blows over the waterlogged basement, the dispute would have become extralegal. Feuds and wars are the best examples of this kind of dispute.

Legal disputes, on the other hand, involve socially approved mechanisms for their settlement. **Law** is the cultural knowledge that people use to settle disputes by means of agents who have the recognized authority to do so. Thus if the argument between neighbors cited previously ended up in court before a judge or referee, it would have become legal.

Although Americans often think of courts as synonymous with the legal system, societies have evolved a variety of structures for settling disputes. For example, some disputes may be settled by **self-redress**, meaning that wronged individuals are given the right to settle matters themselves. **Contests** requiring physical or mental combat between disputants may also be used to settle disputes. A trusted third party, or **go-between**, may be asked to negotiate with each side until a settlement is achieved. In some societies, supernatural power or beings may be used. In parts of India, for example, disputants are asked to take an oath in the name of a powerful deity or (at least in the past) to submit to a supernaturally controlled, painful, or physically dangerous test called an **ordeal**. Disputes may also be taken to a **moot**, an informal community meeting where conflict may be aired. At the moot, talk continues until a settlement is reached. Finally, disputes are often taken to **courts**, which are formally organized and include officials with authority to make and enforce decisions.

Political systems are closely related to legal ones and often involve some of the same offices and actors. The **political system** contains the process for making and carrying out public policy according to cultural categories and rules; **policy** refers to guidelines for action. The **public** are the people affected by the policy. Every society must make decisions that affect all or most of its members. The Mbuti Pygmies of the Ituri Forest described by anthropologist Colin Turnbull, for example, occasionally decide to conduct a communal hunt. Hunters set their nets together and wait for the appearance of forest game. Men, women, and children must work together as beaters to drive the animals toward the nets. When the Mbuti decide to hold a hunt, they make a political decision.

The political process requires that people make and abide by a particular policy, often in the face of competing plans. To do so a policy must have **support**, which is anything that contributes to its adoption and enforcement. Anthropologists recognize two main kinds of support: legitimacy and coercion. **Legitimacy** refers to people's positive evaluation of public officials and public policy. A college faculty, for example, may decide to institute the quarter system because a majority feel that quarters rather than semesters represent the "right length" for courses. Theirs is a positive evaluation of the policy. Some faculty members will oppose the change but will abide by the decision because they value the authority of faculty governance. For them the decision, although unfortunate, is legitimate.

Coercion, on the other hand, is support derived from the threat or use of force or the promise of short-term gain. Had the faculty members adopted the quarter system because they had been threatened with termination by the administration, they would have acted under coercion.

There are also other important aspects of the political process. Some members of a society may be given **authority**, the right to make and enforce public policy. In our country, elected officials are given authority to make certain decisions and exercise particular powers. However, formal political offices with authority do not occur in every society. Most hunting and gathering societies lack such positions, as do many horticultural societies. **Leadership**, which is the ability to influence others to act, must be exercised informally in these societies.

In the first article, Anne Sutherland describes what happens when the substantive laws of two culturally different groups collide in court. A young Gypsy man is convicted of using another family member's social security number although he had no intention of defrauding anyone. The second article, by James Spradley and David McCurdy, uses Zapotec cases collected by anthropologist Laura Nader to illustrate basic anthropological legal concepts, such as substantive and procedural law, legal levels, and legal principles. They show that, for the Zapotec, social harmony is more important than punishment. Elizabeth Eames, in the third selection, looks at the political institution of bureaucracy. Drawing on the theory of Max Weber, she notes that bureaucracy, which is designed to be impersonal and even-handed in Europe and North America, is a personal institution in Nigeria. She introduces Weber's notion of **patrimonial authority** as it pertains to the form of government organized as a more or less direct extension of the noble household, where officials originate as household servants and remain personal dependents of the ruler. The final selection by Carolyn Nordstrom discusses the informal—thus untaxed, unregulated, and illegal—economy among war amputees in Angola as the backbone of the economy.

Key Terms

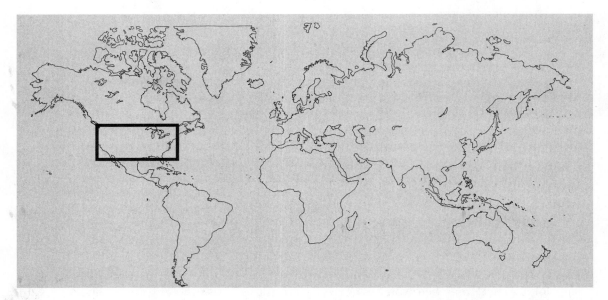

24

Cross-Cultural Law: The Case of an American Gypsy

Anne Sutherland

Every society recognizes a list of legal statutes, which anthropologists call substantive law, *that define right from wrong. In the United States, for example, it is against the law for an individual to marry more than one person at a time. But what is proper in one country may be a crime in another. Unlike the United States, for example, in Iran it is legal for a person to be married simultaneously to more than one person. So what happens when members of one society live within and under the legal jurisdiction of another? This is the question explored by Anne Sutherland in this article on the legal plight of a young Gypsy man who is arrested for using the social security number of a relative on a car loan application. Despite the claim that using different identities of family members is a common Gypsy practice designed to hide their identities, and that he had no intention to defraud anyone by doing so, the young man receives a six-month jail term.**

───────────────────────────────

((•—**Listen** to the **Chapter Audio** on **myanthrolab.com**

It is often the case that a law made for one set of purposes has another, unintended impact on a particular group. A recent law making the use of a false social security number a federal felony is intended to help prosecution of major drug crime syndicates, but it has a special impact on Gypsies in the United States. Gypsies, traditionally a nomadic people, frequently borrow each others' "American" names and social security numbers, viewing them as a kind of corporate property of their kin group or *vitsa*. They also often lack birth certificates and must obtain midwife or baptismal certificates to use for identification purposes when they try to obtain credit, enter school, or apply for welfare.

In this article, I shall examine the case of a nineteen-year-old Gypsy man who was convicted under the new social security law and served six months in jail. Arguments for the defense in the case followed three lines of reasoning: 1) that this law unfairly singled out Gypsies for punishment; 2) that there was no intent to commit a crime; and 3) that in using the social security numbers of relatives, Gypsies were following a time-honored tradition to remain anonymous and separate from non-Gypsy society.

Facts of the Case

In the fall of 1991 in St. Paul, Minnesota, a nineteen-year-old Gypsy man was convicted of the crime of using his five-year-old nephew's social security number to obtain credit to purchase a car. When the purchase was questioned by the car dealership, he returned the car and was arrested on a felony charge of using a false social security number. After he was arrested, police searched the apartment where he was staying. They found lists of names, addresses and social security numbers, leading them to suspect an organized crime ring.

In *The United States of America v. S.N.*,[1] it was "alleged that the defendant, S.N., while in the process of obtaining a new Ford Mustang from a car dealership, used a social security number that was not his own with intent to deceive." Under the statute 42 U.S.C. 408 (g)(2), a person who, with intent to deceive, falsely represents his or her number to obtain something of value or for any other purpose, is a felon.

In Mr. S.N.'s case there is no specific allegation that he intended to deprive another person permanently of property because the focus of the charging statute is false representation of numbers. The underlying purpose which motivates a person to falsely represent his or her number may be an essentially innocent purpose, but the statute, at least as it has been interpreted, does not appear to impose a burden of proof as to wrongful purpose.

The statute punishes the means (false number) which a person may employ to achieve any number of ends and it punishes those means as a felony. The lawyer for the defense argued that the statute's failure to address the nature of the purpose to which false credentials are used is a serious flaw in the law and may punish those who would use the number for petty misconduct as felons. He also argued that there is a potential for discriminatory impact on Gypsies who use false credentials to conceal themselves from mainstream society. A Gypsy household may obtain a telephone by providing a false social security number and even if they pay the telephone bill without fail for years, they are felons under this law. S.N. not only made the payments

---

[1] *United States v. Sonny Nicholas*, U.S. District Court, State of Minnesota, CR 4-91-137 (1991). Quotes from Philip Leavenworth, memorandum in support of a motion to declare 42 U.S.C.408(g)(2) unconstitutional.

for his car, but he returned it when the number was questioned. He is still a felon under this law.

The defense lawyer argued that the law is objectionable for two reasons. First, the law's disproportionate impact on the Gypsies is objectionable under the equal protection guaranteed in the Fifth Amendment of the U.S. Constitution. He argued that the law denies Gypsies equal protection of the law by irrationally and disproportionately punishing at the felony level certain traditional Gypsy actions which cause no positive injury to anyone. As evidence he used material from my book, *Gypsies: The Hidden Americans,* for testimony that Gypsies routinely use false social security numbers to acquire credit but do pay their bills and are available for repossession in case of default of payment. They get phone service, buy houses and cars and other household items on credit and have a record of payment that is probably better than the general population (*United States v. S.N., 1991*). They do this primarily to remain unknown by mainstream society rather than to cause loss or injury to any person.

Second, as the defense lawyer pointed out, there is a Supreme Court decision that requires the government to prove felonious intent when it seeks to punish a person for wrongful acquisition of another's property. S.N. maintained that he used a false social security number because of a Gypsy tradition to remain anonymous and because his own number had been used by other Gypsies. The government argued that there was a "ring" of Gypsies in the area where S.N. was living. At S.N.'s residence a number of false credentials and social security numbers were found which had been used to obtain cars illegally. Some of these cars are still missing. In other words, there was evidence that false identity had been used recently in the area to steal. In this case, however, S.N. had not stolen anything and was not being accused of stealing, but only of using a false social security number.

Because of the evidence of a ring of car thieves in the area, the prosecution hoped to use the threat of prosecution against S.N., the only Gypsy they had been able to arrest, to plea bargain for information regarding the other people involved in the alleged ring. These other people had disappeared immediately as soon as S.N. was arrested.

One of the problems in the case was that both the prosecution and even the defense had difficulty obtaining complete and accurate information on S.N. For example, they had difficulty determining his "real" name, a moot point for the Gypsies since they have a practice of using many "American" names although they only have one "Gypsy" name (*nav romano*). The Gypsy name of *o Spiro le Stevanosko* (or Spiro the son of Stevan) uses the noun declension characteristic of the Sanskrit-rooted Rom language and is not immediately translatable into English since it does not employ a surname. Spiro's identity can be pinned down by finding out what *vitsa* (a cognatic descent group) he belongs to so that he will not be confused with any other Spiro le Stevanoskos. The Spiro of our example is a *Kashtare* which is part of a larger "nation" of Gypsies or *natsia* called *Kalderasha* (coppersmith). For his "American" names he may take any of a number used by his relatives such as Spiro Costello, John Costello, John Marks, John Miller, Spiro John or Spiro Miller. His nickname is Rattlesnake Pete.

The Anthropologist as Cultural Broker

S.N.'s defense attorney contacted me after finding that he was less confused about S.N. after reading my book about Gypsies. He sought my help in determining whether S.N. was a Gypsy, what his name was, and any other cultural information (such as the use of social security numbers by Gypsies) that would help him with his case.

Consequently, one cold autumn day I drove to the federal holding prison, one and a half hours from the city, and met S.N. He was a thin young man, perpetually fearful of pollution from contact with non-Gypsies and suffering from the effects of several months of what for him was solitary confinement since he had not seen any of his people since being incarcerated. The telephone was his only link with people to whom he could relate, people from his own culture who spoke his language. His main contact was with a non-Gypsy woman who lived with one of his relatives. She was his link with the world he had known and the only "American" household he had been in before prison. Since my primary task was to determine if he was a Gypsy, first I talked to him about his relatives in Los Angeles and his *vitsa* (Yowane) and tried to establish what section of the *vitsa* I personally knew. This exchange of information about *vitsa* and Gypsies of mutual acquaintance is a normal one between Gypsies. The purpose was to establish a link between us.

Then I asked him about why he was in Minnesota. He talked about a seasonal expedition he and his brothers and cousins make to Minnesota to buy and sell cars and fix fenders before winter sets in. He claimed not to know where his brothers and cousins had gone or how he got into his present predicament.

For S.N., the most immediately effective action I could take was to see that he got the food he needed to stay "clean" in jail. When I met him he had lost fifteen pounds and was suffering demonstrable distress and nervousness. He was upset at being cut off from his culture and people for the first time in his life. In addition, he was distressed at being incarcerated and fearful for his safety. More importantly, he was worried he would become defiled or *marime*. A major concern of his was that if he ate food prepared by non-Gypsies who did not follow rules of cleanliness considered essential in the Gypsy culture, he would become *marime*, a condition of ritual impurity that would result in his being shunned by his relatives and other Gypsies. To protect himself, he avoided eating prison food in the hopes that when he was released from prison he would be able to return to his family without a period of physical exile, also called *marime* (or "rejected" as the Gypsies translate it into English). I arranged for his lawyer to provide him with money to buy food from the concession because it is packaged and untouched by non-Gypsies and therefore considered clean by Gypsy standards. He bought milk in cartons, candy bars and soft drinks and other packaged foods that, though they may lack in nutrition, at least were not defiling and kept him from starvation.

A further complicating factor for S.N. was that he spoke English as a second language. He had only a rudimentary ability to read, thus straining his grasp of his defense. And his only contact with relatives was by telephone since neither he nor they could write with any ease. Even though his limited English made it difficult for him to follow his own trial, the court did not provide a translator.

The Trial

The trial was held in Federal Court and centered around the constitutionality of a law that unfairly targets a particular ethnic group and the question of intent to commit a crime. My testimony was intended to establish that Gypsies may use false identification for a number of cultural reasons which may have no connection to any intent to commit a crime. For a traditionally nomadic group with pariah status in the wider society and a pattern of secretiveness and autonomy, concealing identity is a long-established pattern.

This pattern is widespread in all Gypsy groups in Eastern Europe, Western Europe, Russia, Latin America and the United States. It is a mechanism they have developed over centuries to protect themselves from a wider society that has persecuted them or driven them away. The recent case of the German government paying large sums to Romania to take back Gypsy refugees is only the latest in a historically established tradition of discrimination against Gypsies. The persecution of Gypsies in the Holocaust, in medieval Europe and in the early part of the 20th century in the United States has been well documented. Current events in Eastern Europe have shown a resurgence of extreme prejudice against Gypsies. Interviews in recent *New York Times* articles have pointed to a hatred of Gypsies so deep that there is talk of extermination.[2]

Because of the history of violence against them, Gypsies have developed elaborate mechanisms of secrecy and have hidden their identity in order to survive. It will not be easy to get them to change this pattern that has stood them in good stead for so many centuries.

The purpose of my testimony was to establish that S.N. *was* a Gypsy and that Gypsies often use false identification without intent to defraud. They do so because as members of a *vitsa*, or cognatic descent group, identification is corporate in nature. Members of the group have corporate access to property owned by other members of the group. That property includes forms of identification.

An additional problem in the S.N. case was the question of identification from photographs. Here we encountered the age-old problem that members of one culture and race have trouble identifying individuals from another culture and race. In simple terms, to many non-Gypsies, all Gypsies look alike. Part of the case involved clearing up erroneous identification of S.N. in photos provided by the prosecution.

I was also asked to testify on my own personal experience with discrimination against Gypsies by the Minneapolis Police Department. One instance of discrimination I related to the court occurred during a talk I gave to some twenty police officers to help them understand Gypsy culture. When I had spoken about the strong sense of family and community among the Gypsies and how much they value their children, a police officer suggested that since the main problem law enforcement officers have is how to detain the Gypsies long enough to prosecute them, removing Gypsy children from their homes on any pretext would be an effective way to keep the parents in town.

Prejudice against Gypsies often goes unrecognized even by culturally and racially sensitive people. The assistant district attorney prosecuting S.N. offered me an article that he used to understand the Gypsies, entitled "Gypsies, the People and their Criminal Propensity,"[3] which quotes extensively from my work, including the fact that Gypsies have several names and that the same or similar non-Gypsy names are used over and over. The article concentrates on "criminal" behavior and never mentions the possibility that there are Gypsies who may not engage in criminal activities. In one section, quotations from my book on the ways Gypsies deal with the

---

[2]See *New York Times*, November 17 and 28, 1993, for recent accounts of extreme prejudice against Gypsies.
[3]Terry Getsay, *Kansas State FOP Journal*, Parts I, II, and III (1982): 18–30.

welfare bureaucracy were placed under the title, "Welfare Fraud," although by far most of the practices I described were legal. These concluding words in Part II are representative of the tone of the article:

> Officers should not be misled into thinking these people are not organized. They are indeed organized and operate under established rules of behavior, including those that govern marriage, living quarters, child rearing, the division of money and participation in criminal acts.

The implication of such statements is inflammatory. Gypsies have a culture, history, language and social structure, but that fact is distorted to imply that their social organization is partly for the purpose of facilitating criminal behavior. Their culture is viewed as a criminal culture. Gypsies have been fighting this view for hundreds of years. It is the view that they still combat in their relations with law enforcement and the criminal justice system. It is the view that was promoted by the prosecution in this case.

In spite of the best efforts of S.N.'s attorney and my testimony that use of a false social security number did not necessarily indicate intent to commit a crime, he was convicted of illegally using a social security number and served about six months in jail.

Conclusions: Anthropology and Cultural Differences in the Courtroom

Anthropologists are often called in as expert witnesses in cases involving cultural difference. Most Native American legal cases, such as the *Mashpee* case reported by James Clifford,[4] center around Indian status, treaties and land rights. In St. Paul, a number of Hmong legal cases highlighted the conflict between traditional marriage (specifically, the age at which children may marry) and the legal status of minors in American law. With the Gypsies, there is yet another set of cultural issues in their contact with American law.

First is the question of the cultural conflict between a historically nomadic group and the state bureaucracy of settled people. Identification—a serious legal issue in a bureaucratic society composed of people with fixed abodes and a written language—has virtually no meaning for the nomadic Gypsies who consider descent and extended family ties the defining factor for identification.

Second is the conflict between Gypsy religious rules regarding ritual pollution and prison regulations. The Gypsies avoid situations, such as a job or jail, that require them to be in prolonged contact with non-Gypsies. Jail presents special problems because the Gypsies can become *marime*, that is, defiled by unclean food and living conditions. The psychological trauma that results from isolation from their community is compounded if they then emerge from jail and have to undergo a further isolation from relatives because of becoming *marime* in jail.

Finally, this case illustrates a cultural clash between the Rom Gypsy value on corporate kinship and the American value on individual rights. The rights and status of an individual Rom Gypsy is directly linked to his or her membership in

---

[4]"Identity in Mashpee," in *The Predicament of Culture* (Cambridge: Harvard University Press, 1988), pp. 277–346.

the *vitsa*. Furthermore, the status of all members of the *vitsa* is affected by the behavior of each individual *vitsa* member. Since they are so intricately linked, reciprocity between *vitsi* members is expected. Members of a *vitsa* and family share economic resources, stay in each other's homes, help each other in work and preparation of rituals, loan each other cars, information, identification, and money. They also share the shame of immoral or incorrect behavior by one member and the stigma (*marime*) attached to going to jail. For the Gypsies, the American ideal of each individual having only one name, one social security number, or a reputation based entirely on their own behavior is contrary to their experience and culture.

The analysis of an event such as a trial, especially an event that brings to the fore cultural difference, can be instructive for both cultures. In this article I have tried to present fundamental differences in the practices of American culture and U.S. law and the practices of Roma law and Gypsy culture. Understanding difference does not necessarily resolve conflict, but it can lead to a more humanitarian application of the law to different cultures. The United States, a country based on immigration and diversity, is in no position to ignore the cultural foundations of different ethnic groups, nor are different cultures in the United States exempt from a law because it is contrary to custom. However, the more aware the legal system is of cultural histories and custom, the greater its capacity for justice.

S.N. chose to pursue his case through the U.S. legal system. He made this choice partly because of the influence and advice of a brother who was married to an American lawyer. The rest of his family strongly opposed this decision, preferring to do it the way they always have, by fleeing or lying to avoid contact with the legal system. While he was in jail, the Gypsies in his community held a *Kris* (formal meeting) to explain his decision to work through the American courts rather than the traditional Gypsy way and to raise money for his defense. The outcome of that trial was that on his release S.N., as well as his brother and brother's wife, who was his lawyer, were "rejected" (*marime*) and totally ostracized by his family. At the same time, the conditions of his probation stipulated that S.N. could not associate with his family, and he was released early into the custody of his brother and his brother's wife. Ironically, in the end, both U.S. and Roma law were in agreement on the consequences of his "crime" but for opposite reasons. The American legal system viewed S.N.'s family as "criminal associates"; his family, on the other hand, viewed S.N. and his brother as *marime* for rejecting Gypsy culture. Nevertheless, the strength of Gypsy culture has always been its ability to keep its closely knit ties, and today S.N. and his brother are back in the bosom of the family.

As the world changes into the next millennium, more people than ever before in human history are on the move as migrants, immigrants, guest workers, refugees and even as tourists. At this time in history, many people are living in places that do not share their cultural and legal traditions. Studies of society and legal systems must search for ways to deal with this cultural encounter. Gypsies have probably the longest recorded history of continuous movement and adaptation to other societies and cultures. Their treatment is a barometer of justice and civilization.

Review Questions

1. What aspect of the "crime" committed by a young Gypsy man is due to cross-cultural difference, according to Sutherland?

2. How did the police interpret the lists of social security numbers and other evidence found in the young man's apartment? How did their interpretation of this evidence differ from the Gypsies'?

3. How does this case illustrate the role cultural anthropologists can play in everyday American life?

4. Can you think of other cases where immigrants or culturally different people run afoul of American substantive law?

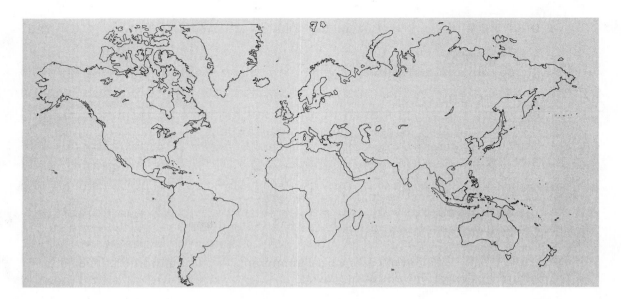

25

Law and Order

James P. Spradley and David W. McCurdy

When we consider U.S. law, we are likely to think of formal written statutes, police, courts, lawyers, strict rules of evidence, the determination of guilt, and punishment. In our large society the system seems technical and impersonal. In this selection, Spradley and Mc-Curdy discuss the structure of law in the context of fieldwork conducted by anthropologist Laura Nader, who did research in the Zapotec community of Ralu'a. They discuss several legal cases to illustrate such concepts as substantive and procedural law, legal levels, and legal principles. They conclude with Nader's argument that Zapotec law seeks "to make the balance," to attempt a settlement between disputants that will promote social harmony.*

((•—|Listen to the **Chapter Audio** on **myanthrolab.com**

The Land Rover disappeared in a cloud of dust on its way back to Oaxaca City. The anthropologist adjusted the shoulder straps on the backpack, turned away from the end of the road, and began to follow the two Zapotec Indian guides. The trail led north, climbing along the edge of steep valleys, crossing over mountain ridges, and winding back and forth to make a steady gain in altitude. Accustomed to living at 5,000 feet above sea level, the two guides walked rapidly, oblivious to the hard breathing of their American companion. In every direction, scattered over much of the 36,000 square miles of Oaxaca State in southern Mexico, the anthropologist knew there were small Zapotec villages. The three of them headed toward the Rincon district, which means "the corner," calling attention to the fact that the area is partially

*"Law and Order" was written by James P. Spradley and David W. McCurdy.

encircled by three high mountain peaks. As they walked, the anthropologist could see the distant and formidable Zempoateptl Mountain reaching to more than 10,000 feet; Maceta and El Machin, the two other peaks, would come into view before they reached their destination, the pueblo of Ralu'a. One of the Zapotec men spoke Spanish and had told the anthropologist as they started, "We are called the people of the corner, *Rinconeros,* because we live between the peaks." The sun was high on this day in early May 1957 and the sky clear; it was several weeks before the rainy season would begin. Wild orchids were in bloom everywhere. The mountains had a kind of awesome beauty for the anthropologist, particularly since she had anticipated the sight for many months. As she walked behind the guides, she wondered why no other social scientist had ever come before to this place, to live and study among these people.

The Zapotec guides pushed on, stopping only for water now and then at the edge of fast-flowing mountain streams. During the first hour they had passed scattered fields of coffee plants in bloom and sugarcane, evidence that a pueblo or homestead was nearby, enfolded in some mountain niche. The anthropologist would like to have stopped to inquire about these settlements and to rest, but the two guides never hesitated, pressing on toward their destination. The sun had already disappeared behind the highest peak when, after a 3½-hour walk, they came to Ralu'a, a pueblo of 2,000 people. Unexpectedly, as they came over a rise, houses appeared everywhere; children played on the paths, and women could be seen carrying firewood. The anthropologist felt a sense of excitement as she looked down on the town that would be her home for many months to come. Here she would live and work and make friends; from here she would travel to other villages and nearby settlements in her efforts to discover the cultural ways of the Zapotec; and here she would try to understand Zapotec law, to describe the cultural rules these people used when settling disputes.

As they entered the edge of the pueblo, she wondered how these people would receive her. Would they understand why she had come? In Oaxaca City she had met an engineer, a government employee who had friends in Ralu'a. He had made tentative arrangements for her to stay with a family while she conducted her field study. All was excitement at the home of her hosts, for a fiesta was in progress to celebrate the return of religious pilgrims from the Sanctuario in Veracruz. Her hosts seemed polite but not enthusiastic as they invited her to join them in the fiesta meal of special foods. After they had eaten, the head of the household came to her and asked, "Are you a Catholic? If you are not a Catholic, you cannot stay here. We do not want Protestants in our town." Surprised by this question, she explained her role and assured him that she belonged to the original Catholic church (Eastern Orthodox).

It would be many weeks before she would fully appreciate what lay behind this simple question about her religion. She was to discover that it concerned authority, conflict, and the process of law and dispute settlement, the very areas she had come to investigate. Before two weeks had elapsed a message came from the priest: she was to come to his house immediately. She entered and, after a brief exchange in Spanish, he said, "You are a Protestant missionary! Why have you come to our pueblo?" Nothing would convince him that it was not so; even the letter of recommendation that she brought from a priest in Oaxaca was dismissed as a fake, and a wire of confirmation from that priest that she was an anthropologist and a good Christian did not convince him. Although others would eventually accept her, the priest in Ralu'a would remain unconvinced, spreading the word from the pulpit and in the streets that she was really a Protestant missionary. Several years earlier some missionaries had come to Ralu'a and, as a result of winning converts, conflicts erupted that led to burning of Protestant homes. The dispute reached enormous proportions for this small pueblo and was only settled through the process of law when the state government forced the town to pay heavy fines for damage inflicted.

When the anthropologist was called to the home of the priest in the Zapotec pueblo of Ralu'a, she became a party to a dispute. He accused her of being a Protestant missionary; she denied it. Although she appealed to another priest to confirm her identity, he did not have the authority to settle the dispute. Like many troubles that beset human interaction, this dispute was never settled, and the anthropologist had to work around the difficulties it created with other individuals in the village. The dispute remained below the level of the law, but it is conceivable that the priest or the anthropologist could have appealed to some agent whose authority was recognized and who could settle the case. It would then have become a legal matter.

One of the earliest disputes that came to the anthropologist's attention occurred at a Ralu'a well several months after she arrived among the Zapotec. She awoke as usual one morning to the sound of the women in the household getting ready to go to the mill. It was 5:00 A.M., and each morning at this time the women in Ralu'a arose to take their corn to nearby mills. The men were still asleep as the anthropologist dressed and prepared to go with the women. It was not yet light at this hour of the morning, but the daily walk to the mill was exhilarating. Other women greeted them and, at the mill, while they waited to have their corn ground, they visited with each other. Soon each would return home to prepare tortillas, fix breakfast for the family, and make lunches for the men who must walk many miles to their fields for a day of work. But now they caught up on the local news and enjoys visiting.

This morning two women were earnestly discussing an argument that had occurred on the previous day at Los Remedies, one of the town wells. Carmen had gone to the well to wash the family clothes, and instead of using the flat slab of stone that belonged to her, she selected one near a friend so they could visit as they worked. Life other women she looked forward to this task because it enabled her to visit and gossip with others in the neighborhood, a pleasant change from working alone inside her house. But hardly 20 minutes had passed when the owner of the washing stone appeared, and instead of taking another place she angrily asked Carmen to move. As Carmen began to gather her wet clothes together, she loudly commented on the other woman's generosity. Insults began to fly, and the situation became especially tense when Carmen "accidentally" splashed water on the newcomer's dress as she went off to finish washing on her own slab. Some said Carmen should have moved to her own stone without, comment; others declared that the second woman was wrong and should have gone quietly to another place to wash. Someone recalled a similar conflict several years earlier when a woman had taken the matter to the *municipio,* or town hall, where the *presidente* had settled the dispute. Some of the women wondered whether the trouble of yesterday would go that far.

It was the end of the summer before the dispute over washing stones reached the boiling point and became a case of law, but it did not happen in the way the anthropologist had expected, for no one took the dispute to the *municipio.* The incident at the well did not die down; the two women continued to make insulting remarks in public, and others began to take sides. Then a similar conflict arose between several other women who were not using the stones that belonged to them. At night in the *cantina* as the men drank *mescal,* an alcoholic drink made from the fermented juice of agave plants, they talked of the disputes they had learned about from their wives. Some men reported that at the wells where their wives washed clothes no such fights had occurred; everyone agreed that the problem was primarily at Los Remedios.

The bickering and fighting continued until one day people noticed that the water at Los Remedios had begun to dry up. Some said this was caused by the fighting.

The men who belonged to the Well Association, a group that worked to maintain the wells, called a special meeting and decided that they must take action to save the water. They formed a work party and improved the well to ensure more water, but they also removed all the slabs of stone used for washing. In place of these privately owned washing places they constructed 24 shallow tubs from cement and announced that no one could own or reserve one of these spaces. They belonged to the well and were to be used on a first-come, first-serve basis. The priest blessed the new well, and the disputes were settled. Although some women complained that they liked the old way better, everyone recognized the authority of the men's Well Association, and the change was accepted. . . .

The ethnographer who investigates the process of law in a non-Western society must collect data on all kinds of disputes. Since any conflict can be transformed overnight into a legal dispute involving some agent with recognized authority, it is important to examine the range of ways that people handle such troubles. By means of various ethnographic discovery procedures, one begins to focus more and more on legal cases, those that are settled by people or groups with authority.

The Structure of Legal Culture

By examining dispute cases, observing their outcome, and questioning the parties involved, one can describe a goodly portion of the law ways of a community. Such legal knowledge can be analyzed into three different aspects. First, the most explicit aspect of legal knowledge includes *substantive law* and *procedural law,* which are interrelated. At a more implicit level, underlying these rules, are the fundamental *legal principles* that determine the shape of the law in a particular society. Finally, there is a common core of *cultural values* that influence the legal principles and link the law of any culture to other domains of that culture . . .

Substantive law

The term "law" is most often used in our own society to refer to substantive law, the legal statutes that define right and wrong. Phrases such as "He broke the law" or "It is illegal to bring liquor across the state line" refer to substantive law. It is easy for us to assume that substantive rules can be equated with written statutes, but this is not always the case in our own society, and most of the world's cultures do not have written laws at all. But all people have agreed on substantive rules. Let us look at an example of an unwritten law from our own society.

Until recently every city in the United States had passed legislation that made it a crime to appear drunk in public. For many years in the city of Seattle this substantive rule was used to make more than 10,000 arrests each year. Although the law against public drunkenness seems clear and simple, ethnographic investigation of individual cases in Seattle shows that many other substantive rules of a complex nature were actually being used. In practice, the police used their own discretion to arrest some drunks but not others. The unwritten rule was, "if you see a poor man on skid row who is drunk, arrest him; those of the middle and upper class who are drunk in other parts of town need not be arrested." A tramp from skid row who had been arrested many times reported the following experience. Standing outside the University Club located several blocks from skid row, he observed men coming out of the club in states of obvious intoxication. A policeman not only saw the same men, but assisted them into cabs for transportation home.

The substantive law of Ralu'a contains many specific rules. Some are part of a written legal code, others must be inferred from what people say and do in dispute cases. Many cases end up in the town hall, the *municipio,* a two-room, adobe building in the center of town. Here certain officials hold a kind of court to settle disputes. Thirteen respected men make up an advisory group for the pueblo, the *principales.* Each year this group nominates three men for the position of village chairman, or *presidente,* one of whom is elected by the village to serve for 1 year. The *presidente,* in turn, appoints these same *principales* for another 1-year term. Working closely with the *presidente is* a man elected to the office of *sindico,* who runs the communal work program of the pueblo and is also head of the town police. There are 12 *policia* who serve under two lieutenants and a chief of police. Each year the outgoing men of this police force nominate other men, generally those who have been the biggest troublemakers during the year, to take over as replacements. They are then elected by the village as a whole, and the roughest man of all becomes the chief of police for the year. The *presidente* and the *sindico,* working together, handle minor disputes such as drunkenness, fighting, flirting, slander, boundary trespass, and theft. There is a third elected official, the *alcalde,* a kind of justice of the peace, who presides over more serious disputes. The *presidente* will often pass more serious cases as well as any cases that he cannot resolve directly to the *alcalde.* More serious cases or those that *alcalde* cannot resolve are passed on to the district court. While the *presidente* and the *sindico* have various duties, the *alcalde* deals only with legal matters. We can see substantive law in action among the Zapotec if we examine two specific cases.

The case of the flirting husband

The first dispute involves a violation of rules that prohibit flirting. An unmarried woman, Señorita Zoalage, came to the *presidente* early on a Tuesday morning. She complained that a married man, Señor Huachic, had flirted with her. He appeared outside her house and made the equivalent of American wolf-calls shortly after dark on Monday night on his way home from the market. The *presidente* talked over the matter with the *sindico,* and someone was sent to notify Señor Huachic to appear in court that afternoon. It was now 2:00 P.M. and the *presidente* sat behind a long table at the front of the *presidencia,* one of the rooms in the town hall. Both Señor Huachic and Señorita Zoalage sat before him. After presenting the complaint to Señor Huachic, the *presidente* waited for his response. "Yes," he admitted, "I did what she said, but only because this woman here, Señorita Zoalage, flirted with me last week! She even invited me to come with her to collect firewood!" After some discussion about the particulars of the case the *presidente* said, "Señorita Zoalage, I am going to fine you 30 pesos for flirting with Señor Huachic. And Señor Huachic, you are fined 60 pesos for flirting with Señorita Zoalage. You are a married man and should have been at home with your wife." After warning them to refrain from further exhibitions of such behavior he dismissed them, they paid their fines, and returned to their homes. Each had violated a substantive rule that holds flirting to be illegal. In some cases individuals refuse to pay fines and, as a result, may be detained in jail or compelled to work on a community project.

The case of the disobedient son

The second case sheds light on substantive rules involving the relationships between parents and children. It was relatively easy to elicit cultural rules for this relationship. For example, one evening after the anthropologist had been in Ralu'a for 8 months, she was having dinner with a Zapotec family. The father had just told the others about a son who had been sent to jail in the district capital because when his father had beat him he had struck back, hitting his father. The anthropologist asked quizzically, "And for this they sent him to jail?"

"Of course," he said, looking rather surprised that she would ask such a stupid question.

"But," she said, seeking to enlarge on the discussion, "many men beat their wives, and they never go to jail for that!"

"Yes," the father responded, "but wives are one thing, fathers another."

It seemed a good place to introduce a hypothetical question and so she asked, "But what if the father beats his son harshly, and the father is in the wrong? Is it still wrong for the son to strike his father?"

The son in the family spoke up, entering the discussion with a serious tone, "Fathers are never in the wrong for beating their sons. They always do it for their own good."

Still not satisfied, the anthropologist asked one last question, "All right, but sons grow up and become men. Under your law could a father ever be proved guilty for doing wrong to a son, even if he is a grown man?"

The father's answer brought looks of agreement from the others, "A father cannot do wrong with his children." There the discussion ended, but several days later she observed a case in the *presidencia* that underscored this substantive rule of Zapotec law.[1]

Señor Benjamin Mendoza Cruz had complained to the court about his son, Clemente Mendoza, who was 25 years of age. Because the complaint had been made several days earlier, both men were sitting before the *presidente*. Señor Cruz repeated his charge. "I have coffee planted on my land near one of the neighboring *ranchos*. Someone harvested some of my ripe coffee beans, and I thought the thief was from the neighboring pueblo, but a woman who has the land next to mine said she saw my son harvesting the coffee. I demand that he repay me for the coffee he has stolen,"

The *presidente* turned to the son, Clemente Mendoza, waiting for him to speak. His eyes were on the floor; he did not look at the *presidente* or his father as he spoke. "Yes," he said, "I admit that I went to his field and cut some coffee. A year ago he allowed me to cut some coffee on his property, and I was confident he would give the coffee to me, but I am at fault, and now he can decide how to punish me. I have committed a crime against him and now I wish he would forgive me." There was a long pause when the son finished speaking. The *presidente* sat silently as the secretary continued writing. Then the father spoke slowly. "I am, as his father, very sad that my son Clemente should have done this wickedness to me. I did not believe that it was he until the woman told me. Now I will leave it to his *Municipio Presidente* to decide what is suitable. As his father I have to help him and look after him, but he should not act this way, disposing of the fruit of my harvest without my consent."

Another period of silence followed; flies buzzed noisily around the room. It was warm and the *presidente* thought about the man and his son, how he would settle the case. He recalled that fathers should provide for their sons when they came asking for a bride price, but Señor Cruz had already given more than once to his son for this purpose; Clemente had spent it on other things. Yes, it was the son who was at fault.

---

[1]This case is presented in the excellent ethnographic film *To Make the Balance*, Berkeley: University of California Extension Media Center, and also in "Styles of Court Procedure: To Make the Balance," in *Law in Culture and Society*, Laura Nader (editor), Chicago: Aldine, 1969.

He turned to him now. "Now you heard what your father said, and I will tell you that your father does not have an obligation to give you, his son, *anything.*" He raised his voice on the last word as if to emphasize the great distance between fathers and sons. He continued, "Nor is a father obliged to give you what is his. If a father loves his son very much, he may give him something, but nobody can force him to do so. Now, you have abused him and, as you have admitted, there is no reason why your father should help you because you committed this wrong." Clemente Mendoza had been afraid of his father all of his life. After his mother died, his father remarried, and he found it even more difficult to get along with the old man. Now he sat in silence, his eyes shifting nervously, focused on the floor most of the time as he listened to the *presidente* ask, "Are you now both ready to come to an agreement?" They would accept his settlement.

"Clemente Mendoza," the *presidente* addressed the guilty son, "you shall repay your father for the coffee that you took without permission. Without delay you have to deliver the 25 pounds of dried coffee to your father, and the deadline is Friday, the 21st of this month, and for the wrong you have committed I impose on you a 200-peso fine, which you have to pay today." The secretary prepared an agreement that finalized the ending of the dispute, and it was soon ready for signing. More than an hour had passed since they first appeared before the *presidente.* The agreement showed the amount Clemente would repay his father as well as the fine payable to the *municipio.* The agreement was shown to both parties, and the *presidente* addressed them one more time.

"Clemente Mendoza, you should realize that both you and your father are bound by this agreement; you should not inflict reprisals on your father or stepmother, and you must realize that your father has the right, as a father, to correct any of your faults. You, as his son, must ask him for full permission to harvest some coffee or give you anything else, to avoid being offensive to your father. You should now go and behave as a good son should behave."

Turning to the father he said, "Señor Cruz, whenever you desire you can dispose of your property and give it to your son, you can help him in mutual agreement, but the father does not have any obligation to give his son anything; on the other hand, the son cannot demand his father to give him any of his property. It is entirely in the hands of the father whether he wants to give or not."

The two men, father and son, signed the agreement and turned to walk out of the *municipio.* It had been a rare occurrence for a father to bring his son to court. Most disputes of this sort are easily settled by the authority of the father. Although all sons feel the constraints of the father's authority, they know they will one day marry and have sons of their own and, like their father, require total obedience.

Procedural law

When a dispute moves into the settlement stage, numerous procedural rules come into play. Procedural law refers to the agreed-on ways to settle a dispute. They guide not only the *presidente,* the *sindico,* the *alcalde,* or other authority agent, but also the parties to a dispute. Take, for example, the unwritten procedural rule about who should bring family disputes to the court. Although a large number of family cases are brought to the *presidente*'s court, only certain classes of persons would think of settling such disputes in the court. The *principales,* for example, are some of the most respected men in Ralu'a, and they take pride in their respectable families. Undoubtedly their authority in the pueblo enhances their authority within their families, giving them the power to arbitrate and settle any disputes that may arise. If any member complained about family problems in court, it would bring shame and dishonor to the entire family. There is, therefore, considerable social pressure to keep members abiding by the unwritten procedural rule that says that *principales and their families should not* use *the court to settle family disputes.* If the wife of a *principale* were to appear in court making a complaint against her husband, the *presidente* would be greatly surprised, and news of this event would quickly spread throughout the pueblo. Everyone would know that she had violated an implicit procedural rule of Zapotec law.

Procedural rules in U.S. society

Procedural rules in our own legal system are not always clearly specified. The ethnographer seeks to make these rules explicit, thereby shedding light on substantive rules and the entire process of law. The ethnographic research among the tramps in Seattle, Washington, mentioned earlier, revealed an implicit procedural rule that held enormous significance for this population. It involves a procedural rule for sentencing that can be stated as follows.

> *If a man is poor and has been arrested many times for being drunk in public, he shall be sentenced with greater severity than those with money or with no record of previous arrests for drunkenness.*

On the basis of this rule, two men could be arrested at 10:00 P.M. on Monday on the same block in Seattle and plead guilty in court to public drunkenness. One would be given a 2-day suspended sentence and would walk out of the courtroom a free man. The other would be given 90 days in jail. Why this difference? The first man had not been arrested for this crime during the preceding 6 months, whereas the other had been arrested seven times.

The most significant part of this procedural rule, however, involves differences in wealth. Take two men, for example, who were arrested 10 to 15 times each year for public drunkenness. Each time they were picked up by the Seattle police they had to spend several hours in the jail "drying out." Then both men were allowed to post a $20 bail, *if they had the money.* Only one of the men had this amount, and he alone was immediately released from jail. He might be arrested again within a few days or weeks and repeat the process. Over the course of 15 or 20 years such a man might spend several thousand dollars for bail, each time walking away from jail after a few hours of sleep. Although a man who posted bail was expected to appear in court for his arraignment, no one did, choosing instead to forfeit this money than face a judge and possible jail sentence. The man who could not post bail, on the other hand, waited several days in the drunk tank, appeared in court, pleaded guilty, received his sentence, and then returned to the jail to serve his time. Thus violation of the same *substantive rule* can lead to enormously different consequences, depending on the nature of related *procedural rules.* . . .

Legal Levels

In every culture the existence of different kinds of authority agents means that disputes can be settled at different levels. In our own society a dispute between a teacher and a student can be settled by the school principal. If the dispute continues, it could go to the town board of education. If still unsettled, it might go to the local court and even be appealed to a series of higher courts.

Among the Zapotec, several levels for settling disputes exist. Disputes can be settled by family elders, witches, local officials, the priest, supernatural beings, or officials in the *municipio*. If all else fails, the dispute can be taken to the district court in Villa Alta. Consider the following case.

Mariano's son Pedro married the only daughter of a family in the Pueblo and went to live with her family. Mariano was pleased with the arrangement because he had helped decide the marriage. But soon trouble began to develop between his son and the new wife. It came to his attention directly when his daughter-in-law came to him and complained, "Your son Pedro is always drunk, he does not work now, and he argues with me all the time in the home of my parents." Mariano talked with her for some time and, on the following day, he warned Pedro that he should drink less and live at peace with his new wife. Like any son in Ralu'a, Pedro promised his father that he would change his behavior. However, within a month Mariano's daughter-in-law was back again with the same complaint. This time Mariano was angry. "She is back again so soon," he thought. "This son of mine does not learn from words." Mariano found his son and this time, amidst stern warnings, he whipped Pedro harshly.

The weeks passed and still Pedro did not change. His wife now turned to the *padrinos de pano*, the godparents of the marriage. But their warnings to Pedro were to no avail, and so she went to the priest. He talked to Pedro several times, and it seemed the penitent husband might change with his intervention. Then one night Pedro came home very drunk and began cursing at his wife and threatening her. Then he beat her, and she lay awake most of the night wondering what to do next. The fact that he had beat her was less important than that it was another stage in their deteriorating relationship and evidence that Pedro had not changed. Early in the morning while Pedro was still asleep she went to the *municipio* and made a complaint to the *presidente*. Pedro was cited and appeared in court later that same afternoon. He told the *presidente* that he had been drunk and did not know what he was doing, that he would change his ways, and that he would begin to work regularly in his fields. Pedro paid a fine of 50 pesos and signed an agreement that he would live at peace with his wife.

Disputes such as this can be resolved at various levels and through various remedy agents such as male family heads, church officials, village officials, and even by appeals directly to supernatural beings and individuals who are witches. For example, a man who is having trouble with his wife may go to a witch and say, "Somebody is gossiping about me and every time I come home my wife is after me because she is so upset. Can you do something about this person who is spreading bad tales about me?" The witch will reply, "Pay me 5 pesos and I'll find out who it is and do something about it." But whether a man goes to a witch or to the *presidente*, or whether a woman goes to her father-in-law is not left to happenstance. The procedural rules of a culture's law help define which authorities should be employed for various kinds of disputes.

Legal Principles and Cultural Values

Underlying the settlement of disputes in every society we find legal principles based on the fundamental values of a culture. A legal principle is a broad conception of some desirable state of affairs that gives rise to many substantive and procedural rules. The witness is asked, "Do you promise to tell the truth, the whole truth, and nothing but the truth, so help you God?" We accept the value of telling the objective truth, getting at the facts, and we believe that humans are capable of telling the truth.

In some societies, however, people hold different assumptions, asserting that it is not possible to tell objective truth. In other cultures the value placed on the facts is small when compared to the importance of restoring amicable relationships. In order to understand the decisions authorities make to settle disputes, we need to grasp the legal principles of a culture.

When the Zapotec talk about the characteristics of those wise men who have settled disputes in the proper way, they say, "He knows how to *make the balance.*" This principle means that fault-finding in a particular trouble case is not as important as balancing the demands of all parties and restoring conditions of peaceful coexistence. The men's Well Association did not concern itself with seeking culprits who had violated rules about the use of private property. Instead, they sought to restore peace and prevent future conflicts at Los Remedios. Their goal—*hacer el balance*—to make the balance, was achieved.

The principle of balance does not mean people are never at fault, never violate substantive rules. Instead, it means that disputes are not settled merely by establishing the facts of the case, finding the guilty parry, and administering punishment. When Clemente Mendoza harvested his father's coffee without permission, he was clearly in the wrong. But the *presidente*, acting as a kind of father to the citizens of Ralu'a, sought to restore the balance, to mend the relationship between father and son, eliciting a signed agreement from them that they would not hold grudges and continue the dispute.

The case of fright

To the Zapotec, making the balance means setting disputes with an eye to the future of the relationships involved, not merely an examination of past events. Disputes create difficulties for people, financial losses, bitter feelings, and disrupted relationships. It would be possible to settle disputes without rectifying any of these conditions, but for the Zapotec this would not be sufficient, although the guilty person were given a life sentence for his or her crime. Take the case of Señora Juan. She complained to the *presidente* that she had been working, cutting coffee in the field of Señora Quiroz, when young boy, Teodoro Garcia, had picked on her 6-year-old boy, hitting him. The experience had been so disconcerting to the smaller boy that he had come down with *susto*, or magical fright, an illness involving the loss of one's soul. "My little boy got frightened," she told the *presidente* "and now he yells during the night and has diarrhea because of the fright. I am asking the *presidente* to help me make my little son well again." The *presidente* asked Teodoro Garcia about the dispute, and he answered that the son of Señora Juan was always calling him names and taunting him while he worked. Back and forth the discussion went, but the *presidente* did not seek to discover what really happened; *his goal was not to find out the facts.* He allowed people to express their feelings in the matter. It was difficult to tell who was at fault, but he could easily see that this upset had disturbed the equilibrium in social relationships of all those involved. A boy had *susto* as a result, and the *presidente* knew he could do something about that, restoring the balance required. The poor mother said she needed 30 pesos for the curer. After negotiation, Teodoro Garcia offered to settle for 20 pesos. The case was resolved, the boy taken to a curer, and the balance restored.

Cultural values

Underlying the legal principles of a society are the values that form the basis of social life. Making the balance in settling disputes is based on a widely held Zapotec cultural value of maintaining equilibrium. Direct confrontation between individuals in which one loses and another wins is unsettling to Zapotecans. As expressed by Laura Nader:

> This concern for equilibrium is evident through Ralu'a. Upon my making inquiries as to the motives for witchcraft in Ralu'a, an informant reported the following as causes: "because one works too much or not enough; because one is too pretty or too ugly or too rich; for being an only child; for being rich and refusing to lend money; for being antisocial—example, tor refusing to greet people." These are all situations that somehow upset the balance as Ralu'ans see it. It is no wonder that the zero-sum game (win or lose) as we know it in some American courts would be a frightening prospect to a plaintiff, even though all "right" might be on his side. The plaintiff need not worry, however, for the *presidente* is equally reluctant to make such a clear-cut zero-sum game decision variety of reasons—among them that witchcraft is an all too possible tool of retaliation for such behavior. If a plaintiff wanted to play the zero-game he would go to a witch and not to the courts, where behavior is far too public.[2]

No doubt on that first day when the anthropologist entered the pueblo she had somehow upset some unseen sense of equilibrium this Zapotec pueblo. A strange woman, dressed in strange clothes, with a strange reason for being there, asking strange questions; she must be a Protestant missionary, a person with supernatural power, at least someone to arouse suspicion. However, after weeks of persistently defining her role and participating in the daily round of life, she had overcome most of the suspicion and fear. Then one warm day when the excitement of a fiesta filled the air of Ralu'a, she had purchased a large barrel of *mescal* and donated it to the pueblo celebrations. It was a simple token, but the citizens of Ralu'a responded with enthusiasm. Public officials lauded her generosity and declared that she was now a true member of the pueblo. Others apologized for their suspicions and unfriendliness as they drank and laughed together. Without calculation she had *hacer el balance*. . . .

Review Questions

1. What are the definitions of *law, substantive law, procedural law, legal levels*, and *legal principles*? What Zapotec dispute cases illustrate these concepts? Can you think of examples from our own society?

2. Based on the examples cited in this selection, how does Zapotec law differ from U.S. law? Illustrate your answer with specific examples.

3. Some anthropologists believe that every society has some *informal* substantive and procedural legal rules. Comment on this assertion using the Zapotec and American cases presented in this article.

4. Why do you think Zapotec law emphasizes "making the balance" while U.S. law seems more concerned with determining guilt?

[2]"Styles of Court Procedure: To Make the Balance," in *Law in Culture and Society*, Laura Nader (editor), Chicago: Aldine, 1969, pp. 73–74.

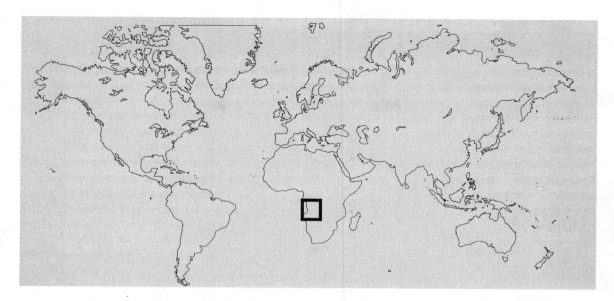

26

Navigating Nigerian Bureaucracies

Elizabeth A. Eames

Anthropologists regularly study different political institutions, from the informal systems of foragers to the more highly structured organization of chiefdomships, kingdoms, and democracies. One important topic of anthropological study is the growth and operation of bureaucracies in complex societies, the subject of this selection by Elizabeth Eames. During fieldwork in Africa, Eames discovered that Nigerian bureaucracies work differently from those found in the West. Whereas the American plan is organized on the principle of what Max Weber called legal domination, one characterized by impersonality and ideally the application of the same rules for everyone, the Nigerian system revolves around patrimonial domination, where transactions depend on establishing and cultivating social relations.*

((•⊣**Listen** to the **Chapter Audio** on **myanthrolab.com**

Americans have a saying: "It's not *what* you know, it's *who* you know." This aphorism captures the usually subtle use of old-boy networks for personal advancement in the United States.

---

*From "Navigating Nigerian Bureaucracies, or 'Why Can't You Beg?' She Demanded," by Elizabeth A. Eames as appeared in *Work in Modern Society: A Sociology Reader,* edited by Lauri Perman (Dubuque, IA: Kendall/Hunt, 1986). Copyright © 1985 by Elizabeth A. Eames. Reprinted by permission of the author.

But what happens when this principle becomes the primary dynamic of an entire social system? The period of three years I spent pursuing anthropological field research in a small Nigerian city was one of continual adjustment and reordering of expectations. This paper discusses a single case—how I discovered the importance personal ties have for Nigerian bureaucrats—but also illustrates the *general process* by which any open-minded visitor to a foreign land might decipher the rules of proper behavior. I was already familiar with Max Weber's work on bureaucracy and patrimony, yet its tremendous significance and explanatory power only became clear to me following the incidents discussed below. Accordingly, the paper concludes with a discussion of Weber's concept of *patrimonial authority*.

I heard the same comment from every expatriate I met in Nigeria—U.S. foreign service officers, U.N. "experts," and visiting business consultants alike: "If you survive a stint in Nigeria, you can survive *anywhere*." The negative implications of this statement stem from outsiders' futile attempts to apply, in a new social setting, home-grown notions of how bureaucratic organizations function. This is indeed a natural inclination and all the more tempting where organizational structure *appears* bureaucratic. Yet in Nigeria, the office-holders behaved according to different rules; their attitudes and sentiments reflected a different moral code. A bureaucratic organizational structure coexisted with an incompatible set of moral imperatives. The resulting unwieldy, inflexible structure may be singled out as one of the British Colonialism's most devastating legacies.[1]

Please bear in mind, the problem of understanding another culture works both ways. Any Nigerian student reading for the first time the following passage by a prominent American sociologist would probably howl with laughter:

> The chief merit of a bureaucracy is its technical efficiency, with a premium placed on precision, speed, expert control, continuity, discretion and optimal returns on input. The structure is one which approaches the complete elimination of personalized relationships and nonrational considerations (hostility, anxiety, affectual involvements, etc.).[2]

Even those well-educated administrative officers who had once been required to incorporate such notions into their papers and exams do not *live* by them.

To many foreigners who have spent time in Nigeria, "the system" remains a mystery. What motivating principles explain the behavior of Nigerian administrative officers? How do local people understand the behavior of their fellow workers? Why do some people successfully maneuver their way through the system while others founder?

Recently I attended a party. As often happens at a gathering of anthropologists, we started swapping fieldwork stories, and meandered onto a topic of our most unpleasant sensation or unsettling experience. That night, I heard tales of surviving strange diseases, eating repulsive foods, losing one's way in the rain forest, being caught between hostile rebel factions or kidnapped by guerrilla fighters. As for me? All that came to mind were exasperating encounters with intransigent

---

[1]One common misunderstanding must be clarified: *bureaucratic organization is not a recent Western invention.* Even during the Han Dynasty (3rd century B.C.), China had developed an efficient bureaucracy based on a system of official examinations. This was the start of a "modern" type of civil service system based on merit. It was almost two thousand years before the West adopted such a system, partly inspired by the Chinese example.

[2]Robert K. Merton, *Social Theory and Social Structure* (New York: Free Press, 1969), p. 250.

clerks and secretaries. I began to ponder why these interactions had proved so unsettling.

My discipline—social anthropology—hinges on the practice of "participant observation." To a fledgling anthropologist, the "fieldwork" research experience takes on all the connotations of initiation into full membership. For some, a vision-quest; for others, perhaps, a trial-by-ordeal: the goal is to experience another way of life from the inside and to internalize, as does a growing child, the accumulating lessons of daily life. But the anthropologist is not a child; therefore, he or she experiences not conversion, but self-revelation.

I came to understand my American-ness during the period spent coming to terms with Nigerian-ness. I found that I believed in my right to fair treatment and justice simply because I was a human being. I believed in equal protection under the law. But my Nigerian friends did not. What I found was a social system where status, relationships, and rights were fundamentally negotiable, and justice was *never* impartial. In the United States, impersonalized bureaucracies are the norm: we do not question them; our behavior automatically adjusts to them. But just imagine spending a year working in a corporation where none of these rules applied.

You see, a Nigerian immigration officer will only sign your form if doing so will perpetuate some mutually beneficial relationship or *if he* wishes to initiate a relationship by putting you in his debt. For those unlucky enough to be without connections (this must necessarily include most foreigners), the only other option is bribery— where the supplicant initiates a personal relationship of sorts and the ensuing favor evens matters up.[3]

Hence, Nigeria becomes labeled "inefficient," "tribalistic," and "corrupt." And so it is.[4] Yet this system exists and persists for a profound reason: Whereas in Europe and Asia, power and authority always derived from ownership of landed property, in West Africa the key ingredient was a large number of loyal dependents. Because land was plentiful and agriculture of the extensive slash-and-burn variety,[5] discontented subordinates could simply move on. The trick was to maintain power over subordinates through ostentatious displays of generosity. This meant more than simply putting on a lavish feast—you must demonstrate a willingness to use your influence to support others in times of need. Even now, all Nigerians participate in such patron-client relationships. In fact, *all legitimate authority derives from being in a position to grant favors and not the other way around.*

Actually, only a minuscule portion of my time in the field was spent dealing with Nigeria's "formal sector." My research entailed living within an extended family house-

---

[3]Bribery exists for several reasons: it initiates a personal relationship, unlike a tip, which terminates all intimacy; if not dedicated to "duty," a worker must be given added incentive to perform a service; the poor salary scale aggravated by the unpredictable nature of extended kin obligations means everyone is desperately in search of extra cash.

[4]Corruption is condemned only in the abstract, when far removed and on a grand scale. But anyone and everyone knows someone "well-placed," and that person is now powerful precisely because he or she has been generous. Moreover, one is more likely to be condemned for going by the book than for corruption. If, for instance, the brother of the man married to one of my cousins (my mother's father's sister's daughter's husband's brother) did not see to it that his colleague signed my tax form with the minimum of fuss, life could be made quite miserable for him indeed!

[5]Also known as shifting cultivation or swidden agriculture: small pieces of land are cultivated for a few years, until the natural fertility of the soil diminishes. When crop yields decline, the field must be abandoned. This has obvious implications for the concepts of private property, ownership, and monopoly.

hold (approximately a dozen adults and two dozen children), chatting with friends, visiting women in their market stalls, even at times conducting formal or informal interviews. And during the years spent researching women's economic resources and domestic responsibilities, I came to understand—indeed to deeply *admire*—their sense of moral responsibility to a wide-ranging network of kin, colleagues, neighbors, friends, and acquaintances. Even now, I often take the time to recall someone's overwhelming hospitality, a friendly greeting, the sharing and eating together. Such warm interpersonal relations more than made up for the lack of amenities.

The longer I stayed, however, the clearer it became that what I loved most and what I found most distressing about life in Nigeria were two sides of the same coin, inextricably related.

The first few months in a new place can be instructive for those with an open mind:

Lesson One: The Strength of Weak Ties

My first exposure to Nigerian civil servants occurred when, after waiting several months, I realized my visa application was stalled somewhere in the New York consulate. Letter-writing and telephoning proved futile, and as my departure date approached, panic made me plan a personal visit.

The waiting room was populated with sullen, miserable people—a roomful of hostile eyes fixed on the uniformed man guarding the office door. They had been waiting for hours on end. Any passing official was simultaneously accosted by half a dozen supplicants—much as a political celebrity is accosted by the news media. Everyone's immediate goal was to enter through that door to the inner sanctum—so far, they had failed. But I was lucky—I had the name of an acquaintance's wife's schoolmate currently employed at the consulate. After some discussion, the guard allowed me to telephone her.

Mrs. Ojo greeted me cordially, then—quickly, quietly—she coaxed my application forms through the maze of cubicles. It was a miracle!

"What a wonderful woman," I thought to myself. "She understands." I thought she had taken pity on me and acted out of disgust for her colleagues' mishandling of my application. I now realize that by helping me, she was reinforcing a relationship with her schoolmate. Needless to say, my gratitude extended to her schoolmate's husband, my acquaintance. As I later came to understand it, this natural emotional reaction—gratitude for favors granted—is the currency fueling the system. Even we Americans have an appropriate saying: "What goes around comes around." But at this point, I had merely learned that, here as elsewhere, connections open doors.

Lesson Two: No Impersonal Transactions Allowed

Once on Nigerian soil I confronted the mayhem of Muritala Muhammad airport. Joining the crowd surrounding one officer's station, jostled slowly forward, I finally confronted her face-to-face. Apparently I was missing the requisite currency form. No, sorry, there were none available that day. "Stand back," she declared: "You can't pass here today." I waited squeamishly. If I could only catch her eye once more! But then what? After some time a fellow passenger asked me what was the problem. At this point, the officer, stealing a glance at me while processing someone else, inquired: "Why can't you beg?" The person being processed proclaimed: "She doesn't know how to beg![6] Please, 0! Let her go." And I was waved on.

A young post office clerk soon reinforced my conclusion that being employed in a given capacity did not in and of itself mean one performed it. Additional incentive was required. Again, I was confronted with a mass of people crowded round a window. Everyone was trying to catch the clerk's attention, but the young man was adept at avoiding eye contact. Clients were calling him by name, invoking the name of mutual friends, and so on. After some time, he noticed me, and I grabbed the opportunity to ask for stamps. In a voice full of recrimination yet tinged with regret, he announced more to the crowd than to me: "Why can't you greet?" and proceeded to ignore me. This proved my tip-off to the elaborate and complex cultural code of greetings so central to Nigerian social life.[7] In other words, a personal relationship is like a "jump-start" for business transactions.

Lesson Three: Every Case Is Unique

Mrs. Ojo had succeeded in obtaining for me a three-month visa, but I planned to stay for over two years. Prerequisite for a "regularized" visa was university affiliation. This sounded deceptively simple. The following two months spent registering as an "occasional postgraduate student" took a terrible toll on my nervous stomach.[8] The worst feeling was of an ever-receding target, an ever-thickening tangle of convoluted mazeways. No one could tell me what it took to register, for in fact, no one could possibly predict what I would confront farther down the road. Nothing was routinized, everything personalized, no two cases could possibly be alike.

Lesson Four: "Dash" or "Long-Leg" Gets Results

This very unpredictability of the process forms a cybernetic system with the strength of personal ties, however initiated. *Dash* and *Long-Leg* are the locally recognized means for cutting through red tape or confronting noncooperative personnel. *Dash* is local parlance for gift or bribe. *Long-Leg* (sometimes called *L-L* or *L-squared*) refers to petitioning a powerful person to help hack your way through the tangled overgrowth. To me, it evokes the image of something swooping down from on high to stomp on the petty bureaucrat causing the problem.

Lesson Five: Exercise Keeps Ties Limber

During my drawn-out tussle with the registrar's office, I recounted my problem to anyone who would listen. A friends grown son, upon hearing of my difficulties, wrote a note on his business card to a Mr. Ade in the Exams Section. Amused by his attempt to act important, I thanked Ayo politely. When I next saw him at his mother's home, he took the offensive, and accused me of shunning him. It came out that I had not seen Mr. Ade. But, I protested, I did not know the man. Moreover, he worked in exams not the registry. That, I learned, was not the point. I was supposed to assume that Mr. Ade would have known someone at the registry. Not only had I denied Ayo the chance

---

[6]It turns out that "begging" means throwing yourself on someone's mercy, rubbing one's hands together, eyes downcast, even kneeling or prostrating if necessary, and literally begging for a favor.

[7]Nigerians coming to the United States are always taken aback by our positively inhuman greeting behavior.

[8]A few years later, I timed my registration as a graduate student at Harvard. The result: three offices in twelve minutes! Even a foreign graduate student could probably register in less than a day.

to further his link to Mr. Ade, but ignoring his help was tantamount to denying any connection to him or—more important for me—his mother.

This revelation was reinforced when I ran into a colleague. He accused me of not greeting him very well. I had greeted him adequately, but apologized nonetheless. As the conversation progressed, he told me that he had heard I had had "some difficulty." He lamented the fact that I had not called on him, since as Assistant Dean of Social Science he could have helped me. His feelings were truly hurt, provoking his accusation of a lackluster greeting. Indeed, things were never the same between us again, for I had betrayed—or denied—our relationship.

Lesson Six: Your Friends Have Enemies

Well, I did eventually obtain a regularized visa, and it came through *Long-Leg*.[9] But the problems inherent in its use derive from the highly politicized and factional-ized nature of Nigerian organizations, where personal loyalty is everything.

Early on, I became friendly with a certain sociologist and his family. Thereby, I had unwittingly become his ally in a long, drawn-out war between himself and his female colleagues. The disagreement had its origins ten years before in accusations of sex discrimination, but had long since spilled over into every aspect of departmental functioning. Even the office workers had chosen sides, and would perform only for members of the proper faction. More significant, though, was the fact that my friend's chief antagonist and I had similar theoretical interests. Though in retrospect I regret the missed opportunity, I realize that I was in the thick of things before I could have known what was happening. Given the original complaint, my sympathies should have been with the other camp. But ambiguous loyalty is equivalent to none. Early in the century, Max Weber, the great pioneering sociologist, articulated the difference between systems of *legal* and *patrimonial domination*.

Within systems of legal domination, organized bureaucratically, authority is the property of a given office or position (not an attribute of the person) and is validated by general rules applying to the whole structure of offices. Assignment to an office is based on merit: rights and duties are properties of the office not its incumbent. The system functions according to routine and is therefore predictable and efficient. Great stress is placed on making relationships impersonal.

In contrast, patrimonial authority (from the Latin term for personal estate) pertains to the form of government organized as a more or less direct extension of the noble household, where officials originate as household servants and remain personal dependents of the ruler. Note how the following passage summarizing Weber s characterization of patrimonial administration fits with my own observations of Nigerian life:

> *First*, whether or not the patrimonial ruler and his officials conduct administrative business is usually a matter of discretion; normally they do so only when they are paid for their troubles. *Second,* a patrimonial ruler resists the delimitation of his authority by the stipulation of rules. He may observe traditional or customary limitations, but these are unwritten: indeed, tradition endorses the principled arbitrariness of the ruler. *Third,* this combination of tradition and arbitrariness is reflected in the delegation and supervision of authority. Within the limits of sacred tradition the ruler decides whether or not to delegate authority, and his entirely personal recruitment of "officials" makes the supervision

[9] I never paid *dash* in Nigeria.

of their work a matter of personal preference and loyalty. *Fourth* and *fifth*, all administrative "offices" under patrimonial rule are a part of the ruler's personal household and private property: his "officials" are servants, and the costs of administration are met out of his treasury. *Sixth*, official business is transacted in personal encounter and by oral communication, not on the basis of impersonal documents.[10]

Weber himself believed that bureaucracy would supplant patrimonial authority. He believed that the world was becoming progressively more rationalized and bureaucratized. But there are several different dimensions along which I dispute this contention:

Bureaucracy has been invented, declined, and re-invented, several times over the millennia.

We have seen how patrimonial ties persisted within a bureaucratic structure of offices in Nigeria. This is also true in America. Within certain organizational structures, personal loyalty remains important, favoritism prevails, connections count, and nepotism or corruption abounds. For instance, urban "political machines" function according to a patrimonial logic. Bureaucracy and patrimonial-ism may be opposite poles on a continuum (Weber called them "ideal types"), but they are *not* mutually exclusive. Most institutions combine both types of authority structures, with a greater emphasis on one or the other. Personal connections can help in either society, but in America, their use is widely perceived as *illegitimate*.

The system I have outlined is not irrational by any means—but rational actions are based on a different set of assumptions.

Ties of kinship and clientship have an ally in human nature.

By the latter, I mean Weber's ideal types cannot be mutually exclusive for emotional/cognitive reasons: an individual's cognitive understanding of hierarchy is necessarily patterned on the relationship between infant and caretaker. Whatever the form of the earliest pattern (and child-rearing practices vary tremendously between and within cultures), it leaves a residual tendency for personal attachment to develop between authority figures and dependents. Clients in the Unemployment Office naturally wish to be considered individuals and resent cold, impersonal treatment. Each bureaucrat wages his or her own private struggle with the temptation to treat each case on its merits.

This is why most Nigerians' finely honed interpersonal skills stand them in good stead when they arrive in the United States. They easily make friends with whomever they run across, and naturally friends will grant you the benefit of the doubt if there is room to maneuver. The psychological need remains, even in our seemingly formalized, structured world, for a friendly, personable encounter. On the other hand, anyone adept at working this way suffers tremendous pain and anxiety from the impersonal enforcement of seemingly arbitrary rules. For instance, a Nigerian friend took it as a personal affront when his insurance agent refused to pay a claim because a renewal was past due.

Once I learned my lessons well, life became much more pleasant. True, every case was unique and personal relationships were everything. But as my friends and allies multiplied, I could more easily make "the system" work for me. As a result of my

---

[10]Max Weber quoted from Reinhard Bendix, *Max Weber: An Intellectual Portrait* (Berkeley: University of California Press, 1960), p. 245; emphasis added.

Nigerian experience, I am very sensitive to inflexible and impersonal treatment, the flip-side of efficiency.

Leaving Nigeria to return to Boston after *2 and a half* years, I stopped for a week in London. I arrived only to find that my old college friend, with whom I intended to stay, had recently moved. Playing detective, I tried neighbors, the superintendent, directory assistance. Tired and bedraggled, I thought of inquiring whether a forwarding address had been left with the post office. Acknowledging me from inside his cage, the small, graying man reached for his large, gray ledger, peered in, slapped it shut, and answered:

"Yes."

"But . . . what is it?" I asked, caught off guard.

He peered down at me and replied: "I cannot tell you. We are not allowed. We must protect him from creditors."

I was aghast. In no way did I resemble a creditor. Noticing my reaction, he conceded: "But, if you send him a letter, *I* will forward it."

Bursting into tears of frustration, in my thickest American accent, displaying my luggage and my air ticket, I begged and cajoled him, to no avail. I spent my entire London week in a Bed 'n Breakfast, cursing petty bureaucrats as my bill piled up. "THAT," I thought, "COULD NEVER HAPPEN IN NIGERIA!"

✓● Study and Review on myanthrolab.com

Review Questions

1. What is the difference between American and Nigerian bureaucracies? How does this difference relate to Weber's concepts of *legal* and *patrimonial domination*?

2. If Nigerians use personal relationships to navigate through bureaucracies, why do such practices as *dash* and *Long-Leg* exist?

3. What are the six features of patrimonial domination suggested by Weber? Do all six apply to the Nigerians?

4. What problems do bureaucracies like the ones found in Nigeria pose for members of the international business world?

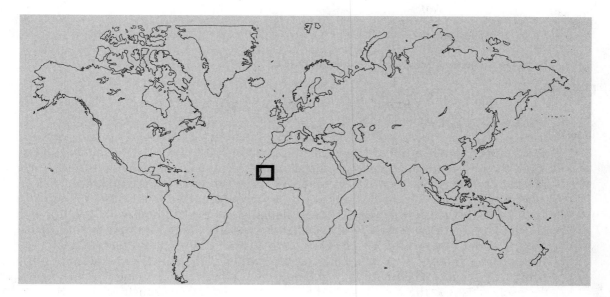

27

Illegal Economies and the Untold Story of the Amputees

Carolyn Nordstrom

Extra-legal networks shape the world around us. In this article by Carolyn Nordstrom, new to this edition of Conformity and Conflict, *we learn about the ability of impoverished people to make a living by engaging in non-legal economic activity. Informal economies— economic activities that are not taxed or monitored by the government, and that are therefore deemed illegal—are often neglected or discounted in attempts to grasp the econo-political dynamics of the world today. Yet in many parts of the world these activities are not only common but are a primary source of income and avenue for the pursuit of financial stability and success. In this chapter, Carolyn Nordstrom takes us to Muleque, Angola, where a group of women united by a shared trauma have banded together in pursuit of this very same goal. All amputees or disabled by land mines, these women may appear to be society's most vulnerable. But Nordstrom and her anthropological lens reveal the ambition, strategy, and impact of their economic efforts in spite of the suffering they have experienced and the crucial role they play in the broader project of national development.*[*]

[*]From Nordstrom, Carolyn. *Global Outlaws: Crime, Money, and Power in the Contemporary World.* 2007. University of California Press. pp. 47–56, "The Untold Story of the Amputee."

((••─Listen to the Chapter Audio on myanthrolab.com

Un-Armed

The truckers quietly moved their diamonds out and loudly moved their beer and commodities into town. The Gov'nor shipped his tomatoes abroad without worrying about how quietly or noisily he worked. The shopkeeper and the street child went about their business, holding down the town's center of commercial gravity. Amid this swirl of activity, other groups of people were redefining the economic landscapes of the country and its worldwide links in ways rarely recognized in business analyses.

These latter business ventures—challenging established notions of legality and nationality, of the divides between civil society, NGOs, and development—are best summed up for me in the example of a group of women amputees I met in Muleque.

The story starts, not with these women, but with the belief that land mines are a military weapon. The mythology of land mines, which is sold along with the mines themselves, is that these explosives deter soldiers and protect sensitive sites. But the truth is that the most common victims arc average civilians looking for food, water, and work. From country to country across the world's militarized zones the same statistics emerge: children playing or going to school, women doing their daily chores, and men engaged in nonmilitary work are those most likely to step on the little metal and plastic units that blow off bits of humanity.

Many people's lives are defined not by whether war continues or peace emerges, but by a chance encounter with violence. A woman who loses her family to attack or a limb to a land mine, finds herself struggling to survive in war and peace alike. These tragedies can happen at the acme of war or long after a peace accord has been signed. In either instance, staying alive suddenly becomes far more tenuous.

Look at me, *the woman said*, I am incomplete for this world. I have no leg, not much of an arm. My heart is strong, and my spirit good. But heart and spirit don't carry water from the river for drinking or firewood for cooking; heart and spirit don't go out and put seeds in the field, get water to irrigate my crops, tend them, and then harvest them. Have you ever tried to do these things with one leg and arm? I have no husband; he left. If I don't do these things, 1 starve and die. There are no wheelchairs out here, no way to get them even if there were. If f have to crawl to carry water, I crawl.

She spits in disgust. This they call war? I won't get into that. There are thousands of us like me around here. But we are going to make a difference.

But Not Defenseless

The group of amputees around Muleque began to congregate, to pool resources, and to help one another. An Irish INGO provided support: seeds and tools, a workshop, and other critical help. The first time I met the women, they had come from far and wide to attend a meeting and seed distribution at their center in town. Walking the long kilometers was the only means of travel they had—a tough ordeal for people who have lost limbs to explosions. The range and barbarity of the land mines available on the world's market was visible in the wounds the women carried. Some had barely the remnants of a leg. Others were missing arms. Some were scarred from face to torso by the shards of metal packed into shrapnel mines. A crutch was generally an impossible luxury; neither the crutches nor the money to buy them were available.

At the center, the women showed me a play they were working on—they had decided to use theater to educate people about land mines. They enacted despair and hope, support and a will to live. They sang of the difficulties of no longer fitting the ideal of a woman—whole in body, capable in limbs, desirable in womanhood—and of the families and men who had stayed to help, and those who had abandoned them; of the suffering and sanguinity entailed in creating a new kind of community of women, with and without families, helping each other. The performance didn't shy away from raw emotions or painful truths. But there was one topic that was left unspoken. Either a person is in the know, or isn't; and thus the knowledge is best left unsaid.

Coming Back from the Dead: Informal Economies and Formal Development

These women had developed survival skills: they cleared farmland and planted crops, built places to live, and established market and barter systems to gain essentials. These are the "informal economies" that governments and INGOs reckon keep the poor alive and the basics of a society intact. This is what the International Labor Organization deems small-scale, low-tech, low-income. But the women had larger plans. They didn't want to eke out the rest of their days hobbling to tiny fields, raising just enough food to keep body and soul together until a drought ended their hopes. They wanted the option to buy prostheses, build decent homes, go into business, and gain the kinds of power that could buy permits and sock away money to cushion them against life's unexpected upheavals.

The Muleque women had several money-making enterprises in mind. They operated what women throughout Southern Africa depend on: a self-run informal banking system. Women who know each other form a group based on stability, trust, and economics. Each month, all the members of the group put a predetermined amount of money into a communal pot, and one woman gets the entire pot that month. The next month the next woman on the rotation gains the entire amount, and so on, throughout the membership cycle. There are no laws or mechanisms to ensure that a member doesn't take her turn to get all the money and then leave the group. That these women's banks are so widespread and enduring is a testimony to the systems of trust and allegiance that can underscore informal economic networks.

With the proceeds of their banking investments, the women amputees were beginning to reap profits: some had been successful at farming and had surplus food. Some began to link into the secondhand clothing industry. And some had plans to begin producing small items to sell, from crafts to business components.

> The trick, of course, is to broaden our markets, *they explained*. Oh, we can sell here. But this is a limited market. We will reach a certain volume and then that's it. We won't grow. We need to be able to sell our products to larger cities. We need to be able to reach Luanda, the capital. We have things that people across the border could use. With these connections, we can really make a go of it.

But as to how they could reach these markets, they remained silent. These were devastatingly poor women, women for whom many days went by when they couldn't scrape together enough to eat. Their impaired mobility made the normally difficult task of walking and trying to hitch rides across the country seemingly impossible. As women, they didn't have the networks of access that men who work in government, transport, or mining and industry have—networks where a friend who is making a flight or a truck run might let him bring his products along. To find the money to pay for such "help" was a distant dream.

The women's silence wasn't due to lack of ideas, but discretion. The story unfolded only when I sat talking to a local coordinator for an INGO working with the amputees. This woman, whom I'll call "Leli," had lived her whole life in the Muleque area and knew it well. She wasn't sure why she had escaped stepping on a mine or stopping a bullet, but she threw herself into helping these women and her community tirelessly. She was a font of enthusiasm, hard work, and dedicated vision. Leli and the hundreds of thousands like her who work beyond the pale of CNN and the *Times* of London give lie to tossed-off statements by Westerners that humanitarian aid produces complacent and dependent populations. I spoke to Leli in the small mud-walled room where she worked. She leaned across the rickety wooden table that served as her desk, taking my hand periodically as if to envelop me in the vitality of her work:

> These are the women who are not supposed to make it—the women who fall off the margins. How does a woman make it in this kind of life . . . a life where a healthy woman with all her limbs finds it hard. There are few precedents for women breaking out of traditional roles and forging new communities of all-women support. So these land-mine victims are sort of expected to fall off the map. But they don't.
>
> They start up farming and making small things they can barter for essentials. And then they start up with the ideas. They have talked with every trader who comes through here, and they know the markets in the next big city, in Luanda, across the border in Congo. They know what is available, what is desirable, and what the prices are. They have tailored their enterprises and products to suit these markets. And they are ready to sell. All they need is transport.
>
> They have come to me to ask if I can take their goods on a flight to Luanda. They know that because I work with the INGO, I have access to flights and cargo rights. They know these flights are safe. And they know they can trust me. They have offered to cut me in on the business for this. I think it's an excellent idea. I am proud of the women. In truth, these INGO flights bring in seeds and tools to keep these women alive. But this is sheer subsistence. They give only enough to keep people alive. They live at the minimum. There is no real way in this scheme to improve, to grow, to gain some prosperity. If the INGO closes shop and moves, these people are left at the margins.
>
> To use my rights as a worker for an INGO, to carry these women's products to the capital, this is development. Now these women have a real chance. I am really moved by what they are doing, they are succeeding where no one expects them to. I'm glad to be a part of it. Now women in my hometown may actually make it.

The women's ambition to group together, form banking and entrepreneurial systems, and move from local and subsistence to inter/national profit making is part of a larger ethos. It is neither haphazard nor reactionary; it follows a carefully crafted plan of development. It is not that the women just want to create a new market for their goods. The market is not the goal, but the means to expanding one's business, one's options, and one's opportunities.

Domingas's Story: From Rags to Riches

After speaking with Leli, I grew increasingly curious about women, survival, and the intricacies of enterprise. At a UN program office for health and education, I spoke with Domingas, the only local woman on staff. Domingas exuded the same vibrant concern for her work and her people as Leli did. Both had seen the worst of war and poverty: Leli in the broken bodies left behind, Domingas in seven-day work weeks dedicated to broken families, communities, and economies.

"How do women and societies on the brink of existence make it?" I asked. It is one and the same thing, *she said with a smile.*

Women, Domingas explained, are the invisible center of gravity of the society. Gravity, because while men move more fluidly, women *are* families, in times when men are there and when they are not. As such, they forge the basic links of society: producing food, daily necessities, communal networks, market systems. Where families are centered, infrastructure, health, education, and trade emerge. Invisibly, because women's role in this is generally overlooked.

If women don't make it, families crumble and communities collapse. And perhaps, she added, economies collapse too; one could argue that the foundations of the economy spin out from here. "Let me give you an example," Domingas said:

No one starts out in this place with anything. Well, if you're a woman that's for sure. They start out below the bottom. They carry water for a penny. You see these poor, hungry women in rags carrying a beaten-up old bucket of water for someone, and you think, "There goes a person all of life has forgotten, a person who will live and die carrying that bucket."

But it is not so. She struggles down the road with a plan. When she scrapes together a few pennies, she will begin to make and sell charcoal.

Domingas grabbed a piece of paper and a pencil and began to draw on it. Her formal "professional in an interview with a stranger" demeanor relaxed into informality; she pushed up her shirt sleeves and hiked a foot up on the rung of her chair as she began to draw, and then stopped to chew thoughtfully on her pencil: "Did I," she wanted to know, "really want to understand the whole thing, the way the economy really worked?" She emphasized the word *really*. Her enthusiasm for her work, and her ideas, was contagious. I remember thinking even a stone would say yes to her question. She began her description, outlining it in a flow chart on paper as she explained it in words:

OK, here's the sequence:

1. You begin with carrying water, or some such hard labor.

2. And then move on to making a product to sell at a little "marketplace"—a patch of swept dirt by the roadside or a spot on the ground in the local open market. Maybe you go out and collect wood and make charcoal, or find food, herbal medicines, whatever, in the bush to sell.

3. You scrape together some few pennies. Enough to get by. Enough to join in a women's informal bank.

4. When your turn comes for the whole banking pot, you invest in a bit of farmland and begin harvesting produce to sell. Bananas, for example. Bananas open the door for you to actually make some money. You start selling in the local markets,

reinvesting everything you can to grow. You check out what they are desperate for in the next country. In the places where the "tourist agencies" fly to. And you begin to plan for that trip.

5. You work the markets, trading and selling, bartering and speculating, to get the dollars to pay for that flight to the neighboring country. One hundred bucks per person per flight, 90 cents a kilo for cargo.

"You know the prices?" I asked.

You're missing the point if you ask this. Of course I know the prices. Everyone knows the prices. The bent-over woman in rags carrying that bucket of water knows the prices. This is where we live our lives. It is the stuff of survival.

6. And then you make the trip into the next country.

"Do you worry about visas, permits, taxes?"

Domingas seemed surprised by my question. The system was so well known that the question seemed irrelevant.

This has nothing to do with that kind of economy. This is informal. Daily life. It works because it is not formal. Entire infrastructures work on this.

7. In the neighboring country, you use the profits of your sales to buy what people need and will spend money for at home. Then you fly back home, sell, and continue the cycle, growing at each turn.

8. At some point, you begin to see real wealth. You build a decent house. You buy a car, hire a driver. You begin to put money into your community, provide jobs, develop the place. You give out goods for poor kids to sell in the streets so they can put together enough money at the end of the day to buy some food to eat. You care about schools and clinics for your kids. Your banking group really carries some weight now.

9. Your horizons expand, and you begin to make flights on commercial airlines to Europe to buy more expensive items to sell to those with real money in your community and country. Often, you bring back suitcases of goods and sell them out of your house.

10. And finally, you purchase a boutique and set up a formal business. You begin to pay some formal taxes. You invest in better education and social development for your country and your home region. But you don't give up your networks. You work them all. You send your children to private schools. And you make your own decisions; you have boyfriends, no husband. Like the Gov'nor's girl-friends who run their own businesses under his "protection."

OK, only the lucky make it all the way down this line, *Domingas added*. But people do. It is how we make the system work. How women make it.

Domingas leaned back in her chair and took a deep breath, saying she could use a cup of coffee. As we strolled over to the rustic kitchen in the UN office to make cof-fee, she confided that she didn't normally take time out of her demanding workday to talk to outsiders. "But this needs to be told." Like Leli, she cared deeply about finding solutions. While we were making coffee we ruminated over the process Domingas had just outlined. I asked her if it was only at the end of this, at point 10, that any of these transactions moved into the formal economy. "Of course" she replied. Points 1 through 9 are invisible to all formal economic reckoning.

Coffee in hand, we walked out to sit on the front stoop of the building. As we looked out over the town—the muddy dirt roads carrying nameless dreams, the women wrapped in bright African cloth hauling heavy burdens on their heads and in their hearts, the children trotting along at their sides—Domingas finished her explanation:

> A huge economy forms the foundations of this country, and much of it runs along these lines—along what people call "informal." Consider: $250 billion of imports comes into this country through the informal economy yearly. Those are UN estimates. What does this say about determining economies? About the way people work? About the impact of women?
>
> And the truth is, while the world talks about diamonds and oil, food and clothing are the real profits. These are where the biggest gains are. Remember: along that line of development from carrying water to a boutique, the leap in profits, the juncture where one can finally move from subsistence to capital ventures, is here—it is food and clothing that builds the houses, buys the cars, and launches the businesses.

Pictures of women who have stepped on land mines and lost limbs—women eking out a subsistence living by farming a small plot of land with a hoe and a crutch—are used worldwide to elicit outrage at perfidious weapons, sympathy for the victims, and money for the organizations helping them. The bananas, or charcoal, they sell constitute another stereotypic image of Africa: women on the margins of the economy offering a small homegrown harvest in neatly arranged piles on a mat in a local open-air market. Their earnings are counted up in single-digit figures, their impact left largely uncalculated because of indifference.

Why their stories, their earnings, their networks, and their contributions to development are not added up becomes an interesting question when we take the UN estimate that S250 billion in informal import earnings is made yearly in the country. The $1 million a day in unauthorized diamond earnings in this country pales in comparison. So too does the $1 billion a year lost from oil profits. Indeed, $250 billion rivals the entire GDPs of the countries of this region of the world.

It would seem the amputee women, and all the women working diligently to earn the money to support their families, are central to the economy. Where, then, are the margins?

And where do we place development? Illicit oil and diamond revenues can be easily channeled into foreign bank accounts and businesses, offering little to help this nation. But in the most basic sense, the work of these women is developing the country. Survival follows their footsteps; infrastructure settles in the imprints they make. They move food, clothing, household and industrial goods, and energy supplies. They set up local and international transport routes, and forge markets across borders and countries.

What they do may be deemed informal and even illegal. It is here that the very notion of "extra-state" becomes most interesting: it would seem that real profits, and real development, are to be found in the places economic analysts are not looking. Perhaps we don't look because we would have to reassess our most fundamental—and cherished—ideas about power, and about the morality and the legality of economics and development.

✓●—[**Study** and **Review** on **myanthrolab.com**

Review Questions

1. What kinds of obstacles do the women face in their desire to attain f̶ bility? What are some of the solutions they have come up with to ad̶ obstacles?

2. What role do communal organizations and social networks play in the sequence of economic growth Domingas describes?

3. What are the stereotypes, Nordstrom says, are often associated with the women she is profiling? In her characterization of them, how do these women defy or not conform to those stereotypes?

4. Why do you think that, as Nordstrom argues, these women and their economic contributions tend to be neglected by many economic analysts? What effect do you think this neglect has on their analysis, its accuracy, and the policies it produces?

5. How do Domingas, Leli, and Nordstrom define development? How might their definition be different from other uses of the term?

PART EIGHT

RELIGION, MAGIC, AND WORLDVIEW

READINGS IN THIS SECTION

People seem most content when they are confident about themselves and the order of things around them. Uncertainty breeds debilitating anxiety; insecurity saps people's sense of purpose and their willingness to participate in social activity. Most of the time cultural institutions serve as a lens through which to view and interpret the world and respond realistically to its demands. But from time to time the unexpected or contradictory intervenes to shake people's assurance. A farmer may wonder about his skill when a properly planted and tended crop fails to grow. A wife may feel bewildered when the man she has treated with tenderness and justice for many years runs off with another woman. Death, natural disaster, and countless other forms of adversity strike without warning, eating away at the foundations of confidence. At these crucial points in life, many people use religion to help account for the vagaries of their experience.

Religion is the cultural knowledge of the supernatural that people use to cope with the ultimate problems of human existence.[1] In this definition, the term **supernatural** refers to a realm beyond normal experience. Belief in gods, spirits, ghosts, and magical power often defines the supernatural, but the matter is complicated by cultural variation and the lack of a clear distinction in many societies between the natural and the supernatural world. **Ultimate problems**, on the other hand, emerge from universal features of human life and include life's meaning, death, evil, and transcendent values. People everywhere wonder why they are alive, why they must die, and why evil strikes some individuals and not others. In every society, people's personal desires and goals may conflict with the values of the larger group. Religion often provides a set of **transcendent values** that override differences and unify the group.

An aspect of religion that is more difficult to comprehend is its link to emotion. Ultimate problems "are more appropriately seen as deep-seated emotional needs," not as conscious, rational constructs, according to sociologist Milton Yinger.[2] Anthropologists may describe and analyze religious ritual and belief but find it harder to get at religion's deeper meanings and personal feelings.

Anthropologists have identified two kinds of supernatural power: personified and impersonal. **Personified supernatural force** resides in supernatural beings, in the deities, ghosts, ancestors, and other beings found in the divine world. For the Bhils of India, a *bhut,* or ghost, has the power to cause skin lesions and wasting diseases. *Bhagwan,* the equivalent of the Christian deity, controls the universe. Both possess and use personified supernatural force.

Impersonal supernatural force is a more difficult concept to grasp. Often called **mana**, the term used in Polynesian and Melanesian belief, it represents a kind of free-floating force lodged in many things and places. The concept is akin to the Western term *luck* and works like an electrical charge that can be introduced into things or discharged from them. Melanesians, for example, might attribute the spectacular growth of yams to some rocks lying in the fields. The rocks possess mana, which is increasing fertility. If yams fail to grow in subsequent years, they may feel that the stones have lost their power.

Supernatural force, both personified and impersonal, may be used by people in many societies. **Magic** refers to the strategies people use to control supernatural power. Magicians have clear ends in mind when they perform magic, and use a set of

---

[1]This definition draws on the work of Milton Yinger, *Religion, Society, and the Individual: An Introduction to the Sociology of Religion* (New York: Macmillan, 1957).

[2]Yinger, p. 9.

well-defined procedures to control and manipulate supernatural forces. For example, a Trobriand Island religious specialist will ensure a sunny day for a political event by repeating powerful sayings thought to affect the weather.

Sorcery uses magic to cause harm. For example, some Bhil *bhopas,* who regularly use magic for positive purposes, may also be hired to work revenge. They will recite powerful *mantras* (ritual sayings) over effigies to cause harm to their victims.

Witchcraft is closely related to sorcery because both use supernatural force to cause evil. But many anthropologists use the term to designate envious individuals who are born with or acquire evil power and who knowingly or unknowingly project it to hurt others. The Azande of Africa believe that most unfortunate events are due to witchcraft, and most Azande witches claim they were unaware of their power and apologize for its use.

Most religions possess ways to influence supernatural power or, if spirits are nearby, to communicate with them directly. For example, people may say **prayers** to petition supernatural beings. They may also give gifts in the form of **sacrifices** and offerings. Direct communication takes different forms. **Spirit possession** occurs when a supernatural being enters and controls the behavior of a human being. With the spirit in possession, others may talk directly with someone from the divine world. **Divination** is a second way to communicate with the supernatural. It usually requires material objects or animals to provide answers to human-directed questions. The Bhils of India, for example, predict the abundance of summer rainfall by watching where a small bird, specially caught for the purpose, lands when it is released. If it settles on something green, rainfall will be plentiful; if it rests on something brown, the year will be dry.

Almost all religions involve people with special knowledge who either control supernatural power outright or facilitate others in their attempt to influence it. **Shamans** are religious specialists who directly control supernatural power. They may have personal relationships with spiritual beings or know powerful secret medicines and sayings. They are usually associated with curing. **Priests** are religious specialists who mediate between people and supernatural beings. They don't control divine power; instead, they lead congregations in ceremonies and help others petition the gods.

Worldview refers to a system of concepts and often unstated assumptions about life. It usually contains a **cosmology** about the way things are and a **mythology** about how things have come to be. Worldview presents answers to the ultimate questions: life, death, evil, and conflicting values.

Finally, anthropologists also study and report on the formation of new religions, especially those that occur as a result of deprivation and stress. These **revitalization movements**, as Anthony F. C. Wallace called them in 1956, are "deliberate, organized, conscious efforts by members of a society to construct a more satisfying culture."[3] Revitalization movements are usually related to rapid change that renders a traditional way of life ineffective. For example, when one cultural group becomes dominated by another, rapid change and loss of authority may make its original meaning system seem thin, ineffective, and contradictory. The resulting state of deprivation often causes members to rebuild their culture along what they consider to be more satisfying lines.

---

[3]Anthony F. C. Wallace, "Revitalization Movements: Some Theoretical Considerations for Their Comparative Study," *American Anthropologist* 58, no. 2 (1956): 264–281.

Wallace argued that revitalization movements go through five stages:

1. *A Steady State.* This is a normal state of society in which people, through their culture, are able to manage the chronic stresses of daily life.

2. *Period of Increased Individual Stress.* Individuals in a society experience new stress caused by such events as culture contact, defeat in war, political domination, or climatic change.

3. *Period of Cultural Distortion.* Stress levels continue to rise as normal stress-reducing techniques fail to work. Social organization begins to break down, causing additional stress, and various cultural elements become distorted and disjointed.

4. *Period of Revitalization.* This period is marked by its own stages. First, a prophet or leader comes forward with a new vision of the culture that requires change. Called a *mazeway reformulation,* this vision is intended to produce a more integrated, satisfying, and adaptive culture. This is followed by the *communication* of the revitalization plan and, if it proves attractive, the plan's *organization* for wider dissemination, its *adoption* by many people, its *cultural transformation* of the society, and its *routinization* in daily life.

5. *A New Steady State.* If no additional stresses occur, the society should attain a new steady state at the end of the process.

Although not all revitalization movements are religious—the Marxist doctrine and communist revolution in Russia exemplify a political revitalization movement—most of the world's major religions probably started as revitalization movements, and many smaller sects and movements fit the revitalization pattern today.

The first article, by Rachel Mueller and written for this edition of *Conformity and Conflict*, describes the spirit world in Senegal. In particular, she highlights the role of boyfriend rabs in society and the various individuals—marabouts, priestesses, doctors—people will consult regarding problems caused by rab. She argues that the rab belief system helps Senegalese make sense of their changing world and are unlikely to fade from public consciousness any time soon. The second article, by George Gmelch*, is the latest revision of his earlier classic piece on the use of magic by American baseball players. He looks in detail at the rituals, taboos, and fetishes employed by the athletes. In the third article, Jill Dubisch illustrates the meaning and impact of ritual and pilgrimage. Using the "Run for the Wall," a motorcycle pilgrimage that involves travel from Los Angeles to the Vietnam Memorial in Washington, D.C., as an example, she shows how this difficult motorcycle ride evokes strong emotions and personal transformation among its participants. The fourth article is Horace Miner's classic article describing the body ritual of a North American group, the Nacirema. The Nacirema's concern for the health and beauty of their bodies has led them to establish an elaborate ritual system including the building of holy fonts in their houses and the presence of a variety of ritual specialists.

*Gmelch, G. *Inside Pitch: Life in Professional Baseball* (Smithsonian Institution Press, 2001).

Key Terms

cosmology p. 255
divination p. 255
magic p. 254
mana p. 254
mythology p. 255
personified supernatural force p. 254
prayer p. 255
priest p. 255
religion p. 254
revitalization movement p. 255

sacrifice p. 255
shaman p. 255
sorcery p. 255
spirit possession p. 255
supernatural p. 254
transcendent values p. 254
ultimate problems p. 254
witchcraft p. 255
worldview p. 255

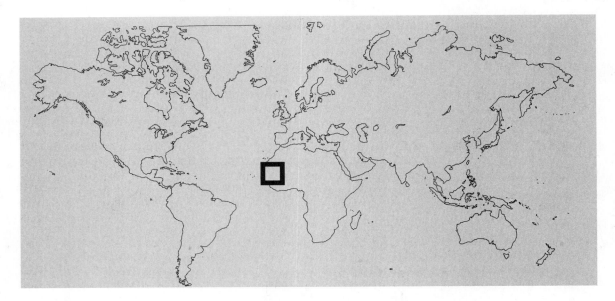

28

The Worst Lover: Boyfriend Spirits in Senegal

Rachel Mueller

The people of Senegal are devout and enthusiastic disciples of Mohammad. But some of them, the Lébou, also claim to live among spirits called rab *who have little to do with Islam. In this article by Rachel Mueller we learn that rab display many of the vices of their human counterparts. Focusing on* faru rab *(boyfriend spirits), Mueller describes how they become attracted to women, their negative effect on women's behavior, and the steps women must take to reject them, including divination, sacrifice, and an expensive dramatic ritual called an* ndepp. *She concludes with a discussion of how rab spirit beliefs fit with Islam and survive in a globalizing Senegal.**

((•─[**Listen** to the **Chapter Audio** on **myanthrolab.com**

During fieldwork in Dakar, the capital of Senegal, I was surprised at how often I talked about lovers. In the city many women, particularly young women and girls, are afflicted by "spirit boyfriends" called *faru rab*. These "rab" spirits have fallen in love with women and, somewhat like their human counterparts, can be possessive, jealous, and vindictive. Their attachment causes their female victims to act strangely and ritual intervention including divination, persuasion, and if necessary, an expensive and dramatic ritual called an *ndepp*, is required to get rid of them.

Senegal has an interesting history that helps explain its present culture and appearance. Around the year 1000, Muslims arrived in Senegal, bringing the Sufi sect of Islam that became the common religion. As a result, Islam is ever present today in the daily life of the city. Most residents pray five times a day and women cover their heads for prayer. Taxis and *car-rapides* (inexpensive public transportation) are decorated with paintings and photos of different *marabout* (Islamic holy men) and other Islamic leaders. Prayer mats lie in the corners of every business.

A second historical influence came about with French colonization in the 1800s. The French established western-style colonial governmental structures that ultimately resulted in the adoption of the French language throughout most of Senegal. Today French is regularly taught in the country's schools and serves as the language of government. Many city residents are bilingual, speaking both French and Wolof. As a result, I was able to conduct interviews in French, a language I speak well, without having to depend upon my beginner level Wolof, the native language of many in the city.

Dakar, which lies on Africa's westernmost coast, is the meeting place between the Sahara desert and the Atlantic ocean. The contrast between the dusty, sandy streets and the heavy, humid air that smells of fish is unsettling at first. The paved freeways with giant concrete overpasses for pedestrians, along with modern-looking hotels and government buildings, speak to the developing infrastructure of a cosmopolitan city. Beachside nightclubs are popular in the evenings, music venues all over the city host a variety of live performances, and Senegalese restaurants (usually with only one menu item per day) can be found at every street corner. Many people have televisions and cell phones.

But there is also a more traditional side to the city. Much of Dakar consists of one and two-story houses that border unpaved sandy streets. A Senegalese culture of *teranga* (hospitality) is predominant. This self-imposed label is fitting as you cannot walk anywhere without being invited to share a meal. No matter your background, your social status, or your destination, the Senegalese will welcome you into their homes and share generously everything they have. Of course you are expected to do the same. It isn't surprising for strangers to ask you to share any food you might be carrying, be it a handful of peanuts or a slice of mango.

Rab Spirits

It is in the Lébou district located in the older part of this bustling city of three million people where I first encountered a rab, although one different from faru rab. My field notes best describe the event.

Khady and I sit together in her living room. The walls are Pepto Bismol pink and seem oppressive in the heat. Khady is a large woman, majestic even, swathed in soft purple fabric. Three teenage girls sit on the floor, taking turns braiding each other's hair in tight cornrows. The TV in the corner displays image after image of wrestling matches, music videos, and news stories. We chat amicably about the unexpected and rapid success of Senegal's newest pop star, Aida Samb.

Abruptly, Khady stops mid-sentence and stares hard out the window. I follow her gaze and see a withered beggar woman standing outside in the street. She is mumbling incoherently and her hands tremble as she steps closer and stretches them in through the window. Khady doesn't move, however. Instead she sits immobile until the tiny woman shivers, turns from the window, and slowly shuffles away.

It isn't until late that evening that Khady told me that the woman was possessed by a rab, a spirit that walks the streets of Dakar. "She resembled a human being," Khady said. "But it [the rab] was not a human. Not totally a human. I did not respond because if you bother him, he can do something to you."

So began my inquiry into the nature of this local Lébou religion. People told me that long ago rab were invisible spirits that inhabited the earth, moving with the wind wherever they pleased. Trees were their homes. Humans lived on earth too, nomadic at this time, migrating with the changing seasons. Soon though, the human communities grew bigger. People learned how to plant crops. More land was needed and people cut down the trees where the rab lived causing the spirits to wander and share the world with humans in a kind of parallel universe.

Rab are thought to resemble people in many ways. They have personalities, genders, professions, and religions, just as humans do. And like humans, rab suffer the same character flaws of jealousy, revenge, and spite. Many rab keep to themselves and don't bother with the human world, but some cross over to establish relationships with people and affect how they feel and act. In some cases they may even possess humans completely. The beggar woman was an example of this type of possession. One Senegalese man told me that when a person is possessed, "you insult people, you hit people, you take off all your clothes, you go around nude. You act like a crazy person, eh!"

The Lébou list several kinds of rab. For example, a "grand rab" named *Madgejuenne* is the protector of Dakar and people search for her benevolent support. *Uyoumouyata* is known to be malicious and is actively avoided. *Luk Daour* is married to *Madgejuenne* and is also a protector. *Mame Diarre* is unpredictable. She seeks positive relationships with humans but is equally likely to attack people. Other grand rab include the females *Kumba Bang, Kumba Castel, Kumba Lamb, Lumbay, Diop,* and *Mboose.* "Tuur" and "rab errant" (or wandering rab) are other kinds of rab. Faru rab are wandering rab that have decided to attach themselves to the human world in the most troublesome ways. They are, in colloquial terms, the worst kind of lover.

Faru Rab

Faru rab fall in love with human beings, particularly women and girls. Although these rab may be attracted to any female, they fall for the same temptations as humans. One of the most common reasons a rab becomes attracted to a woman is based on beauty and her style of dress. For this reason the community advises women and girls to dress conservatively even while sleeping. The following story told to me illustrates this point.

She was a stunningly beautiful woman. Whenever she walked in the streets, heads turned to follow her swinging hips. All the girls were jealous of her. You know what happened to her? Well, her boyfriend came over one day and she said to him, 'I'm coming, just watch T.V.' and she left the room, boiled water, and came back and threw it on him. Just like that! She had a jealous faru rab.

However, as one young woman said to me, following the guidelines in order to avoid the attention of a faru rab isn't easy. "You know the women these days, we don't know how to dress ourselves." She went on to say that rab are especially attracted to women's knees, and if you bare them in public, "they see you in the street, they can love you!" Once they love you, faru rab have otherworldly abilities that affect the lives of the women they are attracted to. They can make a woman refuse to speak to men, give her sexual dreams, trigger infertility, precipitate divorce, or even cause the death of her husband.

Take Laye Fatou for example, a typical Senegalese university student, focusing on her studying, hanging out with friends, and pursuing romantic relationships. When I first met her she was sprawled out on her dorm room bed wearing skinny jeans and a rhinestone studded t-shirt. "He's so cute!" she exclaimed, describing a young man we had seen in the corridor. She feigned fainting and buried her head in her friend's lap. "Did you see how muscular he was?" I nodded and laughed, happy to be welcomed into this gossipy group of Senegalese girls. Four years before, however, Laye Fatou was plagued by a vicious boyfriend spirit who made her life so miserable she had to stop attending school for a year. The faru rab was occupying all of her time. Her life became an endless fight to please him.

She explained how it happened. When she was a teenager, a particularly jealous faru rab fell in love with her. She was swimming at the beach with her friends and attracted him because she was wearing a bikini. "At the beach you go all nude," she told me, clearly exasperated at herself for the obvious oversight. At the time she wasn't convinced that boyfriend spirits could do anything to her, or even that they were real. "But I kept having troubling dreams where he [the rab] would make love to me, sometimes as my friend, sometimes my brother, my father…. And I couldn't get a [human] boyfriend," she said. But after dealing with her strange symptoms for over a year, she had no choice but to believe.

The Marabout

It was then that Laye Fatou visited a *marabout*, or Islamic holy man and healer, in order to determine the source of these mysterious problems. The consultation with the marabout revealed that she had unknowingly become the girlfriend of a spirit. "He had a name, and a face that I could see in my dreams," she told me.

Getting rid of a lover spirit is difficult because love is a strong emotion. One of the skills a marabout has is the ability to communicate with spirits. Through a variety of rituals and divination, the marabout was able to communicate with Laye Fatou's faru rab and determine his likes and dislikes. The marabout found that this spirit, like many spirits, didn't like the color red. Laye Fatou was required to wear red at all times in order to push her boyfriend spirit away. In addition she had to take baths with holy water in the forest several times a day and make two chicken sacrifices. "I didn't even go to school because I was so busy with him [the faru rab]," she explained. Luckily, the marabout persuaded Laye Fatou's rab to leave her without further complications, and she is now a typical engaged college student.

The Ndepp and Ndeppkat

But this wasn't the case for another unfortunate girl, Asu, who was more firmly possessed by a boyfriend spirit. Her family took her to a marabout but his intervention didn't work, which is usual in more serious cases of possession. Convincing a rab to leave its human host alone is a nuanced endeavor, as rab are easily angered. If the marabout does not communicate with the spirit respectfully, the situation can deteriorate, sometimes causing the rab to fully possess a human being. This is what happened in Asu's case.

So what could be done? For Asu the answer was to hold an expensive and elaborate public ritual called *ndepp*. To exorcise a rab, it is necessary to have the expert skills of a priestess called an *ndeppkat*, a kind of female healer who holds one of the most highly respected positions concerning health in Senegal. The rab belief system is one of the only areas where Senegalese women hold this type of power. The priestess employs several disciples who will attend her during the ceremony. She must also arrange to have from three to six drummers to participate at the ritual. She makes arrangements for their housing, food, and clothing for three days.

Priestesses claim they do not choose their profession. They are selected by a rab to be liaisons between the human world and the spirit world. Because of this, they are experts within their work. The ndepp and other ceremonies provide priestesses their only income. This funding source is highly unstable because it is based on the ability of families and individuals to pay. This puts the priestesses in a very uncomfortable situation. "Often you see people who come and have dispensed all of their money at the hospital and they didn't find anything positive. Then they come to [the priestess's] house," one disciple to a priestess tells me. "The priestess calls her disciples. She calls her drummers. She makes arrangements for housing and food and clothing for three days. Afterwards, the family of the sick person still has to give a small fee to them. And the [sick] person doesn't have all of that. So, it's the priestess that has to deal with all of that. She is obliged to heal you," the disciple explains.

The ndepp over which ndeppkats preside are public ceremonies that take place in several different stages. The ndeppkat must first determine what the rab wants (for example, a cow may be sacrificed the day before the ndepp to please the afflicted person's rab). Then as the ndepp begins there will be dancing, drumming, and singing. The rab are called to the circle by the specific rhythm of the drums, which is unique to ndepp rituals. During the ceremony, the ndeppkat priestesses sing various songs, chosen at random though sung in a certain order. A rab will have a song, a *bakk*, which calls to it specifically. This is the moment when the sick person falls into trance. The rab does not possess the individual but rather drives him or her to dance according to the rab's desires. This dancing is pleasing to the rab. All of the steps work together to communicate with the rab, to please him, and put the sick individual's relationship with the rab back into balance. The ndepp ceremony is a delicate process of persuasion that involves convincing the rab to leave the individual alone by discovering what pleases the rab and then offering that to him.

The drumming at an ndepp is overpowering. There are typically three to six male drummers who play several different kinds of drums. The *sabar* is a long, slender drum slung across the body. The drummer stands and walks around playing the sabar with one stick and one hand. He can directly encourage and interact with the dancers because of his mobility. Another drum used is the very small, hour-glass shaped drum called a *tama*. It has strings strung on the outside that when pinched under the arm raise the pitch so the drum seems to 'talk.' This too is used to encourage the dancers. The rhythm for the ndepp drumming is always the same for every ndepp, thus it is easy to know when an ndepp is taking place. However, the choice of songs is determined by the ndeppkat's own rab and thus will vary from one ndepp to the next.

My first exposure to an ndepp involved the effort to cure Asu of her boyfriend spirit. Again my notes reflect the drama of the occasion:

The crowd created a large circle, its edges touching the buildings on either side of the sand covered street. The crowd was seven or eight people deep, the inner circle seated, the rest standing on toes to see over the heads. The roofs of the surrounding houses were full to bursting with people. The sea of faces was made up of women and children. A small altar made of various types of horns stood in the center of the circle in front of the tam-tam (drum) players. The ndeppkat danced around the altar, women frantically singing and clapping hands, encouraging the crowd to do the same. They all wore similar bou-bou dresses, made from the same fabric. Asu's family will have made these dresses for the ndeppkat before the ceremony. La malade, Asu, was dressed in a brown linen robe with a hood. She was seated at the edge of the circle and would occasionally stand to dance. However, she was only able to dance for moments before falling into trance. The head ndeppkat was differentiated from her attendants by the larger number of beads and grisgris she wore across her body. She directed the drummers and the singing, overseeing every movement of la malade. The drums pounded louder and louder, the crowd clapped, sang, and cried out, watching her body shake.

During the course of the ndepp I watched as five different women fell into trance. One woman tried to escape the circle of people as the song changed. "She can feel that this song is the song of her rab and she doesn't want to fall," one young woman told me. Another woman came into the circle, parting the crowd with her flailing arms and legs, already in trance. She danced so quickly and with so much fervor it was clear to the onlookers that something beyond her own body propelled her.

Again my notes describe what happened when Asu eventually fell into trance.

Asu's bare feet pounded the rough concrete. Her dark silhouette danced on the cinderblock walls, thrown into sharp relief from the light of a single florescent bulb outside a neighbor's doorstep. She gathered her ankle-length skirts in her left hand and threw her right hand straight up, palm flat against the sky. The raspy chants sung through the megaphone mixed with the powerful rhythms of the drums reverberated through the crowd. As the sabar drummer pounded the slender instrument with mounting intensity, the woman flung her body into the movements with impossible fervor. It lasted only moments, until her eyes rolled loosely in her head. Her figure was suspended motionless before her arms abruptly fell to her sides and her body began to slump sideways. Before she could collapse to the ground, the other priestesses surrounded her. They carefully supported her weight as they carried her out of the circle of onlookers, drummers, and singers. Asu had fallen into trance. Her boyfriend spirit had called her into the circle to dance. He too had been called to the circle of the ndepp with the rhythm of the drums and possessed Asu when his bakk was sung. Asu danced to please him, to entertain him, while the other priestesses sang and sang.

Unfortunately, I never learned if the ndepp succeeded in driving Asu's boyfriend spirit away.

Can Boyfriend Spirits Co-exist with Islam?

When I first heard about faru rab and other kinds of rab, I couldn't imagine how belief in them could exist in an Islamic nation. Islam dominates religious life in Senegal. The call to prayer echoes off buildings five times a day, competing for space in the listener's ears as multiple mosques project the voices of the imams. The smell of heavy incense wafts out of doorways, reminding believers of the rewards of the afterlife. During prayer time, a delicate suspension takes over as most people cycle through prayer rituals: washing hands, feet, face, kneeling, standing, sitting, fingering lengths of prayer beads, praying softly. The prayer mats are discolored and faded with years of use. During Tamxarit, the Senegalese celebration of the Muslim New Year, families write verses from the Quran on slips of paper to be eaten with the first bite of the evening meal. Islam in Senegal can be heard, smelled, touched, seen, and tasted.

It's useful here to look in broader terms at the nature of Islam and the rab spirit world. In 1964 comparative sociologist Robert Bellah published an article in which he defined general types of religions. One he called *historic*. For Bellah, historic religion is associated with the beginning of cities. It contains two worlds, the natural and divine, and its adherents seek to achieve a divine state when they die through world negation and ritual supplication. Historic religion is led by full-time priests and has congregations. In Senegal, Islam fits this description as does the early Judeo-Christian tradition, Buddhism, and Brahmanic Hinduism in other parts of the world.

Bellah also describes a second religious tradition he called *archaic* religion. This, he felt, was associated with smaller-scale societies that practiced horticulture and agriculture, a single natural divine world, a ritual framed around communication, part-time religious specialists, and cults but no congregations. Rab beliefs in Senegal seem best to fit in this category.

What Bellah didn't discuss was the idea that both of these religious types can exist in the same society without conflict, which I believe is the case in Senegal. As we have seen, rab are present in people's lives and forms of communication including divination and possession are ways to deal with them. In Senegal, if we define this belief as a cult it rests as a peripheral and yet parallel entity in relation to Islam. Islam is the central moral code for people's daily lives in Senegal. Although aspects of the rab cult influence people's behavior, the rab belief system does not offer people an explanation for life, death, or the afterlife. Islam gives counsel on ways to please God and attain a place in Paradise. Islam determines the fate of one's soul. The rab cult, on the other hand, is a religious institution that is a part of life on earth that has no bearing on the afterlife or salvation. It is clearly related to illness and other forms of adversity, and it provides its adherents with a sense of confidence as they seek to manage and control misfortune. In that sense, the two forms of religion complement each other. (Note also that marabout find a role in both religious systems.)

Can Boyfriend spirits survive in the modern world?

Senegal is not isolated and modernization and global ties can conflict with the belief in spirits and its global effects. Young people especially are aware of the modern world through access to the internet and education, and a belief in ever-present spirits does not seem to be part of it. An elder reflected his concern about this:

> *The new generation believes* [in spirits] *less and less. They don't believe in it because they haven't been educated in it. They don't believe in it because they haven't been taken to the places that are impregnated with these African realities. Because this, this is the real reality here. It's not their fault that they don't believe. They don't believe because they do not know.*

The increased availability of Western medicine may also seem to threaten belief in spirits. Many Senegalese with the financial means will visit a doctor of Western medicine at some point and the intervention of doctors may cure some of the maladies once attributed to rab. But most of people's aberrant behavior and feelings occur outside the control of modern medicine. As it turns out, there is strikingly little animosity between healers in the rab cult and Western-trained doctors. In fact, in recent years various non-governmental organizations have attempted to create associations that validate and use all forms of healing.

In sum, belief in the rab spirit world survives because it is firmly engrained in Lébou culture and because there are adversities in life that cannot be explained in any other way. It seems unlikely that the rab belief system will fade into the background, which for many women means dealing with the unwanted affections of lover spirits. "Despite everything, we remain African," an elderly man explained to me. "There are still certain beliefs that sleep in us."

✓●─ **Study** and **Review** on **myanthrolab.com**

Review Questions

1. What aspects of their lives make Senegalese young women prime candidates for spirit possessions in Lébou society?

2. In what ways do rab resemble humans?

3. What prognosis does Mueller provide for the survival of rab in changing Senegalese society?

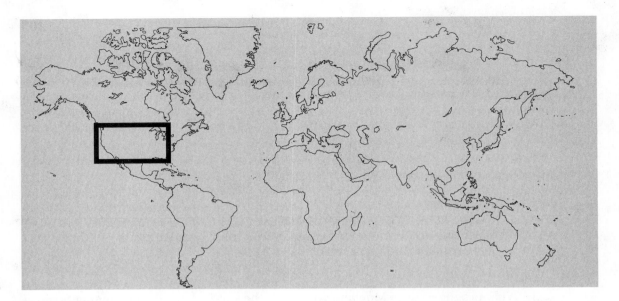

29

Baseball Magic

George Gmelch

Americans pride themselves on what they see as a rational, scientific approach to life and problem solving. But as George Gmelch demonstrates in this updated article, U.S. baseball players, much like people in many other parts of the world, also turn to supernatural forces to ensure success. Following the pioneering analysis of Trobriand magic by Bronislaw Malinowski, Gmelch shows that, like Trobriand Islanders, baseball players use magic, including ritual, taboos, and fetishes, to manage the anxiety generated by unpredictable events that challenge our desire for control.*

((•▪ **Listen** to the **Chapter Audio** on **myanthrolab.com**

On each pitching day for the first three months of a winning season, Dennis Grossini, a pitcher on a Detroit Tiger farm team, arose from bed at exactly 10:00 a.m. At 1:00 p.m. he went to the nearest restaurant for two glasses of iced tea and a tuna fish sandwich. When he got to the ballpark he put on the unwashed sweatshirt and jock he wore during his last winning game; one hour before the game he chewed a wad of Beech-Nut chewing tobacco. On the mound during the game, after each ball Grossini touched the letters on his uniform and straightened his cap. And after every inning in which he gave up a run, he washed his hands.

When I asked which part of his ritual was most important, he said, "You can't really tell what's most important so it all becomes important. I'd be afraid to change anything. As long as I'm winning, I do everything the same." So do many ballplayers. Trobriand Islanders, according to anthropologist Bronislaw Malinowski, felt the same way about their fishing magic.[1] Trobrianders fished in two different settings: in the *inner lagoon* where fish were plentiful and there was little danger, and on the *open sea* where fishing was dangerous and yields varied widely. Malinowski found that magic was not used in lagoon fishing, where men could rely solely on their knowledge and skill. But when fishing on the open sea, Trobrianders used a great deal of magic to ensure safety and increase their catch.

By magic, anthropologists refer to practices, notably the use of *rituals, taboos,* and *fetishes* (good luck charms), designed to gain control over the supernatural. Baseball, America's national pastime, is an arena in which players behave remarkably like Malinowski's Trobriand fishermen. There are three essential activities of the game—pitching, hitting, and fielding. In the first two, chance can play a surprisingly important role. The pitcher is the player least able to control the outcome of his efforts. He may feel great and have good stuff warming up in the bullpen and then get in the game and get clobbered. He may make a bad pitch and see the batter miss it for a strike or see it hit hard but right into the hands of a fielder for an out. Conversely, his best pitch may be blooped for a base hit. He may limit the opposing team to just a few hits yet lose the game, and he may give up many hits and win. And the good and bad luck doesn't always average out over the course of a season. For instance, this season (2013) Boston Red Sox John Lackey gave up slightly fewer runs per game (ERA 3.52) than his teammate Jon Lester (ERA 3.75) but only won 43% of his games (10-13) while Lester (15-8) won 65% of his games. Both pitchers, of course, had the same players on the field behind them. Regardless of how well a pitcher performs, the outcome of the game also depends upon the proficiency of his teammates in scoring runs, the ineptitude of the opposition, and luck. In the words of Red Sox pitcher Kyle Snyder, "There is only so much that is within your control and the rest is left up to the so-called baseball gods." Hitting, which most observers call the single most difficult task in the world of sports, is also full of uncertainty. Unless it's a home run, no matter how hard the batter hits the ball, fate determines whether it will go into a waiting glove or find a gap between the fielders. The uncertainty is compounded by the low success rate of hitting: the average hitter gets only one hit in every four trips to the plate, while the very top hitters average only one hit in every three trips. Fielding, which we will return to later, is the one part of baseball where chance does not play much of a role. How does the risk and uncertainty in pitching and hitting affect players? How do they try to control the outcomes of their performance? These are questions that I first became interested in many years ago both as a ballplayer and anthropology student. I had devoted much of my youth to baseball, and played professionally as a first baseman in the Detroit Tiger organization in the 1960s. It was shortly after the end of one baseball season that I took an anthropology course called "Magic, Religion, and Witchcraft." As I listened to my professor describe the magical rituals of the Trobriand Islanders, it occurred to me that what these so-called "primitive" people did wasn't all that different from what my teammates and I did for luck and confidence at the ballpark.

---

[1]Malinowski, B. *Magic, Science and Religion and Other Essays.* Glencoe, IL: Free Press, 1948.

Routines and Rituals

The most common way athletes in all sports attempt to reduce chance and feelings of uncertainty is to develop a routine—that is, a course of action which is regularly followed. Talking about the routines of ballplayers, former Pittsburgh Pirates coach Rich Donnelly said:

> They're like trained animals. They come out here [to the ballpark] and everything has to be the same, they don't like anything that knocks them off their routine. Just look at the dugout and you'll see every guy sitting in the same spot every night. You watch the pitcher warm up and he'll do the same thing every time. . . . You get a routine and you adhere to it and you don't want anybody knocking you off it.

Routines are comforting; they bring order into a world in which players have little control. The varied elements in following a routine also produce the tangible benefit of helping one concentrate. Ballplayers know that it is easy to "overthink" as opposed to just reacting, and that following a routine can keep them from thinking too much.

But some of what players do goes beyond mere routine. These actions are what anthropologists define as *ritual*—prescribed behaviors in which there is no connection between the behavior (e.g., tapping home plate three times) and the desired end (e.g., getting a base hit). Because there is no empirical relationship between the two, rituals are not *rational*. In fact, they can be quite irrational, as in kissing a medallion to get a base hit.

Baseball rituals are infinitely varied. Most are personal—performed by individuals rather than by a team or group. Most are done in a casual and unemotional manner with no more fanfare than when a player applies eye-black to his cheeks or pine tar to his bat. A player may merely deliberately put on the items of his uniform in a particular order. For outfielder Jim Austin it was always his left sleeve first, then left pants leg, and left shoe before the right. After hitting two home runs in a game, for example, ex-Giant infielder Jim Davenport discovered that he had missed a buttonhole while dressing for the game. For the remainder of his career he left the same button undone. For outfielder Brian Hunter the focus is shoes: "I have a pair of high tops and a pair of low tops. Whichever shoes don't get a hit that game, I switch to the other pair." At the time of our interview, he was struggling at the plate and switching shoes almost every day.

A ballplayer may ritualize any activity that he considers important or somehow linked to good performance. Recall the variety of things that Dennis Grossini does, from specific times for waking and eating to dress. Some players listen to the same songs on their iPods over and over before the start of every game. And that's 162 games a season. Astros infielder Julio Gotay always played with a cheese sandwich in his back pocket. Hall of Famer Red Sox Wade Boggs ate chicken before every game during his career, and that was just one of many elements in his pregame ritual, which also included leaving his house for the ballpark at precisely the same time each day (1:47 p.m. for a night game), running wind sprints at 7:17 p.m., and drawing a Chai—the Hebrew symbol for life—upon entering the batter's box, despite not being Jewish.

Many hitters have a preparatory ritual before stepping into the batter's box. These include tugging on their caps and batting gloves, touching their uniform letters, crossing themselves, and swinging the bat a prescribed number of times. Red Sox third baseman Mike Lowell always took four warm-up swings in the on-deck circle.

Not five. Not three. He did it in a high school game one day and got four hits and never gave it up. Before each at bat, the Giants' Pablo Sandoval draws a cross behind the plate and thanks God for the opportunity to get another hit, then skips through the box and taps his spikes alternately three times for his grandmother, grandfather, and sister who died together in a car crash. Former Cleveland Indian first baseman Mike Hargrove had so many time-consuming elements in his batting ritual that he was nicknamed "the human rain delay." Like most players, Hargrove believed his batting rituals helped him regain concentration, or as some players put it, "get locked in."

But some wonder if players like Hargrove and Sandoval have become prisoners to their elaborate superstitions. Players who have too many or particularly bizarre rituals risk being labeled as "flakes," and not just by teammates but by fans and the media as well. Former Mets pitcher Turk Wendell's eccentric rituals, which included chewing black licorice while pitching only to spit it out, brush his teeth and reload the candy between innings, and wearing a necklace of teeth from animals he had killed, made him a cover story in *The New York Times Sunday Magazine*. Baseball fans observe some of this ritual behavior, such as a player tagging a base when leaving and returning to the dugout between innings, or a pitcher smoothing the dirt on the mound after giving up a base hit, never realizing its importance to the player. The one ritual many fans do recognize, largely because it's a favorite of TV cameramen, is the "rally cap"—players in the dugout folding their caps and wearing them bill up in hopes of sparking a rally.

What are the origins of ballplayer rituals? Most grow out of exceptionally good performances. When a player does well, he seldom attributes his success to skill alone; after all, his skills don't vary much from day to day. So, then, what was different about today which can explain his three hits? He makes a correlation. That is, he attributes his good fortune, at least in part, to a food he ate, or not having shaved, or a new shirt he bought, or just about anything out of the ordinary. By repeating that behavior the next day, he hopes to bring more good luck. Outfielder John White explained how one of his rituals started:

> I was jogging out to centerfield after the national anthem when I picked up a scrap of paper. I got some good hits that night and I guess I decided that the paper had something to do with it. The next night I picked up a gum wrapper and had another good night at the plate. . . . I've been picking up paper every night since.

When outfielder Ron Wright played for the Calgary Cannons he shaved his arms once a week. It all began two years before when after an injury he shaved his arm so it could be taped, and then hit three homers. Similarly, Wade Boggs' routine of eating chicken before every game began when he was a rookie and noticed a correlation between multiple-hit games and poultry plates (by the end of his career his wife had 40 chicken recipes).

Like for Boggs, food often becomes part of a player's ritual, and we're not talking about nutritious foods that might actually enhance performance. Minor leaguer Mike Saccocio got three hits one night after eating at Long John Silver's. After that, he explained, "Whenever we pulled into town my first question would be, 'Do you have a Long John Silver?' " Pitcher Matt Garza goes to Popeyes Chicken on days he is scheduled to start. Detroit Tiger Justin Verlander eats at Taco Bell the night before he pitches, always ordering three crunchy taco supremes, a cheesy gordita crunch, and a Mexican pizza, no tomato. For teammate Torii Hunter, who admits to having "a thousand superstitions but none of which last very long," it's peanut butter and jelly sandwiches before every game, but only as long as he is getting hits. He switches to turkey or another sandwich after an "O-fer" (going hitless). To pitcher Derek Holland it's not what he eats but the amount of money that he spends on dinner the night before he pitches. It must be $30, and at Wendy's.

Almost anything can become ritualized. Take former Yankee manager Joe Torre who during one game stood on the dugout steps instead of sitting on the bench when his team was batting. The Yankees scored a few runs, so he decided to keep on doing it. As the Yankees won nine games in a row, Torre kept standing. Torre explained, "As long as we score, I'll be doing the same thing." Similarly, pennant-winning teams seldom change the design of their uniforms or caps the next season, following the principle of "Never mess with success." Conversely, teams with losing records and/or poor attendance are far more likely to make changes in the design of their uniforms and hats.

When in a slump, most players make a deliberate effort to change their routines and rituals in an attempt to shake off their bad luck. Saccocio, for example, stopped eating at Long John Silver's. Some players try sitting in a different place in the dugout, or driving a different route to the ballpark, or putting their clothes on in a different order. Some shave their heads; others let their beards grow. Jason Giambi took to wearing a gold thong. Hector Martinez put his bat in the trash can for a few innings, as if to punish it, threatening to leave it there if it didn't start producing hits. I played for a manager who routinely rattled the bat bin when the team was not hitting well, as if the bats were in a stupor and could be aroused by a good shaking. Diamondbacks left fielder Luis Gonzalez sometimes placed his bats in the room where Baseball Chapel— a Sunday church service—was about to get underway. Gonzalez hoped his bats would get some benefit, though he didn't usually attend the service himself.

Taboo

Taboos are the opposite of rituals. These are things that you shouldn't do. The word comes from a Polynesian term meaning prohibition. Among the Trobriand Islanders, for example, Malinowski observed that before they went fishing on the open sea, neither men nor women could adorn their bodies or comb their hair or apply coconut oil to their skin. Breaking a taboo, both Trobrianders and ballplayers believe, can lead to bad luck. Most players observe a few taboos. White Sox Adam Dunn, for example, will never stand in the on-deck circle, and during my career I would never hold a baseball during the playing of the national anthem. Many taboos concern behaviors off the field. On the day a pitcher is scheduled to start, he will avoid activities he believes may affect his luck. This can mean not shaving, avoiding certain foods or even not having sex (this notion is probably based on an 18th century belief about preserving vital body fluids, but experts now agree there is no ill effect and there may actually be a small benefit).

Taboos grow out of exceptionally poor performances, which players later attribute to a particular behavior. During my first season of pro ball I ate pancakes before a game in which I struck out three times. A few weeks later I had another terrible game, again after eating pancakes. The result was a pancake taboo: I never again ate pancakes during the season. (But for former Orioles pitcher Jim Palmer, a short stack of pancakes on the day he was to pitch was a requisite and the source of his nickname "Cakes.")

While most taboos are idiosyncratic, a few are universal to all ballplayers and are unrelated to personal misfortune. These taboos are learned as early as Little League and form part of the wider culture of baseball. Mentioning a no-hitter while one is in progress is a well-known example (this is true for almost any pitching or hitting streak; to bring it to the streaking player's attention may "jinx" him). Another universal taboo is not stepping on the white chalk foul lines. The origins of these shared beliefs are lost in time, though the taboo against stepping on the chalk lines may relate to the children's superstition, "step on a crack, and break your mother's back."

Fetishes

Fetishes are charms—usually small objects believed to embody supernatural power (luck) that can aid or protect the owner. Good-luck charms are standard equipment for some ballplayers. These include a wide assortment of items, from coins, chains, and crucifixes to rabbit's feet or a favorite hat or glove. The fetishized object may be a new possession or something the player found that coincided with the start of a streak and which he believes contributed to his good fortune. Pitcher Sean Burnett carries a poker chip in his back pocket, for Al Holland it's a two-dollar bill, and for Mark LaRosa it's a perfectly round stone. My teammate Doc Olms kept a lucky penny for each of his wins in his plastic athletic supporter cup, whose clanging could be heard when he ran the bases. Nyjer Morgan decided that blue argyle socks might help his Milwaukee Brewers break a slump, and after they did he regularly wore them under his baseball socks. Some players have fetishes and rituals that overlap with their religious beliefs, such as touching a Saint Christopher medal, making the sign of the cross before going to bat or the mound, and blowing a kiss to the heavens after some success. Here magic and religion overlap in addressing the universal human need to minimize uncertainty and insecurity.

Some players regard certain uniform numbers as lucky. Often it is a number they wore on a previous team where they had a lot of success. When Ricky Henderson came to the Blue Jays, he paid teammate Turner Ward $25,000 for the right to wear number 24. Don Sutton got off cheaper, convincing teammate Bruce Bochy to give up number 20 in exchange for a new set of golf clubs. Turk Wendell wore number 99 when he was with the Mets, Phillies and Rockies (and in 2000 he asked that his new contract be for $9,999,999.99). Oddly enough, there is no consensus about the effect of wearing number 13. Some players shun it, while a few request it.

Number obsessions can extend beyond the uniform. Former Colorado Rockies [player] Larry Walker's fixation with the number 3 was well known to baseball fans. Besides wearing 33, he took three, or any multiple of three, practice swings before stepping into the box, showered from the third nozzle, set his alarm for three minutes past the hour and was wed on November 3 at 3:33 p.m. Fans in ballparks all across America rise from their seats for the seventh-inning stretch before the home club comes to bat because the number 7 is lucky, although the actual origin of this tradition is uncertain. Fetishes and rituals sometimes intersect. During hitting or winning streaks, for example, players may wear the same clothes day after day. My former teammate, Jim Leyland, now manager of the Detroit Tigers, wore the same pair of boxers to the ballpark every day until his team's winning streak ended. Former manager Art Howe wouldn't wash his socks after his [Oakland] A's were victorious (he would also write the lineup card with the same pen). Once I changed undershirts midway through the game for seven consecutive nights to keep a hitting streak going. Clothing rituals and fetishes sometimes become impractical. Catcher Matt Allen was wearing a long sleeve turtleneck shirt on a cool evening in the New York-Penn League when he had a three-hit game. "I kept wearing the shirt and had a good week," he explained. "Then the weather got hot as hell, 85 degrees and muggy, but I would not take that shirt off. I wore it for another ten days–catching—and people thought I was crazy."

Losing streaks often produce the opposite effect as players discard and try new attire in hope of breaking the "jinx." Most of the Oakland A's went out and bought new street clothes after losing 14 in a row. The Nationals left fielder Matt Swope, mired in a slump, threw away all his Under Armour and went to Dick's [Sporting Goods] and bought new underwear. That night, he began a 26-game hitting streak. In the words of one veteran, "It all comes down to the philosophy of not messing with success—and deliberately messing with failure."

Baseball's superstitions, like most everything else, change over time. Many of the rituals and beliefs of early baseball are no longer observed. In the 1920s and 30s sportswriters reported that a player who tripped en route to the field would often re-trace his steps and carefully walk over the stumbling block for "insurance." A century ago some players spent time on and off the field intently looking for items that would bring them luck. To find a hairpin on the street, for example, was believed to assure a batter of hitting safely in that day's game. A few managers were known to strategi-cally place a hairpin on the ground where a slumping player would be sure to find it. Today few women wear hairpins—a good reason the belief has died out. In the same era, Philadelphia Athletics manager Connie Mack hoped to ward off bad luck by em-ploying a hunchback as a mascot. Hall of Famer Ty Cobb had as a good luck charm a young black boy, even taking him on the road during the 1908 season. It was not uncommon then for players to rub the head of a black child for good luck. None of this would be acceptable today, although Red Sox pitcher Pedro Martinez did have a midget hang around the clubhouse for luck throughout his long career, which only ended in 2009.

To catch sight of a white horse or a wagon-load of barrels were also good omens. In 1904 the manager of the New York Giants, John McGraw, hired a driver with a team of white horses to drive past the Polo Grounds around the time his players were arriving at the ballpark. He knew that if his players saw white horses, they would have more confidence and that could only help them during the game. Belief in the power of white horses survived in a few backwaters until the 1960s. A gray-haired manager of mine in Quebec would drive around the countryside before big games looking for a white horse. When he was successful, he would announce it to everyone in the club-house. One belief that appears to have died out recently is the notion about crossed bats being unlucky, or worse. Several of my Latino teammates in the 1960s took it seriously, and I can still recall Cuban Julio Perez becoming annoyed when during bat-ting practice I tossed my bat from the batting cage and it landed on top of his bat. The brawny outfielder came over and with his foot flicked my bat aside, and asked that I not do it again, explaining that my bat might "steal" hits from his bat. Like Julio, Hall of Famer Honus Wagner, who played in the early 1900s, believed that bats contained a finite number of hits, and that when those hits were used up no amount of good swings would produce any more. While I don't know of any players today who still believe this, other superstitions about bats do survive. Position players on the Class A Asheville Tourists would not let pitchers touch or swing their bats, not even to warm up. Poor-hitting players, as most pitchers are, were said to "pollute" or weaken the bats.

While the elements in many rituals have changed over time, the reliance of play-ers on them has not. Moreover, that reliance seems fairly impervious to advances in education. Way back in the 1890s, in an article I found in the archives of the National Baseball Hall of Fame, one observer predicted that the current influx of better educated players into the game and the "gradual weeding out of bummers and thugs" would raise the intellectual standard of the game and reduce baseball's rampant superstitions. It didn't. I first examined baseball magic in the late 1960s for a research paper; when I returned decades later as an anthropologist to study the culture of baseball, I expected to find less superstition. After all, I reasoned, unlike in my playing days most of today's players have been to college, and therefore with more education should be less superstitious. It wasn't true. I do find that today's players are less willing to admit to having superstitions, but when asked about their "routines" and what they do to give themselves luck they often describe rituals, taboos, and fetishes little different from my teammates in the 60s.[2]

Uncertainty and Magic

The best evidence that players turn to rituals, taboos, and fetishes to control chance and uncertainty is found in their uneven application. As I have noted above, they are associated mainly with pitching and hitting—the activities with the highest degree of chance—and not fielding. Unlike hitting and pitching, a fielder has almost complete control over the outcome of his performance. Once a ball has been hit in his direction, no one can intervene and ruin his chances of catching it for an out (except in the unlikely event of a "bad hop" or two fielders colliding). Compared with the pitcher or the hitter, the fielder has little to worry about. He knows that at least 9.7 times out of 10 he will execute his task flawlessly. With odds like that there is little need for ritual. Clearly, the rituals of American ballplayers are not unlike those of the Trobriand Islanders studied by Malinowski many years ago. In professional baseball, fielding is the equivalent of the inner lagoon, while hitting and pitching are like the open sea.

While Malinowski helps us understand how ballplayers respond to uncertainty, behavioral psychologist B. F. Skinner sheds light on why personal rituals get established in the first place.[3] With a few grains of seed Skinner could get pigeons to do anything he wanted. He merely waited for the desired behavior (e.g. pecking) and then rewarded it with some food. Skinner then decided to see what would happen if pigeons were rewarded with food pellets at fixed intervals, like every fifteen seconds, regardless of what they did. He found that the birds associated the arrival of the food with a particular action, such as walking in clockwise circles. Soon after the arrival of the last pellet, the birds would begin doing whatever they associated with getting food and they would keep doing it until the next pellet arrived. They had learned to link a particular behavior with the reward of being given food.

Ballplayers also associate a reward—wins or base hits—with prior behavior. If a player touches his crucifix and then gets a hit, he may link that gesture to his good fortune and touch his crucifix the next time he comes to the plate. Some psychologists,

[2]In a 2005 cross-cultural comparison, psychologist Jerry Burger and Amy Lynn of Santa Clara University found American baseball players to be more superstitious than their Japanese counterparts. And reflecting a basic cultural difference, the Americans were more likely to believe their superstitions aided their *individual* performance whereas the Japanese players were more likely to believe their superstitions helped *team* performance. (Burger, J. and A. Lynn. "Superstitious behavior among American and Japanese Professional Baseball Players." *Basic and Applied Social Psychology*. 2005 (vol. 27): 1–76.)

[3]Skinner, B.F. *Behavior of Organisms: An Experimental Analysis*. New York: Appleton-Century, 1938. Skinner, B.F. *Science and Human Behavior*. New York: Macmillan, 1953.

like Stuart Vyse[4], offer an evolutionary explanation for such behavior: namely, that humans, like Skinner's pigeons, tend to repeat any behavior that is coincident with success. This tendency, says Vyse, is adaptive: if turning in a circle really does operate the feeder, the pigeon eats and survives another day; if not, little is lost. Likewise for ballplayers. Unlike pigeons, however, most ballplayers are quicker to change their rituals once they no longer seem to work. Skinner found that once a pigeon associated one of its actions with the arrival of food, only sporadic rewards were necessary to keep the ritual going (just as sporadic hits may keep some hitters' ritual going). One pigeon, believing that hopping from side to side brought pellets into its feeding cup, hopped ten thousand times without a pellet before finally giving up. But, then, didn't Wade Boggs eat chicken before every game, through slumps and good times, for seventeen years? Obviously the rituals and superstitions of baseball do not make a pitch travel faster or a batted ball find the gaps between the fielders, nor do the Trobriand rituals calm the seas or bring fish. What both do, however, is give their practitioners a sense of control, and with that added confidence.[5] And we all know how important that is. If you really believe eating chicken or carrying a two dollar bill in your back pocket will make you a better hitter, it probably will.

✓●—⌈**Study** and **Review** on **myanthrolab.com**

Review Questions

1. According to Gmelch, what is magic, and why do people practice it?

2. What parts of baseball are most likely to lead to magical practice? Why?

3. What is meant by the terms *ritual, taboo,* and *fetish?* Illustrate these concepts using examples from this article.

4. How are Malinowski's and Skinner's theories of magic alike and different? What is each designed to explain?

5. Can you think of other areas of U.S. life where magic is practiced? Do the same theories used in this article account for these examples, too?

[4]Vyse, S. *The Psychology of Superstition.* Oxford: Oxford University Press. 1997.

[5]In an experiment conducted in the psychology department of a German university, L. Damisch and several colleagues were able to demonstrate that believing in luck could actually make a group of college students perform better. The students were divided into two groups and taken to a putting green and told to make as many putts as they could. One group was given golf balls that were said to be "lucky" and—surprise—they sank significantly more putts than the comparison group where there was no mention of luck. (Damisch L, Stoberock B, Mussweiler T. "Keep Your Fingers Crossed! How Superstition Improves Performance." *Psychological Science.* 2010 Jul; 21(7):1014–20.)

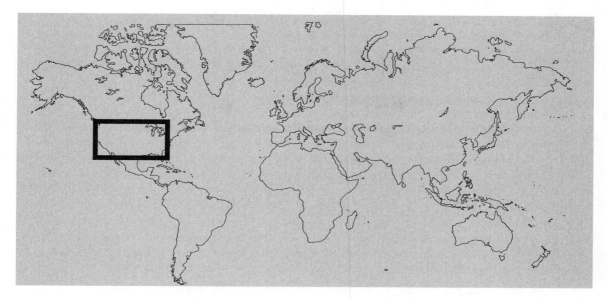

30

Run for the Wall:
An American Pilgrimage

Jill Dubisch

Pilgrimages involve ritually structured travel that physically removes people from their everyday lives as they journey to places that evoke important, often life-changing, emotions. As a ritual, pilgrimages are structured around repetitive acts that symbolize past events, places, stories, and meanings. They involve a ritual of separation, a liminal period, and a final reincorporation into normal life for those who embark on them. We often associate pilgrimages with religion, but they may also occur in more secular contexts with much the same effect. This is the case for a pilgrimage called the Run for the Wall, described by Jill Dubisch in this article. The "run" is a pilgrimage undertaken by motorcyclists who travel for ten days each spring from Los Angeles to Washington, D.C., to commemorate soldiers lost during the Vietnam War. Started years ago by Vietnam veterans, it has grown to include other riders over the years as well. After they leave Los Angeles, riders cross the United States, stopping in towns along the way and occasionally participating in commemorations dedicated to the memory of veterans. Additional riders may join the run along the way, while others may drop out. Those who make it to Washington visit "the wall," their name for the Vietnam War Memorial bearing the names of all those who died in the war. Finally, they participate in "rolling thunder," a parade of thousands of motorcyclists ending at the U.S. Capitol, as a way to honor and "remember" soldiers who were captured, missing, and killed in the

Vietnam War. Dubisch describes the ritual nature of the pilgrimage and details its emotional effect and transformative power for motorcyclists who participate.

((•—Listen to the **Chapter Audio** on **myanthrolab.com**

They roared off the I-40 exit west of Flagstaff, Arizona, a motley crew of leather-clad, long-haired bikers on their Harleys. *Here they are,* we thought, as my partner Ray and I scrambled to pull our Honda Gold Wing motorcycle in behind them. Excitement washed over us, mingled with a large dose of anxiety. Could we really become part of this rough-looking crowd, we wondered, these wild looking riders with their black leather jackets, chains, headscarves, long hair, and beards? After all, these were *real* bikers—not the sort of riders we were used to from our mostly middle-aged Honda Gold Wing motorcycle club. And yet this was the group with whom we planned to spend the next ten days, accompanying them on a cross-country journey from Flagstaff to the Vietnam Veterans Memorial in Washington, D.C., an annual pilgrimage known as the Run for the Wall.

As we parked nervously at the end of the line of bikes on the shoulder of the road, waiting for our police escort for the parade into downtown Flagstaff, little did we know what awaited us in the days ahead. For on this journey across America, both we and the mostly Vietnam veterans with whom we rode would develop emotional bonds that extended well beyond the Run, and we would experience a transformation that would change our lives. Such a transformation was not to be won easily, however, for the journey, a grueling ten-day motorcycle ride, was fraught not only with all the dangers of the road that any motorcycle journey entails, but also with the emotional dangers involved in reawakening memories of a difficult period in our history—the era of the Vietnam War and the political protest and social disruption that were the consequences of that war. What's more, in the course of this journey, our very view of the country in which we lived would change, as we were fed and lodged and greeted with smiles, tears, and ceremonies—and occasionally with hostility or fear—in small communities all across America. The couple that finally returned home three weeks later on their motorcycle were not the same people who left Flagstaff that day in early May of 1996. The ride turned out to be a pilgrimage, a ritual passage that personally transformed both us and those with whom we road.

But who were these people who streamed off the highway and into our lives that day? Why did they term their journey a pilgrimage and why were they making such a pilgrimage so many years after the Vietnam War had ended? And why did they make this journey on motorcycles? Why would those who are not veterans choose to accompany them? And why would communities along the journey's route turn out to feed and celebrate the veterans and to wish them "welcome home"? In order to answer these questions, it is necessary to address not only the issue of the still-unhealed "wounds" of the Vietnam War and to examine the nature of pilgrimage, but also more generally to consider the nature of ritual and its role in American life.

The Run for the Wall: An American Ritual

The Run for the Wall begins every year in mid-May as several hundred motorcycle riders gather at a motel in southern California in preparation for their journey across the United States from California to Washington, D.C. Although many of the riders might be mistaken for outlaw bikers, with their beards, headscarves, boots, and black leather jackets, in fact, most are Vietnam veterans, and the journey they are about to undertake is no mere outing or biker joy ride. Rather, they are at the beginning of a serious, and often emotional and painful endeavor, a journey with a mission, a pilgrimage, whose final destination is the most powerful of American secular shrines, the Vietnam Veterans Memorial—the Wall.

The Run first took place in 1989, when a group of Vietnam veterans decided to ride their motorcycles across the country to the recently inaugurated Vietnam Veterans Memorial. Their intention was, as one of those original riders explained to me, "to say goodbye" to their fallen comrades whose names were on the Wall, and they saw the journey as a one-time event. However, the enthusiastic welcome the group received in the communities where they stopped in the course of their ride, and the ceremonies and hospitality with which they were greeted, as one rider told me, made them realize "we had to do it again." And so the Run for the Wall has taken place every year, and grown every year, so much that recently it has added a more southern route to the original Midwestern route with which the Run began.

During this ten-day journey across the United States, the riders travel several hundred miles a day on their motorcycles. Some go "all the way" to D.C., while others travel shorter distances with the group, replaced by others who join along the route, so that at times the group may have from 200 to 300 riders, forming a line stretching several miles down the highway. During the journey, the riders are greeted with ceremonies performed by local organizations such as veterans' groups and local motorcycle organizations. They visit VFW and American legion halls, Vietnam memorials, local parks and community halls. They are honored and fed and put up for the night at local camping grounds. Few of them pay for a single meal along the way, and camping is always free.

But many of these veterans are making another journey as well—a journey into the past and their own painful memories, to a time of personal danger and fear and grief, and of national dissention and conflict that split a generation—to that painful period of American history, the Vietnam War, a war that (as the 2004 presidential campaign showed) remains controversial to this day. And when the group arrives at its final destination, the Vietnam Veterans Memorial, an arrival always timed for the Friday of Memorial Day weekend, the memories become intensely painful, as the riders confront the names of dead comrades—and the non-veterans the names of dead relatives and friends—and relive once more all the traumatic memories of the war.

And yet the aim of this journey is not simply to confront the past, or to evoke its pain. Rather, the participants describe the aims of their pilgrimage as twofold: as a means of healing the individual wounds of the war and as a ride on behalf of all veterans, but especially those "left behind," the prisoners of war (POWs) and those missing in action (MIAs). Nor are these causes the concern of veterans alone. On this ritual journey, veterans are accompanied by family, friends, and other supporters, and also, since that day in 1996 when we first joined the Run, by two social scientists.

The Anthropology of Pilgrimage

When I joined the Run for the Wall it was not the first time I had been involved with a pilgrimage, however. For a number of years I had done anthropological fieldwork at the shrine of the Madonna of the Annunciation on the Greek island of Tinos, one of that country's most famous pilgrimage sites and the destination of thousands of Orthodox Christian pilgrims every year.[1] Although my work on Tinos was deeply involving and often emotional, I was an outsider, not a Greek Orthodox Christian, and from a different culture, and I did not myself participate in pilgrimage. Thus when I joined the Run for the Wall, it was the first time I had really been a pilgrim myself, and had taken part in a journey with a personal, as well as professional, significance.

"Pilgrimage" is a word that usually conjures up visions of sacred journeys connected with the great world religions—the Muslim pilgrimage to Mecca, Catholic pilgrimage to Lourdes or Santiago, or perhaps a journey of Hindus to the sacred waters of the Ganges in India. But pilgrimage is by no means limited to such religious traditions, and in fact it can take a variety of forms. Pilgrimage can range from large-scale journeys such as those that devout Muslims make to Mecca, to small individual journeys such as the Irish make to a healing well, or Americans to a family reunion. It can be mandated and structured by religious traditions or religious authorities, or undertaken as a purely individual quest. It can be motivated by spiritual needs or by the desire for solutions to such pragmatic physical problems as illness or the inability to bear a child. It is, in short, a highly flexible, variable, and multi-faceted ritual activity.

This notion of a journey, whether it is actual physical travel or metaphoric, is part of what gives pilgrimages their common structure and their widespread appeal. The journey is a powerful symbol and is connected with the idea that one needs to go to a "different place"—to the wilderness, to a sacred locale, to the site of powerful events and away from the place of one's ordinary life—in order to achieve transformation, to touch the sacred, or to receive important messages from the other world. Thus while pilgrimage is a journey, it is not just any kind of journey. It is not taken out of pleasure or simple practical necessity (though it may also include these elements). Rather it is a journey with a purpose, a mission, a ritual act that carries the pilgrim to a place with special meaning or power. Nor need such journeys be strictly religious in nature. The Run for the Wall and journeys to Elvis Presley's home at Graceland or to Ground Zero at the World Trade Center in New York City, for example, do not fit within established religious traditions, yet they are seen by many of their participants as pilgrimages.

Pilgrimage destinations themselves draw people for a variety of reasons. Certain places are special, often by virtue of things that have happened there, whether a human event, such as the Battle of Gettysburg, or the appearance or act of a divine being, such as an apparition of the Virgin Mary at Lourdes in France. In other cases, the origins of the pilgrimage site may be lost in time, and the site simply known for its miraculous powers, as is the case with the healing wells of Ireland. And some pilgrimage sites attract people through the physical powers of place, as with mountains in Chinese pilgrimage, or the red rock "vortexes" of Sedona, Arizona. But journeys are also metaphorical. The idea of life as a moral and spiritual journey is deeply ingrained in the Christian religion. (And it is no coincidence that in the 1960s a psychedelic experience, in which one journeyed in mind but not in body, was termed a "trip"!)

The Anthropology of Ritual

I have spoken of pilgrimage as a "ritual," but what, exactly, are rituals, and why are they important? And what sort of ritual is pilgrimage?

---

[1] See Jill Dubisch, *In a Different Place* (Princeton, NJ: Princeton University Press, 1995).

Robbie Davis-Floyd, in her book *Birth as an American Rite of Passage*, defines ritual as "a patterned, repetitive, and symbolic enactment of a cultural belief or value."[2] According to Davis-Floyd, the primary purpose of ritual is "transformation," and for this reason rituals are often performed to mark important occasions, times, or transitions. From the perspective of those performing the rituals, there are a variety of purposes in carrying out ritual activities: to maintain order in the world, to connect with gods or ancestors, to protect, to express group or individual identity, or because the rituals are mandated by the religious system of the society. Rituals can bring about changes, as when rites of passage such as baptism or marriage transform individuals by moving them from one social status or stage of life to another. Rituals also mark off ordinary life from times when special activities are permitted or required. The carnival period preceding Lent in Catholic cultures both allows creativity and license absent in ordinary life and at the same time signals the beginning of the period of abstinence to follow, a period that itself parallels and dramatizes the sufferings of Christ before the crucifixion and resurrection. Similarly, a pilgrimage is an activity and time set apart, and pilgrimage may take place at times of special significance, such as holy days or national days of commemoration. Thus the Run for the Wall is timed so that its arrival at the Vietnam Veterans Memorial takes place on Memorial Day weekend, a period of remembering the war dead and of patriotic activities.

This brings up another important feature of rituals. As the famous scholar of religion, Mircea Eliade pointed out, rituals often reenact the important myths of society, showing us why they are the way they are. Thus Christian Easter rituals enact the crucifixion and resurrection, while the Jewish Passover meal, the Seder, recounts the Jews' flight from Egypt. Nor need such rituals be religious in nature. The Fourth of July in the United States, for example, commemorates the signing of the Declaration of Independence and serves as an occasion to proclaim American values of freedom, patriotism, and community. Rituals may also seek to rewrite or reshape the past. In the Run for the Wall, as I will show, veterans seek, among other things, to transform the meaning of being a Vietnam veteran from shame to pride, and to give veterans a chance for the homecoming reception most never had when they returned from Vietnam. ("Welcome home, brother" is the ritual greeting extended to these veterans by other veterans on the Run and by those who greet them along the way.)

Symbolism plays an important role in rituals. Victor Turner, an anthropologist who devoted much of his work to the study of ritual, saw symbols as having two poles: the ideological and the sensory. On the one hand, rituals engage our senses of sound, touch, sight, taste and smell (the sensory pole). On the other hand, they also convey important messages about social values (the ideological pole). Although contemporary anthropologists would see these two dimensions as intertwined, with each embedded in the other (rather than as opposite poles), they would agree that it is the combination of the ideological and the sensory that makes rituals so powerful and moving, for they engage more than just our intellects. For this reason, people sometimes find themselves moved by the rituals of other groups or cultures, even when they themselves do not share the values of those performing the ritual.

Although rituals are often perceived as being "traditional," passed on in the same form from generation to generation, the fact is that rituals are an ongoing human activity and must be re-created every time they are performed. Hence rituals are subject to both intentional and unintentional change. Moreover, new rituals are created

---

[2]Robbie Davis-Floyd, *Birth as an American Rite of Passage* (Berkeley, CA: University of California Press, 1992), p. 8.

regularly, and old ones modified. The Run for the Wall has now become a yearly "tradition," the ritual activities carried out in the course of its journey modified and added to every year by both the participants and by those who host them along the way.

It is clear that rituals are a rich source of data for the anthropologist and important windows on the culture in which they occur. For this reason, I like Renato Rosaldo's description of rituals as "busy intersections," places where "a number of distinct social processes interact."[3] It is just such a "busy intersection" that we find in the annual motorcycle pilgrimage known as the Run for the Wall.

Pilgrimage as Ritual

One reason that the journey—as both symbol and as an actual activity—is so powerful is that it has the potential to create what anthropologists call a "liminal" state. Liminality is an important feature of those rituals we call "rites of passage," in which individuals or groups move from one stage or condition to another. Victor Turner and his wife, Edith Turner, saw pilgrimage as one type of rite of passage. When one is on a pilgrimage, the liminal period is marked by the physical separation created by the journey itself. Ordinary duties are left behind, and time and space take on different meanings. This may induce an altered state of consciousness that renders the pilgrim more receptive to both the messages of the journey and the healing or other transformations that pilgrimage can effect. Thus once the pilgrimage is over, the pilgrim often has experienced an inner transformation, such as healing of physical or psychological ills, atonement for sin, or spiritual renewal. Transformation of social status or identity may also take place. Vietnam veterans who participate in the Run for the Wall may return home with newly created identities *as* veterans (an identity they may have previously played down or denied), and they may also find that they have finally begun to heal the long-buried wounds of Vietnam.

To see how these various features of pilgrimage and ritual are represented on the Run for the Wall, let us look at some of the events that take place in the course of this ten-day journey. But before that, it is necessary to address two important elements of American culture that come together to define this pilgrimage: the Vietnam War and motorcycle riding.

The Vietnam War

The Run for the Wall's focus on the POW/MIA issue carries the message that the Vietnam War in some sense is not really over (a message also made clear in the 2004 presidential campaign and the frequent comparisons of the Iraq war to Vietnam). Despite the fact that the Vietnam war officially ended thirty years ago, unresolved conflicts over the meaning of the war, and the fact that it is a war that the United States did not "win," have made the memories of the war difficult and contentious, not only for veterans but for Americans generally. In addition, many veterans are still struggling to come to terms with their own roles in the war, as their faith in themselves—and in the values of their culture—was shaken by the experience. When these veterans returned home, their belief that they would be honored for having fought and risked their lives in defense of their country by those they thought they were defending

[3]*Culture and Truth* (New York: Beacon, 1989), p. 17.

was undermined by the indifference, and sometimes outright hostility, with which a number of homecoming veterans were received.

Because of such a reception, many veterans were reluctant to speak of their experiences in Vietnam or to connect or identify themselves with other veterans. They saw their postcombat symptoms as signs of their own craziness, and not the consequences of a shared experience. Although veterans who ended up in therapy groups in veterans' hospitals had some opportunity to talk about their experiences, many, if not most, Vietnam veterans bore their emotional burdens alone.

Many of these returning veterans thus sought to put Vietnam behind them and to "get on with their lives." It was only later that some of them, at least, began to feel the delayed traumatic effects of their wartime experience and found their carefully constructed postwar lives crumbling. It is from the need to address both the long-term and delayed consequences of the war, both for themselves and others, that many of the participants came to be involved in the Run for the Wall.

But why motorcycles?

Motorcycles in American Culture

Motorcycles have long held an attraction for veterans, from the returning veterans of World War II (some of whom formed the first Hell's Angels club) to current veterans of the Iraq war. For many of those who ride them, motorcycles symbolize important American values of freedom, self-reliance, patriotism, and individualism. Assertion of these values, and particularly patriotism, is evident among at least some groups of bikers—and certainly on the Run for the Wall—in the form of American flags, eagles, and other similar emblems decorating the motorcycles, the jackets, and the tee shirts of the bikers.

Many bikers also see themselves as a breed apart, "rebels" against the norms and restrictions of conventional society (even if only for the weekends they can "escape" on their motorcycles). The sense of marginality that some veterans felt on their return to civilian life, and the difficulty they may experience in adapting to that life, thus fit with the marginality of at least some segments of motorcycle culture, especially that of the "outlaw" bikers and similar groups. Motorcycle riding can also have important therapeutic effects, providing a space in which veterans feel that they can "clear their heads" and find some peace from the memories and emotional traumas that continue to haunt them.

There is a sense of solidarity and "brotherhood" that exists among bikers that is also important in the Run for the Wall. This sense of brotherhood echoes the camaraderie of warriors in combat; indeed, participating in the Run for the Wall is for some like going into battle again—this time for the POW/MIA cause and for the healing of fellow veterans. This is echoed in the military formation of the riders, rolling two by two in a long column down the highway, and in the element of danger present in any motorcycle ride, as well as in the roar of the motorcycles themselves.

By riding motorcycles, the participants in the Run for the Wall also set themselves apart from those making a cross-country journey by ordinary means. The parade of motorcycles (at points numbering several hundred bikes) riding side by side in formation down the highway presents an impressive sight, which is part of the strategy employed by the Run in its political agenda—calling attention to the POW/MIA issue. At the same time, riding motorcycles represents a more conventional element of pilgrimage—the role that hardship and suffering often play in the pilgrim's journey.

Such suffering emphasizes the importance of the journey and leads to a feeling of accomplishment among those who have succeeded in reaching their destination. This sense of accomplishment is reflected in the honoring of those who have gone "all the way," that is, made the entire journey from California to Washington, D.C. The physical sensations of motorcycle riding—the noise, the motion, the riding in formation with several hundred other motorcycles, the hazards of the road—also combine to create a psychological receptivity to the ritual messages imparted along the journey's route.

But what are these messages, and how are they imparted in the course of the Run's many rituals? In order to answer this question, let us look at several of the ritual stops made during the Run for the Wall's long cross-country journey.

The Navajo Reservation and the Brotherhood of Warriors

Since its inception, the Run for the Wall, while maintaining the same basic itinerary (from California to Washington in ten days, arriving the Friday of Memorial Day weekend), has also regularly altered, added, and sometimes eliminated the various stops and ceremonies that punctuate the journey. In 1998, a new stop was added to the Run for the Wall, as the organizers of the Run responded to an invitation from the Navajo Reservation to ride to the still in progress Navajo Vietnam Veterans Memorial at Window Rock on the Run's third day out.

That particular year, the Run had endured snow on its way through the mountains of Northern Arizona and temperatures hovering around forty degrees Fahrenheit as we crossed the high desert along Interstate 40 toward Gallup (with a wind chill close to zero for those riding on motorcycles). As we turned off the interstate toward the Navajo Nation administrative center of Window Rock, we were met by a contingent of Navajo police who escorted us along the narrow two-lane road that led through the reservation. All along the route, groups of Navajo stood next to cars and pick-up trucks, waving and applauding as we rode by. As we pulled into the parking lot beneath the dramatic red rock formation that gives the town of Window Rock its name, we saw crowds of Navajo gathered around the lot and on the rocks above. We rolled to a stop and the crowd burst into enthusiastic applause. In response, the bikers gunned their engines in a collective roar. From the podium at one end of the parking lot, a Navajo leader said, "Look around you, white men—you're surrounded by Indians. We'll take your bikes. You can have our horses." His comment acknowledged both the differences that separated the Navajo from the mostly Anglo group of bikers and the shared military history that connected them. In the ceremonies that followed, Navajo leaders gave the Run a Navajo Nation flag to carry to the Wall, a Navajo folk singer performed a song he wrote in memory of a brother who died in Vietnam, Navajo children took our pictures while balancing precariously on the rocks above, and there was a demonstration by the last living World War II "code talkers" (Navajo who had participated in a secret military operation that used the Navajo language as a code). Then, as the desert light dimmed around the mystical formation of Window Rock, Navajo and non-Navajo warriors saluted while a bugler played "Taps."

At Window Rock what might be seen as an opposition (Anglo/Native American) is transformed into a common culture of the brotherhood of warriors. The horse and the motorcycle are both warrior's symbols, a dead warrior is memorialized (reminding all those present of the common sacrifices made by Navajo and non-Navajo), Navajo are connected to the riders and to the riders' destination—the Vietnam

Memorial—through the presentation of the flag that the riders will carry to D.C., tying the Navajo not only to the pilgrims but also to the powerful symbols of the nation's capital and thus to the nation itself. The cold, grueling ride that preceded these ceremonies for the Run for the Wall participants placed us all in an altered and receptive state that made this ceremony at Window Rock one of the most emotionally powerful events of our pilgrimage.

The Power of Places: Evoking the Memory and Emotion of the Past at Angel Fire, New Mexico

On its fourth day out, the Run stops at the Vietnam Memorial at Angel Fire, New Mexico, high in the mountains near Taos. Although to most people it is best known as a ski area, to those who have participated in the Run for the Wall it will always be one of the most beautiful and powerful places associated with their pilgrimage. Here, high on a knoll and surrounded by a wind-swept alpine valley and snow-topped mountain peaks, stands a beautiful chapel, shaped like a white wing rising against the New Mexico sky. Next to the chapel is a memorial and museum of the Vietnam War, with photographs and exhibits. In the chapel itself, photographs of New Mexican men who died in Vietnam, looking terribly young in their military uniforms, stretches across the wall above a tier of seats descending to the lower part of the chapel and the simple cross that is the building's only ornament. There are often flowers or other offerings at the base of the cross, and on each tier of seats sits a box of tissues, mute testimony to the powerful emotions this stark and simple memorial evokes.

The memorial and chapel were built by Dr. Victor Westphal who lost his son in Vietnam, and who is now himself buried on the memorial's grounds. (Until 2004, Dr. Westphal was there to greet the Run every year, the latter years in a wheelchair.) The first year we were on the Run, there was a service held in the chapel for a veteran who had died the year before and who had been one of the original organizers of the Run. His wife spoke eloquently of what the Run's support had meant to her in her own mourning. Her words had particular resonance with this group of Vietnam veterans, many of whom still grieve for the loss of comrades in a war that was over decades ago. Then a young woman with an incredibly pure voice sang "Amazing Grace." There was not one of those wild tough bikers who had so intimidated us at the beginning of our journey who was not at that point in tears.

Many veterans have spoken to us about the significance of Angel Fire in their own spiritual and psychic journey toward healing. For those who felt they had gotten past the traumas of Vietnam and moved on with their lives, for those who had come on the Run thinking they were "just going for a ride" with fellow biker vets, Angel Fire awakened memories and reopened wounds that had never completely healed. At this point, many began to realize they had much left from the past that they had not confronted, that had continued to affect their lives and the lives of those around them. For these individuals, Angel Fire was not simply a stop on their pilgrimage; rather, it was the beginning of their *real* pilgrimage.

Part of the power of Angel Fire lies in its setting—the remoteness, the beauty, the steep, winding and somewhat hazardous mountain roads that must be traversed to get there. This creates a receptivity to the emotions of the past that are evoked by the memorial. Nor is it only those on the Run who journey here for pilgrimage. Ceremonies are held here on other days as well: on Veterans' Day and on Father's Day, in honor of the men killed in Vietnam whose children never had a chance to know them.

And in between such events, more solitary pilgrimages are made by those drawn by the power of the site.

Limon, Colorado: Remembering the Missing and the Dead

Limon, Colorado is the Run's stop on its fifth night. It is a long day, riding from Cimarron, New Mexico, the previous night's stop, making several ceremonial stops along the way (including, one year, at the Colorado Vietnam memorial in Pueblo), ending up at this small town in eastern Colorado on the edge of the Great Plains. After checking into motels or the local KOA campground (where camping, as everywhere on the Run's journey, is free), many riders mount up again for the half hour ride east to the town of Hugo, where they will be served a wonderful feast prepared by the local women. Afterwards, everyone regroups at the KOA for the evening's ceremony, conducted by members of Task Force Omega, a group of families of POWs and MIAs. Here every year, as dusk falls, the names of the Colorado Missing in Action are read in a candlelight ritual that varies from year to year. On the 1999 Run, a "V" of candelabra was set up in a space near the tents, and we formed into couples, each couple assigned a month and given a list of names of those who had gone missing in Vietnam in that month. As each month was called, the woman read the names on her list. As each name was read in the gathering darkness, the man called out, "Still on patrol, sir!" Afterwards we all joined hands in a "healing circle."

The Run for the Wall's journey is punctuated with rituals such as these, rituals created by Run for the Wall participants and by the individuals and groups that host them along the way. Most of these rituals, in one way or another, commemorate the missing and the dead of the Vietnam War. In the ritual at Limon, it is specifically the missing who are memorialized, providing a ritual for those who have been left in limbo—both the missing themselves and those they have left behind, who have had no space provided for mourning those they have lost. The audience participation in the ritual joins all of us with those who are missing, and with those who mourn. The light of candles, the growing darkness, the open spaces of the looming plains ahead and the mountains behind us create a powerful ritual atmosphere, as do the voices of the dead responding to the calling of their names. They are still here, they remind us, still connected, and we should not forget. ("Missing but not forgotten," we responded in unison another year, as the names of the missing were read at this same ceremony.)

At the Wall: Confronting the Sacred Space

The Vietnam Veterans Memorial, with its two black granite wings engraved with the names of the over 58,000 American soldiers who died in Vietnam, is a particularly powerful symbol in that it memorializes both the individual and the collective dead. For many veterans, it is the Wall, and not individual grave sites, where the spirits of their dead comrades reside. And for many veterans, it is such an emotional and powerful place that they can scarcely bear to think about it, let alone visit. On my first journey with the Run, one veteran, also riding with the group for the first time, told me how terrified he was as we drew closer to our destination. He did manage to complete the journey, but, like many others, he was overcome with grief once he reached the memorial. For many, it is only because they have the support of the other pilgrims on this journey that they are able to make this pilgrimage and to confront its destination at the end.

There are no collective rituals at the Wall. Each of the pilgrims from the Run carries out his (or her) own symbolic acts, whether that be leaving important objects (wreaths, military objects, photographs, letters, and flowers), making rubbings of names, praying, or simply sitting in sorrow and contemplating the many names carved on the black granite surface. Although individual in their expression of grief and remembrance, these are rituals that would be recognized by pilgrims everywhere. Indeed, it is such activities—both the acts themselves and the many physical markers they leave behind—that often mark powerful and popular pilgrimage sites.

For many who are involved with the Run, the Wall has almost mystical powers. People speak of "Wall magic," the force that draws people to the Wall and to each other for healing. To touch a name on the Wall, I was told, is to call forth the soul of the person who died. And some veterans who keep vigil at the Wall the night after the Run arrives (the "Night Patrol") report hearing a cacophony of voices coming from the black granite surface, as if all the dead were trying to speak to them at once. Thus the Wall serves as a place of connection between worlds, between the living and the dead, as well as a place for remembering and for healing.

The Return

There are no special rituals marking the homeward journey of the Run for the Wall participants. Riders return home singly or with groups of friends, make a quick and direct journey or stop to visit friends and family, as they wish. But they return as different people, for the Run for the Wall, like many pilgrimages, is, among other things, a rite of passage and a ritual of transformation. Some have found at least a measure of peace and healing through their journey, through the support of other veterans and of those who host them along the way, and through their confrontation with the Wall and all that it represents. Others have "come out of the woods," out of the shame and guilt and sense of isolation that being a veteran has entailed, and have begun to acknowledge, and even to be proud of, their status as veterans. All have been given an opportunity—and space and support—to mourn the dead for whom the veteran's grief is often still intense and surprisingly fresh. And in a sense, many have been given the opportunity to ritually reenact the Vietnam War by riding for a cause (the POW/MIA issue) with fellow veterans, on an intense, difficult, and sometimes dangerous mission, arriving—this time in triumph—in the nation's capitol. Here, instead of the indifference and even hostility that met them when they returned from Vietnam, they are greeted with warmth and enthusiasm. Thus through ritual, they, in some sense, at least, "rewrite" their own history, as well as that of the war, and become heroes, at last, in what is for many "the parade they never had."

Conclusion: The Journey That Has No End

Pilgrimage, an ancient ritual, continues to flourish today in a range of forms. To understand its continuing popularity, we must also look to the many reasons why people undertake such ritual journeys. One of the answers to this may lie in the creative potential of pilgrimage itself, for, as the Run for the Wall illustrates, it is a ritual readily adapted to a variety of situations and to a range of human needs. Indeed, pilgrimage may be a perfect ritual for a contemporary global world, as it both lends itself to our individual purposes and desires and connects us to the larger world.

Like most rituals, the Run for the Wall also offers itself to many meanings and interpretations. That two individuals who opposed the Vietnam War, and who find some of the kinds of patriotic sentiments celebrated on the Run distasteful, can nonetheless find their participation in the Run for the Wall one of the most moving and powerful experiences of their lives, is testimony to this. It became clearer to me through my own participation the ways in which a pilgrimage, like other rituals, can be many, even contradictory, things at once: a political movement and a personal journey of healing, a celebration of the warrior and a memorial to the tragedy of war, an experience of liminality by the marginal and a mode of integration and the overcoming of marginality, a journey away and a coming home.

As I write this article, the United States is once again engaged in foreign wars, in Iraq and in Afghanistan, and these wars are increasingly reflected in the Run for the Wall and its rituals. (Even prior to these wars, the Run had already attracted some Gulf War veterans, and had begun to broaden its mission to include the veterans, and the missing and the dead, of all American wars.) In 2003, Lori Piestewa, the first Native American woman to die in combat, was memorialized at Run for the Wall ceremonies in Gallup, New Mexico. In the 2004 Run, we were joined by both returning Iraq veterans and those about to be deployed, and prayers were offered daily for the safety of all those serving. Remembering their own treatment when they returned from war, several veterans reminded participants to be sure that today's returning veterans were better received and cared for. As the Vietnam veterans on the Run can testify, the wounds of war are deep and long lasting. For these reasons, then, the Run for the Wall is a ritual journey whose end is nowhere in sight.

✓●—[**Study** and **Review** on **myanthrolab.com**

Review Questions

1. What does Dubisch mean by the term *ritual*? What are the basic parts of rituals?

2. What is a pilgrimage, according to Dubisch? What are the common features of a pilgrimage?

3. What kind of people started the Run for the Wall? Why? What effect does Dubisch say the run has on its participants?

4. Dubisch argues that the Run for the Wall has a strong emotional and transformative impact on those who participate. What appears to generate such intense feelings?

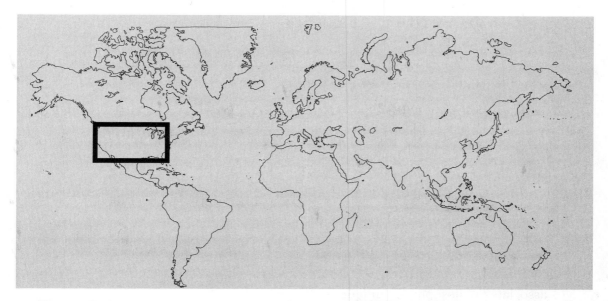

31

Body Ritual among the Nacirema

Horace Miner

Ritual involving repeated symbolic acts can be about many things—the growth of crops, the response to death, movement from one social identity to another, community solidarity, and much more. It can also be about one's body, including how to care for it, how to make it socially acceptable, and how to make it impressive to others. This classic article written in 1958 by Horace Miner describes the extensive body ritual of a North American group, the Nacirema, whose houses contain special shrines in which body ritual takes place. From the article, it is clear that the society's elaborate variety of body rituals reveals important Nacirema cultural values.*

((•—[**Listen** to the **Chapter Audio** on **myanthrolab.com**

The anthropologist has become so familiar with the diversity of ways in which different peoples behave in similar situations that he is not apt to be surprised by even the most exotic customs. In fact, if all of the logically possible combinations of behavior have not been found somewhere in the world, he is apt to suspect that they must be present in some yet undescribed tribe. This point has, in fact, been expressed with respect to clan organization by

*From Horace Miller, "Body Ritual among the Nacirema," *The American Anthropologist,* vol. 58, June 1956. Used by permission of Blackwell Publishing.

Murdock.[1] In this light, the magical beliefs and practices of the Nacirema present such unusual aspects that it seems desirable to describe them as an example of the extremes to which human behavior can go.

Professor Linton first brought the ritual of the Nacirema to the attention of anthropologists twenty years ago, but the culture of this people is still very poorly understood.[2] They are a North American group living in the territory between the Canadian Cree, the Yaqui and Tarahumare of Mexico, and the Carib and Arawak of the Antilles. Little is known of their origin, although tradition states that they came from the east. . . .

Nacirema culture is characterized by a highly developed market economy which has evolved in a rich natural habitat. While much of the people's time is devoted to economic pursuits, a large part of the fruits of these labors and a considerable portion of the day are spent in ritual activity. The focus of this activity is the human body, the appearance and health of which loom as a dominant concern in the ethos of the people. While such a concern is certainly not unusual, its ceremonial aspects and associated philosophy are unique.

The fundamental belief underlying the whole system appears to be that the human body is ugly and that its natural tendency is to debility and disease. Incarcerated in such a body, man's only hope is to avert these characteristics through the use of the powerful influences of ritual and ceremony. Every household has one or more shrines devoted to this purpose. The more powerful individuals in the society have several shrines in their houses and, in fact, the opulence of a house is often referred to in terms of the number of such ritual centers it possesses. Most houses are of wattle and daub construction, but the shrine rooms of the more wealthy are walled with stone. Poorer families imitate the rich by applying pottery plaques to their shrine walls.

While each family has at least one such shrine, the rituals associated with it are not family ceremonies but are private and secret. The rites are normally only discussed with children, and then only during the period when they are being initiated into these mysteries. I was able, however, to establish sufficient rapport with the natives to examine these shrines and to have the rituals described to me.

The focal point of the shrine is a box or chest which is built into the wall. In this chest are kept the many charms and magical potions without which no native believes he could live. These preparations are secured from a variety of specialized practitioners. The most powerful of these are the medicine men, whose assistance must be rewarded with substantial gifts. However, the medicine men do not provide the curative potions for their clients, but decide what the ingredients should be and then write them down in an ancient and secret language. This writing is understood only by the medicine men and by the herbalists who, for another gift, provide the required charm.

The charm is not disposed of after it has served its purpose, but is placed in the charm–box of the household shrine. As these magical materials are specific for certain ills, and the real or imagined maladies of the people are many, the charm–box is usually full to overflowing. The magical packets are so numerous that people forget what their purposes were and fear to use them again. While the natives are very vague on this point, we can only assume that the idea in retaining all the old magical materials is that their presence in the charm–box, before which the body rituals are conducted, will in some way protect the worshipper.

[1]Murdock, George P. 1949. *Social Structure*. New York: The Macmillan Co.
[2]Linton, Ralph. 1936. *The Study of Man*. New York: D. Appleton Century Co.

Beneath the charm–box is a small font. Each day every member of the family, in succession, enters the shrine room, bows his head before the charm–box, mingles different sorts of holy water in the font, and proceeds with a brief rite of ablution. The holy waters are secured from the Water Temple of the community, where the priests conduct elaborate ceremonies to make the liquid ritually pure.

In the hierarchy of magical practitioners, and below the medicine men in prestige, are specialists whose designation is best translated "holy–mouth–men." The Nacirema have an almost pathological horror of and fascination with the mouth, the condition of which is believed to have a supernatural influence on all social relationships. Were it not for the rituals of the mouth, they believe that their teeth would fall out, their gums bleed, their jaws shrink, their friends desert them, and their lovers reject them. They also believe that a strong relationship exists between oral and moral characteristics. For example, there is a ritual ablution of the mouth for children which is supposed to improve their moral fiber.

The daily body ritual performed by everyone includes a mouth–rite. Despite the fact that these people are so punctilious about care of the mouth, this rite involves a practice which strikes the uninitiated stranger as revolting. It was reported to me that the ritual consists of inserting a small bundle of hog hairs into the mouth, along with certain magical powders, and then moving the bundle in a highly formalized series of gestures.

In addition to the private mouth–rite, the people seek out a holy–mouth–man once or twice a year. These practitioners have an impressive set of paraphernalia, consisting of a variety of augers, awls, probes, and prods. The use of these objects in the exorcism of the evils of the mouth involves almost unbelievable ritual torture of the client. The holy–mouth–man opens the client's mouth and, using the above mentioned tools, enlarges any holes which decay may have created in the teeth. Magical materials are put into these holes. If there are no naturally occurring holes in the teeth, large sections of one or more teeth are gouged out so that the supernatural substance can be applied. In the client's view, the purpose of these ministrations is to arrest decay and to draw friends. The extremely sacred and traditional character of the rite is evident in the fact that the natives return to the holy–mouth–men year after year, despite the fact that their teeth continue to decay.

It is to be hoped that, when a thorough study of the Nacirema is made, there will be careful inquiry into the personality structure of these people. One has but to watch the gleam in the eye of a holy–mouth–man, as he jabs an awl into an exposed nerve, to suspect that a certain amount of sadism is involved. If this can be established, a very interesting pattern emerges, for most of the population shows definite masochistic tendencies. It was to these that Professor Linton referred in discussing a distinctive part of the daily body ritual which is performed only by men. This part of the rite involves scraping and lacerating the surface of the face with a sharp instrument. Special women's rites are performed only four times during each lunar month, but what they lack in frequency is made up in barbarity. As part of this ceremony, women bake their heads in small ovens for about an hour. The theoretically interesting point is that what seems to be a preponderantly masochistic people have developed sadistic specialists.

The medicine men have an imposing temple, or *latipso*, in every community of any size. The more elaborate ceremonies required to treat very sick patients can only be performed at this temple. These ceremonies involve not only the thaumaturge but a permanent group of vestal maidens who move sedately about the temple chambers in distinctive costume and headdress.

The *latipso* ceremonies are so harsh that it is phenomenal that a fair proportion of the really sick natives who enter the temple ever recover. Small children whose indoctrination is still incomplete have been known to resist attempts to take them to the temple because "that is where you go to die." Despite this fact, sick adults are not only willing but eager to undergo the protracted ritual purification, if they can afford to do so. No matter how ill the supplicant or how grave the emergency, the guardians of many temples will not admit a client if he cannot give a rich gift to the custodian. Even after one has gained admission and survived the ceremonies, the guardians will not permit the neophyte to leave until he makes still another gift.

The supplicant entering the temple is first stripped of all his or her clothes. In everyday life the Nacirema avoids exposure of his body and its natural functions. Bathing and excretory acts are performed only in the secrecy of the household shrine, where they are ritualized as part of the body–rites. Psychological shock results from the fact that body secrecy is suddenly lost upon entry into the *latipso*. A man, whose own wife has never seen him in an excretory act, suddenly finds himself naked and assisted by a vestal maiden while he performs his natural functions into a sacred vessel. This sort of ceremonial treatment is necessitated by the fact that the excreta are used by a diviner to ascertain the course and nature of the client's sickness. Female clients, on the other hand, find their naked bodies are subjected to the scrutiny, manipulation and prodding of the medicine men.

Few supplicants in the temple are well enough to do anything but lie on their hard beds. The daily ceremonies, like the rites of the holy–mouth–men, involve discomfort and torture. With ritual precision, the vestals awaken their miserable charges each dawn and roll them about on their beds of pain while performing ablutions, in the formal movements of which the maidens are highly trained. At other times they insert magic wands in the supplicant's mouth or force him to eat substances which are supposed to be healing. From time to time the medicine men come to their clients and jab magically treated needles into their flesh. The fact that these temple ceremonies may not cure, and may even kill the neophyte, in no way decreases the people's faith in the medicine men.

There remains one other kind of practitioner, known as a "listener." This witch-doctor has the power to exorcise the devils that lodge in the heads of people who have been bewitched. The Nacirema believe that parents bewitch their own children. Mothers are particularly suspected of putting a curse on children while teaching them the secret body rituals. The counter-magic of the witchdoctor is unusual in its lack of ritual. The patient simply tells the "listener" all his troubles and fears, beginning with the earliest difficulties he can remember. The memory displayed by the Nacirema in these exorcism sessions is truly remarkable. It is not uncommon for the patient to bemoan the rejection he felt upon being weaned as a babe, and a few individuals even see their troubles going back to the traumatic effects of their own birth.

In conclusion, mention must be made of certain practices which have their base in native esthetics but which depend upon the pervasive aversion to the natural body and its functions. There are ritual fasts to make fat people thin and ceremonial feasts to make thin people fat. Still other rites are used to make women's breasts larger if they are small, and smaller if they are large. General dissatisfaction with breast shape is symbolized in the fact that the ideal form is virtually outside the range of human variation. A few women afflicted with almost inhuman hyper-mammary development are so idolized that they make a handsome living by simply going from village to village and permitting the natives to stare at them for a fee.

Reference has already been made to the fact that excretory functions are ritualized, routinized, and relegated to secrecy. Natural reproductive functions are similarly distorted. Intercourse is taboo as a topic and scheduled as an act. Efforts are made to avoid pregnancy by the use of magical materials or by limiting intercourse to certain phases of the moon. Conception is actually very infrequent. When pregnant, women dress so as to hide their condition. Parturition takes place in secret, without friends or relatives to assist, and the majority of women do not nurse their infants.

Our review of the ritual life of the Nacirema has certainly shown them to be a magic–ridden people. It is hard to understand how they have managed to exist so long under the burdens which they have imposed upon themselves. But even such exotic customs as these take on real meaning when they are viewed with the insight provided by Malinowski when he wrote:

> Looking from far and above, from our high places of safety in the developed civilization, it is easy to see all the crudity and irrelevance of magic. But without its power and guidance early man could not have mastered his practical difficulties as he has done, nor could man have advanced to the higher stages of civilization.[3]

✓● Study and Review on myanthrolab.com

Review Questions

1. Where are the Nacirema located?

2. Describe the main body rituals that occur in Nacireman household shrines.

3. What kinds of ritual specialists does Miner describe for the Nacirema in this article? What do they function to do for people?

4. What is the *latipso,* and for what is it used?

5. What do you think the psychological functions of Nacireman body ritual are, and how do these fit with Malinowski's theory about the functions of religion and magic described in the earlier article on baseball magic?

[3]Malinowski, Bronislaw. 1948. *Magic, Science, and Religion*. Glencoe, IL: The Free Press, p. 70

PART NINE

GLOBALIZATION

READINGS IN THIS SECTION

Several times a week, a small island freighter leaves Grenada's Saint George's harbor loaded with fuel drums, crates of processed food, boxes containing manufactured goods, and an occasional motor scooter or car. When its hold is filled, 60 or 70 passengers, many of them women, troop across the gangplank and settle down among the freight or take a seat in a small cabin set aside for them on the upper aft deck. They are bound for their small island home, Carriacou, located about 35 miles by sea to the north. Most are returning from overseas work in New York, Britain, or mainland Europe, where they worked for a few years as maids and cleaners or at other service jobs. Carrying gifts of CD players, clothing, shoes, and other items manufactured outside their island, they will be greeted warmly by their relatives, whom they have alerted by phone or e-mail about the time of their arrival. Most returnees have already wired home money they saved from their off-island work and are beginning to think about using it to build a house or buy items that will make their lives easier and more secure.

The people returning to Carriacou illustrate a major trend that is sweeping the world: globalization. **Globalization** consists of powerful forces that reshape local conditions on an ever-intensifying scale. Although places such as Carriacou may seem peripheral to globalization, the impact of international money, tourists, transportation, goods, communication, media, and the movement of the island's peoples to other parts of the world have all affected the way people live there. And their experience is repeated in many other parts of the world.

Globalization may occur on several levels. In the most general and formal sense, we can talk about it as a world system. The **world system** is often defined in market terms and links nations and people together economically. More accurately, it is **transnational**; it consists of companies and patterns of exchange that transcend national borders and may evade control by individual governments. An international company may have a headquarters located in Bermuda; manufacturing facilities in Atlanta, Mexico, and Shanghai; customer service representatives in Mumbai; and investors from thirty or forty different countries. Japanese cars and motorcycles sold in the United States reflect the transnational world system. So do the tuna caught by American trawlers in the Atlantic and shipped overnight to Japan to make sushi.

The world system affects local conditions by providing goods, stimulating production, and introducing ideas. As a result, local people can easily find themselves both motivated by and at the mercy of world markets. For example, the government of India, through its state and district development offices, encouraged tribals living in Southern Rajasthan to dedicate some of their cropland to sericulture (silk worm production). Local farmers borrowed money to build "cocoon houses," and to underwrite the cost of fertilizing mulberry bushes for the silk worms to eat. The World Bank also advanced money for a small cocoon processing factory. The program was a success—farmers doubled their money each year; women earned wages in the processing plant—until, that is, the Chinese government arbitrarily lowered the price of the silk its farmers produced by half. Unable to compete, the Indian program failed, disrupting the lives of people who embraced it. Stories like this should not come as a surprise to American workers who have lost jobs to "outsourcing," and to factory workers in other countries who are now employed to take their place.

The international movement of people also illustrates globalization. **Refugees**, people who immigrate to other parts of the world because it is too dangerous for them to stay in their homeland, have moved to many countries. **Guest workers** (people granted permission to work in a country other than their own) are found in many parts of the world. Legal immigrants (and illegal or undocumented immigrants) diversify populations in many nations. The result is that many societies are becoming **multicultural**; people with different cultural backgrounds live side by side. Just as companies can be transnational, so can immigrants, workers, and refugees. The movement of people also gives rise to the concept of a **diaspora**, or a scattered population with a common geographic origin. People who originate from the same cultural areas often communicate with one another, phoning, skyping, texting, or e-mailing home, transferring money to each other, and forming a visiting network. Tourism is the world's largest industry and regularly brings people with different backgrounds into contact.

One important aspect of migration is **remittances**. Financial remittances are the most commonly thought of kind of kinds of transfers, or cash that flows from migrants back to their home countries. There are also **social remittances**. This refers to the ideas, practices, and social capital that flow from the host society to the sending society.

Finally, globalization is marked by cultural diffusion. **Cultural diffusion**, or cultural borrowing, represents the movement of cultural ideas and artifacts from one society to another. Coca Cola has diffused from the United States to many parts of the world; sushi has diffused from Japan to the United States and Europe. So have musical styles, forms of dress, words, and a variety of other cultural items.

In almost every case, societies that borrow aspects of another group's culture adapt them to their own ways of life. Borrowed items usually undergo **cultural hybridization**; they are a mixture of the borrowed and the local. A hamburger in China will probably not taste exactly like one cooked on the backyard grill of an American family. Curry in the United States tastes different from the "real thing" prepared in India. (Note that as the local size of immigrant populations rises, more genuine, meaning closer to its ethnic origins, food becomes available to the original residents as well.)

The articles in Part Nine illustrate several of these points. The first, by Theodore Bestor, illustrates the broad scope of globalization by showing the connection between American and European bluefin tuna fishermen and the Japanese love of sushi. The international interdependence between fishing and sushi grows as the Japanese culinary style spreads in popularity around the world. In the second article, Arjun Guneratne and Kate Bjork describe tourism from the locals' perspective. Based on field research among the Tharu living adjacent to Nepal's Chitwan National Forest, they discovered that the tourist industry's portrayal of the Tharus as primitives is false and demeaning, but experience with tourists has created a greater appreciation for their own culture among the Tharu and a way to separate their past from the present. The third article, by Dianna Shandy, describes the ordeal faced by Nuer refugees as they attempt to gain admittance and establish life in the United States. Fleeing civil war that wracked their home in South Sudan, Nuer refugees developed the skill and determination to pass through a series of bureaucratic hurdles to reach and adjust to life in the United States. Personal initiative, education, using U.S. nongovernmental organizations (NGOs), and the sharing of information about what works are keys to their success. In the final article, Barbara Ehrenreich and Arlie Russell Hochschild discuss an important labor trend, the movement of women from poorer societies to take low-paying jobs in rich ones. This is an important illustration of what is called the feminization of migration. Often aided by their countries of origin, women immigrants are expected to send money home and leave their children in the hands of others.

Key Terms

cultural diffusion p. 295
cultural hybridization p. 295
diaspora p. 295
globalization p. 294
guest workers p. 294
multicultural p. 295

refugees p. 294
remittances p. 295
social remittances p. 295
transnational p. 294
world system p. 294

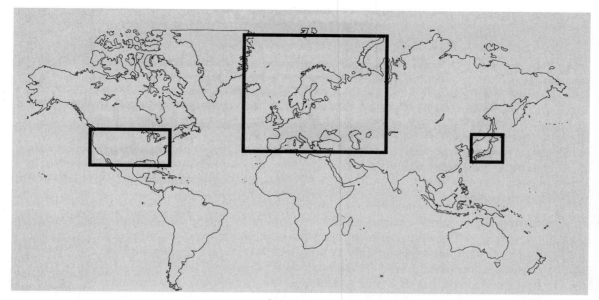

32

How Sushi Went Global

Theodore C. Bestor

International trade, or at least intergroup trade, is nothing new. Tens of thousands of years ago, Upper Paleolithic peoples living in inland Europe made necklaces from shells traded to them from coastal peoples. Semiprecious stones from central India found their way to the Sumerian states by 4000 B.C. However, despite the increased world trade that accompanied more seaworthy oceangoing vessels and steam-powered ships and railroad trains in more recent times, most countries continued to depend largely on homebound manufacturing and commerce. But after World War II, world trade and global economic and cultural inter-dependence exploded. Today this globalization process means a world in which many companies are international conglomerates headquartered in countries other than one's own, communication with almost any place in the world is a keyboard away, and travel across national borders is free and easy. In this article, Theodore Bestor illustrates globalization with an unlikely example: the internationalization of a Japanese culinary custom, sushi, or the eating of raw fish. First, the Japanese love of bluefin tuna as a sushi centerpiece involved fishing industries in North America and Europe. The best bluefins were sent abroad to satisfy Japanese palates. A freak tuna glut depressed the Japanese market just as sushi became popular in the rest of the world, stimulating an increase in tuna fishing and the beginnings of tuna trapping and feeding in the Mediterranean. Despite its global reach, sushi is still a Japanese dish in the minds of most of its connoisseurs.*

*"How Sushi Went Global" by Theodore C. Bestor. Reproduced with permission from *Foreign Policy* #121 (November/December 2000). Copyright 2000 by the Carnegie Endowment for International Peace.

((•—[Listen to the **Chapter Audio** on **myanthrolab.com**

A 40-minute drive from Bath, Maine, down a winding two-lane highway, the last mile on a dirt road, a ramshackle wooden fish pier stands beside an empty parking lot. At 6:00 P.M. nothing much is happening. Three bluefin tuna sit in a huge tub of ice on the loading dock.

Between 6:45 and 7:00, the parking lot fills up with cars and trucks with license plates from New Jersey, New York, Massachusetts, New Hampshire, and Maine. Twenty tuna buyers clamber out, half of them Japanese. The three bluefin, ranging from 270 to 610 pounds, are winched out of the tub, and buyers crowd around them, extracting tiny core samples to examine their color, fingering the flesh to assess the fat content, sizing up the curve of the body.

After about 20 minutes of eyeing the goods, many of the buyers return to their trucks to call Japan by cellphone and get the morning prices from Tokyo's Tsukiji market—the fishing industry's answer to Wall Street—where the daily tuna auctions have just concluded. The buyers look over the tuna one last time and give written bids to the dock manager, who passes the top bid for each fish to the crew that landed it.

The auction bids are secret. Each bid is examined anxiously by a cluster of young men, some with a father or uncle looking on to give advice, others with a young woman and a couple of toddlers trying to see Daddy's fish. Fragments of concerned conversation float above the parking lot: "That's all?" "Couldn't we do better if we shipped it ourselves?" "Yeah, but my pickup needs a new transmission now!" After a few minutes, deals are closed and the fish are quickly loaded onto the backs of trucks in crates of crushed ice, known in the trade as "tuna coffins." As rapidly as they arrived, the flotilla of buyers sails out of the parking lot—three bound for New York's John F. Kennedy Airport, where their tuna will be airfreighted to Tokyo for sale the day after next.

Bluefin tuna may seem at first an unlikely case study in globalization. But as the world rearranges itself—around silicon chips, Starbucks coffee, or sashimi-grade tuna—new channels for global flows of capital and commodities link far-flung individuals and communities in unexpected new relationships. The tuna trade is a prime example of the globalization of a regional industry, with intense international competition and thorny environmental regulations; centuries-old practices combined with high technology; realignments of labor and capital in response to international regulation; shifting markets; and the diffusion of culinary culture as tastes for sushi, and bluefin tuna, spread worldwide.

Growing Appetites

Tuna doesn't require much promotion among Japanese consumers. It is consistently Japan's most popular seafood, and demand is high throughout the year. When the Federation of Japan Tuna Fisheries Cooperative (known as Nikkatsuren) runs ad campaigns for tuna, they tend to be low-key and whimsical, rather like the "Got Milk?" advertising in the United States. Recently, the federation launched "Tuna Day" (Maguro no hi), providing retailers with posters and recipe cards for recipes more complicated than "slice and serve chilled." Tuna Day's mascot is Goro-kun, a colorful cartoon tuna swimming the Australian crawl.

Despite the playful contemporary tone of the mascot, the date selected for Tuna Day carries much heavier freight. October 10, it turns out, commemorates the date that tuna first appeared in Japanese literature, in the eighth-century collection of imperial court poetry known as the *Man'yoshu*—one of the towering classics of Japanese literature. The neat twist is that October 10 today is a national holiday, Sports Day. Goro-kun, the sporty tuna, scores a promotional hat trick, suggesting intimate connections among national culture, healthy food for active lives, and the family holiday meal.

Outside Japan, tuna, especially raw tuna, hasn't always had it so good. Sushi isn't an easy concept to sell to the uninitiated. And besides, North Americans tend to think of cultural influence as flowing from West to East: James Dean, baseball, Coca-Cola, McDonalds, and Disneyland have all gone over big in Tokyo. Yet Japanese cultural motifs and material—from Kurosawa's *The Seven Samurai* to Yoda's Zen and Darth Vader's armor, from Issey Miyake's fashions to Nintendo, PlayStation, and Pokémon—have increasingly saturated North American and indeed the entire world's consumption and popular culture. Against all odds, so too has sushi.

In 1929, the *Ladies' Home Journal* introduced Japanese cooking to North American women, but discreetly skirted the subject of raw fish: "There have been purposely omitted . . . any recipes using the delicate and raw tuna fish which is sliced wafer thin and served iced with attractive garnishes. [These]. . . might not sound so entirely delicious as they are in reality." Little mention of any Japanese food appeared in U.S. media until well after World War II. By the 1960s, articles on sushi began to show up in lifestyle magazines like *Holiday* and *Sunset*. But the recipes they suggested were canapés like cooked shrimp on caraway rye bread, rather than raw fish on rice.

A decade later, however, sushi was growing in popularity throughout North America, turning into a sign of class and educational standing. In 1972, the *New York Times* covered the opening of a sushi bar in the elite sanctum of New York's Harvard Club. *Esquire* explained the fare in an article titled "Wake up Little Sushi!" Restaurant reviewers guided readers to Manhattan's sushi scene, including innovators like Shalom Sushi, a kosher sushi bar in SoHo.

Japan's emergence on the global economic scene in the 1970s as the business destination du jour, coupled with a rejection of hearty, red-meat American fare in favor of healthy cuisine like rice, fish, and vegetables, and the appeal of the high-concept aesthetics of Japanese design all prepared the world for a sushi fad. And so, from an exotic, almost unpalatable ethnic specialty, then to haute cuisine of the most rarefied sort, sushi has become not just cool, but popular. The painted window of a Cambridge, Massachusetts, coffee shop advertises "espresso, cappuccino, carrot juice, lasagna, and sushi." Mashed potatoes with wasabi (horseradish), sushi-ginger relish, and seared sashimi-grade tuna steaks show Japan's growing cultural influence on upscale nouvelle cuisine throughout North America, Europe, and Latin America. Sushi has even become the stuff of fashion, from "sushi" lip gloss, colored the deep red of raw tuna, to "wasabi" nail polish, a soft avocado green.

Angling for New Consumers

Japan remains the world's primary market for fresh tuna for sushi and sashimi; demand in other countries is a product of Japanese influence and the creation of new markets by domestic producers looking to expand their reach. Perhaps not surprisingly, sushi's global popularity as an emblem of a sophisticated, cosmopolitan consumer class more or less coincided with a profound transformation in the international role of the Japanese fishing industry. From the 1970s onward, the expansion of 200-mile fishing limits around the world excluded foreign fleets from the prime fishing grounds of many coastal nations. And international environmental campaigns forced many countries, Japan among them, to scale back their distant water fleets. With their fishing operations curtailed and their yen for sushi still growing, Japanese had to turn to foreign suppliers.

Jumbo jets brought New England's bluefin tuna into easy reach of Tokyo, just as Japan's consumer economy—a byproduct of the now disparaged "bubble" years—went into hyperdrive. The sushi business boomed. During the 1980s, total Japanese imports of fresh bluefin tuna worldwide increased from 957 metric tons (531 from the United States) in 1984 to 5,235 metric tons (857 from the United States) in 1993. The average wholesale price peaked in 1990 at 4,900 yen (U.S. $34) per kilogram, bones and all, which trimmed out to approximately U.S. $33 wholesale per edible pound.

Not surprisingly, Japanese demand for prime bluefin tuna—which yields a firm red meat, lightly marbled with veins of fat, highly prized (and priced) in Japanese cuisine—created a gold-rush mentality on fishing grounds across the globe wherever bluefin tuna could be found. But in the early 1990s, as the U.S. bluefin industry was taking off, the Japanese economy went into a stall, then a slump, then a dive. U.S. producers suffered as their high-end export market collapsed. Fortunately for them, the North American sushi craze took up the slack. U.S. businesses may have written off Japan, but Americans' taste for sushi stuck. An industry founded exclusively on Japanese demand survived because of Americans' newly trained palates and a booming U.S. economy.

A Transatlantic Tussle

Atlantic bluefin tuna ("ABT" in the trade) are a highly migratory species that ranges from the equator to Newfoundland, from Turkey to the Gulf of Mexico. Bluefin can be huge fish; the record is 1,496 pounds. In more normal ranges, 600-pound tuna, 10 feet in length, are not extraordinary, and 250- to 300-pound bluefin, six feet long, are commercial mainstays.

Before bluefin became a commercial species in New England, before Japanese buyers discovered the stock, before the 747, bluefin were primarily sports fish, caught with fighting tackle by trophy hunters out of harbors like Montauk, Hyannis, and Kennebunkport. Commercial fishers, if they caught bluefin at all, sold them for cat food when they could and trucked them to town dumps when they couldn't. Japanese buyers changed all of that. Since the 1970s, commercial Atlantic bluefin tuna fisheries have been almost exclusively focused on Japanese markets like Tsukiji.

In New England waters, most bluefin are taken one fish at a time, by rod and reel, by hand line, or by harpoon—techniques of a small-scale fisher, not of a factory fleet. On the European side of the Atlantic, the industry operates under entirely different conditions. Rather than rod and reel or harpooning, the typical gear is industrial—the purse seiner (a fishing vessel closing a large net around a school of fish) or the long line (which catches fish on baited hooks strung along lines played out for many miles behind a swift vessel). The techniques may differ from boat to boat and from country to country, but these fishers are all angling for a share of the same Tsukiji yen—and in many cases, some biologists argue, a share of the same tuna stock. Fishing communities often think of themselves as close-knit and proudly parochial; but the sudden globalization of this industry has brought fishers into contact—and often into conflict—with customers, governments, regulators, and environmentalists around the world (see Box l).

Two miles off the beach in Barbate, Spain, a huge maze of nets snakes several miles out into Spanish waters near the Strait of Gibraltar. A high-speed, Japanese-made workboat heads out to the nets. On board are five Spanish hands, a Japanese supervisor, 2,500 kilograms of frozen herring and mackerel imported from Norway and Holland, and two American researchers. The boat is making one of its twice-daily trips to Spanish nets, which contain captured Mediterranean tuna being raised under Japanese supervision for harvest and export to Tsukiji.

Behind the guard boats that stand watch over the nets 24 hours a day, the headlands of Morocco are a hazy purple in the distance. Just off Barbate's white cliffs to

BOX 1

Stateless Fish

As the bluefin business grows ever more lucrative, the risk of overfishing has become ever more real. The question of who profits from the world's demand for sushi makes for battles among fishers, regulators, and conservationists.

Bluefin tuna have been clocked at 50 miles per hour, and tagged fish have crossed the Atlantic in about two months. Since bluefin swim across multiple national jurisdictions, international regulations must impose political order on stateless fish.

Charged with writing those regulations is the International Commission for the Conservation of Atlantic Tunas (ICCAT), which assigns quotas for bluefin tuna and related species in the North Atlantic and the Mediterranean and directs catch reporting, trade monitoring, and population assessments. Based in Madrid since its founding in 1969, ICCAT now has 28 members, including Atlantic and Mediterranean fishing countries and three global fishing powers: South Korea, China, and Japan.

In recent years, conservation groups have criticized ICCAT for not regulating more aggressively to prevent or reverse an apparent bluefin population decline in the Western Atlantic. Some activists have campaigned to have bluefin tuna protected under the Convention on International Trade in Endangered Species, or CITLLS. At least in part to keep

that from happening, Japan and ICCAT have implemented new systems to track and regulate trade; "undocumented fish" from nations that fail to comply with ICCAT regulations are now banned from Japanese markets.

Regulations, though, are complicated by how far and fast these fish can travel: No one can say for certain whether there is one bluefin population in the Atlantic or several. ICCAT, the U.S. National Academy of Sciences, the National Audubon Society, and industry groups disagree over how many bluefin migrate across the Atlantic, and whether or not they are all part of the same breeding stock. What's the big deal? If there are two (or more) stocks, as ICCAT maintains, then conservation efforts can vary from one side of the Atlantic to the other.

When ICCAT registered a dramatic decline in bluefin catches off North America, it imposed stringent quotas on North America's mainly small-scale fishing outfits. On the European side of the Atlantic, however, industrial-strength fishing efforts continued. American fishers, not surprisingly, point to evidence of cross-Atlantic migration and genetic studies of intermingling to argue that Europeans need to conserve bluefin more strenuously as well. ICCAT's regulations, they argue, protect bluefin at America's expense only, and ultimately, fishers from other countries pocket Japanese yen.

the northwest, the light at the Cape of Trafalgar blinks on and off. For 20 minutes, the men toss herring and mackerel over the gunwales of the workboat while tuna the size (and speed) of Harley-Davidsons dash under the boat, barely visible until, with a flash of silver and blue, they wheel around to snatch a drifting morsel.

The nets, lines, and buoys are part of an *almadraba,* a huge fish trap used in Spain as well as Sicily, Tunisia, and Morocco. The *almadraba* consists of miles of nets anchored to the channel floor suspended from thousands of buoys, all laid out to cut across the migration routes of bluefin tuna leaving the strait. This *almadraba* remains in place for about six weeks in June and July to intercept tuna leaving the Mediterranean after their spawning season is over. Those tuna that lose themselves in the maze end up in a huge pen, roughly the size of a football field. By the end of the tuna run through the strait, about 200 bluefin are in the pen.

Two hundred fish may not sound like a lot, but if the fish survive the next six months, if the fish hit their target weights, if the fish hit the market at the target price, these 200 bluefin may be worth $1.6 million dollars. In November and December, after the bluefin season in New England and Canada is well over, the tuna are harvested and shipped by air to Tokyo in time for the end-of-the-year holiday spike in seafood consumption.

The pens, huge feed lots for tuna, are relatively new, but *almadraba* are not. A couple of miles down the coast from Barbate is the evocatively named settlement of *Zahara* de los Atunes (Zahara of the Tunas) where Cervantes lived briefly in the late 16th century. The centerpiece of the village is a huge stone compound that housed the men and nets of Zahara's *almadraba* in Cervantes's day, when the port was only a seasonally occupied tuna outpost (occupied by scoundrels, according to Cervantes). Along the Costa de la Luz, the three or four *almadraba* that remain still operate under the control of local fishing bosses who hold the customary fishing rights, the nets, the workers, the boats, and the locally embedded cultural capital to make the *almadraba* work—albeit for distant markets and in collaboration with small-scale Japanese fishing firms.

Inside the Strait of Gibraltar, off the coast of Cartagena, another series of tuna farms operates under entirely different auspices, utilizing neither local skills nor traditional technology. The Cartagena farms rely on French purse seiners to tow captured tuna to their pens, where joint ventures between Japanese trading firms and large-scale Spanish fishing companies have set up farms using the latest in Japanese fishing technology. The waters and the workers are Spanish, but almost everything else is part of a global flow of techniques and capital: financing from major Japanese trading companies; Japanese vessels to tend the nets; aquacultural techniques developed in Australia; vitamin supplements from European pharmaceutical giants packed into frozen herring from Holland to be heaved over the gunwales for the tuna; plus computer models of feeding schedules, weight gains, and target market prices developed by Japanese technicians and fishery scientists.

These "Spanish" farms compete with operations throughout the Mediterranean that rely on similar high-tech, high-capital approaches to the fish business. In the Adriatic Sea, for example, Croatia is emerging as a formidable tuna producer. In Croatia's case, the technology and the capital were transplanted by émigré Croatians who returned to the country from Australia after Croatia achieved independence from Yugoslavia in 1991. Australia, for its part, has developed a major aquacultural industry for southern bluefin tuna, a species closely related to the Atlantic bluefin of the North Atlantic and Mediterranean and almost equally desired in Japanese markets.

Culture Splash

Just because sushi is available, in some form or another, in exclusive Fifth Avenue restaurants, in baseball stadiums in Los Angeles, at airport snack carts in Amsterdam, at an apartment in Madrid (delivered by motorcycle), or in Buenos Aires, Tel Aviv, or Moscow, doesn't mean that sushi has lost its status as Japanese cultural property. Globalization doesn't necessarily homogenize cultural differences nor erase the salience of cultural labels. Quite the contrary, it grows the franchise. In the global economy of consumption, the brand equity of sushi as Japanese cultural property adds to the cachet of both the country and the cuisine. A Texan Chinese-American restauranteur told me, for example, that he had converted his chain of restaurants from Chinese to Japanese cuisine because the prestige factor of the latter meant he could charge a premium; his clients couldn't distinguish between Chinese and Japanese employees (and often failed to notice that some of the chefs behind his sushi bars were Latinos).

The brand equity is sustained by complicated flows of labor and ethnic biases. Outside of Japan, having Japanese hands (or a reasonable facsimile) is sufficient warrant for sushi competence. Guidebooks for the current generation of Japanese global *wandervogel* sometimes advise young Japanese looking for a job in a distant city to work as a sushi chef; U.S. consular offices in Japan grant more than 1,000 visas a year to sushi chefs, tuna buyers, and other workers in the global sushi business.

A trade school in Tokyo, operating under the name Sushi Daigaku (Sushi University) offers short courses in sushi preparation so "students" can impress prospective employers with an imposing certificate. Even without papers, however, sushi remains firmly linked in the minds of Japanese and foreigners alike with Japanese cultural identity. Throughout the world, sushi restaurants operated by Koreans, Chinese, or Vietnamese maintain Japanese identities. In sushi bars from Boston to Valencia, a customer's simple greeting in Japanese can throw chefs into a panic (or drive them to the far end of the counter).

On the docks, too, Japanese cultural control of sushi remains unquestioned. Japanese buyers and "tuna techs" sent from Tsukiji to work seasonally on the docks of New England laboriously instruct foreign fishers on the proper techniques for catching, handling, and packing tuna for export. A bluefin tuna must approximate the appropriate *kata*, or "ideal form," of color, texture, fat content, body shape, and so forth, all prescribed by Japanese specifications. Processing requires proper attention as well. Special paper is sent from Japan for wrapping the fish before burying them in crushed ice. Despite high shipping costs and the fact that 50 percent of the gross weight of a tuna is unusable, tuna is sent to Japan whole, not sliced into salable portions. Spoilage is one reason for this, but form is another. Everyone in the trade agrees that Japanese workers are much more skilled in cutting and trimming tuna than Americans, and no one would want to risk sending botched cuts to Japan.

Not to impugn the quality of the fish sold in the United States, but on the New England docks, the first determination of tuna buyers is whether they are looking at a "domestic" fish or an "export" fish. On that judgment hangs several dollars a pound for the fisher, and the supply of sashimi-grade tuna for fishmongers, sushi bars, and seafood restaurants up and down the Eastern seaboard. Some of the best tuna from New England may make it to New York or Los Angeles, but by way of Tokyo—validated as top quality (and top price) by the decision to ship it to Japan by air for sale at Tsukiji, where it may be purchased by one of the handful of Tsukiji sushi exporters who supply premier expatriate sushi chefs in the world's leading cities.

Playing the Market

The tuna auction at Yankee Co-op in Seabrook, New Hampshire, is about to begin on the second-to-last day of the 1999 season. The weather is stormy, few boats are out. Only three bluefin, none of them terribly good, are up for sale today, and the half-dozen buyers at the auction, three Americans and three Japanese, gloomily discuss the impending end of a lousy season.

In July, the bluefin market collapsed just as the U.S. fishing season was starting. In a stunning miscalculation, Japanese purse seiners operating out of Kesennuma in northern Japan managed to land their entire year's quota from that fishery in only three days. The oversupply sent tuna prices at Tsukiji through the floor, and they never really recovered.

Today, the news from Spain is not good. The day before, faxes and e-mails from Tokyo brought word that a Spanish fish farm had suffered a disaster. Odd tidal conditions near Cartagena led to a sudden and unexpected depletion of oxygen in the inlet where one of the great tuna nets was anchored. Overnight, 800 fish suffocated. Divers hauled out the tuna. The fish were quickly processed, several months before their expected prime, and shipped off to Tokyo. For the Japanese corporation and its Spanish partners, a harvest potentially worth $6.5 million would yield only a tiny fraction of that. The buyers at the morning's auctions in New Hampshire know they will suffer as well. Whatever fish turn up today and tomorrow, they will arrive at Tsukiji in the wake of an enormous glut of hastily exported Spanish tuna (see Box 2).

Fishing is rooted in local communities and local economies—even for fishers dipping their lines (or nets) in the same body of water, a couple hundred miles can be worlds away. Now, a Massachusetts fisher's livelihood can be transformed in a matter of hours by a spike in market prices halfway around the globe or by a disaster at a fish farm across the Atlantic. Giant fishing conglomerates in one part of the world sell their catch alongside family outfits from another. Environmental organizations on one continent rail against distant industry regulations implemented an ocean away. Such instances of convergence are common in a globalizing world. What is surprising, and perhaps more profound, in the case of today's tuna fishers, is the complex interplay between industry and culture, as an esoteric cuisine from an insular part of the world has become a global fad in the span of a generation, driving, and driven by, a new kind of fishing business.

Many New England fishers, whose traditional livelihood now depends on unfamiliar tastes and distant markets, turn to a kind of armchair anthropology to explain Japan's ability to transform tuna from trash into treasure around the world. For some, the quick answer is simply national symbolism. The deep red of tuna served as sashimi or sushi contrasts with the stark white rice, evoking the red and white of the Japanese national flag. Others know that red and white is an auspicious color combination in Japanese ritual life (lobster tails are popular at Japanese weddings for just this reason). Still others think the cultural prize is a fighting spirit, pure machismo, both their own and the tuna's. Taken by rod and reel, a tuna may battle the fisher for four or five hours. Some tuna literally fight to the death. For some fishers, the meaning of tuna—the equation of tuna with Japanese identity—is simple: Tuna is nothing less than the samurai fish!

Of course, such mystification of a distant market's motivations for desiring a local commodity is not unique. For decades, anthropologists have written of "cargo cults" and "commodity fetishism" from New Guinea to Bolivia. But the ability of fishers today to visualize Japanese culture and the place of tuna within its demanding

BOX 2

Tokyo's Pantry

Tsukiji, Tokyo's massive wholesale seafood market, is the center of the global trade in tuna. Here, 60,000 traders come each day to buy and sell seafood for Tokyo's 27 million mouths, moving more than 2.4 million kilograms of it in less than 12 hours. Boosters encourage the homey view that Tsukiji is *Tokyo no daidokoro*—Tokyo's pantry— but it is a pantry where almost $6 billion worth of fish change hands each year. New York City's Fulton Fish Market, the largest market in North America, handles only about $1 billion worth, and only about 13 percent of the tonnage of Tsukiji's catch.

Tuna are sold at a "moving auction." The auctioneer, flanked by assistants who record prices and fill out invoice slips at lightning speed, strides across the floor just above rows and rows of fish, moving quickly from one footstool to the next without missing a beat, or a bid. In little more than half an hour, teams of auctioneers from five auction houses sell several hundred (some days several thousand) tuna. Successful buyers whip out their cellphones, calling chefs to tell them what they've got. Meanwhile, faxes with critical information on prices and other market conditions alert fishers in distant ports to the results of Tsukiji's morning auctions. In return, Tsukiji is fed a constant supply of information on tuna conditions off Montauk, Cape Cod, Cartagena, Barbate, and scores of other fishing grounds around the world.

Tsukiji is the command post for a global seafood trade. In value, foreign seafood far exceeds domestic Japanese products on the auction block. (Tsukiji traders joke that Japan's leading fishing port is Tokyo's Narita International Airport.) On Tsukiji's slippery auction floor, tuna from Massachusetts may sell at auction for over $30,000 apiece, near octopus from Senegal, eel from Guangzhou, crab from Sakhalin, salmon from British Columbia and Hokkaido, snapper from Kyushu, and abalone from California.

Given the sheer volume of global trade, Tsukiji effectively sets the world's tuna prices. Last time I checked, the record price was over $200,000 for a particularly spectacular fish from Turkey—a sale noteworthy enough to make the front pages of Tokyo's daily papers. But spectacular prices are just the tip of Tsukiji's influence. The auction system and the commodity chains that flow in and out of the market integrate fishers, firms, and restaurants worldwide in a complex network of local and translocal economies.

As an undisputed hub of the fishing world, Tsukiji creates and deploys enormous amounts of Japanese cultural capital around the world. Its control of information, its enormous role in orchestrating and responding to Japanese culinary tastes, and its almost hegemonic definitions of supply and demand allow it the unassailable privilege of imposing its own standards of quality—standards that producers worldwide must heed.

---

culinary tradition is constantly shaped and reshaped by the flow of cultural images that now travel around the globe in all directions simultaneously, bumping into each other in airports, fishing ports, bistros, bodegas, and markets everywhere. In the newly rewired circuitry of global cultural and economic affairs, Japan is the core, and the Atlantic seaboard, the Adriatic, and the Australian coast are all distant peripheries. Topsy-turvy as Gilbert and Sullivan never imagined it.

Japan is plugged into the popular North American imagination as the sometimes inscrutable superpower, precise and delicate in its culinary tastes, feudal in its cultural symbolism, and insatiable in its appetites. Were Japan not a prominent player in so much of the daily life of North Americans, the fishers outside of Bath or in Seabrook would have less to think about in constructing their Japan. As it is, they struggle with unfamiliar exchange rates for cultural capital that compounds in a foreign currency.

And they get ready for next season.

✓●—Study and Review on myanthrolab.com

Review Questions

1. How did the Japanese love of bluefin tuna as a centerpiece of sushi dishes affect the U.S. fishing industry?

2. What part does the Tsukiji market play in the international tuna trade?

3. What example does Bestor cite that illustrates the dependence of U.S. fishermen on the Japanese market?

4. According to Bestor, does globalization necessarily mean cultural homogenization? What evidence does he cite to support his view?

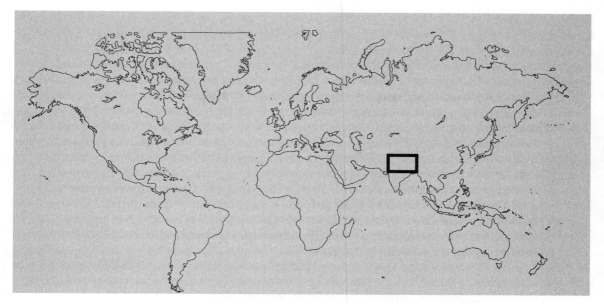

33

Village Walks: Tourism and Globalization among the Tharu of Nepal

Arjun Guneratne and Kate Bjork

What is it like to be the object of the tourist's gaze? That is the topic of this article by Arjun Guneratne and Kate Bjork who regularly witnessed the behavior and impact of foreign tourists and local tour guides on their Tharu neighbors during field research in the Tharu village of Pipariya. Advertised in brochures as the primitive aboriginal inhabitants of Nepal's tarai, the Tharu endured inaccurate and sometimes demeaning descriptions by higher-ranked Brahmin and Chhetri tour guides and the occasionally intrusive behavior of overaggressive tourists. The net effect was to deepen the Tharu's sense of their own cultural identity, introduce them to the broader worlds of the West and Asia, gain employment in the tourist industry itself, and find a way by building a museum to separate their past way of life from the present.*

The blue-painted cart, pulled by a couple of patient and scrawny oxen, rolled to a stop on its two broad rubber tires in the center of the village. It had halted on the dirt road that cut through the heart of the Tharu *tol* or neighborhood in Pipariya,[1] the Nepali village where we had settled for two years of ethnographic fieldwork in 1989. As we watched, the half dozen Western tourists seated in the cart scrambled down and looked curiously around them. In contrast to the khaki drabness of the village and the shabby well-worn everyday clothing of the people who lived there, they looked fresh, new, and well shod. They milled around uncertainly for a moment, and then were taken in hand by their guide, a young man in a green fatigue uniform who moved them off the road and into one of the courtyards adjacent to the road. A few children gathered around to stare. Some women winnowing rice on the verandah of the nearby house soon retreated indoors.

Halting in front of the house, the guide launched into his well-practiced narrative. The Tharu, he told the visitors, were the original inhabitants of the Chitwan valley, living much as their ancestors had done, and were totally dependent on agriculture. They were Nepal's primitive people, he said, warming to his task, and were so ignorant they did not really understand about tourists. Gesturing at the house, he also told his charges that the Tharu had large families and this dwelling housed over 50 people (although as we had already discovered, it was home to only 15). Unlike the women who had gone inside, two young Tharu men remained seated in a corner of the verandah playing chess. They looked up briefly to take note of the visitors, then returned to their game. One of the tourists spotted what the men were doing and, apparently surprised by a sight that seemed to contradict the guide, said, "Look. They are playing chess!" This event, locally called "the village walk," regularly repeated itself during our stay in Pipariya and became a topic of ethnographic interest for us. How, we wondered, did being the object of the tourists' gaze and the guide's depiction of them affect our Tharu neighbors?

Tourism

The village walk is a local example of an important global activity, tourism. Although variously defined, tourism is characterized by several attributes. Above all, it involves temporary travel away from one's permanent home. It often includes recreation and relaxation aimed at separation from the stresses of daily life. It can include a variety of activities such as beach combing, bicycling, sightseeing, gambling, listening to music, sailing, and a host of other amusements. Tourism may also be organized around more serious interests. There is ecotourism, which promotes low impact travel to view natural areas; medical tourism, for people who seek affordable health care; educational tourism involving students and sometimes retirees in study abroad programs; religious tourism defined by pilgrimages to holy sites; and sex tourism for men and women seeking easier and less committed access to sexual activity. The village walk is an example of cultural tourism, which although often associated with visits to museums and historic sites, can also include trips that showcase the traditions and life ways of indigenous communities.

---

[1]Pipariya is not the real name of the village.

Cultural tourism often occurs as part of more broadly defined tours. Such tours typically include a variety of places and activities to view and experience, and most tours to Nepal follow this model. They typically include sightseeing in Katmandu and Pokhara (a picturesque city located about 120 miles west of Kathmandu), a trek to view the Himalayan peaks of Annapurna or Everest, and a visit to the Chitwan National Park. The park's main attractions are its exotic wild animals (especially the Indian Rhinoceros) and forest ecology. However, many tours to Chitwan also offer a visit lasting a few hours to nearby Tharu communities in villages like Pipariya.

Occasionally people ask us why we and other anthropologists feel tourism is a serious topic for study. Many seem to associate tourism only with recreation. What they fail to see is the magnitude of tourism and the globalizing effect it has on people living in almost every part of the world. There were 922 million air arrivals in 2008 providing the tourist industry and local economies with 940 billion dollars. With the world recession and the H1N1 virus scare, the numbers dropped to 880 million arrivals and a 6 percent decrease in sales receipts in 2009. Despite the decline, tourism is still clearly a major world industry and a key source of income for many countries.

But the revenue it generates is not the only measure of tourism's impact: it has a far-reaching social impact as well. This is especially true for people such as the Tharu, who have had to adjust to being gawked at and disturbed by tourists and misrepresented as backward and ignorant people by tour guides and the staff of local tourist hotels and guesthouses. It is the social impact of tourism that especially interested us during our fieldwork in Pipariya.

Pipariya and the Tharu

To understand how tourism has affected the Tharu, we need to look at their physical location and social position in Nepal. Nepal lies on India's northern border. It is roughly divided into three environmental zones: the Himalaya, the tallest mountain range in the world; the central zone, composed of the Mahabharat mountain range (Kathmandu is in this zone); and the *tarai*, a narrow belt of alluvial land that merges into the Indo-Gangetic Plain. In times past, the *tarai* was a thickly forested region fed by heavy monsoon rains. Because of its thick jungle, but especially because of the prevalence of malaria, the region was not densely populated, and was avoided by farmers from North India or Nepalese from the more populated valleys and hills to the north.

The Tharu, however, were able to live in the *tarai*, in small villages around which they cleared the forest to make fields for farming. (One reason for their ability to survive there may be a developed resistance to malaria.) Guarded by their inhospitable environment, they had limited contact with Indians living to their south and Nepalese living to their north, but historically were part of the various hill kingdoms that were united in the 18th century to become modern Nepal.

This isolation changed during the 1950s. The government, with help from the United States, organized an aggressive program of malaria eradication involving the use of the highly effective insecticide, DDT, which was later shown to be environmentally very destructive. As the threat of malaria diminished, immigrants from the mountains of Nepal flooded into the *tarai*. They cleared away much of the forest for farming and came to outnumber the aboriginal Tharu in many parts of their territory. Pipariya has experienced this influx of outsiders and is no longer exclusively a Tharu community. Immigration has shaped two very different and spatially separate social worlds in the village. The central neighborhood *(tol)* represents the original Tharu village; outlying areas around the center are inhabited mostly by Brahmin immigrants. There is limited social interaction between these groups despite their close proximity.

The people of the village, whatever their ethnicity, live in much the same manner. Although a Nepali would be able to distinguish the houses of Brahmans from those of the Tharu, the differences are not obvious to outsiders. When we lived here between 1989 and 1991, all the houses, despite differences in their style, consisted of wooden frameworks supporting thatched or tiled roofs and elephant grass walls plastered over with a mixture of mud and cow dung. Since then, Brahmans have begun to build houses of brick, followed by many Tharu households which prospered from remittances sent home by young men who have gone to the Middle East to work in recent years.

When the park opened in 1972, it was largely the Brahmans, Chhetris, and Newars (high-ranking ethnic groups that also dominate Nepali politics) who built, owned, and ran the tourist facilities near the park entrance. By the time of our fieldwork in 1989, there were luxury wildlife lodges for the wealthy and, for the more budget conscious, guesthouses of differing quality and service. It was these people and facilities that organized village walks to Pipariya, located only two kilometers away, and who framed what tourists would see when they entered the village.

The Tharu as primitives

To attract tourists and entice them to take village walks, the hotel and guesthouse keepers have created a special image of the Tharu. Basing their description on a stereotype held by high caste Nepalese, they represent the Tharu as aboriginal forest dwellers, "co-existing with wild animals." They live apart, they say, from the civilized world and cling to their "primitive" ways. One brochure produced by a hotel in another part of Nepal read this way:

> Living quietly in small clearings in the Terai forests are the little-known Tharu people of southern Nepal . . . they are a primitive native people and one of the last of the indigenous tribes of the sub-continent who remain virtually untouched by civilization. They depend almost entirely on the land for their food and livelihood [,] they still plow with wooden plows, wear clothing that they make themselves, live in big straw-thatched community houses at times with more than sixty people to a house and are, to this day still cut off from the outside world and, by their own choosing independent from it. [Tourists] will spend one day visiting a Tharu village. They will find a colorful, interesting, smiling, friendly and hospitable people and they will be able to visit a Tharu home, view their primitive artwork—painted with their own village made paints and dyes on the mud walls of their homes—and, in the space of a few hours look into another world, one that time and the tide of civilization seem—fortunately—to have forgotten.

Less elaborate brochures are also published by many of the Chitwan tourist hotels. In all of them, the Tharu are presented as a primitive people living a life unchanged for centuries. The terse paragraph under the heading "Cultural Tours" in one brochure reads in its entirety: "The Tharus are the original settlers of Chitwan, co-existing with the wild animals in total isolation until the late 1950's. A visit to their villages is a step back in time, to a way of life hundreds of years old." In short, the Tharus are equated with the other natural wonders of Chitwan. They become part of the valley's natural history and, like the tiger or rhinoceros, exotic creatures living apart from the rest of us to be viewed as a curiosity of nature.

In addition, the way tourists arrive in Pipariya is intended to support this view of the Tharu. They usually arrive in ox-carts hired for the occasion although they may also get there on foot. The ride in the ox-cart is part of the experience, serving to symbolically convey modern visitors into the traditional past, still supposedly present in the Tharu villages of Chitwan.

There are some features of dress and material culture that guides use to mark the Tharu as authentically "primitive." Indeed, the success of the village walk is predicated on the village's appearance of authenticity, meaning that it fits the brochure descriptions. For the village to be authentic, it must look "traditional," and the Tharu *tol* (neighborhood) when we lived there in the early 1990s looked eminently traditional, with houses, as we noted above, constructed of elephant grass (resembling thin bamboo) plastered with a mix of mud and cow dung. In addition, women appear different. Women usually bear the brunt of the village walk because they are the ones most likely to be at home and thus the focus of attention for tourists and guides. Although Tharu men contradict the image—they look more "modern," wearing Western style slacks and shirts and to some extent working as laborers in the tourist hotels and lodges, Tharu women wear lungis (a cloth wrapped around the waist) and short bodices, which contrasts with the sari worn by Brahman women. Indeed, women's appearance, in Pipariya as elsewhere in Nepal, is where ethnicity is most apparent and represented in everyday life. Also, older Tharu women often have tattoos on their forearms and legs (a dying practice now, as few young women will consent to be tattooed these days), distinguishing them from Brahman-Chhetri women. And it is these features that guides are most likely to point out to tourists.

Tour guides adhere to the tourist industry's representation of the Tharu but also reflect the cultural stereotypes of the Tharu that support and relate to their status in Nepal's social hierarchy. Guides come almost exclusively from the high-ranked Brahman, Chhetri, and Newar ethnic groups. Most are local but some, especially those working for the luxury hotels, come from Kathmandu. Brahmans, followed by the Chhetris, occupy the top rungs of Nepal's ethnic hierarchy while the Tharu are ranked low. The guides' high rank gives them a natural sense of superiority that affects how they behave toward the Tharu. They display an unwarranted expertise on Tharu cultural life, and they assume they have a right to treat the Tharu with the lack of respect usually shown to people of lower status. They also rarely ask the Tharu to explain their own cultural artifacts, behavior, and knowledge. This view was confirmed by one of our Tharu friends. He speculated that because they looked down on the Tharu, the Brahman guides did not want to put themselves in the position of asking them (the Tharu) questions. Instead they repeated lore passed down from one generation of guides to another.

An example of a guide's power and insensitivity involved the household of the village's largest and most important Tharu landowner, who had died shortly before we arrived in the village. A guide had brought a group of tourists on a village walk, and, not satisfied with simply showing them the house, had taken them into the kitchen. The intrusion into the kitchen (where strangers should not venture) was a gross violation of Tharu, and in fact, South Asian, etiquette and it imperiled the (ritual) purity of the food that had been prepared. One tourist even stuck his finger into a pot to see what had been cooked. The guide was aware that his actions violated a number of taboos, such as entering the kitchen and touching the food. But given his high opinion of his own status and contempt for the Tharu, he went ahead with the intrusion anyway. In this case, the incensed household head had chased the whole group out with a stick, and had threatened to thrash the guide if he ever did it again. Since then, the village walk has confined itself strictly to the courtyard.

On another occasion a guide who was from Kathmandu asked two Tharu girls why houses were decorated with colored hand prints; considering that he had brought groups through the village many times, he must surely have noticed that the decorations appeared over the festival of Tihar, which had just concluded. The girls, who had been responsible for decorating our house in the same way, brusquely replied that they didn't know. This guide had also started off on the wrong foot in this village when he first arrived by refusing a seat that the wife of the chief Tharu landowner had offered him.

Guides may also use their depiction of the Tharu to symbolize their own higher status. By describing the Tharu as primitive, guides infer that they themselves, and the tourists they address, are members of a more sophisticated modern world. In contrast, the Tharu are presented as backward, primitive, *jangali* (spelled jungly in English but essentially pronounced the same) people, whom "time and the tide of civilization seem to have forgotten." Most Tharu we interviewed about these matters distrusted the guides, believing that a great deal of what guides told tourists about the Tharu was untrue. Some believed this was because the guides held the Tharu in contempt; others attributed it to their ignorance. One man told Arjun, "The guides . . . think we are ignorant and backward so they do not come to us to find out about our culture." Then smiling he said, "Even if they did, we wouldn't tell them."

The guide's power is also amplified by the ignorance of Western tourists. Typically the guides by-pass the houses of Brahman hill settlers and take their charges directly into the heart of the Tharu settlement. Inexperienced foreign tourists may actually find it hard to differentiate between the two village areas because Brahmans and Tharu share much the same material culture and technologies. Indeed, tourists can rarely distinguish between Nepalese groups unless differences are pointed out to them and the task of differentiation falls to the tourist guide.

The Tourists

Most tourists to Nepal come from the United States, Western Europe, Japan, and Australia. Most arrive in Chitwan knowing little or nothing about the Tharu and Nepalese rural life. Most tend to ask questions that reflect their own cultural backgrounds. And most are unsure about how to behave during a village walk when they are in Pipariya. On numerous occasions we witnessed tourists walking slowly through the village, peering at objects, photographing people and animals, and listening to their tour guide as he lectured to them about the Tharu and pointed out objects of interest. "Here come your *didi-bahini-haru* (sisters)" Geeta, our neighbor's daughter, would say to us when she spotted a group of tourists entering the village. This was her favorite joke. Once, when several young American women had entered the family's compound, Geeta's father had called jokingly to Arjun, "There goes your *salt* (sister-in-law)." People in the household enjoyed these jokes based on Kate's supposed shared ethnicity with the tourists.

Some of our most insightful observations of tourists resulted from when they interacted with us. We lived in a Tharu-style house located among other Tharu houses. Although we usually managed to avoid contact with tourists, at times, we, alongside our neighbors, became objects for tourists to observe. As a white American woman, Kate stood out and would attract the attention of tourists by her presence. (Arjun is a Sri Lankan and largely went unnoticed by tourists, for whom one native of South Asia looks very much like another). Upon seeing her, tourists asked why she was there and what it was like for us to live in Pipariya. Questions included, "Are the Tharus superstitious?" "Do they have a church or organized religion?" "Do you eat with your hands?" "Didn't you feel grossed out at first?" "Do you have any American kitchen conveniences?" One woman even told Kate that she was very brave to live in the village, which Kate interpreted as a compliment for being able to put up without the conveniences of Western living.

Although we generally tried to avoid the tourists when they came through, for a brief period Kate went out of her way to engage them. This was when the young men in the village were looking for ways to raise money for a youth club, and hit upon the idea of doing so from tourists. At the request of the club, Kate wrote up a one-page description of the aims of the club: to encourage Tharu youth to study, to preserve Tharu culture, to support Tharu religious ceremonies. Arjun made a sheet to record donations, with columns for the contributors' names, home country, and amounts given.

The next time a group of tourists entered the village, Kate approached them and after some small talk made a pitch for money. In response, one middle-aged man with a video camera asked "What do they need money for?" Kate explained that in addition to building a club house, the young men wanted to buy some sports equipment such as soccer balls and volleyballs. "Why do they need money to build a house?" the man challenged her. "I thought if you wanted to build a house here you just built it. The wood's there; grass is there, mud's there." Kate pointed out how few trees there were outside the national park; "Wood is very precious," she explained. "It's expensive." Ignoring her request for money, the man changed the subject. "If the door's open, can I just look in?" he asked, taking a few steps towards one of the houses. "I don't think they'd appreciate your going into their house," Kate responded. The man turned away and started to film a group of children who had gathered to stare at the visitors. Kate went back to the house in defeat.

Of course not all tourists behave in intrusive, ethnocentric, or uninformed ways. Some seemed discomfited by their role as intruders in Tharu daily life and stayed in the background. Others were careful to be polite at least by their own standards and some seemed better prepared to ask meaningful questions. Many were interested in the initiatives of the youth club and gave money to support them.

Tharu Views of Tourists

Tharu have a very strong ethic of hospitality. There is no Tharu word for tourist, who are referred to with the Nepali word for guest, *pahuna*. As such, the Tharu often treated their visitors with patience and good cheer. Still, there is some disagreement among them on how to respond to the village walk, or even whether or not a response is necessary. Some saw benefit from the occasional tip and children have learned to beg. But many are distressed by the negative way guides portray them to tourists.

Interestingly, Tharu distinguish between tourists who arrive as part of a tour and those who come by themselves without a guide. On one occasion, two college-aged American women had just passed Kate on the dirt road of the village when one of them stepped off into the ditch and bent over to photograph something. Curious, Kate asked her whether she was photographing plants. "Marijuana" she giggled in reply (Cannabis grew wild throughout the village and was smoked by some of our neighbors, especially the elderly.) Further down the road, Kate met our neighbor, Thagawa, and another young Tharu man, who were looking after the retreating figures of the Americans with curiosity. "No guide," Thagawa commented to Kate with approval. "They are pure tourists."

Tharu offer different explanations for why tourists might be interested in visiting a Tharu village. The most positive is to say that tourists are interested in Tharu culture and in the way the Tharu live. For example, one man opined that tourists came on village walks because they were interested in learning about the culture and way of life of Nepal's original inhabitants. Another, a woman, welcomed the village walks. She observed that local people are unable to visit foreign countries, but now they are able to meet foreigners who come to see them.

But many Tharu attributed less flattering reasons for why tourists visited Pipariya. One person suggested that tourists visit the village because they consider the Tharu to be backward and *jangali* people. A Tharu woman was critical of the village walks because, she said, foreigners took pictures of the poverty of the Tharu and then showed that poverty in their own countries, but she also acknowledged that local people made a living off the tourists, with jobs in hotels and through tips and presents when tourists visit their houses.

Many Tharu would prefer that guides acted as interpreters between the village people and tourists. Some of the most positive interaction we witnessed between Tharu and tourists occurred when tourists wandered through the village by themselves and stopped to talk to people. There were a few young men who spoke English well enough to make this meaningful. The Tharu enjoyed these encounters, and our assistant, Surendra, would sometimes invite tourists to eat in his house.

In some ways, anthropologists are like tourists. We are foreigners who come for a limited amount of time, ask endless questions, and take numerous photographs. But unlike tourists, anthropologists don't depend on other people to mediate their relations with the societies they study. A cardinal rule of the anthropological method is that we must learn the language of the people we seek to understand and immerse ourselves in their lives. It is in the nature of modern anthropological fieldwork that anthropologists will build enduring relationships with the people who taught them what it is like to be a Tharu, a Kayapo, or a Barbadian. It is not surprising that the most satisfactory tourist–Tharu encounters, certainly for the Tharu, were those unmediated by guides, in which tourists were sometimes invited to Tharu homes and entertained as guests.

Conclusion

As we watched tourists come and go in Pipariya we concluded several things. First, most tourists, especially those participating in tour groups, knew little or nothing about how the Tharu actually lived and a few treated the Tharu disrespectfully, almost as if they were objects in a museum exhibit. Second, tour operators represented the Tharu inaccurately. Although Tharu do display some ethnic differences from other Nepalese, they are not primitive aborigines that time had forgotten. Instead, they are an integral part of contemporary Nepali society. They till their land in ways characteristic of many Nepali farmers; Tharu men work in the tourist industry, their children attend school, and they see themselves as part of the Nepali nation. In Pipariya, the response of young Tharu men to their disadvantaged position in Nepali society was to form a youth club to promote education for children in a community where many believe it makes more sense for children to work on the farm than attend school. They became aware of their own customs and heritage but also sought to preserve their culture against the changes that were going on around them. Indeed, one of the consequences of cultural tourism is that it makes local people aware of their culture in new ways. Taken for granted ways of living and customary practices become invested with new meanings; art that was once produced for religious or ritual purposes become curios for sale to tourists and dances that might have once been an integral aspect of festivals and life cycle rituals become reconfigured as cultural performances. As culture becomes objectified and transformed, social relationships also undergo change and are understood in new ways.

Postscript

A return to Pipariya in 2009 revealed dramatic changes. The Tharu *tol* had changed almost beyond recognition, with brick houses and TV antennas sprouting everywhere, the fruits of the work of young Tharu men who have gone abroad in recent years as migrant labor. The most significant change however concerned the Tharu response to the village walk. Many years after we had left, the Tharu of Pipariya built a Tharu Culture Museum on land donated by the wealthiest Tharu landowner in the village. The idea for such a museum originated in the youth club for which we had helped to raise money, and its members in turn received advice and financial help from a Nepali conservation NGO. The museum, made of brick, was designed to resemble a traditional Tharu house and consisted of a large hall with two adjacent smaller rooms. The hall had a number of displays all featuring Tharu artifacts once used in different contexts of daily life—fishing equipment, objects used in religious ceremonies, and so on—with murals on the wall behind depicting the contexts in which these artifacts were used. It had been hard to locate these artifacts. Few Tharu own them anymore, as people prefer more durable goods of steel and plastic bought in the bazaar. In the center were three mannequins made by a local artist, wearing traditional Tharu dress, which no one except the very elderly wear anymore. The Tharu museum levies an entrance fee and is now the main focus of the village walk.

It is not a coincidence that the museum emerged here. The press of tourists and the unflattering view of the village that came with them played an important part. So did the curious anthropologist who showed interest in Tharu culture. These forces led local Tharu to think about their customs and practices in new ways. The museum tells the story of the past that the Tharu would like both foreigners as well as their fellow Nepalese to know. But it is also a story that they tell to themselves and especially to their children whose lives no longer depend on the artifacts preserved in the museum.

Chitwan Tharu today have become globalized. Their young men work in places as far afield as the Middle East, Malaysia, and Japan, and some have arrived in the United States as winners of the Green Card lottery. The culture that the Tharu objectify in the museum is not the one that they now live. Instead, it is an image of the past they wish to preserve, because it is closely bound up with their identity. It is the outcome not only of the Tharu encounter with foreign visitors, but also of the changing Tharu relationship with the ethnic groups that dominate Nepal. As Nepal democratizes, historically marginalized communities like the Tharu have begun to assert themselves and to foreground their own identity. An objectified understanding of their culture—as a thing of artifacts and customs—has become a crucial component of the process of distinguishing themselves from other Nepalese. Tourism has played an important role in this change.

✓● Study and Review on myanthrolab.com

Review Questions

1. How did tourist hotels and guides portray the Tharu? Why do you think they did so in this manner?

2. What was the Tharu view of the many tour groups and unaccompanied tourists who traversed their community?

3. In what way did the Tharu manage to separate their past from the present?

4. How have the Tharu become globalized?

5. What role do remittances play in changing Tharu society?

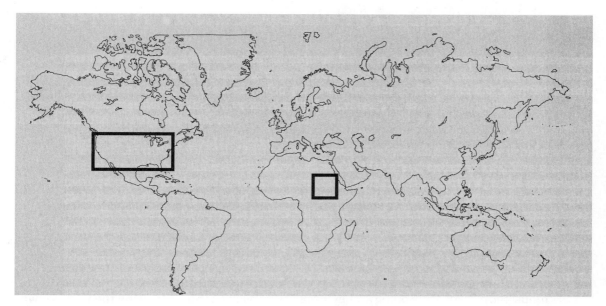

34

Nuer Refugees in America

Dianna Shandy

In the early days of the discipline, anthropologists usually studied non-Western groups that they assumed were bounded and clearly definable. Such groups were named (often by outsiders) and were thought to have territories and a common language and culture. Although anthropologists recognized that many of the groups they studied had outside connections— that they freely traded goods, borrowed culture, intermarried, and migrated—most still felt it was reasonable to talk about groups as if they were bounded units. However, the picture is changing, as this updated article by Dianna Shandy clearly shows. Today people are on the move. Some are migrants looking for economic opportunity; others are refugees. Here, Shandy, using the case of the Nuer from South Sudan, shows how refugees fleeing a civil war manage to gain relocation in the United States and how they have sought to adapt to the demands of life here, while maintaining ties abroad. A key to the process is the role played by the United Nations and social service agencies and the Nuer's own determination to better their lives.*

((•─[**Listen** to the **Chapter Audio** on **myanthrolab.com**

A Nuer youth, Thok Ding (not his real name) lies prone alongside two other boys on the dusty, clay ground on the outskirts of a village in South Sudan. A man crouches over him with a razor blade. Beginning with the right side, the man makes six parallel cuts from each side of the youth's forehead to the center to create scars called gaar. *This ritual scarification, which has been outlawed in Nuer areas since the 1980s, still marks entry into manhood for many Nuer youth.*

A few years later in Minneapolis, Minnesota, Thok sits in pained concentration in front of a computer screen in a driver's license examination office. Still weak in English, he struggles to recall the multiple choice response sequence he memorized to pass the exam, in this stressful, but less painful, American rite of passage into adulthood.

When I began ethnographic work among Nuer refugees living in the United States in 1996, I immediately was struck by the incongruity of their lives. The Nuer are a famous people in anthropology. They were the subject of three books by the well-known late British social anthropologist Sir Edward E. Evans-Pritchard, who described their pastoralist mode of subsistence, complex segmented kinship system, and religion. Evans-Pritchard conducted research among the Nuer in the 1930s. He described the Nuer as a tall, independent, confident people whose existence revolved around the needs of their cattle, especially the requirement to move the animals from high to low ground and back again each year. During the dry season from September to April, the cattle were herded to lower ground where there was still water and grass. During the rainy season, the lowlands became a swampy lagoon and the herds had to be moved to the highlands where rain had restored the range. This transhumant life-style and the need to guard cattle against raiders from nearby tribes had shaped Nuer society. (The Nuer were also the subject of a well-known ethnographic film, "The Nuer," made by Robert Gardner and released in 1970, which showed them to be much as Evans-Pritchard had described them.)

So when I first met Nuer people in Minnesota in the mid 1990s, these African pastoralists seemed out of place. Tall (some men are well over six feet in height) and still displaying the (for men) prominent horizontal forehead scars received at their initiations, the Nuer had come to live in one of the coldest parts of the United States. Why had they left their ancestral home? What did their status as refugees mean and how did they get it? How had they managed to come to the United States? Why had they been settled, as it turns out, in more than thirty different U.S. states? How would a people raised as cattle herders adapt to urban America? Would they remain in the United States on a temporary or permanent basis? How would they maintain relationships with the families they left behind? Would they ever go home? And finally in a broader sense, what does all this tell us about the interconnectedness of a globalizing world and about anthropology's role in it?

Becoming a Refugee

Until recently, most Americans called the people who settled here *immigrants*. No distinctions were made based on the reasons people came here or the circumstances they had left behind. In general, their arrival was encouraged and welcome because the country was spacious and their skills and labor were needed.

Today, things are different. There are immigrants and *refugees*. In the past, refugees were a kind of immigrant. They were people who came here to escape from intolerable conditions in their homelands, such as pogroms, the threat of military conscription, civil wars, and famine. The fact that they were escaping from something, however, did not affect whether or not they could enter the United States. Most people, especially those from Europe, were welcome.

Over the last sixty years, however, refugees have come to occupy a formal status, both in the eyes of the United Nations and U.S. immigration officials. They are not just *internally displaced persons (IDPs),* those who have left their homes but who are still in their own country. Officially, meaning how the United Nations and national governments define them, a refugee is a person who has a "well founded fear of persecution" based on any of five factors: race, religion, nationality, membership in a particular social group, or political opinion, and who has left their home country. How the United Nations or national governments apply this definition when they seek to certify individuals as refugees varies. But the number of people that claim to fit this description and who seek asylum skyrocketed at the end of the cold war in 1989 to an estimated 15 million people in 2013.

Bureaucracies control who can be classified as a refugee. In 1950 the United Nations established a formal agency to help with the refugee "problem" headed by the United Nations High Commissioner for Refugees (UNHCR). The agency recognizes three options, or what it calls "durable solutions," to address the situation of refugees around the world: voluntary repatriation to the country of origin, integration into a country of first asylum, or rarely, third country resettlement, meaning a move from one country of asylum to one that offers possibilities for a more permanent home. Initially sheltered in refugee camps, forced migrants can apply for official refugee status with the hope of resettlement in another country, or that conditions will stabilize in their own country, allowing them to return home.

Many countries have agreed to take in a certain number of refugees as a way of settling them more permanently, and the United States is one of them. To do this, the United States sets a limit on the number of refugees it will accept each year and uses a bureaucratic process to screen prospective refugees it might be willing to take in. In recent years, the United States has resettled an average of about 60,000 refugees here each year, with a sharp dip in numbers in the wake of September 11, 2001. The process is complicated by the fact that the criteria for admission can change, different government officials interpret the criteria dissimilarly, and resettlement policy can shift from one year to the next. It is also complicated by cross-cultural misunderstanding. The U.S. bureaucracy works differently from the way governments operate in the refugee's country of origin or country of asylum. Languages are a major barrier. Categories of meaning are not shared. The screening process is intended to determine "real" refugees, or those who cannot be protected by their home governments, and "economic" migrants who leave their home voluntarily to seek a better life. In practice the distinction is often difficult to establish.

The Nuer living in the United States have managed to come through this process successfully. They have made it to camps that process refugees, discovered how to enter the bureaucratic process designed to certify them as refugees, learned how to tell a sufficiently convincing refugee story to gain certification, and found a way to get on the list to be resettled in the United States.

Thok Ding's life illustrates this process. Thok was born in South Sudan and lived in a small village. As in most Nuer households, Thok lived with his mother, father, siblings, and his father's extended family. Thok had family members who lived in town and attended school, but there was no school in his village. His first memory is of going to the forest to take care of his calves when he was seven or eight. He would leave home in the early morning with other boys his age, taking food with him to eat while he was grazing the cattle and protecting the calves from wild animals. Girls, on the other hand, would stay closer to home and were charged with milking the cows.

When he was in his early teens, he, along with other boys his age, underwent the ritual scarification *gaar* ceremony ushering him into manhood. After undergoing this painful ritual, Thok said that now that he was a man, he could be "free." "You can do whatever you like. You can have a woman. You can have a home by yourself. You can live away from your parents."

Shortly after his initiation, the civil war caught up with him. Fueled by events that extend back much further in time, civil war engulfed Sudan for much of the second half of the 20th century. Sudan gained independence from joint English-Egyptian colonial rule in 1956. Around the same time, the first civil war started, with a brief interlude of peace before the second civil war started in 1983. This conflict in Sudan frequently is attributed to social distinctions based on geography (north-south), ethnicity (Arab-African), and religion (Muslim-Christian). But these are fluid categories. From a southern perspective, northern Muslim Arabs entered their land in the 1800s looking for ivory and slaves. Northerners were favored under colonial rule, which gave them more power and increased tension with people, such as the Nuer, living in the south. In 2005, a peace agreement was signed between southern rebels and the Khartoum government ending what is known as the North-South war in Sudan. And in 2011 South Sudan gained its independence and became the world's newest country.

Nuer society has suffered cataclysmic shifts in the decades since Evans-Pritchard conducted his fieldwork, a fact well documented by anthropologist Sharon Hutchinson in her book entitled *Nuer Dilemmas* published in 1996. For example, instead of merely regulating Nuer seasonal cattle drives, the change of seasons in the southern Sudan also dictated the rhythm of the civil war. The dry season made it possible to move heavy artillery across the clay plains; during the wet season the same plains are impassable. The war and its effects were the major cause of migration.

In the late 1980s, government troops attacked Thok's village, killing many people including his father. Many of the survivors elected to stay and to keep herding cattle. With his father dead, Thok decided to leave Sudan. He traveled on foot for three days with his mother and siblings and their cattle to an Ethiopian refugee camp called Itang.

One feature of camp life was the presence of a Christian mission school, which provided Thok with his first taste of formal education, something that would prove useful later as he sought refugee status. He advanced quickly in school, skipping several grades. Seventh grade, however, stands out for him as the real beginning of his education, because he passed a national exam. As a result, he was transferred to Gambela, another Ethiopian camp, to attend school, leaving his mother and siblings behind. Food scarcity made life in Gambela very difficult. Thok recalls that students were given only a small amount of corn each month. They would grind the grain into flour, cook the mixture with water, and eat it plain without a stew.

His education at Gambela progressed nicely, but was ended when war broke out in Ethiopia. Threatened by the dangers it posed, Thok rejoined his mother and siblings. Together they returned to Sudan where the United Nations had established a temporary camp to care for the Sudanese refugees who were streaming back across the border from Ethiopia. Thok weighed his options and decided to return to Ethiopia on his own. He went to the capital of Ethiopia, Addis Ababa, where he encountered some friends from school who shared information on how to get to refugee camps in Kenya.

He traveled to Kenya by bus, negotiating his way past border and police checkpoints along the way. He was arrested once by Kenyan police and had to spend the night in jail before they turned him over to the U.N. authorities that ran the nearby refugee camp. Once in the camp, he filled out a form that documented his background, and requested that he be considered for resettlement in another country. Since Thok had no relatives who had been resettled in other countries, he applied for resettlement anywhere that would accept refugees from Sudan. These included Australia, Canada, and Sweden as well as the United States, the country that finally admitted him.

Two years elapsed from the time Thok arrived in the camp until he was sent to the United States. Life in the Kenyan camp was much more difficult than the one where he had stayed in Ethiopia. There was nothing to do, no river to fish, no place to keep cattle, and no garden plots. Thok did, however, meet some friends he had made earlier in school, and together they cooked food and found ways to pass the long days in the camp. He and his friends also listened to the stories other Nuer told of their encounters with the refugee officials who interviewed people requesting resettlement. In a tragic commentary on how devastation can seem "normal," they learned that the biggest mistake people made was to invent dramatic stories to make themselves eligible for resettlement. For example, one Nuer man said, *"People feel they need a reason, so they tell the person interviewing them that they killed someone and if they return to Sudan they will be put in jail. But the story didn't work because the interviewer thought the refugee must be a violent man."* The Nuer men who worked as interpreters in the camps believed there was a better approach. *"We told the community, we need to tell them the reality. Don't say you killed someone, just say you were caught in the crossfire."* They had learned that the refugee officials were looking for certain kinds of experiences to determine who fit the criteria for refugee resettlement.

In addition to recounting a plausible story that indicates why they would be persecuted if they returned home, refugees must also pass a medical screening and sign a promissory note to repay the cost of their airfare to the United States once they have settled and found work. Thok passed through this process successfully, and with a ticket provided for him by the International Organization for Migration, flew to the United States. He was met at the airport by a representative from Lutheran Social Services, one of many U.S. voluntary agencies responsible for resettling refugees.

Adapting to America

Some immigrants to the United States rely on family or friends to help them find a home and job in America. But many refugees depend on voluntary agencies or "volags" to help with settlement. These agencies are under contract to the U.S. government and receive a stipend for each refugee that they place. Volags help refugees with such necessities as finding a place to live, getting a job, learning to ride the bus, and buying food. They also help them complete paperwork documenting the existence of family members who were left behind, since there may be a chance to bring them over later. Volags emphasize how important it is for refugees to find a job and become self-sufficient. Volags provide refugees with a small initial cash stipend to help them get established. But the money doesn't last long and refugees are encouraged to start working as soon as possible, often within the first week or two after arrival. An agency helped place Thok in Minnesota, find him an apartment, and secure a job.

There were about thirty refugees from Sudan and Somalia on Thok's flight from Nairobi, Kenya, to New York's JFK International Airport. When Thok boarded the plane, he knew no one. By the time he arrived in New York many hours later, he felt like the eight Sudanese men he had traveled with were his new best friends. In a wrenching sort of dispersal, the eight men were all directed by airline staff to different gates at the airport to await the next leg of their journey to far-flung destinations, like San Diego, California; Nashville, Tennessee; Dallas, Texas; and Minneapolis, Minnesota.

A representative from Lutheran Social Services and a volunteer from a local church greeted Thok when he arrived on his own in Minneapolis. His few possessions fit in a small bag that he carried with him on the plane. The man from Lutheran Social Services gave him shampoo and a toothbrush and took him to Burger King. Thok found the food very strange and difficult to eat. Thok stayed the first night in the volunteer's home—a widower in his mid sixties who regularly helped out Lutheran Social Services in this way. Thok spoke some English, but he relied mostly on gestures to communicate with his host. The next day the volunteer took Thok to Lutheran Social Services to complete paperwork.

When they finished with the paperwork, the case manager who had met Thok at the airport took him to what was to be his apartment. Thok found the place to be very dirty, particularly the carpeting that had not been cleaned after the last tenants departed. There was a strong smell of cigarette smoke, cockroaches in the kitchen, and a very leaky faucet in the bathroom. Despite these problems, Thok would have his own place that would be affordable when he got a job. Later, the man Thok had stayed with the previous night brought over some furniture that had been donated by church members.

Over the coming week, Thok met with his case manager to discuss getting a job. Where refugees work and the kinds of jobs that they can get depend somewhat on the level of education and training they possessed prior to arrival in the United States. Upon arrival, most Nuer have little formal education and can, unfortunately, only find jobs that most people born in the United States do not want such as unskilled factory worker, security guard, parking lot attendant, fast food server, and nursing home assistant. Or, if they do have a degree when they arrive, like many immigrants, they are "underemployed," or work in jobs below their level of credentials. Many of the Nuer who have settled in the Midwest have found work in meat packing plants. Thok first got a job filling beverage trays for airplanes at the airport. His back and arms ached from the lifting he was required to do, and he did not like his boss.

Several weeks later, Thok spotted another Nuer man while shopping at Target. Thok did not know him personally, but after they started talking he discovered that he knew the village where the man was from in Sudan. It was good to see someone from "home," and Thok invited him back to his apartment to cook a meal and eat together. This man had moved to Minnesota from Iowa and was able to tell Thok the names and phone numbers of some Nuer who were living in Des Moines. Thok knew some of these people from the refugee camps in Ethiopia, and the next day he bought a phone card to get in touch. Thok could hardly believe his ears when he heard his friend John Wai answer the phone. After a conversation that lasted until the phone card expired, Thok decided to board a bus and leave Minnesota to move to Iowa. John had talked about the sizable Nuer community living in Des Moines and the good wages paid by a meat packing company. Thok left a message for his case manager saying that he was going. He packed his personal items, left the furniture in the apartment, and boarded a Greyhound bus.

In Des Moines, Thok moved in with John and another Nuer man. Thok worked in a packing plant for a while, but found it very difficult. At first his job was to kill pigs as they entered the processing line. He found it so hard to sleep at night after doing this repeatedly all day that he asked to be transferred to another part of the line. He still found the work exceedingly hard. One motivation to find a job quickly is to make it possible for him to bring over his family members to join him, but Thok has not managed to do this yet.

In addition to his mother and siblings, Thok would also like to bring over a wife. There are roughly three Nuer men for every Nuer woman in the United States, and most of the women are already married or engaged to be married. Thok and other Nuer men struggle with what they perceive as "the unreasonable levels of freedom" afforded to women in U.S. society. One way to marry a wife with more "traditional" Nuer values, or so men think, is to let their family facilitate a marriage in Sudan or in Ethiopia and try to bring the wife over as a spouse or a refugee.

Staying in Touch

Refugee groups are deliberately "scattered" geographically across the United States when they are resettled. Policy makers believe that dispersal increases individuals' ability to adapt successfully to their new environment and that it decreases any disruptive impact on the host community that receives the refugees. However, even though refugees are "placed" in particular locales in the United States, they seldom stay put. Hmong, originally from the highlands of Southeast Asia, and now residents of Minnesota, are a case in point. They, like the Nuer, are well known for moving frequently after arrival in the United States. Nuer, who moved regularly as part of their lives in South Sudan, continue a kind of nomadism in the United States. Nuer move frequently—from apartment to apartment, from city to city, and from state to state. As a result of having been resettled in more than thirty different states in America, Nuer have many residency options to consider and have a tendency to move where they have relatives, friends, or jobs.

Staying in contact is very important to many Nuer refugees. They are adept at devising strategies for remaining in contact with other Nuer dispersed across the United States and those whom they left behind in Africa. The process of incorporation into the United States as a refugee is also about maintaining ties to Africa. One aspect of Nuer life that sets them apart from the experiences of previous waves of immigrants to the United States is the means by which they keep in contact with those who remain at home in South Sudan, in neighboring African countries, and around the world.

Immigrants have always retained some ties with the homes they left. But, in a 21st century context the possibilities for frequent, affordable, and rapid contact are greatly expanded. Anthropologists refer to these crosscutting social ties that span the borders of nation-states as *transnationalism*. For instance, Thok, who wants to marry, could phone his brother in Gambela, Ethiopia, to arrange the event. He can use Western Union to send money, or *remittances*, to his brother to buy cows to give to the prospective bride's father. In Nuer eyes, the groom does not even need to be present for the marriage to be legitimate, but this is not true in the eyes of immigration authorities. Even though the groom can do his part to sponsor the marriage from the United States, he still must travel to Ethiopia for the marriage to be recognized officially for immigration purposes. The bride can apply as a refugee herself but increases her chances of resettlement by also applying as a spouse joining her husband. Now that the war has ended, some men are returning home to South Sudan to look for work and to start a family. Other men who are married are leaving their wives and children in the United States while they return to South Sudan to explore the options for their family's future.

Those in the diaspora maintain close ties with friends and family in South Sudan, in other African countries, and around the world. Therefore, a focus on the lives of Sudanese refugees in Africa is an important part of understanding Nuer refugees' lives in the United States. These transnational linkages influence Nuer people's decisions in the United States.

Conclusion

Refugees are a special category of immigrant to the United States. Often seen as victims of tragic circumstances, refugees are also amazingly skillful at finding ways to survive these same circumstances. Refugees' lives depend on an international and national bureaucracy, and those who pass through the process represent a very small percentage of people who are displaced. Starting a life in a vastly different cultural environment than the one they were raised in presents a number of hardships. Refugees cope with these challenges by trying to maintain their original ethnic group identity. Transnational communication is one way to do this. So is moving to find people they know from their homelands.

Anthropologists, such as Evans-Pritchard, used to journey to faraway places to study distant "others." Nowadays it is often the objects of study that make the journey to the land of the anthropologists. Refugees such as the Nuer are among the latest newcomers to urban and suburban areas in the United States, and anthropologists can play a role in the adaptation process of Nuer in America. For example, some anthropologists work for voluntary agencies where they use their ethnographic research skills to ease refugee adjustment to unfamiliar surroundings. Other anthropologists work at the federal and state levels to advise about the efficacy of the social programs designed to meet the needs of recently arrived populations and suggest ways to improve programs. Sometimes these roles take the form of advocacy.

But through it all, anthropologists still do fieldwork in much the same way. They learn the language of refugee populations; ask open-ended questions in interviews; conduct participant observation at such events as weddings, funerals, graduation ceremonies, and political meetings; and try to understand life from their informants' perspectives.

Although he now knows an anthropologist, Thok Ding goes about his new life in America with the same independent determination that got him here in the first place. He will continue to move his residence if he thinks it will help him, increase his level of education, find better paying jobs, and eventually if all works out, marry a woman from South Sudan, bring his whole family to the United States and in the end, become a new American that maintains ties in the United States and in South Sudan.

Postscript

In December 2013, South Sudan descended into war between rival South Sudanese political factions. And, in April 2014, a lasting solution has not yet been agreed upon.

✓●—[Study and Review on myanthrolab.com

Review Questions

1. According to Shandy, what is the formal United Nations definition of a refugee?

2. What steps do forced migrants have to take to achieve resettlement as refugees?

3. How have Nuer refugees reorganized their lives to live successfully in the United States?

4. In this piece, why do you think we hear so much about men's lives instead of women's lives?

5. How have migrants to the United States changed the way anthropologists define groups they study and the focus of their research?

6. In what ways do social and financial remittances shape Nuer society at home and in the diaspora?

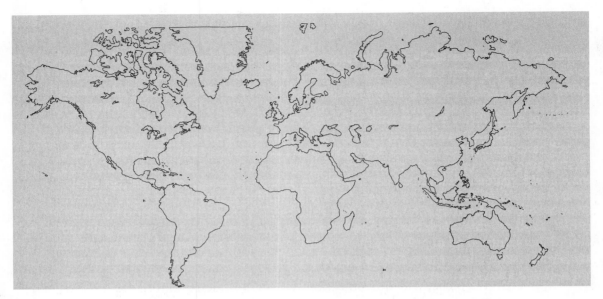

35

Global Women in the New Economy

Barbara Ehrenreich and Arlie Russell Hochschild

Movement is a key feature of today's world economy. Manufacturing jobs move from wealthier nations to poorer ones. An enormous variety of goods and raw materials travels by sea and rail to every part of the world. And more and more, so do people. Most come from poor nations to find work in rich ones. At first most were men; today many are women. In this selection, Barbara Ehrenreich and Arlie Russell Hochschild describe the history of female immigration, the reasons women migrate, the kinds of jobs they take in wealthier nations, the stresses their absence has on their own families, their lives in the families of others when they serve as nannies, and consequences for relative wealth among the world's nations. The authors conclude that women, both rich and poor, seek to better their condition and that migration increases interdependence among nations.*

((•—⎡**Listen** to the **Chapter Audio** on **myanthrolab.com**

"Whose baby are you?" Josephine Perera, a nanny from Sri Lanka, asks Isadora, her pudgy two-year-old charge in Athens, Greece.

Thoughtful for a moment, the child glances toward the closed door of the next room, in which her mother is working, as if to say, "That's my mother in there."

*Introduction and excerpt from Notes from *Global Woman: Nannies, Maids, and Sex Workers in the New Economy* by Barbara Ehrenreich and Arlie Hochschild. Reprinted by permission of Henry Holt and Company, LLC.

"No, you're *my* baby," Josephine teases, tickling Isadora lightly. Then, to settle the issue, Isadora answers, "Together!" She has two mommies—her mother and Josephine. And surely a child loved by many adults is richly blessed.

In some ways, Josephine's story—which unfolds in an extraordinary documentary film, *When Mother Comes Home for Christmas,* directed by Nilita Vachani—describes an unparalleled success. Josephine has ventured around the world, achieving a degree of independence her mother could not have imagined, and amply supporting her three children with no help from her ex-husband, their father. Each month she mails a remittance check from Athens to Hatton, Sri Lanka, to pay the children's living expenses and school fees. On her Christmas visit home, she bears gifts of pots, pans, and dishes. While she makes payments on a new bus that Suresh, her oldest son, now drives for a living, she is also saving for a modest dowry for her daughter, Norma. She dreams of buying a new house in which the whole family can live. In the meantime, her work as a nanny enables Isadora's parents to devote themselves to their careers and avocations.

But Josephine's story is also one of wrenching global inequality. While Isadora enjoys the attention of three adults, Josephine's three children in Sri Lanka have been far less lucky. According to Vachani, Josephine's youngest child, Suminda, was two—Isadora's age—when his mother first left home to work in Saudi Arabia. Her middle child, Norma, was nine; her oldest son, Suresh, thirteen. From Saudi Arabia, Josephine found her way first to Kuwait, then to Greece. Except for one two-month trip home, she has lived apart from her children for ten years. She writes them weekly letters, seeking news of relatives, asking about school, and complaining that Norma doesn't write back.

Although Josephine left the children under her sister's supervision, the two youngest have shown signs of real distress. Norma has attempted suicide three times. Suminda, who was twelve when the film was made, boards in a grim, Dickensian orphanage that forbids talk during meals and showers. He visits his aunt on holidays. Although the oldest, Suresh, seems to be on good terms with his mother, Norma is tearful and sullen, and Suminda does poorly in school, picks quarrels, and otherwise seems withdrawn from the world. Still, at the end of the film, we see Josephine once again leave her three children in Sri Lanka to return to Isadora in Athens. For Josephine can either live with her children in desperate poverty or make money by living apart from them. Unlike her affluent First World employers, she cannot both live with her family and support it.

Thanks to the process we loosely call "globalization," women are on the move as never before in history. In images familiar to the West from television commercials for credit cards, cell phones, and airlines, female executives jet about the world, phoning home from luxury hotels and reuniting with eager children in airports. But we hear much less about a far more prodigious flow of female labor and energy: the increasing migration of millions of women from poor countries to rich ones, where they serve as nannies, maids, and sometimes sex workers. In the absence of help from male partners, many women have succeeded in tough "male world" careers only by turning over the care of their children, elderly parents, and homes to women from the Third World. This is the female underside of globalization, whereby millions of Josephines from poor countries in the south migrate to do the "women's work" of the north—work that affluent women are no longer able or willing to do. These migrant workers often leave their own children in the care of grandmothers, sisters, and sisters-in-law. Sometimes a young daughter is drawn out of school to care for her younger siblings.

This pattern of female migration reflects what could be called a worldwide gender revolution. In both rich and poor countries, fewer families can rely solely on a male breadwinner. In the United States, the earning power of most men has declined since 1970, and many women have gone out to "make up the difference." By one recent estimate, women were the sole, primary, or coequal earners in more than half of American families. So the question arises: Who will take care of the children, the sick, the elderly? Who will make dinner and clean house?

While the European or American woman commutes to work an average twenty-eight minutes a day, many nannies from the Philippines, Sri Lanka, and India cross the globe to get to their jobs. Some female migrants from the Third World do find something like "liberation," or at least the chance to become independent bread-winners and to improve their children's material lives. Other, less fortunate migrant women end up in the control of criminal employers— their passports stolen, their mobility blocked, forced to work without pay in brothels or to provide sex along with cleaning and child-care services in affluent homes. But even in more typical cases, where benign employers pay wages on time, Third World migrant women achieve their success only by assuming the cast-off domestic roles of middle- and high-income women in the First World—roles that have been previously rejected, of course, by men. And their "commute" entails a cost we have yet to fully comprehend.

The migration of women from the Third World to do "women's work" in affluent countries has so far received little media attention—for reasons that are easy enough to guess. First, many, though by no means all, of the new female migrant workers are women of color, and therefore subject to the racial "discounting" routinely experienced by, say, Algerians in France, Mexicans in the United States, and Asians in the United Kingdom. Add to racism the private "indoor" nature of so much of the new migrants' work. Unlike factory workers, who congregate in large numbers, or taxi drivers, who are visible on the street, nannies and maids are often hidden away, one or two at a time, behind closed doors in private homes. Because of the illegal nature of their work, most sex workers are even further concealed from public view.

At least in the case of nannies and maids, another factor contributes to the invisibility of migrant women and their work—one that, for their affluent employers, touches closer to home. The Western culture of individualism, which finds extreme expression in the United States, militates against acknowledging help or human interdependency of nearly any kind. Thus, in the time-pressed upper middle class, servants are no longer displayed as status symbols, decked out in white caps and aprons, but often remain in the background, or disappear when company comes. Furthermore, affluent career women increasingly earn their status not through leisure, as they might have a century ago, but by apparently "doing it all"—producing a full-time career, thriving children, a contented spouse, and a well-managed home. In order to preserve this illusion, domestic workers and nannies make the house hotel-room perfect, feed and bathe the children, cook and clean up—and then magically fade from sight.

The lifestyles of the First World are made possible by a global transfer of the services associated with a wife's traditional role—child care, home-making, and sex—from poor countries to rich ones. To generalize and perhaps oversimplify: in an earlier phase of imperialism, northern countries extracted natural resources and agricultural products—rubber, metals, and sugar, for example—from lands they conquered and colonized. Today, while still relying on Third World countries for agricultural and industrial labor, the wealthy countries also seek to extract something harder to measure and quantify, something that can look very much like love. Nannies like Josephine bring the distant families that employ them real maternal affection, no doubt enhanced by the heartbreaking absence of their own children in the poor countries they leave behind. Similarly, women who migrate from country to country to work as maids bring not only their muscle power but an attentiveness to detail and to the human relationships in the household that might otherwise have been invested in their own families. Sex workers offer the simulation of sexual and romantic love, or at least transient sexual companionship. It is as if the wealthy parts of the world are running short on precious emotional and sexual resources and have had to turn to poorer regions for fresh supplies.

There are plenty of historical precedents for this globalization of traditional female services. In the ancient Middle East, the women of populations defeated in war were routinely enslaved and hauled off to serve as household workers and concubines for the victors. Among the Africans brought to North America as slaves in the sixteenth through nineteenth centuries, about a third were women and children, and many of those women were pressed to be concubines, domestic servants, or both. Nineteenth-century Irishwomen—along with many rural Englishwomen—migrated to English towns and cities to work as domestics in the homes of the growing upper middle class. Services thought to be innately feminine—child care, housework, and sex—often win little recognition or pay. But they have always been sufficiently in demand to transport over long distances if necessary. What is new today is the sheer number of female migrants and the very long distances they travel. Immigration statistics show huge numbers of women in motion, typically from poor countries to rich. Although the gross statistics give little clue as to the jobs women eventually take, there are reasons to infer that much of their work is "caring work," performed either in private homes or in institutional settings such as hospitals, hospices, child-care centers, and nursing homes.

The statistics are, in many ways, frustrating. We have information on legal migrants but not on illegal migrants, who, experts tell us, travel in equal if not greater numbers. Furthermore, many Third World countries lack data for past years, which makes it hard to trace trends over time; or they use varying methods of gathering information, which makes it hard to compare one country with another. . . . From 1950 to 1970, for example, men predominated in labor migration to northern Europe from Turkey, Greece, and North Africa. Since then, women have been replacing men. In 1946, women were fewer than 3 percent of the Algerians and Moroccans living in France; by 1990, they were more than 40 percent. Overall, half of the world's 120 million legal and illegal migrants are now believed to be women.

Patterns of international migration vary from region to region, but women migrants from a surprising number of sending countries actually outnumber men, sometimes by a wide margin. For example, in the 1990s, women make up over half of Filipino migrants to all countries and 84 percent of Sri Lankan migrants to the Middle East. Indeed, by 1993 statistics, Sri Lankan women such as Josephine vastly outnumbered Sri Lankan men as migrant workers who'd left for Saudi Arabia, Kuwait, Lebanon, Oman, Bahrain, Jordan, and Qatar, as well as to all countries of the Far East, Africa, and Asia. About half of the migrants leaving Mexico, India, Korea, Malaysia, Cyprus, and Swaziland to work elsewhere are also women. Throughout the 1990s women outnumbered men among migrants to the United States, Canada, Sweden, the United Kingdom, Argentina, and Israel.

Most women, like men, migrate from the south to the north and from poor countries to rich ones. Typically, migrants go to the nearest comparatively rich country, preferably one whose language they speak or whose religion and culture they share. There are also local migratory flows: from northern to southern Thailand, for instance, or from East Germany to West. But of the regional or cross-regional flows, four stand out. One goes from Southeast Asia to the oil-rich Middle and Far East—from Bangladesh, Indonesia, the Philippines, and Sri Lanka to Bahrain, Oman, Kuwait, Saudi Arabia, Hong Kong, Malaysia, and Singapore. Another stream of migration goes from the former Soviet bloc to western Europe—from Russia, Romania, Bulgaria, and Albania to Scandinavia, Germany, France, Spain, Portugal, and England. A third goes from south to north in the Americas, including the stream from Mexico to the United States, which scholars say is the longest-running labor migration in the world. A fourth stream moves from Africa to various parts of Europe. France receives many female migrants from Morocco, Tunisia, and Algeria. Italy receives female workers from Ethiopia, Eritrea, and Cape Verde.

Female migrants overwhelmingly take up work as maids or domestics. As women have become an ever greater proportion of migrant workers, receiving countries reflect a dramatic influx of foreign-born domestics. In the United States, African-American women, who accounted for 60 percent of domestics in the 1940s, have been largely replaced by Latinas, many of them recent migrants from Mexico and Central America. In England, Asian migrant women have displaced the Irish and Portuguese domestics of the past. In French cities, North African women have replaced rural French girls. In western Germany, Turks and women from the former East Germany have replaced rural native-born women. Foreign females from countries outside the European Union made up only 6 percent of all domestic workers in 1984. By 1987, the percentage had jumped to 52, with most coming from the Philippines, Sri Lanka, Thailand, Argentina, Colombia, Brazil, El Salvador, and Peru.

The governments of some sending countries actively encourage women to migrate in search of domestic jobs, reasoning that migrant women are more likely than their male counterparts to send their hard-earned wages to their families rather than spending the money on themselves. In general, women send home anywhere from half to nearly all of what they earn. These remittances have a significant impact on the lives of children, parents, siblings, and wider networks of kin—as well as on cash-strapped Third World governments. Thus, before Josephine left for Athens, a program sponsored by the Sri Lankan government taught her how to use a microwave oven, a vacuum cleaner, and an electric mixer. As she awaited her flight, a song piped into the airport departure lounge extolled the opportunity to earn money abroad. The songwriter was in the pay of the Sri Lanka Bureau of Foreign Employment, an office devised to encourage women to migrate. The lyrics say:

> *After much hardship, such difficult times*
> *How lucky I am to work in a foreign land.*
> *As the gold gathers so do many greedy flies.*
> *But our good government protects us from them.*
> *After much hardship, such difficult times,*
> *How lucky I am to work in a foreign land.*
> *I promise to return home with treasures for everyone.*

Why this transfer of women's traditional services from poor to rich parts of the world? The reasons are, in a crude way, easy to guess. Women in Western countries have increasingly taken on paid work, and hence need others—paid domestics and caretakers for children and elderly people—to replace them. For their part, women in poor countries have an obvious incentive to migrate: relative and absolute poverty. The "care deficit" that has emerged in the wealthier countries as women enter the workforce *pulls* migrants from the Third World and postcommunist nations; poverty *pushes* them.

In broad outline, this explanation holds true. Throughout western Europe, Taiwan, and Japan, but above all in the United States, England, and Sweden, women's employment has increased dramatically since the 1970s. In the United States, for example, the proportion of women in paid work rose from 15 percent of mothers of children six and under in 1950 to 65 percent today. Women now make up 46 percent of the U.S. labor force. Three-quarters of mothers of children eighteen and under and nearly two-thirds of mothers of children age one and younger now work for pay. Furthermore, according to a recent International Labor Organization study, working Americans averaged longer hours at work in the late 1990s than they did in the 1970s. By some measures, the number of hours spent at work have increased more for women than for men, and especially for women in managerial and professional jobs.

Meanwhile, over the last thirty years, as the rich countries have grown much richer, the poor countries have become—in both absolute and relative terms—poorer. Global inequalities in wages are particularly striking. In Hong Kong, for instance, the wages of a Filipina domestic are about fifteen times the amount she could make as a schoolteacher back in the Philippines. In addition, poor countries turning to the IMF or World Bank for loans are often forced to undertake measures of so-called structural adjustment, with disastrous results for the poor and especially for poor women and children. To qualify for loans, governments are usually required to devalue their currencies, which turns the hard currencies of rich countries into gold and the soft currencies of poor countries into straw. Structural adjustment programs also call for cuts in support for "noncompetitive industries," and for the reduction of public services such as health care and food subsidies for the poor. Citizens of poor countries, women as well as men, thus have a strong incentive to seek work in more fortunate parts of the world.

But it would be a mistake to attribute the globalization of women's work to a simple synergy of needs among women—one group, in the affluent countries, needing help and the other, in poor countries, needing jobs. For one thing, this formulation fails to account for the marked failure of First World governments to meet the needs created by its women's entry into the workforce. The downsized American—and to a lesser degree, western European—welfare state has become a "deadbeat dad." Unlike the rest of the industrialized world, the United States does not offer public child care for working mothers, nor does it ensure paid family and medical leave. Moreover, a series of state tax revolts in the 1980s reduced the number of hours public libraries were open and slashed school-enrichment and after-school programs. Europe did not experience anything comparable. Still, tens of millions of western European women are in the workforce who were not before—and there has been no proportionate expansion in public services.

Secondly, any view of the globalization of domestic work as simply an arrangement among women completely omits the role of men. Numerous studies, including some of our own, have shown that as American women took on paid employment, the men in their families did little to increase their contribution to the work of the home. For example, only one out of every five men among the working couples whom Hochschild interviewed for *The Second Shift* in the 1980s shared the work at home, and later studies suggest that while working mothers are doing somewhat less housework than their counterparts twenty years ago, most men are doing only a little more.

With divorce, men frequently abdicate their child-care responsibilities to their ex-wives. In most cultures of the First World outside the United States, powerful traditions even more firmly discourage husbands from doing "women's work." So, strictly speaking, the presence of immigrant nannies does not enable affluent women to enter the workforce; it enables affluent *men* to continue avoiding the second shift.

The men in wealthier countries are also, of course, directly responsible for the demand for immigrant sex workers—as well as for the sexual abuse of many migrant women who work as domestics. Why, we wondered, is there a particular demand for "imported" sexual partners? Part of the answer may lie in the fact that new immigrants often take up the least desirable work, and, thanks to the AIDS epidemic, prostitution has become a job that ever fewer women deliberately choose. But perhaps some of this demand . . . grows out of the erotic lure of the "exotic." Immigrant women may seem desirable sexual partners for the same reason that First World employers believe them to be especially gifted as caregivers: they are thought to embody the traditional feminine qualities of nurturance, docility, and eagerness to please. Some men feel nostalgic for these qualities, which they associate with a bygone way of life. Even as many wage-earning Western women assimilate to the competitive culture of "male" work and ask respect for making it in a man's world, some men seek in the "exotic Orient" or "hot-blooded tropics" a woman from the imagined past.

Of course, not all sex workers migrate voluntarily. An alarming number of women and girls are trafficked by smugglers and sold into bondage. Because trafficking is illegal and secret, the numbers are hard to know with any certainty. Kevin Bales estimates that in Thailand alone, a country of 60 million, half a million to a million women are prostitutes, and one out of every twenty of these is enslaved. . . . Many of these women are daughters whom northern hill-tribe families have sold to brothels in the cities of the south. Believing the promises of jobs and money, some begin the voyage willingly, only to discover days later that the "arrangers" are traffickers who steal their passports, define them as debtors, and enslave them as prostitutes. Other women and girls are kidnapped, or sold by their impoverished families, and then trafficked to brothels. Even worse fates befall women from neighboring Laos and Burma, who flee crushing poverty and repression at home only to fall into the hands of Thai slave traders.

If the factors that pull migrant women workers to affluent countries are not as simple as they at first appear, neither are the factors that push them. Certainly relative poverty plays a major role, but, interestingly, migrant women often do not come from the poorest classes of their societies. In fact, they are typically more affluent and better educated than male migrants. Many female migrants from the Philippines and Mexico, for example, have high school or college diplomas and have held middle-class—albeit low-paid—jobs back home. One study of Mexican migrants suggests that the trend is toward increasingly better-educated female migrants. Thirty years ago, most Mexican-born maids in the United States had been poorly educated maids in Mexico. Now a majority have high school degrees and have held clerical, retail, or professional jobs before leaving for the United States. Such women are likely to be enterprising and adventurous enough to resist the social pressures to stay home and accept their lot in life.

Noneconomic factors—or at least factors that are not immediately and directly economic—also influence a woman's decision to emigrate. By migrating, a woman may escape the expectation that she care for elderly family members, relinquish her paycheck to a husband or father, or defer to an abusive husband. Migration may also be a practical response to a failed marriage and the need to provide for children without male help. In the Philippines, . . . Rhacel Salazar Parrenas tells us, migration is sometimes called a "Philippine divorce." And there are forces at work that may be making the men of poor countries less desirable as husbands. Male unemployment runs high in the countries that supply female domestics to the First World. Unable to make a living, these men often grow demoralized and cease contributing to their families in other ways. Many female migrants tell of unemployed husbands who drink or gamble their remittances away. Notes one study of Sri Lankan women working as maids in the Persian Gulf: "It is not unusual . . . for the women to find upon their return that their Gulf wages by and large have been squandered on alcohol, gambling and other dubious undertakings while they were away."

To an extent then, the globalization of child care and housework brings the ambitious and independent women of the world together: the career-oriented upper-middle-class woman of an affluent nation and the striving woman from a crumbling Third World or postcommunist economy. Only it does not bring them together in the way that second-wave feminists in affluent countries once liked to imagine—as sisters and allies struggling to achieve common goals. Instead, they come together as mistress and maid, employer and employee, across a great divide of privilege and opportunity.

This trend toward global redivision of women's traditional work throws new light on the entire process of globalization. Conventionally, it is the poorer countries that are thought to be dependent on the richer ones—a dependency symbolized by the huge debt they owe to global financial institutions. What we explore in this book, however, is a dependency that works in the other direction, and it is a dependency of a particularly intimate kind. Increasingly often, as affluent and middle-class families in the First World come to depend on migrants from poorer regions to provide child care, homemaking, and sexual services, a global relationship arises that in some ways mirrors the traditional relationship between the sexes. The First World takes on a role like that of the old-fashioned male in the family—pampered, entitled, unable to cook, clean, or find his socks. Poor countries take on a role like that of the traditional woman within the family—patient, nurturing, and self-denying. A division of labor feminists critiqued when it was "local" has now, metaphorically speaking, gone global.

To press this metaphor a bit further, the resulting relationship is by no means a "marriage," in the sense of being openly acknowledged. In fact, it is striking how invisible the globalization of women's work remains, how little it is noted or discussed in the First World. Trend spotters have had almost nothing to say about the fact that increasing numbers of affluent First World children and elderly persons are tended by immigrant care workers or live in homes cleaned by immigrant maids. Even the political groups we might expect to be concerned about this trend—antiglobalization and feminist activists—often seem to have noticed only the most extravagant abuses, such as trafficking and female enslavement. So if a metaphorically gendered relationship has developed between rich and poor countries, it is less like a marriage and more like a secret affair.

But it is a "secret affair" conducted in plain view of the children. Little Isadora and the other children of the First World raised by "two mommies" may be learning more than their ABC's from a loving surrogate parent. In their own living rooms, they are learning a vast and tragic global politics. Children see. But they also learn how to disregard what they see. They learn how adults make the visible invisible. That is their "early childhood education." . . .

The globalization of women's traditional role poses important challenges to anyone concerned about gender and economic inequity. How can we improve the lives and opportunities of migrant women engaged in legal occupations such as ~~and maids? How can we prevent trafficking and enslavement? More basically,~~ find a way to counterbalance the systematic transfer of caring work from poo tries to rich, and the inevitable trauma of the children left behind? . . .

✓●─[**Study** and **Review** on **myanthrolab.com**

Review Questions

1. What kind of work do most female immigrants do when they move from poorer to richer countries?

2. What are the advantages of working in another country for women immigrants?

3. What are the negative aspects of the work in which female immigrants engage?

4. What are the four main "flows" of immigrants from poorer to richer countries?

5. What do the female immigrants and the women in wealthier societies have in common economically?

6. The authors argue that immigration has actually made rich countries dependent on poor countries. On what do they base their assertion?

PART TEN

USING AND DOING ANTHROPOLOGY

READINGS IN THIS SECTION

Nowhere in the world do human affairs remain precisely constant from year to year. New ways of doing things mark the history of even the most stable groups. Change occurs when an Australian aboriginal dreams about a new myth and teaches it to the members of his band; when a loader in a restaurant kitchen invents a way to stack plates more quickly in the dishwasher; or when a New Guinea Big Man cites the traditional beliefs about ghosts to justify the existence of a new political office devised by a colonial government. Wherever people interpret their natural and social worlds in a new way, cultural change has occurred. Broad or narrow, leisurely or rapid, such change is part of life in every society.

Culture change can originate from two sources: innovation and borrowing. **Innovation** is the invention of qualitatively new forms. It involves the recombination of what people already know into something different. For example, Canadian Joseph-Armand Bombardier became an innovator when he mated tracks, designed to propel earth-moving equipment, to a small bus that originally ran on tires, producing the first snowmobile in the 1950s. Later, the Skolt Lapps of Finland joined him as innovators when they adapted his now smaller, more refined snowmobile for herding reindeer in 1961. The Lapp innovation was not the vehicle itself. That was borrowed. What was new was the use of the vehicle in herding, something usually done by men on skis.

Innovations are more likely to occur and to be adopted during stressful times when traditional culture no longer works well. Bombardier, for example, began work on his snowmobile after he was unable to reach medical help in time to save the life of his critically ill son during a Canadian winter storm. Frustrated by the slowness of his horse and sleigh, he later set out to create a faster vehicle.

The other basis of culture change is **borrowing.** Borrowing—or **diffusion**, as it is sometimes called—refers to the adoption of something new from another group. Tobacco, for example, was first domesticated and grown in the New World but quickly diffused to Europe and Asia after 1492. Such items as the umbrella, pajamas, Arabic numerals, and perhaps even the technology to make steel came to Europe from India. Ideologies and religions may diffuse from one society to another.

An extreme diffusionist view has been used to explain most human achievements. For example, author Erich von Däniken argues that features of ancient New World civilizations were brought by space invaders. Englishman G. Elliot Smith claimed that Mayan and Aztec culture diffused from Egypt. Thor Heyerdahl sailed a reed boat, the *Ra II*, from Africa to South America to prove that an Egyptian cultural origin was possible for New World civilization.

Whether something is an innovation or borrowed, it must pass through a process of **social acceptance** before it can become part of a culture. Indeed many, if not most, novel ideas and things remain unattractive and relegated to obscurity. And, as many a development expert, public health worker, and product development specialist has learned, "target populations" do not always accept or incorporate new ideas or products in the way intended by the government, program, or company. To achieve social acceptance, an innovation must become known to the members of a society, must be accepted as valid, and must fit into a system of cultural knowledge revised to accept it. Anthropologists, skilled in gaining an understanding of systems of cultural knowledge, can contribute to such efforts.

Several principles facilitate social acceptance. If a change wins the support of a person in authority, it may gain the approval of others. Timing is also important. It would have made little sense for a Lapp to attempt the introduction of snowmobiles when there was no snow or when the men who do the reindeer herding were scattered over their vast grazing territory. Other factors also affect social acceptance. Changes have a greater chance of acceptance if they meet a felt need, if they appeal to people's prestige (in societies where prestige is important), and if they provide some continuity with traditional customs.

Change may take place under a variety of conditions, from the apparently dull day-to-day routine of a seemingly stable society to the frantic climate of a revolution. One situation that has occupied many anthropologists interested in change is **cultural contact**, particularly situations of contact where one society politically dominates another. World history is replete with examples of such domination, which vary in outcome from annihilation—in the case of the Tasmanians and hundreds of tribes in North and South America, Africa, Asia, and even ancient Europe—to the political rule that indentured countless millions of people to colonial powers.

The process of change caused by these conditions is called **acculturation**. Acculturation results from cultural contact. Acculturative change may affect dominant societies as well as subordinate ones. After their ascendance in India, for example, the British came to wear *khaki* clothes, live in *bungalows*, and trek through *jungles*—all Indian concepts.

But those who are subordinated tend to experience the most far-reaching changes in their way of life. From politically independent, self-sufficient people, they usually become subordinate and dependent. Sweeping changes in social structure and values may occur, along with a resulting social disorganization.

Although the age of colonial empires is largely over, the destruction of tribal culture continues at a rapid pace today. As we saw in Reed's article in Part Three of this book, hundreds of thousands of Amazonian Indians have already perished in recent years because of intrusive frontier and development programs. Similarly the !Kung that Lee describes in Parts One and Three of this book continue to struggle for their very existence as a people in places like Namibia, South Africa, and Botswana. Following almost exactly the pattern of past colonial exploitation, modern governments bent on "progress" displace and even kill off indigenous tribal populations. The frequent failure of development, coupled with its damaging impact on native peoples, has caused many anthropologists to reassess their role. As a result, more and more anthropologists have become part of native resistance to outside intrusion. These efforts have gone hand-in-hand with the recent 2007 **United Nations Declaration on the Rights of Indigenous Peoples**, which ushers in opportunities for indigenous populations to attempt to resist these efforts under international law.

A less dramatic, but in many ways no less important, agent of change is the world economy. No longer can most people live in self-sufficient isolation. Their future is inevitably tied in with an overall system of market exchange. Take the Marshall Islanders described by anthropologist Michael Rynkiewich, for example. Although they cultivate to meet their own subsistence needs, they also raise coconuts for sale on the world market. Receipts from the coconut crop go to pay for outboard motors and gasoline, cooking utensils, and a variety of other goods they don't manufacture themselves but have come to depend on. Several major American food companies have now eliminated coconut oil from their products because of its high level of saturated fat. This loss has created lower demand for copra (dried coconut meat), from which the oil is pressed. Reduced demand, in turn, may cause substantial losses to the Marshall Islanders. A people who once could subsist independently have now become prisoners of the world economic system.

Anthropologists may themselves become agents of change, applying their work to practical problems. **Applied anthropology**, as opposed to academic anthropology, includes any use of anthropological knowledge to influence social interaction, to maintain or change social institutions, or to direct the course of cultural change. Some anthropologists call themselves "practicing anthropologists." Applied and practicing anthropologists are found in business, government, health, human services and education. They work in companies, congress, and care and educational settings, such as hospitals and schools. Sometimes these anthropologists work as researchers, but often they are involved in identifying problems and developing and managing solutions. They often work in teams and across cultures and disciplines.

There are four basic uses of anthropology contained within the applied field: adjustment anthropology, administrative anthropology, action anthropology, and advocate anthropology.

Adjustment anthropology uses anthropological knowledge to make social interaction more predictable among people who operate with different cultural codes. For example, take the anthropologists who consult with companies and government agencies about intercultural communication. It is often their job to train Americans to interpret the cultural rules that govern interaction in another society. For a businessperson who will work in Latin America, the anthropologist may point out the appropriate culturally defined speaking distances, ways to sit, definitions of time, topics of conversation, times for business talk, and so on. All of these activities would be classified as adjustment anthropology.

Administrative anthropology uses anthropological knowledge for planned change by those who are external to the local cultural group. It is the use of anthropological knowledge by a person with the power to make decisions. If an anthropologist provides knowledge to a mayor about the culture of constituents, he or she is engaged in administrative anthropology. So would advisers to chief administrators of U.S. trust territories such as once existed in places like the Marshall Islands.

Action anthropology uses anthropological knowledge for planned change by the local cultural group. The anthropologist acts as a catalyst, providing information but avoiding decision making, which remains in the hands of the people affected by the decisions.

Advocate anthropology uses anthropological knowledge by the anthropologist to increase the power of self-determination of a particular cultural group. Instead of focusing on the process of innovation, the anthropologist centers attention on discovering the sources of power and how a group can gain access to them. James Spradley took such action when he studied tramps in 1968. He discovered that police and courts systematically deprived tramps of their power to control their lives and of the rights accorded normal citizens. By releasing his findings to the Seattle newspapers, he helped tramps gain additional power and weakened the control of Seattle authorities.

Whether they are doing administrative, advocate, adjustment, or action anthropology, anthropologists take, at least in part, a qualitative approach. They do ethnography, discover the cultural knowledge of their informants, and apply this information in the ways discussed previously. In contrast to the quantitative data so often prized by other social scientists, they use the insider's viewpoint to discover problems, to advise, and to generate policy.

The articles in Part Ten illustrate several aspects of cultural change, especially those associated with applied anthropology. The first, by Hoyt Alverson, details his investigations of problems faced by Peace Corps volunteers assigned to Botswana. Attempting to understand Tswana behavior in terms of their American cultural background, Peace Corps volunteers endured misunderstandings over the perception of time and many other social customs. The second selection by medical anthropologist, Sonia Patten, in an article brought back from an earlier edition, describes her role as an applied medical anthropologist on a program designed to improve women's and children's nutrition. The third article by Rachael Stryker, updated for this edition of *Conformity and Conflict*, introduces the concept of public interest ethnography by describing her and her students' ethnographic research on health care among women incarcerated in two California prisons. The study identified a list of health care problems, including poverty, red tape, and overcrowding, and concluded with a series of recommendations for policy change. The fourth article by David McCurdy, also updated for this edition, discusses the uses of anthropology in a business setting. From studies of General Motors workers to program assessment for people with HIV/AIDS to participation in government health projects to international counseling, professional anthropologists put their discipline to work. Finally, in his article, McCurdy looks at one way in which the ethnographic perspective can be put to work in a business setting. **Business anthropology** is applying anthropological theories and practices to the needs of private sector organizations, especially industrial firms. He argues that anthropology teaches a number of skills that are useful in the world of work.

Key Terms

acculturation p. 337
action anthropology p. 338
adjustment anthropology p. 338
administrative anthropology p. 338
advocate anthropology p. 338
applied anthropology p. 337
business anthropology p. 339

borrowing p. 336
cultural contact p. 337
diffusion p. 336
innovation p. 336
social acceptance p. 336
United Nations Declaration on the
    Rights of Indigenous Peoples p. 337

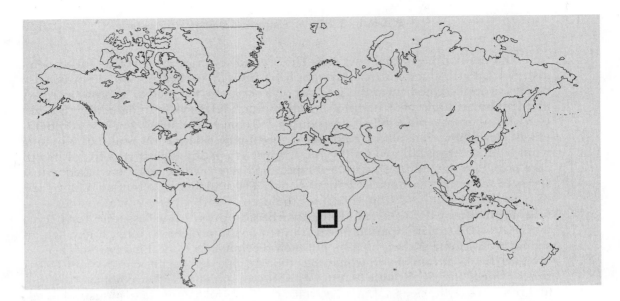

36

Advice for Developers: Peace Corps Problems in Botswana

Hoyt S. Alverson

Anthropologists are sometimes asked to consult about problems experienced by partici-pants in government and nongovernmental programs aimed at helping people in developing countries. Such is the case reported in this article by Hoyt Alverson. Asked to review the program, he learned that Peace Corps volunteers had been trying to introduce development projects among rural Tswana farmers living in Botswana but had found work there dif-ficult. Often unable to successfully teach skills to Tswana and feeling a cross-cultural dis-comfort they could not understand, they tended to isolate themselves, hang out with other Americans or Europeans, and give up, failing to complete their two-year contracts. Frus-trated, they often felt spiteful toward local people. Some experienced nervous breakdowns.

    Alverson, who had already completed fifteen months of fieldwork among the Tswana, discovered an answer to the problem. Volunteers, it was clear, tended to see Tswana behavior in their own, American, cultural terms. Using examples such as the meaning of time, the dif-ferent nature of greetings, and the importance of social obligations, he illustrates the differ-ence between the volunteers' American cultural expectations and those of the local Tswana. His findings helped to inform later Peace Corps Training Programs and could still prove use-ful today as U.S. military personal attempt to "nation build" in Iraq and Afghanistan.*

*Slightly abridged from "Peace Corps Volunteers in Rural Botswana, *Human Organization* 1977, Vol. 36, No. 3, pp. 274–281. Copyright © 1977 by The Society for Applied Anthropology. Reprinted by permission.

((•─│Listen to the **Chapter Audio** on **myanthrolab.com**

Introduction

In 1974, I was engaged by the United States Peace Corps to assist it in developing a training program to help Peace Corps Volunteers (PCVs) adjust to, and effectively live within, the confines of Botswana, a newly developing African country. . . . The Tswana are a constituent of the congeries of southeastern Bantu-speaking peoples. They were, until one hundred years ago, a predominately agricultural people with a very important ancillary tradition of animal (especially cattle) husbandry. Since 1867 they have been incorporated more and more into the vortex of colonial industrialism in southern Africa, a process which continues apace today.

The Peace Corps has been in Botswana only a few years, but has quickly established a conspicuous presence there through its relatively large numbers—about 100 to 200 volunteers at any one time serve a country with a total population of less than 750,000. Also, PCVs usually work either in traditional villages or within small industrial, administrative, or commercial centers, where they form a highly visible constituency of daily community life.

Despite the commitment of time and resources to prepare the volunteers to cope with the exotic surroundings found in Botswana, it became apparent to the Peace Corps that many of the volunteers were not able to meet the three Peace Corps goals as effectively as they might. In particular, some were unable to purvey the skills which they were presumably there to offer. Failing to complete contracts; retreating to enclaves of European settlement; not mixing, nor otherwise establishing rapport with the local people; failing to learn the local language; not understanding the setting of their job, and as a consequence, becoming spiteful of and bitter toward many individuals with whom they had to work; untimely nervous breakdowns; these were among the symptoms of anxiety and stress shown by volunteers.

Part of my job was to work with the volunteers and secondarily with certain host-country nationals (Tswana) to discover whether there existed some fairly straightforward reasons for this state of affairs. Since at this time I had completed 15 months of close participation in a very small and rather isolated Tswana village with my family, I had quite a reservoir of remembered anxieties, doubts, and blunders (as well as successes) to draw upon in formulating hypotheses for beginning my work with the PCV. . . .

A volunteer coming to rural Botswana sees much social behavior around him. Most of this behavior appears to him familiar and meaningful. This is often the volunteer's first serious error in interpretive understanding. He strives to supply the meanings for the behavior he sees by analogically interpolating from his own experience. Very often, he imputes the meanings that a given sequence of behaviors might have if it took place in his home culture and if it were engaged in by familiar types of associates. A trauma for many volunteers stems from the growing realization that the familiar behavior makes no sense, or the wrong sense. What appears to be familiar becomes a puzzlement. Faced with confusion, many volunteers are tempted to provide or express interpretations which often reflect their anguish rather than any serious effort to understand the Tswana. Such well-known rationalizations as: "They're just lazy," "they have no confidence," "they're irrational," "they don't understand time," etc., were frequently encountered. In short, the volunteers often fail to understand the social actions, signaled by the behavior they see. They were unable, during their two-year service, to refer the behavior and performance of Tswana to motives, goals, or evaluations other than those already fixed in their consciousness.

The Peace Corps Volunteers' Projects-of-Action

The following 10 points are a distillation from interviews I conducted with over fifty volunteers in Botswana, all of whom had had at least one year of experience there. Their motives and goals help us to understand the particular difficulties volunteers face in Botswana. Naturally the specific assignments and the specific setting of a particular job are also critically important. The job would be a part—but only a part—of any volunteer's larger project.

(1) Most volunteers see their work in terms of a sacrifice made to serve others. Each believes he has foregone something of the good life to render assistance to those less fortunate.

(2) The "less fortunate" designation is important for the second element in the typical volunteer's project: the volunteer ascribes to himself the status of expert purveying skills among the less knowledgeable.

(3) A central belief of most volunteers is that knowledge is an entitlement to respect and authority.

(4) Most volunteers believe that their knowledge and skills have proven and absolute validity. Hence, there is a right and a wrong—or at least a "best"—way to build a dam, teach English, manage range land, keep books, etc., and the volunteer knows that way.

(5) The volunteer defines his project as one where help has been solicited. "They have asked me to come; I didn't force anything on anyone." The Tswana are supplicants, and the volunteer is a "help-mate" of the Tswana.

(6) Rational behavior (that is, that kind of behavior the volunteer sees himself in Botswana to engage in) is coterminous with Western behavior. The arbiter of rationality in this domain is Western knowledge. The proof for the volunteer lies in the palpable demonstration of success of that knowledge as it has been applied in the West.

(7) Most volunteers' projects take place in contexts where they presume Western norms or rules of performance are in force. The volunteer expects to impart Western ideas to host-country nationals.

(8) For most volunteers the status of expert is sufficient entitlement to purvey skills or technical assistance. The issue of power, however, is problematic. Volunteers are quite ambivalent about influencing host-country nationals in situations where overt resistance is offered. Many volunteers define themselves either as lacking power or as lacking desire to use power to coerce performance on the part of Tswana associates. This self-ascribed lack of power is often used by volunteers as a criterion for distinguishing or distancing themselves from the role of neocolonialist.

(9) The volunteer defines himself, and to a lesser extent the Peace Corps, as engaged in a "human mission." "The Peace Corps is a people organization." Doing good directly for the ultimate intended beneficiaries is a premise held by volunteers as a goal of their actions. Related to this is the volunteer's belief that he should want to work closely with host-country nationals and otherwise get to know them intimately.

(10) Peace Corps service is a personal quest for new experience motivated by a diffusely defined but explicitly claimed idealism. Most volunteers tacitly assume, as a consequence of this, that one cannot know the meaning of being a volunteer unless one has been a volunteer. Outsider interpretations of volunteers' experiences are thus impossible.

In the remainder of this paper I illustrate the points made above by reference to two domains of conflict which affect almost all Peace Corps volunteers. The first concerns the consciousness of time and the second the "presentation of face" in daily interaction. . . .

The Consciousness of Time

The objective conceptualization and the subjective meaning of time in Tswana and Western cultures, respectively, are difficult to compare, since much of anyone's knowledge of time is largely unconscious. . . . Time for the volunteers, as for most of us, is conceived as an autonomous, abstract dimension of lived experience. Time is unrelated to particular events; it is an aspect of all events. Time is unidimensional, and it is linear—witness the equation we all learned in elementary school relating time, distance, and velocity in a linear equation.

For the rural Tswana, time has no such phenomenal constitution. Time is coextensive with events. There is very little unfilled time—time which is extrapolated into the future or past, beyond the points where events are said to exist. Time as duration, as occasion, and as location in a process is defined by events. Thus, the day is defined in terms of the union of daylight and darkness, the rising of women, goats leaving the kraal, men arising, milking, taking morning food, etc. . . . Months, years, generations, and lifespans are events that define time; they are not durations defined by time. In turn, they can be partitioned by still other events: birth, puberty, childbearing, marriage, work, old age, the time of locusts, the reign of King Sechele, etc.

Even the "time for something to take place" is not reckoned in terms of an autonomous continuum, a set of external markers of inner duration. Thus, if a party is to begin at mid-day, this injunction constitutes simply a guide to action for the invited guests. The occasion for beginning the party in question is when the actions of the assembling people create the necessary and sufficient conditions for the party, namely, when they begin to act in a manner called "partying." There is no convenient way in Setswana (the language of the Tswana) even to express the notion that the party (or anything else) is late, early, or on time vis-a-vis a pure time concept. Nothing can be late, because the event is its own time.

Imagine how action predicated on such a view of time would distress volunteers who must organize Tswana labor. Most Tswana will acquiesce to requests for performance defined in terms of clock-time. But the acquiescence often does not entail understanding, especially of the importance of the time component of the performance. For example, if a volunteer requests that a Tswana come see him tomorrow morning at nine to discuss the selection of animals for sale to the abattoir, it could easily happen that the Tswana does not show up until the afternoon or the next day. In such an episode the Tswana is fulfilling the major part of his promise to discuss selection of animals for sale. *When* one discusses such a matter is not that pressing since the

abattoir works year-round, and it makes little difference
the cattle, when the conveyance is executed. The volunte..,
He sees time as something one can lose; something which has definite costs associated with it.

The volunteer may see the Tswana perception of time as an indication of indifference, lack of respect for one's word, or even as laziness. The Tswana, for his part,
considers the volunteer to be compulsive about trivial details. For the Tswana, appearing on the morrow at nine was as incidental to his promise as the surmise that
he would come wearing clothes, or come sober. The important thing is to discuss the
business, which could be done in the afternoon just as well.

Implicit in these notions is the Tswana conception that time cannot be scarce.
If time is made up of events, the only scarcity that could exist would result from conflicts in events. This is most unusual in the daily round of life in a Tswana village.
Hence, the Western notion of an "opportunity cost" associated with the use of time is
anomalous for the Tswana. There are not enough events, nor are they distributed in
such a way, that one must give up doing one thing to do another because one lacks
time. For example, if a volunteer gives instructions to a group of workers concerning a
chore they must do, the salient feature of this episode for the Tswana is to discuss the
details of the assignment, its implications, its significance, its ramification. This may
take half-an-hour. The volunteer is dumbfounded that people would "stand around
bullshitting" about their work while "time is being lost." The Tswana will do the job;
but, if it is not completed that day, tomorrow is still another day, and the world will
still be here in exactly the same shape it is now.

The Presentation of Face

Greeting and "Taking the News"

In a face-to-face group, modes of direct interaction are continuous and crucial features of one's world. The manipulation or presentation of "face" is a matter of importance. What we might call violations of the rules of etiquette or decorum can, in
Tswana communities, be attacks on the bases of social solidarity. Greetings and exchanging or "taking of news" are celebrations of social solidarity and communal life.
These social acts have value that can in no sense be adequately described in terms of
the western notion of being polite. For example, one does not report simply the *new* or
recent as news, since everything is news, whether it is new or heard a hundred times
before. Greeting and newstaking in Botswana is a surface manifestation of *reflection
in a collective mode*—the symbolic, evaluative reconstitution of events.

For the Peace Corps volunteer, saying hello is either a perfunctory, involuntary
habit or an optional act of courtesy. For the Tswana, not to be greeted and solicitously
inquired of is a sign of grievous ill feeling or great depression on the part of the Other.
Being perfunctory or always in a hurry is a sign of many possible problems in the
Other, ranging from being angry to being bewitched. Volunteers see this lengthy greeting and newstaking as a sign of lack of constructive things to do, as laziness, or as a
lack of belief in hard work. "Development will never occur," say many PCVs, "until the
Tswana learn to quit loafing." In Botswana one does not enter an office without greeting and talking with everyone. Indeed, it is considered impolite and crass to get right
down to business. Volunteers injected into this situation perceive this as a waste of
work-time and an impediment to productivity.

In a Tswana community, the sum of greetings and taking-of-the-news during the day is a functional analogy to our reading of the daily paper. It is an aspect of being informed—knowing what is going on. To report one's plans, visits by strangers, deaths, illnesses, and so forth is crucial to the patterned life of a village. Often it is when one greets someone for the first time during the day that this news is best communicated. Opinion—editorial opinion—can often be obtained on the spot and from this, guides to action can be immediately formulated.

This function of newstaking escapes the volunteer's attention. He sees the meaning of "standing around and talking" in terms of our curbside or over-the-back-fence chatter, which he "knows" is not necessary—even a waste of time.

Marking Status in Language Use

In our society, especially in the past three or four decades, we have adopted a pretension of classlessness, which has resulted in a general atrophy of linguistic markers of political and social class. (There are exceptions to this in the patois of certain ethnic groups.) In the United States, generally, face-to-face interaction is characterized by a strain toward the appearance of instant intimacy, camaraderie, superficial amicability; the art of ingratiation is most important in our society. An accompaniment to this is a general use of casual language, and gestures in impression management and expression of emotional tone. In Setswana the contrary prevails. Statuses are clearly marked: male-female, young-old, kinsman-stranger, royalty-commoner. These social antinomies have precise linguistic correlates which carry prescriptions for speech acts in face-to-face contact.

The Peace Corps volunteer typically sees the social encounters before him among Botswana as a kaleidoscopic flux, an unordered round of prattle. Language, especially a second language, for the volunteer just floats around the head waiting to be used by the speaker. The fact that context should dictate what is to be said and how (especially where context is defined by such abstract notions as "social status") is seen as stuffy, needless formalism—a carryover from British rule.

The reputation of the loud, pushy, back-slapping, "ugly American" is sufficient imagery for comprehension of some of the dilemmas volunteers can get into as a result of their informal speech etiquette in face-to-face relations. Many volunteers strive to become friends with Tswana, only to find their jovial and solicitous approach rejected. The prestige inherent in age, for example, is not readily comprehended by many young volunteers who are reared on a steady diet of American veneration of youth and the corollary contempt for age and indifference to the conditions of the elderly. The Tswana values regarding age and other ascribed statuses are coded in the language.

Sincerity and Authenticity

Even more difficult to understand than speech etiquette is the customary violation of Western canons of sincerity in Tswana face-to-face relations. Most Americans place a high value on "telling the truth," "being sincere," "saying what's on one's mind." Even more important is the value of authenticity. We should not simply be sincere, we should attempt to be outwardly what we inwardly genuinely are. The Tswana are quite different. In their society candor has little value; face-to-face relations must be smooth, pleasant, and unharried. Candor which entails rudeness, abrasiveness, or even open deviance cannot be condoned simply by appeals to being honest or telling the truth. Sociability takes precedence over sincerity. (Of course, Americans lie, and Tswana can be brutally candid; I speak here of normative behavior.) How, then, does this affect the volunteer?

When a Tswana makes a request, the most important thing that he can do to make that request plausible and genuine is to have a "good excuse" for making it. To have a good excuse does not imply that the excuse must be the truth. Indeed, on many occasions, it may be necessary to falsify one's statement to come up with a good excuse. While the American may be temporarily assuaged by an excuse, he will, of course, be very upset if he finds out that the excuse was a lie.

Many of the PCVs experience situations where they are confronted with excuses or rationales given by Tswana to elicit or justify some act. Many of these turn out to be falsehoods if interpreted by American criteria (and they are lies even by Tswana criteria). But the value of telling the truth in many situations is subordinate to the value of presenting a reasonable justification. A PCV, for example, may be the employer of a Tswana who will tell a story to justify his request for a day off. He may explain that a relative is sick, or that his cow has wandered off, or that his religious community requires such-and-such conduct. The volunteer may find out later that this is not true. Upon confronting the Tswana with this, the Tswana's reaction is frequently to fabricate yet another story in an attempt to convince the volunteer that the first falsehood was the truth or that he had misunderstood the content of the first excuse. Upon finding out both falsehoods, many PCVs will demand the Tswana admit his errors and apologize. But the mark of personal strength for the Tswana is not to confess to having done wrong; a Tswana must remain stoically silent even in the face of conclusive evidence of culpability, while in American society we believe that to confess error and repent has high value and reflects real strength of character.

Here is another example. A Tswana approaches a volunteer and asks him to interrupt his day to drive him into town. The car after all is idle, making the volunteer seem idle as well. The volunteer's immediate response is, "That's an unreasonable request. The car costs a lot of money to run; petrol is very expensive; and besides, I'm very busy reading." The Tswana is very upset, accusing the PCV of rudeness. Perplexed, the PCV says, "Look, I'm just telling the truth; these are my feelings." The Tswana is insulted. He would have been much happier to hear a lie—that the car was broken; that the only money available for petrol must be used to buy food for the week. The value of smooth, polite face-to-face dealings exceeds the value of sincerity in the conduct of personal transactions.

Space and Privacy

The converse of presentation of face is the absenting of face. Most Americans like their privacy. We celebrate this in word, song, and in architecture. To that end, we bound regions with building space, with walls; we designate areas for escape from public view. Lacking architecturally bounded regions for privacy, volunteers in Botswana often feel like going out in a field to sit and reflect in solitude. To most Tswana this kind of behavior—wanting to be left alone—is considered peculiar, and, at times, indicative of mental problems. As one Tswana once told me: "Children seeing a person sitting alone in a field would become frightened and run away for fear that person is bewitched." The volunteer who craves privacy and obtains it may soon be greeted by a delegation of Tswana concerned about his behavior or state of mind. The meaning of such a simple act as being alone is sufficiently different in the worlds of the

Tswana and the volunteer that the misunderstandings that flow from this difference can create serious frustration for all concerned.

There are few situations in Tswana life where solitude is either sought or prescribed. Where it is, it reflects usually serious personal problems or crises. The normal escape from troubles and the normal mode of reflection is in patterned interaction in a face-to-face group. The lack of opportunity for escapes was a problem many PCVs expressed to me in a very emotional, unequivocal fashion.

Another instance where this lack of escape regions becomes a problem for volunteers is in the task of entering and settling in a village. On such an occasion the Tswana will desire to begin a continual round of calling on and visiting the new arrival. The volunteer, for his part, usually wants to engage himself in village life on his own terms. This means slowly, a little bit every day. The new language, the strange surroundings, and personal insecurity make the sampling of village life something like getting used to very cold water. The Tswana want the volunteer to inundate himself with a round of socializing the very first thing. Another instance of this problem can be found when the volunteer wants to be left alone when he is sick and doesn't feel well. He will then find the community coming to sit and talk with him, when all he wants is peace and quiet. If the PCV spurns any of these visits, it creates puzzlement and antagonism on the part of the Tswana.

The idea of being alone as an intrinsically pleasant experience is foreign to the Tswana. For the Tswana, privacy means a time for "secrets." For the American, it is prophylaxis, a salubrious and reflective mode of being.

Oral Contracts in Speech Acts

For the Tswana, obligations of status generally exceed those of contract. For the Westerner, this is seldom the case. Thus, I can incur a debt to a stranger, which obligates me despite negative consequences for my health, my family, or my duties as a professional. In particular, the obligations of ascribed status among the Tswana have many prescriptions and proscriptions on individual conduct which follow one throughout life. These status obligations can be in conflict with contractual agreements the Tswana makes, as for example, when he sells his labor. They can lead a Tswana to behave in ways that puzzle or disturb volunteers. Among the Tswana what we call demographic markers (age, sex, and kinship status) have detailed and extensive legal elaborations: rights, duties, powers, liabilities, and so forth. In the West these markers have few or no legal elaborations. Volunteers are often puzzled when they find that obligations based on these statuses take precedence over the obligations incurred in wage labor. For the volunteers such wage labor is a central responsibility in life. Yet for the Tswana it is but one of many competing burdens with which he must deal.

A seeming exception to this notion of status taking precedence over contract lies in the domain of oral agreements or oral contracts, found very commonly in Tswana society. The Peace Corps volunteer, like most of us, sees casual conversation as a circumscribed domain—a "language game" apart from other domains. Statements we make in our casual conversations which appear serious, freighted with careful intent, are often no more than "passing the time," "bullshitting," "making time," or "doing a snow job." None of these intentions is directly inferable from the semantic content of the utterances alone. Such is not the case for the Tswana. For example, the semantic content which designates a *promissory* mode has a binding effect on the speaker. Even the mode of possibility in Setswana as reflected in our words "may," "might," or "will," contain in certain uses presuppositions of constraint or binding effect on the speaker. When we say in English: "Yeah, we'll have to get together some time," this will be semantically interpreted by a Tswana as expressing a desire or necessity for "getting together." But in the American context we all know this to be an idle promise, a statement made merely to break off a conversation.

Volunteers share the common American trait of being "giants of the future" in their conversations, especially when they are trying to make an impression. Unfortunately, the typical Tswana gives the volunteer's pseudopromissory speech acts close semantic interpretations. One result of this can be accusations by the Tswana that the volunteer doesn't keep his promises or that he is unreliable. The volunteer, of course, does not believe he has made any promises. All he has done is to engage in a little idle flattery and ingratiation, which, quite unintentionally, the Tswana have interpreted as promises or serious intentions.

The Risks of Intimacy

Because trust is a dimension of friendship for Americans, they feel free to reveal mistakes, indiscretions, or blunders without risking status loss. A friend remains a friend despite the disapproval one might suffer if one's failings became widely known. Americans even engage with friends in rounds of mutual confession and self-incrimination. Mutual confessions bind together individuals by providing each with evidence of the weakness of the other—potential weapons should confidences be broken or misused. This mutuality reinforces the trust of friendship.

Friendship does not have these qualities for the Tswana. Friendship is companionship, but trust is something one expects only from certain kinsmen. For the Tswana, even true friends are subordinate to kinsfolk as trustees of one's secrets and confessions. The Tswana see friendship as a fair-weather transaction. Few Tswana would ever think of weakening their front by confessing to a friend; and a person who by chance or espionage became aware of the misdeeds of another—those of even a friend—would have access to a powerful weapon, which could and might be put to work in the always open arena of gossip or sorcery for one's benefit or another's detriment.

Americans often undertake to initiate ingratiation by offering confessions of weakness, embarrassment, or other trouble. The expectation is generally that such a votive offering of potential weakness will solicit or elicit sympathy or forgiveness followed by an equivalent confession of weakness on the part of the other. This kind of behavior is unheard of for the Tswana. One keeps one's weaknesses to oneself where they will do the least damage. Nothing is worse than having one's problems form part of the humiliating round of gossip and backbiting that forms an endemic part of village life.

Trust for Americans often implies confidentiality. The ease with which Americans reveal something on the strength only of a parole agreement of confidence does not serve the American well in Botswana. One's reputation for good or ill is quickly augmented by ill-conceived conversations with Tswana friends. More importantly, the volunteer finds that statements he makes begin to affect the quality of his relations with Tswana whom he had defined as friends, and hence whom he expected would remain true despite his disclosures or requests. A little reflection on how crucial confidentiality is in the running of our daily lives gives adequate base for imagining the difficulties created for volunteers by their attempts to operate in a Tswana village as they would at home.

Friendship for most volunteers also implies honesty. To be lied to by a friend is a crushing experience for many Americans. Unfortunately the volunteer will find that people he defines as Tswana friends can tell him lies. Nor will they necessarily appear contrite if found out. These and other discrepancies in values create numerous problems for the many volunteers, who generally expect to find friendship in Botswana like the friendships they have known in the United States.

Hospitality and Sociability

In Tswana communal life hospitality and sociability are premier values. The good life is filled with visiting neighbors, entertaining and hosting visitors in the courtyard, giving and receiving gifts of all kinds in an extended network of reciprocities. Involvement in a community means participation in a wide range of obligatory exchanges, including those of giving and receiving hospitality. As I indicated above, there are many important reasons for visiting—like taking the news. The aesthetic satisfaction of effortless and leisurely interaction with one's neighbors is also a very important reason for face-to-face engagement. The pleasures, as well as the social importance of extensive, easygoing interaction, make this an activity which one consciously makes time for, plans for, and sets aside resources to facilitate. The Western phrase "work before play" does not even exist in the lexicon of Setswana.

Time can always be found for work. Such a notion strikes many eager volunteers as vindication of their suspicion that the Tswana know little about hard work. Play and leisure for many volunteers is suspect if it intrudes into work time. Mixing work and play has been proscribed since kindergarten (witness *The Three Little Pigs*). Further, many Americans are self-consciously "private people," not "groupie types." These facts can combine to produce disastrous personal experiences for some volunteers, and less awesome problems for others.

In Botswana one does not turn away a caller. A volunteer, as member of the community, is expected to reciprocate visits. He is expected to drop his work and attend to visiting. When he walks by a neighboring kraal, he is expected to detour from his path, to sit down, and drink beer. It can be a most frustrating experience for a lone volunteer trying to engage himself in reciprocal relations with all of the curious, hospitable people of the village. As stranger, he will be visited, called upon, and presented with gifts. He is expected to reciprocate; yet, one volunteer can hardly do what he defines as his work and attend to the expectations of literally hundreds of Tswana. As he sees work falling behind schedule, coupled with no abatement in the pace of hospitality and sociability, he forms views like: "These people are made for the banana and the sun. Until they learn hard work, they'll never get anywhere."

For the volunteer who is a loner—and most loners I interviewed were very conscious of this need in their lives—life in a Tswana village can be a nightmare. Trying to avoid people creates suspicion, ill-will, or, at least, a lack of readiness to cooperate. The few volunteers who learned to take it easy and to embrace the continual round of drinking and sociability usually found this to be a resource rather than an impediment to the completion of their assignments. But the logic of this step remained counterintuitive for the majority of volunteers.

Conclusions

In my interviews with more than fifty former and experienced current volunteers working in Botswana, I found that the majority had or were experiencing anxiety or puzzlement as a result of conflicts of values. Generally, the meanings the PCVs invested in the behavior they saw were based on simple, analogic reasoning: "X behavior would have such-and-such meaning to me if I were doing it, or if it were occurring in my culture, hence this must be its meaning for the Tswana." My investigations showed that neither physical deprivations nor exotic forms of behavior per se were seen by volunteers as irritations. Rather it was familiar behavior which had problematic meaning that most upset or puzzled the majority of PCVs.

✓●─[**Study** and **Review** on **myanthrolab.com**

Review Questions

1. What problems emerged as Peace Corps volunteers tried to work with rural Tswana in Botswana according to Hoyt Alverson?

2. What are the ten ways Alverson lists that volunteers see themselves and their role as Peace Corpsmen?

3. What is the difference between the way the Tswana and U.S. volunteers culturally conceive of time? What problems does this cause?

4. Why do Tswana sometimes lie to each other and to Peace Corps volunteers? How do volunteers respond to such lies?

5. Why is the American value on privacy a problem for Tswana? How do they respond when volunteers isolate themselves?

6. How do American volunteers make friends and why is this a problem for interaction with rural Tswana?

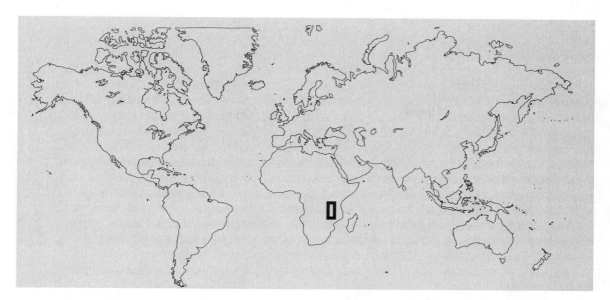

37

Medical Anthropology: Improving Nutrition in Malawi

Sonia Patten

Applied anthropologists work in many settings. They may conduct government program evaluations, work on forest conservation projects, market or advertise products, staff rural development programs, establish foreign offices for nongovernmental organizations or corporations, or advise hospital staff, among other things. In this article, Sonia Patten describes her role as an applied medical anthropologist on a project aimed at the improvement of infant and child nutrition in the African nation of Malawi. As a medical anthropologist, her job was to collect cultural baseline data that would help shape the program and make it appropriate to village conditions in Malawi.

((•─ **Listen** to the **Chapter Audio** on **myanthrolab.com**

Malawi—Welcome to the Warm Heart of Africa. This is the sign that greets travelers when they arrive in this southeastern African republic. The warm, open response to visitors that I have enjoyed each time I have traveled to Malawi contrasts starkly to the poverty that plagues its citizens.

Malawi is a small landlocked nation in southeast Africa that lies south of Tanzania, east of Zambia, and west of Mozambique. The country is long and thin with its axis running north and south along the Great African Rift Valley. Part of the valley holds Lake Malawi, the third largest lake in Africa, which accounts for more than 20 percent of the country's total area of 119,100 square kilometers. Malawi is one of the ten poorest countries in the world. Its economy is based predominately on agriculture, which accounts for half the gross domestic product and virtually all the exports. Cotton, tobacco, and sugar are most likely to be sold to other countries. However, despite exports, food security for both households and the nation is a chronic problem, with annual "hungry seasons" a fact of life and the specter of famine never far from people's minds. Maize, or white corn, is the staple food for the nation, and it is rare when the nation's rain-fed agriculture produces enough of it to adequately feed the population. The Malawi government faces the enormous challenges of strengthening the economy, improving educational and health facilities, and dealing with the serious environmental issues of deforestation and erosion. The country depends heavily on the International Monetary Fund, World Bank, and bilateral and multilateral donor assistance. It was a small project funded by the U.S. Agency for International Development (USAID) that brought me as a medical anthropologist to Malawi several times during the 1990s.

Medical anthropology is difficult to define because it covers such a wide scope of research and practical programming. In the broadest sense, it can be defined as the study of human health in a variety of cultural and environmental contexts. Over the past three decades, medical anthropology has become a distinct and important area within anthropology. Presently it has three major areas of emphasis. One is the study of cultural differences in health beliefs and systems of healing such as alternative therapies, shamanism, and folk concepts of disease. A second consists of biomedical studies of human adaptations to disease, including nutrition, genetics, and demography. The third is applied medical anthropology, which focuses on the application of anthropology to health-related problems and possible solutions.

Medical anthropologists often carry out research as members of interdisciplinary teams, where their main contribution is to discover a people's cultural conceptions of health, illness, and the more general cultural context within which ideas about health are situated. It was as an applied medical anthropologist that I came to be a member of such an interdisciplinary team that would work in Malawi.

In the early 1990s, I was on the faculty at one of three universities that had joined together to apply for a USAID grant under a program called University Development Linkages Program (UDLP). Two of the universities were American and one was the agricultural college that forms part of the University of Malawi system. A major goal of the UDLP was to strengthen developing nation colleges and universities by giving them access to U.S. faculties and other American university resources. The program also sought to increase the involvement of U.S. faculty members with faculty in developing nations so that students at U.S. institutions would benefit from an internationalizing of the curriculum.

In this case, scientists from participating universities were asked to devise and implement a project that would benefit all collaborating institutions of higher education. Many teams of UDLP scientists that applied for grants designed projects intended to strengthen curricula at developing nation institutions. Our team, however, opted to design and implement a project addressing a major problem, child undernourishment in Malawi. We recognized that three out of five children in the country were undernourished. Worse, the mortality rate for children under five was 24 percent or nearly one in four. The problem was caused by the fact that children received insufficient protein and calories, which left them vulnerable to a host of infectious diseases, potential mental impairment, serious deficiency diseases such as kwashiorkor and marasmus, and premature death. This is the story of the people from two central Malawi villages and three universities as we worked to craft a program to reduce child undernourishment and increase child survival on a sustainable basis. Faculty members who were participating in this effort represented a number of disciplines: anthropology, human nutrition, cooperative extension, animal science, veterinary medicine, and crop science. Several of the participating faculty members from Malawi had grown up in small villages, still had extended family in those villages, and were familiar with economic and cultural factors contributing to child undernourishment there. From them and from field research we learned that mothers breastfeed their babies for two to three years, which assured that the children received sufficient protein and calories during these early years. However, that changed when the children were fully weaned. The indigenous weaning food is a gruel of water and maize flour, and babies receive small amounts of it beginning at about four months of age. When mothers wean their toddlers, it is this gruel that the children eat day after day. It is a nutritionally inadequate weaning food and children soon begin to show its effects—swollen bellies, stunted growth, and increased susceptibility to malaria, measles, and other infectious diseases. The weaning food is made from the same crop, maize, that constitutes the staple food for adults, a boiled maize flour dish called nsima. The problem of a nutritionally inadequate weaning food is not unique to Malawi—it plagues many developing nations. In these countries there is often a high-carbohydrate food such as corn or rice that makes up as much as 90 percent of children's daily intake. If people survive into adulthood, their bodies have made an adaptation to this low-protein diet. But young children do not thrive.

As our project searched for ideas about how to create a plan for addressing child nutrition, we decided to focus on a simple approach that would use indigenous resources and be manageable at the local level. This was the introduction of a protein and calorie-rich additive, goat milk, to the local weaning food. Although goats are plentiful in Malawi villages, they are meat goats, not dairy goats. They are like walking bank accounts, to be sold when a family needs money to pay school fees for the children, health care, and rites of passage such as weddings and funerals. It would be a bold step to secure approval from male village political leaders and elders for the introduction of milk-producing goats to provide milk for young children. Dairy goats would be put directly into the hands of women, not men. Would it work? Would women be willing to learn new animal management and food handling techniques? Would they have time to carry out the additional labor that would be required? Would the goat milk be given to the children who needed it? Would husbands or brothers take the valuable animals away from the women? Would the goats and the children flourish? As time went on, we learned the answers to all these questions and more. And the village women contributed very valuable insights and suggestions that made the project a model that has been adopted elsewhere in Malawi.

The Program

Our work began with a series of planning meetings. Our goal was to create a program that would enable women to raise and keep dairy goats on a sustainable and manageable basis, and use the milk that was produced to supplement their children's diets and increase food security for their families. The plan we generated would have three parts: (1) generation of a database on the milk production and biological characteristics of goats; (2) development and implementation of demonstrations and outreach programs for distributing milk goats to rural women and teaching them how to care for the animals; and (3) formation and implementation of outreach programs for rural women so they could learn how to safely handle goat milk and use it as a regular part of the diet, especially for their children who were under five years of age. At our planning meetings we had to figure out what we were actually going to do, and in what sequence.

The animal scientists on the team knew that milk goats introduced into local villages would have to be hardy or they would die. They wanted to try out some breeding experiments using local goats and imported breeds of dairy goats to see just what kind of a crossbred doe would result in the best combination of high milk production and ability to adapt to life in the village. So they worked out a breeding scheme using local Malawi goats and imported Saanen dairy goats from South Africa, Damascus goats from Cyprus, and Anglo-Nubian goats from the U.S. The breeding experiments were carried out at the farm that the Malawi members of our team used for teaching and research.

This kind of research can't be done in a hurry. Arranging for the importation of animals is a complex process because one has to find a supplier, arrange for payment, arrange for shipment (very few airlines are willing to transport large animals internationally), work out how to feed and water the animals while they are in transit, secure permits from the Malawi Ministry of Agriculture, and quarantine the animals for a period of weeks when they arrive in country. Only then can the breeding research begin.

To our dismay, none of the imported Anglo-Nubian goats survived for very long in Malawi. And several of the Damascus goats also died. The Saanens, however, proved to be the hardier—not surprising, since they originated from relatively close by South Africa where environmental conditions were similar to those in Malawi. And when bred with local Malawi goats, the resulting crossbreeds turned out to provide substantial weekly milk yields that would be enough for the goats' kids as well as for the young children of rural families. So the team decided to import more Saanens and continue the crossbreeding program. Crossbred does would be distributed to village women and most of the crossbred bucks would be sold to support the project. As the program developed, team members discovered that some local does produced relatively high average milk yields; this finding became important as the project unfolded.

My work as the team anthropologist involved the human side of the project. With the help of team nutritionists and the extension expert, I designed a survey to collect baseline cultural information in the villages where the milk goats would be distributed. It was important to document such things as women's daily activities, the meaning and use of goats, relationships between men and women, and ways children were fed in the target villages before the milk goats were introduced. Later we would look for changes we hoped would occur after the new goats arrived and for unexpected problems.

To proceed with the social research, we selected three villages, all relatively close to the college campus in a rural setting about 25 km from the capital city of Lilongwe. To proceed, however, it was necessary to obtain permission from the people in each community. To do so we held meetings with the village headmen, men and women elders, mothers of young children who would be affected by our project, and anyone else from the village who was interested in learning about the program.

In the Central Region of Malawi where we were working, most people belong to the Chewa ethnic group. The Chewa have a matrilineal descent system and practice matrilocal residence. Thus, Chewa men and women inherit clan and lineage membership from their mothers. It is this membership that gives people the right to farm plots of land surrounding their villages. When women marry, most continue to live in the village of their birth with a group of related females—mother, maternal grandmother, mother's sisters and their children, sisters and their children, and eventually, adult daughters and their young children. When young men marry, most move to the villages of their brides. The village political leader is usually, but not always, a man. He cannot be the son of the prior headman because a son is not part of his father's matriline. Instead, he is likely to be the son of the prior headman's sister—a maternal nephew. This system creates a situation where almost all of the women and the powerful men in a village are maternal kin to one another.

To introduce the project, we had to recognize the matrilineal nature of village social organization and the need for people's approval. We met with groups of interested women and men and the headmen in two villages. We explained what we were proposing to do. We said we wanted to find out how the young children in the village were doing in terms of growth and health. Then we intended to make milk goats available to women who had children under five years old because we felt the children would benefit from goat milk in their diet. We noted that it would not cost the women any money. (Most rural women lack the means to purchase even local goats, because they cost from $30 to $50. Dairy goats would be much more expensive.) We said that women who received milk goats would be asked to return the first healthy kid, whether male or female, to the college farm and that this would constitute payment for the animal. We told them that women who took the goats would be asked to attend demonstrations to help them learn how to care for the animals, handle the milk, and feed the milk to their children. We also said that someone from the project would come to the village each week to weigh and measure the participants' children to see if goat milk in their diet was having an effect on weight and height of their youngsters.

Village women were uniformly positive about the project—they wanted to participate. But men, including the headmen, were more skeptical. They worried about the impact on social relations of such valuable animals going to women—it didn't seem appropriate—couldn't the goats be given to the men of the village? The goats were not to be sold or slaughtered, we said. They would be there for the benefit of the children, and their care would involve extra work for the women. Everyone knew that children were suffering because of mal-nourishment—sometimes a child would become so seriously malnourished that relatives had to take it to the district hospital for nutritional rehabilitation. This meant a three-week hospital stay with a family member right there to feed and care for the child. The cost to the family was considerable. And the death of a child was a great sorrow. So eventually the men agreed that the project should go forward. The headmen agreed that the goats should belong to the women and said they would resolve any disputes over ownership in favor of the women.

When we were ready to talk with people in a third village about the project, we learned something that quickly dissuaded us from continuing there. It seemed that there was animal theft going on in the area, and the prime suspects were a family living in the third village! Until the local system of justice had solved these crimes and dealt with the perpetrators, we could not take the risk of working in that village. Animal theft became a problem in the other two villages as well. The rural economy in Malawi has weakened in recent years because of droughts, floods, soil depletion, deforestation, erosion, low prices for commodities, and high rates of inflation. The annual hungry season, the period of time between when people consume the last of the food they have stored to the time when the next crops are harvested, used to begin in December and end in March. Now the hungry season often begins in September. People must reduce the amount of food they eat at a time when they have to carry out the heaviest agricultural labor, preparing fields and planting them when the annual rains begin. Both men and women do this work and nearly all agricultural labor is done by hand. In the depth of the hungry season, people may turn to eating maize bran, the portion of the maize kernel that they normally feed to their animals, in order to have something in their bellies to assuage the hunger pangs. Under conditions such as these, it is no surprise that theft of animals is on the rise in the countryside.

Women in the two villages who received milk goats responded vigorously to the threat of theft once a few animals had been stolen. They began to take their milk goats with them as they went to work in the fields, tethering them nearby rather than letting them range free. They built pens against the sides of their mud or brick houses, to provide shade and security. At night they brought the animals into their houses so the whole family could guard them.

Our research team hired two young women who were both native speakers of the local language, Chichewa, and who had grown up in villages. We asked them to administer the baseline survey in the two villages and to continue working on the project. They would help to distribute animals to village women and later pay weekly visits to the recipients to weigh and measure their young children. One of these young women remained with the project throughout, and is dedicated to working with the villagers. She has been a key to the success of our work.

The baseline survey of households with children under five years of age revealed some interesting and useful information. Women headed 30 percent of the households; there was no adult male regularly living with them. Almost 75 percent of the women were nonliterate. A total of 35.4 percent of the children were underweight for their age and 57.7 percent were stunted (short for age). These figures are close to the national averages for a preharvest season, (i.e., the hungry season). A surprising finding was that children in female-headed households were less likely to be undernourished or stunted. We can only speculate about why this was the case. Perhaps it has to do with groups of related women sharing resources in the interest of their children's well being.

We gave women who participated in the baseline survey the opportunity to volunteer to receive a milk goat, with the understanding that they would attend demonstrations that taught ways to manage the animals and keep them healthy, how to milk goats, how to keep the milk from spoiling, and how to add it to their children's food. We also pointed out that they would have to return first-born kids to project personnel so the does could eventually be distributed to other women, but that all kids born after that would be theirs to keep. The female goats would increase their flock of milk-producers, and the males could be sold to give the women much-needed cash. All women who received milk goats would also be provided with a bucket for milking, a pan for cooking, and a measuring cup to help them track milk production.

The program proved popular. Very quickly the project had more participants than it could accommodate, and we had to create a waiting list. We gave priority to those women who had children under five that were most seriously undernourished. Other women on the waiting list agreed to this. We also provided animals to some grandmothers who were raising young grandchildren orphaned when their parents died of AIDS. Care for AIDS orphans has become a major problem in Malawi, and is reflected at the village level. It is common to see women, already struggling to care for immediate family members, stressed to the maximum as they undertake to feed and house children left behind by relatives who have succumbed to the disease.

Team members designed and began to present demonstrations for village women on goat management, goat health, milking, safe milk handling, and incorporation of milk in their children's food. Recipes using local ingredients and goat milk were developed and tested in the home economics kitchens at the college, and taste-tested by the women participants and their children at the village-based demonstrations. The recipes that passed the taste test were routinely used by the women; those that didn't were rejected.

When the women received their animals, all of the does were either pregnant or already had young kids. This is when project field assistants began their weekly visits to the villages. During each visit, the participating women gathered in a central area of the village with their children. Each woman would have her child or children weighed in a sling scale that was suspended from a tree branch. Once a month, team members measured the upper arm circumference and height of the children. The fact of high child mortality was brought home to me in a very graphic way during this process when some women initially objected to having their children's height measured because they thought it was too much like measuring the children for coffins. A few women persisted in their objection. In these cases, our field assistants could only estimate observable changes in height. The field assistants also asked women about the general health of their children during the previous week, the milk production of their goats, and the health of their goats. If a goat was ill, the field assistant arranged for a veterinary assistant or the team member who was a veterinarian to travel to the village and examine the animal. If there was a significant health problem with a child, the field assistant notified faculty team members who would then take the information to the nearest clinic where they could arrange transport of the woman and child to a hospital if that was called for. Almost all the women who received animals were committed to caring for them and using the milk for their children. Ninety-eight percent of the recipients returned the first kid to the project. This is an astonishingly high rate of return and it implies that rural women would be very good risks for other kinds of so-called "payback schemes" that make local efforts to improve economic security sustainable.

We were gratified to see that those children who began to receive even small amounts of goat milk as an ingredient in their daily diets showed steady weight and height gains even when they were sick. In time, however, we began to see children hit growth plateaus or even lose ground temporarily. We learned from village women themselves why this was happening. Women who made up village committees approached the project team with a proposal for a solution. They told us that their milk goats had to have at least two kids before they could get a second high-yield doe, and this meant that there were periods of time when no milk was available for their children. The women asked if we could teach them how to grow soybeans. They were all familiar with soybean flour as a food for undernourished children because this is what they received when they took their malnourished children to maternal and child health clinics for treatment. Their plan was to grow soybeans and grind them into flour to feed their children when no goat milk was available.

Our project team went back to the drawing board and figured out how to incorporate this new effort. The team purchased soybean seed and distributed 5 kg of it to each woman in the two villages. The village headmen approved of this effort and in some instances designated land for use by those women who needed it. Malawi team members developed and presented demonstrations on how to grow and process soybeans. The women agreed to pay back the 5 kg of seed after their first harvest, again a way to perpetuate the program over time and make it sustainable, and all did so.

Women have now completed three or four successful growing seasons with soybeans, and many are growing and storing enough beans to see them through the periods of time when their does produce no milk. They also save enough seed for the next planting season.

It also became clear after a short period of time that we would have to change the goat crossbreeding program. The college farm could not breed enough hardy milk goats to keep up with the demand. The animal scientists on our team looked for local Malawi goats that were the highest milk producers and these, when pregnant or with a kid, were distributed to women on the waiting list. Simultaneously, plans were made to build buck stations in each of the villages and to provide each station with a Saanen or crossbred buck to breed with local goats. Village headmen oversaw the building efforts and other men and women helped to feed and water the buck. When a doe comes into heat, the owner can bring it to the station to be inseminated. In this way the Saanen genes for high milk production spread more rapidly into the village flocks. The villagers know that their bucks must be exchanged for others about every three years in order to avoid inbreeding.

I returned to Malawi for a short visit in the summer of 2004 and found that many positive features of the project were still in place. In discussions with groups of women who had received dairy goats, I learned that two-thirds of them still had their original project animals. The remaining third had lost their original animals to disease or injury, but not before the goats had delivered offspring that survived. Only one woman had sold her animal before it had given her viable kids; this is tantamount to a farmer selling or eating her seed! But the woman's situation was quite difficult. Her husband was seriously ill and could not assist with farm work, and as a consequence she had been unable to raise sufficient maize to provide for household subsistence. She was desperate for cash in order to purchase food, and it was out of this desperation that she sold her milk goat.

Several women had a sufficient number of animals that they were able to meet the nutritional needs of their young children and sell surplus goats, primarily to NGOs planning to launch similar efforts to address child malnutrition. For the most part, money earned in this way was used to buy commercial fertilizer in order to increase the maize harvest. Cooking oil, salt, and clothing were other items commonly purchased with these earnings. The loss of animals to theft had decreased due to the introduction of a community policing effort. Professional police have trained villagers to take turns patrolling the village and its surrounding area at night in order to discourage thieves, and it seemed to be working. But another danger had presented itself. Because the 2004 harvest was not a good one due to erratic rains, people were anxious about their food reserves, most knowing that they would run out long before the next harvest. One result of this is that domesticated dogs (every household has a watchdog) are not fed adequate amounts of cooked maize bran or leftover cooked maize flour. They are hungry, and they have begun running across the fields in packs, attacking kids and young goats belonging to people from villages other than their own. Some people have lost valuable kids in this way and were considering tethering kids while the does free range. Normally tethering occurs only during the rainy season after planting has taken place. There is the possibility that marauding dogs will be shot, but this raises the likelihood of inter-village conflict.

Of the four village buck stations erected as part of the project, three were in good repair and the bucks well cared for. The fourth was somewhat rundown and needed refurbishing. And it was clear that the buck needed better care. After some discussion and investigation, it became apparent that the headman had declared the buck was his personal property and only his relatives could use its services—anyone else would have to pay him a fee if they wished to bring their animals to the buck. Not surprisingly, people did not take well to this proclamation. They more or less boycotted the buck station, which meant that most of the care of the animal fell to the elderly headman and his wife. The station was repaired, the animal was provided with nutritional supplements, the household was provided with a new bucket for the dedicated purpose of bringing water to the buck, and the headman was informed that the buck would die or be returned to the college if it did not receive better care. In the end, it became clear that a miscommunication had occurred between the headman and project personnel, leading the headman to conclude that he was now free to charge for use of the buck station. By the time I left Malawi, the misunderstanding had apparently been cleared up. College personnel will continue to check on the well being of this valuable animal—it would be a great loss to the village if it were to die or be removed.

During group and individual discussions with women, everyone acknowledged the value of goat milk as a component of their children's diets. I was told that, since the milk had become available in the villages, no child had become so seriously malnourished that he or she had to be taken to the hospital for nutritional rehabilitation. This was a real change from an earlier point in time, and a hallmark of success for all of our efforts, researchers and villagers, to promote the health of children.

Conclusion

Our project team designed and tested a locally sustainable approach to alleviate infant and child malnourishment in rural Malawi. Data on changes in the participating children's weights, heights, and upper arm circumferences show that relatively small amounts of goat milk included in the regular diet make a substantial difference in promoting normal growth in children. Results from a rapid appraisal survey that I helped to design indicate that the project is highly valued by rural women. This is confirmed by key village women and by the fact that more women than project resources would permit sought to join the program. Presently some Malawi nongovernmental organizations (NGOs) have introduced similar efforts in other parts of the country. Several district hospitals that provide rehabilitation for severely malnourished children have established flocks of milk goats on their grounds and use the milk as an important part of the rehabilitation treatment. The agricultural college plans to offer training to Malawians and people from other southern African nations who are interested in replicating the program. And the project villages will be demonstration sites for trainees who want to see how the project works "on the ground."

It was important to have an anthropologist on the project team. As the team anthropologist, I participated in every phase of the project, including management duties at times when it was necessary to keep our efforts on schedule. I was responsible for providing an ethnographic account of local culture and using this information to help shape how we could present the program to villagers. I was not trained to manage goat breeding or conduct some of the health measurements, but I could point out how I thought villagers would respond to our plans and to suggest how best to make them full participants in project planning and implementation. It is easy for people from any society to believe that those who are from elsewhere still see the world in the same way they do. Since cultures differ (Americans, for example, find it difficult to understand the ramifications of a matrilineal descent system) anthropologists can translate information about such differences in ways that are useful to other members of interdisciplinary teams. Thus, we can shape programs to fit local conditions and help with cross-cultural communication. That is what I think happened in Malawi.

In July of 2006 I once again traveled to Malawi. A principal motive for this trip was to explore possibilities for securing boreholes and pumps for the villages that had participated in the milk goat project. I had the opportunity to meet with ten women, all project participants, in one of the villages. On this occasion the update that I received was not encouraging. The national and local economies had grown steadily more difficult for Malawians and especially for those who are rural smallholders. Agricultural inputs such as fertilizer and seed had soared in price and many farmers were simply not able to purchase a sufficient amount of fertilizer to assure a harvest sufficient for meeting the subsistence needs of the family. People began to sell off valuable assets in order to secure cash for the purchase of maize. For nine of the ten women with whom I spoke, these assets were their milk goats. The one woman who managed to keep her animals was in the fortunate position of having a husband who was employed, albeit at a relatively low wage, at a government facility. His small but steady income protected the family from having to sell assets such as animals in order to afford staple food. The women who had sold their milk goats were hopeful that, in a year of good harvest, they would be able to purchase a milk doe.

When I expressed my concern and disappointment about these developments to a Malawian who was a key member of the project team, he suggested that I should think about this in another way—if women had not had these valuable animals to sell for a good price in order to see their families through this difficult time, they might have been forced to resort to such dire acts as dismantling their houses to sell the timbers and sheets of metal roofing. This is one of the last resorts of rural dwellers when faced with chronic hunger and the need for cash to purchase food. So the women were buffered from such a drastic move. And they were convinced of the value of milk goats for the physical health of their young children and their own economic well being. They are resilient and resourceful women, and they viewed the setback as only temporary.

✓●─ **Study** and **Review** on **myanthrolab.com**

Review Questions

1. What are the social and environmental conditions that lead to child malnutrition in Malawi, according to Patten?

2. What programs did the project team come up with to improve child nutrition in Malawi, and what steps did they take to implement it?

3. How is anthropology useful for programs such as the one described by Patten in this article?

4. In what ways did team members involve local people in the design and implementation of the program?

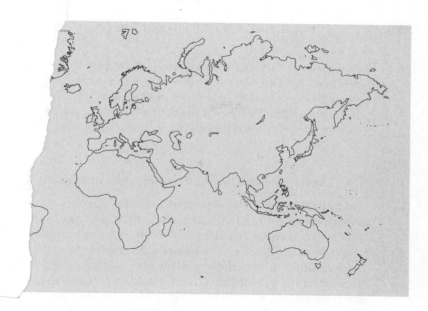

38

Public Interest Ethnography: Women's Prisons and Health Care in California[1]

Rachael Stryker

Public interest ethnography is a branch of applied anthropology that has at least four goals: the study of people affected by public policy, an emphasis on the human consequences of public policy, the production of advice for policy makers, and the empowerment of those affected by policy. In this article, Rachael Stryker describes a public interest study she and six of her undergraduate students conducted in two California women's prisons. Made possible by a U.S. government suit designed to remedy poor health conditions in the California prison system, they conducted ethnographic interviews of numerous female inmates about their health care experiences. They discovered that prison rules and personnel delayed the provision of care, driving many inmates to treat themselves. Women convicts related stories about their health care experiences that revealed a mistrust of prison medical staff, a lack of

[1]Undergraduates Angele Alexander, Natalie Chriss, Kristen Darling, Erin Lucas, Johanna Paillet, and Ali Uscilka authored "Over the Wall: Women Insides' Perspectives on Health Care in California Women's Prisons," the ethnography on which this article is based. They did so in collaboration with Jane Dorotik, Sara Olson, Cynthia Purcell, Angelina Rodriguez, Mary Shields, Sherrie Smith, Silvia Vigil, Annabelle Chapa, and other women inside who have chosen to remain anonymous. Where requested, the names of women inside have been changed.

prison sanitation and food nutrition, the consequences of severe overcrowding, the effects of poverty (co-pays were required) on gaining access to care, and the language barrier faced by the non-English speakers. The research team presented a list of recommendations based on their findings, several of which were incorporated in new prison regulations regarding prison health care.*

((•─┤**Listen** to the **Chapter Audio** on **myanthrolab.com**

"It only takes one bad incident," shared Nicole, a prisoner at Valley State Prison for Women in Chowchilla, California. She was explaining to interviewers why she abstains from contact with prison doctors. "When I feel sick, I go to my cell, kneel in front of the toilet, and pray to God to make me better." Nicole's fear of prison doctors began almost immediately after she was admitted to the prison in 2001. When she first arrived, doctors discovered during a mandatory physical exam that Nicole had high blood pressure. They then prescribed her medication. Unable to speak English in a prison with no translation services, she did not understand what the medicine was for or how it would affect her. After taking the pill, she said, she felt her "heart racing" and sought medical attention. Because of the language barrier, however, no one understood her concerns, and she began to scream in hopes of getting the medical staff's attention. Prison guards, believing she wished to harm herself, stripped and sequestered her for five days. While in isolation, she said, guards walked past her and taunted her. Fearing they might hurt her, she did not want to eat or drink what they gave her. Following her release from isolation, she says, medical staff and guards continuously mocked her. Nicole vowed never to see the prison doctors again.

Nicole's story is not an isolated incident: inadequate health care practices in her prison have been pervasive since it opened in 1995. And although the prison has been recognized as having some of the most advanced medical equipment and capacity in the United States, it, and others like it in California, have been consistently cited for substandard medical delivery, medical neglect, and unnecessary prisoner deaths, especially among those with serious or chronic conditions.

In the light of these problems, it was a common interest in using ethnography to positively impact health care delivery in California women's prisons that provided the seed for the Women's Prison Health Care Project at Mills College in 2006–2007. In collaboration with the San Francisco grassroots organization, California Coalition for Women Prisoners (CCWP), six undergraduates set out to write cultural descriptions of two California women's prisons to answer the questions: (1) What types of experiences do women have in the prisons when they become sick? (2) How do women access health care in the prisons? and (3) What, if anything, do women believe should be changed with regard to the prison health care system? In the process, students learned to use ethnography to render more than just a clearer view of the norms and mores of prison life; they illuminated ethnography as a tool for understanding power, for the humanization of the people involved, and for developing theoretical frameworks and practical protocols for improving people's access to basic needs. In short, they learned to write public interest ethnography (PIE).

*This article was written expressly for *Conformity and Conflict*, Copyright © 2012 and revised in 2014 by Rachael Stryker. Reprinted by permission of the author.

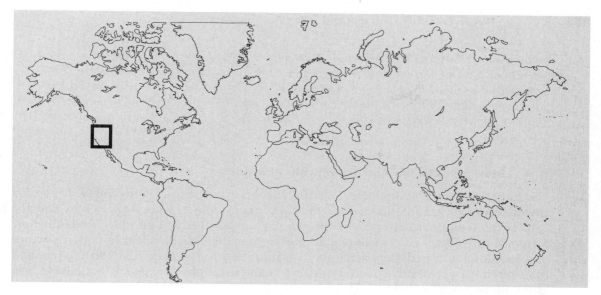

38

Public Interest Ethnography: Women's Prisons and Health Care in California[1]

Rachael Stryker

Public interest ethnography is a branch of applied anthropology that has at least four goals: the study of people affected by public policy, an emphasis on the human consequences of public policy, the production of advice for policy makers, and the empowerment of those affected by policy. In this article, Rachael Stryker describes a public interest study she and six of her undergraduate students conducted in two California women's prisons. Made possible by a U.S. government suit designed to remedy poor health conditions in the California prison system, they conducted ethnographic interviews of numerous female inmates about their health care experiences. They discovered that prison rules and personnel delayed the provision of care, driving many inmates to treat themselves. Women convicts related stories about their health care experiences that revealed a mistrust of prison medical staff, a lack of

---

[1]Undergraduates Angele Alexander, Natalie Chriss, Kristen Darling, Erin Lucas, Johanna Paillet, and Ali Uscilka authored "Over the Wall: Women Insides' Perspectives on Health Care in California Women's Prisons," the ethnography on which this article is based. They did so in collaboration with Jane Dorotik, Sara Olson, Cynthia Purcell, Angelina Rodriguez, Mary Shields, Sherrie Smith, Silvia Vigil, Annabelle Chapa, and other women inside who have chosen to remain anonymous. Where requested, the names of women inside have been changed.

prison sanitation and food nutrition, the consequences of severe overcrowding, the effects of poverty (co-pays were required) on gaining access to care, and the language barrier faced by the non-English speakers. The research team presented a list of recommendations based on their findings, several of which were incorporated in new prison regulations regarding prison health care.*

((∙⸢**Listen** to the **Chapter Audio** on **myanthrolab.com**

"It only takes one bad incident," shared Nicole, a prisoner at Valley State Prison for Women in Chowchilla, California. She was explaining to interviewers why she abstains from contact with prison doctors. "When I feel sick, I go to my cell, kneel in front of the toilet, and pray to God to make me better." Nicole's fear of prison doctors began almost immediately after she was admitted to the prison in 2001. When she first arrived, doctors discovered during a mandatory physical exam that Nicole had high blood pressure. They then prescribed her medication. Unable to speak English in a prison with no translation services, she did not understand what the medicine was for or how it would affect her. After taking the pill, she said, she felt her "heart racing" and sought medical attention. Because of the language barrier, however, no one understood her concerns, and she began to scream in hopes of getting the medical staff's attention. Prison guards, believing she wished to harm herself, stripped and sequestered her for five days. While in isolation, she said, guards walked past her and taunted her. Fearing they might hurt her, she did not want to eat or drink what they gave her. Following her release from isolation, she says, medical staff and guards continuously mocked her. Nicole vowed never to see the prison doctors again.

Nicole's story is not an isolated incident: inadequate health care practices in her prison have been pervasive since it opened in 1995. And although the prison has been recognized as having some of the most advanced medical equipment and capacity in the United States, it, and others like it in California, have been consistently cited for substandard medical delivery, medical neglect, and unnecessary prisoner deaths, especially among those with serious or chronic conditions.

In the light of these problems, it was a common interest in using ethnography to positively impact health care delivery in California women's prisons that provided the seed for the Women's Prison Health Care Project at Mills College in 2006–2007. In collaboration with the San Francisco grassroots organization, California Coalition for Women Prisoners (CCWP), six undergraduates set out to write cultural descriptions of two California women's prisons to answer the questions: (1) What types of experiences do women have in the prisons when they become sick? (2) How do women access health care in the prisons? and (3) What, if anything, do women believe should be changed with regard to the prison health care system? In the process, students learned to use ethnography to render more than just a clearer view of the norms and mores of prison life; they illuminated ethnography as a tool for understanding power, for the humanization of the people involved, and for developing theoretical frameworks and practical protocols for improving people's access to basic needs. In short, they learned to write public interest ethnography (PIE).

*This article was written expressly for *Conformity and Conflict*, Copyright © 2012 and revised in 2014 by Rachael Stryker. Reprinted by permission of the author.

Ethnography and Public Interest Anthropology

What do we mean when we use the term *public interest ethnography*? The answer lies not just in the ethnographic content, but also in the ethnography's intent, context, and possibilities. There are many interpretations of the term, but public interest ethnography is commonly understood as a methodology and product shaped by the principles of the larger subfield of public interest anthropology (PIA). PIA is anthropology that has a problem orientation, that advances knowledge through attention to topics that large groups of people would likely to identify as important to their well-being (although not always, and that is some of its value), that makes clear the relationship between individuals and the broader society, and that expands democracy in the way the research is carried out, is made available, and inspires others.[2]

Put more simply, public interest ethnography is ethnography that might:

1. involve the ethnography of people who are affected by policy.

2. humanize those impacted by policy (and hopefully, policy makers).

3. inform policy.

4. inform the redistribution of power to those affected by policy.

A good example of PIA is also one of the first, carried out during World War II, one of the most prolific periods of applied anthropology in the United States. In 1942, President Franklin Roosevelt appointed several social scientists or "community analysts" to conduct ethnographies of Japanese internment camps that would help shape public policy around the issues of Japanese containment and eventual reintegration into post-war America. Earlier that year, under pressure from Western agriculture lobbies and some high-level members of the U.S. military, Roosevelt had ordered the removal and containment of some 110,000 Japanese-Americans within military camps throughout the western United States. Understanding the controversial nature of his decision, immediately after the order Roosevelt created a civilian agency—the War Relocation Authority (WRA)—to oversee the welfare of the evacuees. In an era that would come to be marked by intense public demand for repressive measures against Japanese-Americans in the name of military defense and national security, the WRA analysts wrote over eighty ethnographic reports or monographs, several illuminating internment as a human rights violation. The ethnographies, which ranged from such topics as Japanese cultural traditions to the results of segregation systems within the camps to perceptions of loyalty among Japanese-Americans, would eventually contribute to policy allowing the mass release in 1945 of those interned as well as the funding for government programs to ease interns' transition into civilian life.[3]

Today, anthropologists write public interest ethnographies to inform policy in a range of areas. Anthropologists document low-income residents' perceptions of production and consumption to reduce environmental pollution in their communities, write collaborative ethnographies with LGBTQ teens to better understand and reduce

---

[2]Peggy Reeves Sanday, "Opening Statement: Defining Public Interest Anthropology" (paper presented at the 97th annual meeting of the American Anthropological Association, December 3, 1998). Available: http://www.sas.upenn.edu/~psanday/pia.99.html

[3]Edward Spicer, "Anthropologists and the War Relocation Authority," in *The Uses of Anthropology*, ed. Walter Goldschmidt (Washington, DC: American Anthropological Association, 1979).

their suicide rates, and work with seniors to write oral histories to improve care for the elderly.[4] Wherever there is policy, there is an opportunity for an anthropologist to creatively use ethnography to influence it.

The Women's Prison Health Care Project

In the 1990s, growing numbers of unnecessary prisoner deaths led several families to bring lawsuits against the state of California to try to improve health care in a variety of areas, including dental care, women's care, HIV/AIDS treatment, custom care for disabled prisoners, and compassionate release. One of the most important of these was a 2001 federal class-action suit (*Plata* v. *Schwarzenegger*), which challenged the general quality of medical care in the state's thirty-three prisons as unconstitutional. The state settled the suit in 2002, agreeing to a range of remedies that would bring prison medical care in line with constitutional standards. However, the state ultimately failed to comply with the court's direction.

In June 2005, upon the discovery that despite the 2002 settlement, California's $1.1 billion-a-year, state-run prison health system was now producing a staggering average of one unnecessary prisoner death per week, Judge Thelton Henderson of the federal court of the Northern California District ruled that the California Department of Corrections and Rehabilitation's (CDCR's) prison health care practices violated the Eighth Amendment constitutional ban on cruel and unusual punishment. In April 2006, in an unprecedented decision, Henderson transferred control of the entire prison medical system from the state of California to his own federal court and named long-time Santa Clara County public hospital administrator Robert Sillen to manage the system as a federal receiver. Sillen's main task was to make appropriate changes to state prison health care infrastructure to accommodate immediate quality of care issues. His tenure as receiver would last until 2008 when he was replaced by lawyer, academic, and former California insurance commissioner J. Clark Kelso.

When Thelton ruled in 2005 that the CDCR would be stripped of its authority to determine issues related to medical care in California prisons, many prisoner advocacy groups saw it as a window of opportunity for prison reform. One of these groups was the California Coalition for Women Prisoners (CCWP), a self-defined grassroots racial justice organization that understands issues such as poor prison health care and unnecessary prisoner deaths as issues of institutional violence.

In January 2006, CCWP director and former prisoner Yvonne Hamdiya Cooks and I met at a Prison Issues roundtable in San Francisco, where she gave a talk that asked, "Given the new receivership, is it possible for female prisoners' voices and experiences to now influence large-scale prison health care reform in California?" I then gave a talk on the value of anthropology and ethnographic method for better understanding prisoners' perspectives on prison life. It was a pretty serendipitous meeting. Within a few weeks, six students in my public interest ethnography class began collaborating with the organization to clarify research questions. Students then worked with CCWP to develop open-ended, yet streamlined and culturally sensitive interview questions that would yield information about how women inside actually responded to illness and the prisons' protocols as well as their women's perspectives, if any, on how to improve health care delivery. In March 2006, CCWP familiarized students with

[4]Meredith Minkler and Nina Wallerstein (eds). 2003. *Community Based Participatory Research for Health.* San Francisco, CA: Jossey-Bass.

the appropriate procedures, conduct, and dress necessary to enter two women's prisons in central California: Central California Women's Prison and Valley State Prison for Women (VSPW). Students each performed five to seven ethnographic interviews with women incarcerated at either prison. The team then collaboratively authored an ethnography based on the findings and presented their results to CCWP and the women inside. In late 2006, CCWP would also present the ethnography to receiver Sillen for his consideration.

Accessing Health Care in Women's Prisons

Interviews with the thirty-seven women highlighted a vast difference between the intent of California prison health care policy and the actual situation. Particularly, women access their health care in ways that are very different from how prison health care delivery is mandated. Amid what women often described as an elusive and unreliable health care system, they had to think and act creatively to access help and treatment. There are at least two different ways that prisoners access medical care at VSPW and Central California Women's Prison. The first is "formal care," which is nonemergency health care received by following the prison's official protocol. The second is "informal care," or care received without the aid of official prison medical staff.

Formal Care

When prisoners are admitted to either VSPW or Central California Women's Prison, they meet with counselors during a fifteen-minute orientation program and are given a Title 15, which is a document that outlines the rules and regulations for everything that happens in the prison, including health care. The orientation and Title 15 are only available in English, although some women mentioned that they had heard of, but never seen, a Spanish version. A new version of Title 15 is supposed to be published whenever prison protocol changes, but women are not given updated copies. In fact, some women didn't recall ever receiving a Title 15, and others said they had access to outdated copies that might be used for reference, but they might be useless, because the information had definitely changed. Since the brief orientation and Title 15 are not reliable sources of information for how to receive health care, many women inside often turned to one another. For example, when asked where she received information about health care, Annabelle, 36, said she asked her cellmates: "You go with the flow and learn by watching or asking." Especially for women who don't speak English, fellow prisoners serve as important sources of information and translation services. Said Sera, who spoke only Spanish, "for women like me, there are things that we just don't know."

Although there are protocols outlined in Title 15, what happens in the prisons often depends on which staff members are working and how they individually respond to a given health situation. As a result, women had different and conflicting ideas about how to navigate the health care system. Despite this fact, there were certain steps they needed to take to obtain the prison's formal care. The first was to fill out a "co-pay," which is a form with boxes to check for symptoms and a pain scale from one to ten. When a co-pay is filed, the prison automatically deducts five dollars from the prisoner's account. Prisoners who require health care, but who have no money in their accounts are not refused care, but these prisoners do accrue debt, which they slowly pay off with a prison job (paid anywhere from eighteen to sixty cents an hour) or if possible, with monetary gifts from family and/or friends outside the prison. After filling out a co-pay, the prisoner waits to receive a "ducat," which is a form of permission to leave a room or normal activity for any reason, including a medical visit. This could take from three days to three weeks to receive one. The women prisoners' responses about the next phase of the procedure varied greatly. Some said they first saw a correctional officer (guard) and then a "Medical Technical Assistant" (MTA, a correctional guard with medical training) who took them to a nurse or doctor, while others said they went to an MTA or a nurse directly. Some women said they had to see a nurse before a doctor, and others said they never saw a nurse.

Informal Care

Since women perceive formal health care protocols as complicated, time consuming, and not always reliable, many women said that they preferred to practice informal forms of care. These included ignoring illness symptoms altogether, self-medicating, sharing medications with each other, or receiving medical care from fellow prisoners. For example, said Hilly, 28, "I'm lucky because [one of my cellmates] was a nurse before she was here. Well, not a nurse. But an EMT? Or trained like an EMT? She knows CPR and what to do if you break something. I dislocate my shoulder sometimes and she pops it in for me." If women are feeling desperate or a sense of urgency, however, they might decide to "fall out," or fake an emergency to get immediate medical attention. Mary, 55, explained the context in which women might resort to falling out: "It doesn't matter how sick you are [prison staff will not offer to bring you to the doctor without going through formal channels]. So, it's a matter of banging on the window of the medical department or passing out where the ambulance has to come and get you." Another reason for falling out had to do with the MTAs. According to many women, the MTA position was problematic: since MTAs' primary duties are correctional and not medical, unlike medical personnel, MTAs are not mandated to "do no harm" and to heal sick prisoners under oath. The custodial aspect of the position thus often trumped the medical aspect, leaving women in correctional units with illnesses and pain longer than they needed to be. Women thus fell out to increase their chances of being tended to more immediately by medical personnel rather than take their chance waiting on an MTA.

Experiences of Formal Health Care in Women's Prisons

What are some themes that characterize the quality of the formal care that women do receive in the two prisons? The most common word women used to categorize their health care experiences was *inefficiency*. All mentioned problems that had to do with the timing and organization of their health care.

Inefficiency

Perhaps the most frustrating experience in this regard, was the delay between the amount of time it took to get ducated after filling out a co-pay and the amount of time it actually took to see a doctor. Women stated that this was the primary reason that they used informal care. And as several women shared, this was usually the reason why anyone would decide to fall out. "It can take from three days to three months to see the doctor," said Sara, 60: "what would you do if you were in pain and you didn't know when you'd get relief?"

Women were also frustrated by inefficient treatment. For example, women sometimes waited years for treatments for simple infections that could be fixed with a prescription for antibiotics, or for necessary surgeries without which women were left for long periods of time in excruciating pain. Inefficiency was also a characteristic of treatment for other chronic, but less serious medical problems. Said Mary, a 58-year-old asthmatic, of her experiences with "the med line" (where women go several times daily to take medication in a supervised fashion): "At night, sometimes the line is so long, that ladies have to miss dinner. So you have to decide, are you going to have dinner or take your meds? Sometimes you have to choose dinner."

According to some women, the problems with inefficiency were not necessarily systemic. Rather, it was individual unresponsive medical staff that caused delays and problems. All women worried that prison medical staff were unqualified and lacking credentials to care for them (a fear flamed by the fact that medical personnel are not required to, and do not, post their credentials in the medical center). There was a general sense that prison doctors only worked at the prisons because they were denied work at other facilities. Many women also stated that medical staff often lost, forgot, or ignored women's health histories prior to incarceration when examining, prescribing, or treating them.

Mistrust of Prison Medical Staff

A second theme among the interviews was fear and mistrust of prison medical procedures and staff. As one woman stated, "Don't assume that everyone even goes to see the doctor. Because then you're not in touch with how bad it might be once you manage to get there." Aside from a basic fear of medical procedures themselves, as we saw at the beginning of this chapter, fear and mistrust of medical procedures can be exacerbated by such things as language barriers and insensitive medical staff members. Nicole's lack of comprehension about her prescription and its effects as well as the derogatory behavior of the doctors and guards created a snowball effect of fear and mistrust of medical personnel that was long lasting. Indeed, most women noted that they had experienced some form of verbal abuse or unwanted sexual advances at their medical centers. For example, Vicky, 45, shared a story about a doctor menacingly and inappropriately flicking her nipples while performing a routine breast exam. She also shared that women in her prison knew which doctors to try to stay away from because they commonly used sexually inappropriate language with, or inappropriately touched, their patients. And as some women noted, disrespect from medical staff might continue even after a prisoner dies. For example, Nicole shared the story of fellow prisoner Martha Fernandez, who had recently died in prison and whose burial was postponed because the prison took weeks to sign her death certificate and release her body to family members. In a similar vein, because little was done to update prisoners' families' contact information, women were also concerned about who the prison would contact if they died. Women thus regularly organized, exchanged, and updated family contact lists with one another to help create a system of family notification should any of them pass away.

Poor Prison Sanitation

In addition, women were very aware of the larger roles that poor sanitation, lack of ability to maintain their hygiene, and poor nutrition and exercise options in the prison likely played in their health trajectory while incarcerated. Women reported that although the prison common rooms and family visiting rooms were kept fairly clean, most found their own living conditions substandard. Much of this was attributed to the fact that it was typical in both prisons for eight women to room together in one cell, which was a problem for several reasons. First, although women said that they were happy to clean up after themselves in their cells (and often wanted to), the prison did not provide an appropriate or adequate amount of cleaning supplies for them to do so. Said Josie, 32, "They should at least give us [dispensable] soap for our hands." In addition, with overcrowded cell conditions at the two prisons, it was of special concern to the women to keep their areas clean to thwart potentially dangerous effects of overcrowding on their health. As Sherrie, 50, stated, "HIV-positive prisoners and other prisoners with infectious diseases are not always housed separately. Because it is unclean inside, you never know what you are sharing with other prisoners and you need to just take their word that they're healthy." She also shared that overcrowding lent its self to hot tempers and physical fights, which resulted in exposure to blood and other bodily fluids. Finally, women shared that such close proximity sometimes lent itself to sexual relations as well. Since there are no sexual education programs at either prison, women inside are not taught about safe sex practices. They also do not receive supplies to help prevent the spread of sexually transmitted diseases.

In addition, women do not receive adequate or enough personal hygiene products. Although the prison supplies them with toilet paper, women said they usually run out quickly. Women who have money in their prison accounts can purchase toiletries, and women who have fewer than five dollars in their account receive a monthly "indigent package" or "fish kit," which includes three small bars of soap, two tubes of toothpaste, a razor, a small bottle of shampoo, laundry soap, deodorant, and 20 envelopes for personal correspondence. The quality of the products is poor, however, and usually not enough to last the entire month. The package also does not include sanitary napkins or tampons.

Poor Prison Nutrition

Several women inside were concerned about the quality of prison food. It was well-known among the women that lifers get stomach problems from eating bad food for so many years. Said one woman, "I try not to eat the food . . . I feel bad for prisoners that come back from eating regular food because they often have to run to the bathroom for diarrhea and stomach aches." Food is pre-frozen and then reheated, and there are few, if any, healthy options. Women with conditions such as diabetes who have special dietary restrictions are also not provided with the specific options they need. And although women with money in their accounts can purchase food at the prison canteen (store), there are no healthy options there either.

Women also fear about the prison's drinking water. Josie, 23, for example, expressed her and other prisoners' suspicions that some of the women's dental problems come from drinking unclean water, and said that some women refrain from drinking water altogether because they are worried about the health effects. This can result in serious stomach problems, because the only other beverages available are coffee with high caffeine content and juices with high sugar content. Another prisoner, Susan, recently had a serious kidney problem because she had been afraid to drink the water and only drank coffee. Linda said that although she knows that drinking water is an important part of staying healthy, she is afraid the water at VSPW will make her even sicker.

Women were also concerned about insufficient access to exercise facilities. Women prisoners have recreation time in the exercise yard, but yard privileges can be revoked as a form of punishment. There is an exercise gym available at VSPW, but it is often closed and has been used for storage, and is therefore inaccessible to the women inside. This restricted access to exercise, combined with poor nutritional quality of food, severely limits the extent to which the women prisoners can manage their own personal health.

Incurring Debt

Finally, women discussed the worry and anxiety they felt about the debt they often incurred as a result of medical treatment. Women prisoners have limited access to money and many of them are indigent. Many also enter the prison with a large amount of restitution debt that results from unpaid court fees and other legal expenses. As mentioned earlier, during their tenure in California prisons, prisoners are assigned "bank accounts," into which family members can deposit funds for prisoners to use for prison expenses or debt. When prisoners perform their paid prison work, however, the prison administration automatically garnishes any wages earned in the amount of 44 percent to pay restitution debt. This severely depletes their resources for health care provision and hygiene products, just to name a few prison expenses. Prisoners often feel that paying $5 to fill out a co-pay is a sacrifice. This sacrifice is compounded by the fact that women work in the prison facility for extremely low wages. As Linda explained, "We get paid eight cents in the kitchen and sixty cents in the laundry room." Thus a $5 co-pay represents almost a week's wages, so some women decide to avoid medical care as a result.

Using Ethnography to Inform Prison Health Care Policy

The Women's Health Care Project elicited several insider suggestions for improving prison health care:

1. *Make Prison Health Care More Efficient*
   a. Provide regular checkups for prisoners
   b. Provide and educate about preventive care for prisoners
   c. Provide opportunities for posttreatment appointments with doctors
   d. Create better access to specialists in a timely manner, especially gynecologists, surgeons, and neurologists
   e. Consider and respond to women's specific health issues (i.e., gynecological, obstetric, and cardiac)
   f. Provide reliable transportation from prisoners' cells to the medical building, especially for disabled prisoners

2. *Make Medical Staff More Reliable and Trustworthy*
   a. Hire more medical staff members, and those with a larger variety of specialties, especially dentistry
   b. Hire medical staff that is compassionate and competent, younger and motivated to heal
   c. Hire medical staff members that are respectful of women's bodies
   d. Mandate that medical staff members post their credentials at the medical center

    e. Eliminate the MTA position in favor of hiring prison guards who can also act as medical staff, to decrease response time to illnesses and emergencies

    f. Hire health educators

3. *Increase Language Accessibility*

    a. Provide prison translation services

    b. Increase knowledge about, and respond to, differences in health care experiences between native English-speaking prisoners and prisoners who can speak little or no English

4. *Improve Nutrition Options*

    a. Provide more balanced and healthier foods in the prison commissary

    b. Offer specific food options for people with diabetes and other health issues

5. *Reduce Debt Accrual*

    a. Eliminate the co-pay necessary to access prison health care

6. *Improve Sanitation and Hygiene*

    a. Decrease number of prisoners assigned to each cell

    b. Allow more access to basic supplies such as soaps and feminine products

    c. Provide sex education and safe sex supplies

7. *Additional Recommendations for Improvements*

    a. Provide grief counseling

    b. Provide a broader array of health issue support groups

Outcome

In late 2006, receiver Sillen read the ethnography in full. He noted that some of the women's suggestions mirrored his own understanding of what would make prison health care more efficient. In particular, he was encouraged by women's understanding and concerns about prison overcrowding. He was also struck by the disparity of health care experiences between English-speaking and non-English-speaking prisoners and by the needless costs of language miscommunication. And like the women inside, he thought that the MTA position was not the most efficient way to manage women's medical emergencies. The women's concerns spoke to Sillen as an administrator: he understood their logic in terms of efficient labor practices and cost-effectiveness.

    In 2008, Judge Thelton Henderson replaced Sillen with J. Clark Kelso. Before the end of Sillen's tenure, however, he increased the number and types of non-English translation services associated with medical care in all California prisons. Although a small step toward constitutionally adequate prison health care, it means that stories like Nicole's might be less likely to happen. Sillen also eliminated the MTA position; guards would now be responsible only for correctional duties, while nursing assistants would conduct triage in custodial units.

    During J. Clark Kelso's tenure as receiver, via the work of CCWP and other prisoner advocacy organizations, the ethnography continues to help identify overcrowding as a serious, "bottom-line" issue for prison health care. In January 2010, a panel of three federal judges authorized by the Prison Litigation Reform Act determined that overcrowding was the "primary cause" of inmates being denied their constitutional rights to adequate medical and mental health care. They also ruled that the state must reduce prison overcrowding in California, and mandated the state to develop a comprehensive plan to reduce the prison population by approximately 40,000 prisoners in two years (reducing California's prison population from an occupancy rate of almost 200 percent of its total design capacity to 137.5 percent.[5] The state reluctantly developed a population reduction plan while then-Governor Arnold Schwarzenegger (and his successor, Jerry Brown) appealed the prison population reduction order to the United States Supreme Court, who agreed in June 2010 to reconsider the lower court's decision. On November 30, 2010, the Supreme Court upheld the decision of the three judge panel by a vote of 5-4, ordering the state of California to reduce its prison population by between 38,000 and 46,000 inmates.[6] From a prison health perspective, this is a favorable ruling that may significantly respond to the concerns about overcrowding expressed by the women inside.

Conclusion

The Women's Prison Health Care Project illuminates the discrepancy between state mandates for prison health care and lived health care experiences of women incarcerated in California prisons. The project also provides a unique and timely description of what constitutionally inadequate medical care to patient-inmates looks like, as well as its effects on prisoners and how prisoners cope. Particularly, it demonstrates that women prisoners must think creatively to access health care in the face of inefficiency, certain forms of discrimination, and insufficient access to resources. Women inside also have many ideas for how to improve their situations.

But like all good public interest ethnography, the project is doing much more than this. It is informing steps toward making constitutionally equitable health care in California prisoners a reality. It has helped inspire state administrators to link the personal experiences and stories of women inside to more efficient prison health care policy, encouraging more translation services for non-English-speaking prisoners seeking medical care, and eliminating what many understand to be one of the causes of delayed medical care and even unnecessary prisoner deaths: MTA positions.

Finally, the ethnography contributes to prisoner advocates' broader efforts to raise ever more public questions and concerns about prisoners' (lack of) access to resources basic human rights. As one woman incarcerated at VSPW put it, the ethnography ". . . shows not only what's happening, but . . . ask[s] people [in charge] to think about *why* it's happening. And make some change." Concerns about overcrowding in California prisons have now been elevated to the federal level. The ethnography thus contributed to larger grassroots and legal movements to make the poor quality of prison health care in California a public interest issue. In the process, it helped connect the micro to the macro, and the personal to the political, planting seeds for possibility and alternate futures.

[5]Richey, Warren. June 14, 2010. "Supreme Court to Hear California Prison Overcrowding Case." *The Christian Science Monitor.* http://www.csmonitor.com/USA/Justice/2010/0614/Supreme-Court-to-hear-California-prison-overcrowding-case

[6]Alicia Bower, *Unconstitutionally Crowded: Brown v. Plata and How the Supreme Court Pushed Back to Keep Prison Reform Litigation Alive*, 45 Loy. L.A. L. Rev. 555 (2012).

((•—Listen to the **Chapter Audio** on **myanthrolab.com**

Review Questions

1. What is the definition of public interest anthropology and public interest ethnography, according to Stryker?

2. What evidence, based on this article, supports the utility of ethnographic interviewing for the construction or revision of public policy?

3. How did inmates' poverty affect their access to effective health care, according to Stryker?

4. What were the major impediments to effective health care revealed by the stories told by inmates?

5. What recommendations did the ethnographers make to California authorities concerning the provision of effective prison health care?

6. What strategies did inmates employ to treat problems with their health?

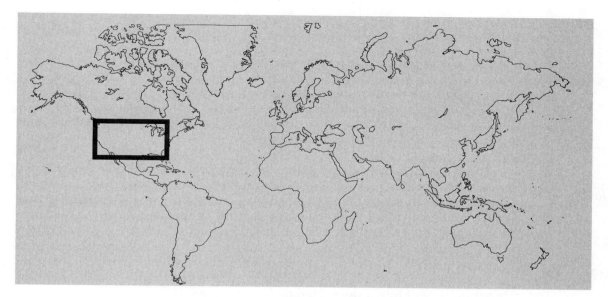

39

Using Anthropology

David W. McCurdy

Some disciplines, such as economics, have an obvious relationship to the nonacademic world. Economic theory, although generated as part of basic research, may often prove useful for understanding the "real" economy. It may seem as though anthropology is not applicable in the same way. In this article, however, David McCurdy discusses some of the professional applications of anthropology, and argues that there is a basic anthropological perspective that can help anyone cope with the everyday world. Using the experience of a company manager as a case study, he asserts that ethnographic and qualitative research is an important tool, not just in diverse professional settings, but in anybody's daily life.*

((•─|**Listen** to the **Chapter Audio** on **myanthrolab.com**

In 1990 a student whom I had not seen for seventeen years stopped by my office. He had returned for his college reunion and thought it would be interesting to catch up on news about his (and my) major department, anthropology. The conversation, however, soon shifted from college events to his own life. Following graduation and a stint in the Peace Corps, he noted, he had begun to study for his license as a ship's engineer. He had attended the Maritime Academy and worked for years on freighters. He was finally granted his license, he continued, and currently held the engineer's position on a container ship that made regular trips between

---

*This article is an updated version of "Using Anthropology," published in *Conformity and Conflict*, 9th ed. Copyright © 2000 by David W. McCurdy. Reprinted by permission.

Seattle and Alaska. He soon would be promoted to chief engineer and be at the top of his profession.

As he talked, he made an observation about anthropology that may seem surprising. His background in the discipline, he said, had helped him significantly in his work. He found it useful as he went about his daily tasks, maintaining his ship's complex engines and machinery, his relationships with the crew, and his contacts with land-based management.

And his is not an unusual case. Over the years, several anthropology graduates have made the same observation. One, for example, is a community organizer who feels that the cross-cultural perspective he learned in anthropology helps him mediate disputes and facilitate decision making in a multi-ethnic neighborhood. Another, who works as an advertising account executive, claims that anthropology helps her discover what products mean to customers. This, in turn, permits her to design more effective ad campaigns. A third says she finds anthropology an invaluable tool as she arranges interviews and writes copy. She is a producer for a metropolitan television news program. I have heard the same opinion expressed by many others, including the executive editor of a magazine for home weavers, the founder of a fencing school, a housewife, a physician, several lawyers, the kitchen manager for a catering firm, and a high school teacher.

The idea that anthropology can be useful is also supported by the experience of many new Ph.D.s. A recent survey has shown, for the first time, that more new doctorates in anthropology find employment in professional settings than in college teaching or scholarly research, and the list of nonacademic work settings revealed by the survey is remarkably broad. There is a biological anthropologist, for example, who conducts research on nutrition for a company that manufactures infant formula. A cultural anthropologist works for a major car manufacturer, researching such questions as how employees adapt to working overseas, and how they relate to conditions on domestic production lines. Others formulate government policy; plan patient care in hospitals; design overseas development projects; run famine relief programs; consult on tropical forest management; and advise on product development, advertising campaigns, and marketing strategy for corporations.

This newfound application of cultural anthropology comes as a surprise to many Americans. Unlike political science, for example, which has a name that logically connects it with practical political and legal professions, there is nothing in the term *anthropology* that tells most Americans how it might be useful.

The research subject of anthropology also makes it more difficult to comprehend. Political scientists investigate political processes, structures, and motivations. Economists look at the production and exchange of goods and services. Psychologists study differences and similarities among individuals. The research of cultural anthropologists, on the other hand, is more difficult to characterize. Instead of a focus on particular human institutions, such as politics, law, and economics, anthropologists are interested in cross-cultural differences and similarities among the world's many groups.

This interest produces a broad view of human behavior that gives anthropology its special cross-cultural flavor. It also produces a unique research strategy, called *ethnography*, that tends to be qualitative rather than quantitative. Whereas other social sciences moved toward *quantitative methods* of research designed to test theory by using survey questionnaires and structured, repetitive observations, most anthropologists conduct *qualitative research* designed to elicit the cultural knowledge of the people they seek to understand. To do this, anthropologists often live and work with their subjects, who are called *informants* within the discipline. The result is a highly detailed ethnographic description of the categories and rules people consult when they behave, and the meanings that things and actions have for them.

It is this ethnographic approach, or cultural perspective, that I think makes anthropology useful in such a broad range of everyday settings. I particularly find important the special anthropological understanding of the culture concept, ethnographic field methods, and social analysis. To illustrate these assertions, let us take a single case in detail: that of a manager working for a large corporation who consciously used the ethnographic approach to solve a persistent company problem.

The Problem

The manager, whom we will name Susan Stanton, works for a large multinational corporation called UTC (not the company's real name). UTC is divided into a number of parts, including divisions, subdivisions, departments, and other units designed to facilitate its highly varied business enterprises. The company is well-diversified, engaging in research, manufacturing, and customer services. In addition to serving a wide cross-section of public and private customers, it also works on a variety of government contracts for both military and nonmilitary agencies.

One of its divisions is educational. UTC has established a large number of customer outlets in cities throughout the United States, forming what it calls its "customer outlet network." They are staffed by educational personnel who are trained to offer a variety of special courses and enrichment programs. These courses and programs are marketed mainly to other businesses or to individuals who desire special training or practical information. For example, a small company might have UTC provide its employees with computer training, including instruction on hardware, programming, computer languages, and computer program applications. Another company might ask for instruction on effective management or accounting procedures. The outlets' courses for individuals include such topics as how to get a job, writing a résumé, or enlarging your own business.

To organize and manage its customer outlet network, UTC has created a special division. The division office is located at the corporate headquarters and is responsible for developing new courses, improving old ones, training customer outlet personnel, and marketing customer outlet courses, or "products" as they are called inside the company. The division also has departments that develop, produce, and distribute the special learning materials used in customer outlet courses. These include books, pamphlets, video and audio tapes and cassettes, slides, overlays, and films. These materials are stored in a warehouse and are shipped, as they are ordered, to customer outlets around the country.

It is with this division that Susan Stanton first worked as a manager. She had started her career with the company in a small section of the division that designed various program materials. She had worked her way into management, holding a series of increasingly important positions. She was then asked to take over the management of a part of the division that had the manufacture, storage, and shipment of learning materials as one of its responsibilities.

But there was a catch. She was given this new management position with instructions to solve a persistent, although vaguely defined, problem. "Improve the service," they had told her, and "get control of the warehouse inventory." In this case, "service" meant the process of filling orders sent in by customer outlets for various materials stored in the warehouse. The admonition to improve the service seemed to indicate that service was poor, but all she was told about the situation was that customer outlet personnel complained about the service; she did not know exactly why or what "poor" meant.

In addition, inventory was "out of control." Later she was to discover the extent of the difficulty.

> We had a problem with inventory. The computer would say we had two hundred of some kind of book in stock, yet it was back ordered because there was nothing on the shelf. We were supposed to have the book but physically there was nothing there. I'm going, "Uh, we have a small problem. The computer never lies, like your bank statement, so why don't we have the books?"

If inventory was difficult to manage, so were the warehouse employees. They were described by another manager as "a bunch of knuckle draggers. All they care about is getting their money. They are lazy and don't last long at the job." Strangely, the company did not view the actions of the warehouse workers as a major problem. Only later did Susan Stanton tie in poor morale in the warehouse with the other problems she had been given to solve.

Management by Defense

Although Stanton would take the ethnographic approach to management problems, that was not what many other managers did. They took a defensive stance, a position opposite to the discovery procedures of ethnography. Their major concern—like that of many people in positions of leadership and responsibility—was to protect their authority and their ability to manage and to get things done. Indeed, Stanton also shared this need. But their solution to maintaining their position was different from hers. For them, claiming ignorance and asking questions—the hallmark of the ethnographic approach—is a sign of weakness. Instead of discovering what is going on when they take on a new management assignment, they often impose new work rules and procedures. Employees learn to fear the arrival of new managers because their appearance usually means a host of new, unrealistic demands. They respond by hiding what they actually do, withholding information that would be useful to the manager. Usually, everyone's performance suffers.

Poor performance leads to elaborate excuses as managers attempt to blame the troubles on others. Stanton described this tendency.

> When I came into the new job, this other manager said, "Guess what? You have got a warehouse. You are now the proud owner of a forklift and a bunch of knuckle draggers." And I thought, management's perception of those people is very low. They are treating them as dispensable, that you can't do anything with them. They say the workers don't have any career motives. They don't care if they do a good job. You have to force them to do anything. You can't motivate them. It's only a warehouse, other managers were saying. You can't really do that much about the problems there so why don't you just sort of try to keep it under control.

Other managers diminished the importance of the problem itself. It was not "poor service" that was the trouble. The warehouse was doing the best it could with what it had. It was just that the customers—the staff at the customer outlets—were complainers. As Susan Stanton noted:

> The people providing the service thought that outlet staff were complainers. They said, "Staff complain about everything. But it can't be that way. We have checked it all out and it isn't that bad."

Making excuses and blaming others lead to low morale and a depressed self-image. Problems essentially are pushed aside in favor of a "let's just get by" philosophy.

Ethnographic Management

By contrast, managers take the offensive when they use ethnographic techniques. That is what Stanton did when she assumed her new managerial assignment over the learning materials manufacturing and distribution system. To understand what the ethnographic approach means, however, we must first look briefly at what anthropologists do when they conduct ethnographic field research. Our discussion necessarily involves a look at the concepts of culture and microculture as well as ethnography. For as we will shortly point out, companies have cultures of their own, a point that has recently received national attention; but more important for the problem we are describing here, companies are normally divided into subgroups, each with its own microculture. It is these cultures and microcultures that anthropologically trained managers can study ethnographically, just as fieldworkers might investigate the culture of a !Kung band living in the Kalahari Desert of West Africa or the Gypsies living in San Francisco.

Ethnography refers to the process of discovering and describing culture, so it is important to discuss this general and often elusive concept. There are numerous definitions of culture, each stressing particular sets of attributes. The definition we employ here is especially appropriate for ethnographic fieldwork. We may define culture as the acquired knowledge that people use to generate behavior and interpret experience. In growing up, one learns a system of cultural knowledge appropriate to the group. For example, an American child learns to chew with a closed mouth because that is the cultural rule. The child's parents interpret open-mouthed chewing as an infraction and tell the child to chew "properly." A person uses such cultural knowledge throughout life to guide actions and to give meaning to surroundings.

Because culture is learned, and because people can easily generate new cultural knowledge as they adapt to other people and things, human behavior and perceptions can vary dramatically from one group to another. In parts of India, for example, children learn to chew "properly" with their mouths open. Their cultural worlds are quite different from the ones found in the United States.

Cultures are associated with groups of people. Traditionally, anthropologists associated culture with relatively distinctive ethnic groups. *Culture* referred to the whole life-way of a society, and particular cultures could be named. Anthropologists talked of German culture, Ibo culture, and Bhil culture. Culture was everything that was distinctive about the group.

Culture is still applied in this manner today, but with the advent of complex societies and a growing interest among anthropologists in understanding them, the culture concept has also been used in a more limited way. Complex societies such as our own are composed of thousands of groups. Members of these groups usually share the national culture, including a language and a huge inventory of knowledge for doing things, but the groups themselves have specific cultures of their own. For example, if you were to walk into the regional office of a stock brokerage firm in 1980, you would have heard the people there talking an apparently foreign language. You might stand in the "bull pen," listen to brokers make "cold calls," "sell short," "negotiate a waffle," or get ready to go to a "dog and pony show." The fact that an event such as this feels strange when you first encounter them is strong evidence to support the notion that you don't yet know the culture that organizes them. We call such specialized groups *microcultures.*

We are surrounded by microcultures, participating in a few, encountering many others. Our family has a microculture. So may our neighborhood, our college, and even our dormitory floor. The waitress who serves us lunch at the corner restaurant shares a culture with her co-workers. So do bank tellers at our local savings and loan. Kin, occupational groups, and recreational associations each tend to display special microcultures. Such cultures can be, and now often are, studied by anthropologists interested in understanding life in complex American society.

The concept of microculture is essential to Susan Stanton as she begins to attack management problems at UTC because she assumes that conflict between different microcultural groups is most likely at the bottom of the difficulty. One microculture she could focus on is UTC company culture. She knows, for example, that there are a variety of rules and expectations—written and unwritten—for how things should be done at the company. She must dress in her *corporates*, for example, consisting of a neutral-colored suit, stockings, and conservative shoes. UTC also espouses values about the way employees should be treated, how people are supposed to feel about company products, and a variety of other things that set that particular organization apart from other businesses.

But the specific problems that afflicted the departments under Stanton's jurisdiction had little to do with UTC's corporate culture. They seemed rather to be the result of misunderstanding and misconnection between two units, the warehouse and the customer outlets. Each had its own microculture. Each could be investigated to discover any information that might lead to a solution of the problems she had been given.

Such investigation would depend on the extent of Stanton's ethnographic training. As an undergraduate in college, she had learned how to conduct ethnographic interviews, observe behavior, and analyze and interpret data. She was not a professional anthropologist, but she felt she was a good enough ethnographer to discover some relevant aspects of microcultures at UTC.

As noted above, ethnography is the process of discovering and describing a culture. For example, an anthropologist who travels to India to conduct a study of village culture will use ethnographic techniques. The anthropologist will move into a community, occupy a house, watch people's daily routines, attend rituals, and spend hours interviewing informants. The goal is to discover a detailed picture of what is going on by seeing village culture through the eyes of informants. The anthropologist wants the insider's perspective. Villagers become teachers, patiently explaining different aspects of their culture, praising the anthropologist for acting correctly and appearing to understand, laughing when the anthropologist makes mistakes or seems confused. When the anthropologist knows what to do and can explain in local terms what is going on or what is likely to happen, real progress has been made. The clearest evidence of such progress is when informants say, "You are almost human now," or "You are beginning to talk just like us."

The greatest enemy of good ethnography is the preconceived notion. Anthropologists do not conduct ethnographic research by telling informants what they are like based on earlier views of them. They teach the anthropologist how to see their world: the anthropologist does not tell them what their world should really be like. This is what happens when a new manager takes over a department and begins to impose changes on its personnel. He does so to fit his preconceived perception of them and their situation. The fact that the manager's efforts are likely to fail makes sense in light of this ignorance. The manager doesn't know the microculture.

But can a corporate manager really do ethnography? After all, managers have positions of authority to maintain. It is all right for professional anthropologists to enter the field and act ignorant; they don't have to maintain an authoritative role. The key to the problem appears to be the "grace period." Most managers are given one by their employees when they are new on the job. New managers cannot be expected to know everything. It is permissible for them to ask basic questions. The grace period may last only a month or two, but it is usually long enough to find out valuable information.

This is the opportunity that Susan Stanton saw as she assumed direction of the warehouse distribution system. As she described it:

> I could use the first month, actually the first six weeks, to find out what was going on, to act dumb and find out what people actually did and why. I talked to end customers. I talked to salespeople, people who were trying to sell things to help customer outlets with their needs. I talked to coordinators at headquarters staff who were trying to help all these customer outlets do their jobs and listened to what kinds of complaints they had heard. I talked to the customer outlet people and the guys in the warehouse. I had this six-week grace period where I could go in and say, "I don't know anything about this. If you were in my position, what would you do, or what would make the biggest difference, and why would it make a difference?" You want to find out what the world they are operating in is like. What do they value? And people were excited because I was asking and listening and, by God, intending to do something about it instead of just disappearing again.

As we shall see shortly, Stanton's approach to the problem worked. But it also resulted in an unexpected bonus. Her ethnographic approach symbolized unexpected interest and concern to her employees. That, combined with realistic management, gave her a position of respect and authority. Their feelings for her were expressed by one warehouse worker when he said:

> When she [Susan] was going to be transferred to another job, we gave her a party. We took her to this country-and-western place and we all got to dance with the boss. We told her that she was the first manager who ever tried to understand what it was like to work in the warehouse. We thought she would come in like the other managers and make a lot of changes that didn't make sense. But she didn't. She made it work better for us.

Problems and Causes

An immediate benefit of her ethnographic inquiry was a much clearer view of what poor service meant to customer outlet personnel. Stanton discovered that learning materials, such as books and cassettes, took too long to arrive after they were ordered.

Worse, material did not arrive in the correct quantities. Sometimes there would be too many items, but more often there were too few, a particularly galling discrepancy since customer outlets were charged for what they ordered, not what they received. Books also arrived in poor condition, their covers ripped or scratched, edges frayed, and ends gouged and dented. This, too, bothered customer outlet staff because they were often visited by potential customers who were not impressed by the poor condition of their supplies. Shortages and scruffy books did nothing to retain regular customers either.

The causes of these problems and the difficulties with warehouse inventory also emerged from ethnographic inquiry. Stanton discovered, for example, that most customer outlets operated in large cities, where often they were housed in tall buildings. Materials shipped to their office address often ended up sitting in ground-level lobbies, because few of the buildings had receiving docks or facilities. Books and other items also arrived in large boxes, weighing up to a hundred pounds. Outlet staff, most of whom were women, had to go down to the lobby, open those boxes that were too heavy for them to carry, and haul armloads of supplies up the elevator to the office. Not only was this time-consuming, but customer outlet staff felt it was beneath their dignity to do such work. They were educated specialists, after all.

The poor condition of the books was also readily explained. By packing items loosely in such large boxes, warehouse workers ensured trouble in transit. Books rattled around with ease, smashing into each other and the side of the box. The result was torn covers and frayed edges. Clearly no one had designed the packing and shipping process with customer outlet staff in mind.

The process, of course, originated in the central warehouse, and here as well, ethnographic data yielded interesting information about the causes of the problem. Stanton learned, for example, how materials were stored in loose stacks on the warehouse shelves. When orders arrived at the warehouse, usually through the mail, they were placed in a pile and filled in turn (although there were times when special preference was given to some customer outlets). A warehouse employee filled an order by first checking it against the stock recorded by the computer, then going to the appropriate shelves and picking the items by hand. Items were packed in the large boxes and addressed to customer outlets. With the order complete, the employee was supposed to enter the number of items picked and shipped in the computer so that inventory would be up to date.

But, Stanton discovered, workers in the warehouse were under pressure to work quickly. They often fell behind because materials the computer said were in stock were not there, and because picking by hand took so long. Their solution to the problem of speed resulted in a procedure that even further confused company records.

> Most of the people in the warehouse didn't try to count well. People were looking at the books on the shelves and were going, "Eh, that looks like the right number. You want ten? Gee, that looks like about ten." Most of the time the numbers they shipped were wrong.

The causes of inaccurate amounts in shipping were thus revealed. Later, Stanton discovered that books also disappeared in customer outlet building lobbies. While staff members carried some of the materials upstairs, people passing by the open boxes helped themselves.

Other problems with inventory also became clear. UTC employees, who sometimes walked through the warehouse, would often pick up interesting materials from the loosely stacked shelves. More important, rushed workers often neglected to update records in the computer.

The Shrink-Wrap Solution

The detailed discovery of the nature and causes of service and inventory problems suggested a relatively painless solution to Stanton. If she had taken a defensive management position and failed to learn the insider's point of view, she might have resorted to more usual remedies that were impractical and unworkable. Worker retraining is a common answer to corporate difficulties, but it is difficult to accomplish and often fails. Pay incentives, punishments, and motivation enhancements such as prizes and quotas are also frequently tried. But they tend not to work because they don't address fundamental causes.

Shrink-wrapping books and other materials did. Shrink-wrapping is a packaging method in which clear plastic sheeting is placed around items to be packaged, then through a rapid heating and cooling process, shrunk into a tight covering. The plastic molds itself like a tight skin around the things it contains, preventing any internal movement or external contamination. Stanton described her decision.

> I decided to have the books shrink-wrapped. For a few cents more, before the books ever arrived in the warehouse, I had them shrink-wrapped in quantities of five and ten. I made it part of the contract with the people who produced the books for us.

On the first day that shrink-wrapped books arrived at the warehouse, Stanton discovered that they were immediately unwrapped by workers who thought a new impediment had been placed in their way. But the positive effect of shrink-wrapping soon became apparent. For example, most customer outlets ordered books in units of fives and tens. Warehouse personnel could now easily count out orders in fives and tens, instead of having to count each book or estimate numbers in piles. Suddenly, orders filled at the warehouse contained the correct number of items.

Employees were also able to work more quickly, since they no longer had to count each book. Orders were filled faster, the customer outlet staff was pleased, and warehouse employees no longer felt the pressure of time so intensely. Shrink-wrapped materials also traveled more securely. Books, protected by their plastic covering, arrived in good condition, again delighting the personnel at customer outlets.

Stanton also changed the way materials were shipped, based on what she had learned from talking to employees. She limited the maximum size of shipments to twenty-five pounds by using smaller boxes. She also had packages marked "inside delivery" so that deliverymen would carry the materials directly to the customer outlet offices. If they failed to do so, boxes were light enough to carry upstairs. No longer would items be lost in skyscraper lobbies.

Inventory control became more effective. Because they could package and ship materials more quickly, the workers in the warehouse had enough time to enter the size and nature of shipments in the computer. Other UTC employees no longer walked off with books from the warehouse, because the shrink-wrapped bundles were larger and more conspicuous, and because taking five or ten books is more like stealing than "borrowing" one.

Finally, the improved service dramatically changed morale in the division. Customer outlet staff members, with their new and improved service, felt that finally someone had cared about them. They were more positive and they let people at corporate headquarters know about their feelings. "What's happening down there?" they asked. "The guys in the warehouse must be taking vitamins."

Morale soared in the warehouse. For the first time, other people liked the service workers there provided. Turnover decreased as pride in their work rose. They began to care more about the job, working faster with greater care. Managers who had previously given up on the "knuckle draggers" now asked openly about what had got into them.

Stanton believes the ethnographic approach is the key. She has managers who work for her read anthropology, especially books on ethnography, and she insists that they "find out what is going on."

Conclusion

Anthropology is, before all, an academic discipline with a strong emphasis on scholarship and basic research. But, as we have also seen, anthropology is a discipline that contains several intellectual tools—the concept of culture, the ethnographic approach to fieldwork, a cross-cultural perspective, a holistic view of human behavior—that make it useful in a broad range of nonacademic settings. In particular, it is the ability to do qualitative research that makes anthropologists successful in the professional world.

A few years ago an anthropologist consultant was asked by a utility company to answer a puzzling question: Why were its suburban customers, whose questionnaire responses indicated an attempt at conservation, failing to reduce their consumption of natural gas? To answer the question, the anthropologist conducted ethnographic interviews with members of several families, listening as they told him about how warm they liked their houses and how they set the heat throughout the day. He also received permission to install several video cameras aimed at thermostats in private houses. When the results were in, the answer to the question was deceptively simple: Fathers fill out questionnaires and turn down thermostats; wives, children, and cleaning workers, all of whom, in this case, spent time in the houses when fathers were absent, turn them up. Conservation, the anthropologist concluded, would have to involve family decisions, not just admonitions to save gas.

Over the past twenty years, anthropology's usefulness in the world of work has been discovered by the United States press. For example, *U.S. News and World Report* carried a story in 1998 entitled "Into the Wild Unknown of Workplace Culture: Anthropologists Revitalize Their Discipline," which traced changing trends in academic anthropology and highlighted the growth of the discipline's penetration of the business world.[1] Included in the article were examples of useful ethnography, such as the discovery by one anthropologist consultant that rank-and-file union members were upset with shop stewards because the latter spent more time recruiting new members than responding to grievances. In another instance, the article reported on the work of anthropologist Ken Erickson. Hired to find out why immigrant meatpackers had launched a wildcat strike, he was able to show that the workers struck because they felt their supervisors treated them as unskilled laborers, not because there was a language problem, as proposed by management. The workers had developed elaborate strategies to work quickly, effectively, and safely that were ignored or unknown to their supervisors.

[1]Brendan I. Koerner, "Into the Wild Unknown of Workplace Culture: Anthropologists Revitalize Their Discipline," *U.S. News & World Report*, August 10, 1998, p. 56.

In 1999, *USA Today* carried a story that further emphasized anthropology's useful-ness. Entitled "Hot Asset in Corporate: Anthropology Degrees," the article began with, "Don't throw away the MBA degree yet. But as companies go global and crave leaders for a diverse workforce, a new hot degree is emerging for aspiring executives: anthropol-ogy."[2] The piece carried numerous examples—the hiring of anthropologist Steve Barnett as a vice president at Citicorp following his discovery of the early warning signs that identify people who do not pay credit card bills; the case of Hallmark, which sent anthro-pologists into immigrant homes to discover how holidays and birthdays are celebrated so that the company could design appropriate cards for such occasions; the example of a marketing consultant firm that sent anthropologists into bathrooms to watch how women shave their legs, and in the process, to discover what women want in a razor.

The article also listed executives who stressed how important their anthropol-ogy degree has been for their business successes. Motorola corporate lawyer Robert Faulkner says that the anthropology degree he received before going to law school has become increasingly valuable in his management job. Warned by his father that most problems are people problems, Michael Koss, CEO of the Koss headphone com-pany, is another example. He received his anthropology degree from Beloit College. Katherine Burr, CEO of The Hanseatic Group, has an MA in anthropology and was quoted as saying, "My competitive edge came completely out of anthropology. The world is so unknown, changes so rapidly. Preconceptions can kill you." The article concluded with the observations of Ken Erickson of the Center for Ethnographic Re-search. "It takes trained observation. Observation is what anthropologists are trained to do." More recently, the March, 2014 edition of *Business Insider* ran an article by Drake Baer entitled "Here's Why Companies are Desperate to Hire Anthropologists." He reports that anthropologists can discover that what customers *want* from a prod-uct can be entirely different from what companies *think* their customers want. As an example, he notes that Adidas was always associated with elite performance and per-formers. Calling in a consulting company called Red Associates to do ethnographic research with customers, Adidas discovered that " . . . after observing their behavior through the lens of anthropology, it became clear that customers wanted products to help them lead healthy lifestyles, not win competitions." This led the company to "change from a sports brand for athletes to an inclusive brand inviting all . . . to join a movement of living a healthier and better life."

In short, cultural anthropology has entered the world of business. I argue that the key to its special utility and value in the commercial world is the ethnographic ap-proach. Anthropologists have this ethnographic field experience and a sense of how social systems work and how people use their cultural knowledge. They have the spe-cial background, originally developed to discover and describe the cultural knowledge and behavior of unknown societies, needed to, in the words of Susan Stanton, "find out what is going on."

✓•⎯ **Study** and **Review** on **myanthrolab.com**

Review Questions

 1. What kinds of jobs do professional anthropologists do?

 2. What is special about anthropology that makes fundamental knowledge of it val-uable to some jobs?

[2]Del Jones, "Hot Asset in Corporate: Anthropology Degrees," *USA Today*, February 18, 1999, section B, p. 1.

3. What is meant by *qualitative research?* Why is such research valuable to business and government?

4. What difficulties did the company manager described in this article face? What solutions did she invent to deal with them? How did her knowledge of anthropology help her with this problem?

5. Why is ethnography useful in everyday life? Can you think of situations in which you could use ethnographic research?

6. List some of the skills acquired by undergraduate anthropology majors that are useful to employers. How can these be translated into résumé language that employers can understand?

Glossary

Acculturation The process that takes place when groups of individuals having different cultures come into firsthand contact, which results in change to the cultural patterns of both groups.

Action anthropology Any use of anthropological knowledge for planned change by the members of a local cultural group.

Adjustment anthropology Any use of anthropological knowledge that makes social interaction between persons who operate with different cultural codes more predictable.

Administrative anthropology The use of anthropological knowledge for planned change by those who are external to a local cultural group.

Advocate anthropology Any use of anthropological knowledge by the anthropologist to increase the power of self-determination for a particular cultural group.

Affinity A fundamental principle of relationship linking kin through marriage.

Agriculture A subsistence strategy involving intensive farming of permanent fields through the use of such means as the plow, irrigation, and fertilizer.

Allocation of resources The knowledge people use to assign rights to the ownership and use of resources.

Applied anthropology Any use of anthropological knowledge to influence social interaction, to maintain or change social institutions, or to direct the course of cultural change.

Authority The right to make and enforce public policy.

Bilateral (cognatic) descent A rule of descent relating someone to a group of consanguine kin through both males and females.

Borrowing The adoption of something new from another group. Also see *diffusion*.

Business anthropology Applying anthropological theories and practices to the needs of private sector organizations, especially industrial firms.

Caste A form of stratification defined by unequal access to economic resources and prestige, which is acquired at birth and does not permit individuals to alter their rank.

Clan A kinship group normally comprising several lineages; its members are related by a unilineal descent rule, but it is too large to enable members to trace actual biological links to all other members.

Class A system of stratification defined by unequal access to economic resources and prestige, but permitting individuals to alter their rank.

Climate change A long-term change in the Earth's climate, especially due to a long-term increase in the atmospheric temperature.

Coercion A kind of political support derived from threats, use of force, or the promise of short-term gain.

Consanguinity The principle of relationship linking individuals by shared ancestry (blood).

Contest A method of settling disputes requiring disputants to engage in some kind of mutual challenge such as singing (as among the Inuit).

Cosmology A set of beliefs that defines the nature of the universe or cosmos.

Court A formal legal institution in which at least one individual has authority to judge and is backed up by a coercive system to enforce decisions.

Cultural contact The situation that occurs when two societies with different cultures somehow come in contact with each other.

Cultural diffusion The passage of a cultural category, culturally defined behavior, or culturally produced artifact from one society to another through borrowing.

Cultural ecology The study of the way people use their culture to adapt to particular environments, the effects they have on their natural surrounding, and the impact of the environment on the shape of culture, including its long-term evolution.

Cultural environment The categories and rules people use to classify and explain their physical environment.

Cultural hybridization The process by which a cultural custom, item, or concept is transformed to fit the cultural context of a society that borrows it.

Culture The knowledge that is learned, shared, and used by people to interpret experience and generate behavior.

Culture shock A form of anxiety that results from an inability to predict the behavior of others or to act appropriately in cross-cultural situations.

Descent A rule of relationship that ties people together on the basis of reputed common ancestry.

Descent groups Groups based on a rule of descent.

Detached observer A researcher who adopts the strategy of detached observation, an approach to scientific inquiry stressing emotional detachment and the construction of categories by the observer in order to classify what is observed.

Diaspora A scattered population with a common geographic origin.

Diffusion The spread of cultural traits from one society to another through a process of contact and borrowing.

Distribution The strategies for apportioning goods and services among the members of a group.

Divination The use of supernatural force to provide answers to questions.

Division of labor The rules that govern the assignment of jobs to people.

Ecology The study of the way organisms interact with each other within an environment.

Economic system The provision of goods and services to meet biological and social wants.

Egalitarian societies Societies that, with the exception of ranked differences between men and women and adults and children, provide all people an equal chance at economic resources and prestige. Most hunter-gatherer societies are egalitarian by this definition.

Endogamy Marriage within a designated social unit.

Ethnocentrism A mixture of belief and feeling that one's own way of life is desirable and actually superior to others'.

Ethnography The task of discovering and describing a particular culture.

Exogamy Marriage outside any designated group.

Explicit culture The culture that people can talk about and of which they are aware. Opposite of tacit culture.

Extended family A family that includes two or more married couples.

Extralegal dispute A dispute that remains outside the process of law and develops into repeated acts of violence between groups, such as feuds and wars.

Family A residential group composed of at least one married couple and their children.

Frames A social construction of a social phenomenon. Social frames are often constructed by media sources, political movements, or other social groups to present a particular point of view about something.

Globalization The process that promotes economic, political, and other cultural connections among people living all over the world.

Go-between An individual who arranges agreements and mediates disputes.

Grammar The categories and rules for combining vocal symbols.

Guest workers Individuals who are given temporary visas to live and work in another country.

Horticulture A kind of subsistence strategy involving semi-intensive, usually shifting, agricultural practices. Slash-and-burn farming is a common example of horticulture.

Hunting and gathering A subsistence strategy involving the foraging of wild, naturally occurring foods.

Incest taboo The cultural rule that prohibits sexual intercourse and marriage between specified classes of relatives.

Industrialism A subsistence strategy marked by intensive, mechanized food production and elaborate distribution networks.

Inequality A human relationship marked by differences in power, authority, prestige, and access to valued goods and services, and by the payment of deference.

Informant A person who teaches his or her culture to an anthropologist.

Infralegal dispute A dispute that occurs below or outside the legal process without involving regular violence.

Innovation A recombination of concepts from two or more mental configurations into a new pattern that is qualitatively different from existing forms.

Kinship The complex system of social relationships based on marriage (affinity) and birth (consanguinity).

Language The system of cultural knowledge used to generate and interpret speech.

Law The cultural knowledge that people use to settle disputes by means of agents who have recognized authority.

Leadership The ability to influence others to act.

Legitimacy A kind of political support based on people's positive evaluation of public policy or positive evaluation of the political structure and process that produces public policy.

Lineage A kinship group based on a unilineal descent rule that is localized, has some corporate powers, and whose members can trace their actual relationships to each other.

Magic Strategies people use to control supernatural power to achieve particular results.

Mana An impersonal supernatural force inherent in nature and in people. Mana is somewhat like the concept of "luck" in U.S. culture.

Market economies Economies in which production and exchange are motivated by market factors: price, supply, and demand. Market economies are associated with large societies where impersonal exchange is common.

Market exchange The transfer of goods and services based on price, supply, and demand.

Marriage The socially recognized union between two people that accords legitimate birth status rights to their children.

Matrilineal descent A rule of descent relating a person to a group of consanguine kin on the basis of descent through females only.

Metaphor A comparison, usually linguistic, that suggests how two things that are not alike in most ways are similar in another.

Microculture The system of knowledge shared by members of a group that is part of a larger national society or ethnic group.

Monogamy A marriage form in which a person is allowed only one spouse at a time.

Moot A community meeting held for the informal hearing of a dispute.

Morpheme The smallest meaningful category in any language.

Multicultural Literally, more than one culture. Usually applied to situations where groups with different cultural backgrounds are part of a larger social aggregate.

Mythology Stories that reveal the religious knowledge of how things have come into being.

Naive realism The notion that reality is much the same for all people everywhere.

Neo-liberalism Redistribution economic philosophy in capitalist countries that emphasize the free movement of goods, capital, and services, with cuts to public expenditure for social services.

Nonlinguistic symbols Any symbols that exist outside the system of language and speech, for example, visual symbols.

Nuclear family A family composed of a married couple and their children.

Ordeal A supernaturally controlled, painful, or physically dangerous test, the outcome of which determines a person's guilt or innocence.

Pastoralism A subsistence strategy based on the maintenance and use of large herds of animals.

Patrilineal descent A rule of descent relating consanguine kin on the basis of descent through males only.

Patrimonial authority Pertains to the form of government organized as a more or less direct extension of the noble household, where officials originate as household servants and remain personal dependents of the ruler.

Personified supernatural force Supernatural force inherent in supernatural beings such as goddesses, gods, spirits, and ghosts.

Phoneme The minimal category of speech sounds that signals a difference in meaning.

Phonology The categories and rules for forming vocal symbols.

Phratry A group composed of two or more clans. Members acknowledge unilineal descent from a common ancestor but recognize that their relationship is distant.

Physical environment The world as people experience it with their senses.

Policy Any guideline that can lead directly to action.

Political system The organization and process of making and carrying out public policy according to cultural categories and rules.

Polyandry A form of polygamy in which a woman has two or more husbands at one time.

Polygamy A marriage form in which a person has two or more spouses at one time. Polygyny and polyandry are both forms of polygamy.

Polygyny A form of polygamy in which a man is married to two or more women at one time.

Prayer A petition directed at a supernatural being or power.

Priest A full-time religious specialist who intervenes between people and the supernatural, and who often leads a congregation at regular cyclical rites.

Production The process of making something.

Public The group of people a policy will affect.

Ramage A cognatic (bilateral) descent group that is localized and holds corporate responsibility.

Rank societies Societies stratified on the basis of prestige only.

Reciprocal exchange The transfer of goods and services between two people or groups based on their role obligations. A form of nonmarket exchange.

Redistribution The transfer of goods and services between a group of people and a central collecting service based on role obligation. The U.S. income tax is a good example.

Refugees People who flee their country of origin because they share a well-founded fear of persecution.

Religion The cultural knowledge of the supernatural that people use to cope with the ultimate problems of human existence.

Remittances Usually refers to cash sent from migrants abroad to home countries.

Respondent An individual who responds to questions included on questionnaires; the subject of survey research.

Revitalization movement A deliberate, conscious effort by members of a society to construct a more satisfying culture.

Role The culturally generated behavior associated with particular statuses.

Sacrifice The giving of something of value to supernatural beings or forces.

Self-redress The actions taken by an individual who has been wronged to settle a dispute.

Semantics The categories and rules for relating vocal symbols to their referents.

Shaman A part-time religious specialist who controls supernatural power, often to cure people or affect the course of life's events.

Slash-and-burn agriculture A form of horticulture in which wild land is cleared and burned over, farmed, then permitted to lie fallow and revert to its wild state.

Social acceptance A process that involves learning about an innovation, accepting an innovation as valid, and revising one's cultural knowledge to include the innovation.

Social groups The collections of people that are organized by culturally defined rules and categories.

Social network An assortment of people with whom an individual regularly interacts but who themselves do not regularly form an organized group.

Social remittances The ideas, practices and social capital that flow from the host society to the sending society.

Social situation The categories and rules for arranging and interpreting the settings in which social interaction occurs.

Social stratification The ranking of people or groups based on their unequal access to valued economic resources and prestige.

Sociolinguistic rules Rules specifying the nature of the speech community, the particular speech situations within a community, and the speech acts that members use to convey their messages.

Sorcery The malevolent practice of magic.

Speech The behavior that produces meaningful vocal sounds.

Spirit possession The control of a person by a supernatural being in which the person becomes that being.

Status A culturally defined position associated with a particular social structure.

Stratified societies Societies that are at least partly organized on the principle of social stratification. Contrast with *egalitarian* and *rank societies*.

Subject The person who is observed in a social or psychological experiment.

Subsistence economies Economies that are local and that depend largely on the nonmarket mechanisms, reciprocity, and redistribution to motivate production and exchange.

Subsistence strategies Strategies used by groups of people to exploit their environment for material necessities. Hunting and gathering, horticulture, pastoralism, agriculture, and industrialism are subsistence strategies.

Supernatural Things that are beyond the natural. Anthropologists usually recognize a belief in such things as goddesses, gods, spirits, ghosts, and *mana* to be signs of supernatural belief.

Support Anything that contributes to the adoption of public policy and its enforcement.

Symbol Anything that humans can sense that is given an arbitrary relationship to its referent.

Tacit culture The shared knowledge of which people usually are unaware and do not communicate verbally.

Technology The part of a culture that involves the knowledge that people use to make and use tools and to extract and refine raw materials.

Transcendent values Values that override differences in a society and unify the group.

Transnational Literally, across national borders.

Ultimate problems Universal human problems, such as death, the explanation of evil, the meaning of life, and transcendent values that can be answered by religion.

Unit of production The group of people responsible for producing something.

United Nations Declaration on the Rights of Indigenous Peoples A UN declaration adopted in 2007 to protect the rights of indigenous people.

Witchcraft The reputed activity of people who inherit supernatural force and use it for evil purposes.

World system The economic incorporation of different parts of the world into a system based on capitalism, not politics.

Worldview The way people characteristically look at the universe.

Photo Credits

Text Credits

Page 2: Edward Burnett Tylor, *Primitive Culture* (New York: Harper Torchbooks, Harper & Row, 1958; originally published by John Murray, London, 1871), p. 1.

Pages 6–12: *Ethnography and Culture* from Participant Observation by James P. Spradley. Copyright © 1980 by Holt, Rinehart, and Winston, Inc. Reprinted by permission of Barbara Spradley.

Page 7: Bronislaw Malinowski, *Argonauts of the Western Pacific* (London: Routledge, 1922), p. 22.

Page 7: George Hicks, *Appalachian Valley* (New York: Holt, Rinehart, and Winston, 1976) p. 3.

Page 9: *Crowd Mistakes Rescue Attempt, Attacks Police*, Minneapolis Tribune, Nov. 23, 1973. Hartford, Connecticut.

Page 11: Herbert Blumer, *Symbolic Interactionism* (Englewood Cliffs, NJ: Prentice-Hall, 1969), p. 2.

Page 12: Charles O. Frake, "Plying Frames Can Be Dangerous: Some Reflections on Methodology in Cognitive Anthropology," Quarterly Newsletter of the Institute for Comparative Human Development 3 (1977): 6–7.

Pages 13–19: *Eating Christmas in the Kalahari*, from Richard Borshay Lee, "Eating Christmas in the Kalahari," Natural History, December 1969, pp. 14–22, 60–64. Reprinted from Natural History December 1969; copyright © Natural History Magazine, Inc., 1969.

Pages 20–30: *Fieldwork on Prostitution in the Era of AIDS*, from Tricking and Tripping by Claire E. Sterk (Putnam Valley, NY: Social Change Press, 2000), pp. 14–20. Reprinted by permission.

Page 21: Claire E. Sterk, *Tricking and Tripping: Prositution in the era of AIDS*. Social Change Press, 2000. Piper, 1987. The names of the women who were interviewed for this study, as well as those of their pimps and customers, have been replaced by pseudonyms to protect their privacy.

Pages 31–36: *Nice Girls Don't Talk to Rastas*, from George Gmelch, "Nice Girls Don't Talk to Rastas." Used by permission of George Gmelch.

Pages 41–48: *Shakespeare in the Bush*, from Laura Bohannan, "Shakespeare in the Bush." Used by permission.

Page 50: Gen. James Lindsay. Gregory C. Sieminski, *The Art of Naming Operations*, From Parameters, Autumn 1995, pp. 81–98.

Pages 50, 51: Gregory C. Sieminski, *The Art of Naming Operations*, from Parameters, Autumn 1995, pp. 81–98.

Page 51: Winston S. Churchill, *The Second World War: Vol. V, Closing the Ring* (Boston: Houghton Mifflin, 1951), p. 662.

Index